HANDBOOKS

TEXAS

ANDY RHODES

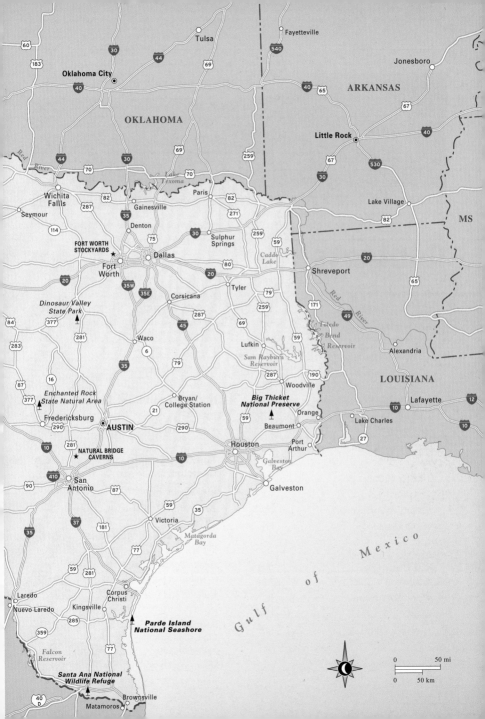

Contents

Discover Texas

Texas has an independent spirit unmatched across the globe. Its people, like its landscapes, are rugged, fiery, captivating, and endearing. The one element that ropes them all together is an immense Texas pride. The Lone Star State's mystique is enormous, and for good reason – Texas is practically a country unto itself, and people continue to be intrigued by its dynamic magnetism.

The proud residents of this vibrant state somehow manage to reflect and defy all stereotypes associated with them. For every good ol' boy set in his ways, there's a progressive genius building her Web-based empire. For every brash oilman making millions, there's a humble educator affecting lives. Intense football coaches coexist peacefully with environmental activists. Like anywhere else, people in Texas have their differences, but there's one thing that transcends obstacles that is wholly unique to this state – the common bond of being Texan.

You can't talk about Texas without mentioning size. It's enormous. It's colossal. It's just a big ol' giant place. No other state can claim mountains, tropics, pine forests, prairies, and mesas all within its borders. Toss in an eclectic mix of regional cuisine, national parks, and real-life cowboys, and you'll find a rich experience representative of Texas's distinct character.

This spirit is evident in the Panhandle plains, where chicken-fried steak is proudly served at diners along old Route 66. It's apparent in the Hill Country, where Texas troubadours play beer-soaked blues guitar on the Luckenbach stage. It's all over the Rio Grande Valley, where Lone Star flags are as abundant as the bountiful groves of grapefruit trees.

Friday Night Lights. Barbecued beef ribs. Austin City Limits. Chisholm Trail cowboys. You can't swing a piñata stick in Texas without encountering a cultural icon. And there's plenty more to discover about Texas's rich heritage: excavated shipwrecks, Spanish missions, majestic courthouses, cattle drives, oil booms, and JFK's assassination all occurred under the state's legendary six flags. This is what makes the state such an enigma and such a fascinating place. You could spend a year exploring the natural and cultural wonders of Texas and still find yourself with dozens of destinations remaining on your must-see list – all certain to become unforgettable future memories.

Planning Your Trip

▶ WHERE TO GO

The Dallas-Fort Worth Metroplex

The towering twin metro cities of Dallas and Fort Worth are only separated by about 35 miles, but their cultural differences are extensive, offering travelers to this region the best of both worlds—glitz and grit, The Big D and Cowtown, the Old South and the Wild West. Though dominated by the "Metroplex," North Texas is also home to a surprisingly large concentration of rivers, lakes, and charming small towns.

Austin and the Hill Country

Dubbed "the Live Music Capital of the World," Austin is the region's—perhaps even the state's—mecca for music and performing arts. Home to the University of Texas at Austin, the city is a hotbed for creative thinkers and entrepreneurs, earning the tech-heavy business nickname "Silicon Hills". Geographically, this region is marked by a convergence of the cotton-rich Blackland Prairie and the granite outcroppings of the Hill Country; culturally, it's known for its German heritage, honky-tonks, and Dr Pepper (invented in Waco).

San Antonio and South Texas

Most of South Texas is defined and unified by its Tejano heritage. The majority of the

IF YOU HAVE...

- **A WEEKEND:** A weekend jaunt to Texas is a tall order, but it can be done. Check out the Dallas-Fort Worth Metroplex, which provides the one-two punch of Southern and Western culture, from cosmopolitans to stockyards.

- **ONE WEEK:** Experience one of Texas's big cities, Dallas and Fort Worth's grit and culture, Houston's Southern metropolitan charm, San Antonio's Hispanic heritage, Austin's creative energy, or El Paso's Wild West spirit.

- **TWO WEEKS:** The wide open landscapes and rugged beauty of West Texas beckon in the Panhandle Plains, Big Bend Region, and El Paso area.

- **A MONTH:** Getting to West Texas can be a fun-filled adventure unto itself. Start your Texas tour in Dallas or Houston before setting your sights to the west to experience the natural majesty of Big Bend and Guadalupe Mountains National Parks.

the Hall of State in Dallas's Fair Park

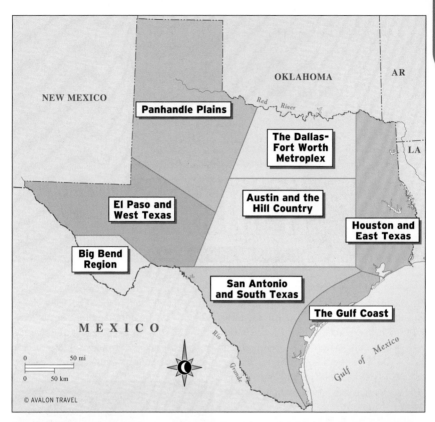

the charming Kinney County Courthouse near Del Rio

St. Ignatius Catholic Church in El Paso

region's culture is tied to Mexico, including the legendary Alamo, constructed with four other San Antonio missions in the early 1700s to help expand Spain's influence in the New World. Tejano heritage is concentrated in the Rio Grande Valley, where the border towns of Laredo, Del Rio, and Brownsville offer a taste of Mexico with a uniquely Texan twist.

Houston and East Texas

From historic oil boomtowns to five national forests to the megopolis of Houston, this enormous region is an ideal place to experience the legacy of the Lone Star State. East Texas has a distinct Southern bayou influence, reflected in the food, heritage, and even the accents. Standing apart is Houston, the fourth-largest city in the country and home to NASA, oil-related industries, and some of the preeminent museums (and humidity) in the country.

The Gulf Coast

Stretching more than 350 miles along the Gulf of Mexico, this region's moderate beaches and waves draw casual beachcombers, salty fishermen, and frolicking families. The biggest city on the gulf, Corpus Christi, offers plenty of recreational activities to accommodate a quick weekend getaway and the ubiquitous Winter Texans. Once a year, students from across the country

the tall ship *Elissa* in Galveston

Fort Leaton's magnificent adobe architecture in Presidio, the Big Bend region

invade South Padre Island for a rollicking Spring Break, but otherwise, the region remains as low-key as the gulf's lightly lapping waves.

El Paso and West Texas

This region is what most people envision when they hear the word Texas—hot and dry with an occasional cactus or cow skull. The Wild West spirit thrives in sun-baked cities like El Paso and Midland, and the Guadalupe Mountains National Park offers stunning views of colorful canyon walls and rugged outcroppings. Local cuisine reflects the personality of the region, ranging from spicy cheese-filled chiles rellenos in El Paso to sweet and hardy helpings of pecan pie in Odessa.

Big Bend Region

Everything about Big Bend is vast—the sky, the views, the mountains, and the canyons. It's a relatively untouched land, where the natural elements dominate the landscape, and the visitors simply marvel at its beauty. The nearby community of Marfa has recently landed on the radar of the international art community, and its neighbors—Fort Davis and Alpine—are equally as compelling for their Old West charm. The rest of the Big Bend area is utterly inviting in its isolation.

Panhandle Plains

The breathtaking views of colorful cliffs and imposing rock towers make Palo Duro Canyon near Amarillo a can't-miss experience, and legendary Route 66—still accessible along portions of I-40—offers a glimpse back in time. This region of the state, including the welcoming wide-open towns of Abilene and San Angelo, is home to many mythical Texas cowboys who branded their way into Texas's mystique by corralling longhorn cattle on the open range.

the U Drop Inn on historic Route 66 in Shamrock

► WHEN TO GO

Texans like to joke about their two distinct seasons: hot and less hot. Summertime can indeed be brutal, with long stretches of 100-plus degree temperatures, and the humidity is usually a factor, too. Austin and San Antonio are mildly comfortable in the summer, but the arid regions of West Texas offer a "cool" respite thanks to the low humidity.

Though seasoned Texans will take summer vacations to the Gulf Coast, most travelers prefer spring in Texas. One of the state's venerable springtime attractions are the abundant wildflowers throughout the entire mid-section of the state. Bluebonnets, daisies, and Indian paintbrushes turn pastures and highway medians into colossal canvases of vivid color with Mother Nature's vibrant brush strokes offering a compelling counterpart to northern states' fall colors.

Spring is also an optimal time to visit Texas parks. Big Bend, Guadalupe Mountains, and the Rio Grande Valley come alive in March and April, with migrating birds and butterflies dotting the landscape as they feed on fresh foliage. This is also a good time of the year to explore the East Texas Piney

Citrus groves are a common sight in the Rio Grande Valley.

Woods—humidity isn't nearly as oppressive as the summer months, and lakes and creeks are brimming with cool, clear water.

Fall can be dicey—it often reaches 90°F

a field of bluebonnets in the Texas Hill Country

as late as November—and winters are surprisingly chilly, with ice storms and snow in the Panhandle and northern plains. That being said, the tropical environs of the Rio Grande Valley are a major draw for Winter Texans from the chilly Midwest, who revel in the comparatively balmy 70°F temperatures while golfing or birding.

▶ BEFORE YOU GO

Texas is far removed from the transportation hubs on the East and West Coast, but it's easily accessible by plane and relatively accessible by car. Air travel is the best option because the state's two largest cities—Houston and Dallas—are primary hubs for major airlines (Continental and American, respectively). It's wise to arrange a rental car reservation before arriving at a Texas airport, and to specify a fuel-efficient vehicle, since you'll likely be driving across widespread areas, whether you're in an urban or rural locale. If you wait to rent a vehicle upon arrival, there's a good chance you'll have to choose from the remaining fleet—typically an SUV or a minivan.

In a state this big, however, a vehicle is virtually a necessity, despite some recent advances in metropolitan public transportation systems. Fortunately, the interstate highway system is pretty impressive—for a state this huge, you can get from most major cities to the others (excluding El Paso) in about three hours.

As for the climate, there's an old saying in Texas that goes, "If you don't like the weather, stick around a few hours, and it'll change." As a result, travelers should always pack plenty of warm-weather gear, including hats, sandals, swimsuits, and especially sunscreen, since much of Texas receives an average of 300-plus sunny days a year. Don't be surprised by Texas's chilly winters, though. For those traveling December through February, make sure to bring jackets, raincoats, and heavy sleeping bags.

Outdoor adventurers don't have to pack anything extra, but a raincoat and tarp are a good idea during the state's rainy months of May and November. A solid pair of hiking boots are essential for the rocky terrain in West and Central Texas.

the vast and stunning Palo Duro Canyon in the Texas Panhandle

Explore Texas

▶ THE BEST OF TEXAS

Texas is an enormous state, but the drives between most of its major cities can be made within a morning. Though it's a daunting task, it's physically possible to capture the essence of Texas over the course of a week if you're expedient and selective. If you'd prefer to move at a more leisurely Southern pace, you better give yourself at least 10 days, especially if you have extra time to explore West Texas.

The following itinerary represents an overview of Texas's distinct cultural attractions. These sites are unlike any others across the country, yet they merely represent the top-layer cream of the state's abundant crop. The West Texas detour is quite a jaunt, but it's absolutely worth it. The wide-open spaces and enormous sky in Marfa and the natural wonders of Big Bend National Park will give travelers a true sense of the Texas mystique.

Regardless, most people find a week-long journey through the heart of Texas will certainly suffice. It offers a somewhat-touristy yet genuinely authentic feel for the Lone Star State's indomitable charm and spirit.

Day 1

Begin in Fort Worth, even if your hotel is in Dallas, in which case the 40-minute drive west on I-30 is still worth the effort. Go directly to the Fort Worth Stockyards and immerse yourself in Texas's cattle-driving heritage. Spend the afternoon at the internationally acclaimed Kimbell Art Museum before devoting the evening to eating and nightlife at Sundance Square.

Day 2

Despite the negative associations, Dallas's lasting legacy is its association with John F. Kennedy's assassination, and the Sixth Floor

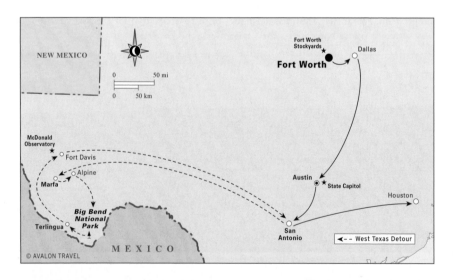

TEXAS'S AWESOME ART MUSEUMS

Texas has an abundance of world-class facilities in its metropolitan areas. Since the state boasts three of the country's 10 largest cities – Houston, Dallas, and San Antonio – the corresponding number of museums and galleries is rather impressive. Fort Worth's Kimbell Art Museum is considered by many to be the best in the state, and contemporary art museums in Dallas and Houston draw artwork and aficionados from across the globe. In addition to these traditional museums, there are several Texas-themed locales worth visiting. Cowboy culture is on display at the Amon Carter Museum in Fort Worth, and the National Center for American Western Art features historic artwork and artifacts in the charming Hill Country town of Kerrville.

FORT WORTH

Fort Worth's **Kimbell Art Museum** is a premiere showcase for art through the ages, from Medieval to millennial. Also worth visiting is the **Modern Art Museum of Fort Worth,** where rotating exhibits from the latest movers and shakers offer visitors a fresh perspective on the creative-art world. Also, the **Amon Carter Museum** is a must for those in search of excellent Western/cowboy-related art.

DALLAS

Dallas is one of the state's major cultural centers, but it's far different than its sibling to the west. Despite is shiny veneer, Dallas is home to several authentically high-quality art museums.

Be sure to visit the **Dallas Museum of Art** and the Meadows Museum. Fair Park makes things easy for visitors by concentrating its eight museums – including the **Children's Aquarium, Museum of Nature and Science,** and automotive museum – in one 300-acre complex.

HOUSTON

You could spend several days exploring Houston's remarkable art museums. At the top of the priority list is the **Museum of Fine Arts,** featuring one of the country's premium collections of art objects, painting, and sculpture. The **Menil Museum** offers an interesting combination of ancient and modern art, and the **Contemporary Art Museum** features ambitious exhibitions.

AUSTIN

Austin may be one of the state's – even the country's – cultural capitals, but it's fairly lacking in visual-art opportunities. Fortunately, the **Blanton Museum of Art** has filled some of the void. Spend the afternoon at the capable **Austin Museum of Art** (downtown or the historic Laguna Gloria grounds) and the intriguing **Umlauf Sculpture Garden.**

SAN ANTONIO

San Antonio boasts several quality art museums offering a refined respite from the hectic Riverwalk scene. Be sure to visit the **San Antonio Museum of Art,** and drop by the impressive collection at the **McNay Art Museum.**

Fort Worth's highly respected Kimbell Art Museum

Marfa's Chinati Foundation is housed in a former army base.

Museum deftly documents its political and cultural implications. After lunch in the historic West End MarketPlace, visit Fair Park, where eight museums tell the story of Dallas's and Texas's rich past. For dinner and drinks, be sure to visit the Greenville entertainment district.

Day 3

Head south on I-35 to Austin for a day and night in Texas's creative hotbed. Visit the

the iconic State Capitol building in Austin

State Capitol, take a stroll down trendy South Congress Avenue, watch a million bats emerge from under a downtown bridge, and experience "the Live Music Capital of the World" in the Sixth Street entertainment district. The following day, head south on I-35 to San Antonio if your time in Texas is limited (jump to Day 8).

WEST TEXAS DETOUR
Day 4

Traverse the Texas Hill Country on Highway 290 West (from Austin) and enjoy the remaining scenic trek on I-10 before heading south on Route 17 to Marfa. The eight-hour drive to get here is *looong,* but the scenic basin and mesa landscape along I-10 is a welcome distraction. Reward yourself for the long drive by enjoying an evening cocktail and dinner at the Hotel Paisano.

Day 5

In the morning, grab a cup of java at the Squeeze Marfa to fuel up for the fascinating Chinati Foundation, which features contemporary art in a former Army base. Later in the afternoon, head over to Alpine for the Museum of the Big Bend and dinner at the

TEXAS'S OVERLOOKED NATURAL WONDERS

Texas is blessed with two particularly dynamic national parks – Big Bend and Guadalupe Mountains – but with a state this large, there are plenty more natural attractions that don't get the attention they deserve. Once you get outside the hustle and bustle of Texas's many major cities, there's an enormous canvas of natural wonders to explore, from forests and canyons to tropics and mountains. The best times to discover these treasures are during Texas's temperate spring months (March and April) and its fleeting fall (November). Seasoned hikers and campers from Texas or those undaunted by the heat will brave the brutally hot summer months to play outside. Whether you're planning a weeklong trek through the canyons or a day hike through the Big Thicket, be sure to bring plenty of water and sunscreen. Winter months can be deceiving, with sun and clear skies one day and ice storms the next.

spring wildflowers in bloom at Palo Duro Canyon in the Texas Panhandle

PALO DURO CANYON

For outdoors enthusiasts, it's well worth the drive (or flight) to the Amarillo area to witness Palo Duro Canyon. The multihued walls, rock towers, and sheer drops appear to be straight out of a Road Runner cartoon, but there's nothing comical about the natural beauty of this otherworldly landscape. Bikes offer an especially rewarding method of experiencing Palo Duro, the second-largest canyon in the country.

ENCHANTED ROCK

The Hill Country's Enchanted Rock State Natural Area is not quite as impressive as Palo Duro, but it has its own charm and an especially large aura of Native American lore associated with it. This massive dome of solid granite is said to have been a location of human sacrifices with "ghost fires" appearing at night. It's a moderate walk to the top, where you'll be rewarded with breathtaking views of the surrounding Hill Country.

NATURAL BRIDGE CAVERNS

Natural Bridge Caverns outside San Antonio is one of the premier caverns in the country.

Experience this natural wonder as part of a regular tour group, or if you're especially adventurous, sign up in advance for the Adventure Tour excursion for some rappelling and exploring in a primitive natural cavern.

BIG THICKET NATIONAL PRESERVE

Covering nearly 100,000 acres, the Big Thicket National Preserve in East Texas features a diverse range of natural features, from pine trees and cactus to swamps and hills. Summertime can be sticky with humidity, but hiking and camping on a cool spring day can be especially rewarding.

DINOSAUR VALLEY STATE PARK

Just outside Dallas lies a prehistoric natural wonder known as Dinosaur Valley State Park. Rock formations from nearly 113 million years ago have been exposed by water erosion, revealing some of the best-preserved dinosaur tracks in the world. It's a fun and fascinating place to visit, whether you're traveling alone or with the family.

the stunning Santa Elena Canyon in Big Bend

Reata. After sundown, be sure to look for the mysterious Marfa Lights.

Day 6

Head south on Route 188 to Big Bend National Park for a day of hiking (the Santa Elena Canyon is a must-see), or simply soak up the beauty of this natural wonder via a scenic drive through the Chisos Mountains. A side trip to the abandoned mining town of Terlingua is also an appealing option. Spend the night camping or in the Chisos Mountains Lodge.

Day 7

Take another Big Bend hike (the Lost Mine Trail is highly recommended) or head back to Fort Davis for a quick visit to McDonald Observatory or Fort Davis National Historic Site before making the long trek back to Central Texas.

BACK TO CIVILIZATION
Day 8

Start your day in San Antonio by visiting Texas's most famous attraction: the Alamo. Afterward, take a stroll along the scenic and bustling Riverwalk, where you can lunch on tacos and enchiladas at Rio Rio Cantina. Afterward, visit the Alamo's historic siblings, the

four other 18th-century structures that make up the Missions National Historical Park, or search for tempting Mexican imports and dinner in the King William Historic District.

Day 9

Head east on I-10 to Houston for an out-of-this-world experience at the NASA Space Center. Visit the Museum District to choose from any of its 14 world-class facilities, or for something completely distinctive, check out the bizarre folk art of The Orange Show.

Houston's Orange Show offers an eclectic collection of folk art.

▶ REMEMBER THE ALAMO!

The Lone Star State's rich heritage is proudly displayed throughout Texas, but several attractions outside the big cities offer authentic windows to the past. For a chronological perspective, start with the San Antonio missions (early 1700s), which tell the story of Spain's role in early Texas history when priests attempted to "civilize" Native Americans by converting them to Catholicism. More than 100 years later, frontier forts were established along the path of westward-bound settlers to help protect the pioneers from the same Indian tribes. In the later part of the 1800s, Texas's cowboy legacy came to life along the Chisholm Trail, where millions of Longhorns and other cattle were herded northward to markets in Kansas. In the 1940s, legendary Route 66 blazed a different kind of trail through the Texas Panhandle, allowing motorists to hit the road in search of adventure and new horizons.

San Angelo's historic Fort Concho

Day 1

You can spend an entire day (or two) along a 5.5-mile stretch of Texas's living history at San Antonio's Missions National Historical Park. Each of these historic stone structures— Mission Concepción, Mission San José, Mission San Juan, Mission Espada, and the famous Mission San Antonio de Valero (a.k.a. the Alamo)—offers a different perspective of the Spanish influence in Texas.

Days 2-3

Texas's frontier forts are spread across the western portion of the state, so it will take a couple days to drive between even the most noteworthy of the bunch. Begin at Fort Concho in San Angelo to get a true sense of what life was like for Army soldiers and ordinary citizens in mid-1800s Texas. Fort Davis, about a four-hour drive west, offers a fascinating look at the Army's Buffalo Soldiers (African-American troops), while Fort Phantom Hill in Abilene, about four hours to the northeast, is one of the most evocative historic sites in Texas.

Days 4-5

Cattle made their way to the Chisholm Trail from Texas's southern tip on the Gulf Coast through the middle of the state and north into Fort Worth and beyond (roughly following present-day I-35). Although it would take an entire day to make the trek by car, several must-see modern-day attractions along the historic trail include King Ranch in Kingsville, San Antonio's Texas Pioneers, Trail Drivers, and Rangers Museum, and the premier Cowtown site, the Fort Worth Stockyards National Historic District.

Days 6-7

"The Mother Road" beckons along legendary Route 66 in Texas's Panhandle. Though it was displaced by I-40 in the 1960s, there are still magnificent stretches of the original Route 66 offering travelers comfort and nostalgia in nearly a dozen small towns along the way. Make a point of visiting Cadillac Ranch and the Big Texan Steak Ranch in Amarillo, the Texas Old Route 66 and Devil's Rope Museum in McLean, the U Drop Inn in Shamrock, and the Midpoint Café in Adrian.

▶ BARBECUE AS A WAY OF LIFE

Barbecue is an art form and a lifestyle in Texas. In other parts of the country, the term "barbecue" is informally used as a general reference to tossing burgers or any kind of meat on a grill. In Texas, barbecuing is a verb referencing the calculated effort of smoking specific meats with the right kind of wood (which creates different flavors of smoke) for the optimal amount of time. It may sound a bit extravagant until you consider two things: the tantalizing taste of a perfectly cooked brisket, and the fact that this is Texas, where a lot of things are over-the-top. Not surprisingly, there are several different styles of barbecue considered to be most authentic, depending on the part of the state you're in. Why not try all of them and decide for yourself which is the best?

the smoke-soaked interior of Louie Mueller's Barbecue in Taylor

Lockhart

Many purists consider Lockhart the Holy Land of Texas barbecue. Hard-core barbecue aficionados insist the ideal experience is at Kreuz Market, where the meat is so perfectly smoked—particularly the pork chop—it would be insulting to slather it with sauce, which isn't even available. Just down the road is Smitty's, which is related to Kreuz's (it's a long story) yet doesn't frown on having sauce alongside their succulent meats. You also can't go wrong with Black's Barbecue or Chisholm Trail, which offer more traditional yet equally tempting fare.

Austin and Environs

Though several joints in Austin's outlying areas are nationally known for their venerable and authentic 'cue (Cooper's in Llano, Louie Mueller's in Taylor, and Southside Market in Elgin), the Capital City boasts its own hotbed of acclaimed barbecue restaurants. At Stubbs' Bar-B-Q, the hickory-smoked barbecue is legendary—the brisket, in particular—and the sauce is the best in town:

a perfect combination of vinegary tang and peppery bite. Just down the road, Franklin Barbecue offers succulent beef brisket, tender pork ribs, and flavorful sausage in a prime downtown location.

West Texas

Not as acclaimed as other approaches, West Texas's open-pit cowboy-style barbecue is still worth sampling, especially if you already happen to be in the area. One of the best examples of this approach is at Jack Jordan's Bar-B-Q in Odessa, where the beef ribs reign supreme and the fiery disposition of the locals is represented in the restaurant's ample supply of jalapeños and Tabasco. While you're out roaming the range, also stop by Western Sky in San Angelo for a better-than-average cowboy-style rib plate.

DALLAS AND FORT WORTH

Houston may be Texas's biggest city, but it doesn't pack the powerful punch of the Dallas–Fort Worth Metroplex. These two North Texas cities encompass much of what Texas represents—the Wild West cattle-driving culture, and the Southern-fried glitzy lifestyle, respectively.

This perfect combination of uniquely Texas elements makes the Metroplex an ideal place to kick off a journey to the Lone Star State. Visitors can immerse themselves in all things Texas and have themselves a good ol' time in the process. Stop by the stockyards. Do the *Dallas* TV show museum. Buy those boots, hats, and belt buckles. And be sure to load up on the trinity of Texas cuisine—barbecue, Tex-Mex, and down-home Southern cookin'—at any of the dozens of top-notch restaurants

throughout Dallas and Fort Worth. After soaking up the Metroplex, discover the genuine charm of the area's outlying communities. Magnificent courthouses anchor downtown squares, which offer distinct Texas antiques, refurbished historic theaters, and perfect pecan pies.

Daily weather reports remind North Texans they're still firmly planted on the southern edge of the Great Plains. Summertime highs regularly reach triple digits, and winters often bring subfreezing temperatures and snowstorms.

Fortunately, Texas's version of the Twin Cities offers plenty of diversions from the weather. World-class art museums, professional sports teams, rodeos, and shopping are first-class attractions in the Metroplex, and side trips to charming nearby towns such as

HIGHLIGHTS

◖ Sixth Floor Museum: John F. Kennedy's legacy survives at this fascinating downtown museum. Informative exhibits and intriguing artifacts tell the story of JFK's powerful political career and his family's mythical version of Camelot (page 26).

◖ Fair Park: A compelling collection of cultural museums awaits in equally impressive art deco buildings in this 300-acre complex, which gained international attention after hosting the grand 1936 Texas Centennial Exposition (page 27).

◖ Mesquite Championship Rodeo: The Mesquite rodeo is a big-time operation featuring the sport's top riders competing in classic events like bareback riding, team roping, bull riding, cowgirl barrel racing, saddle bronco riding, and steer wrestling (page 36).

◖ Fort Worth Stockyards National Historic District: Once an important destination for cattle drivers who rustled steer from ranches across the state, the Stockyards now primarily serve as a cultural attraction, complete with Wild West saloons, historical museums, clothing boutiques, a rodeo arena, and even some genuine livestock activity (page 55).

◖ The Kimbell Art Museum: One of the finest art museums of its kind in the country, The Kimbell is brimming with significant and intriguing works of art in a remarkably designed building. Art ranges from modern masters such as Picasso and Matisse to European classics from El Greco and Rembrandt (page 57).

◖ The Modern Art Museum of Fort Worth: Stunning for its building alone, "The Modern" is a remarkable structure featuring more than 2,600 significant works of international modern art (page 57).

◖ Billy Bob's Texas: Billed as "the world's largest honky-tonk," Billy Bob's in Fort Worth boasts three acres of interior space featuring a bull ring for live bull riding (no mechanical knockoffs here), a Texas-worthy oversized dance floor, a live music venue, arcade and casino games, and 32 individual bar stations (page 64).

◖ Dinosaur Valley State Park: Located in Glen Rose, Dinosaur Valley State Park features 100-million-year-old dinosaur tracks in its limestone riverbeds, including the world's first-discovered tracks from the 30-ton sauropod (page 74).

LOOK FOR ◖ TO FIND RECOMMENDED SIGHTS, ACTIVITIES, DINING, AND LODGING.

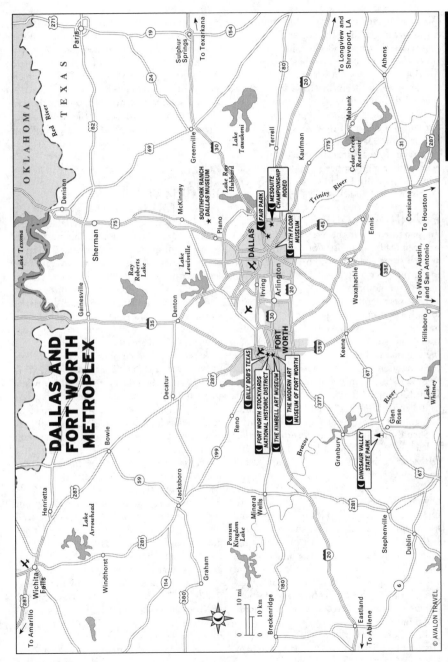

DALLAS AND FORT WORTH METROPLEX

OKLAHOMA

TEXAS

Red River

◄ FAIR PARK
◄ MESQUITE CHAMPIONSHIP RODEO
◄ SIXTH FLOOR MUSEUM
★ SOUTHFORK RANCH DALLAS MUSEUM

DALLAS

Arlington
Irving

FORT WORTH

◄ BILLY BOB'S TEXAS
◄ FORT WORTH STOCKYARDS NATIONAL HISTORIC DISTRICT
◄ THE KIMBELL ART MUSEUM
◄ THE MODERN ART MUSEUM OF FORT WORTH

◄ DINOSAUR VALLEY STATE PARK

To Amarillo
Wichita Falls
To Abilene
To Waco, Austin, and San Antonio
To Houston
To Longview and Shreveport, LA
To Texarkana

Paris
Sulphur Springs
Denison
Sherman
Gainesville
Henrietta
Windthorst
Jacksboro
Bowie
Decatur
Reno
Denton
McKinney
Greenville
Terrell
Kaufman
Mabank
Athens
Corsicana
Ennis
Waxahachie
Hillsboro
Keene
Granbury
Glen Rose
Stephenville
Dublin
Eastland
Breckenridge
Graham
Mineral Wells

Lake Texoma
Ray Roberts Lake
Lake Lewisville
Lake Ray Hubbard
Lake Tawakoni
Cedar Creek Reservoir
Lake Whitney
Possum Kingdom Lake
Lake Arrowhead

Trinity River
Brazos River

271
19
154
24
80
20
82
69
30
175
31
287
75
45
35E
30
20
35W
67
377
281
199
59
114
380
180
6
20

10 mi
10 km

© AVALON TRAVEL

Waxahachie and Denton reveal the community spirit that migrated to the area with its proud pioneers. The region's 30-plus lakes offer additional sources of entertainment and respite, an inviting option on a hot summer day.

The towering twin metro cities have cemented their reputations—Dallas as a financial hub of the South, and Fort Worth as an agricultural center of the West. Though the two are only separated by about 35 miles, their cultural differences are extensive, offering travelers to this region the best of both worlds: glitz and grit, The Big D and Cowtown, the Old South and the Wild West.

PLANNING YOUR TIME

To get a true sense of the intriguing differences between Dallas and Fort Worth, plan to spend at least three or four days in the Metroplex; toss in an other couple of days for side trips to nearby communities.

Dallas is a good place to start, and its downtown is a perfect jumping-off point. Spend the morning in the busy historic commercial district—check out the art deco skyscrapers and the original Neiman Marcus store—and use the afternoon to soak up local history in the West End district, including the essential Sixth Floor Museum. Afterward, drop by the Deep Ellum entertainment district for dinner, clubbing, or live music.

Spend the following day absorbing Dallas culture at Fair Park and the Dallas Arts District. Fair Park, just a few minutes east of downtown, is home to eight worthy museums and the enormous State Fair of Texas each October. The Arts District, meanwhile, features the must-see Dallas Museum of Art and several other notable cultural attractions.

If you have kids or are just playful by nature, plan to spend a day between Dallas and Fort Worth in Arlington, home to several amusement parks (the legendary Six Flags Over Texas, and Six Flags Hurricane Harbor), Cowboys Stadium, and the Rangers Ballpark in Arlington.

The Fort Worth Stockyards National Historic District is an essential stop for any Texas tourist. Spend half a day absorbing the sights, sounds, and even the smells of the Livestock Exchange, Cowtown Coliseum, and Stockyards Museum. Plan to spend an entire day in the Fort Worth Cultural District, which includes the world-class Kimbell Art Museum as well as other essential attractions such as the Amon Carter Museum, the Modern Art Museum of Fort Worth, and the National Cowgirl Museum and Hall of Fame. If you still have time, visit the impressive Fort Worth Zoo.

INFORMATION AND SERVICES

There are plenty of resources available to help make a trip to the Metroplex area hassle free. It may seem daunting to tackle the country's sixth-largest city, but Dallas has several excellent information centers nearby where visitors can inquire about directions, equipment rental, and other travel-related assistance. Likewise, the region's outlying smaller communities have visitors centers offering maps and advice for navigating rural areas.

A handy phone number to keep nearby is **Travelers Aid Dallas/Fort Worth,** 972/574-4420. Rather than providing tips about where to go and how to get there, this service offers specific information about travel-related issues such as foreign-language translation, car seat rental, military assistance, Western Union availability, crisis counseling, and emergency travel assistance. If you're arriving by air, you may also want to jot down the number for **DFW Airport Visitor Information,** 972/574-3694, which provides information about transportation options from the airport and directions to Metroplex-area accommodations and attractions. For international travelers, the DFW Airport has a useful 24-hour foreign-exchange machine that handles 20 different currencies. Detailed information is available at 972/574-4754. Also, the **Texas Department of Transportation** provides emergency road condition information and suggested road-trip routing at 800/452-9292.

For those who wish to drop by a facility and

speak with someone face-to-face, there are several visitors centers throughout North Texas offering detailed maps, brochures, and local know-how about specific travel services in the area. Two of the most comprehensive services for travel in North Texas are located in small surrounding communities. They are: **The Dallas/Fort Worth Area Tourism Council** (701 S. Main St. in Grapevine, 817/329-2438, www.visitdallas-fortworth.com) and the **Texas Historical Commission's Lakes Trail Region** office (116 W. Bridge St. in Granbury, 817/573-1114, www.texaslakestrail.com).

Other North Texas travel centers focusing on specific cities include the **Dallas Tourism Information Center** (100 Houston St., in Dallas, 800/232-5527, www.tourtexas.com/dallas) and the **Fort Worth Visitors Center** (415 Throckmorton St. in the Fort Worth Stockyards, 817/336-8791, www.tourtexas.com/fortworth).

GETTING THERE AND AROUND

Dallas/Fort Worth International Airport is the world's third-busiest passenger airport in operations and serves nearly 152,000 passengers daily to 171 worldwide destinations. For more information, contact 972/973-8888 or www.dfwairport.com. The city's old airport now houses Southwest Airlines' **Love Field**

Airport. It's not nearly as overwhelming as DFW, but its smaller size also means fewer flight options are available (two airlines serve 60 destinations throughout the United States). For more information, contact 214/670-6080 or www.southwest.com. Also, the **Wichita Falls Municipal Airport,** a joint military/civilian endeavor, is served by American Eagle, with four flights daily to the DFW airport. For more information contact 940/855-3621 or www.cwftx.net.

Since the Metroplex is so spread out, renting a car is usually the best option to maximize flexibility while traveling. However, despite being newer Southern cities, Dallas and Fort Worth both have surprisingly popular and well-designed public transportation systems that cater mainly to commuters but offer visitor services as well. The **Dallas Area Rapid Transit** system (referred to as the DART by locals) dashes among 13 area communities with rail, bus, and rideshare services. DART has a line to the DFW International Airport and also to Fort Worth via the Trinity Railway Express (TRE). For more information contact 214/979-1111 or www.DART.org. The **Fort Worth Transportation Authority** (the "T" to locals) provides transportation to the stockyards and the city's cultural district, with access to Dallas via the TRE. For more information, contact 817/215-8600 or www.the-t.com.

Dallas

Dallas (population 1,232,940) prospered and declined at different times compared to most other major U.S. cities, and its downtown buildings reflect these fluctuations. In the course of one city block you'll find everything from late-19th-century commercial structures to Classical Revival buildings to art deco office towers to 1950s modern architecture. Many of Dallas's significant historical events occurred in the mid-20th century, evident in the locales associated with John F. Kennedy's assassination and in Fair Park's stunning edifices.

Downtown Dallas's first transformation occurred in the late 1800s when the city became an increasingly important financial center. Intersecting railroads brought business to and from the city, and Dallas's cotton exchange and agricultural equipment manufacturers added to the city's growth. The city's distinctive historic architecture is displayed in its buildings from the 1936 Texas Centennial Exposition, which brought more than 50 new art deco structures to Fair Park as well as world-renowned science exhibits, music, and attractions for millions of

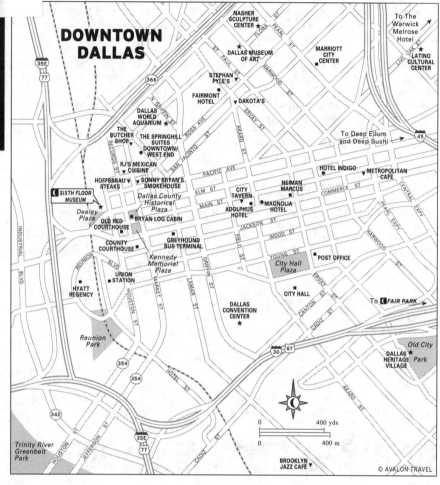

DOWNTOWN DALLAS

visitors to experience. Dallas also has the distinction of introducing the convenience store to suburban America, with the Oak Cliff area south of downtown spawning the 7-Eleven chain (it offered milk and eggs on Sundays and evenings, when most grocery stores were closed).

Above all, the city is remembered as the site of John F. Kennedy's shocking assassination on November 22, 1963, when shots were fired at the president's motorcade in Dealey Plaza. The ramifications of the fatal gunshots would last

for decades, as politicians and citizens deliberated over details while forming and debunking countless assassination conspiracy theories. Add to that the Dallas Cowboys (don't forget the cheerleaders) and the famous *Dallas* TV show, and the result is a fascinatingly diverse Southern city that Texas is proud to call its own.

SIGHTS
⬤ Sixth Floor Museum

The most-visited heritage attraction in North

Texas is the Sixth Floor Museum (411 Elm St., 214/747-6660, www.jfk.org, 9 A.M.–6 P.M. daily, $13.50 adults, $12.50 seniors and children 6–18). The museum is dedicated to the life, death, and legacy of John F. Kennedy, the 35th president of the United States. Upon entering the facility, visitors confront a dramatic quote from JFK: "History, after all, is the memory of a nation." The museum proceeds to jog those memories with exhibits, artifacts, and films providing a slice of American life in the early 1960s and the subsequent impact of JFK's assassination. The most intense and sobering area of the museum is the spot near the sixth-floor window where the fatal shots were allegedly fired. The area remains in its original setting as the school book depository, and its Plexiglas enclosure provides a somewhat creepy window to the afternoon of November 22, 1963. By the time most visitors leave, they've come away with a sense of how the world was affected by the actions in the building on that day, and ideally they've captured the spirit of Kennedy's life to use it in a positive way.

C Fair Park

Fair Park makes things easy for visitors by concentrating its diverse and fascinating mix of museums, exhibit halls, parks, plazas, sports facilities, theaters, parking lots, and livestock facilities in one 300-acre complex. Fair Park was the site of the grand 1936 Texas Centennial Exposition, and it's best known for its 100-plus years as the site of the gigantic State Fair of Texas each October. For those visiting Dallas any other time of the year, Fair Park still has plenty of entertaining attractions. The park's centerpiece is the stunning **Hall of State,** a National Historic Landmark building offering Texas history exhibits along with tours and stage performances providing additional insight into this remarkable art deco structure. Also on the grounds is the 1930 Cotton Bowl, the legendary stadium that served as the first home of the Dallas Cowboys and currently hosts the Cotton Bowl Classic and highly anticipated "Red River Rivalry"—the traditional University of Texas vs. University of Oklahoma

football game each October. Of the museums in the Fair Park complex, the following are most notable:

Texas Museum of Automotive History (1221 Midway Plaza Dr., 214/543-7047 or 469/554-7340, www.tmah.org, Tues.–Sun. 10 A.M.–6 P.M., $10 adults, $6.50 seniors and students, $5 children ages 2–11) is the newest addition to Fair Park's collection of museums, revving up the engines of car aficionados of all stripes, from commuters to professional racers. Opened in late 2010, the museum highlights the relationship between commercial vehicles and race cars, showcasing their design, engineering, and technology. Visitors will marvel at the fancy international race cars as well as the unique creations developed for everyday drivers over the decades. The museum plans to move to a permanent location within Fair Park by 2013, so check ahead to see where you should set your own car's GPS system.

Children's Aquarium at Fair Park (1462 First Ave., 214/670-6826 or 469/554-7340, www.oceansofadventure.org, daily

© ANDY RHODES

the Hall of State in Dallas's Fair Park

JFK'S ASSASSINATION

November 22, 1963, is so momentous, it is the basis of the question "Do you remember where you where on the day . . ." At 12:30 P.M. that afternoon (Texas time), John F. Kennedy was assassinated while riding in a presidential motorcade through Dallas's Dealy Plaza. Ask anyone age 60 or older where they were on that day at that time, and they'll likely be able to tell you their precise location.

The exact location of Kennedy's assassin, however, has been a topic of debate since 1963. Although the official investigation by the Warren Commission concluded the fatal shots were fired from the sixth floor of the nearby Texas School Book Depository by employee Lee Harvey Oswald, several conspiracy theories later evolved. Most involved political-based agendas related to the CIA, FBI, KGB, Fidel Castro, and even the Mafia. Some of these theories were based on several eyewitness accounts of shots being fired from a nearby grassy knoll, though evidence doesn't appear to support the speculation.

The issue still hadn't entirely been put to rest by the late 1970s, when the U.S. House Select Committee on Assassinations determined that Oswald likely was involved with a conspiracy. The subject was again debated when Oliver Stone released his controversial 1991 movie *JFK*.

The sixth floor of the book depository building has since become a museum dedicated to Kennedy's legacy and assassination. It details the best-known conspiracy theories and includes an eerie exhibit preserving the spot by the window where investigators later found three spent shells, a sniper's nest, and a rifle.

9 A.M.–4:30 P.M., $5) houses thousands of aquatic animals selected with kids in mind, including marine and freshwater fish, amphibians, reptiles, and invertebrates in its original art deco building from the Texas Centennial. The aquarium reopened in September 2010 after an $8 million restoration. The aquarium features a good sampling of some of the world's more bizarre aquatic animals, such as the "fishing" anglerfish, poisonous stonefish, albino alligators, and species from popular movies and books. Kids and adults will also enjoy the daily fish feedings at Stingray Bay, where they can interact with rays and small sharks.

The Museum of Nature and Science (3535 Grand Ave. and 1318 S. 2nd Ave., 214/428-5555, www.natureandscience.org, Mon.–Sat. 10 A.M.–5 P.M., Sun. noon–5 P.M., $10 adults, $9 seniors, $7 children 2–11, and $3.50 for the planetarium) is a combination of the former Dallas Museum of Natural History and the Science Place. The natural history component offers more than 200,000 items related to mammals, reptiles, marine life, birds, and insects. Covering approximately 1.7 billion years of earth history, the museum's collection includes mounted animals, four diorama halls featuring Texas wildlife, the Texas Dinosaurs Hall, and regular traveling exhibits. The Science Place portion has more than 200 permanent hands-on exhibits related to physics, astronomy, health, robotics, and nature, and features a public planetarium and IMAX theater.

Texas Discovery Gardens (3601 Martin Luther King Jr. Blvd., 214/428-7476, www.texasdiscoverygardens.org, daily 10 A.M.–5 P.M., $8 adults, $6 seniors, $4 children ages 3–11) strives to teach ways to conserve nature in urban environments with a focus on sustainable and organic gardening. The site's 7.5 acres includes the Rosine Smith Sammons Butterfly House and Insectarium, where guests can meander down a canopy walkway as they view hundreds of free-flying tropical butterflies and plants.

The African American Museum (3536 Grand Ave., 214/565-9026, www.aam-dallas.org, Tues.–Fri. 11 A.M.–5 P.M., Sat.

10 A.M.–5 P.M., free admission) showcases African-American artistic, cultural, and historical materials, and features one of the largest African-American folk art collections in the United States. The 38,000-square-foot structure is made of ivory stone and built in the shape of a cross. To evoke preindustrialized cultures of the African continent, the museum uses natural materials and design motifs throughout the building. Four galleries feature the cultural heritage of African-American art and history along with a research library, theater, studio arts area, and classrooms. The museum's permanent collections include African art, African-American fine art, and historical and political archives.

The **Women's Museum: An Institute for the Future** (3800 Parry Ave., 214/915-0860, www.thewomensmuseum.org, ues.–Sun. noon–5 P.M., $5 adults, $4 senior citizens and students, $3 children 5–12) showcases accomplishments of American women through exhibits, galleries, and programs. The museum, an affiliate of the Smithsonian, uses technology and interactive media to tell the stories of women—both famous and common—who impacted American culture socially and politically. The museum's permanent and traveling exhibits showcase diverse artwork from women across the globe, and its outreach programs provide education and support for women.

Dallas County Historical Plaza

Bound by Elm, Market, Commerce, and Houston Streets, this area is actually divided into two separate parts: **Founders Plaza** and the **Kennedy Memorial Plaza.** Founders Plaza contains an open area with several historical monuments and a reconstruction of Dallas founder John Neely Bryan's original log cabin. The Kennedy Memorial Plaza houses an unusual concrete structure surrounding a small JFK monument. Dallas residents tend to have a love/hate relationship with the structure, and its meaning and value are interpreted differently by each viewer.

One of Dallas's most beloved buildings stands on the western end of the Kennedy plaza: "Old Red," the 70,580-square-foot 1892 Romanesque-style Dallas County Courthouse. The enormous and stately building served a variety of public functions throughout the 1900s, but efficiency concerns resulted in several remodelings. Old Red has been undergoing restoration for many years and reopened as the **Old Red Museum of Dallas County History and Culture** (9 A.M.–5 P.M. daily, $8 adults, $6 students/seniors, $5 children ages 3–16). Its mission is to "inspire and educate visitors about the rich and varied cultural, economic, political and social history of the Dallas County area."

Dallas Museum of Art

The city's crown jewel of cultural museums is the Dallas Museum of Art (1717 N. Harwood, 214/922-1200, www.dm-art.org, Tues.–Sun. 11 A.M.–5 P.M., Thurs. 11 A.M.–9 P.M., $10 adults, $7 senior citizens, $5 students 12 and older), containing more than 24,000 works of world-class international art, from ancient to modern times. Anchoring the city's Arts

© ANDY RHODES

The Women's Museum in Dallas's Fair Park

A FAIR OF THE STATE

To experience the State Fair of Texas's sacred trinity, you'll need to (1) eat a corny dog while (2) watching the University of Texas vs. University of Oklahoma football game in the shadow of (3) Big Tex. Throw in some fried Twinkies and the country's tallest Ferris wheel, and you have a cultural legacy befitting of the Lone Star State.

This venerable autumn event – usually held the first three weeks of October – has been a Texas tradition since 1886, and during that time, it has experienced as many ups and downs as the old Comet roller coaster.

One of the highest peaks was in 1936, when Fair Park served as the site of Texas's mammoth state centennial celebration, featuring science exhibits with items made from a crazy new product called "plastic." The event's edible fare is another custom, with bizarre fried items like cookies, candy bars, and even ice cream drawing people to brazenly sample the newest concoction.

For many, Big Tex is the ultimate representative of the State Fair of Texas. Brought on board in 1952, the big fella is a 52-foot-tall mechanical cowboy figure at the entrance of Fair Park who welcomes visitors with a huge "Howdy, folks!" Big Tex was originally a Santa Claus in Kerens, Texas, and was purchased for $750. After outfitting him with size 70 boots and a 75-gallon hat, Big Tex was transformed into the beloved Texas-sized ambassador for the State Fair of Texas.

For the past decade or so, the fair has become perhaps best known for its featured fried food. Each year, vendors try to top previous experiments by introducing something even more outrageous than before. By 2011, the additions included fried Snickers, fried bacon, fried cola, and fried beer. Yum!

District, the museum covers a lot of ground, from prehistoric Latin American ceramics and sculpture to work from contemporary artists such as Jackson Pollock and Tatsuo Miyajima. The museum's highlight is its remarkable collection of European and impressionist art by Renoir, Van Gogh, Cézanne, and Monet. Also of note is the facility's impressive artwork from Africa, Asia, and ancient Mediterranean history, as well as the outdoor sculpture garden with water walls and contemporary benches. Make a point of visiting the museum's Decorative Arts Wing, which features a re-created Mediterranean villa with lavish furniture and silver furnishings sharing space with masterpieces by Cézanne and Van Gogh. In 2008, the museum opened the Center for Creative Connections, an interactive space that engages visitors in the creative process by experiencing works of art in a more direct way. Of note: Museum admission is free on the first Tuesday of each month, and it hosts "Thursday Night Live!" featuring live jazz music each Thursday 6–8 P.M.

Nasher Sculpture Center

Providing a downtown urban oasis of art and nature in the Arts District is the impressive Nasher Sculpture Center (2001 Flora St., 214/242-5100, www.nashersculpturecenter. org, Tues.–Sun. 11 A.M.–5 P.M., $10 adults, $7 seniors, $5 students, free on first Sat. and for members and children under 5). Located directly across from the Dallas Museum of Art, the facility includes an elegant 54,000-square-foot building by architect Renzo Piano (known for designing Paris's Georges Pompidou Center) featuring the contemporary art collection of philanthropist and collector Raymond Nasher. It's worth making the trip to experience the stunning two-acre sculpture garden, created by landscape architect Peter Walker. The open-air environment offers a distinctive museum experience featuring internationally acclaimed artwork. The Nasher Collection is considered one of the primary collections of contemporary 20th-century sculpture in the world and is comprised of hundreds of works by internationally acclaimed artists. The facility is particularly proud of the depth of perspective it provides for prominent artists such as Henri Matisse (11 sculptures), Pablo Picasso (7), Raymond Duchamp-Villon (7), and Joan Miró (4).

Southfork Ranch (*Dallas* Museum)

The hit TV show *Dallas,* which became a worldwide phenomenon in the late 1970s and early 1980s, spawned an equally popular spectacle when tours opened at the show's filming location, the mythical Southfork Ranch (in the nearby community of Parker, 972/442-7800, www.southforkranch.com, daily 9 A.M.–5 P.M., $9.50 adults, $8 senior citizens, $7 children ages 5–12). Thanks to international syndication, *Dallas* became synonymous with the state of Texas for millions of people across the globe. Whether this did more to help or hurt Texas's reputation remains a topic of debate, but there's no underestimating the pop culture marvel the show became. Therefore, it shouldn't be surprising that hordes of fans descend on Southfork annually to tour the famous Ewing Mansion and view memorabilia such as the gun that shot J. R., Lucy's wedding dress, and Jock Ewing's Lincoln Continental. From U.S. 75 north, take exit 30 and drive east

on FM 2514/Parker Road for six miles; turn right on FM 2551 (Hogge Road) and look for the sign on the left.

Dallas Heritage Village

Located on the southern edge of downtown, Dallas Heritage Village (1515 S. Harwood St., 214/421-5141, www.dallasheritagevillage.org, Tues.–Sat. 10 A.M.–4 P.M., Sun. noon–4 P.M., $7 adults, $5 seniors, and $4 children ages 4–12) is an outdoor museum devoted to the turn-of-the-20th-century's architectural and cultural history. The heritage village is a living-history museum, meaning visitors will encounter people (employees) dressed in period costume discussing the significance of the structures or the time period they represent. Through these interpreters and by soaking up the surrounding scenery, visitors learn about North Texas life from roughly 1840 through 1910. The museum features 38 restored historic structures including Victorian homes, an antebellum mansion, a train depot, a barbershop, a school, a church, and several commercial buildings. The village sits on 13 wooded acres, which feel eerily uninhabited on slow days, and hosts events for children (summer camps, blacksmithing, theatrical performances, animal visits). There are picnic areas and walking trails.

THE *DALLAS* PHENOMENON

In the spring of 1980, *Dallas* was on everyone's mind. And the question on everyone's lips was "Who Shot J. R.?" The country was captivated by the mysterious intruder who fired shots at bullish oil magnate J. R. Ewing. With more than a dozen potential candidates, speculation ran rampant – people even placed Vegas bets on the outcome.

Decades later, most Americans don't remember or even care who pulled the trigger (incidentally, it was Kristin, J. R.'s recent romantic interest), but anyone who watched TV in the early 1980s likely recalls tuning in on Friday nights to keep up with the Ewing clan's latest dramatic adventures.

The Texas mystique played a big role in the show's success, serving as an intriguing backdrop along with the stereotypical big oil, big money, and everything's-bigger-in-Texas sensibilities. The Ewing family's home base was South Fork Ranch, a fittingly sprawling kingdom that, along with the cowboy posturing, came to represent Texas excess to viewers across the globe.

The show itself, which aired from 1978 to 1991, is considered one of TV's most significant prime-time dramas, launching countless other series dedicated to shady business dealings, romantic trysts, dysfunctional families, thrilling season finale cliffhangers, and incredibly poofy hair.

Meadows Museum

The Meadows Museum (on the Southern Methodist University campus, 5900 Bishop Blvd., 214/768-2516, www.meadowsmuseumdallas.org, Tues.–Sat. 10 A.M.–5 P.M., Sun. noon–5 P.M., $8 adults and students 12 and older) is best known for its enormous and impressive collection of Spanish art. The artwork and galleries were a gift to SMU from prominent Dallas businessman Algur Meadows, founder of the General American Oil Company of Texas. The museum includes work from the 15th through 20th centuries by some of the world's foremost painters (who also happen to be Spanish), including El Greco, Velázquez, Goya, Miró, and Picasso. The vast number of works by Goya is particularly noteworthy, as is the museum's collection of 20th-century sculpture. Of note: The museum offers free admission on Thursday 5–8 P.M.

Dallas Zoo

Although the Dallas Zoo (650 S. R.L. Thornton Frwy./I-35E, 469/554-7500, www.dallas-zoo.org, daily 9 A.M.–5 P.M., $12 adults, $9 seniors and children 3–11, parking $7 per car) doesn't have the same top-notch reputation as the Fort Worth Zoo, it's still worth visiting. Beginning with the enormous giraffe sculpture at the front gate, it's clear the zoo's focus is on African animals, and they do a good job bringing the continent to life in their Giants of the Savanna and Wilds of Africa exhibits. Divided by geographical habitat, the Africa area features jungles of monkeys and gorillas (be sure to check out the gorilla conservation center). A monorail ride through woodland, river, and desert regions of the continent provides glimpses of wildebeests, gazelles, and many different bird species. Other areas of the zoo offer up-close views of big cats, elephants, kangaroos, and reptiles, and there's a special treat for those who've always wanted to ride a camel—camel rides! The children's zoo is worth visiting if you have little ones in tow.

Dallas World Aquarium

Not to be confused with the Dallas Aquarium in Fair Park, The Dallas World Aquarium (1801 N. Griffin St., 214/720-2224, www.dwazoo.com, daily 10 A.M.–5 P.M., $20.95 adults, $16.95 seniors, $12.95 children 3–12) is an interesting combination of aquarium and zoo, with monkeys scurrying overhead and sharks lurking nearby. Exotic plants and creatures from around the world add to the sense of being transported to another habitat, especially in the Orinoco—Secrets of the River rainforest exhibit with birds, bats, and reptiles in the company of a 40-foot waterfall. The aquarium's highlight is a 22,000-gallon tunnel with a panoramic view of underwater reef life from the Continental Shelf. Be sure to attend a feeding event (schedules available at admission) or experience a colorful show by the Mayan Performance Troupe (seven times daily on weekends).

Dallas Arboretum

Overlooking scenic White Rock Lake, The Dallas Arboretum (8525 Garland Rd., 214/515-6500, www.dallasarboretum.org, daily 9 A.M.–5 P.M., $10 adults, $9 seniors, $7 children 3–12) offers 66 acres of scenic grounds containing floral, herbal, and vegetable gardens. It's particularly fetching from March through May, when the grounds have an iridescent green glow peppered by floral bursts of red, yellow, and white. Although spring is the best time of year for the vegetation, any season is a good time to escape the hustle, bustle, and concrete of urban life for the arboretum's oasis of nature and peace. Also on-site are the Spanish colonial–style DeGolyer mansion and museum as well as the Camp Estate, which feature 17th- and 18th-century art and furniture.

Latino Cultural Center

Designed by noted architect Ricardo Legorreta, The Latino Cultural Center (2600 Live Oak, 214/671-0045, www.dallasculture.org, Tues.–Sat. 10 A.M.–5 P.M., admission required for some events) is worth visiting for the building itself. Although the 27,000-square-foot facility doesn't offer any large-scale exhibits, it includes a gallery dedicated to Latino art and a courtyard featuring sculpture from international and local artists. The center also has a 300-seat theater that hosts occasional cultural performances, and rooms available for readings, workshops, lectures, and meetings related to Latino culture. Check the Web page for event listings.

Frontiers of Flight Museum

Located at Dallas Love Field, the Frontiers of Flight Museum (6911 Lemmon Ave., 214/350-3600, www.flightmuseum.com, Mon.–Sat. 10 A.M.–5 P.M., Sun. 1–5 P.M., $8 adults, $6 children age 3–17) features aircraft from roughly the past 100 years. The museum covers everything from early aircraft of the 1920s to jets and rockets of the first decade of the new millennium. Of particular interest is the Lighter than Air exhibit, which pays homage to the zeppelins and giant blimps of the past.

ENTERTAINMENT AND EVENTS
Performing Arts

The Morton H. Meyerson Symphony Center (2301 Flora St., 214/692-0203, www.dallassymphony.com) in the Dallas Arts District is the city's premier venue for the performing arts. In addition to housing the prestigious **Dallas Symphony Orchestra,** the impressive facility, with an auditorium designed by world-renowned architect I. M. Pei, also hosts touring shows for the cultured crowd, including a pops concert series and adult contemporary artists.

Another of the city's highly respected performing arts organizations is the **Dallas Opera** (2301 Flora St., 214/443-1000, www.dallasopera.org), which performs its work at the AT&T Performing Arts Center. The company, which performs several high-profile operas each year, has also presented many international stars in their American debuts, including Dame Joan Sutherland and Plácido Domingo.

The ornate **Majestic Theatre** (1925 Elm St., 214/880-0137, www.liveatthemajestic.com) is a 1921 vaudeville-era gem located near the heart of downtown. The 1,700-seat Majestic stages national and local musical productions, dramatic plays, comedy shows, and concerts.

Bars and Clubs

Nightlife in Dallas is a big ol' happenin' scene, and there are plenty of bars, dance clubs, and live music venues for any type of crowd. From Texas chic to student hangouts to gay bars, nightlife is one of the few cultural experiences in the Metroplex that's far superior in Dallas than in Fort Worth. Like most happening entertainment centers, the bars and clubs in Dallas switch names and ownership quicker than a socialite changes trendy sunglasses, so be sure to pick up a *Dallas Observer* (the city's alternative weekly, published every Thursday) to keep up to speed on the latest developments in club names and trends.

UPPER AND LOWER GREENVILLE

One of the city's consistently reliable nightlife areas is along Greenville Avenue paralleling Central Expressway (Route 75). Located just north of downtown near the Southern Methodist University campus, the district is referred to by locals as Upper Greenville and Lower Greenville (Mockingbird Lane is the dividing line). Both have essentially the same offerings, though Lower Greenville has a slightly more concentrated area of taverns, making it a better choice for facilitated bar hopping or ale sipping.

Lower Greenville is anchored by the **Granada Theater** (3524 Greenville Ave., 214/824-9933, www.granadatheater.com), a 1930s movie venue featuring live music, better-than-average food, and occasional special events such as Dallas Mavericks playoff games projected on the big screen. Other options include grabbing a pint and some steak fries down the road at the **Libertine Bar** (2101 Greenville Ave., 214/826-6850) and nearby pubs like the **Dubliner** (2818 Greenville Ave., 214/818-0911) and the neighborhood-friendly **Winedale Tavern** (2110 Greenville Ave., 214/823-5018).

Upper Greenville (extending north of Mockingbird to I-635/LBJ Freeway) is also worth checking out, especially if you're up for grabbing a beer in a comfortable environment where college kids tend to gravitate. The best of the bunch are just off Greenville on Yale and Dyer Streets. **Milo Butterfinger's** (5645 Yale Blvd., 214/363-0660) features an impressive selection of draft brews, **The Across the Street Bar** (5625 Yale Blvd., 214/363-0660) is a popular beer joint with occasional live music, and the **Ozona Bar & Grille** (4615 Greenville Ave., 214/265-9105) offers a comfy beer garden to kick back and enjoy a cold one.

DEEP ELLUM

Although Deep Ellum was ultratrendy more than a decade ago—a hipster district teeming with alternative-music venues and edgy nightclubs—the area is now almost the opposite, which can still have a certain charm if you're looking for a low-key evening where people don't feel the need to dress to impress. Regardless of the destination, there's definitely an appeal to the area's local history, evident in the architecture and signage reflecting its heritage as an African-American hub of business and entertainment in the 1920s. The name Deep Ellum is attributed to the then-locals' pronunciation of the words *deep elm*.

For live music, Deep Ellum's stalwart is the **Sons of Hermann Hall** (3414 Elm St., 214/747-4422, www.sonsofhermann.com, Wed.–Sat.), a remarkable historic building that oozes character while Texas artists perform roots and country music on stage. **Double Wide** (3510 Commerce St., 214/887-6510, www.double-wide.com) is a white-trash-themed bar with a big ol' silver tornado sculpture on the roof and offering bloozy and rough-around-the-edges rock bands and appropriately cheap beer in cans. Or you can edge your way into **Elbow Room** (3010 Gaston Ave., 214/828-9488, www.elbowroomdallas.com) for some tunes from their amazing jukebox, with a side of tasty food and shuffleboard.

COUNTRY AND WESTERN DANCING

Visitors looking for a true taste of Texas should definitely check out the legendary local branch of Houston's "Urban Cowboy" locale, **Gilley's**

Dallas (1601 S. Lamar St., 214/428-2919). It's the ultimate country and western honky-tonk for those who want to test their skills on the dance floor or the mechanical bull. Also worth checking out is the enormous and enormously entertaining **Cowboys Red River Dancehall** (10310 Technology Blvd. W., 214/352-1796), near Arlington, and the modest and genuinely lowdown **Adair's Saloon** in Deep Ellum (2624 Commerce St., 214/939-9900).

DANCE CLUBS

If you'd rather shake your hips than scoot your boots, head to **Lizard Lounge** (2424 Swiss Ave., 214/826-4768), featuring nationally known DJs, electro, neo-Gothic, and plenty of party people. Latin music is the big draw at **Club Babalu** (2912 McKinney Ave., 214/953-0300). One of downtown's best "traditional" dance clubs is **Purgatory Dallas** (2208 Main St., 214/749-5665), offering five levels of dancing, "from hell all the way up to heaven."

GAY BARS

Many of the city's gay bars are located on Cedar Springs Road northwest of downtown. The **Round-up Saloon** (3912 Cedar Springs Rd., 214/522-9611) features gay country & western dancing, and **JR's Bar & Grill** (3923 Cedar Springs Rd., 214/528-1004) and **Sue Ellen's** (3903 Cedar Springs Rd., 214/559-0707) are popular gay and lesbian bars with Dallas flavor.

Events
SPRING
Held each March, **Savor Dallas** is a true feast for the senses, featuring a "wine stroll" in the Arts District, celebrity chef cooking demos, and the International Grand Tasting, offering more than 500 wines and 50 chefs serving samples. Call 888/728-6747 for more information.

The Prairie Dog Chili Cookoff is a big ol' Texas-style event (don't worry, prairie dogs aren't part of the chili recipe), where chili tasting is only part of the fun (be sure to check out the Quail Egg–Eating World Championship).

It's the oldest and largest chili cook-off in the Metroplex area, at Traders Village (2602 Mayfield Rd.). Call 972/647-2331 for more information.

The Cinco de Mayo event in suburban Oak Cliff celebrates Mexico's victory over France in 1862 and features "the Big parade," carnival rides, food, and entertainment. Call 214/650-8381 for more information.

SUMMER
Each August, **Taste of Dallas** features restaurants, retail booths, Kids' Taste Town, and multiple music stages at historic Fair Park. Visit www.tasteofdallas.org for more information.

FALL
The legendary **State Fair of Texas,** held at Fair Park for more than 70 years, runs from mid-September through early October and is an absolute must-see if you're in the city at the time. Experience fried Twinkies, Big Tex, corny dogs, livestock shows, and the tallest Ferris wheel in the Western Hemisphere. Call 214/565-9931 for more information.

ZestFest, a spicy-food festival typically held each October, is now in suburban Irving. It offers plenty of spice for bold, flavor-seeking food enthusiasts. The festival features cooking demos by celebrity chefs, live music, and food samples. Call 972/252-7476 for more information and to confirm event dates.

WINTER
The popular **Trains at NorthPark** runs November–January at the NorthPark Center Mall (1030 North Park Center). The event, completely redesigned with new trains and landscapes in 2010, features more than 35 toy trains and has been a holiday tradition delighting children and toy train lovers since 1987. Visit www.rmhdallas.org for more information.

The Children's Medical Center Holiday Parade features floats, marching bands, and Santa himself. This annual event, complete with reserved bleacher seating, is a Dallas holiday tradition. Call 214/456-0113 for more information.

SHOPPING
Dallas takes its shopping very seriously. Although it doesn't have many well-kept little secrets offering bargain leather goods or Mexican imports like some other Texas cities, it's brimming with trendy boutiques and big-name department stores. In fact, Dallas claims to have more shopping centers per capita than anywhere else in the United States. Regardless, there are several alternatives to the generic shops found in most American cities.

Fashion and Department Stores
The mecca for serious shoppers is the original **Neiman Marcus** store in downtown Dallas (1618 Main St., 214/741-6911). Although it offers the same standard high-quality Neiman Marcus fare as others across the country, the items are housed inside the original department store building, and walking out of its doors onto the hustle and bustle of a busy downtown street is a rare New York City–style experience for shoppers in the South.

The Galleria (13350 Dallas Pkwy., 972/702-7100) is impressive for its mammoth size and its shopping options. A multilevel center with a hotel attached, the Galleria includes four-star restaurants, a year-round ice rink in the center, a five-theater cinema, and nearly 200 stores, including Saks Fifth Ave., Tiffany & Co., Gucci, and Nordstrom.

High-end stores are also the featured attraction at **NorthPark Shopping Center** (8687 N. Central Expwy., 214/890-0908), one of the country's first upscale indoor malls, completed in 1965. NorthPark Center still continues this tradition, offering a mix of luxury retail and fine dining with spacious courtyards and lush landscaping.

Western Wear
Not surprisingly, Dallas has several stores offering Western wear, and the following locations provide plenty of options for a night out at a local honky-tonk. Although some of the city's larger chains have closed, there are several smaller shops worth exploring for authentic cowboy gear. Chuck Norris and Larry

Hagman endorse **Wild Bill's Western** (311 N. Market St., 214/954-1050). On the upper end of the scale is the glitzy and high-quality **Cowboy Cool** (3699 McKinney Ave., 214/521-4500). Also worth visiting for affordable yet well-made cowboy gear—brand-name boots, shirts, hats, and jeans—are **Cavender's Boot City** (2833 LBJ Frwy., 972/239-1375), and the venerable **Shepler's** (18500 LBJ Frwy., 972/270-8811).

SPORTS AND RECREATION

Since it's the sixth-largest city in the country, Dallas has a remarkable selection of spectator sports to keep fans entertained. All the major professional sporting leagues are represented—football, baseball, basketball, and hockey—and several urban and suburban parks offer visitors a chance to get outside for sporting activities of their own. It's the rodeo, however, that sets Dallas's sports apart from other metropolitan areas in the United States.

◀ Mesquite Championship Rodeo

The Mesquite Championship Rodeo is the real deal. Located in the suburb of Mesquite—roughly a 20-minute drive east of downtown Dallas—this is a big-time professional rodeo featuring the sport's top riders with weekly broadcasts on the Nashville Network. The arena packs thousands of fans and families in a football-like environment every Friday and Saturday night from early April through late September.

It's well worth making a visit to experience this Western cultural tradition. Witness time-honored events such as bareback riding, bull riding, cowgirl barrel racing, team roping, saddle bronco riding, and steer wrestling along with rodeo clowns and plenty of cowboy activity. The arena is located in Mesquite on I-635 just off the Military Parkway exit. Tickets range from $7 to $30, and the arena's barbecue buffet is $7 for kids and $11 for adults. Call 972/285-8777 for more information.

AMERICA'S TEAM

Roger Staubach. Troy Aikman. Emmit Smith. All are football legends. All were Dallas Cowboys.

The Cowboys are a love-'em-or-hate-'em kind of team. With their dominant success in much of the 1970s and '90s, the Cowboys garnered their share of bandwagon fans – earning them the nickname "America's Team" – which also had the polarizing effect of creating hordes of Cowboy haters.

The team came to prominence under the helm of legendary coach Tom Landry, the fedora-donning head honcho who shaped and guided the team from their inception in 1960 all the way until 1989. During that time, the Cowboys posted 20 consecutive winning seasons, won 13 division championships, and appeared in Super Bowls V, VI, X, XII, and XIII, winning VI and XII. Overall, they've appeared in eight Super Bowls and won five of them.

Any discussion about the Dallas Cowboys would be incomplete without mentioning their famous cheerleaders. The name alone conjures up images of feathered hair, short white shorts, and, of course, spirited cheers guiding the team to victory. Although they came to prominence during the *Charlie's Angels*-era 1970s, the cheerleaders continue to serve as worldwide ambassadors for America's Team.

The latest chapter in the Cowboys' larger-than-life tale is their fancy new $1 billion (yup, billion) Cowboys Stadium. The enormous facility, nicknamed "Jerry World" or the "Jones Mahal" in reference to team owner Jerry Jones, includes a 60-yard-wide high-def screen inside the world's largest domed stadium.

Regardless of the Cowboys' rank in their division, Texans and other Americans will faithfully follow the team every Sunday during football season. And whatever the final score is, you can bet fans across the Lone Star State will be cheering (or muttering) "How 'bout them Cowboys!"

Professional Sports

FOOTBALL

The Dallas Cowboys, known by football fans as "America's Team," play from August to December at the fancy new $1 billion (yup, billion) Cowboys Stadium in Arlington (925 N. Collins St., 817/892-4161, www.dallas-cowboys.com). New Texas-worthy amenities include a 60-yard-wide high-definition screen inside the world's largest domed stadium. The Dallas Cowboy Cheerleaders are still there, along with their skimpy outfits and big hair.

BASEBALL

The Texas Rangers play from April to October at Rangers Ballpark in Arlington (about 20 minutes west of town at the intersection of I-30 and Hwy. 157, 817/273-5100, www.texasrangers.com) in one of Major League Baseball's most pleasant and aesthetically enjoyable stadiums.

BASKETBALL

The Dallas Mavericks, one of the National Basketball Association's consistently elite teams, play from November through April and often even longer into the playoffs at American Airlines Center (on Victory Ave. off I-35E just north of downtown, 214/665-4797, www.nba.com/mavericks).

HOCKEY

Despite its warm climate, Dallas has a respected hockey team that takes to the ice from October through mid-April. **The Dallas Stars** play at the American Airlines Center (on Victory Ave. off I-35E just north of downtown, 214/467-8277, www.dallasstars.com).

SOCCER

Major League Soccer has a devoted fan base in the Metroplex, and **FC Dallas** is the city's popular franchise (30 miles north of downtown in Frisco at 9200 World Cup Wy., 214/705-6700, www.fc.dallas.com. FC Dallas's (the FC stands for Futbol Club) season lasts from April to October.

Nature Trails

Dallas isn't known for its abundance of green space, but the city boasts several nature and walking trails to help urban dwellers and visitors get a taste of the great outdoors. Most outlying communities have suburban parks, but the following sites offer hiking trails in relatively remote natural surroundings near downtown for jogging, biking, strolling, or people watching.

Boulder Park (3200 W. Redbird Ln., 214/670 4100) includes more than six miles of trails through trees and hilly terrain along Five Mile Creek southwest of downtown. Most of the trails have been created for bike use, but there is a soft-surface hiking trail for nature lovers.

Maintained by the Dallas Off-Road Bicycle Association, this park is conveniently located near I-20 and Highway 67. Hosting approximately six miles of bike trails, Boulder Park offers the perfect ride for everyone. There are sections for beginners and others for advanced riders. Most of the trails have been created for bike use, but there is a soft-surface hiking trail for nature lovers. Here you'll find open sections, wooded areas, rocks, and water. This is truly fun for the entire family.

The L.B. Houston Nature Trail (between Dallas and Irving at Wildwood and California Crossing, 214/670-6244) is a good place to spot wildlife among native plants and trees. The 300-acre area offers four unpaved hiking trails in a dense wilderness area along the Elm Fork of the Trinity River. The trails are in slightly flatter terrain than the hike and bike trails, but the natural surfaces render them virtually impassable after heavy rainfall.

White Rock Creek Greenbelt (Hillcrest and Valley View, 214/670-8895), northeast of downtown, is one of Dallas's natural gems. A seven-mile paved hiking, bicycling, and jogging trail connects to a similar nine-mile trail that circles picturesque White Rock Lake.

ACCOMMODATIONS

Like most big cities, Dallas has a stunning range of hotels, from generic chains on equally uninspiring urban beltways to charmingly restored historic downtown gems. The Big D doesn't have a long list of options for people interested in soaking up nightlife and responsibly hoofing it back to bed, but most of the best hotels (enchanting historic locales in the heart of the city) are a 5- to 10-minute cab ride from the city's hopping entertainment districts. Not surprisingly, the alternatives for those keeping a close eye on their wallets are farthest away from many of the city's main activities. Keep in mind, safe and affordable hotels in one of the nation's largest cities will still cost nearly $100 a night, but it beats getting stuck in an anonymous (and ominous) location.

$50-100

The Courtyard Dallas LBJ at Josey (2930 Forest Ln., 972/620-8000, www.marriott.com, $65 d) is a clean, reliable motel (albeit in a somewhat-marginal part of the city) 12 miles north of downtown and 14 miles from the airport. The Courtyard features free Internet access, an outdoor pool, and whirlpool, and its suites offer microwaves and minifridges. The adjacent Courtyard Café serves a hot breakfast daily.

For a slight step up, consider **Staybridge Suites** (7880 Alpha Rd., 972/391-0000, www.staybridge.com, $85 d), which offers a "well-equipped kitchen" in every suite, free Wi-Fi, and an outdoor pool and whirlpool. The hotel is near the suburb of Richardson—a cab ride to downtown Dallas is fairly reasonable (typically around $20).

If you want to avoid the chains, book a room at the Texas-based **MCM Elegante** (2330 W. Northwest Hwy., 214/351-4477, www.mcmelegantedallas.com, $99 d). The Elegante offers complimentary shuttle service to and from both DFW and Love Field airports, an outdoor splash pool and spa tub, free wireless Internet access, and 27-inch TVs with premium cable.

$100-150

One of the best weekend options for budget-minded travelers is **Hyatt Summerfield Suites Dallas/Lincoln Park** (8221 N. Central Expwy., 214/696-1555, www.bradfordsuites.com, $109 d). The 161 spacious rooms include kitchens, and the hotel offers a continental breakfast daily. Located in the heart of Dallas's tony Park Cities, the Summerfield Suites is only 10 minutes north of downtown and is within walking distance of the fancy NorthPark Mall.

A surprisingly affordable and worthy option downtown is **Hotel Indigo** (1933 Main St., 214/741-7700, www.hotel-dallas.com, $119 d), a 14-story National Historic Landmark that previously served as the Dallas Aristocrat and one of the original Hilton properties. Appealing to travelers who favor the "boutique concept," the Indigo approach is somewhat refreshing, with seasonally updated color schemes and artwork. The hotel offers free wireless access, a fitness center, and guest rooms with hardwood-style flooring and spa-style showers. A breakfast package is available for $10 more per night.

Just north of downtown near the comfy Oak Lawn neighborhood is the **Radisson Hotel Central Dallas** (6060 N. Central Expwy., 214/750-6060, www.radisson.com, $119 d). The 300 rooms feature the chain's signature plush bedding along with free high-speed Internet access. Other amenities include a nice indoor/outdoor heated pool, a fitness center, and free shuttle transportation within a five-mile radius.

Marriott City Center (650 N. Pearl St., 214/979-9000, www.mariott.com, $119 d) is a nice downtown option in the Arts District. *Business* is a key term here—the "City Center" is an atrium with retail shops and an ice skating rink, and the hotel itself is appealing in a corporate way, as opposed to family friendly (you won't find a pool or free buffet or even complimentary Internet service). Notable amenities include an impressive gym facility, maps with suggested jogging routes, and live music during happy hour.

$150-200

The SpringHill Suites Downtown/West End

(1907 N. Lamar St., 214/999-0500, www. marriott.com, $169 d) is in the heart of the Historic West End and just blocks away from the city's Arts District. If you're looking for a hotel among the bustle of an entertainment scene, this a good place to stay. The rooms are spacious and comfortable, and offer an ideal place to relax after a day of sightseeing and shopping. Amenities include an outdoor pool and free breakfast (a hot buffet or "Grab-n-Go" options).

Don't count out the **Grand Hyatt DFW** (2337 S. International Pkwy., 972/973-1234, www.granddfw.hyatt.com, $169 d). Sometimes you gotta get a hotel near the airport, or in this case, at the airport. Aside from offering the ultimate convenience to your flight (the hotel provides free transportation to all terminals via the airport's high-speed train system or an ordinary ol' shuttle bus), the Hyatt features Wi-Fi access, fancy rooms with quality bedding, granite-top desks, minibars, robes, and a free fitness center with heated pool.

The only bad thing about **Westin Park Central** (12720 Merit Dr., 972/385-3000, www.westin.com/dallas, $159 d) is its bizarrely isolated location. Despite being on a major freeway in a busy spot, the hotel itself is an urban island without walking access to restaurants or typical urban amenities. Once inside, however, you'll have everything you need in a reliably high-quality package, including top-notch bedding, a free continental breakfast, Internet access, and a heated rooftop pool.

The **Warwick Melrose Hotel** (3015 Oak Lawn Ave., 214/521-5151, www.warwickmelrosehoteldallas.com, $179 d) is a 1924 historic Dallas landmark located in the city's fashionable Oak Lawn area north of downtown. The Melrose's clean comfort and style is apparent in each of its 184 distinct extra-large guest rooms featuring mahogany furnishings, minibars, marble baths, terry-cloth robes, and incredible views of the downtown skyline. The Melrose has attracted international celebrities for eight decades and has a reputation as one of the city's best hotels. Its award-winning Landmark Restaurant specializes in spectacular Asian food, and its comfy Library Bar is a Dallas tradition offering 100 types of martinis along with live entertainment and late-night dining.

The **Fairmont Dallas** (1717 N. Akard St., 866/540-4427, www.fairmont.com/dallas, $159 d) is a worthy downtown option. Located near the business and arts districts, the Fairmont is somewhat slight on amenities (you have to pay for Internet access and breakfast), but its location is ideal for exploring Dallas by foot. And the hotel itself is stylish, with a fitness center, outdoor pool, and on-site Starbucks café. Also notable is **Hotel Lawrence** (302 S. Houston St., 214/761-9090, www.hotellawrencedallas.com, $139–179 d). The historic hotel is an inviting option in the downtown business district, providing a charming mix of old and new. The rooms are small, but the amenities are impressive, including a free breakfast buffet, complimentary Wi-Fi access, and cookies and milk each evening. Note: Parking is available by valet only.

$200-250

◖ The Adolphus Hotel (1321 Commerce St., 214/742-8200, www.hoteladolphus.com, $239 d) is the best way to experience Dallas. This beautiful Baroque-style 1912 architectural gem from beer magnate Adolphus Busch welcomes visitors with an opulent lobby area, ornate furnishings, fancy bathrooms, flat-screen TVs, and excellent dining for a very reasonable price. Guest rooms—the hotel has 432 available—feature antique furnishings and separate sitting areas, as well as minibars and walk-in closets for those wishing to upgrade. Walls display European lithographs, and feather pillows, deep tubs, and brass-accented fixtures add to the hotel's luxurious feel. Just to top things off, tea is served in the stately Lobby Living Room while beautiful music emanates from an authentic 1893 Victorian Steinway grand piano.

The **Hotel Palomar** (5300 E. Mockingbird Ln., 214/520-7969, www.hotelpalomar-dallas.com, $249 d) is pretty fancy but worth the extra money for the memorable experience. From the time you enter the spacious and impressive lobby, it's evident this is a hotel that pays attention to details—color schemes, geometric patterns, and open atmospheres are prevalent themes throughout the entire building, including the nearly 200 guest rooms. The rooms offer DVD/CD players, 32-inch plasma televisions, minibars, marble bathroom vanities, and bathrobes. The hotel hosts complimentary evening wine hours and serves light fare in the lobby lounge; its restaurant **Trader Vic's** was once a famous Polynesian spot where celebs such as Bob Hope, Kirk Douglas, and Mickey Mantle sampled the bar's inventive cocktails.

$250 and Above

The swanky and über-urban **Hotel ZaZa** (2332 Leonard St., 214/468-8399, www.hotelzaza. com, $250 d) offers spacious, chic rooms with minibars, luxury bedding, and "sensual lighting." The ZaSpa provides body therapies and a tropical pool, and the Dragonfly Restaurant features global cuisine. The hotel's "custom-designed concept suites" include free Wi-Fi access and daily coffee services. On weekends, the hotel shows classic movies projected on a large screen near its outdoor patio.

You can't go wrong at the classic **◖ Magnolia Hotel** (1401 Commerce St., 214/915-6500, www.magnoliahoteldallas.com, $279 d), with its rich history, ornate furnishings, optimal location, and old-fashioned charm. The Magnolia played a vital role in Dallas's history, and the hotel's legendary red-neon Pegasus atop the building is a treasured city landmark. The logo is from the once-dominant Magnolia Petroleum Company, which was headquartered in the hotel's remarkable 1934 art deco building. The Magnolia's 330 guest rooms feature high ceilings, fine linens, oversized soaking tubs, refrigerators, and bathrobes. The hotel also provides some pretty amazing complimentary services, including breakfast at the Magnolia Court, afternoon cocktails and hors d'oeuvres, and even nighttime cookies and milk in the Magnolia Club's library.

The Rosewood Mansion on Turtle Creek (2821 Turtle Creek Blvd., 214/559-2100, www. mansiononturtlecreek.com, $395 d) provides lavish accommodations and has a worldwide reputation for its luxury. If you're looking to splurge on an elegant place in Dallas, this is as sophisticated as it gets. Rooms feature European-style decor containing original artwork, antiques, 480-thread-count linens, fresh-cut flowers, walk-in closets, marble baths, robes, and slippers, along with French doors opening onto private balconies. As expected with a luxury hotel, the Southwestern cuisine–themed restaurant is exquisite and is consistently named one of the top hotel restaurants in the country. The bar offers casual dining surrounded by a hunting-themed decor, and the hotel's Promenade restaurant serves breakfast overlooking the lush landscaped grounds.

Bed-and-Breakfast

For those interested in getting away from the high-rise hotels and chain options in the big city, consider a stay at the historic Uptown **Maple Manor Hotel** (2616 Maple Ave., 214/871-0032, $159–299). A popular wedding destination, Maple Manor offers a romantic getaway for couples at any stage of their relationship. The home features five suites with international themes and garden tubs. Other amenities include free Wi-Fi access, refrigerators, coffeemakers, and, of course, a free breakfast (available in the main dining room or privately in your own suite).

Camping

Located just 10 miles southwest of Dallas, **Cedar Hill State Park** (1570 FM 1382 in Cedar Hill, 972/291-3900, www.tpwd.state. tx.us) is a 1,826-acre urban nature preserve on the 7,500-acre Joe Pool Reservoir. The 355 rural wooded campsites have water and electricity, and the park's facilities include restrooms with showers, four miles of hiking/backpacking trails, and 10 miles of mountain bike trails.

Other nearby camping options include **Dallas Hi-Ho** (18 miles south of town in Glenn Heights, 877/619-3900, www.campingfriend. com), which offers full hookups for motor homes, and spots for trailers, "fifth wheels," campers, and tents. With limited natural space in such an urban area, one of the only other options is a KOA campground, including **Dallas Metro KOA** (2715 S. Cooper, 817/277-6600) and **Dallas Northeast** (903/527-3615, www. koa.com) in Caddo Mills. Both offer RV hookups, cabins, and swimming.

FOOD

Dallas has some of the finest restaurants in the Southwest, featuring an eclectic mix of cuisines. From regional fare like barbecue and Tex-Mex to fancier spots serving French and Italian, there's no shortage of good eats in Big D.

Downtown
MEXICAN AND LATIN AMERICAN

Deep Ellum's **Monica's Aca y Alla** (2914 Main St., 214/748-7140, closed Mon., $9–20) is perhaps best known for its late-night salsa dancing, but the Mexican food with Mediterranean accents is an equally spicy attraction. Regulars return often for the famous Mexican lasagna (chicken, black beans, and corn layered between tortillas), and the spinach and mushroom quesadillas are another flavorful favorite. Be forewarned: Monica's can get extremely loud—especially on weekend nights.

Noteworthy for its convenient West End location, **RJ's Mexican Cuisine** (1701 N. Market St., 214/744-1420, open daily, $6–16) offers a slightly different take on standard Tex-Mex by adding spicy peppers and fresh vegetables to spruce up the tacos and quesadillas. There are even some unconventional Mexican options, such as barbecued ribs and tuna.

Not in the heart of downtown but worth the five-minute drive southwest to Oak Cliff is **Gloria's** (600 W. Davis St., 214/948-3672, open daily, $7–14), known throughout the city for its delectable Salvadoran and Mexican specialties. Start with their signature black bean dip (with tortilla chips) and continue with Latin American favorites like cheese pupusas, fried plantains, yucca, and empanadas. Top it all off with a *horchata,* a sweet Mexican cocktail that can double as a dessert.

Though many visitors are tempted by the flashy neon-lit Mexican restaurant across the street (Iron Cactus), they should resist the colorful lights and jump over to **Sol Irlandes** (1525 Main St., 214/744-9400, www.solirlandes.net, $9–20). Try to arrive at happy hour for the $3 margaritas and appetizers, and settle in for a hearty bout of savory Mexican food, including chicken enchiladas with sour cream sauce, tortilla soup, and fajitas that make it totally worth enduring the sizzling platter experience.

AMERICAN AND SOUTHWESTERN

For those willing to spend a little extra money on a special downtown Dallas meal, consider **Dakota's** (600 N. Akard St., 214/740-4001, open daily, $13–32), a romantic spot featuring New American cuisine and steaks. The wild game mixed grill is a signature dish, and the cuts of beef are dazzling—particularly the bone-in rib eye. For a more affordable option, consider the fixed-price lunch or dinner menu, consisting of an appetizer, a choice of three entrées, and dessert. Reservations are recommended.

Perhaps Dallas's most famous chef is Stephan Pyle, known for his television shows and cookbooks. His namesake restaurant, **Stephan Pyle's** (1807 Ross Ave., 214/580-7000, closed Sun., $15–36), offers all the appetizing reasons why he's become a celebrity. Though he still maintains much of his signature New Millennium Southwestern style, Pyle has also branched out by incorporating some European influences into his out-of-this-world ceviches, tapas, and steaks. Be sure to try the roasted Texas corn soup and/or a Mexican chocolate tamale. Reservations are recommended.

For those seeking something more casual— think shorts and beers—head directly to **City Tavern** (1402 Main St., 214/745-1402, www.citytaverndowntown.com, $9–22). Pub grub is the specialty here, so order a cheeseburger, chicken strips (doused in a flavorful buffalo sauce), and a big ol' plate of fries. One of the Tavern's specialties is fried pickles—prepared with a perfect ratio of crispy batter and pickle nugget.

LUNCH

If you're in the mood for sushi, the best option downtown is Deep Ellum's venerable **❰ Deep Sushi** (2624 Elm St., 214/651-1177, open daily, $5–14). The fresh tuna and spicy volcano roll are highly recommended, and even standard items like avocado-based rolls are bursting with flavor. Weekends are the best time to go, when you'll get bonus enjoyment from the patio's live music and lively pedestrian traffic.

Just south of downtown, check out the **Brooklyn Jazz Café** (1701 S. Lamar St., 214/248-0025, closed Mon., $6–15), where the brunch and sandwiches draw nearly as many patrons as the jazz music does. Especially notable are the Downtown Cheesesteak and veggie burger.

Another good lunch option is Deep Ellum's **Murray Street Coffee Shop** (103 Murray St., 214/655-2808, closed Sun., $5–10). Although the premium coffees are the main draw, Murray Street's tasty sandwiches and hummus are also nice ways to escape the hustle and bustle of downtown Dallas.

For a down-home experience, check out the laid-back **Metropolitan Cafe** (2030 Main St., 214/741-2233, $9–25). This family-run operation (the owner is usually behind the register and serving food while his wife and mother run the kitchen) offers a genuine home-style experience, complete with hearty breakfasts, high-piled sandwiches, savory soups, and, perhaps, best of all, cookies, cakes, and treats.

STEAK

Dallas has fancier steak houses than **Hoffbrau Steaks** (311 N. Market St., 214/742-4663, open daily, $10–23), but this is about as low-key and comfortable as they get. Located in the busy West End district, the Hoffbrau has all the basic cuts of meat (they even process their own beef) without the stuffy atmosphere of other steak restaurants. This is the place to go if you prefer a rib eye and Shiner Bock over a filet mignon and Cabernet.

Another refreshingly laid-back downtown steak house is **The Butcher Shop** (808 Munger Ave., 214/720-1032, open daily, $10–30). All cuts of meat here are above average, but the service can be a little slow. Fortunately, The Butcher Shop pays close attention to the edible details (bread, sides—especially the asparagus), which make it quite recommendable.

Oak Lawn Area
AMERICAN AND SOUTHWESTERN

Since Oak Lawn is one of the tony parts of Dallas, it should come as no surprise that this is where some of the city's most exquisite restaurants are located. For years, the über-exclusive **❰ Mansion on Turtle Creek** (2821 Turtle Creek, 214/559-2100, open daily, $17–43) represented the height of luxury, as Texas's only five-star, five-diamond hotel and five-diamond restaurant. However, times have changed, and the Mansion is loosening up its black tie these days. Jackets are no longer required to partake of the restaurant's famous Southwestern gourmet offerings; in fact, even (gulp) jeans are allowed in the main dining room. Of the many top-notch options, several are supremely spectacular: the filet of tenderloin au poivre, porcini-crusted filet mignon, and Niman Ranch lamb. This meal will set you back a pretty penny, but for some, it pays to dine finely among the elite. Reservations are recommended.

Less glamorous yet nearly as delectable is **Craft** (2440 Victory Park Ln., 214/397-4111, open daily, $16–32), a New York transplant that has cemented a reputation for fine dining without the fuss. The dishes at Craft are extraordinary in their elegant simplicity—the focus is on the pure flavor of the offering (particularly steak or seafood), prepared without an abundance of seasoning or exotic sauces. The mushrooms are especially flavorful. Reservations are recommended.

LUNCH

Technically located just north of Oak Lawn in the Park Cities area, the legendary **❰ Sonny Bryan's Smokehouse** (2202 Inwood, 214/357-7120, open daily, $7–15) is a must for those in search of authentic Texas-style barbecue. Traditional meats are the way to go here—try the triple crown of brisket, pork ribs, and sausage—and the sauce offers the perfect tangy topping that ties it all together. If that weren't enough, the building itself provides an ideal atmosphere, with its smoke-drenched walls and old wooden school desks and picnic tables. There aren't too many places like this outside the Lone Star State, and judging by the long lines of locals clamoring to get in for lunch each day, there aren't many others quite as good in Dallas.

You'll notice the brightly colored **Cosmic Café** (2912 Oak Lawn Ave., 214/521-6157, open daily, $7–14) from blocks away, and the punchy flavors waiting inside will also get your attention. This vegetarian landmark offers excellent traditional Middle Eastern staples such as falafel, samosas, and hummus as well as flavorful sweet treats like brownies, homemade ice cream, and fruit smoothies.

For standard diner fare, check out **Lucky's** (3531 Oak Lawn Ave., 214/522-3500, open daily, $6–12), which offers sandwiches and burgers along with its big draw: chicken-fried steak topped with peppery cream gravy. Pour some of it on a mound of nearby homemade mashed potatoes, and you'll be feeling Lucky (and sleepy) for the rest of the afternoon.

MEXICAN

In the 1970s and '80s, ◖ Mia's (4322 Lemmon Ave., 214/526-1020, open daily, $6–13) drew huge crowds, including the cast of *Dallas,* along with legendary Dallas Cowboys coach Tom Landry and many of his players. Though it's since lost much of its star luster, Mia's still serves some of the city's most authentic and tasty Tex-Mex. Standard fare like enchiladas and chicken tacos are certainly worthwhile, but make a point of trying the perfectly battered and seasoned chiles rellenos or the tender brisket tacos for a truly distinctive Mexican-food experience.

One of Oak Lawn's most popular Mexican restaurants is **Herrera's Cafe** (4001 Maple Ave., 214/528-9644, $4–10). Don't be dismayed by the sketchy exterior—the food awaiting within is high-quality authentic goodness.

The salsa is spicy and garlicky, the cheese is gooey and satisfying, and the beef and chicken are tender and perfectly seasoned.

Outlying Areas
BRUNCH

An ideal place to have a weekend morning brunch is **Dream Café** (2800 Routh St., 214/954-0486, open daily, $6–14), especially if you're with the family. Kids will love the enormous playground, oatmeal, and French toast, while adults will savor the huevos rancheros, cheese grits, and the kids' French toast leftovers. Healthy options abound at this comfortable location north of downtown.

Brunchers will also find home-style goodness in a casual environment at **Bread Winners Cafe and Bakery** (3301 McKinney Ave., 214/754-4940, open daily, $4–12), north of downtown. Snag a spot on the inviting brick courtyard patio and enjoy a cup o' joe while you munch on a fresh pastry or wait for an inspired breakfast dish, like the popular smoked salmon scrambler and French ham Benedict.

MEXICAN

For a feast of the senses, drop by **El Ranchito Cafe & Club** (610 W. Jefferson Blvd., 214/946-4238, open daily, $6–12), in Oak Cliff just south of downtown. From the colorful decor to brassy mariachi bands to the smells and tastes of savory Tex-Mex (emphasis on the Mex), you can't go wrong here. If you're feeling adventurous, try the house specialty of *cabrito* (goat), tender and flavorful meat that tastes surprisingly delicious paired with El Ranchito's buttery tortillas and hearty salsa. The *caldo de pollo* (chicken soup) is also a nice option for lunch or dinner.

Another worthy Tex-Mex spot is **Pepe's & Mito's Mexican Café** (2911 Elm St., 214/461-8357, open daily, $7–13), just east of downtown. This is a great place to stick with the classics—the chicken enchiladas in a tangy green tomatillo sauce, tacos with superbly seasoned beef, and better-than-they-have-to-be pinto beans.

INFORMATION AND SERVICES
Tourist Offices

The Dallas/Fort Worth International Airport has handy visitor information booths to help fresh arrivals get oriented, but it's worth stopping by the **Dallas Convention and Visitors Bureau**'s (CVB) information centers to get personalized information and maps.

The CVB (800/232-5527, www.visitdallas.com) has several information offices and booths throughout the city. The main info center is housed in the city's landmark downtown "Old Red" courthouse (100 S. Houston St., 214/571-1301, daily 9 A.M.–5 P.M.) and features Internet terminals and touch-screen computer information kiosks.

Publications

Entertainment and events are covered in several Dallas publications. The metro daily *Dallas Morning News* is one of the country's most esteemed newspapers and offers thorough coverage of local, state, national, and international news. The best bet for cultural events is the *Dallas Observer,* the city's weekly alternative paper published every Thursday.

GETTING THERE AND AROUND
By Air

Dallas is served by the enormous **Dallas/Fort Worth International Airport** (972/574-8888, www.dfwairport.com) and the smaller **Dallas Love Field** (214/670-6080).

Downtown Dallas is accessible from the DFW airport via **DART** (Dallas Area Rapid Transit) and on the **Trinity Railway Express** (TRE) train Monday through Saturday. To take the TRE, purchase tickets (roughly $3–5) from a vending machine on the train platform.

Cabs are a reliable way to get from the airport to a Metroplex destination, but it will cost at least $30 for the service. Another more-affordable option (averaging around $20) is the **Super Shuttle** (817/329-2000, www.supershuttle.com), available from DFW airport at all hours but occasionally sluggish depending on the number of passengers along for the ride and their destinations. In addition, many airport-area hotels offer pick-up and drop-off services.

Dallas Love Field is more centrally located but is limited in flight options since only Southwest Airlines and one regional airline currently serve it. Love Field is about seven miles northwest of downtown, and local transportation is offered by taxi (approximately $13 to downtown) and the Super Shuttle.

By Bus

The **Dallas Area Rapid Transit** (DART) system operates a bus service throughout the city and will provide personal assistance (how to get from Point A to Point B) by calling 214/979-1111 Monday–Friday 6 A.M.–8 P.M. and weekends 8 A.M.–5 P.M. The basic single-ride fare for most local trips is $1.75. Maps and schedules are available at DART transit centers, libraries, and city hall. More information is also available at DART's headquarters (1401 Pacific Ave., 214/749-3810).

Otherwise, Dallas's main bus activity is at the **Greyhound Bus Terminal** (205 S. Lamar, 214/747-8859) at Union Station, its main downtown train station. Union Station is also serviced by Amtrak's **Texas Eagle** and is connected to the DART system.

By Rapid Transit

DART (214/979-1111, www.DART.org) offers public transportation in and among 13 Dallas-area communities with rail, bus, and rideshare services. In addition to its airport line, DART provides service to Fort Worth via the **TRE** (817/215-8600 or www.the-t.com).

Vicinity of Dallas

The perfect antidote to the hustle and bustle of the Big D is a trip to a small nearby community. Most of these outlying towns began as humble villages out in the country, far removed from the hectic workaday world. Now that they're filled with commuters, they've taken on more of a suburban feel, but their downtowns retain the quaint appeal of their days as mercantile centers and seats of government. You won't find historic courthouses or antiques shops in all of these communities, however. Arlington's big draw is amusement, and it's available in droves at Cowboys Stadium, Six Flags amusement park, and Rangers baseball stadium.

ARLINGTON

Arlington is all about thrills. Whether it's the flittering sensation in the belly from a roller coaster at Six Flags or the rush of adrenaline that comes with a home run at the Rangers' ballpark, Arlington (population 367,197) is a great setting for fun and games. This supersized suburb, occasionally referred to as the "Midway of the Metroplex," is also home to a science center and country music revue, allowing visitors to set up stakes in Arlington for several days' worth of family fun, with side trips to the Metroplex for big-city activities (Dallas and Fort Worth are each 15 miles away on I-30). There is no shortage of hotels near these attractions or major roadways to accommodate those plans.

Cowboys Stadium

Arlington received a major cultural (and economic) boom in 2009, when the Dallas Cowboys' new state-of-the art stadium opened (925 N. Collins St., 817/892-4161, http://stadium.dallascowboys.com/). Constructed for a "mere" $1.2 billion, the 660,800-square-foot stadium is the largest domed structure in the world. Cynically referred to as the Taj Mahal of stadiums or a monument to Cowboys owner

© ANDY RHODES

The gargantuan Cowboys Stadium opened in Arlington in 2009.

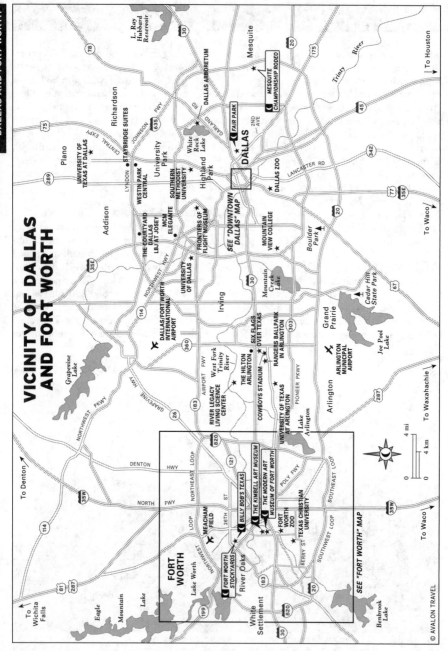

VICINITY OF DALLAS AND FORT WORTH

To Denton

To Wichita Falls

L. Ray Hubbard Reservoir

Trinity River

To Houston

Mesquite

MESQUITE CHAMPIONSHIP RODEO

Richardson

Plano

STAYBRIDGE SUITES

UNIVERSITY OF TEXAS AT DALLAS

University Park

DALLAS ARBORETUM

FAIR PARK

White Rock Lake

DALLAS

WESTIN PARK CENTRAL

SOUTHERN METHODIST UNIVERSITY

Highland Park

DALLAS ZOO

Addison

MCM ELEGANTE

THE COURTYARD DALLAS LBJ AT JOSEY

FRONTIERS OF FLIGHT MUSEUM

SEE "DOWNTOWN DALLAS" MAP

MOUNTAIN VIEW COLLEGE

Boulder Park

To Waco

UNIVERSITY OF DALLAS

DALLAS/FORT WORTH INTERNATIONAL AIRPORT

Irving

Mountain Creek Lake

Cedar Hill State Park

Grapevine Lake

SIX FLAGS OVER TEXAS

Grand Prairie

Joe Pool Lake

To Waxahachie

THE HILTON ARLINGTON

RANGERS BALLPARK IN ARLINGTON

ARLINGTON MUNICIPAL AIRPORT

RIVER LEGACY LIVING SCIENCE CENTER

COWBOYS STADIUM

UNIVERSITY OF TEXAS AT ARLINGTON

Arlington

Lake Arlington

West Fork Trinity River

DENTON HWY

MEACHAM FIELD

BILLY BOB'S TEXAS

THE KIMBELL ART MUSEUM

THE MODERN ART MUSEUM OF FORT WORTH

FORT WORTH ZOO

TEXAS CHRISTIAN UNIVERSITY

NORTH FWY

FORT WORTH

FORT WORTH STOCKYARDS

River Oaks

White Settlement

SEE "FORT WORTH" MAP

To Waco

Lake Worth

Eagle Mountain Lake

Benbrook Lake

0   4 mi

0   4 km

© AVALON TRAVEL

Jerry Jones's ego, the stadium is a marvel to behold. Looming on the horizon like a massive spaceship, the stadium features a retractable roof, luxury suites, and, perhaps most impressive/garish of all, a 60-yard-wide video screen suspended over the field. The stadium's oversized price tag was paid for by city sales tax, which increased by one-half of a percent, an increase in Arlington's hotel occupancy and car rental taxes, and hundreds of millions from the City of Arlington, the NFL, and Jones himself.

For Cowboys (and fancy stadium) fans, the self-guided tour ($17.50) is worth doing, especially to see the locker rooms and toss a football around on the field. For $10 more, you can see the luxury suites and press boxes with a knowledgeable and entertaining guide. Tours are held Monday–Saturday 10 A.M.–6 P.M. and Sunday 11 A.M.–5 P.M.

Rangers Ballpark in Arlington

Rangers Ballpark in Arlington (1000 Ballpark Wy., 817/273-5100, www.rangers.mlb.com)
is a great place to catch a ballgame—even if you're not a big baseball fan (the season runs from April through early October). The stadium opened in 1994 and was designed to capture classic aesthetic elements of old-time ballparks while offering modern amenities. It succeeds on both counts.

Unlike many urban stadiums, the Rangers Ballpark in Arlington sits alone atop a hill surrounded by natural features and parking lots. The 10-minute walk to the front gates takes visitors past lakes and a decked-out miniature stadium used for Little League games and other events. The surrounding greenery is a welcome contrast to the concrete walls and bus exhaust outside baseball stadiums in other metropolitan environments. The exterior of Rangers Ballpark is decorated with relief sculptures depicting Texana scenes such as longhorn cattle, the Alamo, and oil wells.

The most rewarding aspect of the ballpark is the immediate sense of delight experienced upon ascending the walkway into the heart of the stadium—the natural green grass,

© ANDY RHODES

The Rangers Ballpark in Arlington hosted the World Series in 2010.

royal blue sky, and sharp sounds of wooden bats and leather gloves is a baseball fan's Field of Dreams. An extra bonus is the nook-and-cranny-filled outfield underneath deliberately toned-down flat-board advertising (sans flashing neon lights or garish beer billboards). Since the Rangers played in the 2010 World Series, the stadium has become a popular destination for regional sports fans, a rarity in this football-obsessed city and state. Baseball buffs are hoping the kinetic energy encapsulated in the stadium during the 2010 postseason will continue to reverberate for years to come.

Six Flags Over Texas

Named for the six "national" flags that have flown over Texas during its history, Six Flags Over Texas (I-30 at Hwy. 360, 817/530-6000, www.sixflags.com, daily in summer, 10 A.M.–11 P.M., weekends in spring/fall, $35–55, parking $15) has been the king of Texas amusement parks since 1961, when oil tycoon Angus G. Wynne Jr. was so inspired by a visit to Disneyland he commissioned a similar park

for the Lone Star State. Six Flags has evolved over the years by keeping up to speed on the latest roller coasters, rides, and other amusement park diversions. In 2011, the park celebrated the highly anticipated return of the Texas Giant roller coaster, with a state-of-the-art track of steel fabrication, the steepest drop of any wooden coaster in the world (79 degrees), and a record-breaking bank of 95 degrees, steeper than any other wooden coaster on the planet—all in trains that pay homage to the iconic 1961 Cadillac Deville. Other thrill-providers that elicit loud screams (and long lines) are the mammoth 245-foot Titan, the 315-foot Superman Tower of Power, and the famous Mr. Freeze. Six Flags also includes traditional amusement park activities such as theatrical shows, family events, and seasonal festivities in addition to the requisite cotton candy, hot dogs, and lemonade stands.

Six Flags Hurricane Harbor

Just across the street, Six Flags Hurricane Harbor (1800 E. Lamar Blvd., 817/640-

Arlington's Six Flags Over Texas amusement park and Cowboys Stadium

© ANDY RHODES

8900, www.sixflags.com, daily in summer, 10:30 A.M.–7 P.M., weekends in spring/fall, $22–28, parking $10) bills itself as the largest water park in the Southwest. The park's 47 acres are overflowing with water rides, slides, and pools. Millions of gallons of water propel, glide, and douse visitors on more than a dozen rides. Highlights include the Tornado's funnel-shaped waterfall ride, the Black Hole's gushing water tubes, the amusing and appropriately named Mega Wedgie, the 12 levels of activity in Surf Lagoon, and the Bubba Tub inner-tube ride.

The International Bowling Museum and Hall of Fame

Arlington's newest cultural attraction (opened in January 2010) is The International Bowling Museum and Hall of Fame (621 Six Flags Dr., 817/385-8215, www.bowlingmuseum.com, Tues.–Sat. 9:30 A.M.–5 P.M., $9.50 adults, $7.50 seniors and children ages 4–18). The fancy, 18,000-square-foot museum is part of the massive International Bowling Campus, which also opened in 2010. So why is the center of the bowling universe located in Arlington? To be close to all the sports fans and tourists in Fun City, apparently. Though bowling doesn't always get a fair shake as a competitive sport, a visit to the museum and hall of fame will make visitors start taking it much more seriously. Exhibits showcase the sport's past, including a reference to an Egyptian grave from 3200 B.C. that appeared to include objects for an early form of bowling. It also offers plenty of fun interactive kiosks and games, including a virtual bowling lane and a few spots to knock down some real pins.

The Planetarium at UT Arlington

After a full day in the sun waiting in lines to get on rides and water slides, treat yourself to the cool, dark Planetarium at UT Arlington (700 Planetarium Pl., 817/272-1183, www.uta.edu/

BOWLING FOR DALLAS

When someone mentions bowling, do you immediately think of the Dallas suburbs? Well, you should.

In 2010, the city of Arlington became the center of the bowling universe. The **International Bowling Campus** – the sport's educational, governing, and testing center – set up its pins in Fun City to be in proximity to high-profile tourist destinations like Six Flags Over Texas, Cowboys Stadium, and the Rangers Ballpark. This major move to the Lone Star State carried some controversy, however, since the sport's previous headquarters were located in traditional bowling hotbeds – the blue collar, beer-brewing cities of Milwaukee and St. Louis.

When the campus opened in January 2010, representatives proudly announced that "for the first time in the 5,000-year history of the sport, the bowling industry is united under one roof." The massive complex includes a collection of organizations you probably never even knew existed: the International Bowling Museum and Hall of Fame, the International Training and Research Center, the National Headquarters for Bowling Proprietors' Association of America, and the United States Bowling Congress. This is where bowling's best and brightest minds gather to study scientific aspects of the sport, share knowledge with casual and die-hard fans, and test new equipment.

Perhaps most significantly, the campus is home to the new and expanded International Bowling Museum and Hall of Fame. The state-of-the-art museum offers interactive displays and exhibits along with distinctive items from bowling's various eras dating to 3200 B.C.

According to the International Bowling Campus, there are more than 69 million bowlers in the United States alone. These facilities in Arlington are expected to draw many of them for bouts of bowling-related brainstorming.

planetarium, open daily, $6 adults, $4 seniors and children ages 18 and under). The planetarium boasts a 60-foot-wide diameter dome and upgraded to become the only planetarium in the state with a Digistar 4 system with DLP projectors, offering a surprisingly realistic experience of viewing stars as they appear in the night sky. Audiences are transported to various otherworldly locales through shows such as *Spacepark 360, Stars of the Pharaohs,* and *Wonders of the Universe.*

River Legacy Living Science Center

On a much smaller scale is River Legacy Living Science Center (703 NW Green Oaks Blvd., 817/860-6752, www.riverlegacy.org, Tues.–Sat. 9 A.M.–5 P.M., admission free, donations accepted), a popular family destination featuring interactive exhibits with a focus on regional flora and fauna. Visitors experience the North Texas natural environment through the center's terrariums, aquariums, and a simulated raft ride of the Trinity River. Also on grounds is a 950-acre nature park with educational and recreational activities and hiking and biking trails along the banks of the Trinity River. The park is home to a bizarre fungus known as the Devil's Cigar that breaks open with a hiss to issue "smoke" (a cloud of spores).

Johnnie High's Country Music Revue

Running since 1974, Johnnie High's Country Music Revue variety show (224 N. Center St., 817/226-4400, www.johnniehighcountry.com, 7:30 P.M. showtime on Fri. and Sat., $13–17), prides itself on being reminiscent of the Grand Ol' Opry. Country and gospel acts take the stage most weekends at the 1,200-seat Arlington Music Hall, including musicians who went on to become big stars such as LeAnn Rimes and Lee Ann Womack. Johnnie and his group take the stage regularly; check the website for scheduled performances.

Accommodations

Arlington's best choice for moderate rates is

Quality Inn and Suites (1607 N. Watson Rd., 817/640-4444, www.qualityinn.com, $69 d). The hotel is within a few miles of Hurricane Harbor, Six Flags Over Texas, and Rangers Ballpark and features a complimentary breakfast, a pool, and rooms with fridges and microwaves.

A bit closer to Six Flags is the clean and comfortable **Wingate Inn** (1024 Brookhollow Plaza Dr., 817/640-8686, www.wingateinnarlington.com, $89 d), which offers complementary trolley passes to Six Flags, Hurricane Harbor, Rangers Ballpark, and the airport. The hotel also has an outdoor pool and an indoor spa tub, offers free Wi-Fi, and features a complimentary continental breakfast each morning.

◖ The Hilton Arlington (2401 E. Lamar Blvd., 817/640-3322, www.hilton.com, $139 d) is slightly more expensive but offers a step up in the quality of amenities and service. The Hilton provides complimentary transportation to and from the airport and shuttle service within a three-mile radius of the hotel (covering all the major tourist attractions—Six Flags, Hurricane Harbor, the Ballpark). The hotel's outdoor pool includes a splash area for kids and an outdoor lap section for adults.

Food
MEXICAN

Locals love North Arlington's **Mariano's Mexican Cuisine** (2614 Majesty Dr., 817/640-5118, www.marianosrestaurant.com, $8–19), with its tender brisket tacos, spicy Texas Torpedos (stuffed jalapeños), and charmingly dated '70s ambience. Even more impressive, however, is the restaurant owner's claim to fame as inventor of the world's first frozen margarita machine (inspired by a Slurpee machine at the local 7-Eleven store and now housed at the Smithsonian museum).

The consistently commendable **Estella's Mexican Restaurant** (1224 W. Arkansas Ln., 817/276-8226, open daily, $5–10) is a no-frills Tex-Mex treasure in the 'burbs. Locals flock here for breakfast, but the food—particularly the egg dishes—is worth sampling any time of the day. Estella's signature dish is the King Plate, featuring scrambled eggs mixed with chorizo (Mexican sausage), bacon, grilled onion, and jalapeño.

Closer to the theme parks is **Mercado Juarez Restaurant** (2222 Miller Rd., 817/649-0307, open daily, $5–15), a local chain that's earned raves from Dallasites for decades. Known for its distinctive mesquite-fired grill, Mercado Juarez serves up some of the Metroplex's best carne guisada. Wrap it up in a freshly made tortilla with the restaurant's signature warm salsa picante for a classic Tex-Mex flavor combo.

STEAK

The charmingly down-home **Arlington Steak House** (1724 W. Division St., 817/275-7881, open daily, $11–27) is a great place to go if you're looking to unwind with a substantial meal after a day full of amusement. They keep things casual here, and the steaks are consistently flavorful. If you've never tried a chicken-fried steak, this is a good place to start, and if you're already a CFS connoisseur, you won't be disappointed. Locals drop in for the hearty yeast biscuits alone.

Far fancier is the **C Cacharel Restaurant** (2221 E. Lamar Blvd., 817/640-9981, closed Sun., $15–34), offering stunning views of the Arlington area from the ninth floor of Brookhollow Tower Two. This French-inspired elegant restaurant has a reputation for serving some of the finest steaks in the area. The New York strip and bone-in rib eye are reputable favorites, but adventurous diners also have the option of selecting buffalo tenderloin or the grilled fillet of Texas ostrich.

Information and Services

The Arlington Convention and Visitors Bureau's Visitor Information Center (1905 E. Randol Mill Rd., 817/461-3888, www.ar-lington.org, Mon.–Sat. 9 A.M.–5 P.M., Sun. noon–4 P.M.) provides maps, brochures, and additional information about accommodations and restaurants in the area.

The Trolley (817/504-9744, www.arlington-trolley.com) is a free shuttle service running among Arlington's major hotels and attractions.

It occasionally runs a bit slow, but it's hard to complain when the service is complimentary. Cabs are always an option for those who can't stand the idea of being on their feet another 20 or 30 minutes.

WAXAHACHIE

In some ways, Waxahachie (population 21,426) is the opposite of Arlington. It's a quintessentially quaint town (proof: it's known as the "Gingerbread Capital of Texas") and, as such, is appropriately chock-full o' rich history and charming heritage tourism attractions. Located about 30 miles south of Dallas, Waxahachie's name originates from an Indian word meaning "cow" or "buffalo." Prosperity from the area's rich cotton farming industry in the early 1900s resulted in the construction of the attractive downtown buildings and the cotton barons' glamorous Victorian "gingerbread" homes. The city's crown jewel is the enormous and stunning 1897 Ellis County Courthouse, one of nearly 300 Waxahachie structures listed on the National Register of Historic Places. The town's true Texana appeal has resulted in numerous movies being filmed here, including *Bonnie and Clyde, Places in the Heart,* and *Tender Mercies.*

Ellis County Courthouse

The nine-story, red granite and sandstone Ellis County Courthouse (101 W. Main St., 972/825-5000, Mon.–Fri. 8 A.M.–5 P.M.) is an architectural masterpiece and is well worth making the 30-minute drive from Dallas to see. Designed in the Romanesque Revival style, this 1897 building is a true sight to behold— ornate nooks and crannies give way to massive architectural design features, and the entire castlelike element of the edifice is awe inspiring. One of the building's fascinating pieces of folklore involves a face carved atop the sandstone columns. The face begins as an attractive homage to a woman, rumored to be the granddaughter of the stone carver's landlord, but becomes progressively more grotesque, apparently reflecting the unrequited attraction she felt for him. The interior of the building is also a visual spectacle, with intricate detailing, historically accurate color schemes, and ornate woodwork.

Ellis County Museum

Across the street from the courthouse is the Ellis County Museum (201 S. College St., 972/937-0681, www.rootsweb.com/~txecm/, Mon.–Sat. 10 A.M.–5 P.M., Sun. 1–5 P.M.). Housed in a historic 1889 Masonic temple, the museum contains exhibits depicting everyday life in the Waxahachie area from the mid-1880s to the early 1900s.

Gingerbread Trail

Each June, Waxahachie's Gingerbread Trail Tour of Homes celebrates the city's architectural legacy by showcasing historic commercial and community sites. One of the featured attractions is the 1902 Chautauqua Auditorium, an octagonal, 2,500-seat, open-air pavilion built in conjunction with the late-1800s adult education movement in Chautauqua, New York. Other Gingerbread Trail events include an arts and crafts show, street dance, and performances on the downtown square. Call 972/937-0681 for more information.

Accommodations

Holiday Inn Express (984 U.S. Hwy. 287 Bypass W., 972/938-3300, $93 d) is a nice, new hotel that handles the basics effectively with above-average service and amenities, including free buffet breakfast, complimentary Wi-Fi, and a free daily cocktail hour.

Another decent option is **Americas Best Value Inn** (795 S. I-35E, 972/937-4982, www.bestvalueinn.com, $99 d), which includes free continental breakfast and an outdoor pool just a half mile from downtown.

Slightly more expensive and upscale is the **Hampton Inn & Suites** (2010 Civic Center Dr., 972/923-0666, www.hilton.com, $114 d), offering a free hot breakfast and studio suites.

Food

A good spot to soak up local flavor is **Catfish Plantation** (814 Water St., 972/937-9468, closed Mon.–Wed., $10–15). Located in one of the city's trademark Victorian gingerbread homes, the Catfish Plantation is perhaps known better as a haunted house than a restaurant. Although the Cajun specialties and cornmeal-battered catfish fillets are legendary, it's the three resident ghosts that supposedly slam doors, play pianos, and knock on walls that garner the most attention.

A popular place to dine on the historic downtown square is **1879 Chisholm Grill** (111 S. College St., 972/937-7261, closed Mon. and Tues., $7–17). Steak is a specialty here, and the Roxanne Ribeye is a particular favorite. The Chisholm Grill makes almost everything from scratch, and locals have rewarded their efforts by making the restaurant a source of hometown pride.

Also located downtown, just a block off the square, is the popular **BBQ Pit** (106 Water St., 972/938-3677, open daily, $6–12). Bring your appetite, because the Pit packs your plate full of tender smoked meats and classic sides. The Pit Potato is especially popular, the brisket is especially satisfying, and the pork ribs and sausage are noteworthy alternatives.

Information and Services

The Waxahachie Chamber of Commerce/ Convention and Visitors Bureau (102 YMCA Dr., 972/937-2390, www.waxahachie-chamber.com) is a good place to drop by to speak with someone in person about area restaurants and attractions, and to pick up maps and brochures.

MCKINNEY

Located 31 miles north of Dallas off U.S. 75, this town of 107,530 residents was named for Collin McKinney, a signer of the Texas Declaration of Independence and author of a bill establishing North Texas's counties. For more than a century, McKinney primarily served as an agribusiness center (cattle, corn, horses, wheat), but by the mid-1980s it had become a commuter center for residents working in Dallas. It's currently home to nearly 300 businesses, including Collin County Community College, and is one of the fastest-growing cities of its size in Texas, largely due to its proximity to the Metroplex and outlying supersized suburbs like Plano, where many people commute from the comparatively appealing small-town atmosphere.

Historic Courthouse Square

McKinney's Historic Courthouse Square has more than 100 shops—primarily antiques stores, art galleries, restaurants, and specialty spots. **The Old Collin County Courthouse,** the centerpiece of this downtown historic district, was built in 1874 and remodeled nearly 50 years later to include its current neoclassical facade. Just off the square is the **North Texas History Center** (300 E. Virginia St., 972/542-9457, www.thenthc.org, Wed.–Sat. 11 A.M.–4 P.M., $8 family, $4 adults, $2 seniors and children), offering two floors of exhibits related to the pioneer settlers and agricultural heritage of the region. Housed in a remarkable 1911 U.S. post office made of limestone with Italianate detailing, the museum is known for its stunning 1934 Works Progress Administration painted mural and hidden walkways and peepholes once used by postal inspectors.

Heard-Craig House Historic Center

The Heard-Craig House Historic Center (205 W. Hunt St., 972/569-6909, www.heard-craig.org, Tues.–Sat. 8:30 A.M.–4:30 P.M., $5 adults, $3 children.) showcases the life of an affluent owner of a downtown mercantile store from the early 20th century. The Heard family's hospitality made this residence a center of social, business, art, and literary activities. Heard constructed the 7,000-square-foot mansion in 1900, and his family resided in the home for 70 years. Painstakingly restored nearly a decade ago, the grand home is now open for guided tours and private events. Tours are offered on Tuesday and Thursday at 2 P.M., Saturday on the hour from 1–3 P.M., and by appointment.

Bolin Wildlife Exhibit

Exotic animals and agricultural heritage make for strangely effective bedfellows at the eclectic Bolin Wildlife Exhibit (1028 N. McDonald, 972/562-2639, Mon.–Fri 9 A.M.–4 P.M., no admission charge). Located in the headquarters of Bolin Oil Company, this enormous and often just plain bizarre museum was founded by rancher, oilman, and big game hunter W. Perry Bolin in 1980. The wildlife includes a huge amount of taxidermy, mainly from Africa and North America, most bagged by Bolin himself. Other exhibits contain photographs and oil paintings, antique cars, and a collection of walking canes from across the globe.

Accommodations

BED-AND-BREAKFAST

A bed-and-breakfast is an ideal place to spend the night in a historic spot like McKinney, and one of the town's best-regarded establishments is the **Bingham House Bed and Breakfast** (800 S. Chestnut St., 972/529-1883, www.binghamhouse.com, $129). The six-room 1883 Georgian Italianate home is brimming with Southern historic charm, and its romantic ambience is the scene of many weddings and film projects.

HOTELS AND MOTELS

For budget-minded travelers, McKinney's **Super 8 Motel** (910 N. Central Expwy., 972/548-8880, www.super8.com, $65 d) is a decent option with a free continental breakfast. Also worth considering is **Best Western McKinney Inn & Suites** (480 Wilson Creek Blvd., 972/548-3000, www.bestwestern.com, $81 d), offering a complimentary deluxe breakfast and newspaper, outdoor pool, indoor spa, and free Internet access.

Comfort Suites (1590 N. Central Expwy., 972/548-9595, www.choicehotels.com, $104 d) has spacious suites with microwaves, fridges, free Wi-Fi, and free breakfast for a step up from the moderate-range options.

Food

McKinney has several top-notch Mexican restaurants, and one of the city's finest is **El Juarez Mexican Restaurant** (311 E.

Louisiana St., 972/548-9181, open daily, $10–20). El Juarez has lured families, antiquers, and businesspeople to its cantina-esque location on the downtown square for several decades. Traditional Tex-Mex is the main draw here—you can't go wrong with the chicken enchiladas, fajitas, or carne guisada.

The regional chain **Aparicios** (216 E. Virginia St., 214/733-8600, open daily, $8–17) has earned a fine reputation for serving tasty Tex-Mex. Although the sports bar atmosphere at this location can be somewhat distracting, the food is worth enduring the increased decibels. Aparicios has its own tortilleria, so anything wrapped (tacos, burritos) or stacked (enchiladas) have that extra burst of homemade flavor. This is a safe place to get adventurous—try your taco à la carte with pork and pineapple or savory and tender *lengua* (tongue).

Information and Services

For information on McKinney's restaurants, accommodations, and events, drop by the city's **Convention and Visitors Bureau's Visitor Information Center** (1575 Heritage Dr., Suite 100, 888/649-8499, www.visitmckinney.com, Mon.–Fri. 8 A.M.–5 P.M.).

Fort Worth

Fort Worth is the quintessential Texas city—it has a compelling heritage, dynamic culture, and true grit. With a comfortably sized population of more than 650,000, it's easy to get around, which is handy considering there are several days' worth of activities and attractions to experience.

A big part of the city's appeal is its rich history, which began in 1849 when it was established as a military post on the Texas frontier. By the 1860s, Fort Worth was the main destination for cattle drives, which originated on large South Texas ranches and moved along legendary routes like the Chisholm Trail. The city's historical heyday was during the late 1800s and early 1900s, when railroads transformed Fort Worth into a major cattle industry town with a railhead, extensive stockyards, and beef packing facilities. Although the city would continue to grow as an agricultural center, the stockyards remained the most prominent feature of its cultural identity.

The area where most of the activity took place serves primarily as a tourist hub these days, but there's still some honest-to-goodness cowboy-related business in the stockyards. Livestock auctions are held weekly, and there's a rodeo each weekend night at the legendary Cowtown Coliseum. Culture of a completely different variety lies just a few miles down the road, where a collection of world-class museums (The Kimbell, The Modern, The Carter) showcase fascinating artwork from Texas and throughout the world.

INFORMATION AND SERVICES

The **Fort Worth Convention and Visitors Bureau** operates several Visitor Information Centers (The Stockyards: 130 E. Exchange Ave., 817/624-4741; Sundance Square: 508 Main St., 817/698-3300; Cultural District: 3401 W. Lancaster Ave., 817/882-8588). Friendly and helpful staff is on hand to provide information and literature about attractions throughout the city. Pick up brochures and maps while viewing cowboy gear and historic Western artifacts.

GETTING THERE AND AROUND

Dallas/Fort Worth International Airport is located exactly between Dallas and Fort Worth, so Fort Worth visitors arriving by air can take a shuttle service or taxi to their destination for a somewhat reasonable ($40-ish) charge. More information about the airport is available under *Getting There and Around* in

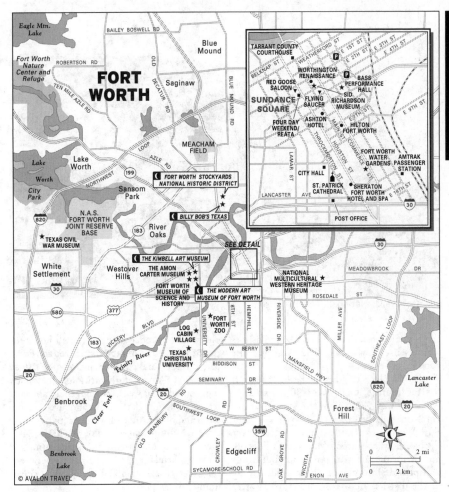

the *Dallas* section. Upon arrival to Fort Worth, visitors can get around town rather swiftly on the transit system (known as "the T"), but a car is perhaps the best option for getting to and from restaurants, attractions, and hotels more conveniently.

SIGHTS
◖ Fort Worth Stockyards National Historic District

Nothing says Fort Worth (or Texas) like a district dedicated entirely to cattle. The Stockyards, located two miles north of downtown in a heritage village-type atmosphere, represent the heart of Fort Worth's cultural history. Make no mistake, this is genuine cowboy stuff—livestock pens, saloons, a rodeo arena, and dozens of other historic structures tell the stories of the cattle drives and the rugged trail hands that followed their trampled tracks 100-plus years ago. Despite some touristy elements (Western-themed trinket shops, Longhorn

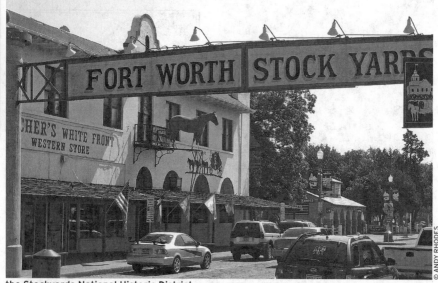

the Stockyards National Historic District

© ANDY RHODES

cattle photo-ops), the Stockyards offer visitors a true sense of what the Wild West was like back in its heyday.

A good place to start is the **Fort Worth Visitor Information Center** (130 E. Exchange Ave., 817/625-9715, www.stockyardsstation. com, open daily), a half mile past the giant Fort Worth Stockyards sign that spans over Exchange Avenue just off Main Street. Friendly and helpful staff will point out buildings and provide information about guided tours of the district. Across the street, the stately 1902 **Livestock Exchange Building** (131 E. Exchange Ave.) captures the business side of Fort Worth's agricultural activity from a historical and modern perspective. Inside, the small **Stockyards Museum** (817/625-5087, www.stockyardsmuseum.org, Mon.–Sat. 10 A.M.–5 P.M.) showcases artifacts and documents related to the area's agricultural heritage. Next door, the 1908 **Cowtown Coliseum**'s (121 E. Exchange Ave., 817/625-1025, www. cowtowncoliseum.com) understated grandeur is a perfect backdrop for one of the world's oldest indoor rodeo arenas. It's still home to the **Stockyards Championship Rodeo** (Fri.– Sat. at 8 P.M.) and occasionally **Pawnee Bill's Wild West Show,** featuring trick roping, shooting, and riding as well as cowboy songs and entertainment. Check the Coliseum's website for dates and times. Another worthy activity is the **Grapevine Vintage Railroad** (817/625-7245, www.gvrr.com), a rustic train ride running most weekends throughout the year between the Stockyard Station and the outlying community of Grapevine.

The Stockyards' **daily cattle drives** (11:30 A.M. and 4 P.M.) showcase a dozen magnificent Longhorn cattle sauntering down the main drag accompanied by period-costumed drivers. The event offers a nice touch of living history, but don't feel compelled to plan your day around the five-minute occurrence.

To make the most of your trip to the Stockyards, visit on a weekend evening for a full slate of events: a stroll through Exchange Street's Western shops, a hearty meal at a steak house, a rodeo at the Coliseum, and top it all

HEAD 'EM UP!

Although historians have debated aspects of the Chisholm Trail's storied past – including the exact route and even its name – none deny its significance in the settlement of the western United States.

The trail was named for Jesse Chisholm, a trader who blazed a route through Kansas and Oklahoma that was eventually used by cowboys to drive Texas longhorns to the northern cattle markets. For roughly two decades – from the end of the Civil War until the mid-1880s – tens of thousands of cowboys rode trails from deep in the heart of Texas to the middle of Kansas, where railroads took millions of cattle east to meat packing centers.

Not surprisingly, Texas is quite proud of its Chisholm Trail heritage. Cattle drives often started from legendary sites such as the 825,000-acre King Ranch near the state's southern tip and continued northwest to San Antonio. From there, cattle moved north through Austin and on to Fort Worth, dubbed "Cowtown," a nickname it still holds.

Although other cattle drive routes existed at the time, none penetrated the heart of popular imagination quite like the Chisholm Trail. Through songs, stories, and mythical tales, the Chisholm Trail has played an important role in developing Texas's Wild West mystique.

donated his art collection and entire personal fortune to the Kimbell Art Foundation, which opened the museum in 1972.

Brimming with significant and intriguing works of art in a remarkably designed building, The Kimbell offers a rewarding visual experience that resonates with visitors long after departing. The Louis I. Kahn–designed building truly enhances the experience by bathing the museum's concrete walls and artwork with indirect natural light emanating from gently sloping overhead barrel-vault arches.

The works contained within range in period from antiquity to the 20th century. The most memorable pieces are from modern notables such as Monet, Cézanne, Picasso, and Matisse. Though lacking in great number, the museum's collection of older European masters is also significant, including masterpieces from El Greco, Rubens, and Rembrandt, as well as an impressive collection of Asian art.

The Kimbell also regularly hosts world-class traveling exhibits highlighting masterworks of painting and sculpture from premier collections. In addition, the museum hosts arts-related lectures, seminars, films, and musical performances throughout the year.

◖ The Modern Art Museum of Fort Worth

Like The Kimbell, The Modern Art Museum of Fort Worth (3200 Darnell St., 817/738 9215, www.mamfw.org, Tues.–Sun. 10 A.M.–5 P.M., $10 adults age 13–59, $4 students and seniors) is stunning for its building alone. Designed by renowned Japanese architect Tadao Ando, "The Modern" is a remarkable structure that appears to float upon a placid pond. Gazing upon the building's dramatic concrete and glass exterior—one of the best views is from the café's patio—reveals the intricate plan and attention to detail (notice how the pool reflects dancing splashes of gilded sunlight onto the underside of the museum's concrete roof).

The visual delights are equally amazing inside, where more than 2,600 significant works of international modern art, from compelling abstract expressionism to recognized pop art

off with a whiskey or cold beer at the legendary White Elephant Saloon.

◖ The Kimbell Art Museum

The cream of the crop in Fort Worth Cultural District is The Kimbell Art Museum (3333 Camp Bowie Blvd., 817/332-8451, www. kimbellart.org, Tues.–Thurs. and Sat. 10 A.M.–5 P.M., Fri. noon–8 P.M., and Sun. noon–5 P.M., no admission charge for permanent collection; varying fees for traveling exhibits), which regularly receives accolades for being one of the finest art museums of its kind in the country. Fort Worth entrepreneur Kay Kimbell

to abstract figurative sculpture, await around each corner of Tadao's own architectural masterpiece. Andy Warhol's familiar silkscreen shares space with Donald Judd's highly stylized artwork, and major traveling exhibits offer even more contemporary imagery.

The Amon Carter Museum

Another of the city's world-class attractions is The Amon Carter Museum (3501 Camp Bowie Blvd., 817/738-1933, www.cartermuseum.org, Tues.–Sat. 10 A.M.–5 P.M., Thurs. until 8 P.M., Sun. noon–5 P.M., no admission charge). Although it's grounded in Western art, "The Carter" covers an impressive range of high-quality American art, from sculptures to paintings to photographs. Through his friendship with Will Rogers, Carter developed an interest in the work of legendary Western artists Frederic Remington and Charles M. Russell, and his extensive collection of their art is the basis for the museum.

Although it's an impressive component, the remainder of the collection is perhaps even more noteworthy. The photography, in particular, is stunning—the black-and-white images of American life are especially profound and gripping, and the paintings are just as mesmerizing, especially the selections from Georgia O'Keeffe, Thomas Eakins, and Winslow Homer. The Carter has a reputation for having one of the foremost collections of American artwork. A visit to the museum confirms this distinctive status.

The Fort Worth Museum of Science and History

The most family-friendly destination in the Cultural District is the Fort Worth Museum of Science and History (1600 Gendy St., 817/255 9300, www.fwmuseum.org, daily 10 A.M.–5 P.M., admission includes access to the adjacent National Cowgirl Museum: $14 adults, $10 children 2–12 and seniors). The museum received a dramatic face-lift in 2009, with a bold, blocky, colorful design. The new Fort Worth Museum of Science and History building is an innovative work of architecture

the Fort Worth Museum of Science and History

designed by the highly acclaimed architectural firm Legorreta + Legorreta of Mexico City. The architect describes the 166,000-square-foot facility as "a very happy environment—a building for kids, young people and adults" with Latin American–based design elements such as bright colors (deep red, yellow, bright pink), courtyards, and extensive use of glass.

The museum's collections and exhibits are equally compelling. Home to more than 175,000 historical and scientific objects with an emphasis on Texas and the Southwest, the museum showcases cultural heritage, botany, entomology, zoology, and paleontology. Popular attractions include the fascinating Cattle Raisers Museum, dinosaur dig/laboratory, the Children's Museum, and IMAX movies.

National Cowgirl Museum and Hall of Fame

Make a point of visiting the National Cowgirl Museum and Hall of Fame (1720 Gendy St., 817/336-4475, www.cowgirl.net, Tues.–Sun. 10 A.M.–5 P.M., $10 adults, $8 children 3–12 and seniors), one of the most recent additions to the Fort Worth Cultural District. Housed in a 33,000-square-foot building designed to mirror Fort Worth's historic Cowtown structures, the museum showcases the important role women played in the American West.

Its origins date to 1975 in the Panhandle community of Hereford, where the small National Cowgirl Hall of Fame honored pioneers, artists, writers, tribal leaders, social activists, and modern ranchers and rodeo cowgirls. These attributes became the basis for the current facility.

Visually stunning in its design and layout, the museum's interior is a dazzling spectacle of open spaces, bright colors, and a 45-foot-high domed rotunda housing the impressive Hall of Fame honoree exhibits, which display changing images on glass screens. Although the museum makes a point of celebrating the heroines it honors, there's also a lot of fun to be had. Check out the media and fashion displays, and be sure to stop by the simulated bronco-

© ANDY RHODES

the National Cowgirl Museum and Hall of Fame

riding exhibit, where visitors are filmed. The resulting digital movie clips are available on the museum's website.

Will Rogers Memorial Center

The Will Rogers Memorial Center (3401 W. Lancaster Ave., 817/392-7469, www.fortworth-gov.org, open to the public weekdays and for equestrian events on weekends, free admission) presides over the Cultural District with its colossal art deco tower. Named by Fort Worth civic pioneer Amon Carter for his friend Will Rogers (the famous cowboy performer), the stately art deco buildings remain significant attractions in the district. The coliseum and auditorium appropriately represent Cowtown culture with livestock shows and theatrical events.

Be sure to note the magnificent architectural elements throughout the complex, including the coliseum's innovative girder support system allowing unobstructed views, and the nearly 200-foot-tall decorative tower. A bronze bust

the Will Rogers Memorial Center in the heart of Fort Worth

of Will Rogers in the facility's lobby is the subject of a popular local legend that claims rodeo cowboys have rubbed a dent into the statue's nose while attempting to bestow Rogers's good fortune on their performance. Although the nose bears a notable impression, it's really there from the statue being accidentally dropped during installation.

Fort Worth Zoo

Set aside an afternoon to experience the remarkable Fort Worth Zoo (1989 Colonial Pkwy., 817/759 7555, www.fortworthzoo.com, daily 10 A.M.–5 P.M., winter months until 4 P.M., $12 adults, $9 children 3–12 and seniors), considered one of the country's premier zoos, and for good reason. This sprawling eight-acre complex feels less like a zoo and more like a collection of habitats, with exotic African and Asian creatures (elephants, rhinos, monkeys, lions, tigers, giraffes, zebra, hippopotamus) often lounging a hundred feet away from visitors with only a pond located between man and beast.

Bamboo and tropical trees are everywhere, giving the impression of walking through jungle trails to hunt down the next attraction. Many exhibits, including the World of Primates, include large Plexiglas windows offering views so close, you can practically feel the beasts' breath. Kids will love seeing parakeets crawl onto their seed-on-a-stick treat (available for a buck each), and adults will be fascinated with the prehistoric marvel and grace of exotic elephants, wrinkly rhinos, and hefty hippos. The Meerkat Mounds are popular, and the Texas Wild! exhibit is a good way to get a handle on the impressive variety of creatures crawling around the Lone Star State.

Fort Worth Botanic Garden

Experience the sensory delight of the Fort Worth Botanic Garden (3220 Botanic Dr., 817/871-7686, www.fwbg.org, Mon–Fri. 8 A.M.–10 P.M., Sat. 8 A.M.–7 P.M., Sun. 1–7 P.M., $1 adults, 50 cents seniors and children ages 4–12), with 2,500 species of native and exotic plants on display in 21 gardens

© ANDY RHODES

the lush Fort Worth Botanic Garden

throughout 109 acres of Trinity Park. Most of the garden has a tropical feel, with waterfalls, ponds, and lushly surrounded pathways offering visitors a welcome respite from the nearby urban environment. The Latin American tropics are highlighted in a 10,000-square-foot glass conservatory with more than 2,500 plants. Other areas worth meandering through are the sweetly scented Rose Garden and the artfully designed Japanese Garden. The garden center and conservatory are open at different times during the week and throughout the year, and various fees apply for different gardens; visit the website for specific information.

Sundance Square

The 20-block Sundance Square Downtown Entertainment District (817/255-5700, www. sundancesquare.com) is filled with restaurants, theaters, art galleries, museums, specialty boutiques, and nightlife. The area is named for the Sundance Kid, who, along with fellow legendary outlaw Butch Cassidy, once hid out in Fort Worth. In the late 1800s and early 1900s,

Fort Worth's downtown area was filled with saloons, gambling parlors, and dance halls, drawing a rough-and-tumble mix of cattlemen and outlaws. Most of Sundance Square's remaining buildings, brick streets, and courtyards from that period have been restored, offering a glimpse into the city's Wild West past. Of particular note are the 1895 **Tarrant County Courthouse** (100 E. Weatherford St.), 1889 **Land Title Building** (111 E. 4th St.), 1901 **Knights of Pythias Castle Hall** (315 Main St.), and circa 1902 **Jett Building** (400 Main St.), the last featuring an enormous and legendary Chisholm Trail mural spanning the building's southern facade.

Fort Worth Water Gardens

If you're downtown, be sure to walk through the Fort Worth Water Gardens (1502 Commerce St., 817/392-7111, water runs 7 A.M.–10 P.M.), a remarkable urban park with water cascading, flowing, bubbling, and sparkling in every direction. Designed by famed New York architect Philip Johnson (who also designed The Amon

COMPELLING COUNTY COURTHOUSES

Texas isn't just bragging when it claims to have more historic courthouses than any other state. Incredibly, more than 225 courthouses still stand that are officially historic (at least 50 years old), and nearly 80 of those were built before the turn of the 20th century.

Although many of them have deteriorated due to abandonment or inadequate maintenance, the Texas Historical Commission developed a statewide program to preserve these majestic architectural gems.

Courthouses served as the centerpieces of most Texas communities, and they often brought striking sophistication to rural parts of the state. Elaborate architectural plans and a variety of styles – Romanesque Revival, Beaux-Arts, Second Empire – contributed to the diversity of Texas's built environment. In addition to holding municipal records and offices, the courthouses also hosted community events and bolstered civic pride.

Several of the state's most impressive courthouses are in small communities just outside the Metroplex. To experience the best examples of the restored dramatic grandeur, visit the Ellis County Courthouse in Waxahachie (south of Dallas), the Denton County Courthouse in Denton (north of Fort Worth), and the Hopkins County Courthouse in Sulphur Springs (northeast of Dallas).

Carter Museum), the Water Gardens are a perfect oasis in a hot, dry, Western town like Fort Worth. Visitors, residents, and nearby office employees gaze upon the pleasant fountains and flowing water as it channels throughout this architectural marvel, which opened in 1974. The open nature of the park has had its drawbacks, however. Over the years, several people have died at the Water Gardens, prompting a major renovation in 2007, with significant enhancements and changes such as interpretive plaques, additional railings, warning signs, seats, and barriers around the pools.

Fort Worth Nature Center and Refuge

Located 10 miles northwest of downtown, the Fort Worth Nature Center and Refuge (9601 Fossil Ridge Rd., 817/392-7410, www.naturecenter.org, daily 8 A.M.–5 P.M., summer hours until 7 P.M., $4 adults, $3 seniors, $2 children ages 3–17) offers 3,600 acres of wilderness, primarily forests, prairies, and wetlands. Residents and visitors can experience the natural side of North Texas through more than 20 miles of hiking trails, an interpretive center, and occasional sightings of bison and white-tailed deer. Located two miles past Lake Worth bridge on Jacksboro Highway (Route 199).

Log Cabin Village

Families will enjoy the Log Cabin Village (2100 Log Cabin Village Ln., 817/392-5881, www.logcabinvillage.org, Tues.–Fri. 9 A.M.–4 P.M., Sat.–Sun. 1–5 P.M., $4.50 adults, $4 children ages 4–17 and seniors), featuring seven authentic pioneer homes built during the mid-19th century and moved to the current site in the 1950s. The site's exhibits include a water-powered gristmill, one-room schoolhouse, and blacksmith shop. Historical interpreters depict the lifestyle of the pioneers who settled in the area.

The Texas Cowboy Hall of Fame

The Texas Cowboy Hall of Fame (128 E. Exchange, 817/626-7131, www.texascowboyhalloffame.org, Mon.–Thurs. 10 A.M.–6 P.M., Fri.–Sat. 10 A.M.–7 P.M., Sun. 11 A.M.–5 P.M., $5 adults, $4 students ages 13–17 and seniors, $3 children ages 5–12) is conveniently located in one of the Stockyards District's historic barns. The museum features impressive exhibits with cowboy and Chisholm Trail memorabilia, a sizable antique carriage collection, and a hall of fame honoring dozens of famous cowboys and cowgirls from Texas.

Sid Richardson Museum

Located in the historic Sundance Square

District, the Sid Richardson Museum (309 Main St., 888/332-6554, www.sidrichardsonmuseum.org, Mon.–Thurs. 9 A.M.–5 P.M., Fri.–Sat. 9 A.M.–8 P.M., Sun. noon–5 P.M., free admission) offers free tours of its remarkable Western art collection. Highlights include paintings of the Old West by Frederic Remington, Charles M. Russell, and other artists in the collection of legendary Texas oilman and philanthropist Sid W. Richardson.

Western Currency Facility Tour and Visitor Center

If you've ever dreamed of making billions of dollars in mere minutes, visit "the money factory," aka the Western Currency Facility Tour and Visitor Center (9000 Blue Mound Rd., 817/231-4000, www.moneyfactory.gov, Mon.–Fri. 8:30 A.M.–3:30 P.M., free admission). An elevated walkway over the production floor allows visitors to preside over millions of freshly printed bills as part of a 45-minute tour including interactive exhibits and an informative theater film. Tours are offered on a first-come, first-served basis, and be sure to allow 30 minutes for everyone to make it through the not-surprisingly heavy security.

Texas Civil War Museum

The Texas Civil War Museum (760 Jim Wright Frwy. N., 817/246-2323, www.texascivilwarmuseum.com, Tues.–Sat. 9 A.M.–5 P.M., $6 adults, $3 students ages 7–12) is one of the largest Civil War museums in the country. Boasting more than 15,000 square feet of exhibits, the museum contains three major galleries: a Civil War collection, Victorian dress collection, and United Daughters of the Confederacy Texas Confederate collection.

National Multicultural Western Heritage Museum

The National Multicultural Western Heritage Museum (3400 Mount Vernon Ave., 817/534-8801, www.cowboysofcolor.org, Wed.–Sat. 10 A.M.–6 P.M., $6 adults, $4 seniors, $3 students ages 6 and up) highlights the important contributions of the state's ethnically diverse cowboys and other prominent African-Americans. Featured exhibits showcase the frontier-era black servicemen known as Buffalo Soldiers, early African-American flying pioneer Bessie Coleman, and significant achievements of Native Americans and Hispanics in Texas history.

Downtown Marker Program

Nearly two dozen bronze markers, known as the **Heritage Trails,** are scattered throughout downtown Fort Worth, offering a historical tour of the people and events that shaped the city's history. Notable markers include JFK, Gamblers & Gunfights, and Architectural Diversity. For more information about the markers and a map of their locations, visit www.fortworthheritagetrails.com.

ENTERTAINMENT AND EVENTS

Nightlife in Fort Worth is generally separated into two hubs of activity: the Stockyards (historic locales) and Sundance Square (historic and hipper locales). Though the Stockyard's saloons are more touristy, you're more likely to have a memorable experience there—even if those memories are of saddle-shaped barstools, period-dressed waitstaff, and longhorns mounted on every wall. Sundance Square draws a younger crowd, and even though the bars are somewhat generic, they're more active and open later. If you're in search of higher culture, the magnificent Bass Performance Hall is a worthy destination even if you're not attending a show.

Performing Arts

For upscale entertainment, it doesn't get much classier than the remarkable **Bass Performance Hall** (525 Commerce St., 877/212-4280, www.basshall.com). Billed as the last great performance hall built in the 20th century, this stately facility is reminiscent of the classic European opera houses. Architectural features include two enormous angels (48 feet tall) sculpted from Texas limestone on the building's facade and a colorfully painted 80-foot-diameter "Great Dome" above the concert theater. Bass is home to the Fort Worth Symphony Orchestra, Texas Ballet Theater, Fort Worth Opera, and the Van Cliburn International Piano Competition. Visit the website for information about touring shows.

The improvisational comedy group **Four Day Weekend** (312 Houston St., 817/226-4329, www.fourdayweekend.com) traffics in interactive entertainment. The audience is invited to become part of the hilarity by submitting ideas for improv routines or by joining the cast on stage for short ad-lib routines. Video, music, and the cast's sharp skills enhance this unpredictable experience. Shows are held Friday–Saturday at 7:30 P.M. and 10 P.M. Tickets are $20.

Bars and Clubs
C BILLY BOB'S TEXAS
The most famous of Fort Worth's entertainment venues is Billy Bob's Texas (2520 Rodeo Plaza, 817/624-7117, www.billybobstexas.com, Mon.–Sat. 11 A.M.–2 A.M., Sun. noon–2 A.M., varying cover charge), billed as "the world's largest honky-tonk." Located just a block north of the main drag in the Stockyards district, Billy Bob's has to be seen to be believed. From the outside, it looks like an enormous arena, and the three acres of interior space are reminiscent of a cavernous Las Vegas casino. There's a bull ring for live bull riding (no mechanical knock-offs here), a Texas-worthy oversized dance floor, a live music venue, arcade and casino games, monstrous gift shop, and 32 individual bar stations. Concerts are held on weekends, as are the bull-riding events. Despite being a bit overboard on the over-the-top Texas atmosphere, Billy Bob's is nevertheless worth visiting just to enjoy a cold Lone Star draft, people watching, and the distinction of experiencing the world's largest honky-tonk.

THE STOCKYARDS
This is a great place to spend a couple nights on the town in Fort Worth. Several area saloons are legendary turn-of-the-20th-century watering holes, where cattlemen bellied up to the bar after a long day of trail driving.

Be sure to catch a glimpse of the boot-scootin' regulars as they two-step and waltz to traditional country and western swing music at other notable Stockyards nightlife venues such as the **White Elephant Saloon** (106 E. Exchange Ave., 817/624-8273, www.whiteelephantsaloon.com, Sun.–Thurs. noon–midnight, Fri.–Sat. noon–2 A.M.). This venerable watering hole is known as the district's most historic saloon and dance hall, and features live music every night of the week. Also worth moseying into is the **Longhorn Saloon** (121 W. Exchange Ave., 817/386-5962), a genuine Western bar that's hosted legendary musicians like Hank Williams and Bob Wills. Another worthy venue is **Pearl's Dance Hall & Saloon** (302 W. Exchange Ave., 817/624-2800), a former bordello commissioned by Buffalo Bill Cody that's been beautifully restored.

SUNDANCE SQUARE
The Stockyards have the history, but Sundance Square has the hip. This comfortably sized area (20 blocks) has an active nightlife scene with plenty of live music venues, dance clubs, and beer joints. Among the best is the **Red Goose Saloon** (306 Houston St., 817/332-4343), a gently worn club with two hoppin' areas inside. Downstairs is a traditional bar with reasonable prices and a welcoming atmosphere. Upstairs is the dance floor, with a rowdy crowd and fun beats. For an amazing beer selection, head directly to **Flying Saucer** (111 E. 4th St., 817/332-5662, www.beerknurd.com/), a laid-back place with more than 100 beers on tap, upper and lower beer gardens, and live local music a couple nights a week. Similar in approach is **8.0** (111 E. 3rd St., 817/336-0880), which has an incredible patio, live music, and a dance floor with a live DJ. For those intent on cutting a rug, take it to **City Streets** (425 Commerce St., 817/335-5400, www.citystreetsfortworth.com.), offering dance floors with rap, pop, and karaoke. If you're looking for a roomy place to watch a ballgame with nightly drink specials, try **Fox and Hound** (604 Main St., 817/338-9200).

Events

WINTER

The Southwestern Exposition and Livestock Show and Rodeo (817/877-2400, www.fwstockshowrodeo.com) is one of the largest events of its kind in Texas. Dating to 1896, this annual 17-day event in January is highlighted by an "all-Western" parade (no motor vehicles allowed) through downtown. Other events include nightly rodeos, cowboy competitions, commercial exhibits, and auctions; most events take place at the Will Rogers Memorial Coliseum.

Held each February, **The Last Great Gunfight** (817/624-8273) is about as Wild West as it gets. In 1887, Luke Short, owner of the White Elephant Saloon, outdrew ex–Fort Worth marshall Jim "Longhair" Courtright on the street in front of the saloon. Deemed the town's last significant duel of its kind, the event is reenacted annually in front of the White Elephant.

SPRING

Mayfest (817/332-1055, www.mayfest.org), which actually begins in late April, is Fort Worth's annual celebration of spring, complete with arts, crafts, live music, sporting events, and food at Trinity Park near the Cultural District.

The Van Cliburn International Piano Competition (817/738-6536, www.cliburn.org) celebrates Fort Worth native Van Cliburn's victory at the first Tchaikovsky International Competition in Moscow in 1958. First held in 1962 and repeated every four years since, the Van Cliburn competition is considered one of the world's most prestigious classical piano contests.

SUMMER

Fort Worth's **Juneteenth Celebration** (214/353-4445), like others throughout the Lone Star State, celebrates the June 19, 1865, announcement of the Emancipation Proclamation, belatedly resulting in the freeing of 250,000 slaves in Texas. Fort Worth's annual event features daylong activities including a downtown parade along with hundreds of vendors lining the streets, as well as cultural activities, carnival rides, and live music.

FALL

The city's **Red Steagall Cowboy Gathering and Western Swing Festival** (800/433-5747, www.redsteagallcowboygathering.com) features three days of cowboy poetry, rodeos, campfire songs, children's events, and a chuck wagon competition, all named for the venerable country and western entertainer.

The National Cutting Horse Association (817/244-6188, www.nchacutting.com) hosts an annual event where sports, music, and media icons ride horseback at Will Rogers Memorial Coliseum, followed by an after-party concert, dinner, and silent auction.

SHOPPING

Not surprisingly, Fort Worth has an impressive collection of authentic Western wear and leather goods (boots, saddles, etc.) in addition to several chic cowboy boutiques. Once again, the two main areas of activity are the Stockyards and Sundance Square.

The Stockyards

The Stockyards and Western wear fit together like leg and denim. A stroll through the district will take you past plenty of shops offering cowboy duds, but two of the most noteworthy are **Luskey's/Ryon's Western Stores Inc.** (2601 N. Main St., 817/625-2391, www.luskeys.com) and **Maverick Western Wear** (100 E. Exchange Ave., 800/282-1315, www.maverickwesternwear.com). Both have authentic selections such as jeans, bolo ties, Western shirts, and vests.

For leather goods, including custom-made boots, saddles, hats, and tack, one of the best options in the entire city is **M.L. Leddy's Boots and Saddlery** (2455 N. Main St., 888/565-2668, www.leddys.com). Just down the street, another local favorite offering similar items is **Ryon's Saddle and Ranch Supply** (2601 N. Main St., 817/625-2391). Other leather and Western goods are available at **Ponder Boot Co.** (2358 N. Main St., 817/626-3523).

Sundance Square

In addition to its top-notch nightlife and restaurants, Sundance Square is a hot spot for shopping. Granted, you'll find some familiar stuff—trendy clothing shops and artsy boutiques—but there are several stores that are good ambassadors of Fort Worth. Perhaps most noteworthy is **Leddy's Ranch** (410 Houston St., 817/336-0800, www.leddys.com), a family business that started in the Stockyards more than 85 years ago. The Sundance Square location deviates slightly from its traditional-minded Stockyards store by offering fashions for cutting-edge cowgirls plus an impressive assortment of jewelry and antiques. Another Cowtown-worthy venue is **Retro Cowboy** (406 Houston St., 817/338-1194), a retail outpost with Western clothing, gifts, and memorabilia.

Outlying Areas

Although most of Fort Worth's authentic and interesting Western shops are in the Stockyards, there are several other spots around town worth visiting for deals and different selections. Most notable is the **Justin Boot Co. Factory Outlet** (717 W. Vickery Blvd., 817/885-8089, www.justinboots.com), where bargains are the draw. Expect 30–40 percent off retail prices for cowboy boots, casual chukkas, steel-toed work boots, or classic lace-up ropers. Another popular destination for shoppers seeking treasures at affordable prices is **Western Wear Exchange** (2809 Alta Mere/Hwy. 183, 817/738-4048, www.weternwearexchange.com), a consignment store with a special concentration on vintage and new pearl-snap shirts (they have nearly 2,500 in stock).

ACCOMMODATIONS
$50-100

Offering the basics at a bargain price is **Microtel Inns & Suites** (3740 Tanacross Dr., 817/222-3740, www.fortworthmicrotel.com, $53 d). Amenities include a free continental breakfast, free Internet access, and a fitness center.

One of the best sub-$100 deals in town is **Quality Inn & Suites** (2700 S. Cherry Ln.,

817/560-4180, www.qualityinn.com, $78 d). For that minor price, consider these major features: free full hot breakfast; free manager's reception (Monday–Thursday evenings) with beer, wine, hot snacks, and homemade cookies; free barbecue get-together in the ranch house living room (Thursday); free Wi-Fi access; outdoor pool and sundeck.

$100-150

Just a few miles up the road from the Stockyards is ▐ **Hilton Garden Inn** (4400 North Frwy., 214/637-9000, www.hiltongardeninn.com, $103 d), a new, comfortable, and family-friendly option. Guests are greeted with warm cookies and cold fruit at the front desk, and the lobby area is stocked with board games. The indoor and outdoor pools and hot tub provide a relaxing way to wind down after a day of sightseeing. Amenities include free Internet access, and microwaves and refrigerators in all rooms.

Located seven miles from downtown, the **Fairfield Inn** (3701 NE Loop 820, 817/232-5700, www.fairfieldinn.com, $116 d) offers a complimentary breakfast and has an indoor pool and spa. The Fairfield includes an exercise room, and minisuites with a private spa, microwave, and refrigerator.

Though it's a bit far from the downtown activity and located on a strangely isolated parcel of land off the freeway, there's much to like about **Country Inn & Suites** (2200 Mercado Dr., 817/831-9200, www.countryinns.com, $139 d). Amenities include suites with a small sink, refrigerator, microwave, and separate room with couch (these are the standard rooms, not an upgrade), as well as free high-speed Internet access, complimentary breakfast, a heated outdoor pool and Jacuzzi, a fitness center, and pet-friendly rooms. Of note: The only other nearby establishment is a Tex-Mex restaurant (**Mercado Juarez Café**) immediately adjacent to the hotel, which happens to be *excelente*.

Farther west of town is **Holiday Inn Express** (2730 S. Cherry Ln, 817/560-4200, www.hiexpress.com, $149 d). Nothing too fancy here, but it's fairly new and offers reliable services such as free Internet access, an outdoor pool and hot tub, a fitness center, and a free hot breakfast bar.

$150-200

Just a few miles away from the Cultural District's attractions is **Residence Inn** (2500 Museum Wy., 817/885-8250, www.residenceinn.com, $150 d), offering complimentary hot breakfasts, free drinks during "hospitality hour" (Monday–Thursday), an outdoor sports court and pool, and whirlpool. The large suites feature separate living and sleeping areas, and stocked kitchens.

A nice downtown option with easy access to most of the city's attractions is **Holiday Inn Express** (1111 W. Lancaster Ave., 817/698-9595, www.hiexpress.com, $171 d). Amenities include complimentary shuttle services anywhere within a three-mile radius of the hotel, an indoor pool and whirlpool, a fitness center, free high-speed Internet access, and a free hot breakfast bar.

One of the best deals for those looking to stay in a fancy downtown hotel is the **(Hilton Fort Worth** (815 Main St., 817/870-2100, www.hilton.com, $189 d). The Hilton is registered as a National Historic Landmark and has the distinction of being the place where President John F. Kennedy spent his final night (he was assassinated in Dallas the following morning). The hotel's large rooms offer all the standard amenities, with the small yet valued bonus of including two complimentary bottled waters daily.

Directly in the middle of all the Stockyards activity atop a small hill overlooking Exchange Avenue is **Hyatt Place Fort Worth Stockyards** (132 E. Exchange Ave., 817/626-6000, www.hyatt.com, $161 d). Amenities include complimentary continental breakfast each morning, an outdoor heated pool, free Wi-Fi, and rooms with 42-inch panel HDTVs.

Another popular downtown option is the **Worthington Renaissance** (200 Main St., 817/870-1000, www.renaissancehotels.com, $189 d), which overlooks Sundance Square.

It features an indoor pool, spa tub, sauna, massage services, and rooms equipped with minibars.

$200-250

If you're planning to plunk down $200 for a night in the Stockyards, you may as well go whole hog and do it right at the historic **Stockyards Hotel** (109 E. Exchange Ave., 800/423-8471, www.stockyardshotel.com, $209 d). Once a hideout for notorious gangsters Bonnie and Clyde, the Stockyards Hotel revels in its heritage, with different Western themes in each room (plus tasty snack baskets) and the charm that comes with a 1907 building listed on the National Register of Historic Places.

Fort Worth's newest downtown hotel is the stunning **Omni Fort Worth** (1300 Houston St., 817/535-6664, www.omnihotels.com, $249 d). Located adjacent to the Fort Worth Convention Center, the Omni has a true Texas feel, with Lone Star–themed art and bedding (saddle blanket throws and stitched pillows). Amenities include a fitness center, full-service spa, and Internet access.

$250 and above

Fort Worth's most elegant downtown option is the beautiful **Ashton Hotel** (610 Main St., 817/332-0100, www.theashtonhotel.com, $269 d). Renovated to its historic grandeur, the Ashton features designer bedding and furniture along with minibars, custom robes, and, perhaps most luxurious for parents, babysitting services.

For those seeking Fort Worth's top-of-the-line accommodations, there's **Sheraton Fort Worth Hotel and Spa** (1701 Commerce St., 817/335-7000, www.starwoodhotels.com, $349 d). This remodeled hotel near the convention center features rooms with 32-inch HD televisions and wireless Internet access, and the hotel's signature spa, including an indoor heated pool, sauna, whirlpool, and fitness center.

Bed-and-Breakfasts

Located in a historic neighborhood southwest

of downtown is the charming **Texas White House** (1417 8th Ave., 800/279-6491, www. texaswhitehouse.com, $125–205). The friendly folks here proudly offer three large rooms in the main house with full private bathrooms, and two suites in the carriage house a fireplace, whirlpool tubs, and sauna. On-site massage services are available, and a tasty breakfast (fancy egg dishes, homemade pastries, fresh fruit) at a time of your choosing starts the day off right. Additional services include early coffee service to your room, free soft drinks, and afternoon snacks.

More historic hotel than typical bed-and-breakfast, **Miss Molly's** (109 W. Exchange Ave., 817/626-1522, www.missmollyshotel. com, $100–175) is one of the only lodging options available in the Stockyards. A former brothel, Miss Molly's was built nearly 100 years ago and reflects Fort Worth's colorful cowboy history in its seven rooms furnished with Old West antiques. Incidentally, Miss Molly's has a reputation for hosting paranormal activity—which can either be fascinating of frightening depending on the traveler—including ghost sightings and unexplained sounds.

Camping

Just six miles southwest of town is **Benbrook Lake** (817/292-2400, www.recreation.gov), where the U.S. Army Corps of Engineers administers six public campgrounds offering sites for utility hookups and primitive camping.

Another option east of downtown is **Sunset RV Park** (5017 White Settlement Rd., 817/738-0567) in the village of Sunset, a rural area surrounded by ranches, farms, and other small towns. The park offers full hookups, free wireless Internet access, showers, and a laundry room.

FOOD

Unless you're a vegetarian, eating a steak is almost mandatory on a visit to Cowtown, and the city has plenty of fine options to choose from, particularly in the Stockyards. Once you've had your fill of steak, order more meat at a legendary barbecue joint or burger counter.

If you're still hankering for a big plate of local goodness, drop by one of Fort Worth's fine Tex-Mex establishments for a beef taco. When in Cowtown . . . .

The Stockyards
STEAK AND AMERICAN

Although the Stockyards have plenty of good steak restaurants to choose from, the best of the bunch is ☑ **Cattlemen's Steakhouse** (2458 N. Main St., 817/624-3945, www.cattlemenssteakhouse.com, open daily, $15–34). Immediately upon entering the weighty doors of this legendary establishment, there's no denying Cattlemen's is all about the beef. The enormous photos of stately bulls adorning the walls and the sound of clanging steak knives are forbearers of the feast that awaits. The popular Rose o' Texas tenderloin is a prime cut of savory charcoal-broiled beef, and the rib eye steaks offer a joyful jolt of succulent flavor. Order the fresh sautéed mushrooms for a perfect flavorful accompaniment, and try to save room for blueberry cobbler.

Just down the street, **Lonesome Dove Western Bistro** (2406 N. Main St., 817/740-8810, www.lonesomedovebistro.com, closed Sun. and Mon., $20–39) offers steaks and Southwestern fare with an eclectic twist. Esteemed chef (and native Texan) Tim Love focuses on steak and wild game, and the results are a true Texas original. It's the only place in the country where can you order huge cuts of Texas steer, grilled Texas quail quesadillas, or braised boar ribs seasoned with inventive rubs or sauces containing European influences. Even the buffalo burgers are exquisite. Food Network fans take note: Chef Love was one of the few competitors on *Iron Chef America* to defeat the esteemed Masaharu Morimoto (in a chile competition). Reservations are recommended.

The new kid on the culinary block in the Stockyards is actually a legendary veteran of Texas barbecue. **Cooper's Old Time Pit Bar-B-Que** (301 Stockyards Blvd., 817/626-6464, www.coopersbbqfortworth.com, open daily, $8–36) is an outpost of the original location in Llano, considered by many barbecue

© ANDY RHODES

the legendary Cattlemen's Steakhouse in Fort Worth

aficionados to be the best in Texas. The similarities to the Llano location are numerous, including the primary focus on quality meats (as opposed to ambience). The signature "big chop" is a must—it's an enormously thick hunk of savory pork with a perfect mixture of flavors from the salt-and-pepper rub and slow-smoked pit. The tender brisket and beef ribs taste like prime rib, and there's even *cabrito* (goat) and ham on the menu.

TEX-MEX
One of the most famous Tex-Mex restaurants in the Metroplex is ((**Joe T. Garcia's** (2201 N. Commerce St., 817/626-4356, www.joets. com, open daily, $7–16). Originally a small room with seating for 16, Joe's has evolved into a gigantic multiwinged facility that accommodates more than 1,000. Even so, there's still usually a line out the door, though it moves pretty quickly. There are no menus for dinner, only a choice between two equally tasty options: the enchilada and taco plate combo or the equally satisfying fajitas. Lunch offers more to choose from, and it's all just as good, including chiles rellenos, tamales, and flautas.

Make sure you don't fill up on the premeal tortillas and butter (or thick chips), and be prepared to bring cash, since Joe T. does not accept credit cards.

Just across the street from Billy Bob's is **Los Vaqueros** (2629 N. Main St., 817/624-1511, www.losvaqueros.com, open daily, $8–16), another enormous (yet less legendary) Fort Worth locale in a charming historic building. The food is standard Tex-Mex fare, with tacos and enchiladas among the best options. Complete your meal with an order of sopapillas, thin puffy pastries dusted with cinnamon and sugar and served with honey.

Downtown
AMERICAN AND SOUTHWESTERN
If you're looking for a fine steak dinner downtown, head straight to **Del Frisco's Double Eagle Steak House** (812 Main St., 817/877-3999, open daily, $22–38). Though it's Chicago-based, everything else about this place is pure Texas, from the huge cuts of succulent meat to the Wild West decor to the colossal chocolate cake. Reservations are recommended.

Far more casual is the aptly named **Cowtown Diner** (305 Main St., 817/332-9555, www.thecowtowndiner.com, $10–20). Comfort food is the main draw here, so bring your appetite for standards like mac and cheese, Salisbury steak, and meatloaf, each with a fancy twist. Entrées are enhanced by subtle yet effective additions such as quality cheese, roasted red peppers, and freshly made sauces. Above-average side dishes (smoked Gouda mashed potatoes, creamed spinach) complete these well-rounded and generously portioned meals.

For those in search of something a bit more upscale, consider **Grace** (777 Main St., 817/877-3388, www.gracefortworth.com, $12–31). This is a great spot for drinks and appetizers, since Grace has developed a well-earned reputation for its quality cocktails and soups. The entrées are also top-notch, but sometimes an appealing dining experience consists of nothing more than an Old Fashioned (or two), a mushroom and cognac soup, and a side of bacon-wrapped onions.

Southwestern cuisine is the main draw at **(Reata** (310 Houston St., 817/336-1009, open daily, $12–29). The Reata is a rare small-town-to-big-city import (the original is in the West Texas town of Alpine), but the food has become a Fort Worth tradition with cuisine inspired by regional cowboy cooking: Tenderloin tamales, barbecue shrimp enchiladas, and smoked jalapeño quail are signature dishes that don't appear on menus in most other cities. Reservations are recommended.

Another erstwhile Texas/American tradition is barbecue, and one of the city's favorite proprietors is **Riscky's** (300 Main St., 817/877-3306, open daily, $9–18). Located on historic Sundance Square, Riscky's offers traditional barbecue (brisket, sausage, chicken), but its biggest draw are the giant beef ribs smoked over a wood fire and rubbed with "Riscky's Dust," a concoction of nearly 20 spices.

MEXICAN

Adjacent to Riscky's on Sundance Square is **Cabo Grandé** (115 W. 2nd St., 817/348-8226, www.cabogrande.com, open daily, $12–23),

an "upscale taqueria" with Mexican and Latin American influences. Although the restaurant offers pricier fare like red snapper and steaks, you're better off sticking with the classics—their queso, chicken enchiladas, and beef tacos are consistently good options.

One of the only other notable downtown Mexican restaurants is **Mi Cocina** (509 Main St., 817/877-3600, open daily, $7–15), a local chain that offers reliable Tex-Mex cuisine. Locals love the Mama's Tacos and fresh guacamole, and you can't go wrong with the pork tamales or quesadillas. Save room for the caramelly flan.

Cultural District
BARBECUE

Located a few miles away from the Cultural District, **Angelo's Barbecue** (2533 White Settlement Rd., 817/332-0357, www.angelos-bbq.com, closed Sun., $8–19) is certainly worth the short drive. This no-frills joint appropriately focuses on the food, a rich, hickory-smoked Texas-style barbecue accompanied by a tangy sauce and savory rub. The brisket is especially tender, and traditional sides like potato salad and coleslaw balance the strong flavors with sweet undertones. Wash it all down with a signature (and gigantic) frosty mug of beer.

Similar yet less rustic is **Railhead Smokehouse** (2900 Montgomery St., 817/738-9808, www.railheadonline.com, closed Sun., $8–18), where ribs and brisket are the top draws. Eschew the usual side dishes for Railhead's top-notch fries, and, if the weather's cooperating, enjoy your plate of smoked and fried goodness on the wholesome outdoor patio. Worth noting: Members of the military receive 50 percent off.

LUNCH

Long lines form early at **(Kincaid's** (4901 Camp Bowie Blvd., 817/732-2881, closed Sun., $6–11), which, according to the reputable surveys noted inside, serves the best burger in the country. That may be a stretch, but they certainly are juicy, flavorful, and immensely satisfying burgers worth waiting 20 minutes in line for. Kincaid's started as a grocery store in 1946, and it retains its old-school charm with produce shelves doubling as countertops and picnic tables near the street-side windows. Instead of fries or onion rings, consider ordering the homemade deviled eggs or jalapeño halves stuffed with pimento cheese.

Just a hop, skip, and a jump away from the museums is the venerable **Paris Coffee Shop** (700 W. Magnolia Ave., 817/335-2041, www.pariscoffeeshop.net, closed Sun., $5–12). The historic building radiates old-urban charm, and the sandwiches are all above average. Locals make a point of stopping by for breakfast—especially the biscuits and gravy—and the Thursday lunch special (delectable home-style chicken and dumplings). Customers are wise to save room for the hearty fruit pies. Note: The restaurant closes at 2:30 P.M.

MEXICAN

For a down-home Tex-Mex experience, head to **La Familia** (841 Foch St., 817/870-2002, www.lafamilia-fw.com, $9–19). Located in an unassuming strip mall just a few blocks east of the Cultural District's unofficial boundaries, La Familia welcomes guests with hearty handshakes and hellos. Be sure to check out the specials scribbled on pieces of butcher paper posted near the front door. The margaritas are highly recommended (they're served with a flaming sugar cube), and you can't go wrong with most of the entrées, though locals tend to gravitate toward the taco plates and beef enchiladas.

Far more Mex than Tex is the somewhat-fancy **Lanny's Alta Cocina Mexicana** (3405 W. 7th St., 817/850-9996, www.lannyskitchen.com, $11–32). Instead of cheese and beef, think squash blossom soup, beets, and lobster. The wine list here is impressive, and although there are many entrées representing interior Mexico, there are still some traditional options for those in search of Tex-Mex, including carne asada (albeit coupled with a swanky asparagus side dish).

Magnolia Avenue

Located just a few miles south of the Sundance Square area is a stretch of fun and funky eateries well worth exploring. Local establishments are on Magnolia's menu, offering everything from vegan (one of the few in town) to upscale urban fare to trendy tacos. The following are among the most popular and highly regarded of the bunch.

Avoiding animal products in Cowtown is a hefty challenge, but vegans and vegetarians now have a habitat at the **Spiral Diner & Bakery** (1314 W. Magnolia Ave., 817/332-8834, www.spiraldiner.com, $8–19). Spiral's is immediately welcoming (omnivores will also enjoy the flavorful options), and the '50s diner decor offers a fun experience. Instead of a standard veggie burger, opt for a McNut burger; enhance chips and salsa with a nacho dish using cashew "cheez" sauce; and spice up ordinary pasta by sampling the tasty curry noodles.

For a different twist on a typical Mexican meal in Fort Worth, head to **Yucatan Taco Stand** (909 W. Magnolia Ave., 817/924-8646, www.yucatantacostand1.com, $9–21). Don't let the counter service fool you: This is quality fare from way south of the border. Start things off with a hefty margarita accompanied by lightly seasoned chips and salsa. Be sure to save room for a burrito bowl, filled with tasty goodness of your choice, from pork to seafood to garlic to peppers.

Authentic Italian meals aren't always easy to find in Texas, but if you're willing to endure a few quirks, you'll be duly rewarded by **Nonna Tata** (1400 W. Magnolia Ave., 817/332-0250, $12–30). First, you'll have to come prepared: bring cash, wine, and a willingness to dine in a tiny establishment only on weekdays. Also, you can expect at least a 30-minute wait (reservations are not accepted). Even with these limitations, Nonna Tata remains one of the most popular and highly regarded restaurants in the city thanks to its spectacular food. Start things off with the antipasti platter (an amazing board full of Italian meats and cheeses) and continue with one of the restaurant's seasonal specialties (pumpkin soup) or one of the tantalizing seafood dishes (calamari or shrimp—served with a homemade pasta and fresh pesto). If you still have room for desert, be sure to order the terrific tiramisu.

Vicinity of Fort Worth

Unlike Dallas, Fort Worth's modest size doesn't prompt visitors to seek a respite from the busy metropolis. Regardless, a couple of its outlying communities offer distinctive characteristics worthy of a day trip. Denton contains a compelling mix of student life and historic charm, and Glen Rose draws visitors from across the state in search of dinosaur tracks and exotic animals.

DENTON

Located 35 miles north of the Metroplex, Denton (population 109,561) offers an intriguing combination of old and new. The charming historic downtown courthouse and surrounding Main Street district offer an interesting juxtaposition to the rollicking Texas Motor Speedway and fresh faces at the University of North Texas and the Texas Woman's University. The universities play a major role in Denton's identity, with a sizable portion of the city's population consisting of college students. The University of North Texas has developed a nationally respected reputation for its premier jazz music program, and Texas Woman's University (yep, it's *woman,* not *women*) is one of the country's largest university primarily for women.

Downtown Denton

Denton is proud of its cultural and architectural heritage, including its association with the Texas Historical Commission's Main Street program and National Register of Historic Places. Visitors come to the courthouse square to browse the antiques shops, art galleries, gift boutiques, and restaurants. Presiding over all the activity is the majestic 1896 **Denton County Courthouse** (110 W. Hickory St.), featuring massive limestone walls and a prominent clock tower. Inside the building on the first floor is the **Denton County Courthouse-on-**

the majestic Denton County Courthouse

the-Square Museum (940/349-2830, www. dentoncounty.com/chos, Mon.–Fri. 10 A.M.– 4:30 P.M., Sat. 11 A.M.–3 P.M.), recalling the town's history through exhibits showcasing historic pottery, pressed blue glass, weaponry, and dolls.

University of North Texas

One of Denton's most popular attractions is the **University of North Texas Sky Theatre Planetarium** (1704 W. Mulberry St., 940/369-8213, www.skytheater.unt.edu, Sat. at 2 P.M. and 8 P.M., $5 adults, $4 senior citizens, $3 children 11 and under). The 40-foot domed theater features a projection system that reproduces the night sky with digital precision, and the planetarium's seating and technology make visitors feel like they're traveling to nearby stars on a celestial roller coaster ride. The facility presents educational and entertainment-oriented features for the general public and UNT students. While on campus, check out a completely different dramatic experience at the nearby **Campus Theatre** (214 W. Hickory St., 940/382-1915, www.campustheatre.com), a beautifully renovated 1940s art deco movie house staging live productions throughout the year.

Accommodations

MOTELS AND HOTELS

Since Denton is a college town, there are more hotel options than normal for a city of its size. Even the budget options are clean and dependable. **Days Inn** (4211 N. I-35, 940/383-1471, www.staydenton.com, $42 d) and nearby **Motel 6** (4125 N. I-35E, 940/566-4798, www.motel6.com, $49 d) offer the basic amenities at an affordable price. For just a bit more, the **Quality Inn & Suites** (1500 Dallas Dr., 940/387-3511, www.choicehotels.com, $74 d) provides a free hot breakfast, free Internet access, and microwaves and refrigerators in every room. At the (slightly) higher end of the chain is Denton's **Comfort Suites** (1100 N. I-35E, 940/898-8510, www.choicehotels.com, $89 d), which offers an indoor heated pool, complimentary Wi-Fi access, and a free hot breakfast.

BED-AND-BREAKFAST

Denton's tree-lined streets and collegiate atmosphere make it a good place to consider staying at a bed-and-breakfast, and one of the best choices available is the **Heritage Inns Bed and Breakfast Cluster** (815 N. Locust St., 888/565-6414, www.theheritageinns.com, $115). The Cluster consists of three separate houses, and each room features a queen-sized bed and private bath. Guests can have a full breakfast in the dining room or privately in bed. The B&B is just down the road from Denton's courthouse square, and well worth the walk after a hearty Italian meal in the downstairs restaurant.

Food

AMERICAN AND BARBECUE

One of Denton's consistently reliable barbecue restaurants is **The Smokehouse** (1123 Fort Worth Dr., 940/566-3073, open daily, $8–17). The brisket plate is one of the most popular items, and it's particularly tasty as a sandwich with onions and pickles. Since The Smokehouse isn't exclusively barbecue, feel free to consider the hearty chicken fried steak. As for sides, opt for mashed potatoes over potato salad, and try to save room for pie or cobbler.

If you have a hankerin' for a meat sandwich, head directly to **Rooster's Roadhouse** (113 Industrial St., 940/382-4227, www.roosters-roadhouse.com, open daily, $8–18). The burgers and sliced beef brisket sandwich are extremely satisfying, and the heaping helpings of side items (beans, coleslaw, potato salad) will have you gladly loosening your belt a notch afterward. Don't forget to order a fried pickle.

MEXICAN

Just southeast of downtown is the festive and fantastic **Fuzzy's Taco Shop** (115 Industrial St., 940/380-8226, www.fuzzystacoshop.com., open daily, $5–13). Be sure to order one of Fuzzy's baja tacos—the tempura fish and shrimp are especially tasty—with feta and garlic sauce. The queso here is legendary, and the corn tortillas are *muy bien*.

Located south of the courthouse square, **El**

Guapos (419 S. Elm St., 940/566-5575, www.elguapos.com/, open daily, $5–15) is a Tex-Mex joint with some gringo fare to boot (chicken fried steak, ribs). Fajitas are the main draw, but you can't go wrong with most of the Tex-Mex items, including chicken enchiladas and beef burritos.

Another downtown favorite is **Mi Casita** (110 N. Carroll Blvd., 940/891-1900, www.micasitafood.com, open daily, $5–12). College students line up for the bargain lunch specials, featuring tacos, nachos, and burritos for a measly $4. The hearty breakfast tacos are also worth sampling, and there's no need to worry about long lines of students in the morning.

Information and Services
For information on lodging, dining, events, and points of interest, visit the **Denton Chamber of Commerce** (414 W. Parkway St., 888/381-1818, www.discoverdenton.com, Mon.–Fri. 8:30 A.M.– 5 P.M.).

GLEN ROSE
Located about 60 miles southwest of Fort Worth, Glen Rose (population 2,122) is a popular getaway for Metroplex residents. Community members joke that humans are latecomers to this region, since evidence of dinosaurs from 100 million years ago is pressed into the area's limestone riverbeds.

By the early 1900s, the town was known for its abundant mineral springs, which attracted doctors and "healers." A modest population increase in the 1980s occurred thanks to the construction of the Comanche Peak Nuclear Power Plant, which became the county's largest employer and main source of tax revenue. One of the community's biggest draws these days is its natural attractions—particularly a wildlife center, fossil park, and camping.

Fossil Rim Wildlife Center
The Fossil Rim Wildlife Center (2155 County Rd. 2008, 254/897-2960, www.fossilrim.org) features some of the planet's most endangered animals along with more than 60 other species on 2,700 acres of protected grasslands. The emphasis is on African animals such as rhinoceros,

giraffe, cheetah, gazelle, and zebra. Fossil Rim's 1,800 acres of open space allow visitors to get close-up experiences with the animals through a self-guided 9.5-mile driving tour.

Along the way are an education center, restaurant, petting pasture, nature store, playground, and picnic areas. Note: The Children's Animal Center is undergoing extensive renovation and is expected to be open by early 2011. The animals, with the exception of the carnivores, rhinos, and a few others, are free to roam across the hill country savannas. Fossil Rim also offers guided tours, mountain bike tours, and hiking tours, and guests can stay overnight at The Lodge or the Foothills Safari Camp. The center's hours of operation and admission fees vary widely throughout the year, so check the website to see what to expect.

◖ Dinosaur Valley State Park
Thousands of visitors annually flock to Dinosaur Valley State Park (254/897-4588, www.tpwd.state.tx.us, daily 8 A.M.–5 P.M., admission $5) to see the 100-million-year-old dinosaur tracks in its limestone riverbeds. This picturesque park along the Paluxy River contains some of the best-preserved dinosaur tracks in Texas. This is where the world's first tracks were found of the sauropod, a plant-eating reptile weighing 30 tons and measuring more than 60 feet long.

Not as impressive in size yet still fascinating from a paleontology perspective are the tracks from two other creatures from the same era—the duckbilled dinosaurs (a mere 30 feet long) and the 12-foot-tall meat-eating theropods. Dinosaur Valley also includes nature trails and areas for camping and picnicking. The park is located approximately five miles west of Glen Rose on U.S. 67, and FM 205 on Park Road 59.

Accommodations
HOTELS AND MOTELS
Glen Rose is a bed-and-breakfast kind of town, but for those who appreciate the familiarity of a standard hotel, try **Glen Rose Inn and Suites** (300 SW Big Bend Trl., 254/897-2940, $79 d)

or **Americas Best Value Inn & Suites** (1614 NE Big Bend Trl., 254/897-2111, www.americasbestvalueinn.com, $89 d), featuring a pool, fitness center, and Internet access.

BED-AND-BREAKFASTS

One of Glen Rose's most popular lodging options is **Country Woods Inn** (420 Grand Ave., 254/897-4586, www.countrywoodsinn.com, $100), which bucks the B&B trend with its kid-friendly approach. Barnyard animals, campfire circles, and walking trails share the 40 wooded acres with century-old guesthouses, charming cabins, a railroad car, and main lodge. You haven't had this much fun since summer camp!

Another good choice is **The Hideaway Ranch and Retreat** (Private Road 1250 Bluff Dale, 254/823-6606, www.thehideawayranch.com, $139–159). Nestled among 155 acres of oak-laden countryside, The Hideaway offers secluded cabins with amenities such as private hot tubs, fully furnished kitchens, and outdoor grills. Activities on the property include horseback riding, swimming, hiking, and fishing.

For those willing to shell out the extra money, consider the beautiful **Inn on the River** (205 SW Barnard St., 254/897-2929, www.innontheriver.com, $159). Built in 1919, the site was originally part of a complex known as Dr. Snyder's Drugless Health Sanitarium, where "Doctor" Snyder, "the magnetic healer," treated patients/guests with mineral waters believed to have curing powers. Whatever the medical outcome, guests were pampered with luxurious accommodations and delectable meals. Those traditions continue at the meticulously restored current complex.

Food
AMERICAN

Despite its limited hours of operation, **Donna K's Catfish Restaurant** (intersection of Hwy. 144 N. and CR 200, 254/897-4305, Thurs.–Sat. 5–9 P.M., $8–16) is a busy and popular restaurant. As the name implies, catfish is what lures most of the crowds, but the seafood (shrimp, oysters, flounder) and standard items (steak and chicken) are also worthy options. The family and community vibe are satisfying intangibles that make Donna K's a fun place to grab a weekend dinner.

Another spot filled with local flavor is **Hammond's BBQ** (1106 NE Big Bend Trl., 254/897-3008, open daily, $7–17). Although Hammond's has had the misfortune of burning to the ground three times, locals have been fortunate to have it rebuilt each time. Demand is high for these perfectly smoked meats, including savory sausage and tender brisket.

For a fancier dining experience, consider **Inn On The River** (205 SW Barnard St., 254/897-2929, open Fri. and Sat. night, $12–35). The restaurant at this popular bed-and-breakfast, a former "health sanitarium" from the 1920s, offers an ever-changing elegant four-course dinner served every Friday and Saturday night. Seatings are available at 6 and 8 P.M.

Information and Services

Contact the **Glen Rose Convention and Visitors Bureau** (1505 NE Big Bend Trl., 254/897-3081, www.glenrosetexas.net, Mon.–Fri. 9 A.M.–5 P.M.) for printed and in-person information about local events, attractions, dining, and lodging.

Wichita Falls

Wichita Falls (population 104,197) isn't really en route to anywhere, but its history as a rough-and-tumble railroad and oil town make it a worthwhile place to visit if you're willing to make the nearly two-hour drive from the Metroplex.

In 1882, the first railroad arrived in Wichita Falls, and the discovery of oil 20 years later established the town as a petroleum headquarters for this region of North Texas. The rugged nature of the agricultural and industrial base brought with it some unsavory characters, and their Wild West exploits in Wichita Falls's growing number of saloons earned the town the nickname "Whiskeytaw Falls." This legacy lives on in the form of "red draws," a dubious concoction consisting of beer and tomato juice, still available at many local watering holes. Oil and agriculture remain important elements of Wichita Falls's economy, as does Sheppard Air Force base, which hosts the only NATO pilot training program in the world.

SIGHTS AND RECREATION
Wichita Falls Waterfall
Naturally, when visitors come to Wichita Falls, they ask, "Where are the falls?" For an entire century the answer was "Well . . . they're gone." Indeed, the town's namesake five-foot-high waterfall on the Big Wichita River was washed away in a flood in 1886. One hundred years later, the town (over)compensated by constructing a 54-foot multilevel cascading waterfall on the south bank of the river. Visitors to the falls, located just north of town adjacent to I-44 South, can also experience the trails, playground, pool, and pavilions at the adjacent Lucy Park. For more information, call 940/716-5500.

Wichita Falls Railroad Museum
Located in the former downtown Union Station building, the Wichita Falls Railroad Museum (500 9th St., 940/723-2661, www.wfrrm. com, Sat. noon–4 P.M., $1) is a showplace

for rail cars and memorabilia associated with "The Katy" (the Missouri, Kansas & Texas Railroad). The museum's vintage equipment includes a 100-year-old Fort Worth & Denver steam locomotive (one of only three in existence), a diesel switch engine, a baggage car, post office car, two World War II troop sleepers, and several cabooses.

Wichita Falls Museum of Art at Midwestern State University
Located on the banks of Sikes Lake, the Wichita Falls Museum of Art at Midwestern State University (2 Eureka Circle, 940/397-8900, www.mwsu.edu, Tues.–Fri. 9:30 A.M.–5 P.M., no admission charge) offers a combination of art, science, and regional history. Renovated in 2010, the facility features works of regional artists during the university's academic year, with an emphasis on student art from May through July. The museum also includes a planetarium and a hands-on science center for children.

River Bend Nature Center
Located on 15 acres in Lucy Park, the River Bend Nature Center (2200 3rd St., 940/767-0843, www.riverbendnaturecenter.org, Mon.–Fri. 9 A.M.–5 P.M., Sat. 10 A.M.–4 P.M., Sun. noon–4 P.M., $3) is an environmental education center featuring a remarkable butterfly conservatory (Thurs.–Sat. 10 A.M.–4 P.M., Sun. noon–4 P.M.). Also on the grounds are a wetland pond habitat, bird habitat, bird-watching, weather station, and a one-mile interpretive nature trail.

Lake Arrowhead State Park
Located approximately 14 miles southeast of Wichita Falls, Lake Arrowhead State Park (228 Park Rd. 63, 940/528-2211, www.tpwd. state.tx.us, $3) is centered on a reservoir on the Little Wichita River. Located on a former oil field, the lake literally reflects the site's past by retaining several of the oil derricks. Local fishermen claim they're the best spots to catch

crappie, perch, and bass. Built primarily as a water supply by the city of Wichita Falls, the lake is also a major recreational site for the North Central Plains. The park offers campsites, restrooms with showers, a boat ramp, an 18-hole disc golf course, fishing, swimming, and waterskiing.

ENTERTAINMENT AND EVENTS
Performing Arts

Wichita Falls residents are proud of their city's performing arts groups, including the **Wichita Falls Symphony Orchestra** (940/723-6202, www.wfso.org), which features more than 70 members who perform a full season of concerts each year at the Wichita Falls Memorial Auditorium (1300 7th St.). The group also offers a popular Children's Concert Series. Also noteworthy is the **Wichita Falls Ballet Theatre** (3412 Buchanan St., 940/322-2552, www.wfbt.org). The company performs traditional ballets such as *The Nutcracker* and hosts guest performers and school demonstrations.

© TEXAS HISTORICAL COMMISSION
the stylish Wichita Theatre

The Wichita Theatre Performing Arts Centre (10th and Indiana, 940/723-9037, www.wichitatheatre.org) is a 1908 historic landmark featuring family-friendly live concerts, touring shows, musical dramas, performing arts, and film events.

Bars and Clubs

Wichita Falls no longer revels in its former reputation as a hard-drinkin' town of rough characters, but there are still several worthy watering holes in town. Those looking for a true authentic local experience should drop by the **Bar L Drive Inn** (908 13th St., 940/322-3400), a tiny downtown spot that claims to have invented the "red draw," a legendary local concoction consisting of beer and tomato juice. If you can't find room in the cramped bar, order a red draw to go via the drive-through service.

Another favorite hangout for locals is the less charming but equally friendly **Iron Horse the Pub** (615 8th St., 940/767-9488), which features live music most weekends and serves cold beers along with darts and pool.

For a neighborhood pub experience—albeit a neighborhood across from a shopping mall—drop by **Toby's Bar & Grill** (2617 Plaza Pkwy., 940/691-5621), where you'll find 50 beers to choose from, televised sports, lots of military servicemen, and decent pub grub.

Events

The city's best-known event is the **Hotter 'n Hell One Hundred** (www.hh100.org), where bicycle racers and fitness-oriented endurance riders come to Wichita Falls each August from across the country to sweat, race, and sweat some more.

Each June, the city hosts professional circuit rodeo as part of the **Red River Rodeo** (940/592-2156). Held at the Wichita County Mounted Patrol Arena, the event draws nearly 10,000 people for the traditional rodeo attractions and a postshow dance.

ACCOMMODATIONS
Motels and Hotels

One of the best lodging deals in Wichita

Falls is the **Budget Host Inn** (1601 8th St., 940/322-1182, www.budgethost.com, $48 d). Located on the western edge of downtown, this modest hotel offers 40 rooms, each including a microwave, fridge, and free wireless service. Just southwest of downtown, the **Fairfield Inn** (4414 Westgate Dr., 940/691-1066, www.marriott.com, $85 d) has an indoor pool and Jacuzzi, a free buffet breakfast, free wireless service, and complimentary access to nearby Gold's Gym.

Located south of Wichita Falls's "urban" core, **Hawthorn Suites** (1917 Elmwood Ave., 940/692-7900, www.hawthorn.com, $89 d) offers various room options, ranging from basic (all rooms have a fridge, microwave, and sofa) to fancy (fireplaces and balconies). The hotel offers free breakfast and wireless service.

Homewood Suites (2675 Plaza Pkwy., 940/691-4663, www.hilton.com, $119 d) is on a lake near Midwestern State University. All rooms have fully equipped kitchens, a full-sized refrigerator, and Internet access, and the hotel features an indoor heated pool and free hot breakfast.

Camping

The best place for camping in Wichita Falls is **Lake Arrowhead State Park.** Another option is the **Wichita Bend RV Park** (300 Central Frwy., 940/761-7490, $17 nightly fee), just a few miles northwest of downtown. The park is located on the Wichita River adjacent to Lucy Park and offers 28 sites with hookups (no tents) along with a pool and nature trails.

FOOD
Mexican

Perhaps the most venerable of Wichita Falls's restaurants is **Casa Manana** (609 8th St., 940/723-5661, closed Sun., $6–13), a 60-plus-year-old downtown institution. The most popular item on the menu is the red soft taco, featuring a rich chile sauce that enhances the seasoned beef

or chicken. Note: As of early 2011, the restaurant was still under renovation following a fire but expected to reopen by the summer.

Another popular Mexican restaurant is **El Gordo's** (513 Scott Ave., 940/322-6251, closed Sun., $7–14), located adjacent to McBride Land and Cattle Co. It's known primarily for its delectable chiles rellenos and cheese enchiladas.

Steak and Barbecue

The McBride family is associated with good cookin' in Wichita Falls, especially when it comes to preparing quality meats. One of the best places to get a steak in town is **Fat McBride's Steakhouse** (4537 Maplewood Ave., 940/696-0250, open daily, $15–29). The saddle blanket sirloin (14 or 16 ounces) is a good choice, as are the ribs and brisket. Be sure to stick with the meat dishes since the Mexican plates don't quite make the grade. The other respected family eatery is **McBride Land and Cattle Co.** (501 Scott St., 940/322-2516, open daily, $13–27), where the food and atmosphere are truly Texan. Enjoy a hearty steak with all the fixins along with the mounted animal heads and enormous fireplace.

For traditional Texas barbecue, locals line up downtown at the small yet satisfying **Branding Iron** (104 E. Scott Ave., 940/723-0338, closed Sun., $8–16), where you can get a tasty lunch—the smoked turkey and spicy sausage are favorites—for under 10 bucks.

INFORMATION AND SERVICES

Drop by the **Wichita Falls Convention and Visitors Bureau** (1000 5th St., 800/799-6732, www.wichitafalls.org) for basic information for travelers, even though it caters more to conventions than individuals. However, visitors will find an abundance of helpful travel-related information—brochures, maps, personal suggestions—at the **Texas Travel Information Center** (900 Central Frwy./I-44, 940/723-7931).

AUSTIN AND THE HILL COUNTRY

This slow-rolling, laid-back area of Central Texas is an ideal destination for a low-key getaway. Austin is a relatively small city, so it feels like an endearing, earnest little sibling compared to urban bullies like Houston and Dallas. The Hill Country, meanwhile, is rustic yet civil enough to have commendable camping and lodging facilities for a nice weekend escape.

Things have always been relatively pleasant in this area of the state, which attracted its first pioneers—mainly from Tennessee, Arkansas, and Missouri—for the same reasons Native Americans had inhabited the land for centuries: a temperate climate and abundant natural resources. By the late 1800s, Germans were arriving in droves. Word got out in Germany that Texas was a land of opportunity, and so

many people jumped at the opportunity that significant portions of Central Texas had a majority German population in the late 19th century. Evidence of their settlement remains in the form of sturdy barns, homes, and dance halls constructed upon their arrival more than 125 years ago. Czech immigrants settled along the Brazos River near Waco, and their cultural legacy is found in the remarkable churches (and kolache pastries) scattered throughout small communities on the fertile Blackland Prairie.

Austin has traditionally attracted another portion of the population not always found in other parts of Texas: intellectuals. The University of Texas has been the main draw, but politicians and lawyers have proliferated ever since the city was named the state's capital in 1846. For the next century, government

AUSTIN

HIGHLIGHTS

(Texas State Capitol: Visitors come to Austin from across the world to experience this architectural and cultural wonder, deliberately designed in true Texas style—15 feet taller than the U.S. Capitol. This magnificent 1888 Renaissance Revival structure is nothing short of stunning (page 83).

(Austin's Bat Colony: Each summer night, more than a million Mexican free-tailed bats emerge from beneath the downtown Congress Avenue Bridge, much to the delight of the hundreds of people who eagerly gather to await their arrival (page 87).

(Sixth Street: This is Austin's party central. Often described as a mini version of New Orleans's Bourbon Street, this half-mile strip draws thousands of students and twentysomethings to dance clubs, shot bars, and live music venues (page 91).

(Kreuz Market: This Lockhart restaurant, a sacred spot for barbecue aficionados, serves traditional, hard-core stuff for serious connoisseurs—there's no sauce, no utensils, and orders are placed at the meat counter (page 120).

(Dr Pepper Museum: Discover what makes the world's oldest major soft drink pop at Waco's Dr Pepper Museum, housed in the bottling building where it was first made more than a century ago. Bonus: The tour ends with a generous sampling from an authentic soda fountain (page 123).

(Fredericksburg: This small Hill Country town of nearly 11,000 people is a favorite weekend destination for travelers interested in Texas's German heritage, with dozens of restaurants and shops specializing in food, drink, and crafts from the Old Country (page 128).

(Lyndon B. Johnson National Historical Park: A highlight of the Hill Country, the LBJ ranch near Fredericksburg offers a fascinating perspective on the legendary Texan who became the nation's 36th president (page 136).

(Enchanted Rock State Natural Area: This enormous pink granite dome has been a mythical natural beacon for more than 11,000 years. Native American tribes believed the rock wove enchanted spells, especially when its iridescent reflections radiated from the sparkling granite on full-moon nights (page 138).

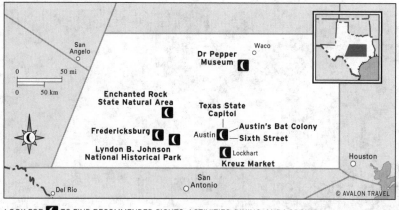

LOOK FOR **(** TO FIND RECOMMENDED SIGHTS, ACTIVITIES, DINING, AND LODGING.

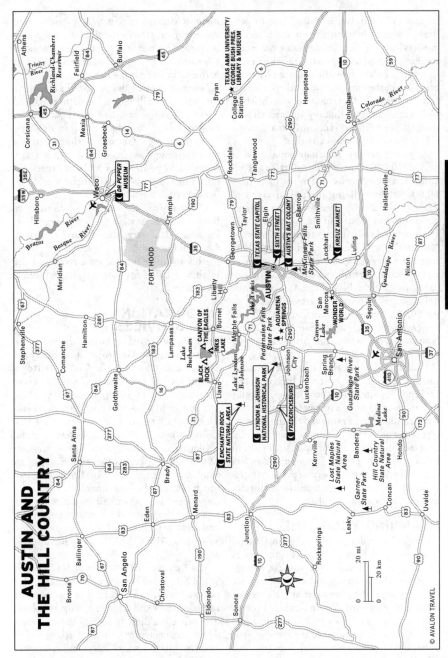

AUSTIN AND THE HILL COUNTRY

© AVALON TRAVEL

entities and the university raised Austin's profile by investing in infrastructure and academic projects (bridges, dams, laboratories, museums, stadiums) aimed at improving the city's quality of life. By the late 20th century, the city became a hotbed for creative thinkers, movers, and shakers, including computer guru Michael Dell, earning the tech-heavy business climate the nickname Silicon Hills while remaining a mecca for musicians and artists.

Despite boasting a current population of nearly 750,000, Austin still maintains a reputation as a college town due to the more than 60,000 students living there. University of Texas grads forced to flee Austin for big corporations and money in the Metroplex and Houston tend to have serious nostalgia for the "40 acres" (the UT campus), so they regularly return for football games or just to comment on how much the town has changed in the decades since they've been there. Austin isn't the only college town in this part of the state, as the 50,000 Aggies in College Station will certainly remind you. Nearby San Marcos is also home to nearly 30,000 students at Texas State University.

Culturally, Central Texas is known for its distinctive heritage, honky-tonks, barbecue, and Dr Pepper (invented in Waco). Geographically, the land is marked by a convergence of the cotton-rich Blackland Prairie and the granite outcroppings of the Hill Country. Communities near the Highland Lakes west of Austin and in small towns like Fredericksburg and Bandera draw hordes of visitors every weekend to experience the region's cooler temperatures, distinct history, and beautiful landscape.

PLANNING YOUR TIME

You could spend a couple weeks in Central Texas and still have plenty of worthy places left to visit, but realistically you can experience everything the region has to offer in six or seven days. Plan to spend at least two or three days exploring Austin's cultural scene. Devote an entire day or two to the area just north of downtown, home to the State Capitol, Texas history museum, LBJ Library, and

Blanton Museum of Art. You'll probably need two nights to take in the live music and club scene, and it's worth devoting an afternoon to a Lockhart day trip just to experience Texas barbecue at its finest.

Set aside another two or three days to drive through the Hill Country, with suggested overnight stops at a bed-and-breakfast in Fredericksburg or a dude ranch in Bandera. Fredericksburg's German heritage offers a memorable getaway, and it's downright sacrilegious to be in Texas without experiencing "The Cowboy Capital of the World," as Bandera proudly bills itself.

Other worthy Central Texas side trips are Bryan–College Station for the George Bush Presidential Library/Museum and the whole Aggieland phenomena, San Marcos for floating on an inner tube down a river, and the Highland Lakes for more traditional water-based recreation.

INFORMATION AND SERVICES

Once you've arrived in Austin, the best place to load up on travel information is a funky old drugstore now housing the **Austin Visitor's Center** (209 E. 6th St., 512/478-0098, www. austintexas.org, Mon.–Fri. 9 A.M.–5 P.M., Sat. and Sun. 9:30 A.M.–5:30 P.M.). Free maps and friendly staffers will help you find your way around town. The office also serves as the headquarters for two worthwhile tour services: **Austin Duck Adventures,** conducted in an amphibious vehicle, and **Austin Overtours,** which take place in the comfort of a van. The corporate office with official information about exploring the city is the **Austin Convention and Visitors Bureau** (301 Congress Ave., Suite 200, 512/474-5171, www.austintexas. org, Mon.–Fri. 8 A.M.–5 P.M.).

The Capitol Visitors Center (112 E. 11th St., 512/305-8400, daily 9 A.M.–5 P.M.) is located adjacent to the capitol in the restored 1856 General Land Office building, the oldest state office building in Texas. Located within the visitors center is the Texas Department of Transportation's travel information counter

(512/463-8586), with staffers offering free maps and literature on travel destinations throughout the state.

For an interesting perspective on Austin and the Hill Country—including customized tours of the city's museums, parks, pubs, galleries, and gardens—contact veteran Austinite and self-proclaimed "Texpert" Howie Richey's **Texpert Tours** (512/383-8989, www.texpert-tours.com, txburb@gmail.com).

Not to be forgotten, the **Waco Tourist Information Center** (106 Texas Ranger Trl., 800/922-6386, www.wacocvb.com, Mon.–Sat. 8 A.M.–5 P.M., Sun. 10 A.M.–5 P.M.) offers free maps, visitors guides, and information about Waco area attractions.

GETTING THERE AND AROUND

Austin-Bergstrom International Airport (512/530-2242, www.ci.austin.tx.us/austinairport/) is surprisingly small and easily navigable. Located eight miles southeast of downtown, the airport is noteworthy for its collection of exclusively local restaurants (where else can you eat a breakfast taco or brisket sandwich while waiting for a plane?) and constant stream of music by Texas artists. There's even a stage with live music at the Hill Country Bar.

Although Austin is a progressive city, its public transportation systems are unimpressive, so you're better off renting a car than relying on a bus or rail line. The city has three major cab companies: **American Yellow Checker Cab** (512/452-9999), **Austin Cab** (512/478-2222), and **Lone Star Cab** (512/836-4900). Fares run around $20 from the airport to downtown. Another option for getting to your destination is **Super Shuttle** (512/258-3826), which offers 24-hour shared-van service for around $10–15 per person.

Waco Regional Airport (866/359-9226) is serviced by American Eagle and Continental Express. The airport received several upgrades after it became the main landing strip for President George W. Bush when he took refuge at his ranch in nearby Crawford. If you feel the need to fly to College Station, **Easterwood Airport** (979/845-8511, www.easterwoodairport.com), owned and operated by Texas A&M University, offers daily service via American and Continental airlines.

AUSTIN

Austin and Vicinity

Austin (population 709,893) is often referred to in Texas as a blue island in the middle of a vast red sea. This progressive and dynamic city stands apart from other parts of the state politically, culturally, and demographically. And Austinites wouldn't have it any other way—they're proud (smug, almost) of their comfortably sized, well-educated, fit, and socially conscious city.

Most people living in Austin are from someplace else—Dallas, Houston, California, the Midwest—which adds to the city's eclectic feel. Although the massive influx of people during the past decade has watered down some of this college town's unassuming vibe, Austin still retains a laid-back quality that out-of-towners find charming and appealing, particularly during the city's enormous music events (South by Southwest Music Festival, Austin City Limits Festival), which annually draw bands and music fans from across the globe.

SIGHTS
◖ Texas State Capitol

The capitol (Congress Ave. and 11th St., 512/463-5495, www.tspb.state.tx.us, weekdays 7 A.M.–10 P.M., weekends 9 A.M.–8 P.M. Free guided tours are offered Mon.–Fri. 8:30 A.M.–4:30 P.M., Sat. 9:30 A.M.–3:30 P.M., Sun. noon–3:30 P.M.) presides over the city and state with a dignified grace. This magnificent 1888 Renaissance Revival edifice, with its captivating exterior of "sunset red" granite (actually a light pink hue) and intricately detailed

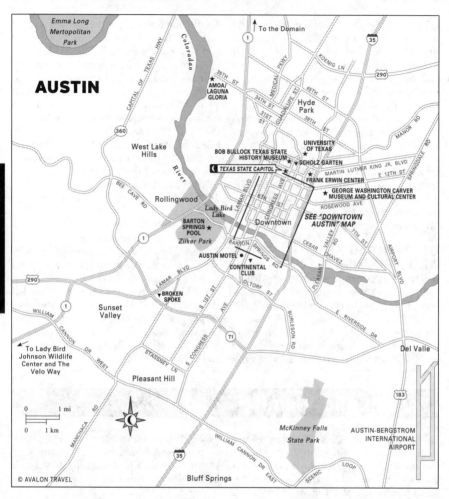

interior, is nothing short of stunning. The capitol building truly represents Texas, from its legislative chambers to the tip of its dome—deliberately designed 15 feet taller than the U.S. Capitol. Visitors from across the world flock to Austin to experience this architectural and cultural wonder, designated a National Historic Landmark for its significant contribution to American history.

The capitol's magnificent architectural features set it apart from its counterparts across the country. Notice the attention to detail, particularly inside the building. Upon close examination, themes and patterns emerge—stars, for instance—that tie all elements of the building together, from floor tiles to staircases to window frames to door fixtures to chandeliers. Statues and paintings exude the magnitude of Texas history, and the sounds of busy legislative aides' clacking heels and tour guides' spirited shtick reverberate around the echoey halls. For an added bonus, order a takeout

© ANDY RHODES

the State Capitol

lunch from the cafeteria and enjoy it on the surrounding 22-acre grounds beneath the massive dome and its stately topper, Lady Liberty, which both received a shiny new coat of paint in late 2010. Majestic oaks tower over the lushly manicured lawn, overlooking the bustling Congress Avenue scene from atop Texas's version of Capitol Hill.

The University of Texas

Not surprisingly, The University of Texas is enormous. With its 357-acre campus and student enrollment of more than 50,000, UT is a major entity in Austin, rivaling the state government for highest profile. Most of the attention is well deserved, since the university, thanks in part to its many affluent and loyal alumni, offers top-notch academic, athletic, and cultural services for students and the community. The public especially benefits from the following campus entities, showcasing Texas's finest cultural resources.

The Blanton Museum of Art (200 E. Martin Luther King Jr. Blvd., 512/471-

5482, www.blantonmuseum.org, Tues.–Fri. 10 A.M.–5 P.M., Thurs. until 8 P.M., Sat. 11 A.M.–5 P.M., Sun. 1–5 P.M., $9 adults, $7 seniors, $5 students 13–21, free on Thurs.) opened its new facility in 2006 to much fanfare in Austin, in part because the city had long been lacking a high-profile quality art museum. The Blanton contains an impressive collection of art from Texas and around the world. The Blanton bills itself as the largest university art museum in the country, with important collections in Latin American art, American art, and European painting, prints, and drawings. The museum boasts more than 17,000 works of art, and its collection of Latin American art is particularly notable, with works from more than 600 artists representing Mexico, the Caribbean, and South and Central America. It's considered one of the oldest, largest, and most comprehensive collections in the country, and it's certainly worth a visit since the Blanton represents Austin's most impressive collection of visual art.

The Harry Ransom Humanities Research Center (21st and Guadalupe Sts., 512/471-8944, www.hrc.utexas.edu, Tues.–Wed. and Fri. 10 A.M.–5 P.M., Thurs. 10 A.M.–7 P.M., weekends noon–5 P.M., free) is an underappreciated gem in Austin and even the nation. Maybe it's the name, which sounds more like an academic facility than a public gallery. Granted, most people impressed by the Ransom Center's holdings are researchers, but there's no denying the impressive magnitude of publicly displayed artifacts such as the world's first photograph, a Gutenberg Bible, and a 1450 edition of Geoffrey Chaucer's *The Canterbury Tales*. Other exceptionally rare holdings at the Ransom Center include the complete working libraries of James Joyce and E. E. Cummings, and manuscripts from Ernest Hemmingway, Walt Whitman, and Mark Twain. Check the website for the latest fascinating exhibit, which could be anything from an Edgar Allan Poe overview to an esteemed Egyptian photo collection.

The Lyndon Baines Johnson Library and Museum (2313 Red River St., 512/721-0200, www.lbjlibrary.org, daily 9 A.M.–5 P.M., free) is dedicated to America's 36th president, a Hill Country native and Texas icon. The facility occupies 14 acres on the University of Texas campus and offers four floors' worth of memorabilia, manuscripts, artifacts, and nearly 45 million documents. Highlights of the museum include the top-floor 7/8th scale replica of the Oval Office and East Room as they appeared during LBJ's tenure, a view of the 1968 "Stretch" Lincoln automobile he used in Washington and Austin, a mint condition 1910 Model T Ford (given to President Johnson by Henry Ford II), and exhibits showcasing political cartoons and campaign items. Be sure to walk through the First Lady's Gallery, dedicated to his beloved wife, Lady Bird, including love letters from their courtship, archival video clips, and Carol Channing's feathered headdress from her White House performance of *Hello Dolly.* The LBJ library has the highest overall visitation of any presidential library and is the only one that doesn't charge admission.

Bob Bullock Texas State History Museum

Located across the street from the Blanton and two blocks north of the capitol, the Bullock Museum (1800 N. Congress Ave., 512/936-8746, www.thestoryoftexas.com, Mon–Sat. 9 A.M.–6 P.M., Sun. noon–6 P.M., $7 adults, $6 seniors and college students, $4 students ages 5–18, additional movie fees) showcases the Lone Star State's proud heritage. The museum welcomes visitors with a gargantuan star out front and showcases the state's enormous history through its front doors. There's a lot to absorb here, but it's well organized and interpreted, leaving visitors with a satisfying crash course in Texas history. Exhibits are presented in chronological order from the ground floor up, starting with artifacts from early Native American tribes and proceeding to Spanish conquistador armor, to lassos and saddles of cowboys and *vaqueros,* to oil rigging equipment and World War II aircraft. The museum is also a destination for multimedia events, including the Spirit Theater, featuring sound and

the Bob Bullock Texas State History Museum

movement special effects, and Austin's only IMAX theater, offering 3-D screenings.

Austin's Bat Colony

Austin's famous bat colony (Congress Avenue Bridge at the Colorado River, 512/416-5700) is a major source of civic pride (and guano). Each summer, more than a million Mexican free-tailed bats pour out nightly from beneath the downtown Congress Avenue Bridge in search of food, and scores of Austinites and visitors from across the world eagerly witness the spectacle. Part of the draw is the anticipation, but the greatest appeal is seeing an undulating mass of chirping mammals flow from their concrete catacomb into the deep blue sky of a pristine Austin evening.

Lady Bird Johnson Wildflower Center

Spanning 178 acres of rolling Texas prairie on the edge of the Hill Country, the Wildflower Center (4801 LaCrosse Ave., 512/232-0100, www.wildflower.org, Tues.–Sat. 9 A.M.–5:30 P.M., Sun. noon–5:30 P.M., $8 adults, $7 seniors and students, $3 children ages 5–12) is well worth the 20-minute drive south of town.

The Wildflower Center is a Central Texas treasure exploding with iridescent colors, especially in the spring. Native flowers, bushes, trees, and grasses exhibit the region's natural beauty in numerous gardens and trails throughout a sprawling meadow, and an interpretive center and signage convey the passion Lady Bird (LBJ's wife) had for Texas's natural resources and educating people about the state's abundant botanical blessings.

The Austin Museum of Art

As the city's premier site for 20th-century and contemporary art, the museum (823 Congress Ave., 512/495-9224, www.amoa.org, Tues.–Sat. 10 A.M.–5 P.M., Thurs. until 8 P.M., Sun. noon– 5 P.M., $5 adults, $4 seniors and students, children under 12 free) hosts permanent and traveling exhibits from internationally acclaimed artists, with much of the space devoted to local and regional works. The museum also offers lectures, films, classes, and performances. The bad news: The museum's digs are in a bland ground-level floor of a nondescript office building. The good news? AMOA has a smaller branch called **Laguna Gloria** (3809 W. 35th St., 512/458-8191, free admission), a gorgeous villa

---

MEXICAN FREE-TAILED BATS

So you've seen the impressive mass of nearly one million bats emerge from under the Congress Avenue Bridge. But what exactly are these creatures?

Considered one of the smaller species of bats, Mexican free-tailed bats have a wingspan of 11-13 inches. They're named free-tails because the lower half of their tail is free of a body-attached membrane. These little critters are typically a dark to light brown color.

Mexican free-tailed bats are found mostly in the western United States and Mexico, and it's estimated that 100 million of them arrive in Central Texas annually to raise their young. Nursing females require large quantities of high-fat insects, so they tend to feast upon egg-laden moths, including bollworm moths, cutworm moths, and other agricultural pests that migrate north from Mexico.

Free-tails usually emerge about 15 minutes after sunset, and the best time to see them in action is in the summer (July-September). They leave the bridge (or, in most other locales, a scary cave) at speeds of up to 35 miles per hour, and they can increase in velocity up to 60 miles per hour. A single bat pup is usually born between June and July, and the little ones take their first flight at nearly five weeks old. Interesting fact: The bats started gathering under the Congress Avenue Bridge in the early 1980s, when engineers designed the crevices that would ultimately become home to the now-famous colony of millions.

WILDFLOWER ROOTS

For decades, Central Texas's highway medians have served as an unlikely springtime photo-op for people with children and dogs. In March and April, these rural grassy knolls are bursting with bluebonnets and brightly blossoming Indian paintbrushes, black-eyed Susans, winecups, goldenrods, and Indian blankets. It's a Texas tradition to dress the kids and/or pets in their Sunday best and place them among the vibrant natural color palate for a prime picture.

Texas's wildflowers have been in existence for more than 130 million years. The species are greatly affected by the vast differences in the state's soils (azaleas thrive in acidic East Texas soil but struggle in the chalky Central Texas earth). Central Texans are fortunate since they're in the middle of several overlapping ecoregions. This biodiversity results in a plethora of springtime wildflowers – nearly 400 varieties in all – and a majority are native species.

Not surprisingly, the best-known type of wildflower in Texas – the iconic bluebonnet – inspires the largest number of stories. The bluebonnet is the subject of a popular tale involving Lady Bird Johnson, wife of President Lyndon B. Johnson. Lady Bird, an active naturalist, described the phenomenon of a bluebonnet's white flowers turning progressively redder as "blushing." She claimed the color change happened after a bee had pollinated the flower, sending a natural signal to

© ANDY RHODES

the Ladybird Johnson Wildflower Center in Austin

other bees to seek out the virginal white blossoms. Lady Bird's legacy endures at her namesake wildflower center in Austin (see entry), where an impressive collection of gardens, trails, meadows, and an exhibit gallery offer a glimpse of Texas's diverse native species.

on Lake Austin featuring a 1916 Italianate mansion and lush grounds containing art exhibits and outdoor sculptures in a serene setting.

The Mexic-Arte Museum

This colorful museum (419 Congress Ave., 512/480-9373, www.mexic-artemuseum.org, Mon.–Thurs. 10 A.M.–6 P.M., Fri.–Sat. 10 A.M.–5 P.M., Sun. noon–5 P.M., $5 adults, $4 senior citizens and students, $1 children under 12) provides much-needed cultural diversity in Austin's largely monochromatic

downtown. Nearly a third of the city's population is Hispanic, but you wouldn't know it based on the Congress Avenue scene. The Mexic-Arte Museum, positioned on a prime piece of downtown real estate at Fourth and Congress, features traditional and contemporary Latin American painting and sculpture, most of it focusing on social aspects of Latino life. The museum also includes a back room dedicated to emerging local artists, who benefit from having a progressive venue for exhibiting their otherwise-overlooked talent.

The George Washington Carver Museum and Cultural Center

Just east of I-35 is the Carver Museum (1165 Angelina St., 512/974-4926, www.carvermuseum.org, Mon.–Thurs. 10 A.M.–9 P.M., Fri. 10 A.M.–5:30 P.M., Sat. 10 A.M.–4 P.M., no admission charge), another much-needed venue dedicated to one of Austin's underrepresented cultural groups. Education gets top billing here, evident in the museum's impressive galleries. The permanent exhibits showcase the significant contributions Austin's African-American families have made to the city, including background information about the people behind the names of parks and streets. The Carver Museum also features a theater, dance studio, archive space, artist's gallery, and a children's exhibit about African-American scientists and inventors.

The Hill Country Flyer

Travel back in time on this slow-rolling, laid-back, completely relaxing trek on a historic train through the scenic Hill Country northwest of Austin (trains depart at 10 A.M. from 401 E. Whitestone Blvd. in Cedar Park, 512/477-8468, www.austinsteamtrain.org, $28–43). Spring is the best time to go for the added bonus of colorful wildflowers and ideal weather beckoning from the open windows of the surprisingly comfortable 1920s coach cars; otherwise, it's worth forking over the extra $15 for a fancy air-conditioned 1950s lounge car in the brutally hot summer months. The gentle clickety-clack of the rails and occasional anecdotes from the seasoned volunteers make for a calming getaway on this peaceful train. After a nearly two-hour ride, the train stops in the sleepy Hill Country community of Burnet (pronounced BUR-nit), where you can grab lunch at the unfortunately named Tea-Licious restaurant, offering surprisingly hearty and tasty cheeseburgers for a tearoom. You'll be back on the train by 2 P.M. and in Cedar Park by 4.

ENTERTAINMENT AND EVENTS

For the most part, the self-proclaimed "Live Music Capital of the World" lives up to its

© ANDY RHODES

The Hill Country Flyer runs between Austin and Burnet.

billing. On any given night you can catch a show ranging in style from blues to reggae to country to punk. Sixth Street retains its distinction as a mini Bourbon Street, the grown-up Warehouse District offers old folks in their 30s a place to gather without screaming their conversations to be heard, and East Austin is emerging as the hipster hot spot.

Performing Arts
THE PARAMOUNT THEATER
This beautiful historic theater (713 Congress Ave., 512/472-5470, www.austintheatre.org) is the city's crown jewel for performing arts events. The magnificent 1915 venue is just four blocks south of the capitol building and originally served as a vaudeville theater and variety house. It continues to stage a wide variety of shows—plays and musicals, comedians, dance shows, lectures, children's programming, and classic films—under a faux sky ceiling and glamorous balconies. The Paramount also operates the adjacent State Theatre (719 Congress Ave.) as part of the Austin Theatre Alliance. The State is a remarkable art deco theater that suffered severe damage from a water main break several years ago. Although it continues to operate in a limited capacity, its status as a fully functional performing arts center remains in flux.

AUSTIN CITY LIMITS

These days, the words *Austin City Limits* may be associated more with the annual music festival than a revered public broadcasting program, but the roots of this world-renowned entity run deep in the city's musical heritage. From the time the twangy opening chords of the show's original theme song, Gary P. Nunn's "London Homesick Blues," hit the airwaves in 1976 (well before MTV), it was evident the program was dedicated to exposing a new brand of quality roots rock music. Willie Nelson was an early regular guest, and each season continued the tradition of showcasing worthy country, blues, and folk to rock 'n' roll, bluegrass, and zydeco artists that weren't getting the radio airplay they deserved.

The show was inspired by Austin's burgeoning live music scene in the early '70s, and it has since featured more than 500 regional and internationally acclaimed artists on its stage. Memorable performances include such diverse acts as Beck, B. B. King, the Pixies, Bob Wills's Texas Playboys, Wilco, Mary Chapin Carpenter, the Flaming Lips, Ray Charles, Leonard Cohen, and Coldplay.

For 25 years, the show was taped in a studio on the University of Texas campus, with a stage containing fake trees and a backdrop of the city skyline. Not surprisingly, many viewers assumed the show was taped outside and were surprised to learn the stage was located on the sixth floor of UT's communications building. The skyline set debuted in 1982 and remained the series' backdrop ever since.

in early 2011, the ACL studio and stage were undergoing an extensive relocation from the UT campus to downtown Austin. The move has been years in the works and is welcomed since it puts the stage in a more prominent and accessible location with a larger capacity. Show tapings will now accommodate 800 (an increase from 320), and the venue can expand to hold 2,750 for a standard concert venue called Austin City Limits Live at Moody Theater. The new ACL stage, custom built adjacent to the fancy new W hotel on West 2nd Street, appropriately opened its new venture with a Willie Nelson concert in February 2011. No word yet on how the famous skyline backdrop will be incorporated into the new venue.

In the past, tickets for the show were extremely hard to come by, since the small studio meant tickets were mainly obtained through connections to the TV station. However, with the increased capacity, more tickets are expected to be available for tapings. Visit the station's blog at http://austincitylimits.org/blog for information about getting tickets to upcoming shows or call 512/475-9077 for more information.

THE UNIVERSITY OF TEXAS PERFORMING ARTS CENTER

The university's primary venue is the Bass Concert Hall (2350 Robert Dedman Dr., 512/471-2787, www.texasperformingarts.org), which brings an eclectic mix of internationally acclaimed performers to the UT campus. Pop legends, dance performances, chamber orchestras, alternative rockers, and world music superstars take the stage throughout the year to the benefit of students and residents. Superior acoustics and comfortable seating make this an especially inviting venue to experience a show.

THE LONG CENTER FOR PERFORMING ARTS

Debuting in 2008, this architecturally stunning facility (701 W. Riverside Dr., 512/457-5100, www.thelongcenter.org) is the city's latest and greatest performing arts venue. The $77 million renovation project of the quirky 1959 Palmer Auditorium on the shores of Lady Bird Lake was 10 years in the making, but locals believe it's been worth the wait. Home to the Austin Symphony Orchestra, Austin Lyric Opera, and Ballet Austin, the Long Center is truly a center stage for Austin's fine arts. With multiple stages and an eclectic mix of performers, this venue will continue to represent Austin's diverse cultural scene well into the future.

(Sixth Street
EAST OF CONGRESS

This is Austin's party central. Shot bars, dance clubs, beer joints, and more shot bars are the featured attractions, and thousands of students and twentysomethings revel in the debauchery each weekend. As an added bonus, the streets are closed to cars on most weekends, allowing revelers to stumble between bars and jabber with their brand new BFFs. One of the premier spots for soaking up the whole scene is the rooftop patio at **Iron Cactus** (606 Trinity St., 512/472-9240, www.ironcactus.com). Their spectacular top-shelf margaritas taste even better on the balcony on a perfect spring

evening. For a genuine sense of the Sixth Street party atmosphere, check out **Spill** (212 E. 6th St., 512/320-8005), a big dance club for the Long Island Iced Tea crowd. The music isn't always trendy, but it's definitely danceable. Take note: There's a dress code, so leave the shorts and flip-flops at home. For a better music mix, head to **Touché** (417 E. 6th St., 512/472-9841), known for its laid-back vibe and hot bartenders. Literally. The specialty of the house is Flaming Dr Peppers, a Southern tradition involving shots of Amaretto and Everclear set ablaze, then dropped in a glass of beer. The kids claim it tastes exactly like a Dr Pepper soda. Back in 2005, the cast of MTV's *Real World Austin* appropriately spent most of their time at two bars with animals in their names. If you insist on doing a body shot where the Real Worlders once held court, stagger to the zoos known as **The Chugging Monkey** (219 E. 6th St., 512/476-5015, www.thechuggingmonkey.com) and **The Dizzy Rooster** (306 E. 6th St., 512/236-1667, www.dizzyrooster.com).

Those looking for a comparatively mellower Sixth Street venue are still in luck. Several bars cater to Austin's laid-back alternative clientele, content to kick back on a patio with tequila on the rocks or a pale ale while the jukebox cranks out Johnny Cash and Interpol. The best of the bunch is **Lovejoy's** (604 Neches St., 512/477-1268), a comfy, tattooy, left-of-center brewpub just a half block from the frenzy of Sixth Street activity. Order a Samson's cask ale and snag a seat on one of the pieces of vintage (ragged old) furniture for an authentic experience. Another alternative venue drawing an eclectic crowd is **Casino el Camino** (517 E. 6th St., 512/469-9330, www.casinoelcamino.net). Don't be too frightened by the graphic S&M scenes painted on the wall or the dungeon decor—even goths like to occasionally whoop it up. Be sure to sample one of Casino's enormous and immensely flavorful burgers (split one with a pal and expect a 20-minute wait) while vintage Clash tunes from the jukebox drown out a Stanley Kubrick movie. Just a couple blocks away is **Club DeVille** (900 Red River St., 512/457-0900), a semi-swanky,

AUSTIN

AUSTIN

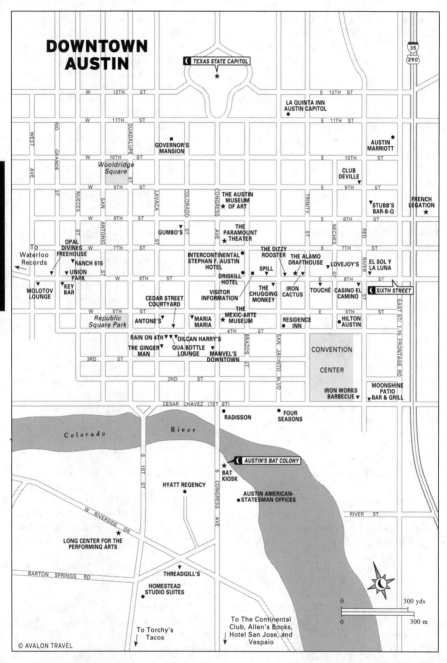

DOWNTOWN AUSTIN

TEXAS STATE CAPITOL

LA QUINTA INN
AUSTIN CAPITOL

AUSTIN
MARRIOTT

GOVERNOR'S
MANSION

*Wooldridge
Square*

CLUB
DEVILLE

THE AUSTIN
MUSEUM
OF ART

STUBB'S
BAR-B-Q

FRENCH
LEGATION

THE
PARAMOUNT
THEATER

GUMBO'S

OPAL
DIVINES
FREEHOUSE

To
Waterloo
Records

RANCH 616

UNION
PARK

INTERCONTINENTAL
STEPHAN F. AUSTIN
HOTEL

THE DIZZY
ROOSTER

SPILL

THE ALAMO
DRAFTHOUSE

LOVEJOY'S

EL SOL Y
LA LUNA

MOLOTOV
LOUNGE

KEY
BAR

DRISKILL
HOTEL

VISITOR
INFORMATION

THE
CHUGGING
MONKEY

IRON
CACTUS

TOUCHÉ

CASINO EL
CAMINO

SIXTH STREET

*Republic
Square Park*

CEDAR STREET
COURTYARD

ANTONE'S

MARIA
MARIA

THE
MEXIC-ARTE
MUSEUM

RESIDENCE
INN

HILTON
AUSTIN

RAIN ON 4TH

THE GINGER
MAN

OILCAN HARRY'S

QUA BOTTLE
LOUNGE

MANVEL'S
DOWNTOWN

CONVENTION

CENTER

IRON WORKS
BARBECUE

MOONSHINE
PATIO
BAR & GRILL

CESAR CHAVEZ (1ST ST)

RADISSON

FOUR
SEASONS

Colorado   *River*

AUSTIN'S BAT COLONY

BAT
KIOSK

HYATT REGENCY

AUSTIN AMERICAN-
STATESMAN OFFICES

RIVER   ST

LONG CENTER FOR THE
PERFORMING ARTS

BARTON SPRINGS RD

0   300 yds

0   300 m

THREADGILL'S

HOMESTEAD
STUDIO SUITES

To The Continental
Club, Allen's Books,
Hotel San Jose, and
Vespaio

To Torchy's
Tacos

© AVALON TRAVEL

super-loungey cocktail bar. Arrive before 11 to grab a prime spot on the big patio beneath the limestone cliff wall. The drinks are strong, the music is perfectly nostalgic, and the scene is always hoppin'—an ideal recipe for a night on the town in Austin.

WEST OF CONGRESS

Like the nearby Warehouse District, this (much smaller) area draws an older crowd that prefers a neat pour of Scotch over a dollar shot of schnapps. Twenty years ago this depressing part of downtown was filled with used car lots and auto repair shops; now it's in the shadow of condo towers and company headquarters. One of the more established and inviting taverns on the street is **Opal Divines Freehouse** (700 W. 6th St., 512/477-3308, www.opaldivines.com). Named for the owner's grandmother, this English-style pub has a magnificent double-decker patio among the towering oak trees and features an impressive Scotch bar on the second floor. Beer lovers will froth over the amazing ale options, and the pub grub—particularly the cracked-pepper fries—is way above average. Venture across the street for the lively singles scene at **Molotov Lounge** (719 W. 6th St., 512/499-0600, www.molotovlounge.com). The Russian theme will compel you to order a vodka drink, which you can keep chilled on the portion of the bar made of ice. Other cool bar features include retractable front doors and a swanky rooftop patio. **Union Park** (612 W. 6th St., 512/478-7275) caters to a similar crowd, with a welcoming rooftop bar featuring foliage and pillowy benches. Mojitos are mainstays here. Next door is the hip-yet-relaxed **Key Bar**, located in a former locksmith shop. The outdoor lounge is a cool place to enjoy a cold beer or a signature cocktail with juice Popsicle garnish.

EAST OF I-35

Most of the hoppin' bar activity on Sixth Street is happenin' just west of the behemoth I-35 freeway, but the hipsters have relocated to a comparatively mellow stretch of venues east of the interstate. These bars are much more laid-back than the raucous shot bars just a half mile away, and they cater to a slightly older crowd. But make no mistake—people here are still dressed to impress, even if that means looking like one of the nearby homeless guys in "vintage" clothes and matted hair. A good starting point in this area is **Rio Rita** (1308 E. 6th St., 512/524-0384, www.riorita.net), offering a large open room with brightly colored walls and curtained-off areas. The drinks are well poured (especially the Bloody Marys), and the quality coffee offers a nice pick-me-up between cocktails. A few blocks away is the welcoming **Shangri-La** (1016 E. 6th St., 512/524-4291, www.shangrilaaustin.com). Known for its spacious courtyard and impressive beer selection, Shangri-La is an ideal place to spend a cool spring evening or warm summer night. For a true East Austin hipster experience, head straight to **Cheer Up Charlie's** (1104 E. 6th St., 512/431-2133, www.cheerupcharlies.blogspot.com), a small bar with a big front yard for lounging, dancing, and smoking trendy cigarettes. The locally brewed kombucha and draft beer are big hits here, as are the nearby food trailers offering a variety of satisfying late-night munchies.

Warehouse District

Compared to Sixth Street, the Warehouse District is downright civil. You won't find too many UT coeds at these bars, but that doesn't mean it's a subdued scene. Instead of angry punk bands, you'll often hear jazz trios. Ladies order cosmopolitans rather than mind erasers. Food options include tapas as opposed to hot dogs from a cart. And if your fifth glass of cabernet makes your feet restless, there are several nearby clubs with crafty DJs playing hoppin' dance music. Besides, Sixth Street is a mere 20-minute walk away if you really want to reconnect with your inner 21-year-old.

Catch some live music and spot the scenesters at **Cedar Street Courtyard** (208 W. 4th St., 512/495-9669, www.cedarstreetaustin.com). One of the district's first successful establishments, Cedar Street features a sunken courtyard with live music and some of the city's

HOLLYWOOD IN TEXAS

For most of the past decade, *MovieMaker* magazine has named Austin among the top moviemaking cities in the country. More than 350 major features and made-for-TV movies have been filmed in Austin over the past 20 years, and hundreds of commercials and independent projects have also used the capital city as a backdrop.

One of the city's first high-profile projects, aside from the classic *Texas Chainsaw Massacre*, was 1989's *Lonesome Dove*, which took full advantage of the Austin area's diverse scenery. Other big-name projects filmed in Austin include *Office Space, Dazed and Confused, Waiting for Guffman, Friday Night Lights, Tree of Life*, the Spy Kids series, and the seminal *Slacker*.

One of the main reasons filmmakers choose Austin is its diverse topography and moderate climate (suitable for year-round filming). The city has rolling hills to the west, flat prairies to the east, crystal-clear lakes, and pine forests all within a half hour of the production office. And because Austin is surrounded by small towns that haven't changed much in the past few decades, there are abundant locations to film period pieces that use historic county courthouses, Main Street storefronts, and vintage homes as scenery. Also, since the area has been a hot spot for filming since the early '90s, there's a deep talent pool of qualified crew members.

Finally, as most Austinites will quickly and enthusiastically claim, the city is a fun place to be on location for a few months. Residents are welcoming without being overly starstruck, the restaurant and bar scene is a fun destination after a hard day's work, there are plenty of outdoor recreation opportunities, and the plethora of actors and directors make for a wealth of qualified available talent.

---

stiffest drinks. Martinis are the specialty here, and the friendly bartenders will gladly help you find your favorite blend. Although the location changed, the vibe is still the same at **The Ginger Man** (301 Lavaca St., 512/473-8801, www,gingermanpub.com), with its almost-overwhelming beer selection. Chalkboards above the bar announce new arrivals, featured selections, and specials among the dozens of brews on tap and in bottles. If it's warm, order a Texas wheat beer and enjoy it in the outdoor beer garden. If it's cold, have a stout inside at the welcoming bar or in one of the comfy nooks and crannies.

The only noteworthy spot remaining from the Warehouse District's once-thriving swanky ultralounge trend is **Qua Bottle Lounge** (213 W. 4th St., 512/472-2782, www.quaaustin. com), complete with a shark tank in the floor. Bottle service, ice tables, waterfalls, and a *shark tank in the floor* await.

Gay Bars

Austin doesn't have a specific downtown area exclusively devoted to gay bars, but several are located in the Warehouse District. One of the city's stalwarts is **Oilcan Harry's** (211 W. 4th St., 512/320-8823, www.oilcanharrys.com), known for its dance scene and bartenders. Though the crowd here is mostly gay, straight folks are welcome. The other venerable gay venue in town is right next door. **Rain on 4th** (217 W. 4th St., 512/494-1150, www.rainon4th.com) features strong drinks and a lively dance floor.

Live Music

Musicians have been drawn to Austin for decades to take advantage of the city's abundant stages, open-minded atmosphere, and (formerly) cheap rent. Several notable artists persevered beyond free meals and tip jar paychecks, including Janis Joplin and Stevie Ray Vaughan, and more recently, acts such as Spoon and . . . Trail of Dead have seen their names ascend from the bottoms of flyers to the tops of marquees. Drop by any of the 100-plus venues in town that host live music, and you just might be lucky enough to discover the next Timbuk 3 or Fastball.

SIXTH STREET

There are still pockets remaining of old Sixth Street—rock 'n' roll venues and comfy dive bars—among the dance clubs, and they're worth checking out for the quality of live music being played most nights. Consistently reliable is **The Parish** (214 E. 6th St., 512/473-8381, www.theparishaustin.com), featuring local and touring indie rock acts. Spoon spent a lot of time here on their rise up the alt-rock ladder, and occasional techno or hip-hop shows appear on the schedule. A couple blocks east is longtime reggae club **Flamingo Cantina** (515 E. 6th St., 512/494-9336, www.flamingocantina.com). The Flamingo is a reliable source for local and national reggae and ska bands as well as cold Red Stripe beer and a lingering haze of green smoke. One of the newest kids on the block is the nearby **Nuno's Bar & Grill** (422 E. 6th St., 512/833-5133, www.nunosonsixth.com), which manages to feel like it's been around a long time. The blues rule at Nuno's, and the nightly drink specials keep things flowing nice and easy.

RED RIVER

Red River Street, at the eastern edge of the Sixth Street district, represents the lifeblood of Austin's live music scene. Once the territory of crack dealers and vagabonds, this four-block stretch is now the vibrant core of the city's rock 'n' roll culture. Anchoring the strip is **⟨ Stubb's Bar-B-Q** (801 Red River St., 512/480-8341, www.stubbsaustin.com), which hosts the city's best road shows on a moderately sized (1,800 capacity) outdoor amphitheater and accommodates smaller acts on an indoor stage. As the name implies, Stubb's also serves some fine smoked meats, but the bands bring the heat most nights. Artists ranging from Wilco and the White Stripes to Snoop Dogg and Interpol grace the main stage, while the more intimate inside stage has hosted local stalwarts such as The Gourds and The Derailers. Incidentally, Stubb's holds perhaps

the most memorable New Year's Eve bash in town. Nearby **Mohawk** (912 Red River St., www.mohawkaustin.com) features indie rock bands from Austin and afar, and draws one of the trendiest crowds in Capital City. The multiterraced outdoor patios offer cool views of downtown and quiet places to drink hipster-approved cans of cheap beer (Pabst Blue Ribbon and Lone Star). Mohawk was named the "coolest bar in America" by *Esquire* magazine in 2008. Three blocks south is the renowned punk club **Emo's** (603 Red River St., 512/477-3667, www.emosaustin.com), featuring several stages and some of the city's craziest artwork—a wall mural depicting famous Texas assassins, depraved posters promoting previous shows, and, suspended over the main bar, the stool Johnny Cash used during his legendary 1994 performance. Bands are largely of the fast and loud variety, but Emo's hosts occasional touring shows from oldies acts such as Cheap Trick and Yo La Tengo. Just down the street are a few down 'n dirty establishments offering local cowpunk and alternative bands along with cheap beer specials most nights of the week. The best of the bunch are **Beerland** (711 Red River St., 512/479-7625, www.beerlandtexas.com) and **Red Eyed Fly** (715 Red River St., 512/476-0997, www.redeyedfly).

WAREHOUSE DISTRICT

By far, the city's most famous nightclub is **⟨ Antone's**, "Austin's Home of the Blues" (213 W. 5th St., 512/320-8424, www.antones.net). Although it's changed locations a few times, Antone's has been a fixture on the music scene for nearly three decades, staging legendary artists like B. B. King along with local blues and roots rock acts such as Pinetop Perkins and Guy Forsyth. Stevie Ray Vaughan got his start here, and people still line up to catch the latest homegrown and national acts rock the big stage. Two doors down is **Lucky Lounge** (209 W. 5th St., 512/479-7700, www.theluckylounge.com), a live music/singles scene combo that actually works. The music kicks off fairly early—around 8 P.M. most nights—and the schmoozing picks up afterward.

AUSTIN

SOUTH AUSTIN

Although this area covers a lot of ground geographically, the soul of this part of town and, consequently, the live music scene, ties the entire South Austin community together. This is perhaps best represented at 【 **The Continental Club** (1315 S. Congress Ave., 512/441-2444, www.continentalclub.com), the venerable South Congress venue that once hosted breezy artists like Glenn Miller in the 1950s. Now the tiny stage is a regular spot for local and national touring acts—most specializing in roots rock, bluegrass, rockabilly, and country. Celebrity sightings are fairly common here, and the happy hours are a great way to experience authentic Austin. Another local favorite is **Saxon Pub** (1320 S. Lamar Blvd., 512/448-2552, www.thesaxonpub.com), featuring blues, singer-songwriters, and Americana. The venue itself isn't remarkable, with its limited seating and small stage, but the sound quality is excellent, and the artists are always far better than you'd expect to hear in a neighborhood bar. If you're looking for a true Texas-style honky-tonk, you absolutely have to check out 【 **The Broken Spoke** (3201 S. Lamar Blvd., 512/442-6189, www.brokenspokeaustintx.com). This is as real as it gets—the music, dancing, and surrounding scenery are purely Texas. On weekend nights, the dance floor is crowded with crisp-jeaned ranchers and tattooed hipsters, all two-steppin' in a smoothly rotating counterclockwise pattern. Legends that've graced this low-ceiling, no-frills establishment during its prominent past include Willie Nelson, Bob Wills, Ernest Tubb, and George Strait, but these days, visitors and locals make a point of seeing local favorites like The Derailers and Gary P. Nunn.

The Alamo Drafthouse

The classic "dinner and a movie" date received a major upgrade when The Alamo Drafthouse opened in 1997 (there are now four Austin locations, listed below). The concept is genius in its simplicity: offer restaurant-quality food to movie patrons. And beer. Each alternate aisle of seats is replaced with narrow tables, allowing waiters to take orders and deftly navigate the theater without disturbing viewers. Menu items include the "Royale with Cheese" burger and "Poultrygeist" pizza, and the cold draft beer and fine wines offer an ideal accompaniment. The food is often paired with the movie (Spaghetti Westerns, or re-creating meals from *Big Night* and *Like Water for Chocolate*), and there are clever promotions galore—screening bad '80s movies with appearances by the starring has-been actors, a karaoke-style movie scene reenactment contest called "videoke," sing-alongs, open screen nights, and rolling road shows. Film festivals are de rigueur, with several hosted by notable industry types such as director Quentin Tarantino and Austin-based online film critic Harry Knowles. If all that weren't enough, *Entertainment Weekly* named the Alamo the "best theater in America." The Alamo's tremendous popularity is a proud Austin success story, and it allowed the franchise to expand from its original location in the Warehouse District to four theaters throughout the city and several others across Texas. The Austin locations are **Alamo Downtown** (320 E. 6th St.), **Alamo South Lamar** (1120 S. Lamar Blvd., 512/476-1320), **Alamo Village** (2700 W. Anderson Ln., 512/476-1320), and **Alamo Lake Creek** (13729 Research Blvd., 512/219-8135). Information about showtimes and events at all locations is available at www.drafthouse.com.

South by Southwest Music Festival

What started as a small collection of bands and industry reps in a single downtown hotel has expanded to one of the largest multimedia festivals in the country. Each March, thousands of musicians and their associated crowds—critics, businesspeople, groupies—flock to Austin for South by Southwest (aka the music industry's spring break) for ideal weather, ice cold beer, barbecue and Tex-Mex, and every kind of music under the warm sun. During this week, Austin becomes the epicenter of the music industry, complete with international

EEYORE'S BIRTHDAY PARTY

The freak flags are always flying at this annual celebration of spring dedicated to A. A. Milne's despondent donkey. Austinites partake in their natural hippie atmosphere by wearing colorful costumes (often nothing but body paint), joining the continuous drum circle, dancing to noodly jam bands, and wandering aimlessly among vendors hawking herbs, tofu, natural sodas, and Texas beer. Artists provide face painting and temporary tattoos, musicians (playing nonamplified instruments) are invited to play, Maypoles are set up, and there's even a forlorn donkey named Eeyore on hand, so everyone can drop by and wish the hapless creature a happy birthday.

Eeyore's Birthday Party has been a traditional springtime event in Austin since the early 1960s, and it's evolved into a major fundraiser benefiting Austin nonprofit groups. The party itself began in 1963 as a spring fling for students attending a fun-loving English professor's class at the University of Texas. The original event featured a trash can full of lemonade, honey sandwiches, and a real flower-draped donkey. Its immense success prompted people to continue the tradition in subsequent years.

The event, typically held the last Saturday in April at the centrally located Pease Park, runs from late morning until dusk. Attendance is free, and shuttle buses transport attendees from downtown garages since parking has become a major issue for the thousands of partygoers.

media coverage, splashy promotional events, and enough black leather to make locals flee in horror. Although the concept is to expose bands and sign contracts for up-and-coming artists (acts getting their first major buzz at the festival include the White Stripes, Norah Jones, and, um, Hanson), SXSW has become such an enormous showcase, it regularly hosts big names and reunion gigs (The Pretenders, Big Star, Morrissey) for the publicity factor among the collaborated industry. Back in the day, visitors and locals could buy an all-access wristband for about $50. Now you need to fork over nearly $1,000 for an unrestricted platinum badge. Fortunately, there are hundreds of fun, worthwhile, and free music options during SXSW week for the common folk, mostly daytime parties featuring lesser-known and some well-known bands who'll play anywhere possible—a back alley, street corner, or front lawn—just to maximize exposure. SXSW organizers also work with the city to stage free shows at the downtown park Auditorium Shores, where past notables include Spoon, Public Enemy, and Cheap Trick. For more information, visit www.sxsw.com or call 512/467-7979.

Austin City Limits Music Festival

This is one of the country's hottest festivals—literally and figuratively. Scheduled annually in the inferno of Austin's mid-September, ACL Fest features searing temperatures and equally scorching bands. Presented by the organizers of the long-running PBS show of the same name, the Austin City Limits Festival is one of those no-brainers that should have been in existence since the show's inception in 1975. Alas, the festival premiered in 2002, and has since become a premier event among music fans of all types. Artists range from American rock legends like Bob Dylan, Tom Petty, and The Eagles to big names such as Pearl Jam, Wilco, and Arcade Fire to up-and-comers (came-and-wenters?) like MGMT, Franz Ferdinand, and the Arctic Monkeys. Over the years, fest organizers have learned some valuable lessons about hosting a successful event by offering the following amenities: dozens of exclusively local food vendors, shade and misting tents, free water stations, and an Austin Kiddie Limits stage. Organizers claim the festival will continue to take place during the blistering month of September since it is the only time to amass the hundred-plus bands that remain on the road wrapping up summer tours. Despite the sweltering conditions, nearly 70,000 fans quickly snap up tickets each year. It's only rock 'n' roll…For more information, visit www.aclfest.com.

The Star of Texas Fair and Rodeo

Most years, the rodeo takes place at the same time as South by Southwest (mid-March). The front page of the newspaper will often feature a photo of a tattooed hipster adjacent to an article about the champion steer. In some ways, it's an apt representation of Austin—the progressive music scene and the old-fashioned livestock show. Even the rockers can enjoy the rodeo, however, with its roping and barrel racing competitions, carnival rides, Texas food vendors, and live music. The rodeo attracts huge crowds from across the state each year, drawn by the excitement of witnessing a bull riding competition—it's far more intense in person than on TV—and by the quality musicians. Past performers include diverse acts such as Merle Haggard, Nelly, Maroon 5, and Lady Antebellum. For more information, visit www. rodeoaustin.com or call 512/919-3000.

SHOPPING

Once home to numerous slacker-y music and bookstores, Austin now has trendy clothing boutiques featured on national TV shows and fashion magazines. Several new upscale malls have also popped up recently, but they haven't displaced too many distinctive local shops—vinyl records, obscure books, and custom-made boots are still available in not-so-trendy places off the beaten path.

South Congress

The über-trendy stretch of South Congress Avenue just south of the Colorado River used to be so desolate, you could easily spot the undercover cops seeking out drug dealers and prostitutes. The area transformed mightily during the 1990s, most notably when a dotcom start-up replaced an aging adult theater. Other new businesses followed suit, and the streetscape soon was revitalized with cafés, galleries, and trendy clothing stores. There were

marketing efforts to brand the strip with the cute moniker "SoCo," but you won't hear many locals referring to it by that name. Two of the strip's anchors are **Lucy in Disguise** (1506 S. Congress, 512/444-2002, www.lucyindisguise. com), the quintessential thrift store featuring the city's coolest vintage threads and accessories along with bodacious costume rentals, and **Uncommon Objects** (1512 S. Congress Ave., 512/442-4000, www.uncommonobjects.com), a fascinating expanse of antiques, curios, folk art, and, well, uncommon objects from across the world. Incidentally, the stock here is always changing since the store showcases many different vendors offering rotating collections of vintage and modern knickknacks.

Clothing-wise, South Congress is a haven for trendy boutiques. Among the most popular is **By George** (1400 S. Congress Ave., 512/441-8600, www.bygeorgeaustin.com), a vibrant shop known for its laid-back vibe, popular designers (Current-Elliot, Madison Marcus), playful accessories, and fairly pricey clothes. Customers are inevitably won over, however, when the staff offers them a beer as they peruse the clothing and jewelry. Nearby, **Maya Star** (1508 S. Congress Ave., 512/912-1475, www.mayastar. com) has developed a strong reputation for its selection of affordable designer clothing, jewelry, and impeccable customer service. Farther down the road, **Creatures Boutique** (1206 S. Congress Ave., 512/707-2500, www.creatures-botique.com) has a hipster edge, particularly with its eclectic selection of purses and shoes.

Though certainly not as trendy, one of the best apparel shops on the entire South Congress strip is **[Allen's Boots** (1522 S. Congress Ave., 512/447-1413, www.allensboots.com), a refreshingly low-key establishment among the much-hyped boutiques. Allen's knowledgeable employees help customers find a perfectly fitting boot and explain the differences among styles and brands. In addition to the extensive selection of boots, Allen's offers a broad range of shirts, hats, jeans, and belts.

The Domain

Austin's newest upscale mall, The Domain

(11410 Century Oaks Terr., 512/873-8099) is considered a godsend by those in search of big-city shopping options, and a threat by those intimidated by big cities. The Domain includes more than 60 stores in a sprawling indoor/outdoor configuration in the rapidly growing northern reaches of the city. There's no denying this shopping center brings a slice of Dallas to Central Texas, but despite the protests of the NIMBY crowd, it has yet to infect Austin with a serious case of City Slickeritis. Appropriately enough, The Domain is anchored by Dallas-born **Neiman Marcus,** known for its quality merchandise and name-brand products—especially women's shoes—with knowledgeable and helpful customer service. Less upscale and certainly less Texan is **Barney's Co-op,** a New York–based enterprise offering affordable quality men's and women's clothing in a distinctive atmosphere. Other high-end retailers include **Tiffany & Co.** and **Calypso.** Since Austin is a computer-savvy town, one of The Domain's most popular establishments is the **Apple Store,** a mecca for gadget geeks and computer connoisseurs who appreciate the latest Apple innovations and, most importantly, want a place to try them personally and gush over them with fellow Mac users.

Sixth and Lamar

It's hard to believe this vibrant and busy intersection was once a collection of used car lots. Now, the vehicles bustling around these streets are hybrids, convertibles, and scooters en route to the city's coolest large-scale stores. In fact, this intersection is a microcosm of Austin's prototypical population—literate, organic, outdoorsy music fans.

The veteran of the group is **❰ Waterloo Records** (600 N. Lamar Blvd., 512/474-2500, www.waterloorecords.com), regularly voted one of the country's top music stores. Waterloo is a music lover's paradise, with tens of thousands of CDs and hundreds of vinyl albums catering to every style, refreshingly categorized in alphabetical order (as opposed to genre). Waterloo hosts in-store appearances by big-name artists on a small stage and is one of the few remaining places where music fans can hang out in person with like-minded souls (and employees) to share their latest musical discoveries.

Across the street is **Book People** (603 N. Lamar Blvd., 512/472-5050, www.bookpeople.com), another nationally recognized independent retailer where customers often find themselves spending an entire afternoon. Billing itself as the largest bookstore in Texas, Book People offers an impressive range of literary works and is a destination for literary types across the state, especially for readings and appearances by world-renowned authors and politicians.

Next door, the gigantic **REI** (601 N. Lamar Blvd., 512/482-3357, www.rei.com) provides the city's weekend warriors with enough outdoor gear to set up an impressive base camp. REI is in the space formerly occupied by **Whole Foods Market,** which moved across the street (512 N. Lamar Blvd., 512/476-1206, www.wholefoodsmarket.com) when it opened its impressive world headquarters and flagship grocery store. At 80,000 square feet, it's a spectacle to behold—stunning displays of colorful produce and delectable foods blend with plentiful islands offering freshly prepared items (salads, seafood, cheese, pastries, coffee) alongside aisles of organic and health food items. Whole Foods draws a large crowd of in-store and to-go diners, and the bustling scene and almost overwhelming abundance of edible options attract foodies and visitors from across the country.

North Austin Western Wear

You're more likely to see flip-flops and ironic T-shirts on Austinites than cowboy hats and big belt buckles, but the city still boasts several big ol' Western shops that remind visitors they're deep in the heart of Texas.

Two of the city's most popular Western wear stores are chains, but considering the products involved are cowboy related, these spots don't carry the stigma of big box retailers. **Sheplers Western Wear** (6001 Middle Fiskville Rd., 512/454-3000, www.sheplers.com) is an enormous store brimming with boots, hats, shirts, belts, jeans, and anything else you'd ever need to make your ride on a mechanical bull appear more authentic. This is perhaps the best place in town for aspiring cowgirls to stock their wardrobe, since many similar stores cater more to men's wear. If you're hankerin' for a pair of affordable boots and jeans, look no further than **Cavender's Boot City** (8809 Burnet Rd., 512/451-7474, www.cavenders.com), which features quality low-priced boots and apparel for cowboys, cowgirls, and cowkids.

SPORTS AND RECREATION

Despite reaching metropolitan status, Austin does not have a major-level professional sports franchise, in large part because the University of Texas dominates many aspects of the city, including sporting events. Fortunately, the boys and girls in burnt orange are perennial contenders for national titles in all sports (they've won nearly 50 championship trophies collectively), so the quality of action on the field is first-rate. Recreation-wise, Austin prides itself on its large amount of natural green space, and residents take full advantage of the city's hike and bike trails and waterways to keep fit and relax.

University of Texas Sports
FOOTBALL
College football is a religion in Texas, and the University of Texas's Royal Memorial Stadium is one of the houses of the holy. As soon as they can walk, little Texans dream of playing there, and anyone who's seen the Longhorns take the field can see why. The atmosphere is exhilarating, especially at late-season games against nationally ranked division rivals, and there's a good chance that many of the enormous players in burnt orange will soon be playing in the NFL. The football program has a tradition of excellence, with four national championships, most recently in 2005 led by current NFL star Vince Young, and previously in 1963, 1969, and 1970 under legendary coach Darrel Royal. Although the Horns' most-hyped game each

year is against the University of Oklahoma, their traditional arch rival is Texas A&M. Even when the Aggies are having another subpar year, the big game—held the day after Thanksgiving alternating between Austin and College Station—is an intense confrontation of strong, scrappy Texans battling for a year's worth of bragging rights.

BASKETBALL
No sport will displace football at the top of the food chain in Austin, but the UT men's basketball team is making a valiant effort to get noticed. They're steadily succeeding, thanks to coach Rick Barnes's impressive skills as a leader and recruiter. The team has produced several highly touted NBA recruits, including Kevin Durant, Daniel Gibson, and LaMarcus Aldridge, and has made regular appearances in the top tiers of the NCAA tournament during the past decade. Although the team's home, the Frank Erwin Center, doesn't get as rollicking as Memorial Stadium, more students and residents are starting to fill the seats and provide the energy found in college basketball arenas in other parts of the country.

Also a formidable force on the Erwin Center court is the women's basketball team, still occasionally referred to as the Lady Longhorns. A longtime powerhouse in women's collegiate basketball, these Longhorns include some of the best athletes in the sport. Legendary coach Jody Conradt retired from the helm and was replaced by legend-in-the-making Gail Goestenkors.

BASEBALL
UT's baseball program doesn't get the exposure and recognition it deserves. Despite taking a backseat to the football and basketball programs, baseball at the university has a long tradition of fielding championship teams. In fact, the baseball program is the winningest in college baseball history and has won more college world series titles than any other school. Many of the players, most notably Roger Clemens and Huston Street, have gone on to successful careers in Major League Baseball. Longtime

coach Cliff Gustafson (1968–1996) led the team to more than a dozen college world series appearances, and current coach Augie Garrido has been at the helm for two national championships. The Horns' home base, Disch-Falk Field, received a much-needed upgrade, although the sight of artificial turf and sound of aluminum bats still makes baseball purists slightly cringe.

Professional Sports

For those who need to see a major sporting event, the big-time professional franchises are just down the road (a three-hour drive in Texas terms). San Antonio, Dallas, and Houston all have top-tier teams, and most Austinites pick and choose their sports allegiances based on their regional backgrounds or history with a franchise and its fan base.

The closest Austin gets to professional sports is the **Round Rock Express** (Dell Diamond, 3400 E. Palm Valley Blvd., 512/255-2255, www.roundrockexpress.com), a minor league affiliate of the Texas Rangers. Since the Express were promoted from AA level classification to AAA (just a step below the major leagues), fans have been treated to quality baseball with plenty of impressive hustle from burgeoning stars. Dell Diamond is a charming and comfy place to watch a game, and even nonfanatics can enjoy the pleasant atmosphere and amusing high jinks of minor league games (kids running the base paths, fans dancing on the dugout, various races on the field). Also just a step below the majors are the **Texas Stars** (512/467-8277, www.texasstarshockey.com), the minor league outfit for the Dallas Stars hockey team. The Stars made an immediate impact upon joining the American Hockey League for the 2009–10 season, when they played in the Calder Cup Finals. Games are played in the sparkling new suburban Cedar Park Center. Locals are also warming up to the **Austin Toros** (512/236-8333, www.nba.com/dleague/austin), the relatively new NBA Development League minor league team affiliated with the San Antonio Spurs. The Toros play at the Cedar Park Center from November through April.

City Parks

Long considered Austin's crown jewel, **Barton Springs Pool** (2201 Barton Springs Rd., 512/476-9044, www.ci.austin.tx.us, daily 5 A.M.–10 P.M., $1–3) in **Zilker Metropolitan Park** is the city's ultimate recreational experience. A source of cool refreshment for nearly a century, the 1,000-foot-long pool is constantly replenished by revitalizing 68°F springwater, a necessary remedy for Austin's triple-digit summer temperatures. The remainder of 350-acre Zilker Park is a sprawling urban oasis, with soccer fields, a hillside theater, sand volleyball courts, a massive playscape, a disc golf course, and picnic sites. Kids of all ages love the **Zilker Zephyr** (512/478-8286, $3.75 adults, $2.75 children), a miniature train that chugs around on several miles of track along the river and through the park. Other family-friendly activities include the serene and stunning **Zilker Botanical Gardens,** featuring the otherworldly Taniguchi Oriental Garden, and the **Austin Nature and Science Center,** a wonderful destination for children, offering glimpses at Texas wildlife (bobcats, owls, reptiles, raccoons), a dinosaur digging pit, science exhibits, and nature trails.

About a mile east as the grackle flies is **Town Lake Metropolitan Park,** spanning the shores of the downtown portion of the Colorado River formerly known as Town Lake (now Lady Bird Lake in honor of LBJ's wife, Lady Bird Johnson). The park contains an extremely popular 10-mile shoreline trail and fields for baseball, football, soccer/rugby, and volleyball. The park stretches east of I-35 and is a favorite spot for gatherings and events at Fiesta Gardens and Festival Beach. The parkland on the south side of Lady Bird Lake is known as **Auditorium Shores,** where numerous concerts are staged throughout the year (most are free public events). Standing in the shadows of the large stage erected for these shows is a statue of Austin's beloved guitarist Stevie Ray Vaughan, who died in a tragic 1990 helicopter accident. Fans pay homage to the legendary bluesman by leaving flowers and memorabilia at the base of the statue.

AUSTIN

One of the city's overlooked recreational gems is **Emma Long Metropolitan Park** (1600 City Park Rd., 512/346-1831, www.ci.austin. tx.us/parks/emmalong, daily 7 A.M.–10 P.M., $5–10). Named for an early member of the Austin City Council, the park is a massive expanse of natural Hill Country beauty, highlighted by a 350-foot-long sandy beach on the north bank of the Colorado River. Visitors bask in the sun or play beach volleyball while ski boats and Jet Skis zoom by. Emma Long is one of the few parks offering a somewhat cool respite on a scorching summer day thanks to the breeze from the water's surface and plentiful shade provided by the row of cypress trees along the riverbank. Incidentally, you'll find some of the tastiest burgers in town along with a full bar and live music on weekends at the adjacent **Ski Shores Cafe** (512/394-7511, www. skishoresaustin.com).

Hiking and Biking
THE TRAIL AT LADY BIRD LAKE
This is the most popular place for Austinites to exercise and flirt in an outdoor setting. The 10-mile-long crunchy and well-worn path offers an ideal representation of the city's physically fit population—healthy hikers, buff bikers, and strolling slackers. Besides being a great place to tone muscles and get in some good cardio exercise, the hike and bike trail is a healthy place to meet people and experience a hot and sweaty date. Recreationers can also get a light workout and enjoy Lady Bird Lake from its serene surface by putting a paddle to the water and soaking up the surrounding greenery, expanding skyline, and clear blue sky. Rent a canoe or kayak at **Zilker Park Boat Rentals** (located east of Barton Springs Pool, 512/478-3852, www.zilkerboats.com, 10 A.M.– dark, rates $10 per hour, $40 per day).

BARTON CREEK GREENBELT
It's hard to believe you're merely minutes from downtown once you've entered a trail and are surrounded by juniper trees, running water, and limestone cliffs. The Greenbelt (512/974-6700, visit www.ci.austin.tx.us/parks/

greenbelts.htm), an eight-mile stretch of preserved space along Barton Creek, draws scores of nature-loving urbanites to its rugged trails, sheer cliff walls, and swimming holes. Two of the most popular and lively access points are **Twin Falls** near Loop 360 and MoPac (Loop 1) and **Campbell's Hole** at the end of Spyglass Drive.

THE VELOWAY
Tucked away in Southwest Austin, The Veloway (4900 LaCrosse Ave., 512/974-6700, dawn–dusk) is a three-mile loop dedicated to wheels only—bikers and in-line skaters, in particular. A sign at the front gate provides a blunt reminder that joggers and walkers are not welcome here, which is fine, since bipeds have exclusive access to the rest of the city. The rolling Hill Country offers a welcoming backdrop to the surrounding 100-acre park, and the Veloway's proximity to Lady Bird Johnson Wildflower Center makes this a pleasantly natural way to get a good workout.

ACCOMMODATIONS
Austin mostly has chain hotels, but its few independently owned spots are big on charm and atmosphere. If you're planning well in advance, book a room at one of the funky South Congress locations—you won't experience anything like them in any other city. Most of the city's downtown options are within walking distance from the entertainment districts, so there's no need to take a cab—in fact, you'll probably want those five minutes on foot to eat your slice of pizza, burrito, sausage wrap, or whatever else seems appetizing enough to consume from a street cart.

South Congress
$100-150
You can't miss the distinctive sign erected in front of this retro establishment, serving as a gateway to the hip South Congress scene. **The Austin Motel** (1220 S. Congress Ave., 512/441-1157, www.austinmotel.com, $100 d) is a SoCo stalwart, particularly for its kidney-shaped pool, surrounded by funky old lounge

furniture and enough vegetation to offer some privacy from the nearby streetscape. Spring for one of the motel's larger rooms overlooking the pool ($137), complete with a fridge, stylish 1950s bathroom, and carport parking. Smaller single rooms overlooking the parking lot go for $80.

$150-200

Considered by many to be the best lodging in Austin, the (**Hotel San Jose** (1316 S. Congress Ave., 512/444-7322, www.sanjosehotel.com, $195 d) is the definition of cool—simple, clean, bright, and relaxing. Vintage and modern furniture rests on smooth concrete floors, fresh-cut flowers and bottled water catch the sun's rays, and intermittent garden areas offer songbirds, citrus trees, and peacefulness as an idyllic backdrop. Enjoy San Jose's cozy pool, movie and music library, free Wi-Fi access, in-room manicure/pedicure service, and charming room-service breakfasts in custom bento boxes with fruit, cereal, juice, and coffee.

Downtown
$100-150

Location-wise, the **La Quinta Inn Austin Capitol** (300 E. 11th St., 512/476-1166, www. lq.com, $115 d) is superb. This is one of the few places in town where having a rental car is not necessary, especially since there isn't any on-site parking. The hotel's prime location is its biggest asset, offering easy access by foot to most of the city's major attractions and entertainment options. Other positive aspects of the hotel include complimentary Internet access, a free continental breakfast, fitness center, and pool.

Commendable primarily for its prime location is **Homestead Studio Suites** (507 S. 1st St., 512/476-1818, www.homesteadhotels. com, $100 d). Situated within walking distance of downtown and Zilker Park, this is an ideal place to stay if you're attending the Austin City Limits festival or if you don't plan to spend too much time hanging out in the mediocre room. Though it's a bit rough around

the edges, Homestead still offers full kitchens with utensils, pet-friendly accommodations, and Wi-Fi for a $5 daily fee.

$150-200

One of the finest downtown options is the new, slick, business-oriented **Hilton Austin** (500 E. 4th St., 512/482-8000, www.hilton.com, $189 d). The hotel is located alongside the Austin Convention Center, so corporate functions are commonplace, but the location is amazing, as are several of the amenities—a fancy health club and spa with outdoor heated lap pool and hot tub, and alarm clocks with mp3 player hookups.

If you're participating in any activities related to the University of Texas or if you just want to stay in a nice, new central location, consider the more-welcoming-than-it-sounds **AT&T Executive Education and Conference Center** (1900 University Ave., 877/744-8822, www.meetattexas.com, $189 d). Located on the southern edge of the UT campus just north of downtown, this often-corporate lodging option is surprisingly one of the few places to stay directly adjacent to campus. Aside from easy access to university attractions (museums, sports facilities, bars), the hotel features fancy bedding, wet bars, 40-inch flat panel TVs, and free Internet access.

You'll find the best skyline view in the entire city at the (**Hyatt Regency** (208 Barton Springs Rd., 512/477-1234, www.hyatt.com, $199 d). Stunning. Sweeping. Expansive. These are all apt descriptions of the vantage point from each of the riverside rooms—one of the only hotels in town offering this experience from the south banks of Lady Bird Lake. Hyatt guests get an eyeful of the ever-expanding city skyline with bonus views of the Hill Country and the bats' celebrated evening emergence. The hotel also includes an outdoor pool, whirlpool, sundeck, and health club facility.

Another notable downtown locale is the **Radisson** (111 E. Cesar Chavez St., 512/478-9611, www.radisson.com, $199 d), overlooking scenic Lady Bird Lake, and, most importantly, the Congress Avenue bat bridge. Take advantage of the backyard view of the city's famous summertime bat-watching festivities, or just enjoy the activity on the water and shoreline hike and bike trail. Amenities include a large outdoor pool, a fitness center, and free Wi-Fi service.

$200-250

The **Residence Inn** (300 E. 4th St., 512/236-8008, www.marriott.com, $209 d) is popular with the business crowd since it's across the street from the convention center. The Marriott is one of the city's newest hotels, and it's just blocks away from some of Austin's premier restaurants and bars. The hotel also features an indoor pool, complimentary hot breakfast, and free wireless Internet access.

$250 AND ABOVE

The spectacular **⬛ Driskill Hotel** (604 Brazos St., 512/474-5911, www.driskillhotel.com, $296 d) exudes history, sophistication, and Texas. Built in 1886 as the showplace of a cattle baron, this historic downtown hotel offers guests a luxurious way to appreciate Austin's charms and attractions. The lobby alone is stunning, with its massive columns, marble floor, and stained-glass domed ceiling, and the rooms contain intricate woodwork, period furnishings, and sweeping views of downtown. Other highlights include the nationally recognized Driskill Grill and a fitness studio with massage tables and a sauna.

Nearby, the magnificent **InterContinental Stephen F. Austin Hotel** (701 Congress Ave., 512/457-8800, www.austin.intercontinental. com, $279 d) provides similar historical luxury on a much larger scale. Originally opened in 1924, the Stephen F. offers opulence in an ideal downtown location and features perhaps the best place in town to enjoy a beverage with a view. The hotel's terrace bar overlooks the busy epicenter of downtown, offering the only publicly accessible balcony with a tremendous view of the Capitol building. Room amenities include minibars, elegant furnishings, and soft bathrobes.

A favorite of celebrities and jet-setters, Austin's **Four Seasons** (98 San Jacinto Blvd., 512/478-4500, www.fourseasons.com, $320 d) is teeming with luxury and exquisite views of Lady Bird Lake, the Congress Avenue Bridge, and the gently rolling Hill Country. Other exquisite amenities the $300-plus tab covers include a luxurious spa, pool, and fitness center overlooking the shoreline; private minibars; thick terry-cloth bathrobes; rental bikes; free newspaper with breakfast; and a Texas authors lending library.

Arboretum Area
$100-150

Though it's far from the typical trendy Austin experience, the Arboretum area offers a pleasant environment adjacent to shops and restaurants with easy access to downtown (a 15-minute drive). An affordable yet reliable option in the Arboretum area is **Courtyard by Marriott** (9409 Stonelake Blvd., 512/502-8100, www.marriott.com, $109 d). Amenities include free wireless Internet access, a breakfast buffet (or add $10 to your nightly rate to include breakfast as part of the package), and a fitness center with indoor pool and whirlpool. Nearby is the slightly more appealing **Staybridge Suites** (10201 Stonelake Blvd., 512/349-0888, www.ichotelsgroup.com, $109 d). Staybridge offers welcoming grounds with grassy hills and an outdoor recreation area, including a heated pool and sports courts. Inside, there's a fitness center, and rooms include free Wi-Fi service. Kids eat free with a standard room reservation; suite reservations include free breakfast for all guests.

A few miles down the road (closer to the newer and fancier Domain "lifestyle shopping center") is **Hampton Inn** (3908 W. Braker Ln., 512/349-9898, www.hamptoninn.com, $119 d). The Hampton's amenities include free high-speed wireless Internet access, a free hot breakfast or to-go bags with a bottle of water (Monday–Friday), a fitness center, and a pool. For a step up in services for only a modest price increase, consider **Homewood Suites** (10925 Stonelake Blvd., 512/349-9966, www.homewoodsuites1.hilton.com, $129 d). This all-suite hotel is located in a tranquil parklike setting, and its one- and two-bedroom suites feature separate living and sleeping areas; kitchens with a refrigerator, microwave, stove, dishwasher, and coffeemaker; and 32-inch flatpanel TVs. Homewood Suites are pet friendly and offer complimentary hot breakfast daily as well as free wireless Internet access.

Camping

Located about 10 miles southeast of downtown Austin, **McKinney Falls State Park** (5808 McKinney Falls Pkwy., 512/243-1643, www.tpwd.state.tx.us, $5 daily ages 13 and older) offers a natural respite just down the road from Capital City. The 744-acre park is a great place to get away for camping, hiking, biking, swimming (in Onion Creek), picnicking, and fishing. Facilities include screened shelters with bunk beds (no mattresses) and dozens of campsites with water and electricity.

Another can't-believe-the-city-is-nearby camping area is **Pace Bend Park** (2501 N. Pace Bend Rd., 512/264-1482, www.co.travis.tx.us, primitive camping $15 per vehicle, improved camping $20 per vehicle). At 30 minutes, it's a bit farther away, but it's well worth the scenic Hill Country drive. This is one of the most popular camping areas in the region, so show up early (and carpool) to take advantage of this beautiful lakeside park. Whether you're in an RV or pup tent, be sure to bring a radio—out here you can catch the rootsy, twangy sounds of Texas Rebel Radio (107.9 KFAN), providing the best campfire music you've ever heard. Ever.

FOOD

Austinites eat out so often, they've been accused of not having kitchens in their homes. Indeed, the city is well known for its diverse mix of quality and affordable restaurant options, and it's quickly become a hot spot for foodies, who enjoy keeping up with the latest trends and chefs without abandoning their traditional favorite comfort-food spots. No matter where you go (airport, hike and bike trail, gas station, friend's house), you'll hear somebody talking about Austin's restaurant scene. Fortunately, most of the talk is good.

Downtown
AMERICAN

Upscale rustic food can be somewhat gimmicky unless it's done right. **Moonshine Patio Bar & Grill** (303 Red River St., 512/236-9599, www.moonshinegrill.com, $10–23) does it right. Down-home favorites like macaroni and cheese, baked chicken, and ribs get the high-end treatment, meaning top-quality ingredients are used with attention to detail. One of the best items on the menu is an appetizer—beer-battered asparagus served with a tangy dipping sauce. Make sure to save room for desert, particularly the chocolate peanut butter pie.

On the other side of downtown, **Ranch 616** (616 Nueces St., 512/479-7616, www.theranch616.com, $10–22) offers American fare with a Texas and Southwestern twist. The Gulf Coast is represented in the seafood options (shrimp quesadillas, fish tacos), and the kitchen does Texas and the South proud with its tasty biscuits, chicken-fried quail, and fried pies. Ranch 616 also draws a lively happy hour crowd, many who come for the dozens of premium tequilas.

You'll find Austin's best Cajun cuisine at **Gumbo's** (710 Colorado St., 512/480-8053, www.gumbosaustin.com, closed Sun., $15–34). It's expensive, but you get what you pay for—top-notch Creole fare such as the tenderloin Michael (Angus beef covered in sautéed crawfish and béarnaise sauce), and blackened shrimp over crawfish étouffée. Save room for the sweet New Orleans–style custard.

BARBECUE

Cold beer, live music, and barbecue: It's a holy trinity for laid-back Southerners, and in Austin, believers flock to the altar, er, bar at **Stubb's Bar-B-Q** (801 Red River St., 512/480-8341, www.stubbsaustin.com, $9–18). The hickory-smoked barbecue is legendary—the brisket, in particular—and the sauce is the best in town: a perfect combination of vinegary

AUSTIN

THE BARBECUE TRAIL

Central Texas is generally accepted as the state's barbecue capital and therefore (in the eyes of Texans) the barbecue headquarters of the world. There's some truly tasty stuff around here, and the smorgasbord of top-notch restaurants to choose from can be mind-boggling. Fortunately, you can't go wrong at most locally owned family-run places, especially if you see the stacks of hardwood logs out back and smell the hearty smoke burning. The good news is, most small towns in Texas are brimming with restaurants like this. Just look for the long lines forming out the door at lunchtime.

Barbecue purists will typically mention three must-taste towns on the barbecue trail – all accessible from I-35. Taylor, just north of Austin, is best known as the home of **Louie Mueller's Barbecue** (206 W. 2nd St., 512/352-6206, www.louiemuellerbarbeque. com, Mon.-Sat. 10 A.M.-6 P.M., $11-26). Open since the late 1940s, Louie Mueller's has been featured on food programs across the globe and is famous for its succulent smoked brisket. The place oozes weathered, smoke-drenched, rustic charm and serves up tender beef with a slightly peppery sauce and accompanying sweet sides (potato salad, coleslaw).

Just down the road is the town of Elgin, known for its delicious "hot guts" (aka sausage). One of the city stalwarts is **Southside Market & Bar-B-Q Inc.** (1212 Hwy. 290 E., 512/281-4650, www.southsidemarket.com, $10-24, Mon.-Thurs. 8 A.M.-8 P.M., Fri.-Sat. 8 A.M.-10 P.M., Sun. 9 A.M.-7 P.M.). Sausage is the main event here, and it's still made with fresh meats in the German tradition and served on butcher paper.

Long considered the holy grail of the barbecue trail is the community of Lockhart. This small town is big on legendary barbecue establishments, each offering a distinctive approach to preparing the meat. Purists swear by Kreuz, which doesn't provide sauce because it would compromise the savory, smoky taste, but others remain loyal to Black's or Smitty's because the sauce and sides provide the perfect complementary flavor. People are usually willing to do the extensive research involved to find out what combination of smoke and meat results in the ultimate Texas barbecue experience.

So, how did Central Texas become such a meat mecca? Food historians believe southern African-American cooking customs and German meat markets primarily influenced the style of barbecue in this area. The concept of barbecued meats on a lunch plate likely came about when African-American and Mexican American cotton pickers, familiar with their own traditional pit-style meat cooking, ordered sausage and ribs from the German butcher shops in small Central Texas towns. The workers weren't allowed in restaurants at that time (early 1900s), so after they got paid, they'd walk over to the market, order fresh smoked meat on butcher paper, and eat it on-site. Before long, picnic tables and side items of vegetables (traditional German fare like potato salad and coleslaw) emerged, giving way to the restaurants that dot the landscape today.

tang and peppery bite. Stubb's Sunday Gospel Brunch (held at the slacker-y hours of 11 A.M. and 1 P.M.) is virtually required for visitors, more for the soulful music than the hearty breakfast. In nonslacker news: Reservations are recommended.

Benefiting from a prime spot next to the Austin Convention Center, **Iron Works Barbecue** (100 Red River St., 512/478-4855, www.ironworksbbq.com, $8–17) has exposed more out-of-staters to Texas-style barbecue than anywhere else in town. Fortunately, it's a worthy ambassador, offering succulent beef brisket, tender pork ribs, and flavorful sausage to barbecue virgins since 1978.

For a true taste of Texas history (and delicious barbecue) drop by **Scholz Garden** (1607 San Jacinto Blvd., 512/474-1958, www.scholz-garten.net, $9–15), a beer garden and dance hall founded in 1866 by August Scholz, a

German immigrant. Now operated by Green Mesquite BBQ, Scholz's serves up Texas-style barbecue (beef brisket and ribs, sausage) and standard German fare like bratwurst, sauerkraut, and even Wiener schnitzel. The back patio biergarten is one of the liveliest places in town during and after UT sporting events.

MEXICAN
With a 30-year history, **Manuel's Downtown** (310 Congress Ave., 512/472-7555, www.manuels.com, $9–19) is an Austin tradition. And for good reason. With an emphasis on fresh seafood dishes (ceviche, shrimp tacos) and interior Mexican (mole enchiladas), Manuel's offers consistent quality. The main drawback: It can get really loud on weekend nights.

Another notable downtown *restaurante* is **El Sol y La Luna** (600 E. 6th St., 512/444-7770, www.elsolylalunaaustin.com, $6–13), relocated from South Congress Avenue. Arrive early to sample a signature Austin breakfast taco (try the potato, egg, and chorizo) or visit at lunch for Tex-Mex with a twist (catfish tacos, veggie tamales). Grab a spot by the window to enjoy the beautiful scenery and colorful Sixth Street scene.

If you're in the Warehouse District, be sure to check out **Maria Maria** (415 Colorado St., 512/687-6800, www.mariamariarestaurants.com, $7–14). Known for its chips, salsa, and famous owner (Carlos Santana), Maria Maria also deserves attention for its enchiladas, carnitas and . . . Smooth margaritas.

South Austin
AMERICAN AND BARBECUE
To get an authentic feel for the old-time Austin that locals pine for, drop by **Magnolia Café South** (1920 S. Congress Ave., 512/445-0000, www.themagnoliacafe.com, $9–16). This chilled-out, veggie-friendly, late-night spot offers Southern charm and hearty breakfasts all day—their famous gingerbread pancakes are especially appealing after a big night on the town. Magnolia's Tex-Mex plates (enchiladas, in particular) are also noteworthy, and their spicy Love Migas will test your heat index.

Another old-school Austin joint is ◖ **Artz Rib House** (2330 S. Lamar Blvd., 512/442-8283, www.artzribhouse.com), serving the best baby back ribs in town. They're fall-off-the-bone tender, and the combination of succulent flavors from the seasoned rub, savory smoked meat, and tangy sauce is tantalizing. Combine them with a cold beer or Dr Pepper, sides of potato salad and pinto beans, and a heaping helping of live music (playing most nights in the main room around 8 P.M.), and you'll have an unforgettably authentic Austin experience. Less laid-back but equally delicious is the **South Congress Cafe** (1600 S. Congress Ave., 512/447-3905, www.southcongresscafe.com, $10–24). Located in the heart of the trendy South Congress scene, this little restaurant is big on style and taste. Most dishes are Southwestern influenced, and all the portions are huge. The pork tenderloin and bluecorn crepes are local favorites.

ITALIAN
Austin was in dire need of a quality Italian restaurant when it was saved by the magnificent ◖ **Vespaio** (1610 S. Congress Ave., 512/441-6100, www.austinvespaio.com, $14–32). This tiny trattoria (as in 15 tables small) is well worth the hour-long wait, since it's impossible to go wrong with any of the impressive menu items or extensive daily specials. The appetizers are incredible—seared tuna and sliced braesola with aged provolone—and the entrées are simply outstanding. The mixed meat plate, seafood grill, spaghetti alla carbonara, and handkerchief pasta are just a few of the delectable options. If you have the time, stick around for a postmeal port or brandy.

JAPANESE
Consistently voted one of Austin's top restaurants, ◖ **Uchi** (801 S. Lamar Blvd., 512/916-4808, www.uchiaustin.com, $9–27) is a must for Japanese-food lovers or anyone who's been looking to explore sushi beyond the basic crab and California rolls. Knowledgeable and friendly waitstaff politely explain and recommend items, and the atmosphere is comfortable

yet romantic. Suggested dishes include the Muscovy duck, striped bass sushi, and baby bok choy. Not surprisingly, sushi is a specialty (the sushi bar is a singles hot spot). Uchi remains one of the city's most popular restaurants, so reservations are highly recommended.

MEXICAN

Consistently serving some of the best Mexican food in the city is South Congress stalwart ◖ **Guero's** (1412 S. Congress Ave., 512/447-7688, www.guerostacobar.com, $8–16). Located in a historic feed store with loads of south-of-the-border and South Austin charm, Guero's draws foodies and celebrities for its delectable Mexican food—perfectly seasoned chicken enchiladas in a tangy tomatillo sauce, savory beef and pork tacos, and a heavenly queso flameado. One of Guero's biggest fans is former President Bill Clinton, and the restaurant has a menu item named in honor of his favorite combo: chicken taco, beef taco, tamale, and guacamole salad.

Perhaps the most popular Tex-Mex restaurant in town is **Chuy's** (1728 Barton Springs Rd., 512/474-4452, www.chuys.com, $8–15), and for good reason. Now a major national chain, this Austin-born, funky, Elvis-obsessed establishment is a reliable source of classic Tex-Mex—enchiladas, tacos, and quesadillas—with a Southwestern flair (blue tortillas, green chiles). The margaritas are highly recommended, and the chips and salsa are so good, you'll find yourself filling up on them before your entrée arrives. It's worth exercising some self control for the whole (stacked) enchilada.

Food Trailers

Food trailers have taken over as Austin's hottest culinary trend. Most of them serve highly inventive food with top-notch ingredients, with the only drawback being the scenery—typically a parking lot or urban streetscape. Regardless, the phenomenon has exploded in recent years (nearly 1,000 trailers joined the city's food fray from 2006 to 2011). The heaviest concentration of options is in South Austin and near downtown. The following locales represent a

sampling of the city's best trailer food, from gourmet doughnuts to authentic Indian cuisine to grits with a soft-boiled duck egg.

1300 BLOCK OF SOUTH FIRST STREET

Visitors may want to start their mobile culinary journey by heading to one of Austin's original "trailer parks," a collection of vendors gathered on South First Street, about a half mile south of the Colorado River. If you only experience one trailer, make sure it's **Torchy's Tacos** (512/366-0537, www.torchystacos.com, $4–7). Though there are nearly a dozen options on the menu, three of them are extra exceptional. The fried avocado taco (hand-battered fresh avocados topped with lettuce, tomato, cheese, and an outstanding poblano sauce on a corn tortilla), the green chile pork (roasted pork carnitas with green chiles topped with queso fresco, cilantro, and tomatillo sauce on a corn tortilla), and the Trailer Park (fried chicken, green chiles, pico de gallo, cheese, and poblano sauce on a flour tortilla)—be sure to get it "trashy," which substitutes the lettuce with a creamy smothering of queso.

Just a few steps away is **Man Bites Dog** (512/445-5591, www.manbitesdogaustin.com, $3–7). You can choose from the special menu or create your own, and all dogs are served on a delicious platter—specially made kolache buns from the Kolache Shoppe in North Austin. Menu highlights include the Reuben (a Vienna beef hot dog with sauerkraut, Swiss cheese, and a punchy Russian dressing sauce), the Abe Froman (a Chicago-inspired hot dog with mustard, onions, relish, tomatoes, and a pickle spear), and the Buffalo Hottie (a hot dog topped with blue cheese and spicy buffalo sauce). Don't forget to complement your order with a sugary-sweet Mexican Coke.

If you'd like to sample one of Austin's famous breakfast tacos (or if the line at Torchy's is just too long), drop by **Izzo's Tacos** (512/326-4996, www.izzoztacos.com, $3–6). The best option here is the miga taco (a South Texas specialty), consisting of a flavorful blend of egg, cheese, peppers, and crispy bits of tortilla chips. You can also order a custom breakfast taco,

TRAILER PARK FOOD

© ANDY RHODES

one of the 1,600-plus food trailers in Austin

Austin certainly didn't invent the concept of a mobile food trailer (taco, hot dog, and gyro carts have been longtime fixtures in nightclub districts across the country), but it can certainly take some credit for taking these food trailers in an unexpected and extraordinary direction.

Most of Austin's food trailers serve highly inventive and high-quality food, from gourmet doughnuts to authentic Indian cuisine to grits with a soft-boiled duck egg. The trailer phenomena took off around 2006, when there were nearly 600 locations. By 2011, there were nearly 1,600 trailers on Austin's streets, garnering national attention and sparking similar trends in other food-obsessed cities.

The appeal of the trailers is the casual approach to excellent food. Though the urban locations and picnic-table ambience aren't too inspiring, the prospect of enjoying a fancy meal alfresco without the ritual of waiting for a table or dealing with a waiter is immensely satisfying (though the prices aren't quite as discounted as you may expect for the lack of overhead costs).

Some of these trailers have become so popular that they went on to open full-fledged restaurant locations complete with roofs, walls, beer, and credit card machines. Though the original locations of places like Torchy's Tacos, Hey Cupcake!, and Franklin Barbecue retain their trailer-park charm, many Austinites have enjoyed having the option of experiencing them in traditional restaurant form.

An important note before venturing out to these popular locales: By their nature, trailers are casual eateries, which means they're not always at the expected location or, more likely, not open when you're there (Austin's slacker-y charm means lunch doesn't happen until about 2 P.M.). Be sure to call ahead or check their websites to ensure everything's rolling by the time you get there. And it's advisable to bring cash since many locations don't have credit card machines. Finally, if you have a smartphone, you can download an app called ATXFoodCart that lets you know where the nearest trailers are and a link to their menus.

with standard items like egg, potato, sausage, cheese, beans, and spinach.

1200 BLOCK OF SOUTH LAMAR BOULEVARD

One of the city's most popular and distinctive trailer destinations is **Odd Duck Farm to Trailer** (512/695-6922, www.farmtotrailer. com, $5–14). Make no mistake, this is haute cuisine. Though the food arrives from a modest trailer, its origins are much more respectable—local farmers. Odd Duck prides itself on using area resources, and diners are rewarded with these efforts through incredibly fresh-tasting menu items. Local favorites include anything made with pork belly (the slider is always a good choice), which packs a lot of rich pork flavor accompanied by a tasty bit of arugula and a garlic mayonnaise. Even more inventive (yet not for everyone) are the grits with a soft-boiled duck egg. This blend of comfort food and haute cuisine includes grits mixed with mushrooms and parmesan topped with a delectable duck egg. Complete your order with a side of turnips and feel free to bring your own bottle of wine (most trailers don't sell alcohol).

Any time of day is a good time for a fancy doughnut, right? Of course. Whether you're in the mood for a meal or a snack, your cravings will be satisfied in completely unexpected ways at **Gordough's** (www.gourdoughs.com, $2–5). Though everything here is surprisingly delicious, locals tend to gravitate toward the Porkey's (Canadian bacon, cream cheese, and jalapeño jelly), the Son of a Peach (peach filling, cinnamon, sugar, and cake mix topping), the Dirty Berry (fudge icing with grilled strawberries), or the Mother Clucker (a fried chicken strip with honey butter). Wet your whistle with an accompanying cup of coffee or, for maximum sweet effect, a Dublin Dr Pepper, made with real cane sugar.

OTHER NOTABLE LOCATIONS

If you're in town for an event at the Austin Convention Center or even if you're anywhere near downtown, make a point of visiting **G'Raj Mahal** (91 Red River St., 512/480-2255, www. grajmahalaustin.com, $4–12). G'Raj Mahal makes the most of its location, offering simple yet classy decorations and a pleasant patio environment. As its name (sort of) implies, this spot specializes in Indian cuisine, and they do a tremendous job with every delectable detail. Start your culinary journey with a samosa appetizer, offering a potato and pea base with spicy green chutneys tempered by the sweet tamarind. Another popular menu item is the chicken tikka masala, blending hearty pieces of white meat accompanied by a savory and slightly spicy tomato cream sauce. Be sure to bring your own wine or beer (alcohol sales aren't permitted) to accompany your memorable meal in this wonderful location.

An especially innovative fusion experience awaits at **Coreanos** (at 7th and Neches St. or 16th and N. Congress Ave., www.coreanostx. com, $4–7). Who knew Korean barbecue and Mexican food worked so well together? Order a tasty burrito (the OG is a favorite, including marinated beef short ribs, french fries, Korean slaw, and kimchi wrapped in a flour tortilla), or a couple of tacos with spicy marinated chicken, garlic spread, and ranchero sauce. The french fries in the burrito work much better than expected, offering a slightly crispy and hearty element to the savory sauces and meats. Hot dogs are also on the menu, complete with a bacon wrapping and caramelized kimchi.

North Austin
MEXICAN

Until the 1980s, the most-admired and highest-profile restaurant in Austin was **Fonda San Miguel** (2330 W. North Loop Blvd., 512/459-4121, www.fondasanmiguel.com, $11–29). It's still a top-notch experience, but the trendy downtowners have overshadowed this North Austin stalwart of late. Fonda San Miguel remains the place to go if you're in search of authentic, flavorful interior Mexican food, and the hacienda-like atmosphere adds to the experience. Start off with a renowned margarita (mango is a popular choice) and continue with a pork, seafood, or enchilada dish (the mole sauce is especially succulent). Fonda San Miguel's Sunday brunches are legendary, so be sure to make reservations.

Far less formal is the campus-area **Changos Taqueria** (3023 Guadalupe St., 512/480-8226, www.changos.com, $5–11). Perfect for a quick quality lunch, Changos offers tacos with some flair—hand-pressed tortillas while you watch, marinated mahimahi, five salsas to choose from—accompanied by a fruity *agua fresca*.

Just down the street is the very untrendy, old-school **El Patio** (2938 Guadalupe St., 512/476-5955, closed Sun., $7–13). It may not be cool, but it's comfort food to the max—cheesy enchiladas, crispy beef tacos, tasty chalupas, and some of the best chips and queso in the city. Although the waiters finally ditched their maroon polyester jackets, they still offer diners a free dessert of their choice: sherbet or candy (a sweet buttery coconut-flavored praline).

AMERICAN

The third component of Austin's holy food trinity is Southern cooking (Tex-Mex and barbecue are the others), and despite South Austin's proud reputation as Bubbaland, two of the city's finest down-home cookin' establishments are located north of the river. The local legend is the original **Threadgill's** (6416 N. Lamar Blvd., 512/451-5440, www.threadgills.com, $8–16). Besides the meat loaf, Threadgill's biggest claim to fame is its role in Janis Joplin's early career—she and other aspiring musicians during Austin's hippie era would reportedly take the stage in exchange for free grub. Threadgill's food has become nearly as famous as Joplin's career was. If you've never experienced a chicken-fried steak—tenderized meat covered in crispy breading and creamy gravy—this is the place to do it. And for a meat-centric place, the veggies are outstanding, even if they're cooked with bacon, mixed with cheese, and doused in butter.

An equally tantalizing brand of Southern cooking is on the menu at **Hoover's** (2002 Manor Rd., 512/479-5006, www.hooverscooking.com, $9–19), just east of I-35 downtown.

Owner/cook Hoover Alexander brings a comprehensive collection of Southern influences to his dishes—his mama's home cooking, East Texas Cajun, pit-style barbecue, and even Tex-Mex. The results are sublime: smothered pork chops, jerked chicken, spicy sausage. The gravy is the best in town, and the sides (mac and cheese, jalapeño creamed spinach) are legendary.

Good burger joints are a must in any college town, and Austin has several noteworthy locales. The king of the old-timers is **Dirty Martin's Kum-Back Place** (2808 Guadalupe St., 512/477-3173, www.dirtymartins.com, $4–9). Much more appetizing than it sounds, Dirty's is a legendary burger stand that still offers carhop service. Inside, a thin layer of grease everywhere lets diners know they're in for the real deal—grilled patties oozing with cheese on a sweet bun accompanied by thin fries or, better yet, tater tots. Washing it all down with a chocolate shake is mandatory.

A few miles north, **Dan's Hamburgers** (5602 N. Lamar Blvd., 512/459-3239, $5–9) is a classic '50s-style burger joint. Utterly unpretentious, Dan's offers a perfect microcosm of Austin's population—rich, poor, old, and young fill this no-frills restaurant daily just to partake of the reliable, tasty burgers. Incidentally, Dan's serves one of the best diner-style breakfasts in town. Biscuits and gravy, breakfast tacos, pancakes, and huevos rancheros provide an ideal way to start the day.

JAPANESE

Opened in 2010, the latest and greatest addition to Austin's culinary scene is the unbelievable ◖ **Uchiko** (4200 N. Lamar Blvd., 512/916-4808, www.uchikoaustin.com, $15–39). An offshoot of the now-legendary Uchi in South Austin (see entry), Uchiko has lived up to Austinites' anticipation and hype by delivering inventive, fresh, and extremely high-quality Japanese-inspired food. Emerging as instant menu classics are bacon onigiri (fried pork belly rice, banh mi pickles) hama chili (yellowtail sashimi, sliced Thai chili, orange), and the take nabe (Japanese mushroom, koshi hikari, farm fresh egg, bushi). Each of the uniquely and unexpectedly crafted dishes are expertly explained by the waitstaff, who politely suggest menu items and recommend dishes based on the level of adventure (and budget) of each individual diner.

INFORMATION AND SERVICES
Tourist Offices
The **Austin Visitor's Center** (209 E. 6th St., 512/478-0098, www.austintexas.org, Mon.–Fri. 9 A.M.–5 P.M., Sat. and Sun. 9:30 A.M.–5:30 P.M.), located in an old drugstore, is a good place to get started with the help of free maps and friendly staffers. The visitors center also contains headquarters for **Austin Duck Adventures,** conducted in an amphibian vehicle, and **Austin Overtours,** which take place in the comfort of a van. Another good place to gather information, brochures, and maps about the city is the **Austin Convention and Visitors Bureau** (301 Congress Ave., Suite 200, 512/474-5171, www.austintexas.org, Mon.–Fri. 8 A.M.–5 P.M.).

Located adjacent to the Capitol, **The Capitol Visitors Center** (112 E. 11th St., 512/305-8400, daily 9 A.M.–5 P.M.) provides helpful information about the magnificent capitol building and surrounding attractions and services.

Publications
Austinites are avid readers—you'll find newspaper racks and free publications available all over town. The city's only metro daily paper is the *Austin American-Statesman,* a fine publication that's known as much for its innovative design as its content. Those looking for up-to-date entertainment news should pick up a Thursday paper, which includes the *Austin 360* supplement. Offering a healthy alternative is the *Austin Chronicle,* published every Thursday. The *Chronicle* is packed with comprehensive, well-written articles devoted to local politics, culture, and entertainment.

GETTING THERE AND AROUND
The only way to arrive in Austin by air is the **Austin-Bergstrom International Airport** (512/530-2242, www.ci.austin.tx.us/austinairport/). Located eight miles southeast of downtown, the small yet easily navigable airport features exclusively local restaurants and music by Texas artists. As a welcome to the "Live Music Capital of the World," check out the bands playing on stage at the Hill Country Bar.

The city has three major cab companies: **American Yellow Checker Cab** (512/452-9999), **Austin Cab** (512/478-2222), and **Lone Star Cab** (512/836-4900). Fares run around $20 from the airport to downtown. Another option for getting to your destination is **Super Shuttle** (512/258-3826), which offers 24-hour shared-van service for around $10–15 per person.

If you're feeling adventurous (aka not renting a car), you can tackle the city's bus system, **Capital Metro** (512/474-1200, www.capmetro.org), which provides service to downtown and the University of Texas campus. Buses run Mon.–Sat. 5 A.M.–midnight, Sun. 6:30 A.M.–10:30 P.M. Fare is 50 cents for an adult one-way fixed route.

Vicinity of Austin

As fun as it is to spend a few days in Austin, there are only so many daiquiris to drink and museums to meander through. Consider taking a weekend road trip to experience more Central Texas culture. In Texas, that means barbecue, and those interested in sampling some of the finest the Lone Star State has to offer should make a pilgrimage to the meat mecca of Lockhart. The region's other college towns offer a fresh take on university life outside a large metro area, and the Highland Lakes are renowned for their placid waters and abundant recreational opportunities.

THE HIGHLAND LAKES

A series of dams was built along the Colorado River in the late 1930s, resulting in the creation of seven lakes. The three most popular (and navigable) are Lakes Travis, LBJ, and Buchanan, 20–60 miles northwest of Austin. These clear, clean bodies of water are a welcome respite from Texas's hot summers, offering an ideal place for residents and visitors to swim, sail, fish, drink, and water-ski.

Lake Travis

Lake Travis is an extremely popular destination for Austinites looking to get away for some r&r on the weekend; so popular, in fact, it's often difficult to navigate around all the party barges and ski boats that descend on the lake during the summer months. Beware (or seek out) Devil's Cove, in particular. Sailors, parasailers, windsurfers, fishers, scuba divers, Jet Skiers, and partiers occupy most of the space, and when things are hoppin' on the lake, it's quite a spectacle to behold. One of the busiest places is **Volente Beach** (16107 FM 2769, 512/258-5109, www.volentebeach.com, $15–20), offering sandy shores (as opposed to the lake's typical limestone banks) along with water slides, a swimming pool, volleyball courts, and a restaurant. Lake Travis boasts 18 parks, eight marinas, more than a dozen restaurants, several nature preserves, and a variety of fishing

and sporting goods businesses providing boat and equipment rental. For more information about these services and a comprehensive listing of upcoming lake events, visit www.laketravis.com.

Lake LBJ

Named after President Lyndon B. Johnson, Lake LBJ is a 21-mile-long constant-level body of water, making it ideal for sailing, boating, and other water sports. Aside from Lake Travis, this is one of the most developed of the Highland Lakes, with hundreds of homes on the shoreline, most of them occupied by retirees and weekenders. If you're looking to rent a condo or lakefront home in a quiet, relaxing environment for a few days, this is the place to be. Anglers flock to Lake LBJ for the abundant largemouth and Guadalupe bass, and the lake's white crappie population is considered the best of any of the Highland Lakes chain. Those angling for a tasty bite to eat have plenty of options at the cafés and Tex-Mex restaurants in the small nearby communities of Horseshoe Bay, Kingsland, Granite Shoals, and Sunrise Beach.

Lake Buchanan

This is a big ol' lake in a sparsely populated area. Lake Buchanan isn't the hot spot destination for partiers or retirees, and that's its appeal. Tree-lined shores and vast open stretches of blue (sometimes brownish) water are welcome scenery for the boaters and fishermen who dot the lake's surface. Lake Buchanan is well known for its striper (striped bass) fishing, and the Texas Parks and Wildlife Department helps keep this reputation thriving by stocking the lake with the species. Fishing guides are available to take visitors to the best spots. Much like the other nearby lakes, accommodations on Lake Buchanan range from campgrounds and RV parks to rental homes and even houseboats.

Those in the area November through March

should consider taking advantage of a unique opportunity to commune with nature. **The Vanishing Texas River Cruise** (800/474-8374, www.vtrc.com, $13–20) offers a rare chance to see one of the largest colonies of American bald eagles. The *Texas Eagle II,* a 70-foot, 120-passenger vessel, has two observation decks and covered viewing areas for catching a glimpse of the magnificent bald eagle in its natural habitat.

Accommodations

The upper Highland Lakes region (northwest of Lake Travis) is surrounded by small communities, most with populations of 5,000 or fewer, so there's a wide range of accommodations to choose from. Many are cheap chains on state highways, others are fancy resorts on the lakeshore, and others are quaint bed-and-breakfasts in historic downtowns. The three "big" cities in the region are Burnet (pronounced BUR-nit), Marble Falls, and Llano. A comprehensive list of accommodations in these communities and outlying areas is available at www.lakesandhills.com. Most visitors to Lake Travis stay in Austin or at one of the nearby campgrounds.

Camping

Camping options in the upper Highland Lakes region are plentiful, but a few parks stand out among the rest. Lake Buchanan's immense size and absence of development make it a good place to enjoy remote, natural conditions (or a comfortable lodge, if you choose). One of the best places to pitch a tent is **Black Rock Park** (on Rte. 261 north of Rte. 29, 512/793-3138, $4 entry fee, call for current campsite and cabin fees). The 10-acre park offers 25 tent sites, 15 RV sites, and 6 cabins with heat and A/C. One of the park's biggest draws is its sandy beach, and the ample shoreline is also popular with bank fishers.

Less rustic is the nearby **Canyon of the Eagles** (16942 Ranch Rd. 2341, 800/977-0081, www.canyonoftheeagles.com, average cottage/room $159, average campsite $14), a 940-acre resort containing a cozy lodge and

campsites. Canyon of the Eagles offers 64 cottage and lodge rooms designed to blend in with the natural beauty of the surrounding Hill Country. Each cabin features wooden rocking chairs on the front porch, some with spectacular views of Lake Buchanan. Camping is also available, with 25 spacious, shaded sites including a paved pad and picnic table. Some of the sites have a limited view of the lake, and all have access to the property's amenities. Those seeking primitive camping have two options—Chimney Slough, located in a peaceful cove on the lake with 23 tent sites and potable water, and Tanner Point, containing 10 sites with no water. Canyon of the Eagles also features a restaurant, swimming pool, and recreation room.

Another popular option is **Inks Lake State Park** (3630 Park Rd. 4 W., 512/793-2223, www.tpwd.state.tx.us, $5 per day). Camping, backpacking, hiking, swimming, and fishing are popular activities, along with the park's guided nature walks and canoe tours. Small cabins and primitive campsites are available, and the park even includes a nine-hole golf course, store (offering boats and bikes for rent), and Wi-Fi access.

Information and Services

The best way to find out about up-to-date lodging and event information is through the various chambers of commerce scattered throughout the Highland Lakes region. They'll also provide plenty of handy maps and brochures with helpful info about places to go and things to do in the area.

For Lake Travis area information, visit www.laketravis.com or contact the **Lake Travis Chamber of Commerce** (1415 RR 620 S., Suite 202, 512/263-5833, www.laketravischamber.com). For the upper Highland Lakes, contact the **Burnet Chamber of Commerce** (229 S. Pierce, 512/756-4297, www.burnetchamber.org), the **Marble Falls/Lake LBJ Chamber of Commerce** (801 Hwy. 281, 830/693-4449, www.marblefalls.org), and the **Llano Chamber of Commerce** (100 Train Station Dr., 325/247-5354, www.llanochamber.org).

SAN MARCOS

Located 26 miles south of Austin, San Marcos (population 47,181), home of Texas State University, can rightfully claim the title of I-35's "college town" now that the metropolis to the north has seemingly outgrown the term. Appropriately enough, it's well known for the laid-back recreational activity of tubing, where young adults lounge around half-dressed drinking beer, all while floating on an inner tube down a refreshingly cold river. Despite the appeal of this pursuit, it doesn't draw nearly as many visitors as the outlet malls on the outskirts of town.

Tubing the San Marcos River

Compared to New Braunfels, San Marcos's tubing scene is pretty tame. Despite the proximity of Texas State, tubing in San Marcos is marketed as a family activity, resulting in fewer booze cruises and less questionable activity than in New Braunfels. Regardless, the appeal remains the same—escaping from the Texas heat by floating in a refreshingly cold river (approximately 71°F) through picturesque countryside with a beverage in hand. For the most part, the pace is slow and relaxing; however, there are occasional swiftly flowing areas, and a river chute on a dam creates a fun rapids effect. The entire trip takes about an hour and a half. The best place to begin your trek (equipment rental, transportation upriver, etc.) is **San Marcos Lions Club Tube Rental** (at City Park off Charles Austin Dr., 512/396-5466, www.tubesanmarcos.com, open daily in the summer, weekends Mar.–May and Sept., tube rental $7–9, $20 tube deposit required).

Aquarena Springs

Serving as the source of the San Marcos River, Aquarena Springs discharges 150–300 million gallons of water daily and is the focal point of Texas State University's **Aquarena Center** (921 Aquarena Springs Dr., 512/245-7570, www.aquarena.txstate.edu, daily 10 A.M.–5 P.M., $7 adults, $6 seniors, $5 children 4–15). For much of the 1900s, the area was a resort and entertainment park known as Aquarena Springs, featuring amusement-park-style rides, water shows with mermaids, and Ralph, a pig that swam around in the river performing amazing tricks. Texas State University purchased the aging theme park in 1994 and transformed it into a nonprofit nature center dedicated to conserving natural resources and educating the public about the role water plays in daily life. The park has a natural aquarium with local endangered species and archaeology exhibits with 12,000-year-old artifacts. One of the most popular attractions is the glass-bottom boat tour, offering a spectacular view of the bubbling San Marcos River springhead and the plants and animals that rely on its cool, clear water.

Wonder World

Take a break from shopping to visit Wonder World (1000 Prospect St., 512/392-3760, www.wonderworldpark.com, 8 A.M.–8 P.M. daily Memorial Day–Labor Day, 9 A.M.–5 P.M. weekdays, until 6 P.M. weekends Sept.–May, $19.95 adults, $14.95 seniors and children 6–12). The main attraction is an enormous cave formed by a prehistoric earthquake along the Balcones fault line, resulting in distinctive geographic formations not found in typical erosion-based caves. At the end of the tour, visitors ascend the 146-foot-tall Tejas Tower via elevator, offering a spectacular bird's-eye view of the region's geographic features. Other park attractions include a train ride through a wildlife park and a wacky antigravity house.

Shopping

San Marcos's outlet stores rank among the top four tourist destinations in Texas. Depending on your perspective, this is either fascinating or depressing. Regardless, shopping for bargains is a phenomena that's unlikely to wane in popularity anytime soon, so people will continue to flock to San Marcos to spend hours or even days sifting through racks of clothes, shoes, accessories, and housewares in search of the ultimate deal at one of the nearly 250 stores in two main centers. The biggest is **Premium Outlets** (3939 I-35 S., 512/396-2200, www.primeoutlets.com, Mon.–Sat. 10 A.M.–9 P.M.,

Sun. 10 A.M.–7 P.M.). Unironically designed after a classic shopping plaza in Venice, Italy, Prime Outlets offers more than 130 luxury and brand-name shops such as Last Call by Neiman Marcus, Giorgio Armani, Lacoste, Salvatore Ferragamo, Polo Ralph Lauren, Barney's New York Outlet, Banana Republic Factory Store, Nike Factory Store, J. Crew, and Saks Fifth Avenue Off 5th Outlet. The other main attraction, located just north of Premium Outlets, is **Tanger Outlet Center** (4015 I-35 S., 512/396-7446, www.tangeroutlet.com, Mon.–Sat. 9 A.M.–9 P.M., Sun. 10 A.M.–7 P.M.). Tanger contains more than 100 stores, including Calvin Klein, Charlotte Russe, Cavender's Boot City, Kenneth Cole, Liz Claiborne New York, Hot Topic, Samsonite Company Stores, and Wilsons Leather Outlet.

Accommodations

If you're looking for an affordable hotel to go with your bargain purchases at the outlet mall, one of the better deals in San Marcos is **Rodeway Inn** (1635 Aquarena Springs Dr., 512/353-8011, www.rodewayinn.com, $69 d). It's quite close to Texas State University—within walking distance of Bobcat Stadium, in fact—and offers a free continental breakfast, Internet access, and an outdoor pool.

If proximity to the outlet malls is a top consideration, it doesn't get much closer than **Baymont Inn and Suites** (4210 I-35, 512/392-6800, www.baymontinns.com, $79 d). The hotel features an indoor pool (heated November–March), a fitness center, free Internet access, and a free continental breakfast.

A bit pricier yet slightly more upscale is **Hampton Inn & Suites** (106 I-35, 512/754-7707, www.stonebridgehotels.com, $129 d), offering free Internet access, a free continental breakfast, an outdoor pool, and exercise room.

Those looking to get away from the hustle and bustle can stay at **Crystal River Inn** (326 W. Hopkins St., 888/396-3739, www.crystal-riverinn.com, $105–150), a bed-and-breakfast and garden complex with 13 rooms in three

buildings. The quaint structures surround a garden with roses, fountains, and stately pecan trees, and Crystal River's gourmet breakfasts offer a wonderful way to fuel up for a day of shopping without dropping.

Food
MEXICAN
One of San Marcos's most popular restaurants is the consistently satisfying **Herbert's Grocery & Taco Hut** (419 Riverside Dr., 866/721-3530, www.herbertstacohut.com, $6–13). Originally a takeout taco stand, Herbert's has evolved into a first-rate Tex-Mex establishment, drawing students and locals with its flavorful tacos and extremely prompt service (food often arrives in mere minutes). The most popular dish is Herbert's Special, a combo plate featuring a taco, enchilada, and chalupa.

Another well-liked Mexican food joint is **Mamacita's Restaurant** (1400 Aquarena Springs Dr., 512/353-0070, www.mamacitas.com, $7–14). This family-friendly spot is a favorite for quick lunches and group outings, and it's an ideal place to take newcomers, since the spices are relatively mild. Popular dishes include the sour cream chicken enchiladas and the beef fajitas.

AMERICAN
There's something to be said for a college-town restaurant that's endured for more than 30 years. **Grin's** (802 N. LBJ Dr., 512/392-4746, www.grinsrestaurant.com, $9–21) is a classic all-American family restaurant that's been (here it comes) putting smiles on people's faces for decades with its tasty burgers, steaks, and sandwiches. The chicken-fried chicken is another signature dish. Located just up the hill from Texas State University, Grin's is popular with students and families, and the huge tree-shaded deck is an ideal place to enjoy a meal.

More student-oriented is **San Marcos River Pub & Grill** (701 Cheatham St., 512/353-3747, www.riverpubandgrill.com, $9–19). Pub grub is the specialty here (anything fried is good), but the other menu items are also noteworthy, including salmon, catfish, and pecan-crusted chicken. The restaurant contains two levels of outdoor decks overlooking the river and features live music most weekends.

Information and Services

San Marcos has two visitors centers offering plenty of helpful brochures and maps about attractions in the area. For general information, contact the **Tourist Information Center** (617 I-35 N., 512/393-5930, www.sanmarcostexas.com, Mon.–Sat. 9 A.M.–5 P.M., Sun. 10 A.M.–4 P.M.). Another reliable source is the **San Marcos Convention and Visitor Bureau** (202 N. C.M. Allen Pkwy., 512/393-5900, www.toursanmarcos.com, open weekdays 8:30 A.M.–5 P.M.).

BRYAN-COLLEGE STATION

Best known as home to Texas A&M University, the Bryan–College Station area is truly representative of the *A* (agriculture) in A&M. Ranches, farms, and rolling prairies surround the two cities, which serve as agricultural supply and market centers for the small surrounding communities. Despite rumors to the contrary emanating from Austin, College Station is actually a cultural asset to the area by drawing educated instructors and students, and regularly scheduling impressive exhibits and speakers.

In fact, College Station's influence—particularly from Texas A&M University—has had a major impact on the region's development. Texas A&M opened in 1876 as Texas Agricultural and Mechanical College, a male-only military institution with Corps of Cadets participation required. During the early 1900s, Texas A&M kept a strong military association, but in 1963 the Texas Legislature approved a bill changing the university's name to Texas A&M, ushering in a new era. Women were officially admitted, and the Corps of Cadets became a voluntary organization. An enrollment surge followed, with a mighty increase from nearly 8,000 students to more than 25,000 in 1976.

The university has positively influenced the region's history and culture by bringing in an impressive range of faculty, students, and ideas from across the globe. Texas A&M has created opportunities that otherwise wouldn't exist in this part of the state, including professional connections, diversity, and a lot of money that have improved the lives of people in Bryan–College Station for the better.

Texas A&M University

Home to more than 49,000 students, Texas A&M University is one of the country's premier schools for agriculture-related studies (veterinary medicine, geosciences, and landscape architecture in particular). Aggieland is truly a phenomena—the immense school pride manifests itself in ubiquitous "Gig 'em Aggies" signs and stickers, the omnipresent color of maroon, and "yell practice," a pep rally event in which the name alone prompts rival students at the University of Texas to guffaw. Aggies' attempts to insult UT (referring to the school as t.u. and calling them "tea sippers") don't tend to rile up the Longhorns, but the Aggies' nostalgic sense of being true to their school is endearing if not commendable.

Texas A&M has a proud history dating back to 1871 as the all-male Agricultural and Mechanical College of Texas. In the 1960s, it opened its doors to women and changed its name to Texas A&M. Until that time, all students were required to undergo military cadet training, and although it became optional afterward, the school still has the largest uniformed cadet corps in the nation (outside the service academies). More than 2,000 male and female students serve as military cadets each academic year, and their Fightin' Texas Aggies Band, which performs mesmerizing precision-filled routines at football halftime shows, is the world's largest military marching band.

Those interested in touring the campus should contact the **Appelt Aggieland Visitor Center** (located on the first floor of Rudder Tower, 979/845-5851, www.tamu.edu/visit, Mon.–Fri. 8 A.M.–5 P.M.).

While on the campus, visitors can also experience the **Sam Houston Sanders**

Kyle Field on the Texas A&M University campus

Corps of Cadets Center (979/862-2862, www.aggiecorps.org/corpscenter, Mon.–Fri. 8 A.M.–5 P.M.), showcasing the proud history of the university's iconic cadets. Dozens of displays feature artifacts and pictures documenting the cadets' occasionally eyebrow-raising rituals such as Fish (freshmen) Drill Team, yell practice, 12th Man, and the Aggie Band.

George Bush Presidential Library and Museum

One of College Station's biggest claims to fame is former U.S. President George Herbert Walker Bush. Although he didn't even attend Texas A&M, Bush was so impressed with the school after accepting an invitation to deliver a commencement address, he agreed to have his presidential archives preserved and displayed there. It's well worth making the trip to Aggieland to experience the George Bush Presidential Library and Museum (1000 George Bush Dr. W., 979/691-4000, http://bushlibrary.tamu.edu, Mon.–Sat. 9:30 A.M.–5 P.M., Sun. noon–5 P.M., $7 adults, $6 seniors, $3 students 6–17).

Renovated in 2007 to add interactive touch-screen and video displays (check out the clip of Bush's first steps in 1925), the museum's main exhibits demonstrate the life and times of Bush Sr. Popular displays include a section of the Berlin Wall, a Gulf War exhibit, an Avenger similar to the plane Bush flew in World War II, and a replica of the White House situation room. One of the most memorable portions of the museum is the Oval Office exhibit that allows visitors to sit in the "seat of power" and have their photo taken behind the president's desk.

Another popular draw is the White House in Miniature, offering visitors a peek into the residence George Bush once called home. Now that Bush and his wife, Barbara, have an apartment on the museum grounds, they make occasional "surprise appearances," shaking hands, signing autographs, and interacting with visitors.

In addition to these exhibits, the site also contains an archives with more than 38 million pages of personal papers and official

© ANDY RHODES

the George Bush Presidential Library and Museum

the area's history along with regular traveling exhibits.

Accommodations

One of the more affordable A&M-area options is the **College Station Super 8** (301 Texas Ave., 979/846-8800, www.super8.com, $80 d). Located three blocks away from campus, the hotel offers free Internet connections and a complimentary breakfast. Another noteworthy spot is the nice, new **Courtyard College Station** (3939 Hwy. 6 S., 979/695-8111, www.marriott.com, $109 d), offering a free healthy breakfast and complimentary Wi-Fi access. The **Comfort Inn & Suites** (2313 Texas Ave. S., 979/680-8000, www.choicehotels.com, $124 d) features free Internet access, a free hot breakfast, an exercise room, and a seasonal outdoor pool.

Just down the road in downtown Bryan is the beautifully restored **LaSalle Hotel** (120 S. Main St., 979/822-2000, www.lasalle-hotel.com, $119 d), a 1928 boutique hotel that's listed on the National Register of Historic Places. The LaSalle exudes vintage charm with a seamless integration of modern amenities, including free Internet access in each room. A complimentary breakfast is also served. Those willing to splurge on a suite ($139) receive the extra benefits of a refrigerator, microwave, Jacuzzi tub, separate living room with pullout sleeper sofa, and three TVs (in the bedroom, living area, and bathroom).

documents from the vice presidency and presidency, an extensive collection of audiovisual and photographic records, and approximately 60,000 historical objects including personal items and gifts from the American people. Of particular interest is the exhibit dedicated to gifts given by international dignitaries and supporters, ranging from small painted rocks to a gilded replica fortress.

The Brazos Valley Museum of Natural History

Regional heritage is on display at Bryan's small yet interesting Brazos Valley Museum of Natural History (3232 Briarcrest Dr., 979/776-2195, www.brazosvalleymuseum.org, Tues.–Sat. 10 A.M.–5 P.M., Sun. noon–5 P.M., $5 adults, $4 seniors and children 4–17). The museum has plugged steadily along since 1961, achieving its mission to increase the public's awareness of the region's cultural and natural heritage. The museum features permanent displays with artifacts, maps, and photos, highlighting the events and people that shaped

Food
AMERICAN

You can't go to College Station without stopping by the **Dixie Chicken** (307 University Dr., 979/846-2322, www.dixiechicken.com, $5–12). Though it's better known as a bar than a restaurant, "the Chicken" can squawk about its tasty food, too. It's mainly pub grub (burgers, sandwiches, fried stuff), but the unique atmosphere certainly enhances the dining experience. Mounted animal heads loom over deeply carved tables and walls, and the place reverberates with the sounds of college students—clinking beer bottles, whoops and laughs, and classic country music. Order a Shiner and soak up the scene. Sister property **Chicken Oil Co.** (3600 S. College Ave., 979/846-3306, $4–9) serves up the best burger in Aggieland. Despite the name (a reference to a former service station), this restaurant offers top-notch beef in a down-home atmosphere.

Slightly more refined is **Blue Baker** (201 Dominik Dr., 979/696-5055, www.bluebaker. com, $5–12), which prides itself on made-from-scratch breads, pastries, and pizza dough. Patrons can watch the bread making and baking process while waiting for a signature brick-oven pizza, mouthwatering sandwich, or homesick-inspiring chocolate chip cookie.

Another classic College Station hangout is **Layne's** (106 Walton Dr., 979/696-7633, www.layneschickenfingers.com, $4–7), which has carved out a distinctive niche in the local culinary scene. Layne's serves one type of food only: chicken. Chicken fingers, in particular. It's also known for its special dipping sauce (a peppery recipe that's sworn to secrecy) and funky, some might even say dumpy, atmosphere. Those feeling adventurous can order one of Layne's only other menu items—a chicken finger sandwich.

For those who still have yet to sample the Southern delicacy known as chicken-fried steak, head straight to Bryan's **Longhorn Tavern Steak House** (1900 Hwy. 21 E., 979/778-3900, $8–24). People come from miles around to satisfy their craving for the Longhorn's famous CFS, but there are other worthy items on the menu—sirloins, rib eyes, T-bones, and New York strips.

MEXICAN

For a memorably fun and tasty dining experience, drop by **Freebird's World Burrito** (original location at 319 University Dr., four other locations, 979/846-9298, www.freebirds. com, $5–9). Enormous burritos are the specialty here, and diners get to choose items—beef, chicken, rice, cheese, veggies, salsa, etc.—as they proceed down the counter. The natural ingredients come with a healthy side of good-natured attitude from the employees,

and patrons are encouraged to create and leave behind the sculptures they make from the left-over tin foil overwrap.

Another popular nearby Mexican restaurant is **Zapatos Cantina** (211 University Dr. W., 979/260-0662, $5–12). Located in the Northgate section of town across the road from A&M, Zapatos serves up fish tacos, fajitas, and an amazing salsa. Look for live music on the patio most weekends.

Down the road in Bryan is local legend **Pepe's Mexican Cafe** (3312 S. College Ave., 979/779-2457, $7–15). Considered the original fast-food restaurant in Bryan, Pepe's still offers freshly made tacos, burritos, enchiladas, and other Tex-Mex specialties.

Information and Services

To learn more about Texas A&M or to take a campus tour, contact the **Appelt Aggieland Visitor Center** (located on the first floor of Rudder Tower, 979/845-5851, www.tamu.edu/visit, Mon.–Fri. 8 A.M.–5 P.M.). For information about the Bryan–College Station area, including maps and brochures related to attractions and lodging, stop by the **Bryan-College Station Convention & Visitors Bureau** (715 University Dr. E., 979/260-9898, www.visitaggieland.com, Mon.–Fri. 8 A.M.–5 P.M., Sat. 10 A.M.–2 P.M.).

LOCKHART

Lockhart (population 14,237) is the true mecca for barbecue lovers, with four legendary restaurants offering enough lore and smoked meat to satisfy connoisseurs of this uniquely Texas food style. In fact, barbecue is Lockhart's biggest draw, making it an ideal place for a quick 30-minute road trip from Austin. Visitors can walk off their brisket-and-sausage laden meal by strolling around the small historic downtown area, punctuated by the majestic and magnificently restored Caldwell County Courthouse.

◖ Kreuz Market

For many barbecue aficionados, this is as good as it gets in Texas, or anywhere else for that

© ANDY RHODES

Kreuz Market in Lockhart

matter. Kreuz Market (619 N. Colorado St., 512/398-2361, www.kreuzmarket.com, Mon.–Sat. 10:30 A.M.–8 P.M., $9–20) is legendary, and among the four famous restaurants in town, it tends to receive the most accolades for "best barbecue" from state and national publications. This is hard-core stuff, so you won't find the typical barbecue combo plates offered at most Texas restaurants. First, there's no sauce, and for good reason—why would you want to taint the perfectly smoked high-quality meat by dousing it in something to mask the taste? Second, orders are placed at the counter, where succulent sausage, thick pork chops, and hearty ribs and brisket are served by the pound on butcher paper. Third, there aren't any utensils. Well, except for the plastic knife that's used for slicing off chunks of meat, cheese, avocado, tomato, and jalapeño. These side items, along with crackers, bread, pickles, and onions, stem from Kreuz's origins as a meat market and grocery store, where patrons—mostly ranchers and farmhands—would buy vegetables, bread, and meat and often eat their purchases on-site,

using a pocket knife to carve the items. The food at Kreuz remains as expertly prepared as it's been since 1900 (even though their new digs slightly resemble an industrial warehouse), and it's worth a visit for the incredible pork chops alone. Wash it all down with a Shiner Bock or Dr Pepper. You'll be singing the praises of this truly Texas experience for years to come.

Black's Barbecue

Vying for the crown of best barbecue in Texas (and therefore the world) is Black's Barbecue (215 N. Main St., 888/632-8225, www.blacks-bbq.com, Sun.–Thurs. 10 A.M.–8 P.M., Fri. and Sat. 10 A.M.–8:30 P.M., $9–24). This is the place to go for time-honored, perfectly smoked, mouthwatering barbecue. There are no pretensions here—no reason to be intimidated by lack of barbecue knowledge or inability to calculate what a half pound of meat translates to on the plate. And there are plates at Black's (as opposed to butcher paper on a tray). There are sides, sauce, and silverware, too. Of course the meat is the main draw, as it's been since

1932. Go directly for the pork—ribs, chops, and loins. They're all fantastic, with the hardwood smoke perfectly accentuating the succulent flavor accented by the basic yet effective salt-and-pepper dry rub. Equal in quality is the sausage, available in a flavorful beef-and-pork combo, garlic blend, and spicy jalapeño version. Most barbecue joints aren't known for their ambience, and Black's is no exception, but the crookedly hung black-and-white photos of bygone high school football teams and the longhorns and antlers looming above them lend a touch of rural charm. The sign outside Black's boasts 8 Days a Week, a reference to the seemingly endless amount of time restaurant staff prepare and dole out their delicious fare (and the fact they're open every day except Thanksgiving and Christmas). Since this is some of the best barbecue available anywhere, it's well worth the extra effort.

Smitty's Market

The business hasn't been around as long as the others (it opened in 1999), but the building itself is legendary at Smitty's Market (208 S. Commerce St., 512/398-9344, www.smittys-market.com, Mon.–Fri. 7 A.M.–6 P.M., Sat. 7 A.M.–6:30 P.M., Sun. 9 A.M.–3 P.M., $9–24). Smoked meat has been a specialty at this rustic locale for more than a century, and people have been continually flocking here to partake of the juicy goodness. Visitors get an up-close view (and feel) of the decades-old fire-and-smoke-spewing brick pits, located adjacent to the long line that snakes out the back door most weekends. By the time you sit down to

eat, you won't even notice your seared skin and smoke-drenched clothes. The brisket and sausage are specialties, and the tender and delicious pork ribs are available on weekends only. Smitty's also offers traditional sides such as potato salad, coleslaw, and pinto beans.

Chisholm Trail BBQ

In a town filled with world-famous barbecue restaurants, the locals' favorite is Chisholm Trail (1323 S. Colorado St., 512/398-6027, daily 8 A.M.–8 P.M., $7–16). A relative newcomer compared to the old stalwarts in town, Chisholm Trail nevertheless holds its own, perhaps because it doesn't have the *New York Times* and Food Network hawking its food across the country. They may want to reconsider, since Chisholm Trail offers quality barbecue that would be a stand-alone knockout in most other Texas towns. Their seasoned sausage is a specialty, and locals line up for the ribs, chicken, and turkey. Chisholm Trail has a large cafeteria-style bar with a plethora of side items, including fried okra, potato salad, coleslaw, pinto beans, green beans, squash, and various salads. What sets it apart from the other barbecue restaurants in town is its expanded menu, offering chicken-fried steak, catfish, and other Southern specialties.

Information and Services

Lockhart doesn't have a convention and visitors bureau or chamber of commerce, but you can direct general questions about area attractions and lodging to the city hall at 512/398-3461 or visit the city website at www.lockhart-tx.org.

Waco

In the late 19th century, cotton was king in Waco (population 121,496), weaving its way through the vivid heritage of this colorful town. The dark, rich soil of the Blackland Prairie proved ideal for growing the crop, and like the oil that would be discovered later, it attracted a rush of immigrants eager to make a living.

Before the advent of river steamers and railroads, cotton buyers employed teamsters to make the overland trek to markets in the east. Eventually, trails and railroads converged in cotton boomtowns like Waco, which became known as "The Crossroads of Texas." Baylor University, the world's largest Baptist university, moved to Waco in the late 1800s, and by the early 20th century, the city's manufacturing base increased from agricultural-related business to include standard service industries, two domino factories, and several soft drink companies (Dr Pepper became nationally famous, while the cream-soda-ish Big Red remained a big sensation primarily in the South).

Waco attained a "Wacko" reputation in 1993 when eccentric Branch Davidian sect/cult leader David Koresh defended his Mount Carmel compound against the U.S. government in a highly publicized attack that drew unwanted worldwide media coverage.

SIGHTS
Dr Pepper Museum

Discover what makes the world's oldest major soft drink pop at the Dr Pepper Museum (300 S. 5th St., 254/757-1025, www.drpepper-museum.com, Mon.–Sat. 10 A.M.–4:15 P.M., Sun. noon–4:15 P.M., $7 adults, $5 seniors, $3 students). This fun museum takes visitors through the history of Waco-born Dr Pepper and Texas's soft drink industry. Dr Pepper (the period after *Dr* was dropped in the 1950s) originated in 1885 at a Waco drugstore, where a pharmacist reportedly concocted the recipe while mixing up medicine.

The museum is housed in the Artesian Manufacturing and Bottling Company

AUSTIN

BE A PEPPER

The Dr Pepper Company bills itself as "the oldest major manufacturer of soft drink concentrates and syrups in the United States" and is proud of its status as a native Texas product. It traces its sweet roots to 1885, at Morrison's Old Corner Drug Store in Waco, where **Charles Alderton,** a young pharmacist, devoted much of his job to mixing up medicine. In his spare time, Alderton liked to serve carbonated drinks at the drugstore's soda fountain, and this is where he reportedly concocted the recipe that would become Dr Pepper.

Alderton was intrigued with the various fruit syrup flavor smells wafting around the pharmacy and soda fountain, so he decided to create a drink that tasted like that smell. He kept a journal, and after many experiments he finally concocted a mixture of fruit syrups to

his liking. Alderton eventually offered his new drink to his customers, and word soon got out about the tasty beverage at Morrison's soda fountain. He knew he was on to something when crowds arrived and began ordering it by asking him to "shoot them a Waco." The origin of the name remains a mystery – one rumor is that Alderton named it after his horse, while another claims that combining its "peppiness" with the "Dr." prefix made it sound healthier.

Dr Pepper continued to gain in popularity throughout the 20th century and went on to have several memorable slogans, including "Drink a bite to eat at 10, 2, and 4," "the friendly Pepper-upper," "Be a Pepper," and the most recent campaign focusing on the 23 flavors that give the drink its distinctive taste.

building, where the product was made in the early 1900s. The mixture of flavors in Dr Pepper remains a closely guarded secret, but visitors can learn about some of the theories and the history of the beverage from the museum's educational and interactive exhibits. The extensive collection of soft drink cans and bottles exhibiting design and logo styles through the ages is particularly fascinating. Appropriately, the tour ends with an authentic soda fountain, serving Dr Pepper in its original incarnation, with pure cane sugar instead of corn syrup.

Mayborn Museum Complex

Baylor University's most noteworthy public entity is the impressive Mayborn Museum Complex (1300 S. University Parks Dr., 254/710-1110, www.maybornmuseum.com, Mon–Sat. 10 A.M.–5 P.M., Thurs. until 8 P.M., Sun. 1–5 P.M., $6 adults, $5 seniors, $4 children 2–12). Waco's crossroads legacy is highlighted through the museum's collection of natural, cultural, and historical exhibits showcasing the convergence of landscapes and people in Central Texas. Features include a Native American grass house, an authentic log cabin from the 1840s, a giant dinosaur model, and a remarkable collection of natural history items. Kids love the museum's hands-on discovery center, and they can even feed the chickens at the outdoor historic village behind the main building.

Texas Ranger Hall of Fame and Museum

You're not going to encounter too many other museums like the Texas Ranger Hall of Fame and Museum (106 Texas Ranger Trl., 254/750-8631, www.texasranger.org, daily 9 A.M.–5 P.M., $7 adults, $6 seniors, $3 children). Stephen F. Austin introduced these legendary hired hands to the state's lexicon in 1823 when they were brought on board to help protect settlers against Native Americans along the westward-expanding frontier. They played significant roles in Texas's history—participating in the revolution against Mexico, bringing

down Bonnie and Clyde—but by 1935, the state government roped them in under the jurisdiction of the Texas Department of Public Safety, where their primary role has been to focus on special investigations.

Although they currently number only about 100 members, the Rangers remain famous for their sharp skills and are considered some of the elite law enforcement officers of the modern era. The museum showcases their legacy through exhibits featuring documents, artifacts, dioramas, and even Bonnie and Clyde's shotguns and the firearms used during the Rangers's ambush. The Hall of Fame honors the most distinguished Rangers in history, and the research center contains archives, books, original clippings, genealogies, and photographs.

Texas Sports Hall of Fame

Another uniquely Lone Star State experience is the Texas Sports Hall of Fame (1108 S. University Parks Dr., 254/756-1633, www.tshof.org, Mon.–Sat. 9 A.M.–5 P.M., Sun. noon–5 P.M., $7 adults, $6 seniors, $3 students 5–18). Sports are an integral part of life in Texas, and the museum pays homage to the state's mythical stories and most accomplished athletes, including Nolan Ryan, Troy Aikman, George Foreman, Roger Clemens, David Robinson, Earl Campbell, and Tom Landry. The facility is divided into four separate wings—the Texas Sports Hall of Fame, the Texas Tennis Hall of Fame, the Texas High School Football Hall of Fame, and the Texas High School Basketball Hall of Fame. Video clips show highlights of Texas sports moments and athletes' achievements, and visitors can view sports artifacts and an interesting display showcasing the evolution of tennis rackets.

Cameron Park Zoo

Similar in approach to the highly respected Fort Worth Zoo is Waco's Cameron Park Zoo (1701 N. 4th St., 254/750-8400, www.cameronparkzoo.com, Mon.–Sat. 9 A.M.–5 P.M., Sun. 11 A.M.–5 P.M., $9 adults, $8 seniors, $6 children 4–12). Dirt paths and wooden bridges

© ANDY RHODES

a busy elephant at the Cameron Park Zoo in Waco

connect habitats featuring animals from Africa, Asia, and the Americas in re-created environments simulating their homelands (they apparently have no idea they're in Waco). The herpetarium is particularly impressive, with lush plants and waterfalls surrounding dozens of species of reptiles and amphibians. Drop by to visit the buffalo, jaguar, and aquarium fish, or check in on the lions, lemurs, and the King Vulture. The zoo represents its Texas roots with the Brazos River Country exhibit, where visitors follow the footsteps of early Spanish explorers who searched for the seven cities of gold through the seven habitats of plant and animal life along the mighty river.

Waco Suspension Bridge

Once the largest suspension bridge in the country, the city's most famous landmark was built in 1870 as a toll bridge spanning the Brazos River along the Chisholm Trail. Traffic crossed under the bridge's lofty towers for a century, but it has been pedestrian-only since 1971. The bridge is considered an icon of Waco history and is the backdrop and centerpiece for festivals and events throughout the year. Access the bridge via University Parks Drive between Franklin and Washington Avenues.

Mount Carmel

In early 1993, Waco received unwelcome international media attention when the U.S. Bureau of Alcohol, Tobacco, and Firearms tried to execute a search warrant at the Branch Davidian ranch at Mount Carmel, about 12 miles northeast of Waco. Gunfire was exchanged, tanks moved in, and the entire complex was eventually burned to the ground. Dozens of people, including Branch Davidian leader David Koresh, died in the incident. Little is left, but what's still there remains a destination for curiosity seekers. Throughout the late '90s and early '00s, representatives of the Branch Davidians, a radical offshoot of the Seventh-Day Adventist theology that have been in Waco since 1935, remained at the site, answering visitors' questions and showing them around. However, in recent years, the property has been taken over by a new group, which doesn't take as kindly to strangers and tends to keep the gates closed to outsiders.

Those still interested in snooping around can check with the Waco Visitors Center (see entry) about possibly getting a map to the out-of-the-way compound. Or you can head there on your own: Take I-35 North to Loop 340 and turn right (east). Continue four miles and take a left onto FM 2491; follow 2491 six miles to Double EE Ranch Road; turn left and you'll see the site about 200 yards up on the right side of the road.

ACCOMMODATIONS
Motels and Hotels

Waco isn't teeming with trendy, historic, or even interesting places to spend the night; in fact, chain hotels are virtually the only option. Fortunately, for the most part, they're clean and affordable. The best of the bunch are down-town near Baylor University, including the **Best Western Old Main Lodge** (I-35 at 4th St., 254/753-0316, www.bestwesterntexas.com, $69 d). The hotel is adjacent to the Baylor U. campus and offers a free continental breakfast, Internet access, and an outdoor pool. Another option is **Ramada Waco** (1001 Martin Luther King Jr. Blvd., 254/753-0261, www.ramada.com, $69 d), which features free hot breakfasts, free wireless Internet access, and what's billed as largest outdoor pool in town. Another good option near Baylor is **La Quinta Inn** (1110 S. 9th St., 254/752-9741, www.lq.com, $79 d), offering free Internet access, a complimentary continental breakfast, and an outdoor pool. The most upscale option in town is the **Hilton Waco** (113 S. University Parks Dr., 254/754-8484, www.hilton.com, $119 d). The recently renovated "high" rise, adjoining the Waco Convention Center, overlooks the mighty Brazos River and is across the street from the city's warehouse en-tertainment center. Rooms include free wireless Internet, and the hotel contains a fitness center, outdoor pool, hot tub, and tennis court.

Bed-and-Breakfasts

Since Waco is overrun with chain hotels, consider staying at one of the city's bed-and-breakfasts as an alternative. Nestled near downtown is the **Cotton Palace** (1910 Austin Ave., 254/753-7294, www.thecottonpalace.com, rooms start at $120), a three-story 1910 Arts and Crafts–style home with seven plush rooms. Guests can relax in rocking chairs on the front porch and help themselves to beverages and homemade treats from the bottomless cookie jar. Luxury robes and marble whirlpool tubs are available in some rooms. For a more rural experience, there's **Let's Go Country B&B** (1182 Spring Lake Rd., 254/799-7947, www.letsgocountry.com, rooms start at $120). Accommodations are located in a renovated 1913 Victorian house on a working farm. The B&B features comfortable rustic fur-nishings, gourmet breakfasts, and the peace and privacy of quiet country living.

Camping

A good camping option along the Brazos River is **Fort Fisher Park** (106 Texas Ranger Trl., 254/750-8696), offering tent and RV sites as well as screened shelters. Also popular are the series of camping areas along the shores of Lake Waco operated by the U.S. Army Corps of Engineers. Sites include **Speegleville Park, Midway Park,** and **Airport Park,** each provid-ing basic drive-in pads and spaces with water and electricity. For information or reservations, call the Corps of Engineers at 254/756-5359.

FOOD

One of Waco's gastronomic specialties is chicken-fried steak, and several spots in town serve up some of the best Texas has to offer, along with regular ol' steak and Continental fare. However, a few restaurants cater to a more refined palate, so fine dining is an option for those seeking a quality meal in Waco.

American

If you're only eating one meal in Waco, make sure it's at the ◖ **Elite Circle Grille** (2132 S. Valley Mills Dr., 254/754-4941, www.elitecir-clegrille.com, $9–24). Formerly known as the Waco Elite Café, this truly distinctive restau-rant has been a favorite place to dine since 1919.

It's nearly as famous for its former clientele—in the late 1950s, Pvt. Elvis Presley, stationed at nearby Fort Hood, frequently ate at The Elite—as its upscale take on Southern food. Not surprisingly, the chicken-fried steak is legendary, but diners also return often for the catfish, salmon, steaks, and ribs. The Elite draws a fairly eclectic mix of customers (for Waco), with Baylor students, blue-collar workers, and hobnobbers sharing space in the restaurant's comfortable yet refined environment.

Another popular upscale yet casual eatery is **1424** (1424 Washington Ave., 254/752-7385, www.1424waco.com, $9–25), one of the few places in town where there can be a wait (due in part to the demand, but also to the limited seating area). Specializing in seafood and Italian dishes, 1424 is an ideal place for a quality meal in a pleasant setting. Nightly seasonal specials are prepared using only natural ingredients, and the head chef often makes the rounds to discuss dishes with the diners.

Seafood

Waco may not be the first place that comes to mind when you think of quality seafood, but **Siete Mares** (1915 Dutton Ave., 254/714-1297, www.elsietemares.net, $8–23) does the ocean justice. Specializing in coastal Mexican seafood, Siete Mares (seven seas in Spanish) offers a tasty blend of flavors that's drawn raves in Waco and was the favorite restaurant of the national press corps covering George W. Bush at his presidential ranch in nearby Crawford. From the delightfully tangy yellow salsa that first arrives at the table, it's evident Siete Mares isn't a traditional (aka boring) Mexican seafood restaurant. Popular dishes include the crab-based nachos, chipotle-seasoned oysters, coconut mango tilapia, and specially seasoned entrées with frog legs and octopus. It's well worth the voyage.

Lunch

Though not technically a college town, Waco does have a fair share of Baylor University students regularly in search of cheap yet decent eats. One of the busiest hangouts for pub grub is **Cricket's Grill and Draft House** (211 Mary Ave., 254/754-4677, $5–13). The emphasis is on the draft, but the pizza and fried food items are worthy companions. Burgers are also a must, and Waco's legendary locale is the not so aptly named **Health Camp** (2601 Circle Rd., 254/752-2081, $4–9). A classic '50s burger joint next to The Elite café downtown, Health Camp offers greasy yet immensely satisfying burgers and perfectly prepared onion rings. Not to be overlooked is **Double-R Burger** (1810 Herring Ave., 254/753-1603, $4–8). Another '50s-style joint, Double-R serves up delicious, meaty handmade patties on soft, sweet buns.

INFORMATION AND SERVICES

The helpful and friendly folks at the **Waco Convention and Visitors Bureau** (254/750-5810 or 800/321-9226, www.wacocvb.com) operate a valuable **Tourist Information Center** (next to the Texas Ranger Museum at I-35 exit 335B, 254/750-8696 or 800/922-6386, daily 8 A.M.–5 P.M.). Pick up free maps, visitors guides, and brochures about Waco attractions or ask the staff for further insight about their city.

GETTING THERE AND AROUND

Waco is practically equidistant from Austin and the Metroplex (nearly two hours from both), so most travelers arrive via I-35, the city's (and state's) main north–south thoroughfare. Those wanting to show up in grand style can utilize the **Waco Regional Airport** (866/359-9226), serviced by American Eagle and Continental Express. Cab service from the airport is available via **Waco Yellow Cab** (254/756-1861). The average fare to downtown Waco is around $15.

The Hill Country

The Hill Country of west Central Texas is a charmingly inspirational landscape, offering rolling vistas, cool breezes, and German heritage as distinctive attractions. City dwellers in Austin and San Antonio often spend summer weekends at bed-and-breakfasts and ranches in the Hill Country, where the slow pace of life and prospect of picking the perfect bushel of peaches provide a welcome getaway. Despite the fanciful moniker, the hills aren't really too dramatic—heights of 1,400 to 1,700 feet are the norm—but the slight increase in elevation and decrease in humidity are welcome respites for heat-drenched lowlanders to the east and south. The views don't quite qualify as breathtaking, but the eye-popping chill of the region's spring-fed rivers will prompt gasps. Cabins, lodges, resorts, and dude ranches dot the landscape, many offering access to a nearby river (Frio, Sabinal, Guadalupe, Medina, and Pedernales) where visitors can swim, canoe,

fish, or tube in the refreshingly cool, crystal-clear water.

FREDERICKSBURG

This small Hill Country town of nearly 11,000 people is a favorite weekend destination for Austin and San Antonio residents looking to add a different cultural spice to their lives. The community's German heritage remains a major draw, with dozens of restaurants and shops specializing in food, drink, and crafts from the Old Country. Several annual events celebrate Fredericksburg's German pioneer past, including the Wild Game Dinner (for men only) and the Damenfest (for women only). Some of the town's longtime residents still speak German as a first language.

Fredericksburg was one of several German settlements to span westward from the Texas Gulf Coast to the Hill Country. The first wagon train of 120 pioneers arrived from New

Bluebonnets color the Hill Country.

© ANDY RHODES

Braunfels in 1846, and soon after, they dubbed their community Fredericksburg after Prince Frederick of Prussia. The town was laid out much like traditional German villages along the Rhine, home of many of the colonists, with one wide main street paralleling Town Creek.

Now, more than 150 years later, this wide road is U.S. Highway 290, which remains the main thoroughfare in town, and it's regularly filled with visitors from across the country, who descend upon Fredericksburg—often via luxury air-conditioned bus—to explore the art galleries, biergartens, German bakeries, and antiques shops.

National Museum of the Pacific War

You can't miss the towering three-story steam-boat-esque tower presiding over the entrance to the National Museum of the Pacific War (340 E. Main St., 830/997-4379, www.pacificwar-museum.org, daily 9 A.M.–5 P.M., $12 adults, $10 seniors/military, $6 students), and you shouldn't miss it. This enormous six-acre site, owned by the Texas Historical Commission, is the only institution in the continental United States dedicated exclusively to telling the story of the Pacific Theater battles of World War II. But why is it in Fredericksburg? The mu-seum was originally known as the Admiral Nimitz Museum, named after Fredericksburg native Chester Nimitz, one of the most re-spected leaders of World War II's Pacific cam-paign (Iwo Jima, Guadalcanal). As a boy in Fredericksburg, Nimitz lived in the family's famous steamboat-shaped hotel, and he went on to have a highly decorated military career, highlighted by his position as fleet admiral during World War II.

In 2009, the museum added the George H. W. Bush Gallery, a state-of-the-art 33,000-foot exhibit focusing on the inspiring story of America's war in the Pacific Theater dur-ing World War II. The new gallery features 40 media installations, approximately 900 arti-facts, and hundreds of historic photographs.

The original portion of the museum offers a fascinating collection of equipment, artifacts,

and models related to the Pacific campaign, including a B-25 bomber, a submarine, battle-ship artillery, and a comprehensive collection of uniforms, weapons, and scale-model destroyers and aircraft carriers. Elaborate walk-through dioramas bring the island combat scenes to life, and, though the Nazi flags and uniforms cause an involuntary shudder, they put the war and the era in context. Even if you're not a his-tory buff, you'll find the well-preserved and simply interpreted artifacts and memorabilia intriguing.

Outside the exhibit halls lie a memorial courtyard honoring war veterans, a Plaza of Presidents dedicated to the 10 commanders-in-chief who served in World War II, and the remarkable Japanese Garden of Peace, an in-viting natural sanctuary containing the three basic elements represented in a traditional Japanese garden: stone, plants, and water. The garden was a gift to the American people from the military leaders of Japan, who held Admiral Nimitz in extremely high regard.

the National Museum of the Pacific War

© ANDY RHODES

AUSTIN

THE HILL COUNTRY'S DANCE HALL HERITAGE

On any given weekend night during the summer, you're bound to hear music, whoops, and hollers emanating from rustic old buildings along the Hill Country's rural ranch roads. Dozens of historic dance halls are still standing throughout the region, where German immigrants built sturdy structures for festivals and community gatherings more than a century ago. The buildings were true feats of engineering. Designed with Texas's hot climate in mind, most included walls comprised mainly of windows, which were propped open with long sticks to catch refreshing breezes.

Thanks to their solid construction, many of the original structures remain standing in rural areas where German immigrants settled, including Fredericksburg, Luchenbach, and near Austin. Although some are in dire need of a face-lift, many still serve their original purpose as community gathering places for friends and family.

There are high-profile places such as **Luckenbach Dance Hall** that draw large crowds on weekends for big-name acts like Robert Earl Keen and Gary P. Nunn, but it's the ramshackle buildings near small communities like **Kendalia, Cherry Spring,** and **Twin Sister** that keep the tradition alive. Up-and-coming artists can still make a name for themselves at these low-profile locales (Pat Green once played the rural Texas dance hall circuit), and families continue to gather at these historic halls to hear country music and dance across the well-worn floors that have supported thousands of pairs of scootin' boots for more than 100 years.

Pioneer Museum Complex

Bookending Fredericksburg's bustling Main Street scene is the city's other major history-related attraction, the Pioneer Museum Complex (325 W. Main St., 830/990-8441, www.pioneermuseum.net, Tues.–Sat. 10 A.M.–5 P.M., $5 ages 18 and up, $3 ages 6–17). This is the kind of museum many small towns have, but most rural communities aren't founded by German settlers who traversed across the hardscrabble environs of the Texas Hill Country to forge a living among the limestone-laden soil, meddlesome cedar trees, and oppressive Texas heat. This collection of late-1800s and early-1900s buildings is based on the original property—a home, smokehouse, and barn—belonging to Henry Kammlah, one of the city's early residents. The home is filled with various pieces of furniture and equipment from pioneer life, but several aspects of Kammlah's home are unique to his heritage—the cool, damp basement contains a large wooden beer keg, and visitors can almost smell the savory scent of sausage emanating from the old smokehouse in the back. The remainder of the complex contains a barn with old farm and kitchen equipment,

a collection of buggies (as in horse-and), and an old schoolhouse complete with desks and a chalkboard with lessons written in German. Serving as an entryway to the complex is the Dambach-Besier House, an 1969 limestone residence relocated to the site and now serving as the welcome center for the museum and Fredericksburg Convention and Visitors Bureau.

Vereins Kirche Museum

If you still can't get enough of the German Hill Country heritage, drop by the small yet interesting Vereins Kirche Museum (in the 100 block of W. Main at the Marktplatz Center, 830/997-7832, Tues.–Sat. 10 A.M.–4:30 P.M., $2). Like the Pioneer Museum Complex, the Vereins Kirche Museum is operated by the Gillespie County Historical Society and features archives and exhibits containing photos and artifacts dedicated to the Fredericksburg area's history, particularly the rugged life experiences of the German settlers and everyday life on the frontier. Housed in a 1936 replica of the 1847 Vereins Kirche (Society Church), the octagonal building honors one of the first structures erected in Fredericksburg and holds the distinction of being the city's first museum.

Shopping

Hill Country heritage aside, Fredericksburg's big draw is the shopping. The town's sidewalks are lined with chalkboard signs, and sweet smells of flowery domestic products entice passers-by with promises of newly imported stock and bargains galore. Though most offer similar types of country-kitchen-style pricey furniture and knickknacks, there are some worthy boutiques and galleries featuring uncommon objects and rustic-without-being-cute home furnishings. Among the more popular establishments is **Homestead and Friends** (230 E. Main St., 830/997-5551, www.homesteadstores.com), specializing in antique and modern furniture, ranging from small sconces to enormous armoires. Just down the street, you'll have to look for the fire-truck-red front door (there isn't a sign) to discover **Something Different II** (221 E. Main St., 830/997-2734, www.somethingdifferent.com). True to its name, this eclectic shop features traditional, contemporary, and downright exotic furniture and accessories. Another popular spot is the nearby **Phil Jackson's Granite & Iron Store** (206 E. Main St., 830/997-4716, www.granite-iron.com), specializing in Mr. Jackson's signature custom tables, most featuring rare granite slabs and intricate ironwork. The home decor items here are also noteworthy, including tasteful lamps, clocks, pottery, and mirrors. Finally, a stroll down ye olde Main Street would be incomplete without stopping by **Fredericksburg Fudge** (105 N. Llano St., a half block north of Main, 830/997-0533, www.fbfudge.com). This traditional candy shop has been doling out thick chunks of rich, sweet, made-from-scratch fudge for decades and provides the perfect souvenir for that special someone who'd rather enjoy a taste of Fredericksburg than have a memento of it sitting on a shelf.

Accommodations

Fredericksburg is the ultimate bed-and-breakfast town. In fact, there are hundreds of options available in the area, ranging from rustic ranch cabins to luxurious posh châteaus to a historic railroad sleeper car. With such a wide selection, many travelers opt to begin their search by providing their particular lodging desires to a B&B locator service, such as **First Class Bed & Breakfast Reservation Service** (909 E. Main St., 888/991-6749, www.fredericksburg-lodging.com). There's even a locator service specifically dedicated to cutting through the infinite possibilities by focusing on the original concept: **Fredericksburg Traditional Bed & Breakfast Inns** (800/494-4678, www.fredericksburgtrad.com).

Of course, not everyone visiting Fredericksburg is required to stay at a B&B. For a dependable and quilt-free evening, book a room at **La Quinta Inn & Suites** (1465 E. Main St., 800/531-5900, www.lq.com, $114 d). The hotel features free Internet access, a fitness center, outdoor pool and Jacuzzi, and a free continental breakfast. A nicer option near the heart of downtown is **Hampton Inn & Suites** (515 E. Main St., 830/997-9696, www.hamptoninn.com, $179 d), offering free Internet access, complimentary breakfast and beverage service, an exercise room, and outdoor pool.

Food

How often do you get to eat authentic German food? Sure, there's the occasional sauerkraut here and Wienerschnitzel there, but when's the last time you sank your teeth into an *uberbacken schweinesnitzel* (pork chop au gratin)? Fredericksburg is the ideal place to explore these indulgences, from fried appetizers to fancy steaks. A good starting point is the **⟨ Fredericksburg Brewing Company** (245 E. Main St., 830/997-1646, www.yourbrewery.com, $9–20). Located smack dab in the middle of all the action, this brewpub provides a remarkable taste of German culture and cuisine. Diners are encouraged to enjoy one of the finely crafted homebrews—made on-site in the shiny copper tanks near the dining room—in the biergarten out back. The beers are immensely satisfying, especially compared to the mass-produced products available at most bars and restaurants. Although the Peacepipe Pale Ale isn't as hoppy as most bitter brews of this type, it has a sweet, full flavor; the Pioneer Porter, meanwhile, is everything a rich, dark beer should be. The menu items are just as flavorful, including German fare such as *jager schnitzel,* sausage, and the incomparable *uberbacken schweinesnitzel* (a tasty pork chop smothered with tangy cheese, colorful peppers, and a sweet apple cider cream sauce), along with local specialties such as chicken-fried steak and venison chili. For a slightly more formal meal, go to **Der Lindenbaum** (312 E. Main St., 830/997-9126, www.derlindenbaum. com, $10–25). Located in a historic limestone building, Der Lindenbaum is the place to go for a truly authentic German dining experience. The standard German dishes (schnitzels, steaks, homemade breads) are worth sampling, but the restaurant's specialties are more traditional meals such as sauerbraten (Rhineland-style sweet and sour marinated roast beef) and *schweinekotelett* (pork chops in mustard sauce). Save room for the strudel. On the other end of the spectrum—in formality, not in quality—is the **Altdorf Biergarten** (301 W. Main St., 830/997-7865, www.altdorfbiergarten-fbg. com, $8–15). This comfortable, noisy establishment feels more like a bar than a restaurant, and for many Fredericksburg visitors, it's a nice way to complement the town's vacation vibe. Altdorf has an impressive selection of German and Texas beers, and the food is quite decent, particularly the schnitzel, sausage, and potato salad.

If a hefty plate of meat and potatoes isn't what you're after, there are nearly a dozen bakers in town serving up pastries and light lunches. One of the best is **C** **Rather Sweet Bakery and Cafe** (249 E. Main St., 830/990-0498, www.rathersweet.com, $5–10). Tucked away in a pleasant courtyard behind busy Main Street, Rather Sweet is a wonderful place to enjoy a sandwich, salad, or especially a delectable pastry. Not surprisingly, the homemade bread is outstanding—especially on the bacon, lettuce, avocado, and tomato sandwich—but

the desserts are the main draw here, and you can't go wrong with whatever suits your fancy. The Mexican chocolate cake is amazing, and customers return regularly for the enormous fried pies, lemon tarts, PB&J cookies, and turbo-charged brownies. Another noteworthy place to pick up some sweets is the **Fredericksburg Bakery** (141 E. Main St., 830/997-3254), which specializes more in homemade goodies than lunches. The cookies are well known throughout town, and people flock here to pick up fresh-baked loaves of bread to enjoy at home, their hotel, or even while hanging out on Main Street.

After having your fill of German fare and baked goods, you may be in search of a fine meal away from all the hustle and bustle of Main Street. If so, head directly to **Hill Top Cafe** (10661 N. U.S. Hwy. 87, 830/997-8922, www.hilltopcafe.com, $10–29). Located about 10 miles west of town, this worth-the-drive restaurant features an upscale Cajun-y take on comfort food. Menu highlights include the rubbed tenderloin with Greek seasoning, fried Port Arthur shrimp, frog legs, and catfish. Try to save room for (or bring home a box of) the peach cobbler and/or raspberry pie. Another nice option outside of town is **Cotton Gin Restaurant & Lodging** (2805 S. State Hwy. 16, 830/990-5734, www.cottonginrestaurant. com, $10–30). Situated in a beautiful outdoor setting with a koi pond and mellow musicians often accompanying your meal, the Cotton Gin features delectable items such as the grande chicken-fried pork steak, jumbo lump crab gratin, and an amazing rib eye steak.

Information and Services
A good starting point to get a handle on Fredericksburg's myriad shopping, eating, and lodging options is the **Visitor Information Center** (302 E. Austin St., 830/997-6523 or 888/997-3600, www.fredericksburg-texas.com, Mon.–Fri. 8:30 A.M.–5 P.M., Sat. 9 A.M.–5 P.M., Sun. noon–4 P.M.). The friendly staff will provide maps and brochures, and as an added bonus, visitors can watch an informative nine-minute DVD about the town and its attractions.

BANDERA

Proudly billing itself as the "Cowboy Capital of the World," Bandera (population 1,216) is a quaint little Western town surrounded by working and guest ranches. This is where city folk and out-of-staters go when they want to get away and experience a somewhat-authentic slice of life on a dude ranch. Bandera is also proud of its rodeo heritage, touting its distinction of having more champions than any Texas town of its size. Visitors can witness this legacy at public rodeo events throughout the summer or get in touch with their inner cowboy or cowgirl through the myriad horseback riding opportunities around town.

Dude Ranches

Bandera's main draw is its dude ranches. Some are hokier than others, but all offer the natural escape most visitors are seeking. Instead of carting the kids or the grandparents around in a car to museums and shows, families, mostly from San Antonio, opt to spend a weekend in the country surrounded by docile horses, wooded trails, swimming holes, outdoor barbecues, campfires, and hayrides. It's a nice change of pace and allows for a different kind of bonding, sometimes with other families at the ranch-style community meals and recreational events. Activities are optional, so guests can choose to spend as much time as they like inside rustic cabins and lodges and outdoors getting in touch with their inner cowpoke.

One of the best known of the Bandera bunch is the **Dixie Dude Ranch** (833 Dixie Dude Ranch Rd., 830/796-7771, www.dixieduderanch.com, adults average $130 each per night, children average $65). Unlike many area locales, the Dixie is an actual working stock ranch, operating since 1901. Guests can partake of planned activities such as horseback riding, swimming, fishing (gear provided), hiking, and hayrides, or they can venture out on their own to explore the ranch on hiking trails, hunt for fossils and arrowheads, or visit the 100-year-old barn and cemetery. Chow time means meals in the family-style dining house, outdoor barbecues, fried chicken, or a cowboy breakfast. Accommodations are in duplex cabins, cottages, a two-story bunkhouse, and a main lodge. All have two or more beds with private baths, air-conditioning, and heat.

Firmly in the resort ranch category (as opposed to working) is the renowned **Mayan Ranch** (off Pecan St., approximately 1.5 miles west of Bandera, 830/796-3312, www.mayanranch.com, adults average $150 each per night, children average $80; three meals and two horseback rides included in the cost). Guests at the Mayan can pony up for a full day of optional activities including a cowboy breakfast cookout, trail rides, a poolside lunch, swimming, cowboy games, tubing on the adjacent Medina River, dancing, and even fireworks. Afterward, guests are certain to sleep soundly in whichever accommodation they choose—individual cottages with up to three bedrooms, or one of the large lodge rooms overlooking the Hill Country.

Another popular Bandera getaway is the **Silver Spur Guest Ranch** (9266 Bandera Creek Rd., 830/796-3037, www.silverspur-ranch.com, adults $135 each per night, children average $70; three meals and two hours of horseback rides included in the cost; minimum two-night stay). Located alongside an enormous state park, the Silver Spur offers many of the activities found at other well-heeled dude ranches, including trail rides, outdoor cookouts, and hayrides, with additional features such as a junior Olympic-sized swimming pool and an arena for barrel racing, pole bending, and other riding activities. The main lodge and cabins offer modern and comfortable amenities.

Bandera boasts nearly a dozen more dude ranches in the general vicinity, each offering a varied range of rustic charm and cowboy-related activities. For a comprehensive list of options and a sneak peek at what they have to offer, visit the Bandera County Convention and Visitors Bureau website at www.banderacowboycapital.com, or to discuss details, call them at 800/364-3833.

AUSTIN

Horseback Riding

Most of Bandera's dude ranches offer horseback riding as part of the package, but not everyone visiting the area is hitching up to the ranch experience. Several independent stables in the area will arrange horseback rides by the hour, day, or even overnight. Options include **Wagon Wheel Horse Farm** (863/634-6397, www.wagonwheelhorsefarm.com), **Lightning Ranch** (830/535-4096, www.lightningranch.com), and **Bar M Guest Ranch** (830/796-9096, www.bar-mranch.com).

Frontier Times Museum

Those looking for a little diversion while in town can visit the Frontier Times Museum (510 13th St., 830/796-3864, www.frontiertimesmuseum.org, Mon.–Sat. 10 A.M.–4:30 P.M., $5 adults, $3 seniors, $2 children 6–17). This is a decidedly old-school museum, so don't expect interactive, hands-on exhibits; instead, you'll find an amazing collection of random stuff deemed important by townspeople since 1933. Western relics abound, including old household items, photos, farming equipment, and rodeo memorabilia, as well as an eclectic mix of "exotic" items from Asia and Europe, such as rare bells, plates, and a gong from the Ming Dynasty. The museum also includes a gallery of Western art.

Hill Country State Natural Area

One of the crown jewels of the Texas parks system is the Hill Country State Natural Area (10600 Bandera Creek Rd., 830/796-4413, www.tpwd.state.tx.us, daily Feb.–Nov., weekends Dec.–Jan., $6 daily 13 and older for day use, $3 daily per person 13 and older for overnight use). Secluded and undeveloped, this ruggedly beautiful 5,400-acre park preserves a magnificent portion of the Hill Country in its natural state. Equestrians, hikers, and mountain bikers traverse trails across valleys, streams, and limestone hills, and primitive backcountry camping areas are available to equestrian and nonequestrian campers.

Most of the parkland was donated by the Merrick Bar-O-Ranch, which stipulated that it "be kept far removed and untouched by modern civilization, where everything is preserved intact, yet put to a useful purpose." The terrain ranges from flat creek bottoms to rocky canyons reaching 2,000 feet in elevation. Several spring-fed streams provide swimming holes and water for horses, but the humans among the herd are encouraged to bring their own drinking water.

Accommodations

MOTELS AND HOTELS

As unbelievable as it may seem, not everyone visiting the Bandera area wants to stay at a dude ranch. Fortunately, there are other worthwhile alternatives, including the charming **River Front Motel** (1004 Maple St., 830/460-3690, www.theriverfrontmotel.com, cabins average $90). The simple, rustic motel has 11 cabins near the river offering a microwave, fridge, coffee, cable TV, private bathroom, and covered front porch. Other nearby options include the **Bandera Lodge** (700 State Hwy. 16 S., 830/796-3093, average $75 d), containing 21 rooms with microwaves and refrigerators as well as free Internet access.

BED-AND-BREAKFASTS

For some, a trip to the country necessitates a stay in a bed-and-breakfast, where gentle breezes land on soft downy pillows and days begin with gourmet coffee and egg dishes. The **Diamond H Ranch Bed and Breakfast** (four miles northwest of Bandera at 5322 Hwy. 16 N., 830/796-4820, www.diamondhbandera.com, rooms average $80) is a comfortable, laid-back locale along the Medina River. The main house has seven Western-style bedrooms with private baths, air-conditioning, heat, porches, and patios, and the main room includes a pool table, games, and a large fireplace. **Cool Water Acres** (3301 FM 470, 830/796-4866, www.coolwateracres.com, $125 nightly) is located on a five-acre spring-fed lake offering crisp, clear water for swimming, snorkeling, fishing, and relaxing. The cabin is part of an 1870 homestead that holds three adults comfortably. Property features include complimentary fruit and farm fresh eggs upon arrival, a private floating dock, and a nearby barn with friendly horses, cats, and chickens.

Bandera is brimming with other B&Bs—a comprehensive list of options is available at the Bandera County Convention and Visitors Bureau's website at www.banderacowboycapital.com.

Food and Entertainment

Despite being a small town of nearly 1,000, Bandera has several noteworthy restaurants catering to locals and the city slickers who invade the community most weekends. To get a true taste of Bandera, drop by the **OST Restaurant** (305 Main St., 830/796-3836, $7–14). The acronym stands for Old Spanish Trail, which used to run through the area, and the Western theme permeates everything from the menu to the John Wayne–inspired decor. The OST's specialty is breakfast, including staples such as biscuits and gravy, hash browns, and huevos rancheros, served at any time. The soups and chicken-fried steak are local favorites. For an authentic experience in the Cowboy Capital, you can literally saddle up to the bar at the OST. Another busy downtown place to get good country vittles is **Busbee's Bar-B-Q** (319 Main St., 830/796-3153, $7–15). Busbee's serves up traditional Texas barbecue—brisket, sausage, and ribs—along with standard side dishes like coleslaw, potato salad, and beans. For a good Tex-Mex fix, visitors can stick close to downtown for their fill of tacos, enchiladas, quesadillas, and breakfast burritos at the tiny **El Jacalito** (1207 Cedar St., 830/460-3853, closed Sun. and Mon., $6–13).

For entertainment, the most famous establishment in Bandera is **Arkey Blue's Silver Dollar Saloon** (308 Main St., 830/796-8826, open daily, with live music Wed.–Sun.). Established in the 1930s, Arkey's is a classic honky-tonk with a sawdust-covered dance floor that's experienced decades of scootin' boots on its well-worn surface. The scene is more authentically Western than many of the nearby resort ranches, and the crowds (especially the veteran two-steppers) will give out-of-towners a true sense of country living. Arkey himself has been tending bar since the late '60s, and

he still occasionally takes the stage with his Blue Cowboys. Over the years, the saloon has hosted many high-profile guest performers, including Willie Nelson, Ernest Tubb, and Bruce and Charlie Robison.

Far less famous yet certainly entertaining in its own right is the **Bandera Saloon** (402 Main St., 830/796–3699, www.banderasaloon.com). Located among the restaurants and bustle of downtown, the saloon hosts live music on the deck overlooking Main Street every Thursday through Saturday. This is a good spot for dancing, drinking, and people watching, and if you happen to arrive on horseback, you're in luck—tie up to the hitchin' post out front, and you'll receive an "I got a horse" discount the whole time you and your horse are there.

Information and Services

For a small town, Bandera has plenty of visitor services to oversee, and this is ably handled by the **Bandera County Convention and Visitors Bureau** (126 State Hwy. 16 S., 830/796-3045 or 800/364-3833, www.banderacowboycapital.com). The website is particularly helpful for comparing available amenities, and the office staff offer expert advice and provide brochures, maps, and directions to the hard-to-find destinations tucked among the hills.

JOHNSON CITY

Most people assume Johnson City (population 1,266) is named for its legendary native son, Lyndon Baines Johnson, the 36th president of the United States. It's actually named after his grandfather's nephew James Polk Johnson, even though he never achieved quite the same level of international acclaim as LBJ. The Johnson family, however, is an ideal representation of the determined, down-to-earth folks who settled in this rugged part of the state more than 150 years ago and whose descendants remain on the rocky yet endearing terrain. A visit to this small town, especially the incredible LBJ Ranch, reveals the gritty and tenacious nature of the region, reflected in the no-nonsense approach of LBJ himself. This was truly far away from Camelot.

◖ Lyndon B. Johnson National Historical Park

Even if you're just passing through the Hill Country, be sure to set aside a couple hours to tour the remarkable Lyndon B. Johnson National Historical Park (two visitors centers—100 Lady Bird Ln. in Johnson City, and at the LBJ Ranch near Stonewall 14 miles west of Johnson City on Hwy. 290, 830/868-7128, www.nps.gov/lyjo, daily 8 A.M.–5 P.M., Texas White House tour $2 adults).

As most visitors soon find out, LBJ remains a larger-than-life figure who brought acclaim (and electricity) to the Hill Country. To get a full appreciation for this mythical man, start at Johnson City's State Park and Historic Site—his boyhood home and the Johnson Settlement—which put his formative years in the context of his environment.

Afterward, make the relatively quick 14-mile drive west to the LBJ Ranch near Stonewall. Beginning in 2008, the National Park Service opened the family residence, aka the Texas White House, to the public. Visitors can view the president's office, living room, and dining room (additional rooms are being renovated). The self-guided driving tour on the ranch property lets visitors learn about what made LBJ the legendary figure he became by experiencing everything from the one-room schoolhouse he would sneak into as a four-year-old to the small graveyard with the modest granite blocks marking the graves of Lyndon and his beloved wife, Lady Bird. The ranch's interpretive center includes informative exhibits about the history of LBJ and the Hill Country, including a post office display with audio versions of letters describing the harsh environs of the region to relatives on the East Coast and in Germany.

Exotic Resort Zoo

There's plenty of land in the Hill Country, and apparently it's somewhat similar to the environment of the creatures that roam the spacious grounds of the Exotic Resort Zoo (located four miles north of Johnson City at 235 Zoo Trl., 830/868-4357, www.zooexotics.com, daily 9 A.M.–6 P.M., $11.95 adults, $9.95 children).

© ANDY RHODES

the Lyndon B. Johnson Ranch, near Stonewall

Visitors take a guided open-bus tour through the expansive property while guides describe the characteristics of the zoo's animals, including giraffes, lemurs, kangaroos, zebras, bears, ostrich, and buffalo. Some of the friendly beasts will even let visitors pet them (the treats handed out by the guides offer an extra incentive). The Exotic Resort Zoo also operates several cabins, three with kitchenettes, for those who really want to experience life on the range.

Pedernales Falls State Park

One of the most pleasant and scenic spots in Central Texas is Pedernales Falls State Park (nine miles east of Johnson City at 2585 Park Rd. 6026, 830/868-7304, www.tpwd.state.tx.us, $5 daily per person 13 and older, $3 daily per person 13 and older staying overnight). Located on more than 5,200 acres of rolling hills and flowing water, the park's main attraction is its namesake Pedernales Falls, visible from a scenic overlook at the north end of the park.

Park activities include camping, hiking, swimming, tubing, mountain biking, fishing, and, most popular of all, bird-watching. The park has a covered bird viewing station with feeders (food is provided year-round) and a drip bath. Quails, doves, rufous-crowned sparrows, western scrub jays, and the endangered golden-cheeked warbler nest in the park and visit the feeders. Facilities include campsites with water and electricity, primitive campsites, restrooms with and without showers, 20 miles of hiking and mountain biking trails, and 14 miles of backpacking trails.

Accommodations

For a pleasant rural experience, stay in a cabin at **Country Cabins B&B** (793 Lange Rd., 830/868-7447, www.countrycabinsbnb.com, $100–140 nightly). The guest rooms are rustic without being shabby and pleasant without being too quaint. If you're looking for a simple, quiet place to stay on a working cattle ranch, this is a good spot.

Those looking for a reliable hotel experience have limited options, and the best among them is the **Best Western Johnson City Inn** (at the intersection of Hwys. 281 and 290, 830/868-4044, www.bestwestern.com, $99 d). The hotel offers free Internet access, a complimentary continental breakfast, and an outdoor swimming pool.

Food

For a town of 1,000, Johnson City has several worthy restaurants, perfect for fueling up before a day at the LBJ ranch or Pedernales Falls Park. The best of the bunch is **Silver K Cafe** (209 E. Main St., 830/868-2911, www.silverkcafe.com, $11–26). Housed in a historic lumberyard alongside several antiques shops, the Silver K offers upscale country fare in a pleasant environment. Choose from standards like chicken-fried steak, bronzed catfish, crab cakes, or tenderloin steak. Sunday mornings feature a sumptuous brunch buffet with egg casseroles, fried green tomatoes, and carved roasts. Local singer-songwriters such as John Arthur Martinez and Mike Blakely enhance the Hill Country experience with their mellow acoustic tunes from the small corner stage.

The other reliable local restaurants in town serve standard Tex-Mex fare. You can't go wrong with either **El Charro Restaurant** (502 N. Hwy. 281, 830/868-7040, $7–12) or nearby **El Rancho** (408 S. Hwy. 281, 830/868-0812, $7–12). Both feature classic cheesy and beefy Tex-Mex dishes such as enchiladas, tacos, quesadillas, and burritos.

Information and Services

Information about accommodations, restaurants, and other visitor needs, including maps and brochures, is available at the **Johnson City Chamber of Commerce** (830/868-7684, www.lbjcountry.com).

HILL COUNTRY SIDE TRIPS

Visitors often turn a Hill Country excursion into an extra long weekend, with day trips to one of the region's scenic parks for hiking and biking, or an afternoon cruising down a canyon-walled river in a canoe, kayak, or inner tube. Fans of outlaw country music—particularly Willie, Waylon and the boys—are

AUSTIN

virtually required to make a pilgrimage to the tiny yet fabled Luchenbach.

⟪ Enchanted Rock State Natural Area

Serving as a mythical natural beacon for millennia is the enormous pink granite dome at the heart of Enchanted Rock State Natural Area (18 miles north of Fredericksburg at 16710 Ranch Rd. 965, 830/685-3636, www. tpwd.state.tx.us, $6 per person day-use fee). Although visitors have only been visiting the state park since 1984, people have been drawn by its surreal magnitude for more than 11,000 years. The rock itself is a massive granite exfoliation dome rising 1,825 feet above sea level and is one of the largest batholiths (an underground rock formation uncovered by erosion) in the country.

Tonkawa Indians believed the rock wove enchanted spells, and Spanish explorers in the mid-1700s were equally intrigued by the natural structure. Legend has it Comanche Indians held human sacrifices at the base of the rock, but this has been disputed. However, most anthropologists agree the Native Americans were fearful of the rock because they believed it to be haunted. These days, there are occasional New Age types who seek spiritual power from the iridescent reflections emanating from the sparkling granite on full-moon nights.

The rock's intrigue continues to draw hundreds of visitors on weekends for hiking, rock climbing, backpacking, camping, and stargazing. In fact, the park itself often reaches parking capacity on weekends and closes early, sometimes by 11 A.M. Call ahead to gauge accessibility.

The park contains a four-mile hiking trail that snakes through the granite formations, and a short yet steep trail leading to the top of the rock (those not on a regular workout regimen will likely have to take several breaks along the way). Park amenities include an interpretive center, hike-in primitive sites, restrooms with showers, tent pads, picnic sites for day-use with tables and grills, and a group picnic area with a pavilion and restrooms. Vehicular camping is not permitted. Contact the park regarding camping fees and restrictions, which vary depending on the number of people and type of use.

Frio and Sabinal Canyons

If the word *canyon* brings to mind sheer cliffs and towering vertical rock formations, then perhaps the geological structures along the Frio and Sabinal Rivers should be referred to as "mini canyons." Even though they're not dramatic in size, these canyons remain beautiful wonders of nature. Since most Texas rivers traverse through hills and across plains, these are spectacular scenes in comparison—especially from the vantage point of a canoe or inner tube. And, true to its name, the Frio River (*frio* means cold in Spanish) is refreshingly brisk on a 100°F summer day. Visitors to this area relish the rural scenery and the abundant opportunities to camp in primitive areas or stay in rustic hillside cabins and lodges.

GARNER STATE PARK

One of the most popular year-round destinations in this area of the Hill Country is Garner State Park (eight miles north of Concan at 234 Ranch Rd. 1050, 830/232-6132, www.tpwd. state.tx.us, $6 daily per person 13 and older day use, $4 per person 13 and older staying overnight). Boasting 1,420 acres of natural beauty along the Frio River, the park attracts hundreds of thousands of visitors annually to swim, boat, tube, and fish in the chilly water; hike the park's remarkable nature trails; dance at the nightly concession stand gatherings during the summer season; and even get in a few rounds at the nearby miniature golf course (lighted for nighttime playing). Most visitors camp at the primitive tent sites, although there are a limited number of high-demand cabins are available for rent (renovations were continuing in 2011; call ahead for availability). The park is open year-round, seven days a week, but it's busiest Memorial Day through Labor Day. Like Enchanted Rock, the popularity of this park occasionally results in parking capacity issues, forcing officials to close the gates by noon. Also contact the park regarding camping fees and restrictions, which vary depending on the number of people and type of use. The popular summertime dances can reach maximum parking capacity as well, so call ahead before putting your dancing boots on.

LOST MAPLES STATE NATURAL AREA

Northerners take note: Fall colors—particularly crimson reds and brilliant oranges—are virtually nonexistent in Texas, so don't be surprised to hear about frenzied and overcrowded conditions at Lost Maples State Natural Area (five miles north of Vanderpool at 37221 Ranch Rd. 187, 830/966-3413, www.tpwd. state.tx.us, Oct.–Nov. $6 daily per person 13 and older day use, $3 per person 13 and older staying overnight; Dec.–Sept. $5 daily per person 13 and older day use, $3 per person 13 and older staying overnight). The main-attraction maples add a welcome splash of color to the region's normally uninspired fall palate of browns and yellows. They're deemed "lost" since they grow hundreds of miles away from their native habitats, primarily due to the cooler and wetter conditions provided by the surrounding canyon walls. The trees hit their colorful peak in late October and early November, resulting in huge crowds and parking-capacity issues (limited to 250 vehicles), so visitors are advised to call ahead regarding accessibility, or, better yet, arrive on a weekday when it's less full.

Even when the fall foliage isn't taking center stage, visitors are attracted year-round to the park's limestone canyons, cool spring-fed streams, and wooded trails. Since the beloved maples have a shallow root system, hikers are encouraged to stay on the trail to avoid damaging the trees. Park amenities include campsites with water and electricity, restrooms with showers, and primitive camping areas. Camping fees are $8 per night for primitive campsites, $18 per night for campsites with water and electric hookups.

CANYON COMMUNITIES

This region of the state is dotted with small riverside towns filled with resort guests, retirees, and the descendants of the German settlers who migrated to this area in the 1800s. **Concan** is a tiny community (population 490) surrounded by gorgeous scenery in the form of tree-topped hills and cliffs overlooking the crystal-clear Frio River. The meandering drive along Highway 83 leading to and from the town is unlike any other in Texas, with the adjacent canyons beckoning drivers to pull over and explore their scenic overlooks. Perhaps the best place to experience this view is the one-of-a-kind **Neal's Lodges** (located approximately three miles southwest of Concan on Hwy. 127, 830/232-6118, www.nealslodges. com, cabins cost $60–250 daily for up to eight people; three-night minimum stay during summer months). Established in 1926, Neal's offers 62 cabins, ranging from funky to fancy. The most basic options are one-room wooden structures with "evaporative coolers," and the nicest of the bunch are upscale Hill Country lodges. In between are cinder-block-based structures overlooking the Frio and the "best swimming hole in Texas." All but four of the cabins have kitchenettes. Other on-site amenities include a grocery store, restaurant, and Laundromat. RV hookups and tent sites are also available, and Neal's rents inner tubes for floating on the Frio, with a return stop on the property's riverbank.

Just up the road on Highway 83 is **Leakey** (pronounced Lay-key), another small community (population 387) with riverside lodging and multigenerational Hill Country settlers. This is one of the closest towns to Garner State Park, so visitors often stay in a reliable Leakey cabin at night and visit the park during the day. One of the more interesting lodging options in town is the **D'Rose Inn and Cabins** (527 S. Hwy. 83, 830/232-5246, www.droseinn.com, $65–145). The D'Rose caters to motorcyclists and bicyclists only (guests must be riding or have their bikes on a trailer). The three-acre property includes four rooms and 11 cabins along with free wireless Internet service, a lounge, pool, covered pavilion, barbecue grills, and picnic tables.

Kerrville

This charming Hill Country town (population 20,425) isn't quite as quaint as it used to be, but it's still well worth visiting—especially for the arts scene. It may not seem like a likely site for a cultural mecca, but artists, musicians, and writers are continually drawn to its rolling hills, cool breezes, and laid-back lifestyle.

KERRVILLE FOLK FESTIVAL

Kerrville is best known for the annual Kerrville Folk Festival (830/257-3600, www.kerrville-music.com), held for 18 days in late May and early June. The fest draws more than 100 singer-songwriters specializing in folk, Americana, country, and roots rock from across the globe for nearly three weeks of scheduled concerts and improvisational jams on stages and around campfires in the hills. Several big-name artists played Kerrville early in their careers, including Willie Nelson, Lyle Lovett, Robert Earl Keen, Lucinda Williams, and Nancy Griffith. Other nationally known artists like Arlo Guthrie, Judy Collins, and Janis Ian make regular appearances at the festival. While many people attend just the evening main stage shows, the true soul of the festival is in the campgrounds, where artists and amateurs spend hours singing and strumming in guitar circles under the majestic oaks and starry sky.

MUSEUM OF WESTERN ART

One of the city's proudest and most impressive attractions is the Museum of Western Art (550 Bandera Hwy., 830/896-2553, www.museumofwesternart.org, Tues.–Sat. 9 A.M.–5 P.M., Sun. 1–5 P.M., closed Mon., $5 adults, $3.50 seniors, $2 students 15–18, $1 children 6–14). The first thing visitors notice is the building itself—hearty timbers and rugged limestone frame the exterior, and life-sized bronze statues occupy the grounds. Inside, the Wild West comes to life through artwork featuring cowboys, cowgirls, Native Americans, and frontier settlers. A 5,000-volume library of art and history draws students and scholars, and the museum features distinguished artists in permanent and rotating exhibits following the tradition of Remington and Russell in their celebration of the Old West.

ACCOMMODATIONS

Kerrville offers a wide range of accommodations, from guest ranches to river cabins to bed-and-breakfasts to hotels, motels, RV parks, and campgrounds. The **Kerrville Convention and Visitors Bureau** offers a comprehensive list of lodging options at www.kerrvilletexascvb.com. The friendly staff is also happy to lend a hand via phone or in person. Call them at 800/221-7958 or drop by for a visit at 2108 Sidney Baker Street Monday–Friday 8:30 A.M.–5 P.M., Saturday 9 A.M.–3 P.M., Sunday 10 A.M.–3 P.M.

Luckenbach

Luckenbach (population 25) is perhaps best known as the subject of a classic 1977 Waylon Jennings tune called "Luckenbach, Texas (Back to the Basics of Love)." The song painted a mythical picture of a simple place to unwind "with Waylon and Willie and the boys." Decades later, people are still making a pilgrimage to this tiny Hill Country town, located on Ranch Road 1376, 52 miles northwest of San Antonio and 75 miles west of Austin.

The thriving "downtown" contains three buildings—a blacksmith shop, rustic tavern/general store, and a historic dance hall. During the summer months, you'll find Texas troubadours gathered 'round beneath the outstretched arms of the enormous oak trees picking tunes on their banjos and guitars. Shows are held several times a month, with themes such as Wacky Waylon Wednesday and the Thursday Songwriters' Circle. Tickets for these shows run anywhere between $15 and $25. For more information, visit www.luckenbachtexas.com or call 830/997-3224.

Finding the town can be a challenge, since people often steal the Luckenbach signs pointing the way. From Fredericksburg, head east on Highway 290 for about six miles to FM 1376, then head south for another four miles or so to Luckenbach. Take the second left (Luckenbach Road).

SAN ANTONIO AND SOUTH TEXAS

Most of South Texas is defined and unified by its Tejano heritage. Though it contains a scattering of German and other European settlers' communities, the majority of South Texas culture is tied to Mexico, including the legendary Alamo, constructed along with four other San Antonio missions in the early 1700s to help expand Spain's influence in the New World. Despite the well-known phrase, people typically don't remember The Alamo in its correct historic context. The 1836 siege at the Alamo site, by then an abandoned mission complex, resulted in a loss for the Texans, who subsequently used the defeat as a motivational rallying cry ("Remember the Alamo!") in their victorious battle at San Jacinto a month later.

Settlers continued to descend upon this sun-drenched, tropical region throughout the 19th and 20th centuries, many from Mexico, and others—Germans, Czechs, and French, to name a few—from ports on the Gulf Coast. The Mexican cowboys known as *vaqueros* had a cultural impact on the region that would ultimately affect the entire state's image. These professional ranch hands passed along their knowledge of roping, branding, and riding to the Anglos who arrived in droves in the mid-1800s and acquired vast amounts of South Texas ranch land. The evacuation of longhorn and other cattle from area ranches to San Antonio, Fort Worth, and markets to the north along the legendary Chisholm Trail was the largest migration of livestock in history.

The urban (not quite cosmopolitan) intrigue and abundant business opportunities in San Antonio made it a destination point for

© ANDY RHODES

HIGHLIGHTS

◖ **The Alamo:** This "Shrine of Texas Liberty" is a world-recognized cultural icon for a reason: It stands as a proud monument to the valor and sacrifice of a few brave men who were willing to fight to their deaths in defense of Texas. Don't forget to remember the Alamo (page 148)!

◖ **San Antonio Missions National Historical Park:** Four magnificent colonial mission buildings (including the Alamo) transport visitors to the mid-1700s, when Spain ruled the region and attempted to civilize the native population at these stunning historic structures (page 149).

◖ **San Antonio River Walk:** Also known as *El Paseo del Rio*, the River Walk spans a downtown portion of the San Antonio River and is flanked by lush foliage, cobblestone walkways, and an impressive assortment of shops, restaurants, and nightclubs (page 151).

◖ **Pearl Brewery Development:** Housed in historic buildings from San Antonio's former Pearl Brewery, this stunning adaptive reuse project features several top-notch restaurants, a culinary institute, residential lofts, a retail center, and enough eye-catching architectural details to make for a memorable evening out (page 172).

◖ **Gruene Historic District:** Take a step back in time in Gruene, a small historic district just outside of New Braunfels featuring Texas's oldest operating dance hall, a top-notch rustic restaurant, and enough shopping options to keep the family stocked with jewelry and T-shirts for years (page 177).

◖ **Tubing the Guadalupe River:** Grab an inner tube and a cooler full of beverages, and plop into New Braunfels's stretch of the Guadalupe River—kick back and let the current lazily carry you down a refreshing tree-lined waterway on a hot summer day (page 178).

◖ **Seminole Canyon State Park:** Located west of Del Rio, Seminole Canyon State Park contains a fascinating collection of ancient Native American rock art featuring mystic shaman figures and mysterious handprints, some dating back more than 4,000 years (page 182).

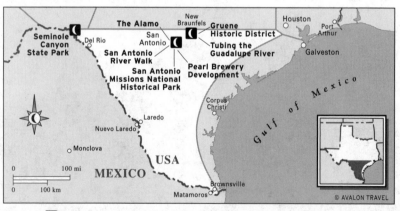

LOOK FOR ◖ TO FIND RECOMMENDED SIGHTS, ACTIVITIES, DINING, AND LODGING.

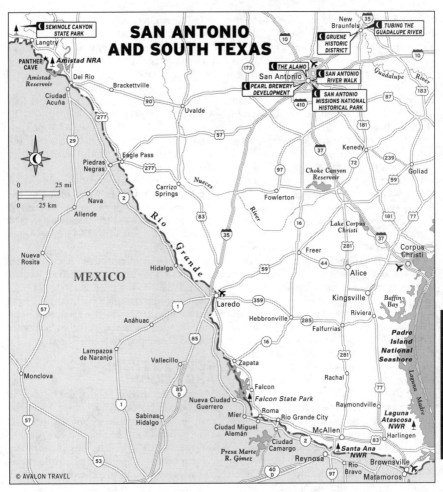

immigrants throughout the 1800s and 1900s, but the cities receiving the most significant population booms recently are along the Texas-Mexico border. Brownsville and McAllen, in particular, have experienced population explosions thanks to the manufacturing jobs at major factories built on the banks of the Rio Grande.

Also having an economic impact on the region are the snowbirds, aka Winter Texans. These retirees migrate from cold northern climes to roost in the Lower Rio Grande Valley and along the Gulf Coast. They frequent the region's many Tex-Mex restaurants and are particularly fond of the abundant birding and ecotourism opportunities as well as the museums and historic sites scattered throughout the region.

PLANNING YOUR TIME

Most visitors to this region either stay exclusively in San Antonio or near the Mexican border. Although the three-to-five-hour drive from San Antonio to the Lower Rio Grande Valley may seem lengthy, it's worth making just to experience the tremendous border culture. South Texas food (from *sopapillas* to citrus) is especially outstanding. Now that Mexico is virtually off-limits to tourists, the closest many people will get to a genuine Mexican meal is along the border.

Allow at least two or three days in San Antonio. The city's genuinely friendly atmosphere draws visitors into its laid-back vibe, where the next attraction or event can always wait for another margarita. And The Alamo and the nearby River Walk are definite must-sees, despite being two of the most touristy places in the country. Weekdays are less crowded at these sites; save the weekend for visiting the missions, the Institute of Texan Cultures, and the San Fernando Cathedral, or take an extra day to enjoy the amusement at SeaWorld or Six Flags.

For those planning to stay in the San Antonio area, the historic charm of New Braunfels offers a nice destination for a day trip, especially if there's a show at Gruene Hall. Otherwise, the pleasant yet small city of Del Rio is a somewhat more ambitious yet manageable day trip (about two and a half hours away). Del Rio's counterpart on the Mexican side is the enticing Ciudad Acuña, one of the safer border towns along the Rio Grande.

For a true taste of border culture, plan to spend several days in the Valley, especially Brownsville and McAllen. Brownsville offers the history and traditions of two countries, while McAllen features newer attractions related to ecotourism and the arts.

INFORMATION AND SERVICES

One of the best places to get started on your hunt for San Antonio information is the **San Antonio Visitor Information Center** (317 Alamo Plaza, 210/207-6700 or 800/447-3372, www.sanantoniovisit.com, daily 9 A.M.–5 P.M.), located in the historic Crockett building between The Alamo and the River Walk. Maps,

guides, brochures, souvenirs, and expert advice from the professional staff are available. You can also drop by the Convention & Visitors Bureau's corporate offices (203 S. St. Mary's St., second floor, 210/207-6700 or 800/447-3372, daily 8 A.M.–5:30 P.M.).

Another useful resource is the **Greater San Antonio Chamber of Commerce** (602 E. Commerce St., 210/229-2100, www.sachamber.org), which offers a comprehensive website with extensive listings of hotels, restaurants, attractions, and events.

For those seeking specific information about the famous River Walk, including the status and location of the many businesses, contact the **Paseo del Rio Association** (110 Broadway, Suite 500, 210/227-4262, www.paseodelrio.com).

For a regional perspective, check with the fine folks at the **Texas Tropical Trail Region** in Kingsville (635 E. King Ave. #102., 361/592-4603, www.texastropicaltrail.com). They'll offer an informed perspective along with maps and brochures on heritage tourism and other cultural destinations in South Texas.

GETTING THERE AND AROUND

Most travelers arrive to South Texas by plane at San Antonio International Airport. However, there are several smaller regional airports in Del Rio, Laredo, and Brownsville. San Antonio and the midsize cities have bus and taxi services; otherwise, travelers in this region tend to navigate the long stretches between (and even within) cities by car. San Antonio's freeway system was well designed and built with the anticipation of increased traffic volume, unlike other cities that chose to take a "if you don't build it, they won't come" approach to highways (yes, Austin, this is aimed directly at you). As a result, rush hour traffic isn't too much of a nightmare, since the abundance of interstate and bypass loop options adequately distribute the mass of vehicles.

The **San Antonio International Airport** (9800 Airport Blvd., 210/207-3411, www.sanantonio.gov/aviation) is relatively small for the seventh-largest city in the country, but it's a good-looking facility and easy to navigate. Located about 12 miles north of downtown, the airport offers flights from eight U.S.-based airlines and four Mexican companies.

Most travelers choose to rent a car since they'll likely explore beyond downtown. Most of the major companies are represented—Alamo (of course), Budget, Enterprise, Dollar, etc. After picking up a vehicle, it's a straight shot down U.S. 281 to downtown, which takes about 15–30 minutes, depending on the time of day.

Another transportation option from the airport worth considering is **SA Trans** (210/281-9900, www.saairportshuttle.com), offering shared van service to downtown hotels for a mere $18 one-way (with a round-trip purchase). The company operates booths outside both airport terminals, and service runs 7 A.M.– 1:30 A.M. Call 24 hours ahead for return service from the hotel.

Taxis cost about $25 and take approximately 15 minutes between the airport and downtown. Stations are located outside the airport terminals, and, a bonus not found in most cities, up to four people can share a cab for the same price without paying additional charges per person or luggage.

Also fairly unique to San Antonio is the respectable public transportation system, which is considered rather efficient, inexpensive, and easily accessible. **VIA Metropolitan Transit** (210/362-2020, www.viainfo.net) runs about 100 bus lines and a downtown street car service. Fares run from as low as 55 cents to several dollars.

A unique way to get around town is via river taxi with **Rio San Antonio Cruises** (tickets available at Rivercenter Mall and Holiday Inn, 210/244-5700 or 800/417-4139, www.riosanantonio.com, $7.75 adults, $5 seniors, $2 children 1–5), which specializes in tours but can also arrange for transportation.

For those in search of more traditional travel services, San Antonio is accessible by train (**Amtrak** operates a depot on the east side of downtown at 350 Hoefden St., 210/223-3226) and bus (the **Greyhound** station is downtown at 500 N. St. Mary's St., 210/270-5824).

Several smaller airports also serve this region of the state, including the **Laredo International Airport** (5210 Bob Bullock Loop, 956/795-2000, www.ci.laredo.com/airport), which offers daily flights to Dallas/Fort Worth, Houston, Las Vegas, and other cities on three major airlines. **Del Rio International Airport** (1104 W. 10th St., 830/774-8538, www.cityofdelrio.com) provides a Continental Airlines flight to and from Houston several times daily, and the **Valley International Airport** in Harlingen (3002 Heritage Wy., 956/430-8600, www.flythevalley.com) offers Southwest Airlines and Continental Express as the main airline carriers.

San Antonio and Vicinity

San Antonio is a mythical city, and for good reason. Its beginnings predate the founding of the United States by more than half a century, the legendary Alamo is a cultural icon, and the city's missions represent an era of Spanish colonialism that becomes more fascinating as each new detail is learned. Add to that the lure of the River Walk, amusement parks, and the city's welcoming lack of pretension, and it should come as no surprise that San Antonio regularly appears in top-10 lists of favorite travel destinations in Texas and the United States.

San Antonio (population 1,296,682) is the seventh-largest city in the country, according to the U.S. Census Bureau, but it's certainly not evident to visitors savoring long lunches at downtown patio cafés alongside casually dressed office workers. Nor is it obvious when you're sitting atop the Tower of the Americas, surveying the modest skyline, devoid of egocentric glass monuments dedicated to power

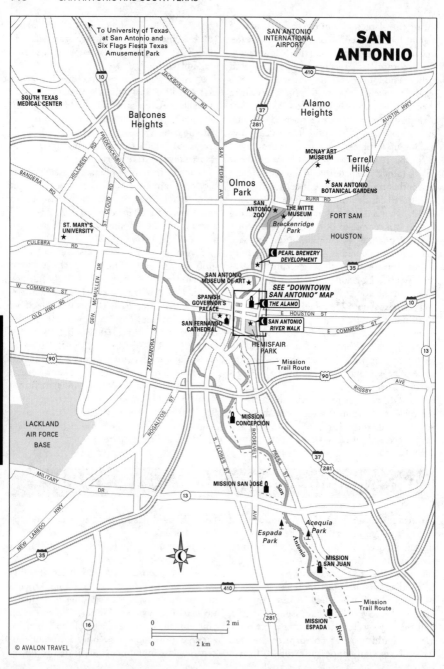

SAN ANTONIO

To University of Texas at San Antonio and Six Flags Fiesta Texas Amusement Park

SAN ANTONIO INTERNATIONAL AIRPORT

SOUTH TEXAS MEDICAL CENTER

Balcones Heights

Alamo Heights

MCNAY ART MUSEUM

Terrell Hills

Olmos Park

ST. MARY'S UNIVERSITY

SAN ANTONIO BOTANICAL GARDENS

SAN ANTONIO ZOO

THE WITTE MUSEUM

Brackenridge Park

FORT SAM

HOUSTON

PEARL BREWERY DEVELOPMENT

SAN ANTONIO MUSEUM OF ART

SEE "DOWNTOWN SAN ANTONIO" MAP

SPANISH GOVERNOR'S PALACE

THE ALAMO

SAN FERNANDO CATHEDRAL

SAN ANTONIO RIVER WALK

HEMISFAIR PARK

Mission Trail Route

LACKLAND AIR FORCE BASE

MISSION CONCEPCIÓN

MISSION SAN JOSÉ

Acequia Park

Espada Park

MISSION SAN JUAN

MISSION ESPADA

Mission Trail Route

0 — 2 mi
0 — 2 km

© AVALON TRAVEL

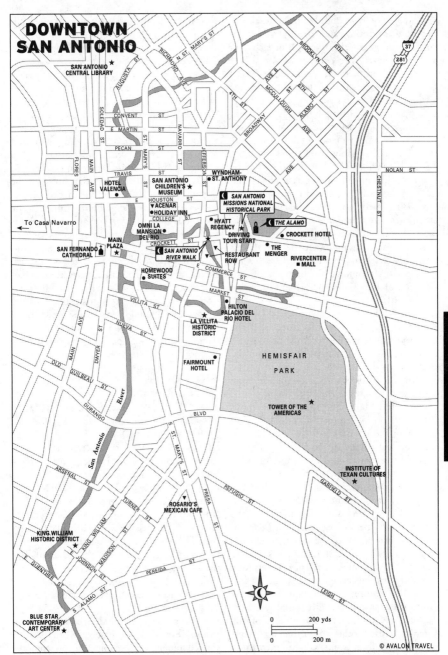

DOWNTOWN SAN ANTONIO

SAN ANTONIO CENTRAL LIBRARY ★

RICHMOND AVE

N ST MARY'S ST

AUGUSTA ST

SOLEDAD ST

CONVENT ST

E MARTIN ST

PECAN ST

FLORES AVE

MAIN AVE

TRAVIS ST

ST MARY'S ST

NAVARRO ST

4TH ST

BROADWAY

AVE B

McCULLOUGH AVE

8TH ST

9TH ST

ALAMO ST

BROOKLYN AVE

RTL ST

37 281

NOLAN ST

CHESTNUT ST

JEFFERSON ST

HOTEL VALENCIA ●

SAN ANTONIO CHILDREN'S MUSEUM ★

HOUSTON ST
▼ACENAR ★
●HOLIDAY INN

E COLLEGE

OMNI LA MANSION DEL RIO ●

CROCKETT ST

SAN FERNANDO CATHEDRAL ⛪

MAIN PLAZA ★

To Casa Navarro →

WYNDHAM- ● ST. ANTHONY

🌙 SAN ANTONIO MISSIONS NATIONAL HISTORICAL PARK

HYATT ● REGENCY

🔒 THE ALAMO ☾

● CROCKETT HOTEL

DRIVING TOUR START

🌙 SAN ANTONIO RIVER WALK

▼ RESTAURANT ROW

● THE MENGER

RIVERCENTER ■ MALL

HOMEWOOD ● SUITES

VILLITA ST

NUEVA ST

E COMMERCE ST

MARKET ST

▼ HILTON ● PALACIO DEL RIO HOTEL

LA VILLITA HISTORIC DISTRICT ★

HEMISFAIR PARK

San Antonio River

MAIN AVE

S ST

DWYER

OLD GUILBEAU ST

DURANGO

FAIRMOUNT HOTEL ●

TOWER OF THE AMERICAS ★

BLVD

ST MARY'S ST

ARSENAL ST

REFUGIO ST

GARFIELD ST

INSTITUTE OF TEXAN CULTURES ★

TURNER ST

PRESA ST

ROSARIO'S ▼ MEXICAN CAFE

KING WILLIAM HISTORIC DISTRICT ★

KING WILLIAM ST

MADISON ST

JOHNSON ST

E GUENTHER ST

PEREIDA ST

S ALAMO ST

LEIGH ST

BLUE STAR CONTEMPORARY ART CENTER ★

0   200 yds
0   200 m

SAN ANTONIO

© AVALON TRAVEL

and prosperity. It's certainly not noticeable in the genuine greetings and friendly eye contact you'll encounter on the other side of each door and around every street corner.

It's the kind of town ideally suited for a getaway—no stressful hustle and bustle, just a steady flow of activity among an impressive infrastructure of historic buildings and modern conveniences. Most visitors come to San Antonio on a pilgrimage to see The Alamo, even though they likely couldn't tell you about its significance in U.S. history. The nearby River Walk is one of the top tourist destinations in the entire state, and even though its tantalizing smells, colorful sights, and vibrant energy are entertaining, the stretch of restaurants, shops, and hotels along the San Antonio River doesn't truly represent the soul of this city. Though it may come as a surprise to some tourists, San Antonio thrived between the construction of The Alamo (1724) and the River Walk (1961).

The city's origins are tied to the 1718 San Antonio de Bexar Presidio (fort) and the nearby village of San Fernando de Bexar, chartered in 1731 by a group of people from the Canary Islands. Around this time, several of San Antonio's most significant structures were constructed on two of the city's major plazas, Military and Main. The Spanish Governor's Palace was completed in 1749, and, nearly 10 years later, the San Fernando de Bexar Church was built just around the corner.

San Antonio became a major hub of activity during the Texas Revolution and was the site of several notable clashes, including the 1835 Siege of Bexar and the memorable 1836 Battle of the Alamo. Once Texas entered the Union in 1845, people began arriving in droves from the eastern part of the country and from European nations via Gulf Coast ports (mainly Galveston). Many of the city's newcomers were involved with the cattle industry, and aspects of city life soon revolved around the agriculture business since most early trail drives went through San Antonio. A good portion of this ranching activity centered on the city's main plazas, especially at banks, saloons, mercantile

stores, and fancy hotels like the Menger, St. Anthony, and Gunter. The more prosperous ranchers had homes in the tony King William District just south of downtown.

The cowboys who gathered at the plazas and stockyards were appropriate ambassadors of San Antonio's multicultural makeup, since their skills and equipment were largely based on the *vaqueros* who rustled cattle and worked the ranches in Mexico before Anglos started arriving in Texas. From branding to roping to riding, the Mexican influence on ranching in Texas was profound, and in San Antonio, the impact reached far beyond the barbed wire.

San Antonio would go on to flourish in the late 1800s and early 1900s, thanks in large part to the railroads and highway systems that kept the economy strong with agricultural trade and the military bases that proliferated in the area. By the middle of the 20th century, the city had gained a reputation as a major travel destination due to its moderate climate and dynamic history. San Antonio became one of the country's most-visited cities as a result of its abundant attractions and appealing midcontinental location for industry conventions.

SIGHTS
◖ The Alamo

The Alamo (300 Alamo Plaza, 210/225-1391, www.thealamo.org, Mon.–Sat. 9 A.M.–5:30 P.M., Sun. 10 A.M.–5:30 P.M., free admission) is appropriately referred to as a shrine. Upon entering, visitors are asked to remove their hats and refrain from taking photos "out of respect for the shrine," and it's been referred to as the "Shrine of Texas Liberty." If this word conjures up images of a mythical and sacred fortress drawing faithful devotees, then The Alamo certainly qualifies. Once visitors get past the site's unexpected urban setting—apparently most textbooks include a rustic sketch of The Alamo in its frontier-era isolated state—they can appreciate its historical significance.

To get a true understanding of The Alamo's role in Texas and U.S. history, be sure to devote 20 minutes to the compelling presentation

© ANDY RHODES

the intricately carved door of The Alamo

offered continuously inside the main Alamo building. Without lecturing to or boring the assembled visitors, Alamo experts discuss the complex series of events leading to the famous battle. From the site's original role as Mission San Antonio de Valero, established in 1718 to teach Catholicism and protect Spain's colonial interests, to its subsequent incarnations as a hospital and cavalry post, The Alamo's historic context begins to take shape. A detailed and engaging explanation of the specific occurrences leading to the March 1836 Alamo siege make for gripping drama, from thousands of Mexican troops descending on San Antonio raising a red flag of "no quarter" (no mercy), to the few hundred Texans and Tejanos valiantly proclaiming to fight until death "in the cause of liberty and humanity," to the final, brutal early-morning hand-to-hand combat, the vivid presentation is an essential component of an Alamo visit. By the time it's over, the walls seem even more sacred, and the already-buoyant sense of Texas pride becomes even more inflated.

The Alamo site was in pretty bad shape in 1905 when the Texas Legislature entrusted the care and maintenance of the grounds to the Daughters of the Republic of Texas. Since then, this nonprofit group has done an adequate job of retaining the site's status as a cultural icon. In addition to the famous mission building, The Alamo grounds include the **Long Barrack Museum,** featuring a small theater with a fascinating film about The Alamo and an impressive collection of historic artifacts (weapons, vernacular items, and models), a lush courtyard with a well dating to the mission era (1724–93), an informative timeline displayed on large outdoor panels, and a jam-packed gift shop befitting of a worldwide tourist destination. You'll find the entire spectrum of visitors—from old women in head wraps to young boys in coonskin caps—making their pilgrimage to remember The Alamo.

◖ San Antonio Missions National Historical Park

The extraordinary San Antonio missions stand proudly among common urban scenery. The five structures (including The Alamo) were built during the era of Peter the Great and Johann Sebastian Bach, and serve as testament to the important role Texas played in international history during the early 18th century. By helping expand Spain's religious and secular influence in the New World, the missions became a focal point for European powers and their quest to lay claim to the land that would eventually become Texas.

The first to be developed was San Antonio de Valero (The Alamo), in 1718. As the overachieving older sibling, it went on to achieve much fame and is therefore designated as its own separate historic site. The remaining missions—Concepción, Espada, San José, and San Juan—were established between 1720 and 1731, and offer a fascinating window to the past, particularly in a state where the words *historic structure* conjure up images of Main Street buildings and Victorian homes from the early 1900s.

Way back in 1690, Spain established six

SAN ANTONIO

MISSIONS ACCOMPLISHED

The five fascinating Spanish missions are unlike any other historic structures in Texas. Representing a bygone era of the Lone Star State's storied past, these magnificent structures transport visitors to a time when Native Americans still occupied the land and European powers were staking claims in the New World. The following brief descriptions offer an overview of the individual compounds and their contributions to Texas history.

SAN ANTONIO DE VALERO

Now known as **The Alamo,** this mission was founded in 1718 and was the first to be established on the San Antonio River. Like the other missions, it served to protect the interests of Spain and teach Catholicism; however, it is best known as a fort that was attacked during Texas's War for Independence from Mexico in 1836.

CONCEPCIÓN

The mission **Nuestra Señora de la Purísima Concepción** was relocated from East Texas in 1731, and the church still appears as it did in the mid-1700s, when it served as the mission's center of religious activity. The mission was once covered with colorful geometric patterns on its exterior and interior surfaces, but they have long since faded.

ESPADA

This is the oldest of the original East Texas missions (founded in 1690 as San Francisco de los Tejas). In 1731, the compound was moved to the San Antonio River and renamed **San Antonio de la Espada.** This mission's church appears almost as remote today as it did in the mid-1700s since it's the farthest south from the urban environs of San Antonio.

SAN JOSÉ

Known as the "Queen of the Missions," this compound's enviable size and organization gave it a reputation as being a model of mission life. San José was a major social center, featuring distinctive architecture and plentiful pastures.

SAN JUAN

Mission **San Juan Capistrano** was originally established in East Texas as San José de los Nazonis. In 1731, it was relocated to the San Antonio River and renamed San Juan. Decades later, it became a major regional supplier of agricultural produce thanks to its rich farmlands.

missions in East Texas to help establish its presence in the New World and, while they were at it, convert the area's "savage" Native Americans to Catholicism. Before long, a midway point was needed between the new settlements and the main supply source south of the Rio Grande, so plans were made to construct the new missions along a natural stopping point on a meandering river, where the Spanish often gathered to celebrate the feast of Saint Anthony (San Antonio).

Meanwhile, the missions farther north were struggling due to drought and disease, so several of these settlements relocated to the San Antonio River valley in 1731. From the 1740s through the 1780s, the missions thrived, and the Native American "recruits" hunted, built structures, gardened, cooked, and learned how make soap. Although they were trained to be good Catholics and even adopted many Spanish customs, the Native Americans continued practicing their traditions, typically under the pretext of Catholic festivals.

By the late 1700s, mission life became more difficult, with Apache and Comanche tribes encroaching on Spanish territory, and political maneuvers in Europe threatening the missions' roles. A secret treaty involving Napoleon Bonaparte was apparently the last straw for the missions, eventually resulting in the famed Louisiana Purchase to support his military ventures in Europe.

By this point, the missions were beginning to decline for other reasons—European diseases decimated much of the Native American population, and acculturation of local tribes made the missions' original objectives become obsolete. In 1824, the missions were secularized, the land was redistributed, and the chapels in the complexes transferred to the secular clergy.

◖ San Antonio River Walk

It's easy for people to dismiss the River Walk (210/227-4262, www.thesanantonioriverwalk. com), referred to by some locals as the *Paseo del Rio*, as a crowded, touristy attraction. And it is, to a degree. But like many things touristy, there's a reason people flock to this location, and it's not just to spend money on unnecessary trinkets and experience unnatural thrills. This is a genuinely festive environment punctuated by bouts of laughter, spiky yucca plants, and riverboats packed with people wearing silly hats and sunglasses. The immediate access to so many different types of authentic high-quality Texas food is alone worth the visit.

The unifying force is a scenic horseshoe-shaped stretch of the San Antonio River, flanked by tropical foliage, cobblestone walkways, and a fascinating collection of shops, restaurants, and nightclubs. The whole blissfully detached scene exists a level below the busy streets and sidewalks used by bustling businesspeople, allowing River Walkers to operate in their own private San Antonio.

For those looking to stretch their legs beyond the main loop, the River Walk extends throughout downtown, linking many of the city's main tourist attractions, including Alamo Plaza, La Villita, Hemisfair Park, the King William Historic District, and Rivercenter. The River Walk also plays a major role in the city's annual Fiesta San Antonio, with a river parade featuring flower-bedecked "floats" that actually float on the water.

In 2009, a $72 million overhaul doubled the size of the River Walk by transforming a previously unsightly area north of the existing section into a manicured waterway. Referred to as the museum reach of the River Walk, this 1.5-mile jaunt features footpaths lined with artwork, benches, and fountains en route to attractions upriver, including the San Antonio Museum of Art and the magnificent Pearl Brewery redevelopment project.

The modern-day version of the River Walk began taking shape in 1961, when one of the companies responsible for designing Disneyland drafted a plan recommending the buildings be developed with riverside access in an early Texas or Mexican colonial style. Soon after, the city developed a River Walk District, and the parks department completed a major landscape project by adding 17,000 assorted tress, shrubs, vines, and ground cover. Next came the hotels, which brought the pedestrian traffic that boosted the restaurants and retail establishments along the nearly three miles of scenic riverside walkways. Before long, word spread across the state and country about this distinctive attraction, annually drawing hundreds of thousands of visitors, mainly business conventioneers and families, to its tree-lined banks.

One of the most popular ways to experience the River Walk is via boat. To get on board, contact **Rio San Antonio Cruises** (210/244-5700 or 800/417-4139, www.riosanantonio. com, $8.25 adults, $6 seniors, $2 children 1–5). The boat rides are about 30 minutes long and include a narrated description of sites along the San Antonio River. Visit the website for boat stations and ticket counters.

Institute of Texan Cultures

The 50,000-square-foot gargantuan structure located just east of downtown is the magnificent Institute of Texan Cultures (801 E. Durango Blvd., 210/458-2300, www.texancultures.utsa.edu, Mon.–Sat. 9 A.M.–5 P.M., Sun. noon–5 P.M., $8 adults, $7 seniors, $6 children 3–12). The building's main ground-floor exhibit reveals that Texans are a remarkably diverse bunch, with cultural and ethnic backgrounds from all corners of the globe. Although more than 250 distinct ethnic and cultural groups currently exist in the Lone

Star State, merely 26 are showcased in the exhibits. A large sign announcing each group's name hangs from the ceiling, and the display cases below feature objects and artifacts representing the culture, with a focus on their Texas connection. An enormous globe at the entryway not-so-subtly conveys the message that Texas, like the rest of the country, is a big ol' melting pot (or perhaps a really flavorful stew or chili).

The institute offers other resources in the halls above and beyond the massive main exhibit space. They include a research library, which contains books, oral histories, and an extensive photo archive devoted to Texas's diverse cultural background, and offices related to special events, most notably the annual Texas Folklife Festival. This immensely entertaining multicultural event is held annually during the second weekend in June, when people from across the globe are recognized and honored via ethnic food, music, dance, arts, and crafts as a way of celebrating Texas's unique heritage. The 22-acre institute is also home to a museum store and a living-history area known as the Back 40.

San Antonio Museum of Art

A world-class facility truly befitting of the nation's seventh-largest city is the San Antonio Museum of Art (200 W. Jones Ave., 210/978-8100, www.samuseum.org, Tues. 10 A.M.–9 P.M., Wed.–Sat. 10 A.M.–5 P.M., Sun. noon–6 P.M., $8 adults, $7 seniors, $5 students and military, $3 children. Free Tues. 4–8 P.M.). The museum contains a fascinating collection of artwork from across the world, representing all eras and formats. It's perhaps best known for its distinct and colossal holdings in Latin American art. Located in the Nelson A. Rockefeller Center for Latin American Art (the former vice president provided his extensive collection to the museum), the facility includes an overview of more than 3,000 years of creative offerings from Mexico, Central and South America, and countries of the Caribbean. The museum's pre-Columbian collection is particularly fascinating,

A historic mansion houses the McNay Art Museum.

with stone, ceramic, and metal objects from early Latin American groups as well as more recent works from the Maya, Aztec, Zapotec, and Inca cultures.

Another noteworthy museum section is the Egyptian gallery, where an enormous statue of the goddess Sekhmet from circa 1350 B.C. greets visitors. Ceramics and stone objects testify to the longevity of the artwork (many of these beautiful objects were crafted by human hands more than 3,000 years ago), and the fascination continues with the museum's remarkable Greek and Roman art.

McNay Art Museum

Well worth the five-mile jaunt north of downtown is the remarkable McNay Art Museum (6000 N. New Braunfels Ave., 210/824-5368, www.mcnayart.org, Tues., Wed., and Fri. 10 A.M.–4 P.M.; Thurs. 10 A.M.–9 P.M.; Sat. 10 A.M.–5 P.M.; Sun. noon–5 P.M.; $8 adults; $5 seniors, students, and military; children 12 and under free). The museum is named for Ohio-born heiress Marion Koogler, who moved to San Antonio in 1926 and lived in the 24-room Spanish Colonial Revival mansion that would become the core of the museum. Marion collected 19th- and 20th-century European and American paintings and Southwestern art, ultimately leaving her collection of more than 700 works, her house, the surrounding 23 acres, and an endowment to establish "the first museum of modern art in Texas." The McNay opened its doors to the public in 1954 and has since expanded to nearly 20,000 works, including Medieval and Renaissance art, and an impressive collection of 19th–21st-century European and American paintings, sculptures, and photographs. The 19th- and 20th-century paintings are especially notable, with famous names and images beckoning around each corner of the mansion—don't be surprised to encounter a Picasso, Cézanne, Matisse, Van Gogh, or Pissarro. Be sure to spend time strolling through the magnificent and lush Spanish-influenced courtyard, and check ahead to see if the museum is hosting a compelling exhibit like the New Image Sculpture.

© ANDY RHODES

the King William Historic District

SAN ANTONIO

King William Historic District

To get a sense of what San Antonio's high society was like at the turn of the previous century, take a walking tour through the King William Historic District (located just south of downtown on the east side of the San Antonio River). Stately and ornate Victorian, Greek Revival, and Italianate homes stand on pleasant tree-lined streets in this 25-square-block area, one of the first Texas neighborhoods to be listed on the National Register of Historic Places. Even on a hot day, it's worth taking a walking tour of the neighborhood (the enormous trees provide a shady canopy over most streets), guided by a handy brochure available at the **San Antonio Conservation Society**'s headquarters at the northern edge of the neighborhood (107 King William St., 210/224-6163, www.saconservation.org, Mon.–Thurs. 9:30 A.M.–3:30 P.M.).

Although a majority of the district's homes are privately owned or renovated as bed-and-breakfasts, two significant sites are open to the public for tours. The 1859 **Guenther House** (205 E. Guenther St., 210/227-1061, www.guentherhouse.com, Mon.–Sat. 8 A.M.–4 P.M., Sun. 8 A.M.–3 P.M.) is the outstanding home of the family that founded Pioneer Flour Mills—you can't miss the gigantic factory behind it with *Pioneer* on the tower. The house features a small yet informative museum of milling history and a popular restaurant. A block north is **Steves Homestead** (509 King William St., 210/225-5924, daily 10 A.M.–4:15 P.M., $6 admission 12 and older), a stunning three-story 1876 mansion. Guided tours showcase the home's ornate furnishings as well as the carriage house, servants' quarters, and the city's first indoor swimming pool.

San Fernando Cathedral

The magnificent San Fernando Cathedral (115 Main Plaza, 210/227-1297, www.sfcathedral.org, Mon.–Fri. 8 A.M.–5 P.M., Sat. 8 A.M.–7 P.M., Sun. 8 A.M.–6:30 P.M.) was organized in 1731 by a group of Canary Island families and has been a centerpiece of San Antonio ever since. This stunning building went through several incarnations before

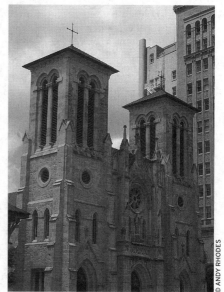

the San Fernando Cathedral

© ANDY RHODES

construction on its current Gothic Revival appearance was consecrated in 1873. The enormous cathedral has a distinctive European feel, with lofty Gothic arches, a gilded 24-foot-tall altar, and gigantic stained-glass windows. People gather at the church throughout the day for tours, to light candles, pray in the pews, or simply sit in wonder as they gaze upon the serene surroundings. The cathedral doesn't function exclusively as a Catholic church; rather, it bills itself as "a center of unity and harmony for all the God-loving people of San Antonio and beyond," drawing more than 5,000 parishioners to Mass every week.

The Spanish Governor's Palace

Just around the corner from the cathedral is the circa 1749 Spanish Governor's Palace (105 Military Plaza, 210/224-0601, Tues.–Sat. 9 A.M.–5 P.M., Sun. 10 A.M.–5 P.M., $4 adults, $3 military/seniors, $2 children ages 7–13), which served as the headquarters and residence of the presidio of San Antonio de Bexar's captain, the ranking representative of

© TEXAS HISTORICAL COMMISSION

the Spanish Governor's Palace

the king of Spain in the absence of the governor. The National Geographic Society has called the palace "the most beautiful building in San Antonio," and although it doesn't conjure up images of princes and turrets, the building's three-foot-thick stuccoed stone walls are particularly striking, as are its eclectic mix of historic furniture and artifacts. The palace's highlight, by far, is the magnificent courtyard, a natural patio with a canopy of live oaks stretching over lush tropical plants. Chirping birds, a soothing fountain, and gentle breezes transport visitors to an oasis far away from the surrounding urban environment.

SeaWorld of Texas

When you need a break from Texas history, head directly to SeaWorld (10500 SeaWorld Dr., 800/700-7786, www.seaworld.com, hours vary by season, $50–59). This 250-acre park offers a perfect destination on a hot summer day—water rides, water shows, and water games will keep the entire family entertained and slightly refreshed. The main attraction is the activity at Shamu Stadium, where star Shamu and several other killer whales perform impressive tricks—leaping to great heights, splashing the audience, and serving as surfboards—all to an accompanying overwrought choreographed soundtrack. The spectacle may be a bit over-the-top, but witnessing the whales' grace and power is an ultimately rewarding experience.

One of the park's most popular summertime attractions is the Lost Lagoon area, a mini water park featuring a giant wave machine, a mellow tube ride, and several twisty water slides. Kids 1–6 years old will love Shamu's Happy Harbor, a small area in the center of the park with several rides, a large ship festooned with climbing and crawling features, an infant play area, and a water zone with every kind of soaking device imaginable. Adults can have their fun in the sun, too, by experiencing SeaWorld's various water rides and roller coasters. Be sure to smile sweetly (or hold back your lunch) at the bottom of the first big hill since a camera captures everyone's expressions for fun souvenir keepsakes.

Of course, animals are a featured attraction at SeaWorld, particularly at the exhibit areas and shows featuring sea lions and dolphins. The penguin habitat with its replicated Antarctic environment is especially fascinating. Throughout the park families will also find (or avoid) typical amusement park fare such as midway-style games, snack stands, and gift shops.

Casa Navarro

The smooth whitewash stucco blanketing Casa Navarro (228 S. Laredo St., 210/226-4801, www.visitcasanavarro.com, Tues.–Sun. 9 A.M.–4 P.M.) doesn't quite mesh with the blocky correctional facilities nearby. Once inside, however, this cozy home of Tejano patriot Jose Antonio Navarro radiates a charm not found in the urban fortresses beyond the house's thick adobe walls. Navarro's home reflects his simple yet refined environment, including interpretive panels, Texas law books, a rustic desk with an inkwell, and other period furnishings offering insight about his family and city during the mid- to late 1800s. Most of the home was constructed circa 1848, and its acquisition by the Texas Historical Commission has helped raise the profile of the deservingly significant complex. Navarro's service to Texas is legendary—he served in the legislature under Mexico, the Republic of Texas, and the state of Texas, and he signed the Texas Declaration of Independence in 1836 representing San Antonio. Most historians consider Navarro to be the first Tejano to write about Texas history. Of note: Casa Navarro was undergoing extensive renovation throughout most of 2011; please call in advance to ensure exhibits are open.

The Witte Museum

The Witte Museum (3801 Broadway St., 210/357-1900, www.wittemuseum.org, Mon.–Sat. 10 A.M.–5 P.M., until 8 P.M. on Tues., Sun. noon–5 P.M., $8 adults, $7 seniors, $6 children 4–11) focuses on South Texas history and science, and features impressive permanent and rotating galleries and hands-on exhibits. This

COMO SE LLAMA?

In Spanish classes across the United States, one of the first things most students learn is the question "*Como se llama?*" ("What's your name?"). The wording literally translates as "What do you call yourself?" a question many Mexican Americans are being asked (and asking themselves) these days thanks to the various categorical terminology being used.

San Antonio's Museo Alameda has been credited as a media source to help clear up some of the confusion. Although Alameda representatives claimed it's ultimately up to the individual to determine what they want to be called, they offered the following definitions with the stipulation that ethnic identifiers vary by region:

- **Mexican American:** A U.S. citizen of Mexican descent whose roots trace to the racial mixture that resulted from the 16th-century conquest of Mexico.

- **Hispanic:** A term created by the U.S. Census Bureau to denote people of various Latin American and Spanish origins.

- **Latino:** A U.S. resident with cultural and historical ties to Latin America and the Caribbean.

- **Chicano:** A generational designation rooted in the idea of self-determination. The term arose from the civil rights movement in the 1960s.

- **Tejano:** A Texan of Mexican descent.

is an ideal place to bring the kids—they're omnipresent at this museum, especially during school hours—to learn about Texas culture. Adults will benefit from the experience, too. Not surprisingly, dinosaurs take up a big portion of the ground floor, along with other animals and fascinating aspects of nature. The second floor is devoted to permanent exhibits, including displays related to mummies and the

4,000-year-old rock art of Texas's Lower Pecos region. Outside are several historic buildings and, top on the list for kids, a four-story "tree house" featuring science experiments, demonstrations, hands-on activities, and an observation deck overlooking the San Antonio River.

La Villita Historic District

The downtown La Villita Historic District (bound by Durango, Navarro, and Alamo Sts. and the San Antonio River, 210/207-7235, www.lavillita.com, most shops open daily 10 A.M.–6 P.M.) reflects the Spanish, European, and Anglo influences that helped shape San Antonio's history. Once the site of a Coahuiltecan Indian village, La Villita subsequently thrived as a residential area containing Mexican houses of caliche block or stucco-covered brick and German (and later Swiss and French) vernacular structures before the neighborhood deteriorated into a run-down barrio in the early 1900s. In 1939, La Villita was restored by the city, and, following another major renovation in the early 1980s, the neighborhood now houses scores of tourist-friendly boutiques, art galleries, and restaurants. One of the most popular attractions is the historic "Little Church," a 19th-century stone chapel that frequently hosts weddings and festival activities.

San Antonio Central Library

Libraries typically aren't tourist attractions, unless they're historic or contain rare volumes of work. The exception is San Antonio's Central Library (600 Soledad St., 210/207-2500, Mon.–Thurs. 9 A.M.–9 P.M., Fri.–Sat. 9 A.M.–5 P.M., Sun. 11 A.M.–5 P.M.). Known around town as "Big Red," the library is indeed enormous (240,000 square feet) and dons the color of a red enchilada. For these reasons, it's generated much attention (not always good) and is considered one of the city's most important architectural accomplishments. The six-floor library was designed by renowned Mexican architect Ricardo Legorreta and rests on the footprint of an old Sears department store. Legorreta used natural light, color, water, and some unexpected angles and sight lines to create this urban cathedral of knowledge, which also features an intriguing mural by San Antonio artist Jesse Treviño, depicting a slice of life in the city during World War II.

Six Flags Fiesta Texas Amusement Park

One of the city's biggest draws for family fun is Six Flags Fiesta Texas (at the intersection of I-10 W. and Loop 1604, 210/697-5050, www.sixflags.com, Mon.–Sat. 10 A.M.–9 P.M., Sun. 11 A.M.–9 P.M., late May–late Aug.; weekend hours vary in off-season, $55 adults, $40 children under 48 inches). Most of the rides and attractions at this 200-acre facility are standard amusement park fare, but Six Flags' nine roller coasters are the main draw, with the "floorless" Superman Krypton Coaster generating the most buzz, along with the rapidly rotating Tony Hawk's Big Spin. The old wooden-coaster standby, the Rattler, still remains a crowd pleaser, even though park officials had to reduce the length of its first downward plunge after too many complaints about it being "too intimidating and aggressive." The park contains several Texas-themed areas with shows and rides related to different aspects of the Lone Star State's history (German heritage, oil boomtowns, 1950s small towns), and the entire complex is partially surrounded by 100-foot cliffs from a former limestone quarry. Six Flags Fiesta Texas also operates a water park on the grounds (included in the admission fee) called White Water Bay, which features water slides, family raft rides, and a lazy river tube ride. The park also stages a variety of shows and concerts.

San Antonio Zoo

With all the other attractions San Antonio has to offer, visitors often overlook the worthy San Antonio Zoo (3903 N. St. Mary's St., 210/734-7184, www.sa-zoo.org, open 9 A.M.–5 P.M. daily, $10 adults, $8 seniors and children ages 3–11). The 56-acre zoo, located among the cliffs of an old limestone quarry in Brackenridge Park, is home to more 3,500 animals representing 600 species. The facility's extensive exhibits include an impressive bird collection (make a point to visit the penguins), an African antelope collection, a monkey and ape area, and the only American exhibit of the endangered whooping crane. The children's area, called the Tiny Tot Nature Spot, is a great place for kids under 5 years old to get out of their strollers (and shoes and socks) to interact with the natural world by digging up worms and bugs and occasionally feeding them to non-threatening animals like the guinea pig.

San Antonio Children's Museum

On hot summer days when an entire scorching afternoon at Six Flags or SeaWorld sounds unbearable, there's a cool indoor alternative at the San Antonio Children's Museum (305 E. Houston St., 210/212-4453, www.sakids.org, Mon.–Fri. 9 A.M.–5 P.M., Sat. 9 A.M.–6 P.M., Sun. noon–5 P.M., $7 admission ages 2 and up). With more than 80 exhibits to experience, kids will be entertained most of the day, often far outlasting their parents' patience. Fortunately, the interactive activities are well maintained and even educational. Highlights include the miniature bulldozer that kids can actually operate to some degree (a dream come true for any three-year old and their father), a large supermarket area where kids can play customer and cashier, a music stage that captures future *American Idol* stars on video monitors, a kid-sized airplane complete with knobs and buttons in the cockpit, and several areas (Tot Spot, Power Ball Hall) for toddlers to play with blocks, spheres, and soft sculptures.

Blue Star Contemporary Art Center

Located in an enormous former warehouse complex on the city's south side is the eye-catching and thought-provoking Blue Star Contemporary Art Center (116 Blue Star St., 210/227-6960, www.bluestarart.org, Tues.–Sat. noon–6 P.M., Thurs. until 8 P.M., free admission). Anchored by the Contemporary Art Center, Blue Star embodies the word *eclectic*—from performance art to trendy jewelry to avant-garde photography and everything in between. Although the exterior of the complex is somewhat uninspiring, visitors are intrigued as soon as they step inside and are greeted by colorful, bizarre, and beautiful artwork in various mediums. Local and nationally known artists grace the walls, floors, and halls of the many distinctive galleries throughout the complex.

ENTERTAINMENT AND EVENTS

San Antonio's music scene may not get the same attention as Austin's, but it should, especially considering its eclectic mix of wide-ranging styles—conjunto, country, blues, punk, and even German polkas. For a truly authentic taste of the San Antonio's culture, however, visit the city during one of the annual festivals, where locals celebrate the many spices of life their community has to offer.

Performing Arts

San Antonio doesn't have an abundance of professional performing arts groups, which is odd for the seventh-largest city in the country, but not surprising considering many of its residents prefer their cultural experiences to be country or conjunto dancing. For a highbrow evening, however, it doesn't get much better than the **San Antonio Symphony** (performances held at the Majestic Theatre, 224 E. Houston St., 210/554-1010, www.sasymphony.org). The symphony's season runs from late September until June and features a diverse mix of classical, pops, family, and community programs, often with high-profile guest artists.

Long considered the crown jewel of San Antonio's performing arts venues is the stunning **Majestic Theatre** (224 E. Houston St., 210/226-5700, www.majesticempire.com). This magnificent 1929 facility was originally constructed as an "atmospheric" palace for vaudeville shows and the emerging motion-picture trend. It now serves as the home of the San Antonio Symphony and hosts an eclectic schedule of touring shows, from Broadway productions to world-renowned concert artists. A recent schedule of events reflects this mix:

Messiah, A Tribute to the Music of John Denver, Homage to Mexico, and *Young People's Concert: the Anatomy of an Orchestra.*

The Majestic features an alluring interior described as "a Mediterranean amphitheater in a Moorish-Baroque style." The main lobby includes ornately decorated plaster sculptures and a colossal ornamented chandelier, and the elaborate auditorium contains colorfully illuminated alcoves and grottos topped off by a simulated night sky, complete with twinkling stars and floating clouds.

Country Music Venues
LIVE MUSIC
Though it's a bit out of town—about 15 miles northwest toward Bandera—there's no other place in or near San Antonio quite as authentic as **Floore Country Store** (14492 Old Bandera Rd., 210/695-8827, www.liveatfloores.com). A sign outside this historic honky-tonk reads

Willie Nelson Every Sat. Nite, and although those days are long gone, the Red-Headed Stranger still makes a point of playing semi-regular gigs at this big ol' Texas dance hall. The walls are covered with photos of other country legends who have graced the stage (Ernest Tubb, Hank Williams), and the venue still hosts contemporary and classic country acts such as Lyle Lovett, Dwight Yoakum, Jack Ingram, and Bruce Robison.

Another legendary honky-tonk on the outskirts of town is the **Hangin' Tree Saloon** (just northeast of San Antonio in the community of Bracken at 18424 2nd St., 210/651-5812, www. hangintree.com), which opened in 1915 as a two-lane bowling alley for nine-pin, a game popular in German pioneer communities. In 1989, mythically named Texan Big John Oaks converted the bowling alley into a roadhouse honky-tonk, using wood from the lanes to construct the bar. The stage stands where the pins

THE SAN ANTONIO SOUND

Ask a Texas musician about the San Antonio sound, and many will mention heavy metal. Over the past few decades, the city has developed a reputation for rocking hard, serving as a regular tour stop for bands in black leather.

Rewind 50 years, and you'll hear the city's best-known sound is much sweeter. Dubbed "Chicano soul" or the "West Side sound," the music is tremendously enjoyable yet tragically overlooked.

Emerging from the late-1950s influences of rhythm and blues and doo-wop, the San Antonio sound captured an innovative blend of soulful Motown-style harmonies and melodies with Mexican-influenced accents from brass and reed instruments. The combination is instantly catchy, and it remains puzzling why the style never caught on much beyond the San Antonio city limits.

One song – Sunny and the Sunglows' "Talk to Me" – found a broader audience, and it peaked at No. 11 on the Billboard charts in September 1963. But similar songs from bands

with quaint names like Danny and the Dreamers, the Royal Jesters, and Little Jr. Jesse and the Teardrops were mostly unknown.

Though this Tejano take on R&B music never gained a national following, the Mexican influence on pop music made a splash several years later in California, where acts like Richie Valens ("La Bamba"), the Champs ("Tequila"), and even ? and the Mysterians ("96 Tears") had hit singles. San Antonio's only contribution to the national music scene at the time was the garage-rocker "She's About a Mover" by the Sir Douglas Quintet.

Still, the city's Chicano soul movement was celebrated locally, and the style has experienced a resurgence and newfound appreciation thanks to music blogs and online radio programs. For those interested in lending an ear to these delightful sounds, several sweet-sounding compilations were released in the early 2000s – pick up a copy of *Chicano Soul: San Antonio's Westside Sound* Vols. 1-3.

were once placed. This classic venue hosts local country bands on the weekends and occasionally features well-known regional acts such as Johnny Bush, Gary P. Nunn, and Johnny Rodriguez. To get there, take FM 2252 north from Bracken, turn right at the first road past the railroad tracks, go four blocks, and then turn left.

It doesn't book country acts exclusively, but there's still a lot of rustic charm to **Casbeers** (1150 S. Alamo, 210/271-7791, www.casbeers. com), a fairly small venue (relocated to a historic downtown church) that's known almost as much for its tasty food as its quality music. Every seat in the house offers a close-up view of the stage, and the church's acoustics are spectacular, which works out nicely when popular acts such as Alejandro Escovedo, The Mescaleros, and Mary Cutrufello perform. Casbeers features live music nearly five nights a week, and their Sunday-morning Gospel Brunch is an ideal way to ease into the day. On another food-related note, Casbeers's downstairs café offers some of San Antonio's most popular onion rings and burgers.

DANCING

For those who'd rather have their conversations drowned out by prerecorded sounds instead of a live band, San Antonio has several popular clubs that cater to the country and western crowd. The biggest of the bunch is **Midnight Rodeo** (12260 Nacogdoches Rd., 210/655-0040, www.midnightrodeosanantonio.com, closed Mon.–Tues.), an enormous complex drawing singles and couples from across South Texas. People get gussied up for a night out at the Midnight Rodeo, meaning they have their pressed jeans, Western shirts, and best boots for line dancing and two-stepping to songs from current and classic country artists.

Another heavy hitter is **Cowboys Dance Hall** (3030 NE Loop 410, 210/646-9378), which features a cavernous dance floor with a bonus: bull riding. Saturday nights feature a rodeo with live bull riding, and urban cowboys and cowgirls can try their eight seconds of luck on the mechanical bull at any time. The music

is the big draw here, and live shows (including a bona fide house band) have thankfully replaced DJs in recent years.

Conjunto and Tejano Clubs

San Antonio's conjunto clubs, which specialize in accordion-based Tejano dance music, are typically found in neighborhood bars that appear unassuming during the week but get mighty spicy on weekend nights. In fact, two of the city's most popular venues are sports bars that just happen to have large dance floors and disco balls for the occasion. One of the best known is **Arturo's** (3310 S. Zarzamora St., 210/923-0177), which features local and regional bands most weekend nights. Another is **Reptilez Sports Bar** (5418 W. Old U.S. Hwy. 90, 210/433-5552), where conjunto reigns on Sunday, thanks to the bouncy beats of house band Fred Saldana y Los Camaroneros. Other established venues include the tiny yet colorful **Salute!** (2801 N. St. Mary's St., 210/732-5307, www.saluteinternationalbar.com) and the occasionally rowdy **Cool Arrows** (1025 Nogalitos St., 210/227-5130).

River Walk Bars

The River Walk is a touristy area by design, so it's not surprising that the bars here lack some scruffy neighborhood charm. Still, when you're out on the town in a big city, it's often nice to have a slick place to enjoy a fancy drink and check out the nightlife. One of the best places to accomplish this along the river is the swanky **V Bar** (150 E. Houston St., 210/227-9700), located on the second floor of the alluring Hotel Valencia. Shimmery beaded curtains and silky couches give the place an air of sophistication, and the sprawling scene—particularly the inviting stone terrace overlooking the River Walk—makes for a romantic yet vibrant experience.

Not quite as chic yet equally savory is **Havana** (1015 Navarro St., 210/222-2008), at the Havana Riverwalk Inn. This is an ideal place to mellow out on a soft leather couch with some light jazz music and a heavy martini. The tapas are worth ordering, particularly the empanadas, or if you're in the mood for dessert, consider the handmade chocolate sampler.

Those not interested in getting their swank on should head to **Howl at the Moon** (111 W. Crockett St., 210/212-4770), a raucous dueling piano bar where tourists regularly let loose with the abandon of being anonymous in an unknown city. Patrons "sing" along with their favorite tunes (think "Sweet Caroline," "Crocodile Rock," and, of course, "Piano Man") as they're pounded out on the ivories along with some good-natured banter. Complement the boisterous scene with a Jell-O shot or fuzzy navel.

Downtown Dance Clubs and Lounges

San Antonio's Latino culture takes center stage at **Azuca** (713 S. Alamo St., 210/225-5550), a restaurant by day and bar by night. Arrive around 10 and take advantage of both—the classic Latin American fare and contemporary dance scene. Have a drink at the Nuevo Latino bar and shake a leg on the dance floor. Nearby is the slightly upscale yet decidedly low-key **Bohanan's Bar** (221 E. Houston St., 210/271-7472), the lounge associated with an adjacent steak house. The patio is a perfect place to chill out on a warm summer evening, or belly up to the long black granite bar for a hearty cocktail. Just down the block is the trendy **Suede Lounge** (231 E. Houston St., 210/485-1100). This is a place to see and be seen, but since it lacks pretension, the atmosphere is refreshingly comfortable. Leave the flip-flops and ball caps at home, however, since Suede enforces a fairly strict dress code (to be safe, guys should wear collared shirts and long pants).

Events

SPRING

The winters aren't too harsh in San Antonio, but that doesn't stop people from enthusiastically celebrating the warmer spring weather with festivals and gatherings. One of the city's first major annual events, **Remembering the Alamo Weekend** (210/273-1730), is held the first weekend of March. A stirring sunrise

ceremony honors the Texans who died at the siege of The Alamo, and much of the daytime activity involves living history reenactments, music, demonstrations, and food. Another distinctive event in March is the St. Patrick's Day **River Parade** (210/273-1730, www.thesanantonioriverwalk.com). City officials use 35 pounds of environmentally safe green dye to tint the San Antonio River the color o' the Irish and rechristen it River Shannon. Residents and visitors celebrate Celtic culture throughout the weekend with a pub crawl, river parade, and Irish music and dance.

The city's biggest and best annual celebration, **Fiesta San Antonio** (210/227-5191, www.fiesta-sa.org), is held in April. This massive 10-day event is the cultural highlight of the year for the city and the 3.5 million people who attend the festivities, which range from colorful parades to fashion shows to art exhibits, concerts, and a legendary oyster bake. The pageants and parties are important social events, and the carnivals and galas celebrate the city's proud Latino heritage.

SUMMER

Another major event drawing nearly a million people annually is the **Texas Folklife Festival** (at the Institute of Texan Cultures, 801 S. Bowie, 210/458-2224, www.texancultures.utsa.edu), held each June. This event celebrates the Lone Star State's cultural diversity through art, crafts, music, and plenty of amazing food. Cultures not always associated with Texas proudly represent the state each year, including Scotland, China, Norway, India, Greece, and the Canary Islands.

September is still summertime in San Antonio, and the biggest cultural events of the month are related to **Fiestas Patrias,** particularly Mexican Independence Day, also referred to as Diez y Seis (for September 16). Celebrations including dances, food booths, and carnivals take place at Market Square, La Villita, and Guadalupe Plaza.

FALL AND WINTER

Those in the San Antonio vicinity on

November 2 shouldn't be afraid to take part in the events of **El Dia de los Muertos** (Day of the Dead). This Mexican custom welcomes back departed family members and friends for one day through offerings (skulls made of sugar, marigolds), parades (many participants dress as skeletons), and grave decoration. Call 210/432-1896 for details about specific event information.

The Christmas season in San Antonio officially kicks off with the **Holiday River Parade and Lighting Ceremony** (210/227-4262) on the Friday after Thanksgiving. More than 122,000 colorful lights are simultaneously lit, bathing the River Walk in bright festive hues, while decorated floats glide along the sparkling water.

This is Texas after all, so San Antonio residents proudly head 'em up and move 'em out to the **Stock Show and Rodeo** (3201 E. Houston St., www.sarodeo.com) for two weeks in early February. All the traditional events are here—calf roping, barrel racing, bull riding—as well as popular children's' events such as the calf scramble and mutton bustin' (sheep riding).

SHOPPING
River Walk

The River Walk is truly on the beaten path, so it shouldn't come as a surprise that the shopping options are run-of-the mill tourist spots offering T-shirts, knickknacks, overpriced art, and decorative furnishings. For some reason, the most popular shopping experience along the River Walk is the **Rivercenter Mall** (849 E. Commerce St., 210/225-0000, www.shoprivercenter.com), a three-story structure that offers a cool respite on hot days, but that's about the only refreshing thing here. Rivercenter contains all the shops and food options found at most malls across the country, but there are a couple distinguishing features—the Rio San Antonio River Cruises depart from a "lagoon" on the ground level, and the IMAX theater showcases an Alamo movie to complement the real deal just around the corner.

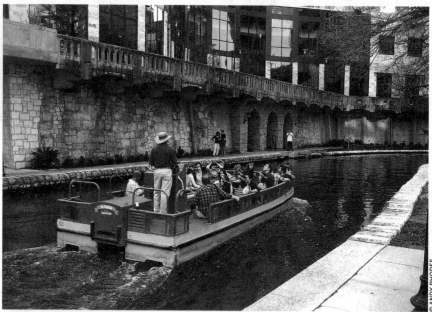

a barge on the San Antonio River along the River Walk

© ANDY RHODES

Market Square

For a more authentic San Antonio shopping experience than the River Walk, head about six blocks west to Market Square (514 W. Commerce St., 210/207-8600), referred to as the largest Mexican marketplace outside of Mexico. This bustling pedestrian area has a south-of-the-border appearance, with roaming mariachis and hordes of street vendors selling pottery, blankets, handmade crafts, and authentic Mexican food. Speaking of food—a trip to Market Square, also referred to as *El Mercado* by locals, would be incomplete without stopping by **Mi Tierra Bakery and Cafe** (218 Produce Row, 210/225-1262, www.mitierracafe.com). Whether you're in the mood for a sweet snack of their famous *pan dulce* or a hearty meal—everything from huevos rancheros to charbroiled steak—this 24-hour establishment is a must. Next door is the welcoming Mexican craft shop **Los Pueblitos** (202 Produce Row, 210/212-4898, www.lospueblitos.com). This stylish two-story building is packed with colorful clothing and Latin American objects.

La Villita

Falling somewhere between the River Walk and Market Square (tourist-wise, not geographically) is La Villita (418 Villita St., 210/207-8610, www.lavillita.com, daily 10 A.M.–6 P.M.). Located adjacent to the River Walk, La Villita is known as much for its interesting heritage as its shopping opportunities, which run the gamut from trendy boutiques to upscale galleries to comfy cafés. The vernacular architecture adds a charming appeal to this "little village," as do the working artisans—glass blowers, pottery spinners, and the like—who create their wares for all to see. One of the more popular shops is **Casa Manos Alegres** (418 Villita St. #600, 210/224-5107), offering Mexican and Guatemalan imports such as enormous colorful papier-mâché animals, quaint woodcarvings, and pottery. Another intriguing shop is **The Village Gallery** (502 Villita St., 210/226-0404), specializing in handmade stoneware and porcelain pottery. One of the best places to eat lunch in La Villita is **La Villita Cafe** (418 Villita St. #900, 210/223-4700), which serves fresh sandwiches and frosty ice cream.

Mexican Goods

Since Market Square is one of the largest Mexican markets outside of Mexico, it shouldn't come as a surprise that it's home to several of San Antonio's best Mexican import shops. Visitors looking for Mexican goods—everything from popular *guayaberas* (the short-sleeved, open-collared shirts worn in most tropical locales) to copper sinks and tin ornaments to Mexican wrestling masks—have plenty to choose from around here. For the basics, head to **Perales Mexican Imports** (210/223-4802) or **Naturaleza** (210/227-9254). For something unique, drop by **Aztec Mexican Imports** (888/522-8434, www.old-mexicoinc.com), which specializes in *talavera* goods. *Talavera* is a white glazed ceramic with simple or colorfully decorated designs on everything from plates and bowls to tile and furnishings. The jewelry selection is impressive at **La Perla** (210/299-8108), and shoppers can find sterling silver jewelry, Latin American embroidered clothing, and handcrafted products at **Cozumel Arts & Crafts** (210/228-0445).

Western Wear

In a city famous for its Western heritage, it's quite a compliment to be considered a highly respected boot maker. Such is the case with **Lucchese** (255 E. Basse Rd., 210/822-2177, www.lucchese.com), which claims to have outfitted "all the great cowboys, including Gene Autry and John Wayne" with their handsome boots. This fancy footwear has been custom made since 1883 with top-notch leather, lemon-wood pegs, and quality finishing (you can ask for your initials to be stitched or inlayed). These boots take time, but customers claim it's totally worth it—especially considering how many years they'll last. Lucchese has a retail store in the Alamo Quarry Market with stock-sized boots, shirts, cowboy hats, belts, and other Western accessories.

Another local legend is **Little's Boots** (110 Division Ave., 210/923-2221, www.davelittleboots.com), another family operation that's been in business for nearly a century. Little's specializes in custom boot making but also provides special makeups and made-to-measure boots. Customers can choose from a variety of non-PC materials—kangaroo, ostrich, alligator, lizard, and eel—or simply have their worn-out boots repaired here.

If you're on Alamo Plaza, drop by the Menger Hotel to take a gander at the impressive Western apparel at **Silver Spur** (212 Alamo Plaza, 210/472-2210, www.silverspurstore.com). If sparkly things catch your eye, this is the place to go—much of the clothing is embedded with rhinestones and crystals, perfect for a night out on the town. Silver Spur also has a limited selection of clothing for men as well as an extensive jewelry collection, hats, belts, handbags, and other accessories.

Not quite as charming but appealing in its immense size and selection is the chain option of **Shepler's** (two locations: 4911 Whirlwind St., 210/656-3010 and 6201 NW Loop 410, 210/681-8230, www.sheplers.com). These stores are practically warehouses of Western clothing items, including decent yet moderately priced boots, cowboy hats, jeans, shirts, belts, and the obligatory big buckles.

SPORTS AND RECREATION

San Antonio's warm weather throughout most of the year makes it an ideal place for outdoor recreation. The city's biggest claim to sports fame, the four-time NBA champion San Antonio Spurs, play indoors at the raucous AT&T Center, but residents also enjoy attending or participating in sporting events outside, including the Missions minor league baseball team, golfing, hiking, biking, and strolling through the city's colorful gardens.

Mexican Rodeo

Who needs all four major sports leagues in town when you have Mexican rodeo? This exquisite custom captures everything essential about a sporting event—drama, heroics,

compassion, and grace. The **San Antonio Charro Association** (210/846-8757, www.sacharro.com) promotes monthly *charreadas* from March through October. Don't miss seeing the daring and graceful charros in action on horses, bulls, and wild mares. One of the most jaw-droppingly suspenseful acts is *el paso de la muerte* ("the pass of death"), where a charro tries to leap from his own bareback horse to a wild bareback horse (all without reins) and ride it until it stops bucking. The death-defying element? All the while, three other mounted charros are chasing the wild mare around the arena. As if all this weren't enough, sometimes the charros perform this act backward just for show. This event, along with other macho roping and riding feats, are tempered with the beauty and grace of the Escaramuza equestriennes. Check the website for show dates and locations.

Professional Sports

The **San Antonio Spurs** are the city's only professional sports franchise, and they're beloved by most residents. The team was very successful in the '00s, so it's still quite common to see Spurs stickers, banners, T-shirts and hear the chant "Go! Spurs! Go!" across town, especially when they're in the playoffs. In their three decades on the court, the Spurs have won 15 division titles (the most in the NBA during that time), yet they're often frustratingly overlooked as a basketball powerhouse on the national sports scene. The team plays at the AT&T center in northeast San Antonio near the intersection of I-35 and Walters Street. Visit www.nba.com/spurs or call 210/444-5000 for information.

The **San Antonio Missions** are a minor league baseball team in a city that has a major affinity for baseball. Despite efforts to lure a major league team to San Antonio, the only professional outlet for fans is the Missions, which play in the Texas League at the AA level (two below the big leagues) and are affiliated with the San Diego Padres. The team remains a popular draw, with fans regularly filling 6,300-capacity Wolff Stadium just west of town (5757 U.S. Hwy. 90 W.), although a handful in attendance will admit to being there simply to see "Henry the Puffy Taco" race the kids around the bases during the seventh-inning stretch. For more information about the Missions or to find out their schedule of upcoming games (the team plays April through September), visit www.samissions.com or call 210/675-7275.

Golf

Golf is apparently popular everywhere across the country, but in semitropical areas like San Antonio, where the game can be played year-round on fairways lined with palm trees, it's even more of an obsession. The city boasts more than two dozen golf courses—private, public, and municipal—drawing hordes of golfers, often the husbands of wives who spend the day shopping on the River Walk.

For a comprehensive list of courses throughout the city, including directions, ratings, greens fee information, and golfers' comments, visit www.sanantoniogolf.com. Those looking for a scenic and somewhat-challenging round of golf may want to consider the following San Antonio stalwarts.

One of the most popular courses in the region is **The Quarry** (444 E. Basse Rd., 210/824-4500, www.quarrygolf.com), rated one of America's Top State Golf Courses by *Golf Digest* and located just 10 minutes from downtown. The front nine has long, open holes with several water hazards, and the back nine winds through a former rock quarry, with 100-foot walls as a backdrop. Another noteworthy public course near downtown is **Pecan Valley** (4700 Pecan Valley Dr., 210/333-9018, www.pecanvalleygc.com), which, as its name implies, contains groves of giant pecan trees along a scenic winding creek. Locals make regular tee times to take advantage of the challenging course layout and well-maintained grounds.

City Parks and Gardens

One of the city's most pleasant destinations is the inviting **San Antonio Botanical Garden** (555 Funston Pl., 210/207-3250, www.sabot.

org, daily 9 A.M.–5 P.M., $8 adults, $6 seniors/military/students, $5 children ages 3–13). Texas's diverse landscape is well represented here, with native wildflowers, grasses, bushes, and trees demonstrating the variety of foliage in the Lone Star State. Visitors experience individual environments, a large courtyard, and pond. The 33-acre complex also includes a tearoom, gift shop, and impressive conservatory, offering nearly 100,000 square feet of display space, which visitors access through a tunnel leading 16 feet below ground to several greenhouse areas dedicated to tropics, the desert, palms, and ferns.

Another popular expanse of public green space is **Brackenridge Park** (3910 N. St. Mary's St., 210/207-7275, daily 8 A.M.–11 P.M.). This century-old, 344-acre park is a busy place on weekends, but there's plenty to do, so crowds are well dispersed; however, most tend to congregate in the three main areas—the San Antonio Zoo, Brackenridge Golf Course, and the Japanese Tea Gardens. The Tea Gardens are well worth visiting. This natural oasis contains lush foliage, stone bridges, a 60-foot waterfall, carp ponds, and shaded walkways. The name was changed to "Chinese Tea Gardens" during World War II, and it was also known as Sunken Gardens before reclaiming its original name. Other park highlights include a 3.5-mile miniature train known as the Brackenridge Eagle; the Skyride, a cable car system providing aerial views of the city and zoo; and a 60-horse carousel. Otherwise, the park offers standard features such as hike and bike trails, plenty of sport courts and fields, playgrounds, and picnic facilities.

ACCOMMODATIONS

San Antonio is perhaps the best city in Texas for downtown lodging within walking distance from major tourist attractions. The River Walk is teeming with a wide range of accommodations, and although the city's historic downtown hotels are somewhat more expensive, it's worth the extra $30–40 for a memorable experience in a vibrant urban environment. For those looking to save a few bucks, there are myriad affordable chain options about 20 minutes outside of downtown on Loop 410, especially on the north side of the city near the airport.

The River Walk-Alamo Vicinity
$50-100
It's difficult to find a worthy bargain hotel in downtown San Antonio, but there are a few options that offer basic amenities. Be forewarned: These spots tend to be pretty noisy due to freeway, train, and munchkin traffic. Regardless, the best of the bunch is **Red Roof Inn** (1011 E. Houston St., 210/229-9973, www.redroof. com, $99 d), about a 10-minute walk (under the freeway) from Alamo Plaza. The hotel offers complimentary Wi-Fi Internet access in all rooms, a free continental breakfast, and an outdoor pool.

Within a mile of the River Walk are two other budget options that feature prime locations more than top-notch amenities and service. They are **Days Inn Downtown** (1500 S. I-35, exit 154B, 210/271-3334, www.dayssanantonio.com, $88 d), including a free breakfast, outdoor pool, and free wireless Internet access. The other is the minimal and micropriced **Microtel Inn & Suites** (1025 Frio St., 210/226-8666 or 800/771-7171, www.microtelinn.com, $59 d), offering complimentary wireless Internet access and a heated outdoor pool.

$100-150
If you're planning to stay downtown, you may as well be in a hotel directly on the River Walk, where all the activity is merely a step away from the hotel lobby. Fortunately, there are several moderately priced options offering reliable service and clean, compact rooms. A longtime family favorite is **Holiday Inn** (217 N. St. Mary's St., 210/224-2500, www.holidayinn.com, $135 d), located smack dab in the middle of the action. The hotel has a small yet comfortable heated outdoor pool and whirlpool, free Internet access, an exercise facility, and on-site parking. A nicer alternative is the towering **Crowne Plaza Hotel** (111 Pecan St.

E., 210/354-2800, www.ichotelsgroup.com, $136 d), offering Internet access in all rooms, a heated rooftop pool, sauna, whirlpool, and full fitness center.

$150-200
Most of the River Walk hotels fall in this price range, although it's worth checking the discount travel websites since many of the following recommended locations are often available for $30–40 less. For those who like a little touch of home with their hotel experience, consider the fully equipped kitchen suites at **Residence Inn** (425 Bonham St., 210/212-5555, www.marriott.com, $159 d). Located near The Alamo, the hotel also offers complimentary Internet access, a free breakfast buffet in the morning, and a weekday special (5–7 P.M.) providing complimentary beverages and a light dinner.

Another nice option in the middle of all the action is the **Drury Plaza Hotel** (105 S. St. Mary's St., 210/270-7799, www.druryhotels.com, $189 d). Located in the stately 24-story Alamo Bank Building, the hotel covers an entire city block and retains much of its 1929 elegance and style (lofty ceilings, travertine flooring, chandeliers, and stained-glass windows) along with its legendary rooftop weather spire. The Drury offers free wireless Internet service in all rooms, a complimentary hot breakfast, free evening beverages from 5:30 to 7 P.M. daily, and an outdoor rooftop whirlpool and swimming pool, billed as the highest swimming pool in San Antonio.

A little bit further up the luxury ladder is **Homewood Suites** (432 W. Market St., 210/222-1515, www.homewoodsuitesriverwalk.com, $189 d). This prime location is ideal for those traveling with kids since it includes fully equipped kitchens for snack storage and storing/reheating leftovers, separate living and sleeping rooms to facilitate earlier bedtimes, plus complimentary Internet access in all rooms and a free hot breakfast every morning.

$200-300
If you're willing to shell out some extra cash,

the upscale lodging options along the River Walk will ensure a memorable stay in San Antonio.

One of the most distinctive and classy locations is the stylish **℃ Hotel Valencia** (150 E. Houston St., 210/227-9700, www.hotelvalencia.com, $200 d). This 213-room contemporary luxury hotel bills itself as "classic meets hip," and rightfully so. Corridors and rooms are shadowy (if too dark at times) with dramatic lighting and trendy detailing. Guests won't want to leave their room thanks to the exceptional city views, minibar, free Internet access, and luxurious linens; even the bathrooms are welcoming, with their classic bathtubs and waffle-weave robes. Another bonus: The Valencia is at the end of the River Walk, so crowds aren't much of an issue (unless the adjacent nightclub is thumping into the wee hours of the night). This is a good romantic spot for couples, not families looking for a fun getaway.

A popular mainstream option is the **Hyatt Regency** (123 Losoya St., 210/222-1234, www.sanantonioregency.hyatt.com, $204 d). Located at the gateway to the River Walk just a block away from The Alamo, the Hyatt is a modestly sized hotel with a 16-story atrium and rooftop terrace offering an outdoor swimming pool, spa, and adjoining 2,800-square-foot health club. Rooms are decked out in Southwestern-style decor and include a fridge, microwave, and Wi-Fi access. The hotel also has a swingin' jazz club on the riverbank with cool outdoor seating.

Another clean, reliable, amenity-filled choice is **AmeriSuites** (601 S. St. Mary's St., 210/227-6854, www.amerisuites.com, $229 d), located downtown on the San Antonio River, just not in the thick of the River Walk activity. The rooms here are fairly large and feature microwaves, refrigerators, a separate workspace, and free wireless Internet access. The hotel also offers a free hot breakfast buffet, an outdoor heated swimming pool, and free parking (a bonus for a downtown establishment).

A consistently reliable and oft-recommended option is the welcoming **Westin** (420 W.

Market St., 210/224-6500, www.starwoodhotels.com, $299 d), which distinguishes itself from other chain options on the River Walk by showcasing the region's Latin American culture. Guests are greeted with Venezuelan specialty chocolates; a traditional *la merienda* (high tea) features roasted Mexican coffees, hot cocoas, *aguas frescas,* and Mexican cookies in the lobby (Tuesday–Saturday, 3:30–5:30 P.M.); and a Spanish classical guitarist croons on weekends. The rooms are inviting, too, with historic Texas decor, big comfy beds, marble bathrooms, and views of the river and city. The Westin also features an outdoor heated pool, a fitness center, and a sauna.

Historic Downtown Hotels
$100-150
Housed in the fancy 1883 Dullnig Building is the 17-room **Riverwalk Vista** (262 Losoya St., 210/223-3200, www.riverwalkvista.com, $120 d and up), a luxury boutique hotel located less than a block from the River Walk. The more-affordable rooms are pretty small, but the hotel's historic decor and thoughtful amenities make it an extremely worthwhile experience. Rooms include bottled water (always a nice touch) as well as feather blankets, cordless phones, ottomans, and fancy bathrooms containing bathrobes, slate showers, lighted makeup mirrors, and plush cotton towels. The Vista's food is also a big draw—fresh-baked cookies are served every afternoon (along with glasses of wine), and the mega breakfasts include empanadas, quiche, muffins, cereal, and fruit.

Located directly behind The Alamo is the remarkable **℃ Crockett Hotel** (320 Bonham St., 210/225-6500, www.crocketthotel.com, $139 d). Renovated in 2007, this magnificent downtown historic establishment is in the heart of all the action, just steps away from The Alamo (18 paces, according to hotel reps) and a five-minute leisurely stroll from the River Walk. The lobby area is modest yet welcoming, and the rooms are tastefully decorated, with soothing colors and boutique-style features such as interior shutters and regional artwork.

The Crockett's amenities include free Internet access and a complimentary breakfast offering a tasty egg casserole, pastries, fresh fruit, and cereal.

$150-200

The second-most famous building on Alamo Plaza is the outstanding hotel referred to simply as **The Menger Hotel** (204 Alamo Plaza, 210/223-4361, www.mengerhotel.com, $159 d). This significant and highly recommended 1859 hotel sits just across the street from The Alamo and has been a destination for travelers, ranchers, and dignitaries throughout its illustrious 150-year history. The busy Victorian-era lobby conjures up memories of bygone days in San Antonio's bustling heyday, when famous guests such as Babe Ruth, Mae West, and Theodore Roosevelt walked the halls (some claim their ghosts now do the roaming). Roosevelt's experience at the hotel is well documented with photos and news clips, especially in the Menger Bar, where he recruited Rough Riders and shot a couple bullets in the wall (the holes are still there). The hotel proudly boasts having downtown San Antonio's largest heated swimming pool, a wonderful place to take a dip at night under the stars. Aside from these distinctive amenities, the hotel also features charming historic rooms, most with extremely high ceilings, antique furnishings, quality bedding, and fantastic views of The Alamo, courtyard, or pool. Additional amenities include a full-service spa, fitness room, Jacuzzi, and free Wi-Fi access.

Another well-regarded historic downtown hotel is the **Wyndham-St. Anthony** (300 E. Travis St., 210/227-4392, www.wyndham.com, $159 d), an ornate yet refined Victorian property located three blocks from The Alamo and one block from the River Walk. Built in 1909, the hotel is designated a National Historic Landmark and is legendary for its "Peacock Alley" lobby, decked out with eight-foot-wide crystal chandeliers and original artwork by Remington, Cartier, and DeYoung. The rooms feature Queen Anne–style decor with custom-tailored bedspreads and antique replicas. The

The Menger Hotel is located across the street from The Alamo.

© ANDY RHODES

bathrooms have a touch of style with black-and-white-tiled baths and pedestal sinks. All rooms feature wireless Internet access, and the hotel has a pool and spa tub.

$200-250

Billing itself as the "Jewel of San Antonio" is the **Fairmount Hotel** (401 S. Alamo St., 210/224-8800, www.thefairmounthotel-sanantonio.com, $200–219 d). This magnificent 1906 Victorian-style hotel is a block away from La Villita, the historic neighborhood turned shopping area, and just down the street from the River Walk and The Alamo. The Fairmount features 37 individually decorated rooms and suites enveloped in a stately brick building with wrought-iron verandas. The lobby area overlooks a jeweled granite and marble courtyard with a fountain and palmetto trees, offering a romantic place for garden seating. Most of the Fairmount's rooms are intimate suites featuring period furnishings, silk fabrics, fancy tiling, canopy beds, and Internet access.

One of San Antonio's fanciest lodging options is the luxurious **Omni La Mansion Del Rio Hotel** (112 College St., 210/518-1000, www.omnihotels.com, $219 d). Locals stay here for a special night out, and travelers return regularly to experience this Spanish Colonial hacienda-style accommodation on the banks of the historic San Antonio River Walk. Those who can't afford the nightly rates are still drawn to La Mansion for its excellent margaritas. Hotel amenities include a magnificent courtyard with a heated swimming pool and spa along with historically stylish rooms offering Internet access, minibars, and plush robes.

Bed-and-Breakfasts

San Antonio has dozens of fine bed-and-breakfasts, especially in the charming King William Historic District (see entry) just south of downtown. To help narrow down the options (location, price, required interaction with other patrons), visit the San Antonio Bed & Breakfast Association's website at www.sanantoniobb.org.

Considered by many to be the finest B&B in town is the **Brackenridge House B & B Inn** (230 Madison St., 210/271-3442, www.brackenridgehouse.com, $120–160), in the King William district. The Brackenridge prides itself on being comfy and cozy without being too cute—there are the requisite antique furnishings in each room, but they're accompanied by a microwave, fridge, and free wireless Internet service. The B&B also offers a few added amenities, such as drinks, chocolates, and sherry in the guest rooms, and the breakfast portion of this package is legendary—a three-course feast in the formal dining room. Also distinctive to this B&B is the backyard pool and hot tub.

Rivaling the Brackenridge for the coveted title of San Antonio's supreme B&B is the remarkable **Oge Inn** (209 Washington St., 210/223-2353, www.ogeinn.com, rooms start at $159). This 1857 elegant mansion is located on the banks of the scenic San Antonio River, and its architectural significance has resulted in two coveted Texas Historical Commission designations: listing on the National Register of Historic Places and as a Texas Historical Landmark. Once the home of pioneer Texas Ranger, cattle rancher, and businessman Louis Ogé, the home now contains 10 guest rooms luxuriously decorated with period antiques, private baths, fireplaces, and refrigerators, all with free Internet access. Non–morning people will appreciate the Oge Inn's private tables, where a full breakfast is served in view of the fireplace or on the majestic front veranda.

Camping

San Antonio isn't a big destination for campers, but there are several notable state parks within a half-hour drive of downtown. The best of the bunch is **Guadalupe River State Park** (29 miles north of downtown in Spring Branch, 3350 Park Rd. 31, 830/438-2656, www.tpwd.state.tx.us, $7 daily 13 and older). The main attraction is the beautiful namesake Guadalupe River, and a nine-mile stretch of it crosses over four natural rapids and two steep limestone bluffs in the park. The Guadalupe is known for its crystal-clear water, and the park takes full advantage of this natural resource by offering easy access to canoeing, fishing, swimming, tubing, picnicking, hiking, and camping. The park also has a 5-mile equestrian trail that's also open to mountain biking.

For those who want to stay closer to town in an RV-type park, there's the **KOA Campground** (602 Gembler Rd., 210/224-9296, www.koakampgrounds.com), located just a few miles east of town. The KOA offers free Wi-Fi and is adjacent to a lake and golf course, so there's plenty of recreational activity even if you aren't in a recreational vehicle. Another option fairly close to town is **Travelers World RV Park** (2617 Roosevelt Ave., 210/532-8310, www.carefreervresorts.com). Located three miles south of the city, Travelers World offers a city bus line at the main gate, a nearby hike and bike trail, a heated swimming pool, and wireless Internet access.

FOOD

The food is fabulous in San Antonio, and not surprisingly, the focus is on Mexican restaurants. The sheer number of Mex-related eateries (Tex-Mex, Cal-Mex, Interior Mex, etc.) can be overwhelming, so check out www.sae-ats.com or pick up a *San Antonio Current,* the city's alternative weekly tab, to get a better handle on the latest restaurants in each category and where they're located. Fortunately, several well-regarded eating establishments have additional locations on the touristy River Walk, and other downtown areas offer some of the highest-quality Mexican food in Texas.

River Walk
AMERICAN AND SOUTHWESTERN
Just because you're in proximity to the Rio Grande doesn't mean you have to eat Mexican food all the time. At least one meal a day can be set aside for other gastronomical considerations, and in a touristy area like the River Walk, the best bet is a good ol' American-style restaurant with a local twist. One of the most popular destinations for this kind of family-friendly fare is **Zuni Grill** (223 Losoya St., 210/227-0864, www.zunigrill.com, $11–24).

Splashes of bright colors are everywhere, from the mosaic tiles on the tables to the brightly colored walls inside. Request a seat on the patio for a wonderful view of the river, and order a signature cactus 'rita while you're waiting for your entrée. Noteworthy options include a glazed pork loin, grilled salmon, and chicken quesadillas. Incidentally, this is one of the few restaurants on the River Walk that serves breakfast.

For a fancy dining experience, consider **Boudro's** (421 E. Commerce St., 210/224-8484, www.boudros.com, $13–33). Not many places on the river can entice locals to wade through the throngs of walkers, but since Boudro's does, be sure to call ahead for a reservation. If you're looking for a little local flavor, start with a prickly pear margarita accompanied by chips and fresh-made guacamole prepared at your table (note the fresh squeeze of orange as opposed to lemon or lime—the difference is subtle yet spectacular). Entrées run the gamut from seafood to steaks to upscale Southwestern dishes, and Boudro's desserts, including bread pudding, flan, and crème brûlée are legendary.

Another upscale eatery drawing townies through its doors is **Biga on the Banks** (203 S. St. Mary's St., 210/225-0722, www.biga.com, $14–36). Located off the trampled path in the city's former central library, Biga's has established a reputation for serving some of the finest cuisine in the state (the late *Gourmet* magazine named it one of the top five restaurants in Texas). Enjoy complimentary champagne upon arrival as you browse the impressive menu of savory items, including smoked pork chops, seared tuna, roasted lamb, grilled steaks, and wild game. Many dishes are accompanied by bold touches such as curry sauces and foie gras. Be sure to make reservations to ensure a seat at this exquisite establishment.

The River Walk would be an incomplete Texas tradition without a barbecue restaurant in the mix. Some of the best San Antonio has to offer is at the **County Line** (111 W. Crockett St. #104, 210/229-1941, $9–18). This is authentic Texas-style 'cue, so load up on tender brisket, meaty beef ribs, and flavorful sausage, accompanied by classic sides like potato salad and coleslaw. Wash it all down with a cold Shiner Bock or Dr Pepper.

MEXICAN

It's difficult to narrow down the ultimate Mexican food in the restaurant capital of a Hispanic-flavored town like San Antonio, but several spots float to the top of the River Walk scene due to their long-standing reputation for consistent quality and service. Among them are **Casa Rio** (430 E. Commerce St., 210/225-6718, www.casa-rio.com, $9–20). Considered the first-ever restaurant on the River Walk (open since 1946), this venerable institution is a great place to get started on your Tex-Mex adventure in San Antonio. Interior walls and patio umbrellas radiate festive colors, complementing the equally tantalizing food. You can't go wrong with the basics here—their beef tacos, chicken enchiladas, pork tamales, and cheesy quesadillas are *perfecto,* especially

when accompanied by a refreshing margarita or Mexican cerveza. Snag a seat on the patio for optimal people watching and ambience, and be sure to arrive early since the standard wait at noon and 6 p.m. is typically 30–45 minutes.

Another classic Tex-Mex spot with an amazing deck overlooking the riverbank is **Rio Rio Cantina** (421 E. Commerce St., 210/226-8462, www.rioriocantina.com, $9–22). Bring your appetite, since the portions here are enormous. Fortunately, they're tasty, too, especially the chicken enchiladas with green salsa, the camarones Yucateco (spicy shrimp), and even the standard fajita plate, containing enough beef and chicken to feed an entire crew on one of the passing river barges. Kids will love the quesadillas, and their parents will appreciate the noisy chatter drowning out their incessant questions about the pervasive pigeons.

Those looking for a step up from the standard Tex-Mex fare should head directly to the remarkable █ **Acenar** (146 E. Houston St., 210/222-2362, www.acenar.com, $13–29).

MEXICAN DELICACIES

Mention Mexican food, and people immediately think of tacos and burritos, the standard Tex-Mex fare from south of the border that fills diners' combo plates (and bellies) at Mexican restaurants across South Texas. There's typically not much room left for dessert, which is unfortunate since Mexico is home to many delectably sweet delicacies often known as *dulces* (sweets or desserts).

One of the most popular is *tres leches,* (three milks), a cake soaked in three kinds of . . . milk: evaporated, condensed, and whole. Tres leches is a very light cake filled with lots of air bubbles, so the "soaking" doesn't tend to bog down the consistency; rather, it complements the sweet creamy taste.

Another popular dessert served in Tex-Mex restaurants are *sopapillas,* a fried pastry made from a flat bread. These puffy treats are made by deep frying the pressed bread, causing it to expand with a large air pocket in the cen-

ter and creating its distinctive pillowy shape. *Sopapillas* are typically served with honey or a mixture of powdered sugar and cinnamon sprinkled on top.

Not quite as widespread yet uncommonly delicious are *marranitos,* aka *cochinos* or even "gingerbread pigs." These moist and rich cakey cookies have a spicy undertone from the molasses and cinnamon, and are a perfect accompaniment to a mug of strong, steaming coffee.

Several other standard Mexican delicacies don't authentically qualify as native products, but you'll find them on the dessert menus of most Mexican restaurants. Two have Spanish origins – flan and *churros* – and have long been associated with postdinner indulgences in Mexico. The other, pecan pralines, is tied to New Orleans via France, but the buttery confections have long graced the dessert plates of many fine Tex-Mex restaurants in the Lone Star State.

This is one of the largest restaurants on the River Walk, and its multiple levels and tables are consistently packed with diners enjoying the stellar view and stunning Mexican food with a distinctive twist. Tacos are packed with unconventional fillings like crab and oyster, and any dish with the savory mole sauce is magnificent. The duck crepes are well worth trying, and the entomatadas (a chicken and sweet potato filled tortilla covered in an astounding roasted tomato sauce with queso fresco) are a culinary highlight. Accompany your meal with one of Acenar's signature "hand-shaken" margaritas, and try to save room for the exquisite *tres leches* cake or coconut flan.

◀ PEARL BREWERY DEVELOPMENT

Technically located at the far northern edge of the River Walk (even though it's a couple miles from downtown and beyond I-35), the new Pearl Brewery complex was still getting off the ground in early 2011. Although the historic brewhouse is still undergoing restoration, the surrounding facilities (eateries, in particular)

are well on their way to attracting local regulars and out-of-town visitors. Note: Several establishments are closed on Monday.

Garnering much attention and rave reviews is ◀ **La Gloria Ice House** (100 E. Grayson St., 210/267-9040, www.lagloriaicehouse. com, $9–24). Now that Mexico is essentially off-limits to tourists, one of the safest ways to experience authentic Mexican "street food" is at a restaurant like La Gloria. Designed like a Mexican mercado taco stand (despite the fact it's near a historic brewhouse alongside a river with a miniwaterfall), La Gloria specializes in delicious tacos, gorditas, and tortas prepared in the regionally diverse styles of street vendors from across Mexico. A key thing to keep in mind before ordering: Tacos come three per order, so resist the temptation to sample everything on the menu and start with just one or two (they'll get cold if they arrive all at once, and you're encouraged to place additional orders during your visit). Though everything here is just as good as it sounds on the menu, some of the more notable dishes include the

the Pearl Brewery Development

al pastor pork tacos, the crispy-battered fish tacos, the tacos Potosinos (rolled tortillas in chile sauce with fried carrots and potatoes), and the avocado *tlayuda* (pizza). Another immensely popular and flavorful menu item is the tamal del dia, featuring a seasoned meat combined with spices (cinnamon, cloves) and fruit (apricots, dates) all wrapped up in a banana leaf. *Que sabor!*

Across the street is the tasty **Sandbar Fish House & Market** (200 E. Grayson St., 210/222-2426, $11–34). Though San Antonio is far from the ocean, that doesn't mean the landlubbers in town can't appreciate a quality plate of seafood. In fact, one of the most popular items in the menu is oysters (offered East Coast or West Coast style). If you're looking for something with a little more local flair, opt for the bold ceviche. Other popular items include the creamy lobster bisque and pan-seared scallops with a surprisingly tasty cauliflower puree.

Also on-site at the Pearl complex is the contemporary Italian restaurant **Il Sogno** (200 E. Grayson St., 210/223-3900, www.pearlbrewery.com, $9–28). This somewhat-small locale is always bustling with activity, thanks in large part to the open kitchen and closely placed tables. Menu highlights include a diverse cheese and antipasti plate, a wide variety of fresh pizzas (the margherita is especially flavorful), and duck ravioli.

If you're not in the mood for a lengthy meal, head to the nearby **CIA Bakery Café** (312 Pearl Pkwy., 210/554-6400). Featuring baked goods from the Culinary Institute of America's kitchen (the institute has a branch of its campus at the Pearl complex), the bakery and café offer a casual place to sample the tasty fare from students, including light entrée options for lunch and dinner (sandwiches, soups, salads). The café is also a great spot to grab an espresso, coffee, or tea (or a beer or wine).

If you're visiting on Saturday morning or Wednesday afternoon, be sure to stop by the **Pearl Farmers Market** (between La Gloria and the Sandbar Fish House, Sat. 9 A.M.–1 P.M. and Wed. 4–7 P.M.). Market vendors are from the area and offer their own fresh, local, and seasonal products. Booths include a bevy of vegetable stands as well as fruits, meats, herbs, baked goods, and other local edibles (pecans, goat cheese, eggs, jams, and salsas).

Downtown Area
AMERICAN

Although it's no longer in its off-kilter, slantedly enchanted location, San Antonio's **Liberty Bar** (1111 S. Alamo St., 210/227-1187, www.liberty-bar.com, $11–26) still merits mention for its creative and high-quality food. Fortunately, the food remains straight-up tremendous, even in its salmon-colored former-convent building, with a focus on sauced and seasoned meats (pot roast, lamb sausage, herbed chicken). Little things done extremely well—bread, spreads, iced tea—make a big impression, and the vegetables are always perfectly prepared. The Liberty draws its largest crowds on Sunday morning for its legendary brunch (served 10:30 A.M.–2 P.M.), with sumptuous egg dishes and the perfect piece of French toast.

The stunningly sweeping views are the main course at **Chart House** (600 Hemisfair Plaza Wy., 210/223-3101, www.chart-house.com, $11–29), the revolving restaurant atop the Tower of the Americas. Normally, these eateries in the round aren't known for their top-notch food, but the selections here are impressive. Since the restaurant is owned by Landry's, a respected seafood establishment, most of the menu options are of the surf and turf variety, including the tasty shrimp dishes. Incidentally, the tower is 750 feet high and was built in 1968 especially for the HemisFair. A "4-D" multisensory theater is located on the ground level.

It may be a Midwestern chain, but when it comes to preparing a perfect steak, Texans and visitors from across the globe line up for **Morton's** (300 E. Crockett St., 210/228-0700, www.mortons.com, $16–39). Morton's looks, smells, and tastes exactly like an upscale steak house should—dark wood, tuxedoed waitstaff, clanging steak knives, and delectable cuts of prime beef. Highlights include the porterhouse, double-cut filet mignon, and the bonein prime rib.

MEXICAN

The *gigante* selection of fine Mexican restaurants In San Antonio is overwhelming; fortunately, there's an ideal combo plate for everyone. The fun part is the discovery. A great place to start is ◖ **Rosario's Mexican Cafe** (910 S. Alamo St., 210/223-1806, www.rosariossa.com, $8–20), on the edge of the King William Historic District. The food here is a bit more contemporary than traditional cheesy enchiladas and tacos, and that's what's so appealing about it. Instead of greasy beef, there's fresh avocado. Many dishes contain pleasant surprises (diced cactus, exotic peppers, a touch of cinnamon) rather than bland standbys (rice, beans). The deliciously smoky roasted-pepper salsa that comes to the table with the tortilla chips is a good indication of the quality to come. The spectacular chile relleno contains a tantalizing blend of flavors—a slight bite from the ranchero sauce is tempered by the sweet raisin undertones—and the chile itself is perfectly breaded. You'll eat it all the way to the stem. On weekend nights, Rosario's becomes a hot spot for the singles scene, with salsa, merengue, and jazz bands playing for enthusiastic dancing crowds.

More traditional yet similarly compelling is **Mi Tierra Cafe & Bakery** (218 Produce Row, 210/225-1262, www.mitierracafe.com, $8–19), the legendary 24-hour Market Square restaurant. The scene here is worth the visit alone— the ceilings are decked out with Christmas lights, and mariachis stroll the grounds crooning their *canciones*. A lot of people come here just for the tasty *dulces* (sweet breads) and impressive tequila selection, but the food is worth sticking around for, too. Pastry fans should order an empanada de calabaza (a pumpkin turnover). The homemade tortillas are soft and flavorful, and the standard combo plates with enchiladas, tacos, and tamales are an ideal way to get a classic Tex-Mex fix. Be sure to get a perfect pecan praline or a to-go pastry for a tasty late-night snack.

Azuca Nuevo Latino (713 S. Alamo St., 210/225-5550, www.azuca.net, $10–25) specializes in Latin American and Caribbean food, a nice change of pace for those fed up with the typical Mexican dishes. Located in the King William Historic District, Azuca is a busy spot that consistently ends up on annual "best-of" lists. Locals and out-of-towners drop by regularly for the contemporary take on Latin classics, such as the mixed meat grill (chicken, beef, pork, and sausage), pork loin, and just about anything with plantains and coconut shrimp. The curry Latino offers an intriguing blend of spices and seafood, and even the steaks have a Caribbean marinated flavor. Stick around for the salsa, mojitos, and merengue bands on weekend nights.

Another local Tex-Mex institution is **La Fonda On Main** (2415 N. Main Ave., 210/733-0621, www.lafondaonmain.com, $9–20). Be sure you go to the Main Avenue location, since other (unaffiliated) La Fondas in town don't offer nearly the same quality of food. This excellent restaurant is located in a historic building on the near-north side of town, and it's an ideal place for people who want to explore the Mexican-food scene without getting too adventurous. The menu features standard Tex-Mex, albeit with a slightly more upscale approach (fancier tortillas, sauces in zigzag patterns), and classic interior Mexican fare (mole dishes, black beans). The margaritas are some of the best in town, and if the weather's nice, be sure to grab a spot on the patio.

LUNCH

You can't subsist merely on Tex-Mex dinners and hearty steaks, so make a point of checking out a few of San Antonio's unique lunch and brunch spots. The funkiest of the bunch is **Madhatters** (320 Beauregard St., 210/212-4832, www.madhatterstea.com, $5–11). A teahouse turned lunch locale, this *Alice in Wonderland*–inspired café is a little warped, in a metaphorical sense. The incredible variety of teas are still the focal point here, but the healthy salads and tasty sandwiches are causing customers to avoid being late for an important date at Madhatters. One more: The spinach mad scramble with a side of fresh-squeezed orange juice will leave you grinning like the Cheshire Cat.

Seemingly better suited for Austin than San Antonio is the organic-minded **Twin Sisters Bakery & Cafe** (124 Broadway St., 210/354-1559, www.twinsistersbakeryandcafe.com, $5–15). Although it has a strong veggie focus, carnivores can still find some meat to devour at this comfy spot near the Alamo. Favorites among the herbivore crowd include a tasty avocado sandwich and Greek salad, while meat eaters enjoy the enchiladas and stews. Omnivores will love the fresh-baked items, including muffins, breads, pies, and cookies. On weekends, Twin Sisters transforms into a mellow hangout with live acoustic music.

Outside of Downtown

Sometimes, the hustle of a downtown urban area can be too much of a bustle, especially if you're looking for a fancy meal in a quieter environment. One of the favorite destinations for locals is the expensive yet consistently excellent **Silo Elevated Cuisine** (434 N. Loop 1604 E., 210/483-8989, www.siloelevatedcuisine.com, $11–36). It's called *Silo* and *Elevated* for a reason—this stylish restaurant sits in a lofty second-story perch accessible via elevator, and the quality of the food ascends beyond the city's other upscale options. Not surprisingly, the wine selection is superb (the waitstaff will bring several sample glasses if you're feeling indecisive), as are the entrées, including premium steaks, shrimp and grits, seared yellowfin tuna, and Silo's famous chicken-fried oysters. Silo also features live entertainment several nights a week. Reservations are strongly recommended.

For some of the best craft beer in the region, head directly to **Freetail Brewing Co.** (4035 N. Loop 1604 W., 210/395-4974, www.freetailbrewing.com, $8–23). Named after Texas's official flying mammal (the Mexican free-tail bat), this locale aptly represents the state's eclectic culture and influences. The brews are largely seasonal here, so expect some hearty homemade porters during the cooler winter months and crisp pilsners on the patio in summertime. Local favorites include the Rye Wit (a flavorful wheat beer), the smoky Rubio Fumando, and a purple-tinged prickly pear variety. The waitstaff is knowledgeable and friendly, so be sure to ask them for suggestions based on your experience and willingness to experiment. While there, you may also be interested in eating. Fortunately, Freetail's food is on par with its beers, so load up on quality pub grub like nachos, pepper fries, mac and cheese, and pizza (the barbecue brisket pie is especially cheesy and delicious).

San Antonio is teeming with can't-miss Mexican restaurants, but it's well worth making the 15-minute drive north from downtown to experience **Los Barrios** (4223 Blanco Rd., 210/732 6017, $8–14). Start things off with a smooth and tangy margarita to accompany the warm chips and Argentina-style garlicky pesto salsa. Puffy tacos are the specialty here, and the enchiladas are highly recommended—opt for the rich and flavorful chicken mole or hearty Mexicana sauce. The fresh homemade tortillas and flautas are also excellent choices. Food Network fans will appreciate the fact that Bobby Flay "Threw Down" with Los Barrios (and lost). Don't be surprised if the owners drop by to make sure everything is *perfecto*.

Named by *Texas Monthly* as one of the top five Mexican restaurants in the state, **SoLuna** (7959 Broadway St., 210/930-8070, www.solunasa.com, $12–30) offers consistently tasty cuisine with an emphasis on the country's interior influences. The chile en nogoda (a poblano pepper with beef or pork seasoned with spices and cooked fruits) is an especially memorable dish, and the *pescado veracruzana* is a simple yet exquisite snapper fillet with capers, olives, and tomatoes. SoLuna's takes enchiladas to a whole new level, and the best way to sample the goodness is via the SoLuna special, featuring three enchiladas with tantalizingly different cream-based sauces.

INFORMATION AND SERVICES
Tourist Offices
Drop by the **San Antonio Convention and Visitor's Bureau** (203 S. St. Mary's St., 210/207-6700 or 800/447-3372, www.visitsanantonio.com, weekdays 8 A.M.–5:30 P.M.) to get the scoop on where things are and how to get there. Staff members will provide you with a stack of brochures, maps, and travel guides. Another handy service organization is the **Greater San Antonio Chamber of Commerce** (602 E. Commerce St., 210/229-2100, www.sachamber.org), which offers a comprehensive website with extensive listings of hotels, restaurants, attractions, and events.

If you're looking for specific information about River Walk businesses, including hours of operation and location, contact the **Paseo Del Rio Association** (110 Broadway St., Suite 440, 210/227-4262, www.thesanantonioriverwalk.com).

Publications
San Antonio's daily newspaper, the *San Antonio Express-News,* is a good source of information about South Texas politics and culture. The *San Antonio Current* is the city's alternative newsweekly, featuring local writers and critics covering politics, arts, music, and food. It's distributed every Wednesday at more than 850 locations citywide, including most downtown coffee shops and bars.

GETTING THERE AND AROUND
The **San Antonio International Airport** (9800 Airport Blvd., 210/207-3411, www.san-antonio.gov/aviation) is located about 12 miles north of downtown and offers flights from 10 U.S.-based airlines and three Mexican companies. Most travelers pick up a car at the airport from one of the major rental companies. Another transportation option from the airport is **SA Trans** (210/281-9900, www.saairportshuttle.com), providing shared-van service to downtown hotels for only $18 one-way (with a round-trip purchase). The company operates

booths outside both airport terminals, and service runs 7 A.M.–1:30 A.M. Call 24 hours ahead for return service from the hotel. Taxis cost about $25 and take approximately 15 minutes between the airport and downtown. Stations are located outside the airport terminals.

San Antonio has a reliable public transportation system, **VIA Metropolitan Transit** (210/362-2000, www.viainfo.net), which runs about 100 bus lines and a downtown streetcar service. Fares start around $1.

A popular and uniquely San Antonio way of getting around downtown is via river taxi. **Rio San Antonio Cruises** (tickets at Rivercenter Mall and Holiday Inn, 210/244-5700 or 800/417-4139, www.riosanantonio.com, $7.75 adults, $5 seniors, $2 children 1–5) specializes in tours but can also arrange for transportation.

NEW BRAUNFELS
New Braunfels is synonymous with German heritage and tubing (the "sport" of floating in an inner tube on the river). This town of 49,969 people just northeast of San Antonio has been relying on its natural resources for more than 150 years, starting when German immigrants used the dependable, strong-flowing Comal Springs and Guadalupe River as a source for power and navigation. By the mid-1800s, New Braunfels had emerged as a growing agricultural area and manufacturing center supplying wagons, farm equipment, clothing, and furniture for Central Texas pioneers. The subsequent population boom resulted in New Braunfels being the fourth-largest town in Texas in 1850. People continued to arrive after the Civil War, and the agriculture industry grew along with the population. By the mid-1900s, the area became a recreational hot spot catering to San Antonio residents who bought weekend or retirement homes on nearby Canyon Lake or the scenic Guadalupe River. Motels, resorts, and tubing companies soon followed, cementing New Braunfels's reputation as a unique spot to relax on the water or spend time at the numerous antiques shops and German restaurants.

◖ Gruene Historic District

Quaint can have negative connotations (think frilly quilts, tea sets, doilies), but when combined with authentically rustic, it can be downright charming. The modest Gruene Historic District (Gruene is pronounced "green"), located just a few miles northwest of downtown New Braunfels, is one of the finest heritage tourism destinations in the region. Resisting the temptation to go overboard and "cute" things up, this several-block area retains much of its authentic character from the late 1800s, when German immigrant Henry D. Gruene built a mercantile store and later a cotton gin and dance hall to serve the sharecroppers who settled in the area. The small community was bustling until the 1920s, when the Great Depression and a nasty plague of boll weevils wiped out the cotton business and, consequently, the town. In the 1970s, several San Antonio and New Braunfels entrepreneurs determined the abandoned buildings had potential, and their instincts proved right when recreational tourists on the nearby Guadalupe River added shopping and dancing to their weekend itineraries.

The district's most remarkable structure is **Gruene Hall** (1281 Gruene Rd., 830/606-1281, www.gruenehall.com), the oldest continually running dance hall in Texas. This magnificent 1878 building is a Hill Country treasure—the sturdy German-constructed wooden floors and long tables have witnessed more than a century of honky-tonkin' boot-scootin' country and roots-rock music. Overlooking the scene are authentically reproduced beer and soft drink ads offering two-steppers a step back in time. Americana artists play Gruene Hall several nights a week and include some well-known regional acts (Robert Earl Keen, Bruce and Charlie Robison, Delbert McClinton) and some heavy hitting national stars (George Strait, Lyle Lovett, Jerry Jeff Walker). Check the website for upcoming performances.

Shopping in Gruene isn't too overwhelming—there are only a couple main streets, and the historic buildings are spaced fairly far apart. One of the highlights is the 1875

SAN ANTONIO

© ANDY RHODES

Gruene Hall

Gruene General Store (1610 Hunter Rd., 830/629-6021, www.gruenegeneralstore. com), containing everything you'd expect to find in an old-time mercantile business, from Texas-made candy, coffee, jams, and trinkets to home decor items and clothing. Other noteworthy shops in the district include the adjacent **Grapevine** (1612 Hunter Rd., 830/606-0093, www.grapevineingruene.com, daily 10 A.M.–9 P.M.), a wine-tasting store featuring quality Texas wines, specialty beers, and gourmet gifts and food; **The Gruene Antique Company** (1607 Hunter Rd., 830/629-7781, daily 10 A.M.–9 P.M.), an enormous space containing antiques and collectibles housed in H. D. Gruene's 1903 mercantile building; and the **Tipsy Gypsy** (1710 Hunter Rd., 830/625-4431), a funky boutique with colorful and flashy new and consignment items.

McKenna Children's Museum

One of the best places in South Texas for kids to play and learn is the McKenna Children's Museum (386 W. San Antonio St., 830/606-9525, www.mckennakids.org, Mon.–Sat. 10 A.M.–5 P.M., closed Sun., $5.50 adults and children over 1 year old). Rivaling big-city facilities in San Antonio and Austin, this museum will keep kids occupied and educated for hours on end. On hot days, head to the outdoor area, where a raised water canal offers innumerable opportunities for kids to be entertained—fountains, hoses, bridges, movable dams, and so many boats and rubber ducks you'll hardly hear the common parental command of "share." Nearby, there's an old Volkswagen bug surrounded by paint buckets, brushes, and smocks, allowing children to fulfill their fantasies of painting the car however they choose. Inside, an imagination world awaits with miniature environments offering kids the chance to play in a town square, grocery store, hospital, tool shed, ranch house, and campground. There's also a Tot Spot for barely walking babies, an outer space area, and a large hall for traveling kid-oriented art and educational exhibits.

◖ Tubing the Guadalupe River

Grab an inner tube (a cooler full of beverages is standard or optional, depending on who you ask), plop it in the Guadalupe River, kick back, and let the current lazily carry you down a refreshing tree-lined waterway. It's a pleasant way to spend a hot summer day in South Texas, even though city officials are making efforts to deflate some of the fun, particularly for the younger crowd who consider it an excuse to get loaded while catching some rays. The party-on-the-water atmosphere was indeed getting a bit out of hand, with empty beer cans and bottles littering the scenic river, and reports of several types of questionable activity taking place along the banks. To combat the excess, lawmakers adopted ordinances that prohibit tubers from carrying coolers with capacities of more than 16 quarts. This allows the college-age crowd to continue their shenanigans without requiring a case of beer to do so, and, in the process, keep the scene clean and more family friendly.

Dozens of companies provide tube rental service. To do some comparative shopping, check out the River Outfitters link at the New Braunfels Chamber of Commerce website (www.nbcham.org). The following sites come recommended by veteran tubers.

A good place to get your tube in the water is **River Sports Tubes** (12 miles west of town at 12034 FM 306, 830/964-2450, www.riversportstubes.com, Sun.–Fri. 9 A.M.–7 P.M., Sat. 8 A.M.–7 P.M.). River Sports has a prime spot on the Guadalupe right in the middle of the busy Horseshoe Loop, making access to the river simple and quick. Tubers have the option of taking short, medium, or long floats, and when they're done, the shuttle returns them back to home base. Tube rental runs $15, or upgrade to a tube/cooler combo for $23.

For those setting up base camp in Gruene, the local hot spot is **Rockin' R River Rides** (1405 Gruene Rd., 800/553-5628, www.rockinr.com), billing itself as the only river outfitter in New Braunfels with locations on both the Guadalupe and Comal Rivers. Call for rental options and costs.

Another popular rental spot is **Roy's Rentals & Campground** (6530 River Rd., 830/964-3721, www.roysrentals.com). Campsites are available, and, in addition to tubes, Roy's provides inflatable canoes, regular canoes, and rafts.

There's also the downtown option of **Felger Tube Rental** (161 S. Liberty Ave., 830/625-4003). Tube rental is a respectable $8 (with $10 deposit), and the shuttle charge to the pick-up/drop-off point is $10. Be forewarned: Parking is a hefty $7 per vehicle, and the owner can be a bit rude to customers if he's had a few beers.

Schlitterbahn Waterpark

For three months a year, the German word *Schlitterbahn* is on every South Texas kid's lips. The word translates as "slippery road," but around here it means "the hottest, coolest time in Texas," the company's ubiquitous summertime slogan. Schlitterbahn Waterpark (381 E. Austin St., 830/625-2351, www.schlitterbahn.com, daily June–Aug., weekends Apr., May, and Sept., $49.98 adults, $41.98 children). The words *water park* don't begin to describe this summer wonderland, featuring more than three miles of tubing "trails," 17 water slides, seven children's water playgrounds, the world's first surfing machine, and three unique "uphill water coasters." Attractions include dueling speed slides, tube chutes, and soft slides for toddlers. Schlitterbahn is an ideal family destination, since teens can get their adrenaline rush on the speedy downhill racing slides, the parents can spend their time leisurely floating in an inner tube on the slow-moving Kristal River ride, and the little ones can splash in the kiddie pools. Admission fees cover costs for tubes, life jackets, and a souvenir cup with free refills.

Natural Bridge Caverns

About 12 miles west of town, an otherworldly experience transports visitors to a different dimension. The subterranean Natural Bridge Caverns (26495 Natural Bridge Caverns Rd., 210/651-6101, www.naturalbridgecaverns.com, daily 9 A.M.–4 P.M. Oct.–Feb., summer hours

vary, $18–27 adults, $10–15 children ages 3–11) is a good way to escape the Texas heat in the summer (the caverns' temperature is a steady 70°F, although the 99 percent humidity feels like Houston). Visitors descend nearly 200 feet below ground via cement walkways to a surreal world of ancient natural formations with expressive names like soda straws, chandeliers, flowstones, and cave ribbon. Parents be advised: Wait until the kids are at least four or five years old since strollers are difficult to operate and toddlers might not have the patience or interest. Two tours are available. The standard North Cavern Tour, a 75-minute half-mile trek past oooh-inducing stalagmites, stalactites, flowstones, and other formations, some with descriptive titles such as the King's Throne and Sherwood's Forest. The other option, the Jeremy Room Flashlight Tour, takes place in a 120-foot-deep chamber filled with some of the more delicate formations—particularly the brittle yet mesmerizing soda straws. Each person gets a flashlight to check out the nooks and crannies of this space at their leisure. For those who really want to get up close and personal with the cavern, sign up for one of the Adventure Tours ($100), a physically demanding three-plus-hour excursion allowing visitors to climb, rappel, and explore the cavern. Caving gear is provided.

Sophienburg Museum

Those interested in learning more about New Braunfels's cultural history should visit the Sophienburg Museum (401 W. Coll St., 830/629-1572, www.sophienburg.org, Tues.–Sat. 10 A.M.–4 P.M., $5 adults, $2 students, $1 children ages 6–12). Not surprisingly, the town's German heritage takes center stage, with hundreds of artifacts dedicated to telling the story of the hearty folks who settled here in the mid-1800s and persevered through difficult times. Docents describe how the original village was founded by Prince Carl of Solms Braunfels, and historic photos and documents chronicle these events. A replica town containing a castle, general store, pharmacy, doctor's office, and saloon help transport visitors to this bygone era.

Accommodations
BED-AND-BREAKFASTS

New Braunfels is a B&B kind of town, especially its Gruene Historic District. San Antonio and Austin residents often make weekend getaways to New Braunfels, using a Gruene B&B as home base while they tube and shop. One of the most popular destinations is **Gruene Mansion Inn** (1275 Gruene Rd., 830/629-2641, www.gruenemansioninn.com, rooms start at $190 and most weekends have a two-night minimum stay). This is where the town's namesake, Henry D. Gruene, once lived; his Victorian home and outbuildings are now listed on the National Register of Historic Places. Gruene's mansion has been converted into 30 guest rooms, each with its own entrance, private bathroom, and porch, and the rooms are decorated with a heavily furnished "Victorian rustic elegance." Free Wi-Fi service is available, and breakfast consists of a buffet with several hot items, pastries, breads, and fruit.

Another highly regarded option is **Gruene Homestead Inn** (832 Gruene Rd., 830/606-0216 or 800/238-5534, www.gruenehomesteadinn.com, rooms start at $140), a collection of historic farmhouses on eight acres. Amenities include private baths and porches, free wireless Internet, and a full breakfast. Guests also have access to the swimming pool and hot tub, and family accommodations on this former German homestead are available in cottages and guesthouses that sleep up to five people. Catch a local blues or Americana band on the inn's grounds at Tavern in the Gruene, a live music venue featuring a full bar, shuffleboard table, and horseshoe pit.

HOTELS

New Braunfels has several decent nonchain accommodations, including the fancy **Faust Hotel** (240 S. Seguin Ave., 830/625-7791, www.fausthotel.com, $129 d). Built in 1929, this elegant hotel has an added bonus: an on-site microbrewery. The Faust Brewing Company, the only microbrewery in New Braunfels, is located in the hotel's original beer garden and serves some tasty brews, including

a crisp hefeweizen wheat beer. The rooms are pretty nice, too, with period furnishings and free Wi-Fi. The hotel also provides a free breakfast.

Not nearly as upscale is the tuber-friendly collection of cottages on the river at **The Other Place** (385 Other Place Dr., 830/625-5114, www.theotherplaceresort.com, cabins range from $180 to more than $300). This natural spot has been around since 1910, when it was founded as Camp Giesecke, and its four wooded acres are bordered by 1,400 feet of river frontage in the horseshoe bend of the Comal River. Each unit has central air/heat, a full kitchen with dishes and utensils, a dining area, Wi-Fi access, and a private porch overlooking the river. Be forewarned: There are no phones or TVs in the rooms, so guests have to rely on good ol' fashioned conversation and game playing (or their iPhones) for entertainment.

Food

The Gristmill (1287 Gruene Rd., 830/625-0684, www.gristmillrestaurant.com, $8–23) is a must if you're in Gruene. Located in a historic cotton gin building beneath the iconic Gruene water tower, The Gristmill embodies the district's appeal: tastefully done rustic comfort. The fabulous scenery at this multilevel establishment overlooking the scenic Guadalupe River is almost as good as the food. Start with an order of perfectly breaded sweet onion rings and proceed to enjoy anything on the Southern-tinged menu. The beef tenderloin sandwich with avocado and horseradish sauce is especially tasty, as are the burgers, fried catfish, and tomatillo chicken. Good luck saving room for the delectable fudge pie.

For a true German experience in this authentically German town, try **Friesenhaus** (148 S. Castell St., 830/237-8862, www.friesenhausnb.com, $9–21). The name references the family's native stomping grounds in northern Germany, and the food proves they know their stuff. Breaded pork schnitzel is the specialty here, but the other menu options, from steaks to sausage to seafood, are equally tempting. Be sure to sample some of the flavorful breads and rolls made daily in the restaurant's bakery, and stick with the German tradition by accompanying everything with a local beer or two.

Although it's better known as a national phone/online meat delivery company, the **New Braunfels Smokehouse** (140 S. State Hwy. 46, 830/625-2416, www.nbsmokehouse.com, $11–27) has a restaurant just off the freeway that serves savory hickory-smoked meats on a plate rather than in a box. Sausages are the most popular items here, but locals make regular returns for the beef brisket, ham, ribs, and chicken and dumplings. If you're in the area at breakfast, don't miss their eggs and smoked sausage or pork chop combos. Lunches feature smoked ham, turkey, pastrami, and Canadian bacon sandwiches on homemade bread.

For those who've had enough of the German and Hill Country scene, head directly to New Braunfels's popular downtown **Huisache Grill & Wine Bar** (303 W. San Antonio St., 830/620-9001, www.huisache.com, $10–26). Housed in a modest late-19th-century building with beautiful woodwork and abundant natural light, Huisache features freshly prepared, eclectic cuisine in a comfy setting. You can't go wrong with their mixed grill (beef tenderloin kabobs, wild boar sausage, seared duck) or baked salmon.

Information and Services
The sheer number of tubing and German-related tourist activities can be mind-boggling. To help get a handle on what's available and where, drop by the **Greater New Braunfels Chamber of Commerce** (390 S. Seguin Ave., 830/625-2385 or 800/572-2626, www.nbcham.org). Friendly staffers will gladly provide brochures and directions.

Del Rio

Del Rio (population 36,491) bills itself as the "Best of the Border," and that's a fairly accurate statement in Texas. It's certainly a worthwhile destination, primarily for the fascinating Native American pictographs and archaeological sites in Amistad Recreation Area and Seminole Canyon State Park. Although it appears to be in the middle of nowhere, Del Rio is actually a fairly quick (almost two-hour) road trip directly west of San Antonio. It's worth making a quick day trip or an overnight trek for the prehistoric Native American rock art alone.

Del Rio's history is tied to the San Felipe Springs, which still gush nearly 100 million gallons of clear, cool water each day. Early Native American tribes and Spanish settlers used the springs to forge crude irrigation systems, eventually developing a canal system that diverted water to 1,500 acres of surrounding land.

Soon after the canal system was formalized in 1871, two major railroads linked up just west of the city, and the resulting economic boom established Del Rio as a burgeoning border town, becoming a division headquarters for the railroad. By the 1900s, a healthy portion of Del Rio's economy was government based, with the border patrol, Laughlin Air Force Base, customs offices, and a federal courthouse here.

Del Rio's cultural legacy also has an intriguing tale worth broadcasting: the border blaster radio saga. In the late 1950s, "Dr." John R. Brinkley made international waves when he advertised his controversial hormone-enhancing medical procedures (involving goat gland transplants) from his radio station in Ciudad Acuña across the border from Del Rio. American radio stations had federal limitations on the amount of power they could use to broadcast their signals, but Brinkley's Mexican station XER had 250,000 watts (five times the U.S. limit). In the early 1960s, he hired a gravelly voiced deejay named Wolfman Jack, who, thanks to the insane amount of voltage beaming his sonic sounds throughout the continent, became a vital figure in early rock 'n' roll history.

SIGHTS
◖ Seminole Canyon State Park

The steep, narrow canyons of the Rio Grande and Pecos River have provided shelter for thousands of years and, in the process, preserved prehistoric materials by offering protection from the elements. Some of the most impressive examples are of ancient Native American artwork, the focal point of Seminole Canyon State Park (located 38 miles west of Del Rio on Hwy. 90, 432/292-4464, www.tpwd.state. tx.us, open daily, $3 daily fee ages 13 and up). The park's main attraction is Fate Bell Shelter, containing an amazing array of ancient pictographs, including mystic shaman figures, animal images, and soul-stirring handprints.

The meaning of the mesmerizing paintings is buried with the people who painted them nearly 4,000 years ago, but that's what makes them so utterly intriguing. What were they communicating with these crude drawings? What do the mystic shaman figures represent? What were conditions like in this region so many millennia ago? What's known is that the various Native American tribes, collectively referred to as the people of the Lower Pecos River, lived in small groups and subsisted off small animals and wild plants. The pictographs, made with rust-colored paint derived from animal oils and plant materials, depict many of these animals, along with shaman figures. Some historians suggest the shamans are symbols of medicine men or spiritual beings connecting them to different levels of consciousness via hallucinogenic herbs and plants.

The park's **Fate Bell Shelter Tour** is held Wednesday–Sunday (at 10 A.M. June 1–August 31, 10 A.M. and 3 P.M. September 1–May 31) and involves a fairly rugged hike to the bottom of the canyon and then up to the art-filled rock shelter. Volunteers with the nonprofit Rock Art Foundation (888/762-5278, www.rockart.org) conduct tours of the shelter, and the group also offers weekend trips to the region's

a shaman statue at Seminole Canyon State Park

© TEXAS HISTORICAL COMMISSION

LOWER PECOS ROCK ART

© TEXAS HISTORICAL COMMISSION

the namesake panther pictograph in Seminole Canyon's Panther Cave

Panthers, shamans, deer, and abstract figures adorn the walls of hundreds of rock shelters in the Lower Pecos region of South Texas just west of Del Rio. Known as rock art or pictographs, these ancient images – many believed to be between 3,000 and 4,000 years old – are considered among the finest in the world and represent possibly the largest collection in North America. This fabled region of the state, where the Pecos and Devils Rivers join the Rio Grande, is prized by archaeologists and historians worldwide for its impressive collection of these mostly red figures representing centuries of mysterious and compelling artwork.

Although evidence of human habitation in the Lower Pecos region dates back at least 10,000 years, archaeologists estimate the rock art was created between the years of 3000 B.C. and A.D. 1880. This era includes several distinct types of pictographs, including the Archaic-age Pecos River style, with scenes depicting stylized figures and humans, the Late Archaic period's tiny dark-red rock art, the Late Prehistoric period's multicolored (red, orange-ish, and yellow) solid human and animal figures, and the Historic style, including drawings containing European influence.

Though it remains somewhat controversial, some archaeologists cite the influence hallucinogenic plants (peyote, mountain laurel beans, jimson weed) may have had on the artists' work. Many depicted shaman figures, which served an important role in the Native American tribes as healers, diviners, and guardians who journeyed to the spirit world through altered states of consciousness.

other noteworthy rock art sites, including the Galloway White Shaman Preserve, the Casper Site, and the Curly Tail Panther Site.

Although Seminole Canyon is primarily devoted to ancient pictographs, there are other things to do there between visits to rock shelters. The park also includes an insightful and well-researched interpretive center, campsites with water and electricity, eight miles of multiuse trails for hiking and mountain biking, and nature/interpretive trails.

Panther Cave

Panther Cave has been referred to as the Sistine Chapel of American Rock Art, and those who have experienced it understand why. This mesmerizing rock shelter featuring 4,000-year-old (!) Native American pictographs is only accessible by boat, and even at a choppy 45 miles per hour it takes nearly an hour to get there. For those fascinated by ancient people and their lifeways, it's well worth the effort.

After traversing the enormous Lake Amistad, a man-made reservoir on the Rio Grande just west of Del Rio, visitors ascend a steep steel staircase along the canyon wall to see this spectacular panorama of rock art.

Stretched across a 100-foot-wide canvas of limestone are more than 100 rust-colored images depicting animals and magnificent shaman (medicine man) figures, most created by Native Americans long before ancient Egyptians placed the first stones of the Great Pyramids. The centerpiece is the cave's namesake 10-foot-long panther, a reddish-brown profile of a massive cat raised on its hind legs with spiky hairs on its back and an unusually long tail. Visitors will be transfixed by its allure, repeatedly muttering "wow" as they try to comprehend its ancient origins. A chain-link fence limits up-close interaction with the cave's paintings, but the protection it provides, along with nearby informative panels, ensure the site will remain a fulfilling destination well into the future.

The National Park Service manages Panther Cave with Seminole Canyon State Park, and it should be noted that recent droughts have resulted in lowered lake levels and an occasional loss of access to the cave. To plan a visit to Panther Cave, first get your bearings by obtaining a map at one of the local visitors centers or via the Amistad Recreation Area website (www.nps.gov/amis). This will help you get a sense of where the marinas are in relation to the cave; to reach it, boaters should launch at the Pecos River boat ramp. Boat rental options include **Lake Amistad Marina** (830/774-4157 or 800/255-5561, www.lakeamistadmarina. com) or **Rough Canyon Marina** (830/775-8779). For a list of marinas, see the Amistad Recreation Area entry.

Amistad Recreation Area

Lake Amistad (Spanish for friendship) was created in 1969 by Amistad Dam, an enormous structure containing two bronze eagles at the center symbolizing the spirit of cooperation between the United States and Mexico. The National Park Service manages the Amistad National Recreation Area (830/775-7491, www.nps.gov/amis) and its impressive 67,000 surface acres of water along 540 miles of U.S. shoreline. The lake is a popular destination for year-round boating, fishing, swimming, scuba diving, waterskiing, and bird-watching. Most of the water activity originates at one of the lake's main marinas, where visitors can arrange boat and slip rentals and purchase fuel, bait, ice, snacks, and beverages. They include **Lake Amistad Marina** (830/774-4157, www. lakeamistadmarina.com), **Rough Canyon Marina** (830/775-8779), **Diablo East Marina** (830/774-4157), or the **Air Force Marina** (830/775-7800).

FISHING

Professional anglers are hooked on Amistad Reservoir's high-quality year-round fishing, especially for largemouth, smallmouth, and striped bass. By boat or on shore, fishermen also cast lines for channel and blue catfish, crappie, various species of sunfish, and alligator gar. A catch-and-release policy is encouraged. What's required, however, is a valid Texas fishing license (for the U.S. side of Amistad

Reservoir). Mexico also requires a fishing license for boaters in their waters. Numbered buoys running along the main channel of the Rio Grande indicate the border with Mexico. The permits are available at **Amistad Marine** (7410 Hwy. 90 W., 830/775-0878) or at **Fisherman's Headquarters** (in the Chevron at the intersection of Hwy. 90 W. and Rte. 277 N., 830/774-5670).

BOATING

At any given time of the year you'll see boats punctuating the surface of Amistad Reservoir's clear surface. Personal watercraft, ski boats, sailboats, and houseboats are commonly seen on the lake thanks to the mild weather in this part of the state. A lake use permit is required for the U.S. side of Amistad Reservoir, and Mexico also requires a boat permit for use of their waters. Boating permits can be purchased at **Amistad Visitor Information Center** (located five miles west of the park headquarters on Hwy. 90 W., 830/775-7491, daily 8 A.M.–5 P.M.). Permits are also available at ATM-type machines located at Diablo East,

Rough Canyon, Box Canyon, and the Pecos. The NPS also charges a lake use fee for all watercraft requiring state registration. The fees are $4 daily or $10 for a three-day pass.

CAMPING

Don't expect any fancy camping accommodations at Amistad. The lake's four campgrounds are for hard-core campers only, with site pads, covered picnic tables, and grills about the only amenities available (no RV hookups). In fact, the only campground offering potable water is **Governors Landing,** containing sites suitable for tents or RVs less than 28 feet. Each site costs $4 per night.

Historic Buildings

Like other border towns, Del Rio has retained an impressive number of historic structures, although it doesn't have as much to do with a strong preservation ethic as much as the economy. Since much of the region has struggled financially, it hasn't been in a position to afford the luxury of tearing down old buildings to replace them with fancy new

BORDER RADIO

Way before MTV and blogs, people relied on the radio for exposure to new music. Most cities had AM stations with news and religious broadcasts, but a different sort of animal took to the airwaves in the 1960s. Wolfman Jack became a legendary growly voiced DJ spinning records from a small radio studio just across the Rio Grande from Del Rio.

Known as border radio or border blasters, these stations became powerful ambassadors of early rock 'n' roll because their mega wattage – often operating with nearly five times the amount of power allowed by U.S.-regulated stations – transmitted the broadcasts across the entire hemisphere. In the 1930s, Americans as far away as New York and Seattle were exposed to Western swing and Mexican folk music; by the '50s and '60s the sounds of Southern blues artists and early rhythm and

blues bands were reaching cotton fields and backseats of cruisers via transmitter radios.

The most famous (or infamous) of the border radio stations was XER (later called XERA), home of Wolfman Jack and controversial "goat gland doctor" James Brinkley. Brinkley made a fortune from his bizarre yet popular medical procedure – a gland transplant operation from goat to man to supposedly increase libido – and used his wealth to open the radio station in neighboring Ciudad Acuña and a hospital in Del Rio. The 300-foot-tall border blaster transmitters in Mexico advertised the procedure across the continent and brought occasionally unwanted attention to Del Rio. Regardless, the country and rock music had a lasting cultural impact on America and inspired many would-be musicians to pick up a

modern facilities. It's ultimately proven to be quite beneficial, since border communities like Del Rio contain magnificent vernacular structures from the early 1900s that were bulldozed in most other areas of the state and country during the 1950s as part of the out-with-the-old Modern architectural movement. For a handy guide detailing the location and background of more than 30 historic buildings in town, drop by the Del Rio Chamber of Commerce downtown office (1915 Avenue F).

One of the city's gems is set in the heart of downtown, the 1887 **Val Verde County Courthouse** (400 Pecan St.). Noted for its distinctive tan-colored limestone, the courthouse features handsome stonework forged by Native American masons. Del Rio celebrated the restoration of this magnificent Classical Revival structure as part of its association with the Texas Historical Commission's Texas Historic Courthouse Preservation Program. The nearby **Sacred Heart Church** (320 Mill St.) is another spectacular example of regional architecture. Construction of this native limestone church began in 1891, and the Gothic Revival structure was enlarged and remodeled in 1929. Historic for very different reasons is the **Brinkley Mansion** (512 Qualia Dr.). Built in the early 1930s, this Spanish Eclectic–style residence was home to the infamous "goat-gland doctor" John R. Brinkley of border radio fame. The house serves as a monument to one of the country's biggest medical frauds, a procedure known as the "Brinkley operation," where a gland transplant from a goat supposedly restored virility in men. Patients and money rolled in, and Brinkley used his profits to establish a 250,000-watt radio station across the border (the legendary XER, where Wolfman Jack and early rock 'n' roll were introduced to the continent). He also enhanced his home with flashing colored lights, elaborate water features, and speakers connected to a pipe organ inside. Locals would gather outside this local landmark to dance to the music and enjoy the light show.

Whitehead Memorial Museum

Local history is the main draw at the Whitehead Memorial Museum (1308 S. Main St., 830/774-7568, www.whitehead-museum.org, Tues.–Sat. 9 A.M.–4:30 P.M., Sun. 1–5 P.M., $5 adults, $4 seniors, $3 students ages 13–18, $2 children ages 6–12). Named for a local ranching family who preserved the historic 1871 Perry Store, the museum contains a three-acre frontier village featuring the store and 20 other exhibit sites. The open-air museum includes a replica of local legend Judge Roy Bean's famous combined saloon/courtroom building, as well as Bean's actual gravesite. Also featured are a portion of the San Felipe irrigation canal, an exhibit on the Black Seminole Indian tribe, and a building dedicated to border radio.

Val Verde Winery

Just down the road is Val Verde Winery (100 Qualia Dr., 830/775-9714, www.valverdewinery.com, Mon.–Sat. 10 A.M.–5 P.M.), considered the oldest continuously running winery in Texas. Italian immigrant Frank Qualia discovered Lenoir grapes thriving in the Del Rio sun when he arrived in 1883, and his original adobe winery building is still in use today. Third-generation vintner Thomas Qualia operates Val Verde Winery, and its products, particularly the Don Luis Tawny Port, have won medals from Texas to New York. Most of the wines are sold at the winery itself, but bottles can be shipped throughout the state or are available at specialty shops in the Hill Country, Austin, and Houston. The winery offers complimentary tours and tastings Monday through Saturday.

San Felipe Springs

Del Rio's San Felipe Springs have been a source of nourishment and refreshment for ages. They were a vital watering stop for prehistoric people and settlers on the historic Chihuahua Road. Nearly 100 million gallons of clear clean water emanate from the springs daily, and although they no longer fill the historic irrigation canals that run throughout town, they still sustain the city of Del Rio and nearby Laughlin Air

Force Base. Most local residents will tell you the springs are an ideal destination for cooling off on a hot summer Texas afternoon. Moore City Park has stone banks offering a safe and shallow place for kids to play, and the swimming hole at Horseshoe Park remains a popular place to take a refreshing dip. To reach the source of San Felipe Creek, take Highway 90 West into town; look for San Felipe Country Club on your right. The road through the golf course, San Felipe Springs Road, leads to the source of San Felipe Creek.

Brackettville

Take a few hours on your way in our out of Del Rio to visit Brackettville (about 30 miles east of town on Hwy. 90). One of the town's (population 1,784) main attractions is **Fort Clark Springs** (830/563-2495, www.fortclark. com, call in advance for reservations/accessibility), a spectacular site combining military history and modern-day recreation. This hotel/pool/museum/golf course combo is located at the site of a U.S. Army fort that was in operation for nearly a century. Its historical significance lies in its role as home base for the Army's Seminole-Negro Indian Scouts, a band of displaced East Coast slaves who gained respect as soldiers along the Mexican border. The **Seminole Indian Scout Cemetery** honors their legacy just west of Brackettville on FM 693.

ACCOMMODATIONS
Hotels

Although Del Rio has several independently owned lodging options, travelers often find the city's uninspiring yet reliably consistent chains to be the best options due to their . . . reliable consistency. Among them are **Best Western Inn of Del Rio** (810 Veterans Blvd., 830/775-7511, www.bestwesterntexas.com, $59 d), offering "the largest rooms in the area," complete with microwaves and refrigerators, along with free Wi-Fi access, a free breakfast, and an outdoor pool and hot tub. Another worthy option

the charming courthouse in Brackettville

is **La Quinta Inn Del Rio** (2005 Veterans Blvd., 830/775-7591, www.lq.com, $74 d), featuring free Internet access in all rooms, a free deluxe continental breakfast each morning, and an outdoor pool. A modest step up in price and quality is **Hampton Inn & Suites** (2219 N. Bedell Ave., 830/775-9700, www.hamptoninn. com, $89 d). The Hampton's amenities include a free hot breakfast, free Internet access and lap desks, an outdoor swimming pool, and a fitness center.

Camping

Del Rio's camping options are generally divided into two types: no-frills campsites for fishers and hunters, and full-service parks for RVs. For tent camping, the best place to be is close to the action at **Amistad National Recreation Area** (see entry). For the RV crowd, there's **Holiday Trav-L Park** (11490 W. Hwy. 90, 830/775-7275, www.holidaytrav-l-park.com), with free Wi-Fi access (with tech support), bathhouses, a swimming pool, free coffee and breakfast, and car rentals. Another option is **Lonesome Dove RV Ranch** (4832 W. Hwy. 90, 830/774-1823, www.lonesomedovervranch.com), offering full hookups, showers, a swimming pool, and laundry room.

FOOD
American

Located in a faux log cabin, **Cripple Creek Saloon** (Hwy. 90 W., 830/775-0153, $8–22) is one of the best places in town for standard steak and seafood dishes. Although the mesquite-grilled steaks are popular, locals head here for the seafood, including lobster, swordfish, shrimp, and crab. This is a great place to bring the family since Cripple Creek has a small outdoor petting zoo to keep the kids entertained before, during, and after the meal. A bonus for locavores: Cripple Creek serves wine from Del Rio's very own Val Verde Winery.

Another favorite local hangout is **TB's Bar and Grill** (3806 Veterans Blvd., 830/775-3005, $7–16), a no-frills establishment (the *T* and *B* stand for Todd and Bullet) that focuses more on hearty food than quaint atmosphere. The Corona Chicken is a signature menu item, and other popular dishes include TB's barbecue sandwich and the meaty burgers and steaks.

Mexican

Since nearby Ciudad Acuña's border-crossing appeal is no longer a safe option for sampling authentic Mexican food in its country of origin, most visitors opt to sample Del Rio's wares. Although they don't quite match the appeal of eating at a true Mexican café, Del Rio has several *restaurantes* worth experiencing. At the top of the list is **Memo's** (804 E. Losoya St., 830/774-1583, www.memosrestaurant.com, closed Sun., $7–18). Known more for its history than its food, Memo's has developed a reputation for serving respectable Tex-Mex fare and steaks in a scenic setting on San Felipe Creek. Since 1936, the restaurant has been operated by the Calderon family, including a decades-long stint by "Blondie" Calderon, who achieved fame as the lead piano player and conductor for Ray Price's Cherokee Cowboys Band. The restaurant continues its musical traditions with Latin-themed jam sessions on Thursday nights. There's food here, too, including local favorites like the Tampiqueña dinner (tenderized steak in a spicy sauce with a cheese enchilada on the side) and Blondie's guizado (carne guizada and an enchilada).

One of the newest options is **Manuel's Steakhouse** (804 1312 Veterans Blvd., 830/488-6044, www.manuelssteakhouse. com, $8–18). Also straddling the border between Tex and Mex, Manuel's offers visitors the rare opportunity to experience a Mexican restaurant (the original location is in Ciudad Acuña) without having to cross into Mexico. Steaks are the specialty here, but the Mexican menu is extensive and delicious, with Northern Mexico favorites such as pericos (fancy nachos), quail legs, and mollejas (sweetbreads). The fresh guacamole is some of the best the border has to offer.

Known more for its food than its charm is **Chinto's Super Taco** (400 E. 6th St.,

830/774-1592, $5–10). Located in the heart of downtown, Chinto's is a hot spot for Tex-Mex breakfast and lunch, primarily serving the business crowd. Locals line up for the tasty breakfast tacos and lunch specials (crispy beef tacos, bean burritos). Just don't expect attentive service—orders are placed and picked up at the front counter.

Finally, if you're in the mood for a no-frills Tex-Mex meal, drop by **Taco Torito** (2110 Veterans Blvd., 830/775-6176, $5–9). Locals love this place, and it's easy to see why—the pork adobo tacos are delectable (consider sharing this dish since three tacos is more than enough for one person), and the fresh salsa bar is highly commendable.

INFORMATION AND SERVICES

The **Del Rio Chamber of Commerce** (1915 Veterans Blvd., 830/775-3551, www.drchamber.com) distributes maps and brochures, and provides visitor information about the area. Check with them for details about walking and driving tours of Del Rio, and information about the latest news in Ciudad Acuña.

Laredo

Although Laredo's (population 215,484) reputation as a fun tourist destination has been tarnished by the drug cartel violence in neighboring Nuevo Laredo, the city is still safe to visit, with authentic Mexican culture, historic buildings, and abundant birding opportunities.

From a historical perspective, Laredo has a very Texas-worthy distinction—it's the only area in the state's current borders to have served under seven flags. This seventh flag flew over short-lived yet fiery Republic of the Rio Grande, a district created in 1840 by a constitutional convention after several prominent Laredoans joined a revolt to protest the Mexican government. During its existence, several violent clashes erupted, including one especially brutal battle that ended with the execution of the republic's Chief Army lieutenant Antonio Zapata. His severed head was later displayed as an ominous warning. Representatives ultimately surrendered later that year, marking the end of the Republic of the Rio Grande after merely 283 days.

Unlike many border towns in the lower Rio Grande Valley, Laredo has retained its Hispanic culture without yielding to the religious, architectural, and governmental influences European settlers imposed on other Texas cities. Anglo settlers typically married into Mexican families and assimilated into their culture, rather than enforcing theirs on the natives. Local historians refer to it as a comfortable "Hispanicization," with newcomers easily picking up the language and customs.

This assimilation resulted in the Rio Grande being considered more of a psychological dividing line than a physical border, at least until the recent episodes of gang-related violence in Nuevo Laredo made Mexico a dangerous destination. Laredo's ties to Northern Mexico are long-standing, dating back to 1755, when the city was divided in half after the Rio Grande was established as the international boundary.

Until the past decade, families freely traversed the border, living and working on both sides of the river. This binationalism is reflected in the city's architecture, referred to as border vernacular, with downtown buildings often containing traditional Mexican adobe or mission elements combined with American neoclassical style.

SIGHTS
San Agustin Plaza

One of the city's centers of historical activity is the San Agustin Plaza, a formerly thriving town square near the Rio Grande with traditional Mexican elements such as a cathedral, hotel, mercantile stores, and a central park. The most striking feature is the **San Agustin**

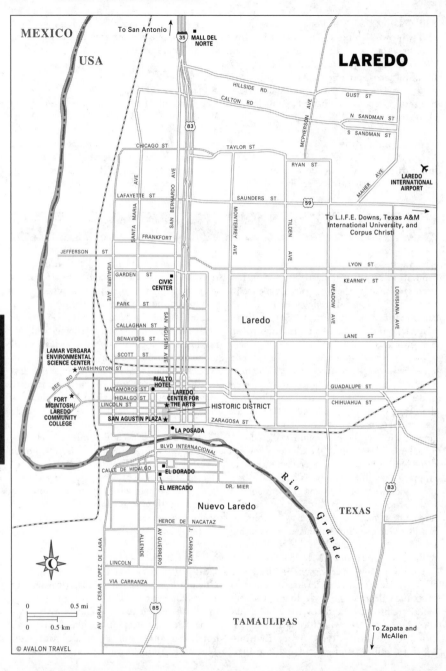

SAN ANTONIO

Cathedral (214 San Bernardo Ave., on the east side of the plaza). Although the parish was established in 1778, the current building dates to 1872. A focal point of the plaza, the masonry Gothic Revival structure boasts a spectacular five-story tower and spire, making it the second-tallest building in Laredo. The cathedral serves as the seat of the Catholic Diocese of Laredo.

On the south side of the plaza is the equally compelling **La Posada** (1000 Zaragoza St.), an upscale hotel. The building's remarkable Spanish Colonial–style architecture makes it another focal point. The building site dates to 1767, when it served as a city hall. It later became Laredo's first convent before transforming into Laredo High School and subsequently a hotel in 1966.

Also on the La Posada grounds is the **Washington's Birthday Celebration Museum,** featuring costumes, photos, and exhibits related to Laredo's 115-year-old fiesta honoring George Washington. The city holds the "father of our country" in high regard for his role in making the United States a welcome location for the many cultures that influenced Laredo's heritage. The celebration itself is held each February, drawing nearly 400,000 people for the festive parades, carnival, concerts, fireworks, and traditional exchange of *abrazos* (hugs) representing the "friendly" relationship between the United States and Mexico.

Directly next door to La Posada is the **Republic of the Rio Grande Museum** (1005 Zaragoza St., 956/727-3480, Tues.–Sat. 9 A.M.–4 P.M., $2), located in a circa-1830 Mexican vernacular home that served as the capitol building for the short-lived republic. The museum features artifacts related to the republic, which existed for a scant 283 days in the year 1840, along with other documents and photos showcasing Laredo's history.

Local history is also on display at the nearby **Villa Antigua Border Heritage Museum** (810 Zaragoza St., 956/727-3480, www.webbheritage.org, Tues.–Sat. 9 A.M.–4 P.M., $5).

San Agustin Plaza is also the starting point for a **trolley tour** (956/727-3480, Tues.–Sat.

© TEXAS HISTORICAL COMMISSION

the Republic of the Rio Grande Museum on the south side of San Agustin Plaza

© TEXAS HISTORICAL COMMISSION

San Agustin Cathedral in historic downtown Laredo

9 A.M.–2 P.M., $10 ages 13 and up) of Laredo's historic districts, including Victorian-era St. Peter's district, the Old Mercado downtown area, and the restored Fort McIntosh. Other stops include the nearby San Agustin Cathedral, a Victorian mansion in the St. Peter's district, and optional stops at the 1909 Webb County Courthouse and the Laredo Center for the Arts. The price includes admission to the Republic of the Rio Grande Museum and the Villa Antigua Border Heritage Museum.

Laredo Center for the Arts

Laredo isn't considered a hotbed of artistic activity, but any city of more than 200,000 has a creative community in need of a major facility. In Laredo, their nucleus is the Laredo Center for the Arts (500 San Agustin Ave., 956/725-1715, www.laredoartcenter.org, Tues.–Sat. 11 A.M.–4 P.M., free). Located in Laredo's historic City Hall in Market Square, the facility's mission is to "promote the artistic creativity of all people" by hosting artistic and cultural events such as international art exhibits, dance performances, art history lectures, musical performances, and art education classes for adults and children. The Center for the Arts is also home to the Webb County Heritage Foundation and hosts a gallery for the Laredo Art League. The center manages three galleries: the Lilia G. Martinez Gallery, the Goodman Gallery, and the Community Gallery, showcasing the work of local student artists.

Fort McIntosh

Fort McIntosh (on the campus of Laredo Community College, west end of Washington St., www.laredo.edu) was established by the U.S. Army in 1848 following the Mexican War and was among a series of border forts guarding against attacks. Its years of service far outlasted Texas's other border forts, which protected settlers for several decades in the mid- to late 1800s. Because of its position on an international border, Fort McIntosh was in continuous use for nearly a century. The fort is now part of Laredo Community College, which has incorporated several of the historic buildings—barracks, chapel, infirmary, guardhouse, commander's house, and commissary—as administrative facilities and housing for faculty and students. Fort McIntosh is marked by four distinct architectural eras: early Fort McIntosh (1848–61), Civil to Spanish-American War (1861–98), modern Fort McIntosh (1900–45), and Laredo Community College period (1946–present). The street names honor fort commanders, officers, and soldiers.

Lamar Vergara Environmental Science Center

Also located on the Laredo Community College campus is the Lamar Vergara Environmental Science Center (west end of Washington St., 956/764-5701, www.laredo.edu, Mon.–Thurs. 8 A.M.–6 P.M., Fri. 8 A.M.–noon), dedicated to plant and animal life in the Rio Grande watershed. The property features four ponds containing alligators, turtles, and fish, and a garden area with more than 50 types of native vegetation, including cacti, wildflowers, and

MEXICO: NOT FOR NOW

Several years ago, people were able to easily cross the Rio Grande sans passport, free to roam the pleasantly slow-paced Mexican border towns in search of cheap treasures and tasty tacos. These days, it's too dangerous for border-town residents, let alone tourists, to brave the once-simple jaunt across the bridge.

People in border communities are rightfully wary of the violence across the river associated with warring drug cartels, which don't always limit their kidnappings and killings to people they know. Fortunately, law enforcement retains a strong presence on the U.S. side, where cities tend to be some of the safest in the state, while the opposite is true just a few miles away in Mexico.

As of early 2011, the violence and unrest in Mexico was severe enough to warrant state-wide warnings against visits to the neighboring country. Since this affects most tourists, it is advisable for travelers in Texas to remain in the state for safety's sake. Even longtime residents of Texas's border communities are reluctant to cross the border, unless a family or business emergency necessitates it.

If the volatile conditions in Mexico subside (as most border communities hope, since their tourism has historically been tied to border hops), visitors will once again return to Mexico's *restaurantes* and *tourista* areas. Meanwhile, many of these destinations (restaurants, in particular) have addressed the drop in business by opening new locations on the Texas side of the Rio Grande. It may not offer the same international flavor, but it provides visitors with something equally as palatable: safety.

---

regional brush species. Indoor exhibits showcase amphibians, reptiles, rodents, and fish.

Birding

Like many of the border towns along the Rio Grande, Laredo has built a strong reputation for its abundant birding opportunities. Birders flock to this part of the state during migratory periods in search of their feathered friends, who arrive from across the country en route to Mexico and other warm climes. The birds' geographical diversity provides an interesting blend of species, including the rare green parakeet and similarly colorful-named white-tipped dove, green jay, and white-collared seedeater. The city's hot spots for bird-watching include River Road on the **Laredo Community College** campus, the **Paso del Indio Nature Trail** (accessible through the Lamar Vergara Science Center), and areas near the **Laredo Independent School District**'s central office (1702 Houston St.).

SHOPPING

Laredo doesn't boast an impressive collection of trendy boutiques, but it has several interesting spots worth checking out for that potentially elusive treasure—especially since border-hopping trips are no longer a safe option. A good starting place is **San Bernardo Avenue,** a stretch of road between Hidalgo and Matamoros near downtown with several quality import stores. Most carry similar products—ceramics, glassware, furniture, paiper-mâaché artwork, small musical instruments, leather goods, home furnishings, and metalwork—though some are higher-quality locales than others. Among them are **Martinez Imports** (3302 San Bernardo Ave., 956/727-9828), **Laredo Mexican Imports** (2905 San Bernardo Ave., 956/791-8020), and **Vega's Imports** (4002 San Bernardo Ave., 956/724-8251). Those looking for larger items, furniture in particular, should drop by one of the city's noteworthy antiques shops. Back in the olden days, you'd probably spend less money across the border for alluring items such as rustic Mexican-style tables, chairs, and cabinets, but the Laredo prices are still reasonable. Check out **Oscar's Antiques** (1002 Guadalupe St., 956/723-0765) or the **Victorian Antique**

Gallery (3202 San Bernardo Ave., 956/727-1231). Far less spectacular yet hands-down the most popular shopping destination in Laredo is **Mall Del Norte** (5300 San Dario Ave., 956/728-1536, www.malldelnorte.com), featuring Macy's, Dillard's, Sears, and more than 150 other retail stores along with a kids' play area, food court, and movie theater.

ACCOMMODATIONS

If you're planning to be in Laredo for a few days, your best bet is to stay in one of the downtown historic hotels, where you'll get a true sense of the city's culture. Compared to other Texas cities, their rates are rather affordable. Hotels are downright cheap in other parts of the city, particularly the reliable chains on I-35 a couple miles north of downtown.

Downtown

Located on the banks of the Rio Grande in the heart of the city is the **Rio Grande Plaza Hotel** (1 S. Main Ave., 877/722-2411, www.venturastreet.com, $89 d). It's not the fanciest place in town, but the location is ideal, and it offers a pool, exercise facility, and Internet access in the rooms.

The best way to experience Laredo is at (**La Posada** (1000 Zaragoza St., 956/722-1701, www.laposadahotel.com, $139 d). With its remarkable Spanish Colonial–style architecture, the hotel is a focal point on the San Agustin Plaza. The building site dates to 1767, when it served as a city hall, and its hacienda appearance makes it a welcoming regional building. Completely renovated in 2007, La Posada features a fully equipped fitness center, lush courtyards, and free wireless Internet access in all rooms.

Another worthy downtown option is the historic **Rialto Hotel** (1219 Matamoros St., 956/725-1800, www.rialtohotel.net, $119 d), offering classic features with modern amenities. This 47-room boutique hotel includes a fitness center and free Internet access in all rooms, along with a microwave and refrigerator.

North of Downtown

One of the best budget options in town is the independently owned **Family Garden Inn & Suites** (5830 San Bernardo Ave., 956/723-5300 or 800/292-4053, www.familygardeninn.com, $65 d). Amenities include a free continental breakfast and evening social gathering, an outdoor pool, fitness center, playground, and rooms with refrigerators and microwaves.

Nearby is the **Courtyard Laredo** (2410 Santa Ursula Ave., 956/725-5555, www.marriott.com, $79 d), catering to business travelers and featuring free Internet access, a swimming pool, breakfast, whirlpool, and exercise room.

Those looking for the comforts of home, including a fully stocked kitchen and several large rooms, should consider **Residence Inn Laredo del Mar** (310 Lost Oaks Blvd., 956/753-9700, www.marriott.com, $98 d), which also offers a complimentary breakfast and free Internet access in all rooms.

Camping

The best place to camp near Laredo is just east of town at **Lake Casa Blanca International State Park** (6101 Bob Bullock Loop off U.S. Hwy. 59, 956/725-3826, www.tpwd.state.tx.us, $4 daily per person 13 and older). The park offers restrooms with showers, campsites with water and electricity, and playgrounds, sports courts, an amphitheater, boat ramp, and two miles of mountain bike trails.

FOOD

Laredo has some of the best Tex-Mex in the state, with its own distinctive variety (norteño) of standard fare such as nachos (panchos), breakfast tacos (mariachis) as well as some of the best cabrito (goat) in the state. There are other types of restaurants in town, but most of them are chains or spots not really worth recommending. The following locales offer a good sampling of the many different sabores (flavors) of Mexican food in this bountiful border town.

Skip the free hotel breakfast and start your day instead at **Maria** (5904 McPherson Ave., 956/729-9878, open daily until 2 P.M., $5–15). The Texas version of a Mexican institution, this place does breakfast right—migas (eggs with crispy tortilla chips and savory peppers) and biscuits topped with beans are true eye-openers.

For lunch, head just down the street to **Tacolare** (6102 McPherson Ave., 956/753-0116, closed Sun., $4–10), which takes the seemingly ordinary taco and elevates it to a lofty delicacy. Some have crafty ingredients (ham, sausage), while others are uniquely constructed, like the *sincronizada,* a sandwichlike stacked tortilla concoction.

A good spot for any meal is the semiswanky **Tono's Bar & Grill** (1202 E. Del Mar Blvd., 956/717-4999, www.tbglaredo.com, closed Sun., $8–28), one of the best places in town to get an authentic interior Mexican-style meal. Entrées range from *huevos montados* (sunnyside up eggs over tortillas, beans, cheese, and sausage) and beef milanesa (a "Mexican-fried steak" with chipotle sauce in place of gravy) to upscale meat and seafood dishes like tenderloin medallions and sea bass. Look for live music in the bar area most weekends.

Two of Laredo's legendary establishments are within a few miles of each other on McPherson Road. **El Rancho Su Majestad El Taco** (9720 McPherson Rd., 956/725-2553, www.elranchosumajestad.com, $8–24) is an import from Nuevo Laredo, where it has enjoyed obligatory dining status for decades. The Laredo version hasn't quite ascended to these heights yet, but the food and experience are still memorable. Mariachi bands often serenade diners as they enjoy traditional Tex-Mex favorites (enchiladas, tacos, quesadillas) and fancier fare like the parrillada platter (sausage, ribs, fajita meat) and roast quail. Just down the road is **Fonda Don Martin** (9652 McPherson Rd., 956/723-7778, $8–24) an amazing restaurant in an uninspiring location (strip mall). Upon entering and seeing the tortilla-making stand, however, you know you're in for a treat. Order the enchiladas *callejeras* (cheese-filled goodness topped with a spicy sauce) or the heftier *cortadillo del res* (seasoned beef).

INFORMATION AND SERVICES

The **Laredo Convention and Visitors Bureau** (501 San Agustin Ave., 956/795-2200 or 800/361-3360, www.visitlaredo.com, Mon.–Fri. 9 A.M.–5:30 P.M., Sat. 9 A.M.–1 P.M.) is a good place to pick up maps and brochures, and the staffers can handle most inquiries regarding businesses and services related to border crossing. The CVB also has a booth at the airport.

GETTING THERE AND AROUND

Although most Laredo visitors arrive via I-35, there's also the **Laredo International Airport** (5210 Bob Bullock Loop, 956/795-2000, www.cityoflaredo.com/airport). The small airport offers daily flights to Dallas–Fort Worth, Houston, Las Vegas, and several other cities on three major airlines.

Rio Grande Valley

Known throughout the state as simply "the Valley," this four-county area in South Texas extends from the mouth of the Rio Grande and continues for nearly 100 miles upriver. For most of its history, semidesert coastal plains occupied the land, but things dramatically changed when irrigation and railroads were introduced to the region in the early 20th century. Property in the area near present-day McAllen was selling for 25 cents an acre in 1903; three years later an acre was going for $50. The subsequent migration of farmers from the Midwest and immigrants from Mexico led to an enormous population growth in this once-desolate land.

The combination of irrigation and fertile river delta soil resulted in ideal conditions for farming, citrus in particular. Texas grapefruit, including the famous ruby red, and several varieties of oranges became big-time cash crops

VAQUEROS

The mythical American cowboys would be all hat and no cattle if it weren't for the Spanish and Mexican *vaqueros* who preceded them. These colonial herdsmen and 19th-century ranch hands set the stage for the modern cowboys by passing along the tricks of the trade to Anglo settlers on the South Texas plains.

Spanish *vaqueros* in colonial times were generally considered rough and rowdy dudes acknowledged for their cattle-rustling skills and horsemanship. As ranching progressed northward through Mexico to Texas, these herdsmen were the on the front line of Hispanic colonization. They often became associated with a *patrón* (a big-time rancher with a land grant from the king) and stayed with the ranch and family for generations.

When Anglos arrived on the scene in the early 1800s, the *vaqueros* were the experts in the field, and they passed along their ranching techniques to the newcomers. Items associated with cowboys of the Wild West – saddles, lassos, spurs, sombreros, bandanas, and chaps – came from the *vaquero* traditions. These elements of the ranching and cattle-driving culture eventually became attached to Texas cowboys, reaching fabled heights in books and movies celebrating the rugged rustlers of the plains.

for the Valley. To this day, several counties in the region remain tops in the state in acres of fruit and vegetables harvested.

The Valley's mild year-round climate also draws tourists and seasonal residents to its nearby beaches and resorts. McAllen, Brownsville, and other Valley communities have become winter homes for more than 125,000 northerners (outnumbering most cities in the area). Still, the local population remains the leading cultural force, with recent population figures showing nearly 85 percent of Valley residents being Hispanic.

BROWNSVILLE

Brownsville (population 172,437) offers the history and traditions of two countries in one border destination, and its towering palm trees and warm Gulf Coast breezes provide an ideal complement to its bird-watching and beach-combing opportunities. The city is also one of the few in the Valley with a deep history, dating to the mid-1700s (most other border communities are tied to the development of the railroad in the early 1900s).

Brownsville was the site of two important battles—Palo Alto and Palmito Ranch—of the U.S.–Mexican War (1846–48), which many historians consider a particularly significant war since its outcome resulted in the United States extending from sea to shining sea. The city also played a vital role in the Civil War thanks to its access to the Gulf of Mexico, allowing trade to continue with Europe without Union retaliation.

Agricultural trade was essential to Brownsville and the region, particularly its cotton industry. Cotton merchants and riverboat entrepreneurs such as Charles Stillman, Mifflin Kenedy, and Richard King made fortunes in their business dealings, resulting in massive land purchases leading to the birth of Texas's ranching industry. Citrus farming later became a major industry, and the construction of a bridge over the Rio Grande led to increased trade with Mexico. In the 1930s, a ship channel was constructed, connecting Brownsville to the Gulf Coast. By the 1960s, the city's industry received another economic boost via the Border Industrialization Program, which helped bring more than 100 manufacturing companies to Brownsville.

Museums

The city's multicultural past is on display at the **Historic Brownsville Museum** (641 E. Madison St., 956/548-1313, www.historicbrownsvillemuseum.org, Tues.–Fri.

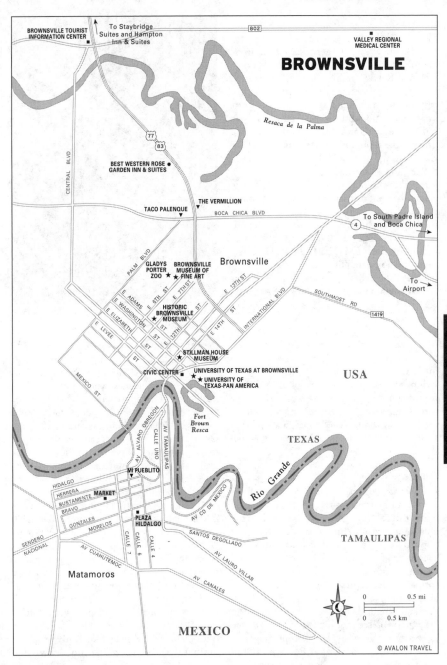

BROWNSVILLE

BROWNSVILLE TOURIST INFORMATION CENTER

To Staybridge Suites and Hampton Inn & Suites

802

VALLEY REGIONAL MEDICAL CENTER

CENTRAL BLVD

77
83

Resaca de la Palma

BEST WESTERN ROSE GARDEN INN & SUITES

THE VERMILLION

TACO PALENQUE

BOCA CHICA BLVD

4

To South Padre Island and Boca Chica

PALM BLVD

Brownsville

GLADYS PORTER ZOO

BROWNSVILLE MUSEUM OF FINE ART

E 13TH ST

To Airport

E ADAMS ST

E 6TH ST

E 7TH ST

INTERNATIONAL BLVD

SOUTHMOST RD

1419

E WASHINGTON ST

HISTORIC BROWNSVILLE MUSEUM

ST

E 14TH ST

E ELIZABETH ST

E 12TH ST

E LEVEE ST

ST

ST

USA

MEXICO ST

STILLMAN HOUSE MUSEUM

CIVIC CENTER

UNIVERSITY OF TEXAS AT BROWNSVILLE

UNIVERSITY OF TEXAS-PAN AMERICA

Fort Brown Resca

TEXAS

AV ALVARO OBREGON

CALLE UNO

AV TAMAULIPAS

Rio Grande

MI PUEBLITO

HIDALGO

HERRERA

BUSTAMANTE

MARKET

BRAVO

AV CD DE MEXICO

TAMAULIPAS

GONZALES

PLAZA HILDALGO

CALLE 7

CALLE 6

CALLE 4

MORELOS

SANTOS DEGOLLADO

SENDERO NACIONAL

AV CUAUHTEMOC

AV LAURO VILLAR

Matamoros

AV CANALES

0   0.5 mi

0   0.5 km

MEXICO

10 A.M.–4 P.M., Sat. 10 A.M.–2 P.M., $2 adults, 50 cents children under 16). Housed in the remarkable 1928 Southern Pacific Railroad Depot (the city's best example of Spanish Colonial Revival architecture), the museum's abundant informative exhibits feature the history of city namesake Fort Brown, historic artifacts, regional artwork, and a Baldwin railroad engine. Local history is also the main draw at the **Stillman House Museum** (1325 E. Washington St., 956/542-3929, Tues.–Sat. 10 A.M.–4 P.M., closed noon–2 P.M., $4). Located in the 1850 downtown home of town elder Charles Stillman, the museum features plenty of historic images and items depicting the city's ranching, education, and religious heritage as well as mid-19th-century Stillman family furnishings. The facility also offers tours and a research library.

One of the Valley's preeminent art museums is the **Brownsville Museum of Fine Art** (600 Ringgold St., 956/542-8909, www.brownsvillemfa.org, Wed. 10 A.M.–8 P.M., Thurs.–Sat. 10 A.M.–4 P.M., $5 adults, $3 children ages 6–12). Located next to the Gladys Porter Zoo, the museum prides itself on its regional and international art as well as its daily art classes. Exhibits range from local school competitions to renowned paintings and works of sculpture. Classes in different medias are held in the historic 1850 Neale House, and the museum is also home to the original Fort Brown Bandstand.

Birding

Ecotourism (visitation dedicated to environmental and cultural awareness) is one of the biggest draws for visitors to the Brownsville area, and bird-watching is perhaps the most popular activity. Virtually all migratory bird species from the eastern United States and the Midwest pass through the region in the spring and fall, and an increasing number of area nature preserves and sanctuaries host exotic and rare birds not typically not found in other parts of Texas or the United States. One of the best places to get a grip on the local birding scene is the **Sabal Palm Audubon**

Sabal Palm Audubon Center and Sanctuary near Brownsville

© TEXAS HISTORICAL COMMISSION

Center and Sanctuary (8400 Southmost Rd., 956/541-8034, www.sabalpalmaudubon.org, daily 9 A.M.–5 P.M., $6 adults, $3 students, $2 children 6 and under). Owned by the National Audubon Society, the center offers 557 acres of preserved land, harboring many endangered species of birds and plants, including the marvelous sabal palm. Visitors can take self-guided tours on the sanctuary's three miles of nature trails, allowing bird-watchers to have face-to-beak contact with long-billed thrashers, buff-bellied hummingbirds, and chacalacas.

Another place to find fine-feathered friends is **Los Ebanos Preserve** (north of Brownsville in San Benito at 27715 Hwy. 100, 956/399-9097, www.losebanospreserve.com, call for hours and to make a bird-watching appointment, prices vary). This 82-acre park is a haven for local bird and butterfly species. Tropical landscaping and gardens entice the winged wonders to frolic in the preserve while visitors track their activity through binoculars. Several trails include self-guided tours and the opportunity to see the elusive and tiny Brownsville common yellowthroat, previously thought to be extinct.

Just west of town is the **Resaca de la Palma State Park** (four miles west of Brownsville at 3301 S. International Blvd./FM 1015, 956/585-9156, www.worldbirdingcenter.org, tours by appointment and reservation only), offering the World Birding Center network's largest tract of native habitat. The 1,700 acres of semitropical property provide an especially rich birding environment, with colorful species such as the yellow-breasted chat and American redstart making occasional appearances. The birding opportunities are currently available via guided tour only, but a World Birding Center visitors center and nature trails are currently being developed.

Palo Alto Battlefield National Historic Site

Brownsville's enduring military legacy is the centerpiece of the National Park Service's Palo Alto Battlefield (five miles north of downtown Brownsville at the intersection FM 1847 and FM 511, 956/541-2785, www.nps.gov/paal, daily 8 A.M.–5 P.M., free admission). On May 8, 1846, this unassuming site, marked by prickly pear cactus, spiky yucca plants, and miles of sandy soil, was the scene of a violent clash in the U.S.–Mexican War (1846–48), a conflict that played an important role in shaping America's history. The desolate field may not seem significant now, but its place in history is put in context in the visitors center's small theater, with the 15-minute video *War on the Rio Grande.* Although visitors center movies can occasionally be as inspiring as a middle school history lecture, this one is actually insightful and interesting, thanks to the National Park Service's thorough research and quality production.

Gladys Porter Zoo

One of the city's most popular attractions is the small yet satisfying Gladys Porter Zoo (500 Ringgold St., 956/546-2177, www.gpz. org, daily 9 A.M.–5 P.M., with extended summer hours, $9.50 adults, $8 seniors, $6.50 children ages 2–13). The zoo features more

than 1,600 animals representing nearly 400 species in four geographic areas: Africa, Asia, Indo-Australia, and tropical America. It also takes pride in its successful endangered-species breeding program. Built on an old channel of the Rio Grande River, the Gladys Porter Zoo is designed to allow the animals to live in open exhibits surrounded by natural flowing waterways. Creatures drawing the largest crowds are the gorillas, bears, sea lions, and the myriad tropical birds that live in the zoo's foliage. Kids will love Small World, featuring a nursery and petting zoo where they can touch and interact with domesticated animals.

Accommodations

Like other border towns, Brownsville's accommodations are relatively affordable, although the lower-tier options tend to be pretty scary. To be safe (not as many cockroaches), go with one of the more expensive chains along Highway 77/83.

For inexpensive downtown lodging in Brownsville's historic district, consider the **Colonial Hotel** (1147 E. Levee St., 956/541-9176, $75 d), which doesn't offer too many amenities, except for rooms with stylish Western decor and refrigerators. On the northern edge of downtown is the reasonably priced **Best Western Rose Garden Inn & Suites** (845 N. Hwy. 77/83, 956/546-5501, www.bestwesterntexas.com, $79 d), offering a free breakfast buffet, outdoor pool, and Internet access.

Farther north of downtown on Highway 77/83 are several higher-end options (in Brownsville terms), which tend to be newer and oriented toward business clients. For fully furnished rooms, consider **Staybridge Suites** (2900 Pablo Kisel Blvd., 800/970-4654, www.staybridge.com, $95 d), with equipped kitchens, living room areas, and office space along with free Internet access, a complimentary breakfast buffet and evening happy hour, a fitness center, and outdoor pool. A bit closer to town is **Hampton Inn & Suites** (3000 N. Hwy. 77/83, 956/548-0005, www.hamptoninn.com, $89 d), featuring a free hot breakfast buffet, swimming pool, whirlpool, fitness center, and wireless Internet access.

Food

Not surprisingly, Brownsville's best eating establishments are Mexican restaurants. If you're looking for the best available Mexican food (making a run for the border to experience the real deal is no longer an option), there are several noteworthy Tex-Mex spots in Brownsville. At the unique **Trevino's Restaurant** (54 Boca Chica Blvd., 956/544-7866, $5–12), visitors know they're getting fresh-made fare since the restaurant doubles as a tortilla factory and bakery/grocery store. Another popular spot near downtown is **Mejia's Easy to Go** (2974 East Ave., 956/544-7266, $5–12), specializing in consistently tasty standards such as tacos, enchiladas, tostadas, fajitas, and flautas. Another local favorite is **Taqueria Rico's** (714 Hwy. 281, 956/546-0014, closed Tues., $4–9). You can't go wrong with any of the beef-based items (bistec tacos, fajita tacos, and beef flautas are highly recommended), and the fresh avocados on the plates and in the guacamole are alone worth the trip.

Just north of downtown is **The Vermillion** (115 Paredes Line Rd., 956/542-9893, $7–16), a long-standing institution (since 1934) offering a bit more than the typical Tex-Mex specialties. Down-home Southern-style menu items such as chicken-fried steak, charbroiled chicken, and fried catfish still make this a true Tex-Mex option. Brownsville residents and Winter Texans alike flock here for the fully loaded nachos and beef tacos.

For basic yet consistently reliable Mexican dishes, go to the nearby **Taco Palenque** (1803 Boca Chica Blvd., 956/544-8400, $7–15). Locals line up for the breakfast tacos here, as well as the tasty tortillas, enchiladas, tostadas, and fajitas.

For big flavor at a small price, head to **Taqueria Ultimo Taco** (938 N. Hwy. 77/83, 956/554-7663, $4–8). Like most *restaurantes* in the area, meals begin with a small serving of *frijoles* (charro beans), but be sure to save room for the tacos. At 97 cents, you can order

a handful (they're fairly small, so four or five per order is fairly common). Try the barbacoa and al pastor, and be sure to ask for them *con todo* (with everything), including avocado and queso fresco.

Information and Services

The best place to stock up on maps and brochures about area attractions is the **Brownsville Convention & Visitors Bureau** (2305 N. Hwy. 77/83, 956/546-3721, www.brownsville.org). Offering info about businesses in the area is the **Brownsville Chamber of Commerce** (1600 University Blvd., 956/542-4341, www.brownsvillechamber.com).

MCALLEN

One of the fastest-growing cities in the country, McAllen's (population 126,411) initial development was so slow, the town actually ceased to exist about 100 years ago. The railroad and citrus industries helped keep the burgeoning village afloat, and it eventually went on to become an important agricultural center with one of the busiest access points between Mexico and Texas.

Like other Valley cities, McAllen's mild temperatures and subtropical climate is a destination for Winter Texans and birders. It doesn't have the dense historical fabric of other border towns, but McAllen's newest residents have had a distinct cultural impact on the community. Wildlife refuges, a renowned art museum, and the city's status as the "Square Dance Capital of the World" reflect the values of the seasonal and newly arrived population. But why square dancing? Many Winter Texans enjoy retirement by grabbing their partners and do-si-do-ing while expert callers direct the action at dance halls open nightly throughout town. Things get even crazier the first Saturday of February, when thousands of people converge on McAllen for the Texas Square Dance Jamboree.

Unfortunately, McAllen isn't all fun and excitement. One of the reasons it's growing so fast is the tremendous influx of Mexican immigrants, many living on the outskirts of town in substandard conditions. In fact, McAllen is bordered on all sides by *colonias* (neighborhoods without basic services such as water and streets) primarily inhabited by agricultural workers.

International Museum of Art and Science

The finest cultural experience in the region awaits at McAllen's International Museum of Art and Science (1900 Nolana Ave., 956/682-1564, www.imasonline.org, Tues., Wed., Fri., and Sat. 9 A.M.–5 P.M.; Thurs. 9 A.M.–8 P.M.; Sun. 1–5 P.M.; $7 adults, $5 seniors 55 and older, $4 children ages 4–12). Spanning several centuries' worth of artwork ranging from European masters to Mexican folk art to enormous sculptures, the museum is a destination for those intrigued by intellectual endeavors. The fine art and pre-Columbian objects are joined by items in the Earth Science Gallery, including fossils, geological samples, and dinosaur prints. The museum's primary focus is its impressive collection of objects from the Americas, represented by folk art such as masks and ceramics.

Los Ebanos Ferry

Though border-hopping is discouraged these days, visitors may still be interested in viewing the operation of Los Ebanos Ferry (west of McAllen off Hwy. 83 at FM 886, daily 8 A.M.–4 P.M.). This "ancient" (1954) mode of transport is the last hand-pulled ferry on the Rio Grande. Crew members use ropes and pulleys to carry a maximum of three cars and a small number of pedestrians across the river on this modest metal barge. Customers are welcome to take part in the fun by yanking on the rugged, thick ropes if they choose. Border inspection stations are set up on both banks of the river, and the journey across takes a scant five minutes.

Birding

The McAllen area is home to several acclaimed birding sites catering to the thousands of visitors who arrive annually to keep an eye on their feathered friends. The city helps operate the World Birding Center's **Quinta Mazatlan** (600 Sunset Ave., 956/688-3370, www.worldbirdingcenter.org, Tues.–Sat. 8 A.M.–5 P.M., $2 adults, $1 seniors and children). Located near downtown on the grounds of Quinta Mazatlan (Spanish for country estate), the site is an urban oasis offering 15 acres of tropical gardens, native woodlands, and a beautiful 10,000-square-foot historic Spanish Revival adobe hacienda. Naturalists enjoy the walking trails, butterfly garden, nature exhibits, birding feeding stations, and bird meadow, where they can spot elusive local bird species such as the lack-bellied whistling duck, buff-bellied hummingbird, and olive sparrow.

A few miles east of town near the community of Alamo is the highly regarded **Santa Ana National Wildlife Refuge** (off Hwy. 281 at FM 907, 956/784-7500, www.fws.gov, trails open daily dawn–dusk, driving tour open summer weekends 9 A.M.–4 P.M., $3 per vehicle). Nearly 400 bird species live in this 2,000-acre refuge, established in 1943 to protect the thousands of birds that funnel through the region as they migrate to and from Central and South America. This small patch of semitropical thorn forest that once dominated the area also hosts nearly half of all butterfly species found in the United States. The refuge contains a visitors center offering field guides, insect repellant, bird lists, and binoculars, and many visitors opt to experience the property via a 90-minute interpretive tram tour (three daily trips from Thanksgiving to the end of April, $3 adults, $1 children).

The **Bentsen-Rio Grande Valley State Park** (2800 S. Bentsen Palm Dr., 956/585-1107, www.worldbirdingcenter.org, daily 7 A.M.–10 P.M., $5 adults 12 and older, $3 seniors) bills itself as the "crown jewel of Rio Grande Valley parks." Located just west of McAllen in the town of Mission, its lofty claims are supported by the World Birding Center, which is headquartered at this one-of-a-kind 760-acre park. Birders flock here for the "Valley specialties" and "Mexican vagrants" (the species found exclusively in this region).

Park officials strive to retain the natural state by maintaining the distinctive woodlands and re-creating the flooding that previously nourished the land. These conditions (and the park's feeding stations) draw species popular with the birding crowd, such as the chacalaca, green jay, broad-winged hawk, and the awesomely named northern beardless-tyrannulet. Visitors can ride the tram, bikes, or walk through the park, which offers observation decks, bird blinds, bike rentals, nature programs, and a visitors center surrounded by butterfly gardens and hummingbird feeders.

Accommodations

Because it's a relatively new city, McAllen doesn't have many funky/interesting historic lodging options. However, there's a fairly wide range of relatively affordable chains to choose from offering standard amenities. One of the few independently owned options is **La Copa Hotel** (2000 S. 10th St., 956/686-1741, www.lacopainn.com, $67.40 d), featuring a free hot Belgian waffle breakfast, free Internet access in all rooms, as well as a heated pool, fitness room, and Jacuzzi. Similarly priced is the **Pear Tree Inn** (300 W. Hwy. 83, 956/682-4900, www.druryhotels.com, $89 d), offering a free hot breakfast, free Internet access in every room, and an outdoor pool.

A step up in price and quality is the remarkable **◖ Renaissance Casa de Palmas** (101 N. Main St., 956/631-1101, www.marriott.com, $109 d), a stunning Spanish Revival structure in the heart of downtown. Lush tropical landscaping on the surrounding grounds and inviting interior courtyard set this hotel apart from the rest, along with its state-of-the-art fitness center, minibars, Spanish Room restaurant, and wireless Internet access.

One of the nicest and most expensive places in town is **Embassy Suites** (1800 S. 2nd St., 956/686-3000, www.embassysuites.com, $159 d), with its welcoming tropical courtyard and fountain, fitness room, pool, free cooked-to-order breakfast and nightly manager's reception, and rooms featuring refrigerators, microwaves, and free wireless Internet access.

Food

There's no shortage of quality food in McAllen, so visitors shouldn't feel obligated to cross national boundaries in search of a good meal. Although the city's Mexican food is predictably commendable, there are other worthy locales in town offering fresh takes on American classics.

MEXICAN

A reliable local hangout, **La Justica Restaurante y Tacqueria** (5421 N. 23rd St., 956/928-1905, $6–14), offers a dose of rustic charm. Start with the *caldo de pollo*, a savory chicken soup loaded with meat and potatoes and fresh veggies (jalapeño, onion, cilantro) on the side. Then feast on a sumptuous entrée, such as the chicken mole with its smooth yet spicy sauce. Somewhat more upscale is the fantastic **Costa Messa** (1621 N. 11th, 956/618-5449, $9–22), where authentic Mexican meals are accompanied most weekend nights by a trio of guitarists or even a mariachi band. The best way to sample many of Costa Messa's delectable menu items is via the botana platter, a tantalizing mix of fajitas, quesadillas, flautas, and fried zucchini. Be sure to order the fresh guacamole, served with crispy fried tortilla halves.

Those searching for a reliably tasty lunch should visit **La Casa del Taco** (1100 W. Houston Ave., 956/631-8193, $5–10), a Valley stalwart featuring better-than-average standards such as tacos, burritos, and enchiladas. The margaritas here are particularly popular (and potent).

Considered one of the finest Mexican spots in town is the slightly more expensive **Palenque Grill** (606 E. Hwy. 83, 956/618-5959, www.palenquegrill.com, $8–28). Fancy fajitas are a specialty here, and not just because they spare you the spectacle of bringing them out on a sizzling skillet. The quality of the beef, shrimp, and chicken is top-notch, and the fresh flour tortillas provide a tasty wrapping. Other fine options include pork al pastor and the sarandeado fish. Not nearly as fancy is local mainstay **Delia's** (4800 S. 23rd St., 956/630-3502, $4–10), known for its tamales . . . and tamales.

Tucked in a shopping center corner, Delia's offers tasty tamales of all types, from chicken to pork to sweet and spicy varieties.

AMERICAN

You'll feel right at home (if you live on a ranch) at the **Republic of the Rio Grande Grill and Cantina** (1411 S. 10th St., 956/994-8385, $10–26). This knickknack-stocked establishment specializes in down-home cuisine, including steaks, seafood, chicken, and the enormous Lone Star Burger, doused in tangy homemade barbecue sauce. Snag a seat on the patio by the fountain if possible, and be sure to save room for the almond taco dessert (a sweet shell filled with fruit and cream). Just up the road is **Fresco** (7017 N. 10th St., 956/683-8800, $7–19). Owned by a Long Island native, this local favorite offers American (New York) style Italian specialties, including fancy pasta dishes (gambretto, penne rustica), hand-tossed pizza pies, and fresh seafood dishes. This is a great spot to bring the family since Fresco features dishes appealing to all ages.

Information and Services

The **McAllen Convention & Visitors Bureau** (1200 Ash Ave., 956/682-2871, www.mcallenchamber.com, Mon.–Fri. 8 A.M.–5 P.M.) is a great source of information for places to go locally, including a variety of friendly personal service along with maps, brochures, and guides.

HARLINGEN

Some locals would prefer if Harlingen (population 64,202) was referred to as a Valley city instead of a border town. There's quite a difference. Harlingen has a proud connection to its neighboring Mexican culture, but its small-town American sensibility—with a traditional grid-patterned Main Street–style downtown based on the railroad—differs from the nearby rough-around-the-edges border communities.

In fact, residents of those border towns often go to Harlingen specifically for its folksy Americana. Jackson Street, the main drag of the city's historic commercial district, hosts traditional downtown shops and

© TEXAS HISTORICAL COMMISSION

Jackson Street in historic downtown Harlingen

restaurants. What sets it apart from other Main Street communities in Texas are the towering palm trees and occasional sounds of Tejano music drifting from a lunch counter or passing vehicle.

Geographically, Harlingen is part of the Valley region, but the Lower Rio Grande is actually considered a rich river delta. The fertile soil was the main draw for the farmers (citrus, especially) who came here in the late 1800s/early 1900s. Harlingen grew even more when the railroad arrived in 1904, connecting it to larger coastal cities like Brownsville and Corpus Christi.

The railroad put Harlingen on track for development, particularly with the region's plentiful produce being packed in the city's icehouses and shipped north on the rails. Harlingen didn't see a notable population increase until the 1920s, when land developers allegedly hoodwinked some Yankees to the Texas tropics. Local legend claims the railroad companies advertised the Harlingen area's fertile and affordable land before loading Northerners on trains to see this "land of opportunity." When the trains got to the dry, dusty, and desolate King Ranch area, developers would lower the window shades and open bottles of booze so potential property buyers would be in good spirits by the time they arrived in Harlingen's tropical environs. Many people enthusiastically purchased plots of land immediately on sight, and the region's population went from around 1,700 people to nearly 12,000 in a 10-year period.

Harlingen Arts and Heritage Museum

Located at the former Harlingen Army Air Field site, the Harlingen Arts and Heritage Museum (2425 Boxwood St., 956/216-4901, Tues.–Sat. 10 A.M.–4 P.M., Sun. 1–4 P.M.) complex contains several facilities representing Harlingen's colorful past. One of the main attractions is the Lon C. Hill Home, a relocated 1904 structure where Harlingen's founding father lived with his eight children. The home features a compelling collection of historic

photos and period antiques chronicling family and frontier life in the early 1900s.

The palm-lined complex also includes the Historical Museum, located in the former police headquarters of the Harlingen Air Force Base. Exhibits chronicle Harlingen's military history through artifacts (uniforms, flags, weapons, and maps) and a fascinating photo gallery. The Harlingen Arts and Heritage Museum also contains a modern main building with rotating cultural exhibits and touring art shows.

Iwo Jima Memorial and Museum

Harlingen's most recognizable attraction is its Iwo Jima Memorial and Museum (320 Iwo Jima Blvd., 956/421-9234, www.mma-tx.org). This massive structure is the original working model used by sculptor Dr. Felix de Weldon while casting the official bronze version in Washington, D.C. Not surprisingly, the monument is just as powerful as the true rendering, with its six inspirational figures stirring patriotic emotions among the veterans and visitors

The model for the Iwo Jima Memorial is in Harlingen.

who make regular pilgrimages here. The structure was donated to the nearby Marine Military Academy to inspire young cadets and also to acknowledge the regional connection to one of the soldiers depicted in the monument.

The nearby museum and gift shop (associated with the Marine Military Academy) feature exhibits and displays primarily related to the U.S. Marine Corps. Other attractions include an educational film about the Battle for Iwo Jima and the Iwo Jima Veterans Hall of Fame.

Rio Pride Orchard

A visit to the Valley would be incomplete without paying homage to the citrus industry that paved the way for the region's development. The famous ruby red grapefruits come from this area, and one of the best-known and most-visited sites in the Valley is the Harlingen-based Rio Pride Orchard (14748 Hoss Ln., 956/423-1191, www.riopride.com). The orchard is at its peak from November through March, when succulent grapefruit and plump oranges burst from the groves, much to the delight of farmers and tourists. Drop by the orchard for some flavorful fresh fruit and a history lesson about the agricultural industry that put the Rio Grande Valley on the map.

Hugh Ramsey Nature Park

One of Harlingen's top natural attractions is the spectacularly lush 55-acre Hugh Ramsey Nature Park (1001 S. Loop 499, 956/216-5951). This is a paradise for nature tourists who flock to this pristine swath of Valley vegetation, containing dozens of varieties of rare birds, subtropical plants, and colorful butterflies. Although the park peaks during winter months, its peaceful gardens and pleasant walking paths are a welcome natural attraction throughout the year. Just be sure to bring plenty of bug repellant since the mosquitoes are relentless in this naturally lush area.

Accommodations

One of the best lodging deals in Harlingen is **Country Inn & Suites** (3825 S. Expwy. 83, 956/428-0043, www.countryinns.com, $63 d). Amenities include an outdoor pool and whirlpool, on-site fitness center, free wireless Internet access, complimentary hot breakfast daily, and, as an added bonus, free 24-hour coffee, cookies, and candy in the lobby. Another affordable option is **Holiday Inn Express** (501 S. P St., 956/428-9292, www.hiexpress.com, $87 d). The hotel features an outdoor heated pool with adjacent Jacuzzi, a fitness center, and free breakfast bar.

For a slight increase in price and quality, consider **Hampton Inn and Suites** (1202 Ed Carey Dr., 956/428-9800, $109 d). The Hampton offers Internet access, a free breakfast, an exercise room, and an outdoor pool. For those in search of the sparkling new hotels, there's **Best Western Casa Villa Suites** (4317 S. Expwy. 83, 956/412-1500, www.bestwestern.com, $110 d). Amenities include a complimentary hot breakfast Monday through Friday (continental breakfast on weekends), free newspaper, outdoor pool and hot tub, exercise room, and free Wi-Fi service.

Food

Since border-hopping is no longer an option in the Valley, the closest most visitors will get to Mexican food is in Texas. Fortunately, Harlingen has several worthy options, including **Pepe's Mexican Restaurant** (117 S. 77 Sunshine Strip, 956/423-3663, $6–13). Don't skip the chips and salsa here, since they're one of the highlights, using crispy tortillas and slightly spicy salsa. That's not to say the rest of the menu is lacking; in fact, the entrées are some of the best in the region. The chicken mole, in particular, perfectly captures the rich flavor you'd expect in a traditional mole sauce, and the enchiladas verdes offer the perfect balance of tangy tomatillo sauce and heartily seasoned chicken.

Another mostly authentic Mexican option (more Mex, less Tex) is **La Playa Mexican Café** (502 S. 77 Sunshine Strip, 956/421-2000, $7–15). The first thing you may notice is that the queso isn't the Velveeta-y yellow color most people expect; instead, it's a white cheese

SAN ANTONIO

served with fried flour tortilla chips. Main dishes are inventive and flavorful, ranging from shrimp amarrados (cheese-and jalapeño-stuffed shrimp wrapped in bacon), chipotle chicken enchiladas, and shrimp-and scallop-stuffed eggplant.

If you're looking for more traditional Tex-Mex in a casual atmosphere, go to **Los Asados** (210 N. 77 Sunshine Strip, 956/421-3074, $5–11). If you happen to be with a group, be sure to order the botana, a platter crammed with beef and chicken fajita meat, beans, cheese, guacamole, and jalapeños. Other specialties include verde enchiladas, crispy beef tacos, and chicken burritos.

Information and Services

The **Harlingen Convention and Visitors Bureau** (311 E. Tyler St., 956/423-5440 or 800/531-7346, www.visitharlingentexas.com) can assist travelers with brochures, maps, and personal advice. Another helpful resource is the knowledgeable **Downtown Harlingen** (956/216-4910, www.myharlingen.us), which helps visitors discover local businesses and hard-to-find resources.

HOUSTON AND EAST TEXAS

Like the mountains more than 800 miles to the west, the pine forests of East Texas are another natural wonder not typically associated with the Lone Star State. Not surprisingly, the cultural gap between the two regions is as wide as their distance apart.

East Texas has a distinct Southern bayou influence, reflected in the region's food, heritage, and even the accent. Locals are much more likely to regale visitors with long stories in their laiiid-baaack, draaaawn-out speaking style than their twangy tight-lipped West Texan counterparts. Standing apart from this rural Southern character is the megapolis of Houston, the fourth-largest city in the country and home to NASA, oil-related industries, and some of the preeminent museums (and humidity) in the country.

East Texas has long been the gateway to the Lone Star State because its earliest inhabitants—Native Americans, European explorers, Anglo settlers, and African-Americans—arrived primarily from Eastern locales. One of the first things they encountered was the dense acreage now known as the Piney Woods, which includes several national forests and the Big Thicket Preserve.

One of the first groups to inhabit the area was the Caddo Indians, an advanced tribe with sophisticated trade networks throughout the region. The Caddos are credited with inspiring the name Texas, since they welcomed the Spanish explorers by referring to them as *tejas,* meaning friends or allies. By the 1700s, Spain attempted to fortify its presence in the area by establishing a series of missions to protect their

HIGHLIGHTS

◖ **NASA Space Center:** For a true otherworldly experience, shoot over to NASA, Houston's preeminent tourist attraction. Don't miss the awe-inspiring Mission Control building (page 213).

◖ **Contemporary Arts Museum of Houston:** One of the country's most respected modern art facilities, the Contemporary Arts Museum offers a compelling collection of paintings, sculpture, and objets d'art in a stunning stainless-steel building (page 217).

◖ **The Orange Show:** Postman-turned-artist Jeff McKissack glorified "the perfect food" by devoting thousands of square feet to orange-related folk art, including sculptures, masonry, and bizarre buildings (page 218).

◖ **The Kemah Boardwalk:** Located southwest of Houston on Galveston Bay, the boardwalk is pretty touristy but offers nostalgic fun with amusement park rides, a massive aquarium, and a train along with restaurants, shops, and fountains at the water's edge (page 221).

◖ **Spindletop-Gladys City Boomtown Museum:** The 1901 oil gush heard 'round the country erupted at this site chronicling Beaumont's boomtown days (page 241).

◖ **Big Thicket National Preserve:** This swath of East Texas Piney Woods contains a gaggle of species from the Gulf Coast, Central Plains, and Southeastern forests coexisting with critters from the deserts, bayous, woods, and swamps (page 247).

◖ **Texas State Railroad:** Experience the old-time feel of riding the rails on this rickety yet enchanting locomotive, which chugs, clanks, and charms its way through the East Texas Piney Woods (page 257).

◖ **Caddo Lake:** Though it's way up in the northeast corner of the state, Caddo Lake, the only natural lake in Texas, is worth a visit for its scenic backdrop of wispy Spanish moss and outstretched cypress trees while hiking, swimming, fishing, or boating (page 266).

LOOK FOR ◖ TO FIND RECOMMENDED SIGHTS, ACTIVITIES, DINING, AND LODGING.

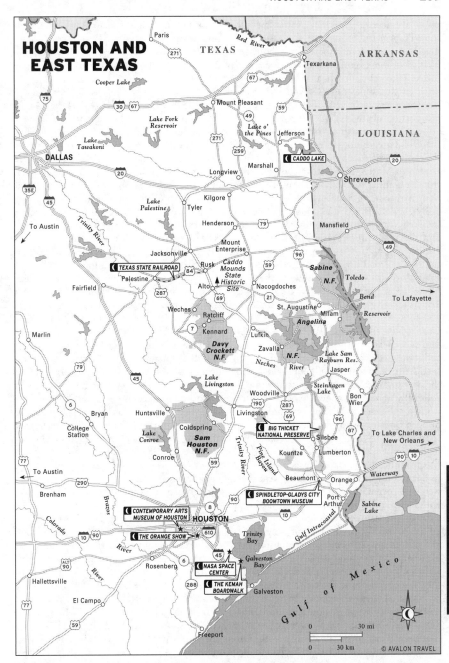

HOUSTON AND EAST TEXAS

© AVALON TRAVEL

political interests (especially against meddle-some France) and to "civilize" the native pop-ulation by converting them to Catholicism. Neither of these ventures was very successful, so the land remained relatively unoccupied until Anglo homesteaders began arriving in large numbers in the early 1800s. In the south-ern portion of this region just west of mod-ern-day Houston, a group of settlers known as the Old Three Hundred established Stephen F. Austin's initial colony. After the fall of the Alamo in March 1836, droves of frightened frontier families fled to East Texas in an event known as the Runaway Scrape.

By the late 1800s, the region became as-sociated with industry. Railroad expansion and European immigration brought an in-creased population and entrepreneurs, and the new railroad lines provided access to the Piney Woods's interiors, allowing the lum-ber industry to flourish. A few decades later, Texas's identity was forever changed when the 100-foot-high oil spout known as the Lucas Gusher blew in (the industry term for erupt-ing) near Beaumont. As soon as word spread about the gusher's subterranean Spindletop oil field, tens of thousands of people flocked to the area to make (or lose) their fortunes. The colorfully named roughnecks and wildcatters worked the fields, while the entrepreneurial-minded investors made the money.

In 1901, the first year of the boom, three major oil companies—Gulf, Humble (later Exxon), and Texas (later Texaco)—formed in Beaumont, and by the following year there were 500 corporations in town. The impact of Spindletop and other oil fields discovered near Tyler is immeasurable, as it brought billions of dollars to Texas through oil company profits and related industry endeavors. Houston per-haps benefited the most, since the oil business ultimately shifted most of its headquarters and shipping operations to the city, which grew at phenomenal rates throughout the mid-1900s.

As a result of this intriguing history, East Texas has a remarkable number of heritage tourism and cultural destinations for visitors to explore. From Caddoan Indian burial mounds

to historic logging towns to Southern planta-tion homes, oil boomtowns, and five national forests, this widespread region is an ideal place to experience the enormous legacy of the Lone Star State.

PLANNING YOUR TIME

Houston is often considered more of a business obligation than a tourist destination, which is unfortunate, since many of the city's museums and cultural attractions are first-rate. Those who make the effort to visit, be it for personal or professional reasons, will discover several days' worth of intriguing activities. NASA is a must, and the downtown museum district and restaurants will keep visitors occupied for at least two if not three days. History buffs should devote half a day to the state park 20 miles east of town containing the impressive San Jacinto Monument and Battleship *Texas*.

The remaining vast expanse of East Texas is worth spending three or four days explor-ing, depending on the amount of time and energy available for seeking adventure among the Piney Woods and Deep South surround-ings. Beaumont is a fun day trip from Houston (less than two hours away), especially for those who want to learn everything they ever wanted to know about Texas's oil legacy. Naturalists should set aside a day or two to explore the Big Thicket National Preserve and other nearby national forests, and visitors interested in old-fashioned Southern culture are encouraged to spend a few days in the northern portion of the Piney Woods, where the cities of Tyler, Lufkin, and Jefferson exude Texas's true heritage.

INFORMATION AND SERVICES

Since Houston isn't a big-time vacation desti-nation, it doesn't have an abundance of travel-ers' bureaus offering maps and brochures. In fact, it only has one. Fortunately, the **Greater Houston Convention and Visitors Bureau** (901 Bagby St., Suite 100, 713/437-5200, www. visithoustontexas.com, daily 9 A.M.–4 P.M.) can handle just about everything. The CVB's impressive offices at City Hall (Bagby Street location) are chock-full of literature and knowledgeable staff members, and the bureau offers similar services at satellite offices at the Bay Area Houston Visitors Center (on Hwy. 45 about 15 miles southeast of town, 281/338-0333) and a kiosk at Katy Mills Mall (on I-10 about 15 miles west of town).

Tours of Houston and the surrounding area are also available. Contact **HoustonTours. net** (888/838-5894, www.houstontours.net) to choose from activity types or location. The site also offers a selection of "most popular tours," including motorcycle rentals and helicopter rides in the area. Another company, **Houston Tours, Inc.** (8915 Bellaire Blvd., 713/988-5900, www.houstontours.com, daily 8 a.m.–8 p.m.) features traditional bus tours of downtown, outlying neighborhoods, and treks to Galveston.

For something more educational (and quirky), consider taking part in one of the Orange Show Foundation's **Eyeopener Tours** (713/926-6368, www.orangeshow.org/eyeopener-tours, typically held the second weekend of the month). Inspired by "places that made you stop, look and look again," Eyeopener Tours are dedicated to itineraries involving compelling food, stories, and sightings in the Houston area and beyond. Tours typically involve a fancy bus with snacks and drinks (averaging around $65 for the entire package) en route to the interesting objet d'folk art, architectural wonders (or disasters), and enigmatic ethnic enclaves of the city.

For those venturing beyond Bayou City, the **Texas Forest Trail Region** (headquarters 202 E. Pilar St. #214, Nacogdoches, 936/560-3699, www.texasforestrail.com) is an ideal place to prepare for a Piney Woods adventure. Check out the website or drop by the main office to get help with determining an East Texas itinerary. For detailed information about travel options in the region's smaller communities, contact the local convention and visitors bureau or chamber of commerce, listed at the end of the corresponding sections in this chapter.

If you're entering East Texas by vehicle from Louisiana, look for the Texas Department of Transportation's **Travel Information Center** at two spots on the state border. The largest facility is in Orange (1708 E. I-10, 409/883-9416) on I-10 en route from New Orleans. The other is in Waskom (1255 N. I-20 E., 903/687-2547) on I-20 from Shreveport. Visit www.dot. state.tx.us for road-related travel information, or check out www.tx.roadconnect.net to find out about the nearest rest area or travel center with free Wi-Fi access.

The best source for news and information in Houston and southeast Texas is the *Houston Chronicle* (www.chron.com), containing thorough coverage of city and state happenings, as well as detailed listings of restaurants and entertainment venues. For specific information about local politics, touring shows, and movie listings, pick up a free copy of the *Houston Press* (www.houstonpress.com) at bars, coffee shops, and bus stations across town.

GETTING THERE AND AROUND

Houston is so big, it has two airports. The rest of the cities in East Texas aren't that big, but several have small regional airports to save travelers the long drives through forests and marshy grasslands.

The major air hub in this part of the country is **George Bush Intercontinental Airport** (2800 N. Terminal Rd., 281/230-3100, www.fly2houston.com), located just north of Houston. This is one of Continental Airlines's major hubs, and since it offers nonstop service to and from more than 170 cities around the world, it's typically hustling and bustling at all hours of the day and night. The city's old airfield, **William P. Hobby Airport** (7800 Airport Blvd., 713/640-3000, www.fly2houston.com) is now the center of activity for Southwest Airlines and hosts flights from several other major carriers. Located 10 miles southeast of downtown, Hobby is more accessible than Bush, but it's showing its age. That's often forgivable by travelers who prefer the facilitated accessibility and cheaper cab fares (nearly $20 less than the trek from Bush to downtown Houston).

SuperShuttle (281/230-7275, www.supershuttle.com) offers shuttle service to and from area hotels and Bush Intercontinental and Hobby Airports. Look for the company's ticket counters in the lower level baggage claim areas of Bush and Hobby. Many downtown-area hotels offer free shuttle service to and from Bush Intercontinental Airport, but check first to make sure they're running.

Another option is a cab. Ground transportation employees outside each terminal of Bush Intercontinental Airport and near the lower level baggage claim area (Curbzone 1) of Hobby Airport will half-heartedly hail travelers a taxi. All destinations within Houston's city limits to/from Bush Intercontinental are charged a flat zone rate or the meter rate, whichever is less. For more information on zone rates, check out the Ground Transportation section at www.fly2houston.com. To arrange for cab pick-up service from within the city, contact one of the following local companies: **Liberty Cab Company** (281/540-8294), **Square Deal Cab Co.** (713/444-4444), **Lonestar Cab** (713/794-0000), and **United Cab Co.** (713/699-0000).

Many travelers prefer to rent a car, and the powers that be at Bush Intercontinental have attempted to make things easier by establishing the **Consolidated Rental Car Facility** (281/230-3000, www.iahrac.com). All the major rental car companies are accessible from this shared location about five minutes away from the terminals. The rental companies share a shuttle system, designated by the white and maroon buses marked "Rental Car Shuttle" located outside the terminal.

Houston is large enough to make accessibility by bus and train a viable option (thanks to the frequency in arrivals and departures). Those interested in traveling by bus can contact **Houston Greyhound** (2121 Main St., 713/759-6565 or 800/231-2222, www.greyhound.com). Passenger trains arrive in town via **Amtrak's Sunset Limited** line, which runs cross-country between Orlando and Los Angeles. Look for arrivals and departures at the Houston Amtrak station (902 Washington Ave., 713/224-1577 or 800/872-7245, www.amtrak.com).

Houston has a decent public transportation system, but it can be confusing for out-of-towners who haven't yet developed a strong sense of direction. Regardless, a little homework can be helpful in strategizing plans via the Metro, aka the **Metropolitan Transit Authority of Harris County** (713/635-4000, www.ridemetro.org), which offers local and commuter bus service. Tickets are available in vending machines located at each station. Metro's red line services 16 stations near downtown's busiest commercial and recreational sites.

Houston

A city as big as Houston (metro population 2,144,491) deserves to be named after a larger-than-life figure: Sam Houston, president of the Republic of Texas who, as general of the Texas army, led the fight for independence from Mexico. Everything about Houston is huge—with more than five million people in the area, it's the largest city in Texas and fourth largest in the country. The Bayou City is notorious for its lack of zoning ordinances and its high humidity, resulting in unmitigated sprawl and unbearably hot summers. But it's not without its charm—Houston has world-class cultural and medical facilities, and its immense international population contributes to a truly cosmopolitan setting with world-renowned corporations, services, and restaurants.

The city even started out with grand ambitions. In the late 1830s, New York City brothers and entrepreneurs Augustus and John Allen claimed that the town would become the "great interior commercial emporium of Texas," with ships from New York and New Orleans sailing up Buffalo Bayou to its door. For most of the late 1800s, Houston was a typical Texas town, fueled by cotton farming and railroad expansion. Unlike other cities, however, Houston received a major financial and identity boom when oil was discovered at nearby Spindletop in 1901. The oil industry changed Houston forever, with major corporations relocating to the city and using its deep ship channel for distribution.

Houston received another identity change and financial surge in the mid-1900s, when it became a headquarters for the aerospace industry. NASA established its Manned Spacecraft Center in 1961, which eventually became the epicenter of the country's space program with its earth-shattering Gemini and Apollo missions.

With the proliferation of air-conditioning around the same time, Houston's brutal humidity was no longer a year-round deterrent, resulting in corporations and their associated workers relocating from colder climes. The population boomed even more in the 1970s when the Arab Oil Embargo caused Houston's petroleum industry to become one of the most vital assets in the country. The world oil economy in the 1980s caused a recession in Houston, and although the city eventually recovered, it received another black eye in the late 1990s as a result of the Enron accounting fraud scandal.

Texans typically don't consider Houston a viable travel destination, but they should. Most people within the state prefer to visit natural wonders such as Big Bend or South Padre Island, but a dose of cosmopolitan life is good for the soul. Houston's sense of style is a step ahead of the Lone Star State's masses, its restaurants often specialize in the regional cuisine of lesser-known countries (offering tantalizing taste-bud sensations beyond standard eatery fare), and the city's public transportation system is surprisingly comprehensive in its coverage. Incidentally, you'll be able to identify a native by the way they say their city's name—locals don't always pronounce the *H* (resulting in "yoo-ston") for some reason.

A drive through Houston's inner-core neighborhoods reveals what happens when a city doesn't prioritize zoning regulations. Depending on who you ask, it's good (Texans in particular don't like to be told what they can or cannot do with their property) or bad (significant historic neighborhoods and homes are routinely leveled to make room for McMansions). Regardless, it's part of Houston's character, even if that means a 150-year-old home sits in the shadow of a monstrous contemporary house across the street from a gargantuan pseudo-historic retail and residential complex.

Houston may never equal San Antonio in visitation numbers, but its distinctive characteristics—a Southern cosmopolitan city with an independent spirit befitting of Texas—make it a worthy destination for more than just business travelers.

SIGHTS

A city of Houston's size offers countless attractions, most of them cultural in nature. The Museum District is a loose collection (not logically planned, but what in Houston is?) of facilities dedicated to art, science, and children's sites located just southwest of downtown. The urban core features occasional historic buildings and theaters among the modern skyscrapers, and the city boasts several offbeat spots outside of town worth checking out for fun, including the folk-art wonder of the Orange Show, and the historically significant state park featuring the San Jacinto Battleground site and the Battleship *Texas*.

◖ NASA Space Center

Light years away from ordinary cultural attractions is NASA's Space Center (1601 NASA Pkwy., 281/244-2100, www.spacecenter.org, weekdays 10 A.M.–5 P.M., weekends 10 A.M.–6 P.M., extended summer hours, $19.95 adults, $18.95 seniors, $15.95 children ages 4–11). NASA is about as big as it gets for Houston tourist attractions, and it's one of the only cities in the United States to host such a distinct icon of contemporary American history. However, this might not be apparent when you step through the front gates. There

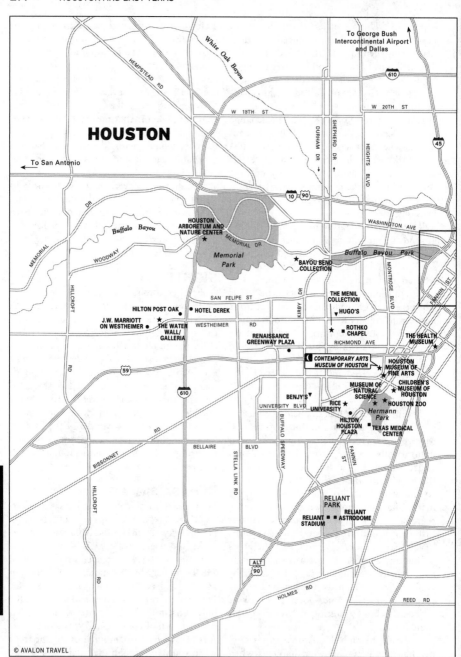

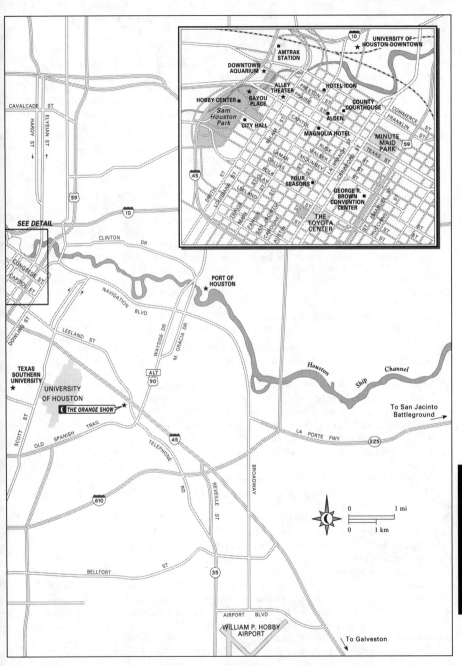

SEE DETAIL

HOUSTON AND EAST TEXAS

HOUSTON, WE HAVE A LEGACY

Space exploration used to be major international news; now, we hardly know when a mission is taking place. Throughout the past four tumultuous decades, NASA's Johnson Space Center in Houston has been the hub of America's celestial activity.

The facility was established in 1961 as the Manned Spacecraft Center and renamed in honor of former president and Texas native Lyndon B. Johnson in 1973. The Johnson Space Center will forever be associated with its earth-shattering early missions with mighty extraterrestrial names, such as Gemini and Apollo.

The famous Mission Control Center is known as the nerve center of America's human space program, and the facility's remarkable guided tours shed light on the fascinating activities that took place here. Grainy TV footage from the manned Apollo missions comes to life as visitors absorb the significance of being in the same room where the words "The Eagle has landed" and "Houston, we have a problem" were first heard.

For the past decade or so, Mission Control has handled all the activity related to the space shuttle and International Space Station programs. Training for these missions took place at an adjacent building, where astronauts and engineers prepared for their time in orbit by using the Space Vehicle Mockup Facility. This enormous edifice houses space shuttle orbital trainers, an International Space Station trainer, a precision air-bearing floor, and a partial gravity simulator. Although the future of the space program remains unclear, NASA expects to play a role in exploring the outer reaches of our known universe, however that may occur. As of late 2010, Johnson Space Center's workforce consisted of about 3,000 employees, mostly professional engineers and scientists. Of these, approximately 110 are astronauts. For the past 40 years, these men and women have helped humans transcend the physical boundaries of Earth to enhance our knowledge about the universe.

To learn more about Johnson Space Center, visit www.nasa.gov/centers/johnson/home/.

are no time lines or text panels dedicated to the history of America's proud space program; instead, there's a 40-foot-tall playground and exhibits about nature's slimiest animals. At this point it becomes apparent that NASA is about two very distinct experiences: kids and adults. Fortunately, it works well.

Those who want to experience the significance and history of the facility should go directly to the tram tour at the far end of the main building. The open-air tram transports visitors to the space center's significant buildings, including the remarkable Mission Control Center. Here, visitors can learn (or relive) the fascinating saga of the Apollo manned spacecraft missions. A knowledgeable and entertaining guide takes you on a descriptive tour of the extraordinary manned spacecraft experience as you peer through a glass partition at the dated yet iconic original gray-paneled equipment and flat monitor screens.

Goosebumps involuntarily rise on your neck as you realize you're in the exact same room where the words "The Eagle has landed" and "Houston, we have a problem" were first heard. Next door, you'll get to see real astronauts in action at the Space Vehicle Mockup Facility, containing space shuttle orbital trainers, an International Space Station trainer, a precision air-bearing floor, and a partial gravity simulator.

Children may not understand the historical significance of Mission Control, but they'll certainly appreciate Kids Space, a massive collection of exhibits, games, and hands-on activities. Most of NASA's main facility features educational and entertainment-related elements, including an enormous playground for kids, interactive flight simulators for young adults, and the compelling Starship Gallery for all ages, offering life-sized models and an educational effects-filled film.

🄲 Contemporary Arts Museum of Houston

As big-city museums go, this is one of the best, with intriguing and captivating (and sometimes head-scratching) objets d'art down every hall. Located in the heart of the Houston Museum District, the CAM (5216 Montrose Blvd., 713/284-8250, www.camh.org, Wed. and Fri. 11 A.M.–7 P.M., Thurs. 11 A.M.–9 P.M., Sat. and Sun. 11 A.M.–6 P.M., free admission) is unmistakable, housed in a distinctive stainless-steel building designed by prominent architect Gunnar Birkerts.

As a noncollecting museum, the facility focuses on current and new directions in art, with regularly changing exhibits and acclaimed education programs. The museum grew steadily in the 1970s and '80s to reach significant status in the nation's art world with celebrated exhibits featuring contemporary still-life painting, thematic installations, performance pieces, and other mediums.

If you're visiting on the last Friday of the month, be sure to drop by the museum's Steel Lounge for an "art"ini while you browse the exhibits and visit the amazing shop, featuring whimsical toys and objects, large posters, decorative items, and exceptional gifts.

Museum of Natural Science

One of the best places in Houston for a family adventure is the science museum (1 Hermann Circle Dr., 713/639-4629, www.hmns.org, Mon.–Sat. 9 A.M.–5 P.M., Sun. 11 A.M.–5 P.M., $15–36 adults, $10–29 seniors and students, based on exhibits). The museum features an almost overwhelming array of exhibits and artifacts covering everything from dinosaurs to gems and minerals to ancient Egypt. Its permanent collection is especially impressive, most notably the Hall of the Americas, with its compelling exhibits depicting the stories of how people arrived on the continent (including Native American, Mayan, and Aztec cultures) and their lifeways once they became permanent residents.

Children will never want to leave the museum's Discovery Place on the lower level,

the Museum of Natural Science

featuring interactive exhibits dedicated to light and sound waves; machines with levers, pulleys, and gears; and a simulated weather studio. The museum's butterfly exhibit is a bit pricey ($7–8) but worthwhile, especially to see the thousands of colorful, lithe winged creatures peacefully meander throughout the towering domed Mayan rain forest habitat. A lengthy waterfall flows gently in the background, and the butterflies occasionally drop by for a personal visit. The museum also contains a McDonald's, but be forewarned: At lunch and dinner the scene gets about as crazy as Times Square on New Year's Eve.

Houston Museum of Fine Arts

Another Museum District hot spot is the fine arts museum (1001 Bissonnet St., 713/639-7300, www.mfah.org, Tues.–Wed. 10 A.M.–5 P.M., Thurs. 10 A.M.–9 P.M., Fri.–Sat. 10 A.M.–7 P.M., Sun. 12:15 P.M.–7 P.M., $7 adults, $3.50 seniors and students 6–18, free on Thurs.). Billing itself as "the largest art museum in America south of Chicago, west of

Washington, D.C., and east of Los Angeles," the Houston Museum of Fine Arts contains two major buildings offering 300,000 square feet of display space and 18 acres of public gardens drawing more than two million people annually. The museum's collection contains nearly 63,000 pieces of art representing all major continents and dating from antiquity to the present. Highlights include the impressively bold Italian renaissance paintings, the mesmerizing French impressionist works, stunning photographs, vintage jewelry, and renowned works of sculpture.

◖ The Orange Show

You know that occasional burst of inspiration that enters your brain? The one that encourages you to take an idea, no matter how ambitious, and follow through with it? Jeff McKissack, a Houston postman-turned-artist, actually did it. He built an enormous folk-art monument dedicated to oranges. McKissack glorified his favorite fruit with 3,000 square feet of space filled with orange-related folk art now known as The Orange Show (2402 Munger St., 713/926-6368, www.orange-show.org, open most weekends noon–5 P.M., $1). Standing among modest suburban homes just east of downtown Houston, this bizarrely compelling artwork is comprised primarily of brick and concrete, accompanied by metal sculptures, mosaic tilework, and various random objects (birdhouses, windmills, statues). McKissack once delivered oranges throughout the South, and he apparently became obsessed enough with them to fashion this whimsical collection of objects found along his mail route. The absurdity-bordering-on-lunacy factor is rather fascinating, and the devotion to his subject is admirable in a disturbing kind of way. McKissack apparently believed his life work (it took him nearly 25 years to assemble his collection into a publicly accessible venue) would become a major tourist destination, but somehow it never quite caught on with the masses. Regardless, it remains an intriguing folk art environment unlike any other you'll ever encounter.

San Jacinto Battleground-Battleship *Texas* State Historic Sites

Two distinctly different yet remarkably significant historical attractions lie adjacent to each other near the Houston Ship Channel 20 miles east of the city. The San Jacinto Battleground and the Battleship *Texas* (3523 Hwy. 134, 281/479-2431, www.tpwd.state.tx.us) tell the stories of valiant warriors in disparate settings fighting for freedom.

Perhaps most significant to Texas history is the San Jacinto Battleground site, with its remarkable 570-foot-tall monument (15 feet taller than the Washington Monument) commemorating Texas's victory for independence. The 1,200-acre site and its adjoining San Jacinto Museum of History preserve and interpret the legendary battleground where Texian troops under Gen. Sam Houston defeated the Mexican Army in an 18-minute battle on April 21, 1836. The magnificent monument—topped by a 34-foot star symbolizing the Lone Star Republic—is dedicated to the "Heroes of the Battle of San Jacinto and all others who contributed to the independence of Texas."

The ground level houses the San Jacinto Museum of History, containing nearly 400,000 objects, documents, and books spanning 400 years of Texas history. Be sure to watch the fascinating 30-minute movie *Texas Forever! The Battle of San Jacinto*. The site's highlight is the observation deck, a 490-foot-tall vantage point offering stunning sweeping views of the battlefield, ship channel, reflecting pool, and surrounding scenery.

Just across the street lies an important piece of the state's history: the Battleship *Texas*. This impressive 1911 vessel is unique—it's the only remaining battleship to serve in both World Wars I and II and was the first U.S. battleship to mount antiaircraft guns and launch an aircraft.

The mighty ship's multiple decks reveal what life was like for the crew, who bravely defended the stars and stripes during crucial combat situations while enduring overcrowded conditions. The elaborate system of massive guns remains

the Battleship *Texas*

impressive, and visitors can occupy one of the artillery seats to get a feel for the challenging precision required to operate the heavy machinery. Head below deck to see the cramped cots, officers' quarters, galley, engine room, medical facilities, and other slices of life to get a true appreciation for the distinguished service provided by the men of the *Texas*.

Since the ship has been moored at the site (in the brackish water of the Houston Ship Channel) since 1948, it has experienced significant weakening in its hull. The approval of a 2007 bond package included funds for dry-berthing the ship, expected to be completed in time for its centennial celebration in 2014.

The Health Museum

Since Houston is one of the country's leading medical centers, it makes sense there's a corresponding health museum (1515 Hermann Dr., 713/521-1515, www.mhms.org, Tues.–Sat. 9 A.M.–5 P.M., Sun. noon–5 P.M., $8 adults, $6 seniors and children ages 3–12, occasional fees for traveling exhibits). Located in the Museum

District, this modest-sized facility is dedicated to educating visitors (kids, mostly) about the importance of good health. The museum includes one of the best exhibits in town, the Amazing Body Pavilion, where you can experience a human body by walking through it. Start by entering through the mouth and exploring the various systems and organs via innovative interactive displays. Vocal chords, lung capacity, stomach acids, and blood content are portrayed through games, hands-on activities, and informative models. The museum also features traveling exhibits related to children's health issues and a fancy gift shop with fun toys, games, and knickknacks.

Houston Zoo

Consistently rated one of the city's top attractions is the lush, welcoming, and occasionally stinky Houston Zoo (6100 Hermann Park Dr., 713/533-6500, www.houstonzoo.org, daily 9 A.M.–6 P.M., $11 ages 12–64, $7 children ages 2–11, $6 seniors). Five thousand animals keep adults and children entertained

HOUSTON'S HUGE HEALTH CENTER

Houston has become a worldwide destination for people in search of a cure. The **Texas Medical Center,** southwest of downtown, bills itself as the largest medical center in the world.

The sheer size of the complex – 1,000-plus acres (billed as "approximately the same size of Chicago's inside loop") – is impressive, as are the number of patients: 160,000 daily visitors with more than six million annual patient visits.

The medical center's origins date to the 1930s, when businessman Monroe Dunaway Anderson proposed a medical center consisting of hospitals, academic institutions, and support organizations. Land was provided free of charge to institutions as an incentive to build within the complex.

Over the decades, the medical center has flourished, with dozens of facilities and specialists flocking to the enormous complex. It now contains one of the world's highest densities of clinical facilities for patient care and medical research. The center contains 49 medicine-related institutions, including 13 hospitals, 2 medical schools, 4 nursing schools, and several schools for other health-related practices (pharmacy, dentistry, public health, etc.).

In true Texas braggadocio style, the Texas Medical Center proudly touts many of its accomplishments and acumens, including:

- Performs more heart surgeries than anywhere else in the world

- Has delivered 19,500 babies

- Has 21,000 physicians, scientists, researchers, and other advanced degree professionals

- Has 71,500 students, including those in high school, college, and health profession programs

- Has 93,500 employees

- Boasts $7.1 billion in approved building and infrastructure for future growth

in 55 acres of various worldwide ecosystems. Be sure to drop by the World of Primates, the Asian Elephant habitat, the lion and tiger exhibit, and the grizzly bear habitat. Kids will also love the Children's Zoo, featuring a petting area with various farm animals, and the "Meet the Keeper" program, offering behind-the-cage insight. Families with children will want to set aside time for a little excursion on the train, which takes a short journey through the park along the zoo's border. Also, if you have children in tow, consider bringing some extra clothes since most kids love the water play area and will undoubtedly get soaked.

Children's Museum of Houston

A must-see if you're in the Museum District with kids is the Children's Museum of Houston (1500 Binz St., 713/522-1138, www.cmhouston.org, Tues.–Sat. 10 A.M.–6 P.M., Thurs. until 8 P.M., Sun. noon–6 P.M., $8 adults and children age 2 and up, $7 seniors). The building itself is a sight to behold—an appropriately playful take on classical architecture with giant colorful details. The fun continues inside, where nine galleries engage children's minds through various subjects including science, geography, performing arts, and history. One of the most popular and informative attractions is the multilevel exhibit How Does It Work? Parents may even pick up a few pointers on how mobile phones function and how turning a key gets an engine running. Younger kids will relish the opportunity to sit in a model car with the freedom to push and pull every button and lever in sight. Other fun activities include an interactive Mexican village, art stations, live shows, and a café with healthy snacks. An added bonus: The Teacher and Family Resource Center has loads of books and items related to child development and parenting for the grown-ups

the playful facade of the Children's Museum of Houston

who may need a break from all the incessant noise and questions.

The Menil Collection

What do you do when you have too much fine art to handle? If you're renowned art collectors John and Dominique de Menil, you open your own museum (1515 Sul Ross St., 713/525-9400, www.menil.org, Wed.–Sun. 11 A.M.–7 P.M., free admission, parking at 1515 W. Alabama St.). Located in the middle of the city's Museum District, the Menil is an ideal place to spend a few hours soaking up some magnificent art spanning many ages. The Menils have passed on, but they left a legacy of approximately 16,000 paintings, sculptures, prints, drawings, photographs, and rare books. Most of the works are modern with an emphasis on the surrealist movement, but there are also African pieces and works from the Byzantine period on display. Be sure to check around each nook and cranny since some of the Menils' most rewarding experiences are in solitary areas where artwork and gardens are

bathed in natural light. The Menil compound also includes several noteworthy structures near the main museum building. Make time for the octagonal Rothko Chapel and the beautiful Byzantine Fresco Chapel.

◖ The Kemah Boardwalk

Located about 25 miles southeast of downtown on Galveston Bay, the popular Kemah Boardwalk (215 Kipp Ave., 281/535-8100, www.kemahboardwalk.com, open daily, all-day ride passes are available: $20 for adults, $17 for children) features restaurants, shops, fountains, and an impressive collection of amusement-park-style rides at the water's edge. Though it's touristy by nature (and draws suburbanites by the thousands for an escape from their 'hoods), the boardwalk offers a much-needed summertime diversion for families along with a nostalgic sense of fun. The restaurants are more notable for their bayside views than adventurous fare, but there's plenty of excitement nearby in the form of rides—including a bona fide roller coaster, Ferris wheel, and double-decker carousel along with bouncy, swingy, and spinny diversions. Other attractions include a 50,000-gallon aquarium with more than 100 different species of tropical fish, a marvelous meandering train, and an interactive stingray reef.

The Water Wall

Houstonians take immense pride in their beloved water wall (2800 Post Oak Blvd., 713/621-8000, weekdays 8 A.M.–6 P.M.). Located southwest of downtown near the Galleria, this six-story structure is exactly what it sounds like—a giant wall of cascading water. But it needs to be experienced to be truly appreciated. The structure is semicircular shaped, and the hypnotic sound of falling water is especially mesmerizing. The gentle mist provides a soothing respite from a hot summer day, and the experience is even cooler at night thanks to the dramatic lighting (and "cooler" temperatures in the 80s). Considered by many to be the most romantic spot in town, the water wall is typically bustling with couples on dates or even getting married. The nearby colossal 64-story-tall Williams/Transco Tower offers a nice urban complement to the scene. Parking can be a hassle—try to snag a spot in the nearby West Drive parking garage, which doesn't charge a fee after 9 P.M. weekdays or on weekends.

Houston Arboretum and Nature Center

Experience Houston's oft-forgotten natural side at the Arboretum and Nature Center (4501 Woodway Dr., 713/681-8433, www.houstonarboretum.org, trails and grounds open daily 7 A.M.–7 P.M., Discovery Room open Tues.–Sun. 10 A.M.–4 P.M., free admission). Located on the west side of near-downtown Memorial Park, the 155-acre nature sanctuary is a green oasis in a city known for its sprawling concrete. Native plants and animals are the focal point, with interactive exhibits and activities educating residents and visitors about the importance of not paving over everything. The park area is beautifully landscaped, and kids will love the Discovery Room's pondering pond and learning tree. Stroll the five miles of trails, hear the sweet sounds of birds, and get a glimpse of Houston's version of the natural world.

Downtown Aquarium

Mingle with marine life at the modestly sized downtown aquarium (410 Bagby St., 713/223-3474, www.aquariumrestaurants.com, Sun.–Thurs. 10 A.M.–9 P.M., Fri.–Sat. 10 A.M.–11 P.M., $9.25 adults, $8.25 seniors, $6.25 children ages 2–12, additional fees for rides and parking). Not as extensive or awe-inspiring as some other big-city aquariums, Houston's version is focused on fun, and there's plenty to be had here. The highlight is the Shark Voyage, where a train takes visitors into a clear tunnel surrounded by blacktips, whitetips, and zebra sharks. Other notable exhibits are the Gulf of Mexico tank with barracuda and snappers, and the Discovery Rig, where kids can get a handle on horseshoe crabs and stingrays. The Ferris wheels (above and below water) are fun, but, like the Shark Voyage, cost a few bucks extra. The aquarium also includes a seemingly unrelated yet interesting exhibit area with several majestic white tigers. Incidentally, the adjacent aquarium restaurant is known for its slow service and mediocre food, so plan accordingly.

Bayou Bend Collection

The affluent home of unfortunately named Ima Hogg, a respected Texas philanthropist,

LITTLE SAIGON, THE SEQUEL

In the 1960s, hundreds of Vietnamese residents fled their country and settled in and around Houston, where they found jobs as fishermen and shrimpers (and working in manufacturing and retail) in a humid coastal environment reminiscent of their homeland. Today, Houston's Vietnamese community of approximately 70,000 is the third largest in the nation, according to U.S. Census figures.

During the past few decades – particularly in the '00s – tens of thousands of Vietnamese residents relocated from California and their native country to purchase homes and open businesses, mostly along a four-mile stretch of Bellaire Boulevard in southwestern Houston. Comparatively cheap housing drew the Californians, many who lived in Los Angeles's famed Little Saigon district.

Word soon got out that Vietnamese families were selling their pricey L.A. abodes and purchasing homes in Houston for a third of the cost. Their remaining funds were often invested in new Vietnamese-centered enterprise businesses, including restaurants, real estate firms, medical facilities, and supermarkets.

The result is a vibrant community, and its neighboring enclaves – shops and residences representing cultures from Chinese to Latino to Pakistani – add to Houston's cosmopolitan and diverse atmosphere. What was once the Vietnamese "best-kept secret" is quickly becoming a high-profile area.

now houses the Bayou Bend Collection (1 Westcott St., 713/639-7750, www.mfah.org, Tues.–Thurs. 10 A.M.–11:45 A.M., Fri.–Sat. 10 A.M.–11:15 A.M., guided tours $10 adults, $8.50 seniors, $5 students ages 10–17). This spectacular 1928 home is one of Houston's cultural treasures, and it's filled with an impressive collection of nearly 5,000 antique objects showcasing American decorative arts from 1620 to 1870. "Miss Hogg," as she was known, also had a hand in the design of the opulent home and grounds, featuring lush gardens and distinctive decorations spanning from the colonial to antebellum eras. Visitors are encouraged to call in advance to make tour reservations, and it should be noted that children under age 10 are not permitted in the home (apparently some old-fashioned customs are still retained along with the objects).

George Ranch Historical Park

For a step back in time and away from the urban pace, consider a jaunt to George Ranch Historical Park (10215 FM 762 in Richmond, 281/343-0218, www.georgeranch.org, Tues.– Sat. 9 A.M.–5 P.M., $9 adults, $8 seniors, $5 students ages 5–15). Located about 30 miles southeast of downtown near the community of Richmond, the site showcases four generations of family members on a 484-acre living-history site. Visitors discover what life was like for Texans on a working cattle ranch through exhibits and displays at the 1820s pioneer farmstead, an 1890s Victorian mansion, and a 1930s ranch house.

Smaller Museums

The Museum District is rife with attractions, including several smaller museums worth visiting for their focus on a particular aspect of the city's culture. They include the following.

THE BUFFALO SOLDIERS MUSEUM

This museum (1834 Southmore Blvd., 713/942-8920, www.buffalosoldiermuseum.com, Mon.–Fri. 10 A.M.–5 P.M., Sat. 10 A.M.–4 P.M., $5 adults, $3 students) is somewhat small, but its significance is enormous. Its name is derived from the term associated with the African-American troops who served in the U.S. Army and protected the Texas frontier in the late 1800s. The Native Americans reportedly referred to them as Buffalo Soldiers due to their immense bravery and valor. Fittingly, the museum honors the legacy of African-Americans' contributions to military service for the past 150 years. This is a unique collection of materials dedicated to a compelling aspect of Texas and America's heritage. Two stories of exhibits feature artifacts, photos, and maps detailing the importance of legacies being passed on to future generations. It's a true learning experience, and it's inspiring to see the groups of area students making connections with their past as interpretive guides offer insight about the uniforms, flags, and equipment. Note: As of early 2011, the museum was planning to move to a new location yet to be determined. Call in advance regarding its current location.

THE HOLOCAUST MUSEUM

A somber subject is handled admirably at the Holocaust Museum Houston (5401 Caroline St., 713/942-8000, www.hmh.org, Mon.–Fri. 9 A.M.–5 P.M., Sat.–Sun. noon–5 P.M., free admission). The museum's mission is to educate people about the dangers of prejudice and hatred in society, and it certainly makes an impact on everyone who walks through its doors. Visitors learn about the historical and personal stories associated with the Holocaust in the museum's permanent exhibit called Bearing Witness: A Community Remembers, which focuses on the stories of Holocaust survivors living in the Houston area. Displays chronicle the Nazi rise to power and the imprisonment in concentration camps. Artifacts, photos, films, informative panels, and a research library serve as testament to the suffering, with the hope that this educational experience will help prevent future atrocities from occurring.

HOUSTON CENTER FOR PHOTOGRAPHY

One of the best little museums in the region is the Houston Center for Photography (1441

W. Alabama St., 713/529-4755, www.hcponline.org, Wed.–Fri. 11 A.M.–6 P.M., Sat.–Sun. noon–5 P.M., free admission). Located in a funky building at the edge of the Museum District, the HCP's mission is to encourage and educate people about art and photography. Exhibits showcase local and national photographers, and programs and services strive to stimulate dialogue about the art form through digital workstations, presentations about methods and critique, and community collaboration.

ENTERTAINMENT AND EVENTS

The Urban Cowboy legend was born in Houston in the early 1980s, and in some parts of town, it's never left. Visitors can get a good feel for the true (and tired) honky-tonks by sampling a few of the city's many nightlife options. Houston has a healthy blues scene, and the bars and dance clubs are reminders of the city's cosmopolitan culture. Speaking of culture, the performing arts in Houston are truly befitting of the nation's fourth-largest city, particularly its internationally renowned opera and ballet companies and spectacular symphony.

Performing Arts
THE HOUSTON GRAND OPERA

A big-time city deserves a big-time opera company, and Houston has one in The Houston Grand Opera (713/228-6737, www.houstongrandopera.org). Performances are held at the downtown Wortham Theater Center (501 Texas Ave.), and the opera is considered one of the city's cultural crown jewels. It's the only opera company on the planet to win a Tony, two Emmys, and two Grammy awards, and it has a reputation for commissioning and performing new works, with dozens of world premieres in more than 50 years. The company tours extensively, bringing productions to Europe, Japan, and Egypt, and on the home front, it's been lauded for its accessibility (tickets for some shows start at $15, and the casual dress series is popular among the younger crowd).

THE HOUSTON BALLET

Another world-class performing arts company is The Houston Ballet (713/523-6300, www.houstonballet.org). Also utilizing the beautiful Wortham Theater Center, the ballet has developed a national reputation for making stars of principal dancers and staging contemporary, edgy ballets. In recent years, the company has been an important diplomat for the city by taking its impressive show on the road to China, London, Canada, and Washington, D.C.'s Kennedy Center.

THE HOUSTON SYMPHONY

Also highly respected in the city's performing arts scene is The Houston Symphony (713/224-4240, www.houstonsymphony.org). The symphony has been impressing audiences at the magnificent downtown Jones Hall (615 Louisiana St.) for more than four decades, and it currently performs more than 170 concerts attended by nearly 350,000 people annually. Shows include a classical season, pops series, *Messiah* performances at Christmas, and family concerts. In the summer, the symphony performs outdoor shows and stages children's performances throughout the region.

THEATER

Houston boasts several high-quality theater companies, but two consistently emerge as the top of the playbill. The **Alley Theatre** (615 Texas Ave., 713/220-5700, www.alleytheatre.org) stages its productions in a facility that's a sight to behold—a medieval-type fortress in the heart of downtown separated into two stages. The Alley is known and respected throughout Houston for its ability to embrace the old and the new. Their classic and contemporary performances consistently draw wide audiences. Also drawing rave reviews is the **Ensemble Theatre** (3535 Main St., 713/520-0055, www.ensemblehouston.com). Billed as the largest African-American professional theater company in the country with its own productions and facility, the Ensemble regularly stages acclaimed dramas, comedies, and musicals for enthusiastic crowds. The company also runs an educational touring program and a popular summer training program for youth.

Live Music

BLUES

Mention blues towns and most people think of Memphis or Chicago, but Houston definitely belongs in the mix. It has a long-standing tradition of serving up swampy bayou blues, and some of the state's grittiest and most soulful players have emerged from the city's downtown African-American neighborhoods. One of the best places to see them play is the legendary **Etta's Lounge** (5120 Scott St., 713/528-2611). You'll have to seek Etta's out since there's no sign out front, a testament to its unassuming vibe. Inside, you'll find the real deal—a no-frills, cavernous room allowing the focus to be on the stage. The refreshingly diverse clientele isn't there to be seen (just to hear). Etta's shines on Sunday nights, when Grady Gaines wows the crowd with his soulful sax. Bring your appetite for a tasty meal, too, since Etta's serves some fine soul food in the restaurant up front.

The **Continental Club** (3700 Main St., 713/529-9899, www.continentalclub.com) doesn't stage blues exclusively—roots and alternative rock acts are often on the bill—but the local and touring blues bands that play here are typically the best around. An offshoot of the legendary Austin venue, Houston's version of the Continental is appropriately more sprawling but still dedicated to offering some of the most soulful music in Bayou City. Bring your dancing shoes, since patrons often shake a leg to work off their meal.

COUNTRY AND WESTERN

Houston is the true home of the Urban Cowboy, so grab those boots if you're fixin' to head out for some two-steppin' at one of these fine dance halls. For a real-deal honky-tonk experience, go straight to **Blanco's** (3406 W. Alabama St., 713/439-0072). Located near downtown just north of the Rice University area, Blanco's is small in size but huge on character. Some of the best live acts in the state play

here, and there's always a fascinating array of couples gliding across the dance floor, from old-school octogenarians to new-school college students. The music is classic country, transporting all ages to a bygone era of bolo ties and beehive hairdos.

Less charming yet more appealing to the masses are the city's big-box country music venues. Located near the Galleria among the trendy upscale dance clubs is the refreshingly unhip **Firehouse Saloon** (5930 Southwest Frwy., 713/977-1962, www.firehousesaloon.com). There's some flashiness here—big ol' shiny belt buckles, fancy light machines, Vegas-style video games—but the crowd is genuinely friendly. Although cover bands take the stage most nights, you'll find the occasional worthy local band looking to catch their big break.

For an overwhelming dose of Lone Star State culture, drop by the **Big Texas Dance Hall and Saloon** (803 E. NASA Blvd., 281/461-4400, www.bigtexassaloon.com). It's a bit hokey—the decor is pseudo-rustic with cacti and Western "artifacts"—but the scene is vibrant, especially for singles. Live music is the big draw on Thursday, when regional acts get boots scootin', but DJs fill the dance floor most weekends.

JAZZ

One of the many benefits of being a music fan in a big city is access to quality jazz clubs. Houston is a major player on the jazz circuit, and it's a hotbed for some of the genre's rising stars. The stalwart on the scene is **Sambuca** (909 Texas Ave., 713/224-5299, www.sambucarestaurant.com). Located in the stunning historic Rice Hotel, Sambuca is a jazz fan's dream—a classy downtown venue offering nightly performances from local and national performers. Accompany your ideal evening with a juicy steak from the acclaimed restaurant and a postmeal or set-break visit to the cigar room.

For a truly intimate experience, visit **Cezanne** (4100 Montrose Blvd., 713/522-9621, www.blacklabradorpub.com), a 40-seat venue in the trendy Montrose district. Cezanne's is considered Houston's premier jazz club, which is nice for the aficionados who get a chance to sit merely feet away from national acts but unfortunate for the hundreds or even thousands of other music lovers who'd like to see the show. Regardless, every seat in this cozy spot is a good one, and you'll hear, see, and feel every note being played.

CONCERT VENUES

Since Houston is such a business- and convention-oriented city, visitors often find themselves in town for a few days in search of familiar rock acts or with an expense account to afford some pricey tickets. Virtually every touring act makes a stop in Houston, so out-of-towners also have an opportunity to catch shows that may not make it to their home turf until the second or third leg of the tour. These folks will likely want to browse the online calendar for the downtown entertainment complex **Bayou Place** (500 Texas St., 713/227-0957, www.bayouplace.com). The Bayou's **Verizon Wireless Theater** (713/230-1600, www.verizonwirelesstheater.com) covers the gamut from rock and country to comedy and musicals, while the adjacent **Hard Rock Cafe** (713/227-1392, www.hardrock.com) offers its venerable blend of music and memorabilia. Nearby is the more club-oriented **Rocbar** (713/236-1100, www.rocbartx.com), where DJs and live acts keep the party going until 2 A.M.

If you still want to rock but prefer to roll away from the hassle of downtown, head to the classic Houston venue **Fitzgerald's** (2706 White Oak Dr., 713/862-3838, www.fitzlivemusic.com). Housed in an enormous historic Polish dance hall, Fitz's features indie rock acts, classic Americana groups, and comfy local bands. The all-ages policy can rub some old-timers the wrong way, but they can always escape to the spacious back patio for a fresh breath of smoky air. Also housed in a historical venue is the folky **Anderson Fair** (2007 Grant St., 713/528-8576, www.andersonfair.com). This tucked-away club in the Montrose area has been hosting up-and-coming folk and roots rock acts for decades and continues to stage some of Texas's most popular Americana acts. Note: Anderson Fair is only open on weekends and only accepts cash.

Bars and Clubs
BARS

One of the most popular spots to open in the past several years is **Max's Wine Dive** (4720 Washington Ave., 713/880-8737, www.maxswinedive.com). "Dive" is a misnomer, since the trendy locale caters to an upscale clientele, but the pairings of drink and food are incredibly down 'n' dirty. You never realized a glass of red wine would complement a burger so well. Or a flute of champagne with fried chicken. More than 150 wines are available by the glass or bottle, and wines are available to go. An added bonus: Most of the beverages and food are Texas organic products. Max's was spawned from the outstanding Uptown establishment **The Tasting Room** (1101 Uptown Park Blvd., 713/993-9800, www.tastingroomwines.com), a big hit with the hip oenophiles (wine aficionados) who frequent the place. The amazing Wine Wall offers hundreds of options for less than $30, or you can descend to the cellar for the more expensive varieties. Drop a $6 corking fee, and you can sip your purchase on-site. Much like its son Max's, The Tasting Room offers perfect pairings of wine and food, including cheeses, olives, salamis, tapas, and pizzas.

One of the more distinctive spots in town to grab a cocktail is **Dean's Credit Clothing** (314 Main St., 713/227-3326, www.deanshouston.com). Nope, that's not a misprint. Housed inside a historic downtown 1930s clothing store, Dean's strives to maintain a much of its early charm as possible. Original features include the elevator (one of the first in Texas), the ornate flooring, and checkout area that's been transformed into a bar. Even the clothing racks remain stocked with vintage items, available for purchase at the bar. Local fashion shows are held here on occasion, and best of all, the drink prices are almost as dated as the surroundings—$2 for cans of Pabst Blue Ribbon and $5 well drinks. Nearby is the low-key and comfy **Warren's Inn** (307 Travis St., 713/247-

9207). A longtime downtown lounge, Warren's is a dark and mellow place where the regulars look like they've occupied their spots at the bar for decades. Be sure to check out the jukebox with appropriate soundtrack music from the 1940s to 1960s.

Many Houston residents associate pub crawls with the **Rice Village** area, where a collection of English-style brewpubs has kept nearby university students out of libraries for decades. The following locales are ideal spots for grabbing a freshly poured pint, finding the jukebox of your dreams, and soaking up the freewheeling college scene: **The Ginger Man** (5607 Morningside Dr., 713/526-2770, www.gingermanpub.com), **Hans' Bier Haus** (2523 Quenby St., 713/520-7474, www.hansbierhaus.com, be sure to play some bocce ball out back), and **Two Rows Restaurant & Brewery Pub** (2400 University Blvd., 713/529-2739, www.tworows.com).

CLUBS

Like most metropolitan areas, Houston's club scene is an ever-changing animal, leaping from spot to spot with an unpredictable life span. One that's managed to stay alive for a while is **Grasshopper** (506 Main St., 713/222-1442, www.grasshopperhouston.com). Located in a swanky late-1800s downtown building, Grasshopper has an Amsterdam vibe, with two separate areas—one for dancing and one for lounging. The thumping hip-hop and R&B tracks keep people jumping on the dance floor, and the alcoves offer a safe escape from the hordes. Just a few blocks away is **Club Venue** (719 Main St., 713/236-8150, www.venuehouston.com). Locals have been lining up here for years to dance the night away to über-trendy house and techno beats. Call in advance for bottle service or to reserve a VIP table.

The appropriately named **Next** (2020 McKinney St., 713/221-8833, www.whatsnexthouston.com) is one of the city's up-and-coming spots where eager line-waiters clamor to be next in line. Located in an obscure building in the city's Warehouse District, the club feels like an L.A. or NYC hot spot with its elevated dance floor, shiny DJ booth, and glass box of beautiful dancers above the bar. Those not as interested in keeping up with the latest trends or worrying about specifically appropriate footwear should head to **La Carafe** (813 Congress St., 713/229-9399). Known for its laid-back vibe and legendary jukebox, La Carafe is in a historic brick building that exudes character. Order some wine, punch in a little Otis Redding on the jukebox, and settle in for a long and cozy evening.

It would be a downright shame to not include a country and western venue in Houston's club listings, so if you're up for some line dancing or people watching head 'em up to **Wild West** (6101 Richmond Ave., 713/266-3455, www.wildwesthouston.com, closed Mon. and Tues). Though it's a bit huge for a club, there's plenty to see and do here, including soaking up the Urban Cowboy scene and even taking dance lessons (offered for just $3 on Sunday afternoons).

GAY BARS

Houston has perhaps the largest gay scene in the South, and most of it is centered on the city's Montrose District west of downtown. This is where most of the gay bars are, drawing all walks of life, from the understated to the overblown. One of the newer clubs on the scene is **JR's** (808 Pacific St., 713/521-2519, www.jrsbarandgrill.com), drawing a semiprofessional crowd for drink specials, karaoke, and male dancers. Parking is hard to come by, so consider using the valet service across the street at the old-school (and somewhat outdated) **Montrose Mining Company** (805 Pacific St., 713/529-7488). Next door to JR's is the popular **South Beach** (810 Pacific St., 713/529-7623, www.southbeachthenightclub.com), a hot spot for dancing. South Beach attracts a primarily gay clientele, but everyone is welcome on the dance floor, where suspended jets spray liquid ice on the crowd to keep things cool. A bit farther away, yet still in the Montrose area, is **EJ's** (2517 Ralph St., 713/527-9071, www.ejsbar.com). Pool is a popular draw here, as are the cheap drinks and a second-floor martini bar.

Events

WINTER

Each year in mid-January, the Antioch Missionary Baptist Church of Christ hosts the **Gardere Martin Luther King Jr. Oratory Competition** (713/867-3286) in honor of Dr. Martin Luther King Jr. The event also includes a highly anticipated performance by the Salvation Army Choir. In mid-February, the **Texas Home and Garden Show** (800/654-1480) offers interactive displays and more than 1,500 exhibitors at the Reliant Center to help Houstonians and visitors get their spring gardening plans growing.

SPRING

Every March, the University of Texas Health Science Center presents the popular **Brain Night at the Museum** (713/521-1515), featuring presentations about how the brain works, a gross yet fascinating dissection of a sheep's brain, an informative video, and other brainy activities. In April, don't miss the **Bayou City Cajun Fest** (281/890-5500) at Traders Village. Patrons enjoy crawfish, po'boys, zydeco bands, and all kinds of Cajun culture. Another popular annual springtime event is the **Asian Pacific Heritage Festival** (713/784-1112), featuring an impressive parade, food booths, and cultural activities at the Alief Community Park in southwest Houston each May.

SUMMER

It gets downright sweltering in Houston during the summer months, but that doesn't deter locals from celebrating. One of the city's best-known annual events is **Juneteenth** (713/558-2600), commemorating the day in June that enslaved Texans learned about their freedom via the Emancipation Proclamation. Juneteenth activities include national gospel, blues, and jazz acts taking the stage at Hermann Park, along with plenty of good eats and revelry. Paper-folding aficionados won't want to miss the annual **Origami Festival at Tansu** (713/880-5100), held each July in Houston Heights. Participate in the interactive workshops, exhibits, and demonstrations.

September is still the height of the summer in Houston, and residents celebrate by enjoying hot jazz at the **Houston International Jazz Festival** (713/839-7000). Let the smooth sounds of local and nationally known jazz artists provide a cool breeze to beat the September heat.

FALL AND HOLIDAY

Get your ghoul on with the city's annual **Ghost Walks** (713/222-9255) throughout October. Hauntees ride on the Metro to different downtown locales where they can get freaked out by various urban legends and authentic historical death scenes. Speaking of deceased, locals and visitors descend en masse on downtown neighborhoods on November 2 as part of the **Day of the Dead Festival** (713/343-0218). Parades and festivals honor the former lives of family and friends. In early December, City Hall becomes the gathering place for **Chanukah Fest** (713/774-0300). The Chabad Lubavitch Outreach of Houston sponsors this annual event featuring traditional food, live music, craft demonstrations, and holiday activities.

SHOPPING
Downtown

Several years ago, the big news in Houston's downtown shopping scene was the transfer from Foley's to **Macy's** (1110 Main St., 713/405-7035, www.macys.com) in the venerable five-story department store in the heart of the historic business district. The building housed the original Foley Bros. store, an establishment that went on to become a mall mainstay across the country. Now that it's been in place for a few years, Macy's ably continues the tradition of offering quality clothing, perfume, and accessories in a cosmopolitan environment. For a real urban experience, take the Metro to the Main Street rail stop and step out near Macy's grand front doors.

Another popular downtown shopping destination is the pleasantly modest **Shops at Houston Center** (1200 McKinney St., 713/759-1442, www.shopsathc.com), comprised of nearly 50 specialty stores and boutiques beneath a canopy-style atrium. Look for jewelry, home decor items, and a quick bite to eat as you stroll the two-block complex among meandering visitors and bee-lining professionals. The shops are connected to Houston's bizarre yet fascinating **Downtown Tunnels** (713/650-3022, tour info at 713/222-9255, www.downtownhouston.com), a six-mile system of air-conditioned subterranean walkways. More than 82 downtown buildings are linked via the tunnels, which started as a small system to connect three downtown theaters in the 1930s. Now, tunnelers can find scores of services, ranging from banks to restaurants to clinics to clothing boutiques, 20 feet below the surface. The tunnel system is accessible from street-level stairwells, and elevators and escalators inside buildings situated above the passageways. The only building offering direct access to the tunnels from the street is the Wells Fargo Plaza (1000 Louisiana St.).

Uptown

One of the city's most popular tourist and shopping destinations is the colossal **Galleria** (5085 Westheimer Rd., 713/622-0663, www.galleriahouston.com). This city within a city—the fourth-largest mall in the country—draws more than 24 million visitors annually. Noted for its remarkable glass atriums and suspended balconies, the Galleria contains a popular ice-skating rink, two Westin hotels, and more than 375 shops, including top-notch retailers such as Nordstrom (the only location in Houston), Saks Fifth Avenue, Neiman Marcus, Cartier, Gucci, and Tiffany & Co. The best time to experience the Galleria is Saturday afternoon. It's an absolute madhouse, and you probably won't get much shopping done, but the people watching is the best the city has to offer. Grab a latte and keep an eye out for the Hispanic girls in their flashy gowns celebrating their Quinceaneras (a cultural rite of passage dedicated to a girl's 15th birthday).

Across the street is the slightly more eclectic **Centre at Post Oak** (5000 Westheimer Rd.), offering a good mix of corporate giants and smaller independent stores. Barnes & Noble

and Marshalls peacefully coexist alongside specialty shops such as J. Tiras Classic Handbags & Jewelry and Jeffrey Stone Ltd. Upscale dining options are also a part of this pedestrian-friendly environment.

Nearby is the charming **Uptown Park** (1400 Post Oak Blvd., 713/850-1400, www.uptownparkhouston.com). Billed as "Houston's Italian-style piazza," Uptown Park features pleasant European-esque buildings, lush landscaped walkways, and soothing fountains. Coffee shops, upscale clothing retailers, fancy jewelry stores, and luxury spas add to the ambience.

Rice Village-Kirby District

Aside from the Galleria, one of Houston's most popular and venerable shopping destinations is **Rice Village** (Rice Blvd. and Kirby Dr. just west of Rice University, www.ricevillageonline.com). This 16-block complex has been a favorite place for bargain hunting, browsing, and people watching since the 1930s. The Village features scores of independent shops and eclectic boutiques along with local restaurants and services, some located in historic homes, others in modest 1950s strip centers. The nearby **Highland Village** (4055 Westheimer Rd., 713/850-3100, www.shophighlandvillage.com) is considered a more subdued version of the galleria. It's an upscale collection of shops, but the stucco buildings and breezy palm trees give it a more relaxed feel than other high-end plazas. Home furnishings are big here, including retail giants such as Williams-Sonoma, Crate & Barrel, and Restoration Hardware, along with dozens of fancy clothing stores and restaurants.

Southwest Houston

An eclectic mix of Asian shops and restaurants awaits on **Harwin Drive,** roughly between Gessner and Fondren Streets. The area offers an epic mash-up of typical American suburban sprawl (strip malls, gaudy signs) and cultural diversity (Thai, Pakistani, Indian, and Chinese vendors, authentic eateries). Plan to spend an afternoon browsing for unexpected gems and bargain clothes, accessories, furniture, and knickknacks. Just a couple miles west on Harwin is **Chinatown,** a concentrated collection of Chinese establishments, including a mall with bookstores, music, gifts, and cooking items.

Katy Outlet Stores

Located about 25 miles west of Houston is the immensely popular **Katy Mills** (5000 Katy Mills Cir., 281/644-5015, www.katymills. com), a destination for bargain hunters who thrive on finding discounted clothing and products from big-time retailers. Katy Mills goes a step beyond other outlet malls, however, by including a 20-screen movie theater, a merry-go-round, and rock wall. It's the brand-name stores that offer the true thrills, however, including Tommy Hilfiger, Off 5th Saks Fifth Avenue, Books-A-Million, Bass Pro Shops, Last Call Neiman Marcus, Cole Haan, and Polo Ralph Lauren.

SPORTS AND RECREATION

Houston is home to several professional sports franchises as well as myriad opportunities for year-round outdoor activities, including golf, hiking, and biking. Pro sports teams are the big draw, especially since so many Houston residents are transplants from other parts of the country in search of opportunities to see their hometown heroes on the field. Natives have had reason to jump on the bandwagon for several sports, most notably the Astros baseball team and Rockets basketball squad, both with postseason appearances in the past decade.

Professional Sports

Houston is a football town, but since the relatively new Houston Texans have been rather punchless since their inception, sports fans are drawn to the venerable (by this city's standards) **Houston Astros.** In 1965, the Astros became the primary occupants of the then-futuristic Astrodome, referred to as the Eighth Wonder of the World. Indeed, it was a sight to behold and an especially welcome respite from Houston's horrendous humidity. The Astros assembled some worthy teams in the 1980s,

the Astrodome, a.k.a. the Eighth Wonder of the World

most notably with hometown hero Nolan Ryan, and two decades later, they attained similar success with another local legend at the helm, Roger Clemens, and a powerhouse offense featuring the "Killer Bs"—Craig Biggio, Jeff Bagwell, and Lance Berkman. By this time, the Astros had fled the Eighth Wonder for the comfy confines of the downtown Minute Maid Park (501 Crawford St.), a classic urban ball field with a modern retractable roof. For Astros ticket and schedule information, contact the team at www.houston. astros.mlb.com or 713/259-8000.

Once home to the storied Houston Oilers football franchise (before they bolted for Tennessee and became the Titans), the city is now the home to the NFL's **Houston Texans.** As an expansion team, the Texans were slow to gain their footing in the NFL, and despite passing on hometown hero and University of Texas standout quarterback Vince Young with their number-one draft pick in 2006, the Texans are building a formidable franchise that, regardless of their spot in the standings, continues to draw substantial crowds to Reliant Stadium (1 Reliant Park). For Texans ticket and schedule information, contact the team at www.houstontexans.com or 832/667-2000.

Basketball isn't as big a draw in Texas as other sports, but the **Houston Rockets** have always had a considerable following. Their successful 1990s teams, featuring top-notch talent such as Clyde "The Glide" Drexler and Hakeem "The Dream" Olajuwon, were the talk of the NBA during their glory years, when they won the NBA title in 1993 and '94. Though they've been less threatening lately, they boast Yao Ming, a 7-foot, 6-inch-tall superstar from China who draws a sizable international fan base. The Rockets hold court at the downtown Toyota Center (1510 Polk St.). For ticket and schedule information, contact www.nba.com/rockets or 713/627-3865.

Parks

Most big cities have a showcase central park offering an inviting natural oasis among the harsh urban environs. Houston's version is **Hermann Park** (6001 Fannin St., 713/524-5876, www.houstontx.gov). Located in the heart of the Museum District just southwest of downtown, Hermann Park is a 400-acre magnet for joggers, dog walkers, bikers, and families in search of some rare green space in a city known for its rampant development. Trails and trees are abundant here, as are the amenities and services, including a theater, golf course, and garden center. The park is filled with statues, too; look for monuments to Sam Houston, Mahatma Gandhi, and namesake George Hermann.

Farther outside of town but worth the 30-minute drive is **Armand Bayou Nature Center** (8500 Bay Area Blvd. in Pasadena, 281/474-2551, www.abnc.org, Tues.–Sat. 9 A.M.–5 P.M., Sun. noon–5 P.M., $3 adults, $1 seniors and students ages 4–12). Located near NASA on the west side of Galveston Bay, the nature center offers residents and visitors a chance to learn about native plant and animal species, hike on the discovery trails, or see the live animal displays featuring the likes of bison, hawks, and spiders. The main area of the park contains a boardwalk traversing the marshes and forests, and providing a glimpse of the beautiful bayou region of East Texas. The best way to experience this natural wonder is by boat—consider taking a tour on the Bayou Ranger pontoon boat or signing up for a guided canoe tour.

Hiking and Biking

Rivaling Hermann Park for crown jewel of Houston's public green space is **Memorial Park** (6501 Memorial Dr., 713/845-1000, www.houstontx.gov, daily 6 A.M.–11 P.M.). What sets Memorial Park apart is its recreational facilities, primarily the hike and bike trails. Located on 1,400 acres formerly dedicated to World War I–era Camp Logan, Memorial Park is now a magnet for all varieties of athletes and exercisers.

The three-mile Seymour Lieberman Exercise Trail is popular with residents who have a daily workout routine and utilize the exercise stations and restrooms along the route. More dedicated runners use the nearby asphalt timing track to work on speed and develop skills, while the Memorial Park Picnic Loop offers a smooth surface for in-line skaters, traditional roller skate enthusiasts, and hikers. Dogs are welcome and even encouraged at the park—canine drinking fountains are conveniently located at ground level along the jogging trails. Just remember to keep your pooch on a leash and to bring a doggie bag.

Mountain bikers race to the park for the miles of challenging terrain along the Buffalo Bayou. The southwest section of the park contains color-coded trails with maps at the trailheads, and Infantry Woods provides an advanced trail for those with superior skills. The park's other recreational opportunities include a full-service tennis center, swimming pool, golf course, fitness center, baseball diamonds, a croquet field, and sand volleyball courts.

Just east of Memorial Park is the pleasantly modest-sized **Buffalo Bayou Park** (1800 Allen Pkwy., 713/845-1000, www.buffalobayou.org), an urban greenbelt with the namesake waterway as its centerpiece. With the towering Houston skyline as a backdrop, the park draws bikers, joggers, art lovers, and walkers from across the city who relish its riverside trails and bustling activity. In addition to the smooth, wide trail system, the 124-acre park contains exercise stations, a recreation center, disc golf course, children's playground, and popular dog recreation area. Public art abounds along the jogging trail, from stainless-steel objects representing tree roots on an overpass to the large stone-blocks-turned-sculpture that remain from the city's demolished civic auditorium. Visit the park's website to download PDFs of trail maps.

Golf

Houston's Parks and Recreation Department (www.houstontx.gov) runs seven respectable municipal golf courses, a worthy city service in an urban environment that features year-round moderate temperatures and developers ready to capitalize on any available open space. Three of the most popular courses are located within the loop, drawing golfers and hackers to the links' well-maintained grounds and affordable greens fees.

The gem of the downtown-area muni courses is **Memorial Park Golf Course** (1001 E. Memorial Loop Dr., 713/862-4033), a 600-acre oasis of rolling fairways and challenging greens. Originally constructed as a nine-hole sand green course for soldiers at Camp Logan (now Memorial Park), the links feature lush landscapes, putting and chipping greens, a golf museum, contemporary clubhouse, and always-packed driving range offering shade and lighting.

Located adjacent to the city's Museum District, **Hermann Park Golf Course** (2155 Cambridge St., 713/526-0077) is another natural escape from the surrounding urban scenery. Lengthy fairways, snug out-of-bounds, and occasional water hazards make Hermann a favorite among serious golfers, who appreciate the shade of the ancient oaks and steady surface of the Bermuda-grass greens. While at the turn, be sure to order a hot dog or two from the clubhouse kitchen.

Farther south of town is **Wortham Park Golf Course** (7000 Capitol St., 713/928-4260), a former private course now operated by the city. The sportiest of the three downtown-area courses, Wortham Park features hilly terrain, tight turns, and several short par fours. The course also offers a practice green and bunker, a chipping green, and a full driving range.

ACCOMMODATIONS
Downtown
$100-150

One of the best ways to experience Houston—at an affordable rate, no less—is at the fabulous ((**Magnolia Hotel** (1100 Texas Ave., 713/221-0011 or 888/915-1110, www.magnoliahotel-houston.com, $143 d). This historic downtown gem hosts many business guests and events, and the bustling activity adds to the cosmopolitan aura of the grand 1926 building. The Magnolia offers an impressive number of complimentary services, including wireless Internet access, downtown car transportation, a continental breakfast, and, even better: free happy hour drinks and milk and cookies at bedtime. The rooftop fitness center, lap pool, and hot tub make the Magnolia one of Houston's top-notch lodging options.

At the complete opposite end of the chronological scale is the eco- and tech-minded **Westin Houston Vintage Park** (14555 Vintage Preserve Pkwy., 281/379-7300, www.starwoodhotels.com, $113 d). Part of a "lifestyle center" in the bustling northwestern part of town, Element touts its environmentally friendly design and construction, as well as its thorough provision of widespread wireless access for computers, phones, and portable online devices. Other amenities include a hot breakfast, open-flow guest rooms with fully equipped kitchens, and an evening reception (Monday–Thursday 6–7:30 P.M.) with hand-selected regional wines and beers, soft drinks, and appetizers.

$150-200

For a deluxe downtown lodging experience in

a major city of Houston's size, it doesn't get much better than the **Alden** (the former Sam Houston Hotel at 1117 Prairie St., 832/200-8800, www.aldenhotels.com, $150 d). The Alden offers near-luxury accommodations without charging outrageous prices. Pamper yourself in this contemporary setting with amenities such as fancy bathrooms (granite walls and glass-walled showers with plush robes and towels), quality bedding (400-thread-count sheets, down comforters and pillows, pillow-top mattresses), as well as DVD libraries, gourmet snacks, a minibar, and free Wi-Fi service.

For a modest price increase, consider **Hilton Americas** (1600 Lamar St., 713/739-8000, www.hilton.com, $167 d), a humongous hotel with more than 1,200 rooms towering over downtown. This is a big-time business destination since the Hilton is attached to the convention center, but weekends are a nice (and cheaper) time to stay since the hotel's many amenities are even more accessible. Highlights include three restaurants, several bars and lounges, and an impressive spa and health club with downtown views. Rooms feature free wireless Internet access, fancy linens (300 thread count), and an in-room refreshment center.

Another worthwhile option is the clean and spacious **Best Western Downtown Inn and Suites** (915 W. Dallas St., 713/571-7733, www.bestwestern.com, $159 d). Rooms and suites include microwaves, fridges, and free Wi-Fi service, and the hotel offers a free full breakfast every morning, happy hour cocktails (Monday–Thursday), a fitness center, spa, and outdoor pool.

Those seeking the comforts of home in a historic urban setting will enjoy the **Residence Inn Houston Downtown** (904 Dallas St., 832/366-1000, www.marriott.com, $169 d). The building itself is spectacular—the 1921 Humble Oil Building features well-restored Classical Revival details such as brass elevator doors, tall ceilings, and stately rose marble. Hotel amenities include free Internet access, free drinks at the evening social hour, a large pool, fitness center, and spacious suites with fully equipped kitchens and separate sleeping and living areas. Check out this over-the-top service: You can leave a grocery list at the front desk and return in the evening to a stocked kitchen.

$200-250
Sometimes a visit to a cosmopolitan city requires a cosmopolitan lodging experience. In Houston, look no further than the (**Hotel Icon** (220 Main St., 713/224-4266, www.hotelicon.com, $219 d), offering dynamic contemporary lodging in the heart of downtown. This 12-story hotel is filled with bold colors and lavish details, including marble countertops, antique claw-foot tubs, luxury robes, and plush linens. In the mood for a bubble bath? Simply summon the Bath Butler for a perfectly drawn sudsy experience. Other amenities include free Wi-Fi service, Web TV, a stocked minibar, and fresh-cut flowers.

If a historic setting is more your style, consider the elegant **Lancaster** (701 Texas St., 713/228-9500, www.thelancaster.com, $219 d), considered Houston's original small luxury hotel. The Lancaster's posh aura is immediately apparent upon entering the lobby, decorated with large oil paintings, beveled glass, and dramatic lighting. There's a sense of European opulence in the hotel's decor, and the guest rooms capture this charm with dark wood two-poster beds, feather pillows and duvets, and brass furnishings. The Lancaster also offers free wireless Internet service, plush bathrobes, and free car service to nearby attractions.

$250 AND ABOVE
Those in search of five-star accommodations have several downtown options, including the reliably luxurious **Four Seasons** (1300 Lamar St., 713/650-1300, www.fourseasons.com, $275 d). The skyline views are outstanding here, as are the services, including the exquisite spa and salon, a spacious pool and fitness center, complimentary downtown car service, a tasty antipasti bar, and rooms featuring plush bathrobes, minibars, and Wi-Fi access. Some of the most expensive lodging in town is at the

mediocre-sounding **Inn at the Ballpark** (1520 Texas St., 713/228-1520, www.innattheballpark.com, $279 d), located within earshot of the cracks of the Houston Astros' bats. The location is one of the prime amenities here, since the other services (aside from being five-star in quality) are as inspiring as the hotel's name. The Inn at the Ballpark offers free transportation services around town as well as complimentary Internet access and a light breakfast.

Uptown

$50-100

Some of the best bargains in the city are in the busy Uptown area west of downtown near the Galleria. Among them are **Drury Inn and Suites** (1615 W. Loop S., 713/963-0700, www.druryhotels.com, $89 d), offering a free hot breakfast, evening social hour, a fitness center, indoor/outdoor pool, and whirlpool. Guest rooms feature free Internet access, microwaves, and refrigerators. Similarly priced and amenity packed is the adjacent **La Quinta Inn and Suites** (1625 W. Loop S., 713/355-3440, www.lq.com, $85 d), with a heated pool and spa, a fitness center, free deluxe continental breakfast buffet, and rooms with free Internet access.

$100-150

For a modest increase in price, consider the impressive **Hilton Post Oak** (2001 Post Oak Blvd., 713/961-9300, www.hilton.com, $129 d). Each room includes a balcony offering impressive skyline views, as well as Wi-Fi access, minibars, and refrigerators. The hotel also offers complimentary shuttle service to destinations within a three-mile radius. Another option favored by many Galleria shoppers is the **JW Marriot on Westheimer** (5150 Westheimer Rd., 713/961-1500, www.marriott.com, $149 d), a stately 23-floor hotel featuring wireless Internet access, a fitness center, indoor and outdoor pools, and a whirlpool.

$150-200

It's a bit more expensive, but you'll certainly enjoy a unique and memorable experience at ℂ **Hotel Derek** (2525 W. Loop S., 866/292-4100, www.hotelderek.com, $150 d). This independent option is contemporary and sophisticated, with consistently reliable service. Hotel Derek's highlights include an outstanding pool with gushing waterfall, day-spa treatments, and the Derek Mobile, a black stretch SUV providing free transportation to the Galleria's nearby shopping locales (or business meetings). Rooms feature free Wi-Fi access, minibars, CD players with extensive libraries, bathrobes, and beds with goose-down duvets. The hotel's restaurant, Bistro Moderne, is a destination itself, with remarkable French cuisine.

Galleria visitors also enjoy setting up shop at **Embassy Suites** (2911 Sage Rd., 713/626-5444, www.embassysuites.com, $169 d). Guests are immediately greeted by an almost-overwhelming lobby featuring a lofty atrium with a jungle-themed waterway containing swans. Hotel amenities include an indoor pool and whirlpool, a large fitness center, a free cooked-to-order breakfast, and an evening social reception. Rooms offer a private bedroom and separate living area with a sofa bed, minibar, refrigerator, microwave, and Internet access.

The Galleria draws some big spenders, and the surrounding area accommodates them with several pricey lodging options. Among them are **Doubletree Guest Suites** (5353 Westheimer Rd., 713/961-9000, www.doubletree.com, $159 d). In addition to its ideal location, the hotel offers spacious one- and two-bedroom suites with wireless Internet access, a fancy fitness center, and a large outdoor pool area with sundeck and whirlpool.

$200-250

If shopping is a priority, consider staying in a hotel connected to the country's fourth-largest mall. The **Westin Galleria Houston** (5060 W. Alabama St., 713/960-8100, www.starwood-hotels.com, $200 d) is in a prime location, allowing guests to walk straight from the hotel to the massive attached shopping center. After a full day of browsing stores (or even leaving the hotel to explore nearby restaurants, taverns, and cultural attractions), you can unwind in a spacious room with Internet access (for a fee) and high-quality bedding. Another worthy option is **Staybridge Suites Houston Galleria Area** (5160 Hidalgo St., 800/465-4329, www.ichotelsgroup.com, $209 d), featuring full kitchens, separate sitting and work areas, free Internet access and printing capacities, a fitness center, and outdoor pool.

Kirby District-Rice Village

Downtown is pretty quiet most nights, but Rice Village is usually hoppin'. Visitors often opt to stay here for the abundant nearby nightlife and cultural attractions. One of the best deals in the area is the **Courtyard Houston West University** (2929 Westpark Dr., 713/661-5669, www.marriott.com, $119 d), offering an outdoor pool/whirlpool, exercise room, book-filled library, and free Internet access. Similarly priced yet slightly more upscale is the **Renaissance Greenway Plaza** (6 Greenway Plaza E., 713/629-1200, www.marriott.com, $129 d), featuring spacious rooms with walk-in closets, luxury bedding, Internet access, a fitness center, and outdoor pool.

Another worthy option is the **Hilton Houston Plaza** (6633 Travis St., 713/313-4000, www.hilton.com, $139 d). The Hilton includes large suites, minibars, Internet access, a fitness facility, heated swimming pool, and free transportation within a three-mile radius of the hotel.

The lodging jewel of the city's Museum District crown is **Hotel ZaZa** (5701 Main St., 713/526-1991, www.hotelzaza.com, rooms start at $179). Billed as an "urban resort with a mix of glamour and warmth, high style, and creature comforts," the ZaZa is in a league of its own. Amenities include a poolside retreat and outdoor bar with private cabanas, the luxurious ZaSpa and fitness center, nightly turndown service, cordless phones, free Wi-Fi service, ZaZa guest robes, fancy linens, refrigerators, and an in-room "grab and go gourmet refreshment bar."

Camping

Houston's best camping is about 30 miles southwest of the city at **Brazos Bend State Park** (21901 FM 762, 979/553-5102, www.tpwd.state.tx.us, $4 daily per person 13 and older). Covering roughly 5,000 acres, this popular state park offers biking, biking, equestrian trails, and fishing on six easily accessible lakes. However, visitors are cautioned about alligators (seriously), which are numerous in some areas of the park. Facilities include restrooms with showers, campsites with water and electricity, screened shelters, primitive equestrian campsites, and a dining hall. Many visitors make Brazos Bend a weekend destination due to its abundant activities, including free interpretive programs and hikes. A nature center with informative displays contains a "hands-on" alligator discovery area, a model of the park, a freshwater aquarium, live native snake species, and the George Observatory (open Saturday 3–10 P.M.).

Closer to town is the unremarkable yet convenient **Alexander Deussen County Park** (12303 Sonnier St., 713/440-1587, call for reservation information). Named after a respected Houston geologist, Deussen Park offers basic camping services, including site pads, fire pits, picnic areas, and restrooms. Pets are allowed, but they must be kept on a leash.

FOOD

Houston has more than 8,000 restaurants (that's not a misprint). People here love eating out, and the array of options is overwhelming, from lowly fast food to lofty haute cuisine. Visitors and residents benefit from the city's enormous international population, offering authentic fare from all corners of the globe, including specific regional styles not found in most midsize cities. This being Texas, the options also include a fair number of home-grown varieties, including some of the state's finest barbecue, Tex-Mex, and good ol' fashioned down-home Southern cookin'.

Downtown
STEAK
A steak house doesn't have to be stodgy. The scene is certainly more swank at **Strip House**

(1200 McKinney St., 713/659-6000, www. striphouse.com/houston, $11–42). The name references the venue's red meat and red decor, a nod to the burlesque theme, but the food is the restaurant's main hook, with sumptuous steaks taking center stage. Featured cuts include the double-cut strip, filet mignon, and porterhouse. The meat is perfectly prepared and the sides (they cost extra but are well worth it) are ideal accompaniments, including the popular goose-fat potatoes, truffled cream spinach, and roasted wild mushrooms.

Another well-heeled yet nontraditionally bedecked downtown steak house is **Vic & Anthony's** (1510 Texas St., 713/228-1111, www.vicandanthonys.com, $15–40). Chic, minimalist, and tightly packed, Vic & Anthony's wisely sticks with the basics—a simple menu offers high-quality cuts of meat and a few seafood and chicken options. The salads and appetizers here are outstanding (the pear salad and oysters, in particular), and the wine selection is impressive, if a bit pricey. The steaks are enormous, and the bone-in rib eye is considered among the best in town.

CAJUN

Houston is one of the few places in the country that serves authentic Cajun cuisine. The Bayou City has direct access to the seafood, sauces, spices, and swamps—the style's integral ingredients. It doesn't get much better than the legendary New Orleans family establishment **Brennan's** (3300 Smith St., 713/522-9712, www.brennanshouston.com, $10–36). Located in a historic brick mansion, Brennan's offers classic Louisiana flavors such as étouffee, lump crab cakes, and pecan-crusted amberjack. The breakfasts at Brennan's are legendary, and the eggs and delectable sauces taste even better paired with live jazz music during the weekend New Orleans Jazz Brunch. Less formal is the popular downtown lunch chain **Treebeard's** (several locations, including 315 Travis St., 713/228-2622, www.treebeards. com, $6–13, weekdays 11 A.M.–2 P.M.). All the Creole classics are here—shrimp étouffee, jambalaya, gumbo, and a hearty dose of red

beans and rice. Be sure to order a side of jalapeño corn bread, and save room for the bread pudding with whiskey sauce. The only drawback: Treebeard's isn't open on weekends or for dinner.

Uptown
LEBANESE

One of the benefits of being in a cosmopolitan environment is the abundance of international cuisine in various formats. Houston's Uptown area contains several noteworthy informal lunch venues, and the best among them serve savory Lebanese food. One of the favorites is **Mary'z Lebanese Cuisine** (5825 Richmond Ave., 832/251-1955, www.maryzcuisine.com, $6–15). It's a tiny place, but the tastes are huge, especially in fresh-made favorites like kabobs, falafel, shawarma, and baba ghanoush. Complement your meal with a Lebanese beer like Almazo. At night, Mary'z becomes a hot spot for young adults who toke on hookahs and exchange phone numbers. A larger and more traditional option is **Café Lili Lebanese Grill** (5757 Westheimer Rd., 713/952-6969, www. cafelili.com, $7–16). This mom-and-pop establishment is a no-frills operation that focuses on the most important things: exemplary food and service. Start off with spinach pie, hummus, or tabouleh, and proceed to the kafta kabobs or lamb dishes. Top it all off with their signature strong coffee.

CONTINENTAL

One of the most popular restaurants in the food-filled Uptown area is **DaMarco** (1520 Westheimer Rd., 713/807-8857, www.damarcohouston.com, $11–32). Known for its splashy colors and equally bold food, DaMarco's is the showcase of renowned Italian-born chef Marco Wiles. Diners are faced with the daunting task of choosing from Tuscan- to Texas-inspired dishes, including savory Chianti-braised pork ribs, sea bass with grilled grapefruit, flavorful lamb chops, and roasted Texas quail. Locals also can't get enough of the classy **RDG+Bar Annie** (1728 Post Oak Blvd., 713/840-1111, www.rdgbarannie.com, $12–39). Elegance exudes from the decor and the dishes, starting with tantalizing appetizers such as goat cheese crepes and continuing with entrées like the cinnamon-roasted pheasant and cocoa-roasted chicken. Haute Texas cuisine is well represented in the cilantro-enhanced mussel soup and barbecued sweet potatoes. Take note: Many locals still refer to this locale as Café Annie, its previous name. Reservations are highly recommended.

Montrose and Kirby Area
MEXICAN

A visit to the Galleria is incomplete without a meal at the tremendous **(Hugo's** (1600 Westheimer Rd, 713/524-7744, www.hugos-restaurant.net, $12–33). This open-air, chic hacienda serves trendy Mexican dishes sizzling with *sabor* (flavor). Start with Hugo's signature velvety margarita, paired with a tantalizing appetizer, such as the squash-blossom quesadillas or one of four varieties of ceviche. Entrées range from savory pork carnitas to tender snapper Veracruzana. Desserts are legendary at Hugo's, especially the options containing freshly roasted and ground cocoa beans (flan, Mexican hot chocolate).

Another trendy spot with fantastic food is **Armando's** (2630 Westheimer Rd., 713/520-1738, $10–22). Hipsters and regulars arrive early for the potent happy hour margaritas and stick around for the classic Tex-Mex dishes with a twist. Enchiladas are filled with crab and vegetables, and beef dishes are prepared with savory sauces. Unfortunately, the beans are bland, but Armando's is known around town for its tasty *sopapillas* (pillowy pastries topped with honey and powdered sugar).

More traditional in approach yet equally commendable in taste is **Molina's** (7901 Westheimer Rd., 713/782-0861, www.molinasrestaurants.com, $8–15). A Houston institution for nearly seven decades, Molina's is the ultimate destination for old-school Tex-Mex. The signature Mexico City Dinner captures it all: chili con queso, tamale, tostada, taco, and enchilada with requisite rice and beans. Similar in approach and quality is **El Patio**

Mexican Restaurant (6444 Westheimer Rd., 713/780-0410, www.elpatio.com, $8–18). El Patio is also known for its rollicking bar Club No Minors, named for the legal notice posted on the door. The other main draw here is the fajita plate, a steaming dish of savory beef and chicken accompanied by cheddar cheese and piquant pico de gallo. The chicken enchiladas and chiles rellenos are also popular menu items.

AMERICAN

Houstonians go berserk over **Backstreet Café** (1103 S. Shepherd Dr., 713/521-2239, www.backstreetcafe.net, $10–26). This wildly popular two-story New American venue is revered for its crafty chef (Hugo Ortega of Hugo's), who specializes in quality comfort food. Backstreet is particularly known for its "crusted" dishes, including mustard-crusted salmon and sesame-crusted shrimp. The most popular entrée is the meat loaf tower, an aptly named stack of seasoned meat, garlic mashed potatoes, sautéed spinach, and mushroom gravy. Backstreet breakfasts are also legendary, as is the Sunday jazz brunch (11 A.M.–3 P.M.).

Also popular with the locals is **(Benjy's** (2424 Dunstan Rd., 713/522-7602, www.benjys.com, $11–28), a contemporary venue with outstanding food and service. Things change often here, from the artwork to the menu, keeping things fresh for the regulars and kitchen staff. Seafood is the specialty (smoked salmon, seasoned shrimp), but Benjy's also serves comfort food with modern flair, including distinctive sandwiches and entrées such as the pecan- and pistachio-crusted chicken with mixed potato gratin. Locals flock to Benjy's for brunch, and their Bloody Marys are some of the best in the city (they use wasabi instead of regular horseradish).

Another trendy and tasty option is **Mockingbird Bistro** (1985 Welch St., 713/533-0200, www.mockingbirdbistro.com, $11–32), nestled in a dark yet comfy historic building in a well-heeled neighborhood. Diners can elect to go small (the "bar bites" offer mini portions of ribs, risotto, and mussels) or large (the entrées

HOUSTON AND EAST TEXAS

are generously sized). Popular menu items include the onion soup, seared tuna steak, pork chop, and steak au poivre. Save room for the chocolate-themed desserts.

LUNCH

Most restaurants in this traditionally trendy part of town have impressive lunch menus, but a few places are noteworthy for their vibrant scenes. Among them is **Goode Co. Barbeque** (5109 Kirby Dr., 713/522-2530, www.goodecompany.com, $9–19), a funky spot that's always packed with students, young professionals, and working-class carnivores. Goode's specializes in classic 'cue—sausage, ribs, chicken, and the signature tender and juicy brisket—all topped with a succulent and smoky sauce. The side items are better than average, including a sweet coleslaw and bitey jalapeño corn bread.

On the opposite end of the cultural and social spectrum is the sleek **Ra Sushi** (3908 Westheimer Rd., 713/621-5800, www.rasushi.com, $5–17). Drawing a young crowd of busy singles, Ra is known for its stylish social scene as much as its hip sushi rolls. Popular items include the spicy lobster roll, scallop dynamite, and Viva Las Vegas roll with light tempura, crab, tuna, and lotus root. Consider ordering one of the seaweed salads or a more substantial item from the Pacific Rim–themed full menu. Stick around for the happy hour scene at Ra's Flying Fish Lounge.

Outlying Areas
AMERICAN

Burger fans take note: **Becks Prime** (2615 Augusta Dr., 713/266-9901, www.becksprime.com, $7–18) is just about as good as it gets. Upscale burgers with top-quality meat and sensational seasonings are typically found only in fancier restaurants with tablecloths and wine menus. Not here. The fast-food vibe tricks your senses with lowered expectations, but the massive burger you hold in your hands has all the makings of a classic: thick, juicy high-quality ground beef and fresh toppings on a soft, sweet bun. You'll never want to bite into a chainstore burger again. Becks also serves equally tantalizing steaks (and milk shakes). Becks operates several downtown-area restaurants, but the Augusta Drive location has especially pleasant scenery, thanks to several colossal outstretched oak trees on the grounds.

Meat is also the main attraction at **Pizzitola's Bar-B-Cue** (1703 Shepherd Dr., 713/227-2283, $9–18), a legendary barbecue joint with a forgettable exterior and name. This old-fashioned locale has been around since the 1930s, when it was known as Shepherd Drive Barbecue, and the decades of hickory-smoked goodness have lingered ever since. Tender ribs and brisket are the big draw here, and the spicy sauce subtly enhances both. Another bonus: Warm towels are available for post-eating sauce removal. Be sure to save room (or place a takeout order) for the amazing desserts, particularly the coconut pineapple cake and banana pudding.

Those craving fresh seafood won't regret the 30-mile drive to **TopWater Grill** (815 Ave. O in the small town of San Leon, 281/339-1232, www.topwatergrill.com, $8–24). Nestled in an unassuming building on the bay, Top Water is high on the list of fishermen's favorites, thanks to the quality fresh catches and understated yet effective seasoning and preparation. Start with the plump and flavorful peel-and-eat shrimp (or fried, or grilled), and complete your feast with the snapper, swordfish, or redfish. It's advisable to fill up on the fresh seafood only and not waste valuable stomach space with the iceberg lettuce salad or fried side items (hush puppies and fries).

CHINESE

Houston has a sizable Chinese population, and the plethora of restaurants provide an impressive representation of the various styles of national cuisine. Topping most foodies' lists is **Fung's Kitchen** (7320 Southwest Frwy., 713/779-2288, www.fungskitchen.com, $10–36), a haven for fresh seafood. This is fancy stuff, so don't be surprised by the somewhat lofty yet completely worthwhile prices. Many of the seafood items are still swimming in tanks when you order them, including the soon-to-be lightly seasoned and heavily flavorful lobster, crab, and cod. With more than 400 items to choose from, the menu is somewhat overwhelming but ultimately tantalizing in its impressive array of items. Dim sum fans will be pleasantly surprised and rewarded with the vast number of quality options.

Less distinguished yet more appealing to the masses is **Yao Restaurant & Bar** (9755 Westheimer Rd., 832/251-2588, www.yaorestaurant.com, $10–29), run by the parents of Houston Rockets basketball star Yao Ming. This upscale establishment focuses on the classics—Peking duck, Szechuan prawn, and mu shu pork—in a modern Asian setting with several large-screen televisions broadcasting sporting events. The food isn't very adventurous, but it's high-quality stuff. In fact, it may be one of the best meals you'll experience while watching a game on TV.

An interesting place to go for dim sum—the traditional Chinese custom of ordering individual items from roving carts—is **Kim Son** (2001 Jefferson St., 281/222-2461, www.kimson.com, $10–30). Though it's technically a Vietnamese restaurant, the dim-sum custom, like many families in Houston, crosses cultures. If you've never experienced this unique approach to enjoying a meal, this is the place to do it: Pan-fried and steamed seafood dumplings, sticky rice, seaweed-wrapped shrimp, and mushroom-capped meatballs are just a few of the dozens of enticing items awaiting your selection at Kim Son.

MEXICAN

Not too far away from downtown is the fantastic **Pico's** (5941 Bellaire Blvd., 713/662-8383, www.picos.net, $9–23). Billing itself as "Mex-Mex," Pico's offers interior Mexican food with some flair. Specialties include the bacon-wrapped shrimp with poblano pepper stuffing, pollo pibil (marinated chicken wrapped in banana leaves), and smooth yet spicy mole sauces. Things get a bit festive here, especially on weekends, when diners enjoy margaritas and mariachis on the palapa-covered patio.

For a more traditional Tex-Mex experience, head to **Doneraki Restaurant** (300 Gulfgate Mall, 713/645-6400, www.doneraki.com, $9–20), a classic joint complete with a massive Diego Rivera mural. The taste is huge here, too, especially in the perfectly seasoned meat dishes. Try the beef fajitas and chicken enchiladas, and appreciate the fact that the chips, salsa, and bowl-scraping chili con queso are free at lunch.

For some of the best Mexican home-style cooking in Houston, visit **Otilla's Mexican Restaurant** (7710 Long Point Rd., 713/681-7203, www.otilias.com, $8–19, closed Mon.). What Otilla's lacks in atmosphere (it's housed in a former fast-food drive-in) it makes up for in spectacular-tasting food. Like most interior-leaning locales, the velvety mole sauce is outstanding here, but it's the á la carte items that make a visit to Otilla's imminently worthwhile. Load up on gorditas, chiles rellenos, cochinita pibil, and the tres leches cake for an unforgettable experience in a forgettable building.

VEGETARIAN

Houston is generally more about beef than veggies, but there are a few safe havens for vegetarians. The most acclaimed spot, **Baba Yega** (2607 Grant St., 713/522-0042, www.babayega.com, $8–21), is not exclusively vegetarian, but the meat-free dishes are considered some of the city's finest. The salads, pasta, and sandwiches here are legendary, including the tasty veggie club (turkey, fake bacon, and provolone) and Tuesday Italian Special (pasta and wine combo). The owner's adjacent herb shop is the source for many of Baba Yega's fresh and flavorful seasonings.

Also not technically a full vegetarian restaurant, the popular **Hobbit Cafe** (2243 Richmond Ave., 713/526-5460, www.myhobbitcafe.com, $7–17) serves earthy fare in a forestlike setting surrounded by a white picket fence. Soups and salads are the specialty here, including the ambrosial fruit salad and tropical chicken salad, and the veggie burgers are as charming as the mystical decor. The Hobbit Cafe also has a well-deserved reputation for serving delicious desserts, including moist carrot cake and tangy Key lime pie.

For a cheap and flavorful veggie meal, drop by the magnificent **Shri Balaji Bhavan** (5655 Hillcroft Dr., 713/783-1126, $4–12). This is hot stuff, but for the price—most entrées average around $5—you can't go wrong. The cuisine is primarily South Indian, including spicy yet well-balanced dishes such as rasam soup, chole, and dal.

INFORMATION AND SERVICES

For detailed information about specific companies and service agencies offering Houston visitor information, see the *Information and Services* section at the beginning of the *Houston and East Texas* chapter. Meanwhile, here's a quick overview: The **Greater Houston Convention and Visitors Bureau** (901 Bagby St., Suite 100, 713/437-5200, www.visithoustontexas.com, daily 9 A.M.–4 P.M.) can handle most visitor needs. The CVB operates brochure- and map-filled offices at City Hall (Bagby Street location), Katy Mills Mall (just off I-10 about 15 miles west of town), and the Bay Area Houston Visitors Center (off Highway 45 about 15 miles southeast of town).

To find out what's going on in the city and beyond, pick up a copy of the respected *Houston Chronicle* (www.chron.com), the city's only metro daily. The *Chronicle* provides detailed coverage of city and state news, as well as detailed listings of restaurants and entertainment venues. For information about local politics and arts happenings, pick up a free copy of the *Houston Press* (www.houstonpress.com) at businesses and bus stations across town.

GETTING THERE AND AROUND

Houston's major airport is **George Bush Intercontinental Airport** (2800 N. Terminal Rd., 281/230-3100, www.fly2houston.com), located just north of town. The city's old airport, **William P. Hobby Airport** (8183 Airport Blvd., 713/640-3000, www.fly2houston.com), is now the major hub for Southwest Airlines.

SuperShuttle (281/230-7275, www.supershuttle.com) provides shuttle service between both airports and downtown-area hotels. To arrange for cab pick-up service from within the city, contact the following local companies: **Liberty Cab Company** (281/540-8294), **Square Deal Cab Co.** (713/444-4444), **Lonestar Cab** (713/794-0000), and **United Cab Co.** (713/699-0000). To rent a car from the airport, contact the **Consolidated Rental Car Facility** (281/233-3000, www.iahrac.com). All the major rental car companies are accessible, and they share a shuttle system.

To reach the city by bus, leave the driving to **Houston Greyhound** (2121 Main St., 713/759-6565 or 800/231-2222, www.greyhound.com). Trains arrive and depart at the Houston Amtrak station (902 Washington Ave., 713/224-1577 or 800/872-7245, www.amtrak.com) via Amtrak's Sunset Limited line.

Houston's public transportation system, the Metro, aka the **Metropolitan Transit Authority of Harris County** (713/635-4000, www.ridemetro.org), offers local and commuter bus service. Tickets are available in vending machines located at each station.

BEAUMONT AND VICINITY

Beaumont (population 109,856) isn't your average Texas midsize city. It's more connected to the eastern United States than other Southern communities, it's a working-class union town (due to the propensity of oil riggers), and it has a denser historic downtown than its wide-open West Texas brethren. Its proximity to New Orleans and the Gulf Coast along with its two nearby sister cities of Port Arthur and Orange have earned the area the nickname "the Cajun Triangle."

The city's (and state's and country's) fate was forever changed on the morning of January 10, 1901, when the Lucas Gusher erupted from the Spindletop oilfield. Tens of thousands of people flocked to Beaumont to capitalize on the oil boom and, in the process, built an impressive collection of churches, civic buildings, and residences. The impact on Beaumont resulted in a true American melting pot, with Italian and Jewish influences combined with Cajun and African-American inspirations. The city's architectural treasures remain an integral part of downtown's distinctive historical charm.

Although the corporate oil scene would eventually move to nearby Houston (about 90 miles to the southwest), Beaumont's petroleum-related legacy remains its true identity. In 1901, the first year of the boom, three major companies formed—the Gulf Oil Corporation, Humble (later Exxon), and the Texas Company (later Texaco). One year later, more than 500 Texas corporations were doing business in Beaumont.

However, the boom soon went bust, as Spindletop quickly fell victim to an overabundance of wells. Two decades later, new advancements in the oil industry allowed riggers to dig wells deeper, resulting in another Spindletop boom. In 1927, the oilfield yielded its all-time annual high of 21 million barrels.

The Beaumont area never experienced another major surge, but the city had landed on the map, with corporations and families from across the country relocating to the region. During World War II the city prospered as a shipbuilding center, and the petrochemical industry continued to sustain the economy for decades to come.

Meanwhile, the nearby coastal communities of Port Arthur and Orange benefited from Beaumont's corporate and cultural activity. Although the oil money never made the Golden Triangle as prosperous as its name implies, the region benefited by opening several art museums, forging a soulful music identity, and capitalizing on its Cajun culture by developing fabulous food establishments.

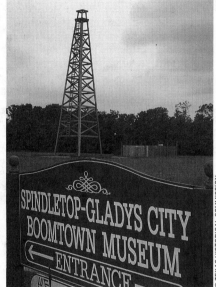

© TEXAS HISTORICAL COMMISSION

the Spindletop-Gladys City Boomtown Museum

offers a self-guided tour of 15 clapboard building replicas from the oil-boom era, including a general store, saloon, post office, stable, and blacksmith shop. The buildings and associated photos and interpretive panels tell the story of the massive and unprecedented boomtown saga, where Beaumont transformed from a village of several hundred to a city of nearly 30,000 in a matter of weeks. The museum also features wooden oil derricks of the era, including a life-size water-spewing gusher that keeps families entertained and refreshed during the hot summer months.

McFaddin-Ward House

One of the city's top tourist destinations is the remarkable 1906 McFaddin-Ward House (1906 Calder Ave., 409/832-2134, www.mcfaddin-ward.org, Tues.–Sat. 10 A.M.–3 P.M., Sun. 1–3 P.M., closed at lunch, $3 guided tours, $1 self-guided tour; reservations recommended). This impressive neoclassical, Beaux-Arts–style mansion features beautiful decorative exterior detailing and opulent interior furnishings

◖ Spindletop-Gladys City Boomtown Museum

To get a true sense of the craziness that befell Beaumont upon the discovery of the Spindletop oilfield, visit the intriguing Spindletop-Gladys City Boomtown Museum (5550 University Dr., 409/835-0823, www.spindletop.org, Tues.–Sat. 10 A.M.–5 P.M., Sun. 1–5 P.M., $3 adults, $2 seniors, $1 children). Located near the site of the famous Lucas gusher, the museum reflecting the lifestyle of William McFaddin, a member of one of Texas's oldest and wealthiest families. McFaddin was a Texas Army veteran who created a cattle and oil empire from the land he received for his military service. The guided tours of his family's fabulous home and adjacent carriage house provide anecdotal and architectural background information along with up-close views of furniture, artwork, and mementos showcasing this prominent Texas family.

Texas Energy Museum

Somewhat surprisingly, Beaumont boasts nearly 20 museums. Among the best is the downtown Texas Energy Museum (600 Main St., 409/833-5100, www.texasenergymuseum. org, Tues.–Sat. 9 A.M.–5 P.M., Sun. 1–5 P.M., $2 adults, $1 seniors and children ages 6–12). This spacious two-story facility features a fascinating collection of exhibits dedicated to, appropriately enough, oil-based energy sources. Interactive displays highlight the history of oil as a versatile resource and provide vital information about the global significance of this local commodity. Though the name is somewhat misleading—there aren't any power plants or light bulbs here—the museum succeeds in educating visitors about the remarkable history and relevance of the petrochemical industry.

Fire Museum of Texas

The nearby Fire Museum of Texas (400 Walnut St., 409/880-3927, www.firemuseumoftexas. org, Mon.–Fri. 8 A.M.–4:30 P.M., free admission) is another unexpected gem. The small museum, housed in the 1927 Beaumont Fire Department Headquarters Station, is practically dwarfed by the massive black-and-white-spotted "world's largest fire hydrant" in front of the building. Now considered the third largest in the world, this 24-foot-tall hydrant was donated to the museum by Disney Studios in conjunction with the release of the animated movie *101 Dalmatians*. Inside, the facility showcases the importance of firefighters in Texas and across the country through vintage

the 24-foot tall fire hydrant at the Fire Museum of Texas

© TEXAS HISTORICAL COMMISSION

fire engines and equipment, educational exhibits, and the Texas Firefighter Memorial.

Babe Didrickson Zaharias Museum

Babe who? You'll be telling everyone about her after experiencing the captivating Babe Didrickson Zaharias Museum (1750 I-10 E., 409/833-4622, www.babedidriksonzaharias. org, daily 9 A.M.–5 P.M., free admission). Port Arthur native Zaharias was a pioneer in women's sports who was voted the world's greatest woman athlete of the first half of the 20th century in a poll conducted by the Associated Press. Nicknamed "Babe" after swatting five home runs in one baseball game, Zaharias was an accomplished Olympic athlete, tennis player, basketball player, diver, bowler, and, most notably, golfer. She won every major professional golf championship at least once and is credited with single-handedly popularizing women's golf. The museum features trophies, golf clubs, photos, newspaper clippings, Olympic medals, and films representing her fascinating and enormously successful athletic career.

Accommodations

For a small city, Beaumont is surprisingly lacking in recommendable rooms at discounted rates as well as downtown hotels within walking distance of the city's many museums and cultural attractions. Regardless, one of the better deals in town is **La Quinta Midtown** (220 I-10 N., 409/838-9991, www.lq.com, $69 d), located about five minutes from the city center on busy I-10. La Quinta offers a free continental breakfast, free Internet access, and an outdoor pool.

A popular and reliable option is **Sleep Inn & Suites** (2030 N. 11th St., 409/892-6700, www.choicehotels.com, $79 d), featuring free wireless Internet access, a free deluxe continental breakfast, fitness center, and an outdoor pool.

The best bang for the buck is **⟨ Holiday Inn Beaumont-Plaza** (3950 I-10 S., 409/842-5995 or 800/465-4329, www.holidayinn.com, $89 d). An enormous three-story cascading waterfall greets guests as they enter the spacious garden atrium, and the renovated rooms provide clean and comfortable accommodations. The Plaza location (not to be confused with Holiday Inn Midtown) features free Wi-Fi service, an indoor pool and whirlpool, full-feature fitness center, and free meals for kids 12 and under.

Representing the upper tier of Beaumont's lodging options is the regional chain **MCM Elegante** (2355 I-10 S., 409/842-3600, www. mcmelegantebeaumont.com, $139 d). The hotel features a tropical outdoor pool, a fancy fitness center, free Wi-Fi access, refrigerators, and microwaves.

Food
CROCKETT STREET DISTRICT

It's only one city block, but the historic Crockett Street District is a fun little stretch of downtown that gives Beaumont an extra dash of flavor. The area was once the center of illicit activity, with bordellos and bars

© TEXAS HISTORICAL COMMISSION

the Crockett Street entertainment district

keeping roughnecks and port visitors plenty entertained. These days, most of the establishments are respectable bars and restaurants. If you're only in town one day, go to **(Spindletop Steakhouse** (290 Crockett St., 409/833-2433, $10–29). Housed in the city's historic oil exchange building, the restaurant is a worthy representation of Beaumont, with photos, artifacts, and decor harkening back to the boomtown days. The real draw, however, is the food—a hearty sampling of local favorites, from thick, flavorful steaks to perfectly prepared pasta to thick, spicy gumbo. A word of caution: The soft, warm bread served before your meal is so tasty, you'll be tempted to eat the whole loaf before your meal arrives. Enjoy it in moderation.

Just a few doors down is **Rio Rita's Mexican Food & Cantina** (230 Crockett St., 490/833-0750, $8–16). Be sure to request a table on the balcony, a pleasant wrought-iron second-story setting reminiscent of New Orleans. If it's full (which it often is), the backup plan is perfectly acceptable: a table on the pleasant ground-floor patio with fountain. You can't go wrong with the food here, either. Rio Rita's specializes in classic Tex-Mex, with sizzling fajitas, stuffed enchiladas, and seasoned nachos among the locals' favorites. Enhance your experience with a smooth and potent house margarita.

CAJUN AND SEAFOOD

Beaumont is one of the best places in Texas to get authentic Cajun food, and the city's proximity to the Gulf means the seafood is always immensely fresh and flavorful. A favorite among locals is the no-frills **Sartin's West** (6680 Calder Ave., 409/861-3474, closed Mon., $9–20). Beaumonters can't get enough of their fantastic barbecued crabs, and for good reason: These tasty morsels are succulent and slightly spicy, an ideal representation of Beaumont's distinctive cuisine. Other popular menu items include the broiled seafood platter and any variety of shrimp (fried, grilled, or peel-and-eat).

Another spot where locals line up is the consistently delectable **Vautrot's Cajun Cuisine** (13350 Hwy. 105, 409/753-2015, www.vautrots.com, $7–18, closed Sun. and Mon.). Start with the tasty crawfish étouffée or jam-packed gumbo, or go crazy and proceed directly to the ridiculously large and immensely flavorful Uncle Emrick's Seafood Sampler, containing the gumbo and étouffée along with fried crawfish, fried catfish, fried shrimp, fried oysters, onion rings or French fries, and a healthy salad.

Floyd's Cajun Seafood (2290 I-10 S., 409/842-0686, www.floydsseafood.com, $8–19) is a small regional chain that's huge on authentic flavor. You'll find all the reliable standards here, from crawfish and shrimp to oysters and catfish.

Information and Services

To get a handle on the layout of the city and where things are in relation to your hotel, contact the friendly folks at the **Beaumont Convention & Visitors Bureau** (505 Willow St., 409/880-3749 or 800/392-4401, www.beaumontcvb.com). Maps, brochures, and staff members are available at the CVB's information centers. The main office, 505 Willow Street, is open Monday–Friday 8 A.M.–5 P.M. The other visitors center is at the Babe Zaharias Museum at 1750 I-10 (exit 854), 409/833-4622, open daily 9 A.M.–5 P.M.

Port Arthur

With three major oil refineries in operation, the coastal city of Port Arthur's (population 55,745) economy remains primarily petro-centered. Named for Arthur Stillwell, a Kansas City businessman who brought the railroad to town, this low-key community has been tied to the shipping industry since a navigable canal was dredged in the early 1900s.

Aside from oil and ocean commerce, Port Arthur is known for churning out music stars (Janis Joplin, the Big Bopper, Johnny Winter, and Tex Ritter are area natives) as well as its Cajun food, fishing, and legendary Mardi Gras celebration, drawing tens of thousands of people each February for the festive atmosphere.

SIGHTS

Get a grasp on the Golden Triangle's illustrious history at the **Museum of the Gulf Coast** (700 Proctor St., 409/982-7000, Mon.–Sat. 9 A.M.–5 P.M., Sun. 1–5 P.M., $4 adults, $3 seniors, $2 students ages 6–18). Located in a large downtown two-story former bank building, the museum covers a lot of ground. From prehistoric items to Texas Revolution artifacts to modern mementos, the Museum of the Gulf Coast offers a comprehensive representation of cultural events in the region. Be sure to check out the replica of Janis Joplin's painted psychedelic Porsche in the museum's music exhibit, where visitors can play songs on a jukebox (for free) and browse among the displays dedicated to the surprising number of musicians from the area, including Joplin, George Jones, the Big Bopper, Tex Ritter, and members of ZZ Top. Nearby, a similarly large (head-scratchingly so) number of sports legends and celebrities are featured in the pop culture exhibit, including Jimmy Johnson, Bum and Wade Phillips, and two *Police Academy* stars (G. W. Bailey and Charles "Bubba" Smith).

The **Sabine Pass Battleground** (6100 Dick Dowling Rd., 512/463-7948, www.visitsabinepassbattleground.com), 12 miles south of town, is worth visiting even if you aren't a history buff. Acquired by the Texas Historical Commission, this 58-acre site tells the story of a fierce Civil War battle where severely outnumbered Confederate troops prevailed over a formidable Union fleet. Interpretive panels and a big bronze statue help portray the conflict, and visitors have access to walking trails and camping facilities overlooking the Sabine Ship Channel.

For a unique experience, drop by the **Buu Mon Buddhist Temple** (2701 Procter St., 409/982-9319, www.buumon.org). Established as the first Buddhist center in Beaumont (an inspiration for the name), the temple is now located in a former Baptist and Vietnamese Catholic church. Where there was once a steeple, a stupa now exists. Instead of a crucifix, a seven-foot-tall gilt bronze Buddha now rests on the altar. The temple's annual spring garden

Buu Mon Buddhist Temple

© TEXAS HISTORICAL COMMISSION

tour attracts hundreds of Texans in search of pleasing colors and smells in the lotus garden. Monks are always on hand to enthusiastically guide visitors through the temple and the garden, and even offer a cup of freshly brewed green tea.

FOOD

Port Arthur is known across Texas for its excellent seafood and Cajun restaurants. One of the best spots in town is the bland-looking yet consistently tasty **Bruce's Seafood Deli** (6801 9th Ave., 409/727-3184, $8–18). You can't go wrong with the basics here—shrimp, crawfish, and catfish. Another favorite Bayou-style eatery is **Larry's French Market and Cajun Cafeteria** (3701 Atlantic Hwy. in nearby Groves, 409/962-3381, www.larrysfrenchmarket.com, $7–19, closed Sun.), offering an ideal all-inclusive combo (the Captain's Platter), featuring fresh and flavorful shrimp, catfish, oysters, barbecue crabs, fried crawfish, seafood gumbo, and Cajun fries. Alternate menu options include the "boiled water critters"

HOUSTON AND EAST TEXAS

(crawfish and crab) served with corn, potatoes, and a dipping sauce, as well as fried critters (alligator, frog legs).

Locals tend to loiter at traditionally minded and decorated **The Schooner** (1507 S. Hwy. 69, 409/722-2323, $8–23). Seafood is the main catch here, ranging from fresh fillets to fried platters. Popular menu items include the broiled fillet of snapper, stuffed crab, and oysters.

Orange

One of Texas's easternmost and oldest cities is Orange (population 18,113), a border town (with Louisiana) named for orange groves along the Sabine River. It never experienced the same gushing levels of successful oil activity as Beaumont and Port Arthur, but it was an important industrial port during the two World Wars, boasting an all-time-high population of 60,000 in the mid-1940s.

Decades earlier, Orange was infamous for its red-light district and outlaw reputation. Its respectability increased when shipbuilding kept the local economy afloat during wartime. Though many residents fled to larger cities in subsequent decades, Orange continues to draw hordes of fishermen and outdoors enthusiasts for its abundant hunting, birding, and fresh- and salt-water fishing.

SIGHTS

You're already in the bayou, so why not *really* get into the bayou? **Adventures 2000-plus Swamp and River Tours** (409/883-0856, www.swampandrivertours.com, several tours offered daily [call for reservations], $25 adults, $20 seniors and students, $15 children 11 and under). Adventures 2000-plus educates locals and visitors about the fascinating biodiversity of the region, so don't look for any high-powered, speedy water vessels here. Instead, the boats are designed for comfort and relative quiet, allowing a better chance of seeing wild alligators, eagles, rare birds, and various swamp plants and creatures. Note: As of early 2011, the company was still operating tours regularly but was in search of new ownership. Check

beforehand regarding a potential change in name, hours of operation, etc.

On the opposite end of the cultural scale is the highbrow **Stark Museum of Art** (712 Green Ave., 409/886-2787, Tues.–Sat. 10 A.M.–5 P.M., free admission). Named for Orange native Henry J. Lutcher Stark, a successful lumber baron and entrepreneur, the museum showcases the family's extensive collection of art related to the American West. Paintings, prints, and sculpture depict the breathtaking landscapes and natural features of the West, along with other artistic mediums such as bronze Remington sculptures, Native American pottery and baskets, and Steuben crystal.

To learn more about the intriguing life of the Stark family, visit the remarkable **W.H. Stark House** (610 W. Main St., 409/883-0871, www.whstarkhouse.org, Tues.–Sat. 10 A.M.–3 P.M., $5 adults, $2 seniors and children ages 10–17). The magnificent 1894 Queen Anne mansion contains 15 rooms of opulent furnishings, artwork, carpet, and silver and porcelain settings. The family's financial success afforded them the rare luxury (in this part of Texas) of purchasing expensive housewares and artwork, including fancy cut glass, imported bronzes, and Asian antiques. The Stark House is listed on the National Register of Historic Places and is designated a Recorded Texas Historic Landmark by the Texas Historical Commission.

FOOD

Like the other apexes of the Golden Triangle, Orange is known for its top-notch Cajun food. Though the options here are slightly more limited, they're still quality locales. Among them is the **Original Cajun Cookery** (2308 Lutcher Dr., 409/670-1000, www.cajuncookeryorange.com, $9–17). The best menu items are the Cajun classics such as blackened catfish, fried alligator, and hearty gumbo. The lunch and dinner buffets are the way to go—sample the dozens of tasty options for a reasonable price.

Another popular option is **Crazy Jose's** (110 Strickland Dr., 409/883-6106, $7–16). As the name implies, Crazy Jose's is an eclectic mix of Mexican, Cajun, and seafood items, providing a welcome mix of tantalizing flavors, from the superb chiles rellenos to the spicy seafood gumbo to the flaky catfish fillets.

If you're more in the mood for turf than surf, belly up to the consistently reliable **J.B.'s BBQ Restaurant** (5750 Old Hwy. 90, 409/886-9823, $7–16, closed Sun. and Mon.). J.B.'s doesn't offer table service (customers place and pick up their orders at the counter), and that's good news—it means less time to wait on the fabulous food. You can't go wrong with any of the classics here. Ribs, brisket, sausage, and chicken are all perfectly smoked and smothered in a sweet and spicy sauce.

Another popular local hangout is **Spanky's Restaurant** (1703 N. 16th St., 409/886-2949, $6–17). Noteworthy menu items include the mega one-pound "Flookburger" and the deep-fried peppers stuffed with crabmeat and cheese.

Piney Woods

The Piney Woods are the natural heart of East Texas. Comprised of several national forests and not much else, most of this vast area remains as it has for centuries, when Native American tribes and pioneers hunted wild game in the dense woods by day and slept under the canopy of pine boughs by night.

The moniker "Piney Woods," a Texas colloquialism, is an endearing term describing this forested region, an image many visitors don't associate with the stereotypical desert landscape of the Lone Star State. Regardless, these aren't dense, lush, groves of evergreens—they're mainly shortleaf and loblolly pines, sprinkled liberally with hardwoods such as oak, elm, ash, and maple. The combination is especially appealing in autumn, when, in another unexpected Texas scene, occasional bursts of changing colors offer a scenic outdoor escape.

There's no shortage of recreational activities in this portion of East Texas, particularly in the national and state forests and parks, which annually draw tens of thousands of campers, bikers, hikers, fishers, and boaters to their natural playscapes. Texans accustomed to their state's hot summers and unpredictable winters will frequent the recreation areas throughout the year, while out-of-staters prefer to enjoy them during the temperate months of spring and late fall.

These wooded areas provided shelter and sustenance for the region's earliest inhabitants, the Native American tribes that were largely displaced by Westward frontier expansion. The legacy of the Caddo Indians is evident in the rich history of Piney Woods communities like Nacogdoches, and the Alabama-Coushatta tribe remains a vital cultural presence on its reservation in the Big Thicket National Preserve.

The forests also had a significant impact on East Texas's economy when the lumber industry became a major contributor to the state's agricultural output in the late 19th and early 20th centuries. Though much of the area was initially overharvested, the industry eventually recovered and remains an essential economical element today. The Piney Woods community of Lufkin contains several cultural attractions related to the area's timber-oriented past.

◖ BIG THICKET NATIONAL PRESERVE

The Big Thicket National Preserve's name is somewhat misleading. Sure, there are areas of dense forest seemingly impenetrable by man or beast. But for the most part, this National Park Service property is merely woodsy, with pines, oaks, and swamplands dominating the landscape. It's what occupies this flora that makes the Big Thicket a national treasure.

Species from the Gulf Coast, Central Plains, and Southeastern forests coexist with critters from the deserts, bayous, woods, and swamps. Birds from all regions of the country that should never be sharing air space pass through the area on migratory routes. There are 85 tree species, nearly 186 kinds of birds, and 50 reptile species, including a small, rarely seen population of alligators. In short, the tremendous variety of habitats coupled with the thicket's geographic location result in a unique destination for nature lovers and wildlife enthusiasts.

A good place to start is the Big Thicket's visitors center located seven miles north of Kountze at the intersection of U.S. Highway 69 and FM 420 (409/951-6725, daily 9 A.M.–5 P.M.). The center provides brochures and maps, and includes a discovery room with interactive and educational exhibits related to the history and scope of the Big Thicket. Visitors can also view a 30-minute orientation film and have access to a NPS nature guide offering a short excursion to several of the ecosystems found in the preserve.

Those planning to stick around awhile can take advantage of the Big Thicket's many recreational opportunities, including hiking, with eight trails offering more than 45 miles of mild terrain through the muggy forest.

Bikers should head to the preserve's Big Sandy Creek Unit. One of the most popular activities at Big Thicket is bird-watching, and the Big Thicket Loop offers ideal opportunities. Bird migrations peak between March and May, and some of the most sought-after species include the brown leaded nuthatch, the red cockaded woodpecker, and the Bachman's sparrow. Camping is also available, but only at primitive sites (no hookups). Campers must have a valid Backcountry Use Permit, available at the visitors center or headquarters offices.

The preserve is also known for its water-based activities, particularly fishing, popular along the Neches River, Village Creek, and Pine Island Bayou. Preserve rangers require fishers to have a valid State of Texas fishing license. The Big Thicket also contains two major canoe trails, the scenic Neches River and naturally rustic Pine Island Bayou. Find out about other canoeing, kayaking, and boating opportunities throughout the preserve by checking with the visitors center for maps.

The Big Thicket does not charge fees for

LOGGING TIME WITH THE COMPANY

From the 1880s until the 1920s, East Texas's Piney Woods became a lot less piney. And woodsy. During these four decades, the "lumber bonanza" resulted in 18 million acres worth of timber being cut.

Lumber production started out with small owner-operated sawmills and eventually evolved into sophisticated operations that dominated the East Texas economy in the early 1900s. These corporations built their own railroads into the forests and connected their isolated sawmills with major cities and shipping points for their wood products.

One of the more fascinating aspects of this era was the establishment of lumber "company towns." The men who worked in the sawmills and on the cutting crews were encouraged to remain with a company for the long haul, and one of the main incentives was the promise of caring for their wives and children.

The companies would choose a location on a rail line and construct a makeshift town, complete with all the basic necessities, including homes, schools, churches, stores, and hospitals. The workers were often paid with credits they could use for food, merchandise, and services in the company town facilities.

Sometimes, the towns would pick up and move along with the ever-changing frontier of virgin forest. Homes located in rail cars allowed for easy mobility, leaving behind a ghost town of clapboard buildings and dirt roads.

By the 1920s, the depletion of the East Texas timber resources combined with the effect of the Great Depression caused the decline of the lumber bonanza. Some of the companies went into bankruptcy, while several of the larger timber corporations moved to the fertile forests of the Pacific Northwest.

park entrance, activities (aside from fishing and camping permits), education programs, or hunting permits. Naturalist activities are available with reservations, or on selected weekends. Call 409/951-6725 or visit www. nps.gov/bith to learn more about the park and its activities or to find out more about making reservations.

NATIONAL FORESTS

Nearly 750,000 acres of East Texas pine forests remain standing as a result of the involvement of the federal government. The trees were mostly clear-cut during the zealous timber harvesting of the early 1900s, but the U.S. Forest Service eventually became involved as an "administrator" of the vast woodlands, allowing them to be responsibly maintained through professional oversight of harvesting and replenishing.

The four national forests of East Texas are ideal destinations for a natural weekend getaway. Campers will want to pack more than hiking boots and mountain bikes—these woods are filled with rivers and lakes ideal for canoeing and fishing. Many nearby communities have small shops offering boat rental, fishing supplies, and fishing licenses to address most weekenders' recreational needs.

Angelina National Forest

Located just east of Lufkin, the 153,179-acre Angelina National Forest is one of the most popular East Texas forests for fishing and boating excursions. Angelina completely encapsulates most of the massive Sam Rayburn Reservoir, an 114,500-acre lake on the Angelina River formed when the Sam Rayburn Dam was constructed in the early 1960s.

The forest itself is like most of its East Texas brethren, with gently rolling landscapes covered mostly with shortleaf and loblolly pine, hardwoods, and a swath of longleaf pine in the southern portion. When it was acquired by the federal government in 1935, Angelina was in pretty bad shape—most of the property had been forested and left without adequate protection. The Texas Forest Service's fire prevention

© TEXAS HISTORICAL COMMISSION

ruins of the Aldridge Sawmill in Angelina National Forest

efforts resulted in much of the land "seeding in" naturally, a practice that continues to this day.

Though Angelina is focused primarily on water-based activities, there are several hiking trails available, including access to the historic **Aldridge Sawmill,** where huge concrete structures remain as reminders of the region's timber-industry heritage. To get there, take the 5.5-mile Sawmill Hiking Trail, which follows an old tramway used in the early 1900s to haul logs to the sawmills.

The park's two main recreation areas, Caney Creek and Sandy Creek, offer camping, boating, and fishing on or near the shores of Sam Rayburn Reservoir. Camping and fishing are also popular at Bouton Lake Recreation Area and Boykin Springs Recreation Area, including historic structures built by the Civilian Conservation Corps and offering camping, swimming, fishing, and canoeing.

The Sam Rayburn Reservoir is a popular destination for anglers, who return regularly for the lake's abundant largemouth bass, crappie, and catfish. Recreational boating is also a major activity, with water-skiers, sailboats, and personal watercraft dotting the water's surface.

Visitors also flock to Angelina to view the hundreds of wildlife species, including deer, wild turkey, woodcock, quail, and the year-round resident population of wood ducks. During the winter, bald eagles occupy the area surrounding the reservoir, and the forest is also home to the endangered red-cockaded woodpecker, a small black-and-white bird that visitors often make (largely unsuccessful) quests to locate.

To learn more about campsite availability and fees, lake access points, and trail maps, contact the Angelina National Forest park office (111 Walnut Ridge Rd. in Zavalla, 936/897-1068, www.fs.fed.us/r8/texas, Mon.–Fri. 8 a.m.–4:30 p.m.).

Davy Crockett National Forest

Like to hike? Then the Davy Crockett National Forest's wild frontier is right up your trail. With

Davy Crockett National Forest in East Texas

more than 160,000 acres of scenic woodlands just west of Lufkin, the Davy Crockett forest has some of the region's best opportunities for hiking and horseback riding.

Most popular among bipeds is the Four C National Recreation Trail, named after the Central Coal and Coke Company that logged the forest's stately trees from 1902 to 1920. The 20-mile trail traverses moderate terrain amid lofty pines, swampy bogs, and hardwood forests. Horses and hikers share the woodsy, mossy, and boggy 50-mile Piney Creek Horse Trail.

Visitors are also drawn to the Ratcliff Lake Recreation Area, built in 1936 by the Civilian Conservation Corps around a 45-acre lake that was once a log pond and source of water for the Central Coal and Coke Company Sawmill. The area offers camping, a swimming beach and bathhouse, interpretive trail, showers, boating, and fishing.

Camping is also available along the Four C trail at the Walnut Creek campsite (five tent pads, a shelter, and pit toilet) and at another small campsite, farther north on the trail, with two tent pads. Campers comfortable with primitive sites should head to the nearby Neches Bluff Overlook at the north end of the trail, where they can enjoy a panoramic view of pine-hardwood forests in the Neches River bottomlands.

While hiking, be on the lookout for the forest's abundant wildlife, including deer, turkey, dove, quail, and various waterfowl. The endangered red-cockaded woodpecker also lives in a managed habitat within the forest.

To obtain a map or to learn more about camping and boat accessibility, contact the Davy Crockett National Forest headquarters near Kennard at Route 1, Box 55 FS (936/655-2299). To find out more about the forest and its seasonal activities, visit www.fs.fed.us/r8/texas. The ranger district office is located near Ratcliff on Highway 7, approximately 0.25 mile west of FM 227.

Sabine National Forest

The 160,656-acre Sabine National Forest is the easternmost of Texas's four national forests and is dominated by the massive Toledo Bend Reservoir along the Louisiana border.

Considered the second-largest lake in Texas and the fifth-largest man-made reservoir in the United States, Toledo Bend offers extensive recreational opportunities, from boating and fishing to swimming and lakeshore camping. For a comprehensive list of lake services—fishing guides to private resorts to boat launch sites—visit www.toledo-bend.com.

Outdoor recreation opportunities in the Sabine National Forest include fishing, hunting, camping, hiking, horseback riding, and mountain biking. One of the most popular destinations in the forest is the 12,369-acre Indian Mounds Wilderness Area, designated by the U.S. Congress as a site "to allow the Earth's natural processes to shape and influence the area." Unfortunately, it was misnamed since the mounds are actually just normal hills; fortunately, these natural formations shelter beautiful flora, including American beech, southern magnolia, yellow lady's slipper orchids, and broad beech ferns.

Less primitive is the Ragtown Recreation Area, offering opportunities for hiking, fishing, and bird-watching atop a bluff that facing the lake. Camping with electrical hookups is available only at Red Hills Lake and Boles Field.

Hikers should hoof it to the 28-mile Trail Between the Lakes, extending from the Toledo Bend Reservoir's Lakeview Recreation Area to Highway 96 near Sam Rayburn Reservoir. Contact park headquarters for a map showing the many miles of roads throughout the forest that are open to mountain bikers and horseback riders.

Anglers have many opportunities for fishing, and although the massive reservoir seems to be the best spot to catch large volumes of big fish (a striped bass fishery on Toledo Bend spawns fish reaching upward of 30 pounds), it's the forest's rivers and creeks that draw many recreational anglers. Crappie, bass, and bluegill are prevalent in the upper Sabine River, and the approximately 18 miles of perennial

© TEXAS HISTORICAL COMMISSION

Sabine National Forest

streams in the forest support populations of warm-water fish.

Birding is also popular with forest visitors, who flock to the area during the spring and fall to catch a glimpse of migratory waterfowl and other species of neotropical migratory birds such as songbirds, hawks, and shorebirds. Like the other East Texas forests, the red-cockaded woodpecker, an endangered species, receives special habitat management.

To learn more about campsite availability and fees, lake access points, and trail maps, contact the Sabine National Forest headquarters at 201 South Palm in Hemphill (409/787-3870). To learn more about the park's recreational opportunities and seasonal news, visit www. fs.fed.us/r8/texas.

Sam Houston National Forest

Located approximately 40 miles north of Texas's largest city, Sam Houston National Forest contains 162,984 acres of short- and long-leafed pine, hardwood forests, and abundant recreational opportunities appealing to visitors, big-city dwellers, and small-town folk. Camping is the main draw here, complemented by daytime activities on Double Lake and Lake Conroe and the 140-mile-long Lone Star Hiking Trail.

Sam Houston National Forest contains three developed campgrounds (Cagle, Double Lake, and Stubblefield Recreation Areas). Cagle Recreation Area is a campground with 48 camping units offering electric, water, and sewer connections; hot showers; lakeshore hiking, biking, and equestrian trails; fishing; and swimming. Double Lake Recreation Area, constructed in 1937 by the Civilian Conservation Corps, surrounds a 24-acre lake and includes family camping units (a tent pad, parking area, picnic table; some with water, sewer, and electrical hookups), swimming area and beach, and a concession stand with bathhouse. Stubblefield Recreation Area has 28 camping units, hot showers, and access to fishing and hiking. Double Lake facilities are available by reservations, while Cagle and Stubblefield are available on a first-come, first-served basis only.

For reservation information, call 877/444-6777 or go to www.recreation.gov.

The Lone Star Hiking Trail contains approximately 140 miles of walkways open to foot travel only. The trail traverses the entire Sam Houston National Forest through woodlands, swamps, and meadows via five loops to accommodate various starting points and parking for day hikers or overnight backpackers. Trail maps and brochures are available at the park headquarters in New Waverly (contact information follows).

Cyclists will enjoy the eight-mile trail on the east side of the forest custom built by mountain bikers. Though most of the East Texas forests are devoid of significant slopes, this hilly trek offers terrain-filled passages winding through the pine forests.

The 22,000-acre Lake Conroe is one of the biggest draws to Sam Houston forest, particularly for its swimming, boating, fishing, and sailing. The lake is stocked with bass and bluegill, and boats are available for rent at various marinas along the lakeshore.

For more information about recreational opportunities at the forest, including all-important maps, contact the headquarters, located two miles west of I-45 and New Waverly at 394 FM 1375 (936/344-6205 or 888/361-6908, www.fs.fed.us/r8/texas, Mon.–Fri. 8 A.M.–4:30 P.M.).

ALABAMA-COUSHATTA INDIAN RESERVATION

One of only three Indian reservations in Texas, the Alabama-Coushatta reservation represents the distinctive heritage of this small yet proud group. At one time the tribe offered tours, a museum, and cultural events for tourists; unfortunately, they are no longer operating. Regardless, visitors are encouraged to spend time at the reservation's campground or fishing on Lake Tombigbee (information follows).

Located on 4,600 acres of dense woodland close to the center of the Big Thicket National Preserve, the Alabama-Coushatta reservation was established in 1854 by Sam Houston as a reward to the tribes for their courage in remaining neutral during the Texas War for Independence from Mexico. Both groups had been living in the Big Thicket area since circa 1800, when they migrated westward to hunt and build homes out of the abundant East Texas timber.

White settlers displaced countless tribe members, prompting many Coushattas to relocate near Kinder, Louisiana, where a majority still resides today. Malnutrition and disease took their toll on the Alabama-Coushatta, resulting in a disturbingly low population of 200 members in the late 1800s.

By the 1920s, the state and federal government recognized their poor living conditions and appropriated funds to purchase additional land, construct frame houses to replace meager log cabins, dig wells to help eliminate long water treks to natural springs, and provide medical and educational resources.

Despite the closing of the tribe's cultural facilities, the reservation still operates the popular Lake Tombigbee Campground, offering primitive sites, full-capacity RV stations, restrooms with bathhouses, swimming areas, and hiking and nature trails.

Call 936/563-1221 or 800/926-9038 for camping information and to obtain a map of the facilities. For additional information about the tribe, call 936/563-1100 or visit their well-organized and regularly updated website: www.alabama-coushatta.com.

LUFKIN

Lufkin (population 33,863) is worth visiting for its unique role as a major logging town in Texas's history. Founded in 1882 as a stop on the Houston, East and West Texas Railway, the town was named for Abraham P. Lufkin, a Galveston cotton merchant and close friend of the railroad company president.

The construction of railroad lines in the early 1880s allowed access to the forests' interiors, and the lumber industry and regional economy began to flourish. In fact, between 1890 and 1900, the forest industry contributed more to Texas's economy than any other industry, including the traditional stronghold markets of cattle and cotton.

As a result, lumber "company towns" flourished in the Lufkin area. The corporations provided jobs for men and prioritized family life by building and advocating schools, churches, and medical facilities. Often, the workers were paid in coupons and credits redeemable for merchandise and services in the company town facilities. Although some sawmill workers were later drawn to the oil fields for higher wages, many men chose to stay with their families in the lumber company towns since they were good places to raise a family in a community environment.

The lumber industry continues to play a significant role in Lufkin's economy. Each year, the region produces more than a million board feet of saw timber as well as a significant manufacturing of pulpwood from the nearby pine and hardwood forests.

Visitors, especially antiques shoppers and history buffs, are drawn to downtown Lufkin's quaint mix of restaurants and retail shops. A walking tour showcases several remarkable historic buildings, including the 1925 Pines Theater and the location of the first Brookshire Brothers grocery store. Along the way, look for the five colorful murals by artist Lance Hunter depicting historic businesses and stories from the area.

Texas Forestry Museum

An essential stop in Lufkin is the incomparable Texas Forestry Museum (1905 Atkinson Dr., 936/632-9535, www.treetexas.com, Mon.–Sat. 10 A.M.–5 P.M., Sun. 1–5 P.M., free admission). The museum offers a look at historic and contemporary growth of the region's lumber industry in two main areas—the forest history wing and resource/management wing.

Highlights include a compelling exhibit about life in a lumber company town, complete with model buildings and a large collection of artifacts from early logging camps. Historic equipment, a fire lookout tower cab, paper mill room, and an educational exhibit detailing the natural succession of a forest are other noteworthy attractions at the Texas Forestry Museum. Visitors can learn more about the region's natural resources on the scenic Urban Wildscape Trail located behind the main building.

Museum of East Texas

Despite its all-encompassing name, the Museum of East Texas (503 N. 2nd St., 936/639-4434, Tues.–Fri. 9 A.M.–5 P.M., Sat. and Sun. 1–5 P.M., free admission) isn't as grand as it sounds. Built in 1976, the museum primarily features exhibits showcasing the talents of regional artists. Though there are occasional traveling shows and science or children's exhibits, the museum devotes much of its attention to the work of locals, which is certainly commendable yet somewhat limited in scope. The museum also hosts occasional lectures, performances, classes, kids' art camps, and publications dedicated to the character and heritage of East Texas.

The History Center

Located just 11 miles outside Lufkin in the small town of Diboll is a fascinating attraction known simply as The History Center (102 N. Temple St., 936/829-3543, www.thehistorycenteronline.com, Mon.–Fri. 8 A.M.–5 P.M., Sat. 9 A.M.–1 P.M., free admission). Appropriately situated in Diboll, the oldest continually operated forest company site in Texas, the 12,000-square-foot History Center is technically a public archives facility dedicated to East Texas history. But that makes it sound rather boring, which it's not.

The vaguely named History Center did not get a specified moniker because organizers did not want it to be classified as simply a museum or a library. Although it contains many reference materials, it's more than a research center. Likewise, it features artifacts, but it is not really a museum. It's best described as a public history and archive center that collects, preserves, and explores the heritage of East Texas.

Visitors are immediately drawn to the facility by its exquisite woodwork, consisting of cypress walls preserved from the 1950s along with floors of locally harvested yellow pine. Exhibit panels feature remarkable century-old photos showcasing Diboll's dynamic past as a lumber company town, an impressive collection of archives (including 70,000 photos, decades' worth of community newspapers, lumber company log books), and an authentic 1920 Baldwin 68-ton steam locomotive where kids and adults can climb aboard to experience the immense satisfaction of sounding the authentic steam whistle.

Accommodations

Lufkin's lodging options are somewhat limited, but there are several chains offering reliable accommodations and amenities. Those looking for an affordable rate in a commendable hotel should consider **La Quinta** (2119 S. 1st St., 936/634-3351, www.lq.com, $95 d). Features include an outdoor pool, free continental breakfast, and free Internet access. A step up on the price and quality ladder is **Best Western Crown Colony Inn & Suites** (3211 S. 1st St., 936/634-3481, www.bestwesterntexas.com, $109 d), offering spacious rooms with microwaves and refrigerators, free Internet access, a deluxe continental breakfast, outdoor pool, and fitness room. Similar in price and scope is **Hampton Inn & Suites** (4400 S. 1st St., 936/699-2500, www.hamptoninn.com, $139 d), featuring a free hot breakfast, to-go breakfast bags (on weekdays), and free Internet access.

A suggested alternative to the chain hotels is the welcoming **Wisteria Hideaway** (3458 Ted Trout Dr., 936/875-2914, www.wisteriahideaway.com, rooms start at $95). Located in a 1939 Colonial-style home, this B&B provides genuinely charming Southern hospitality without being too fancy. Or frilly. Rooms are tastefully decorated, and the breakfasts are outstanding, starting with the freshly made buttermilk biscuits and continuing with fluffy and flavorful egg casseroles and sausage or bacon. Enjoy the feast in the dining room or the privacy of your own quarters.

Food
AMERICAN
Like most small towns in Texas and across the United States, Lufkin has many generic chains

and a few admirable local down-home eateries. One of the most popular is **Mom's Diner** (900 W. Frank Ave., 936/637-6410, $6–14). As its name implies, this semirustic spot specializes in comfort food, including one of the best chicken-fried steaks in the area, as well as juicy burgers, fried chicken, and outstanding peppered cream gravy. Take note: Mom doesn't accept credit cards, just cash.

For old-time greasy and tasty burgers, head to **Ray's Drive In Cafe** (420 N. Timberland Dr., 936/634-3262, $5–9). Locals love the classic '50s feel and fare of this original drive-in restaurant, including the mouthwatering bacon cheeseburger with onion rings, mushroom burger, chili dog, and chocolate milk shake. The surrounding sound of classic oldies music completes this nostalgic scene.

BARBECUE
To experience a classic East Texas barbecue joint, go directly to **Bryan's Smokehouse Bar-B-Q** (609 S. Timberland Dr., 936/632-2255, $8–17). This small, rustic smokehouse has everything a barbecue place should—smoke-stained photos of local and regional musicians, hearty portions of succulent meat, and a sticky, tangy sauce. Brisket and pork ribs are the favorites here, and you can't go wrong with the better-than-average sides, particularly the savory beans and sweet potato salad. For those feeling adventurous, give the fried cabbage a try. **Lufkin Bar B Q** (203 S. Chestnut St., 936/634-4744, $8–17) isn't quite as strong on character, but the food is nearly as good. Tasty brisket and spicy sausage are the way to go, or try a chipped beef sandwich if you're not in the mood for quantity. The sides here are rather average, but a cold Dr Pepper will always enhance your meal.

MEXICAN
Lufkin is known more for its barbecue than Mexican food, but there are several places in town that draw sizable lunch crowds. One worth visiting is the consistently reliable **Cafe Del Rio** (1901 S. 1st St., 936/639-4471, $7–15). From the crispy chips and spicy salsa to the

loaded nachos and sizzling fajitas, Cafe Del Rio doesn't disappoint. Also recommended is **Casa Ole** (2109 S. 1st St., 936/632-2653, $6–14), offering tasty tacos and hearty enchiladas. Another local hot spot is **El Taurino Mexican Grill** (3774 Hwy. 69 N., 936/699-3344, www. eltaurinomexicanrestaurant.com, $5–14), featuring classic Mexican combo dishes with enchiladas, tacos, chiles rellenos, and burritos.

Information and Services
To get the scoop on additional lodging and dining options or to pick up a handy map or brochure, stop by the **Lufkin Convention & Visitors Bureau** (1615 S. Chestnut St., 936/633-0349 or 800/409-5659, www.visitlufkin.com, Mon.–Fri. 8:30 A.M.–5 P.M.).

NACOGDOCHES AND VICINITY
Nacogdoches (population 31,135) claims to be Texas's oldest town, and though some historians debate this, there's no denying the wealth and breadth of its East Texas heritage and culture.

Named for the Caddo tribe (the Nacogdoche) that lived in the area, Nacogdoches was an active Native American settlement until 1716 when Spain established a mission at the site. In 1779, Nacogdoches received official designation from Spain as a pueblo (village), prompting locals to deem it Texas's first official "town."

Soon after, Nacogdoches became a hotbed of trading activity, most of it illicit, primarily among the French and Americans, with much of the action centered around the Old Stone Fort. The frequent activity coupled with the town's prime location on several major trade routes made Nacogdoches prominent in early military and political arenas.

By the mid-1800s, Nacogdoches lost its distinction in these areas due to its lack of modern transportation facilities such as steamboats and railroads. Growth remained relatively stagnant until the 1920s, when Stephen F. Austin State Teachers College (now Stephen F. Austin State University) opened its doors, bringing fresh faces, jobs, and cultural activities to town. With a current enrollment of nearly 12,000 students, the university remains the lifeblood of Nacogdoches.

Old Stone Fort Museum
The Old Stone Fort Museum (1936 North St., 936/468-2408, www.sfasu.edu/stonefort, Tues.–Sat. 9 A.M.–5 P.M., Sun. 1–5 P.M., free admission), located on the Stephen F. Austin State University campus, is a 1936 replica of the home of Don Antonio Gil Y'Barbo, considered the founder of present-day Nacogdoches. The original facility, dating to the 1700s, was considered the oldest standing stone structure in Texas before it was torn down amid much protest in 1902. Now officially historic itself, this replica remains an important Nacogdoches landmark, featuring a permanent exhibit on the fascinating history of the building that served as a trading post, church, jail, private home, and saloon but never an official fort. The Old Stone Fort Museum also contains artifacts related to the early history of East Texas, with a special focus on the Spanish and Mexican periods (1690–1836).

Sterne-Hoya House
One of the oldest homes in East Texas is the 1830 Sterne-Hoya House (211 S. Lanana St., 936/560-5426, Tues.–Sat. 10 A.M.–4 P.M., free admission and tours). Built by Adolphus Sterne, a prominent leader of the Texas Revolution, the modest yet stately home is still standing on its original site, a rare claim for many structures of this era, which were either moved or demolished. Prominent figures of the time, including Davy Crockett, Sam Houston, and Cherokee chief Bowles, visited the Sterne home in the mid-1800s. Tour guides explain the significance of the period antiques and the prominent families who occupied the home, which is now listed on the National Register of Historic Places.

Stephen F. Austin Experimental Forest
Looking for a quiet retreat to the surrounding

woodlands? Then hoof it to the Stephen F. Austin Experimental Forest (eight miles southwest of Nacogdoches at 6598 FM 2782, 936/564-8924, www.srs.fs.usda.gov). Not quite as compelling at its name implies, the forest is dubbed "experimental" for its crazy variety of tree species planted in the 1940s. A century ago, the area was logged and abandoned for use as cotton fields, but the U.S. government's purchase of more than 600,000 acres of East Texas property—eventually becoming the region's national forests—allowed for the reforestation of hardwoods and pines that would eventually populate the area. The Experimental Forest contains three miles of trails with interpretive signs. Visitors and locals regularly traverse the wooded trails to catch a glimpse of the more than 150 species of birds and 80 kinds of butterflies throughout this peaceful site.

◖ Texas State Railroad

The rich throaty sound of a steam train whistle beckons visitors to the Texas State Railroad (Park Rd. 76 off Hwy. 84 W., 888/987-2461, www.texasstaterr.com). The nearest depot is located in Rusk, approximately 30 miles northwest of Nacogdoches, where passengers get all aboard on a historic journey through the East Texas Piney Woods. Trains have rolled on these 25 miles of rustic yet sturdy tracks between Rusk and Palestine since 1881, when the state prison system began constructing the railway to transport iron ore and timber.

The 90-minute trek between the two towns is a thoroughly enjoyable and relaxing journey into the past, with gently rolling train cars clickety-clacking over bridges and through the dense green forest. Sit back and let time slowly slip by while the steam locomotive's whistle bellows and the genial conductor checks your ticket. Before you know it, you'll be at the Victorian-style depot at the end of the line, where you'll find historical exhibits, gift shops, and food service.

Round-trip excursions depart each weekend year-round from both the Rusk and Palestine depots at 11 A.M. and return to their point of

© TEXAS HISTORICAL COMMISSION

the Texas State Railroad

HOUSTON AND EAST TEXAS

origin by 3:30 P.M. Adult tickets run $36.50, and child (ages 3–11) fares are $19. A 90-minute layover is scheduled at the opposite train depot, where a variety of lunch options are available. Snacks, beverages, and restrooms are provided on the train.

Caddo Mounds State Historic Site

Just south of Rusk near the small town of Alto is the compelling Caddo Mounds State Historic Site (1649 State Hwy. 21 W., 936/858-3218, www.visitcaddomounds.com, Tues.–Sun. 8:30 A.M.–4:30 P.M., $4 adults, $3 students). Caddo-speaking farmers built these ceremonial burial mounds more than 1,200 years ago, and historians now realize they are the southwestern-most structures of the legendary Mound Builders of the eastern North American woodlands. Three of these earthen mounds, used for burials, temples, and religious ceremonies, still rise from the East Texas forests. Visitors can walk among the gently sloping structures, explore the interpretive center's exhibits and displays, and view a reconstructed Caddo house built with Stone Age tools.

Accommodations

Like Lufkin, Nacogdoches's lodging options are primarily chains, with most located near the Stephen F. Austin campus. The best budget choice is **Best Western Inn of Nacogdoches** (3428 South St., 936/560-4900, www.bestwestern.com, $85 d), offering rooms with free Internet access along with microwaves and refrigerators, a free continental breakfast, and an outdoor pool. One of Nacogdoches's few locally run establishments is the pleasant downtown six-story **Fredonia** (200 N. Fredonia St., 936/564-1234, www.fredoniahotel.com, $89 d). In operation since 1955, the Fredonia features Wi-Fi access, a large outdoor pool, and a fitness center.

CADDO COMMUNITIES

Most of East Texas was originally occupied by the remarkable Caddo Indians, a large tribe consisting of dozens of distinct groups or "families" occupying an enormous area covering portions of modern-day Texas, Oklahoma, Arkansas, and Louisiana.

When Europeans first arrived in the 1500s and 1600s, they encountered many Caddo communities along streams and rivers. The tribe members were farmers who grew corn, beans, squash, sunflowers, and other crops that flourished in the humid and semiarid East Texas environment.

Although the Caddo people were in remote river and stream valleys, their tribal leaders usually lived in larger villages, where tall temples built of poles and thatched grass often stood atop earthen mounds. These were ritualistic centers where tribe members gathered for festive activities or during times of crisis.

The vast territory occupied by the Caddo provided them much protection, but they also had a reputation as fierce and skillful warriors.

When threatened, the groups would band together and form a formidable force.

The Caddo were also known for their pottery skills. Caddo women made everything from three-foot-tall storage jars to tiny bowls as well as smoking pipes and earspools. In addition to pottery and wooden bowls, the Caddo traded buffalo hides and horses for French guns and merchandise.

Today, descendants of this great group make up the Caddo Nation of Oklahoma, with nearly 4,000 members on its official tribal roll. The tribe's headquarters is approximately 45 miles west of Oklahoma City in the town of Binger.

In Texas, a 1,200-year-old village and ceremonial site now known as Caddo Mounds State Historic Site was once the southwestern-most ceremonial center for the tribe. Three earthen mounds still rise from the East Texas landscape near the small town of Alto, where visitors can learn about the everyday lives and heritage of this ancient civilization. For more information, call 936/858-3218 or visit www.visitcaddomounds.com.

Moving into the triple-digit range is the clean and comfortable **Holiday Inn Express Hotel & Suites** (3807 South St., 936/564-0100, www.hiexpress.com, $109 d), with amenities such as free wireless Internet service, a fancy fitness center, and an outdoor pool. A popular option with business travelers is the nearby **Hampton Inn & Suites** (3625 South St., 936/560-9901, www.hamptoninn.com, $119 d), offering free Internet access, a complimentary hot breakfast buffet, an outdoor pool, and a fitness center.

Food
AMERICAN
If you're in the downtown area at lunch, drop by the wonderful **Shelly's Bakery Cafe** (112 N. Church St., 936/564-4100, www.shellys-bakerycafe.com, closed Sun. and Mon., $5–14). The salads are a big draw here, as are the hearty sandwiches. Billing itself as a European-style Bistro, Shelley's is one of those tucked-away little places that's ideal for grabbing a midmorning coffee and pastry while perusing the local paper. Another popular lunch spot is the campus-area **Stacy's Deli** (3205 N. University Dr., 936/564-3588, closed Sun., $4–8). Students and professors line up at this shopping-center deli for tasty BLTs, Reubens, and meatball subs accompanied by salty chips and a large iced tea. Stacy's spicy pickles are legendary among SFASU students. Locals also love the regional chain **Clear Springs Cafe** (211 Old Tyler Rd., 936/569-0489, www.clear-springsrestaurant.com, $6–19). Seafood is the main draw here, including popular dishes such as the pan-seared tilapia, salmon or crawfish salad, and catfish étouffée.

BARBECUE
Don't let the shiny new decor fool you at the **Barbecue House** (704 N. Stallings Dr., 936/569-9004, cash only, $8–16). Just because the building is new, it doesn't mean the food is fancy. This is classic East Texas–style barbecue done right: sweet tomato-based sauce smothering delicious brisket, savory sausage, and meaty pork ribs. Instead of pinto beans and coleslaw,

opt for the red beans and rice. Houston-based **Harlon's Bar B Que** (603 Old Tyler Rd., 936/564-4850, $7–14) isn't quite as tantalizing, but it'll satisfy your craving. The brisket and chicken are popular here, as are the weekend late-night gatherings, where blues music, karaoke, and dancing are often on the menu.

MEXICAN
Nacogdoches isn't really known for its quality Mexican restaurants, but there are a couple options in town if you need a fajita fix. **San Miguel Mexican Restaurant** (2524 South St., 936/569-2082, $6–15) offers all the classics: chicken enchiladas with green sauce, tacos, burritos, and even fried ice cream. Another option is **Restaurant El Ranchero** (123 King St., 936/569-2256, $7–14), featuring some of the hottest and heartiest salsa in town, along with traditional favorites such as quesadillas, fajitas, and flautas. Call in advance to see if they're offering their semiregular "two free margaritas" special.

Information and Services
While strolling historic downtown Nacogdoches, drop by the town's two main tourism offices. The **Nacogdoches Convention & Visitors Bureau** (200 E. Main St., 888/653-3788, www.visitnacogdoches.org, Mon.–Fri. 9 A.M.–5 P.M., Sat. 10 A.M.–4 P.M., Sun. 1–4 P.M.) to learn about the city's history and to pick up information on local sites of interest. Just around the corner is the office headquarters of the **Texas Forest Trail Region** (202 E. Pilar St., 936/560-3699, www.texas-foresttrail.com, Mon.–Fri. 8:30 A.M.–5 P.M.). Operated by the Texas Historical Commission, the Forest Trail Region oversees heritage travel destinations and cultural activities in Nacogdoches and the entire East Texas Piney Woods region. Drop by to pick up brochures, maps, and to talk to the friendly and knowledgeable staff.

TYLER
Slow-moving Tyler will never be confused with fast-paced Austin, but this large town/

© TEXAS HISTORICAL COMMISSION

downtown Tyler

small city (population 94,146) certainly has a distinctive feel: Southern. From stately plantations to hospitable residents to deep-fried cooking, Tyler has a strong cultural connection to the Deep South.

The city's biggest draw is its roses. Once responsible for more than half of the country's rose bush supply, Tyler now provides 20 percent of the roses in the United States. The Tyler Municipal Rose Garden contains more than 35,000 rosebushes representing nearly 500 varieties. The gardens attract bees, butterflies, and more than 100,000 people annually from across the world. Many visitors come especially for the Texas Rose Festival, a tradition held each October since 1933, featuring events such as the queen's coronation, the rose parade, the queen's tea, and the rose show.

Tyler changed dramatically in 1930, when the discovery of the nearby East Texas oil field turned this small agricultural and railroad city into a major destination for workers and corporations. The town received an added boost in the 1940s when Camp Fannin was established

nearby, including a troop capacity of 19,000 at the height of World War II.

In the following decades, Tyler's economic base shifted from agriculture to industry. Most were petroleum related, but other manufacturing plants soon followed, including metal and fabricating companies, railroad and machine shops, furniture and woodwork manufacturers, aluminum foundries, and air-conditioning and refrigeration plants.

In the 1970s and '80s, Tyler was best known as the hometown of football legend Earl Campbell, who earned the Heisman Trophy at the University of Texas and went on to become a Hall of Fame running back in the National Football League. Campbell's nickname, "The Tyler Rose," forever linked him with his hometown.

Tyler Municipal Rose Garden and Museum

The region's most popular tourist attraction is the Tyler Municipal Rose Garden and Museum (420 Rose Park Dr., 903/597-3130,

BOOM! GOES THE TOWN

In the early 1900s, East Texas was a land of opportunity, with prospectors speculating about the location of the next big oil field. More often than not, their efforts were unsuccessful. But when they guessed correctly and tapped into a fertile patch of petroleum, the fortunes of everyone associated with the discovery exploded like the gusher of oil that burst into the East Texas sky.

The wildcatters working at the base of Beaumont's Lucas gusher certainly couldn't have predicted the global impact they'd helped create on January 10, 1901. Once word spread about the gusher's subterranean Spindletop oil field, tens of thousands of people flocked to Beaumont to make their fortunes.

Everyone wanted a piece of the action, from engineers and riggers to real estate companies and saloon owners. Virtually overnight, the oil discovery transformed Beaumont from a small village of several hundred rice farmers and cattle raisers to a big ol' boomtown of petroleum barons, field workers, and the people who provided services to them.

A lesser-known East Texas boomtown was Kilgore, about 30 miles east of Tyler. Kilgore's glory years began in 1930, when the first oil gusher arrived; within weeks, the town's population surged from 500 people to more than 10,000. Before well-spacing regulations were adopted, Kilgore boasted a small section of downtown that became known as the "World's Richest Acre," where 24 oil wells once stood.

At the height of Kilgore's boom, residents woke up to find their yards filled with strangers covered with boxes, sacks, and newspapers. People installed iron doors on their homes for protection from the influx of newcomers, and they stopped hanging their clothes out to dry since they'd be stolen right off the line.

Not surprisingly, the oil boom also brought professional undesirables such as con men, criminals, and prostitutes to these small East Texas towns. The Texas Rangers were assigned to clean up the area, and they often had to resort to unorthodox means – like the time they "remodeled" an old church into a makeshift prison with padlocked prisoners lining the interior walls – to address the newfound population of ne'er-do-wells.

These stories, along with photos and artifacts, are often on display at local history museums in East Texas. For a full-fledged step back in time to the region's oil boomtown glory years, visit Kilgore's comprehensive and compelling **East Texas Oil Museum** (at the intersection of Hwy. 259 and Ross St., 903/983-8295, www.easttexasoilmuseum. com, Tues.-Sat. 9 A.M.-4 P.M., Sun. 2 P.M.-5 P.M., free admission).

www.texasrosefestival.com, Mon.–Fri. 9 A.M.–4:30 P.M., Sat. 10 A.M.–4:30 P.M., Sun. 1:30–4:30 P.M., $3.50 adults, $2 children ages 3–11). The museum is well worth visiting, with numerous displays showcasing the elaborately jeweled, hand-sewn gowns worn by rose queens dating back to 1935. Be sure to check out the scrapbook pages from each rose queen, including memorabilia, personal recollections, and photos (including one with a queen and her freshly killed deer). Visitors can also view videos about the history of Tyler's rose industry and rose festival, and experience an interactive "attic" exhibit with a bizarre collection of antiques and collectibles from Tyler's past.

The municipal garden is the primary draw, however, with its sea of colorful roses—more than 35,000 bushes representing the nearly 500 distinct varieties. Though the blooming period is from May through November, early May is the peak of the flowers' natural growing cycle. This is when the garden's 14 acres burst with the bright sight and sweet scent of fresh roses.

Plantation Museums

Tyler's heritage is on full display at Tyler's three plantation museums, where the Old South comes to life through historic furniture, artifacts, and photos. This lifestyle, typically associated with the Deep South, wasn't prevalent in most of Texas, so it's worth dropping by one of these sites just to get a feel for the ornate homes and luxurious grounds. If you're lucky, the docents and tour guides may even be dressed in period costume.

The Goodman Museum (624 N. Broadway Ave., 903/531-1286, www.cityoftyler.org, Tues.–Sat. 10 A.M.–4 P.M., free admission) was the home of Dr. W. J. Goodman, a local doctor and Civil War surgeon for 72 years (1866–1938). Originally built in 1859, the house is Tyler's first property to be listed on the National Register of Historic Places. The museum features original furnishings, including hand-carved tables and chairs, a grandfather clock from the colonial era, surgical tools and medical cases, and fine silver and china. It's open for walk-in tours.

Just as impressive is the 1854 **Dewberry Plantation** (14007 FM 346 W., 903/825-9000, www.dewberryplantation.com, open daily, tours are $8 adults, $7 seniors, $5 children ages 6–18). The plantation site served as a campground for the officers of the Army of Republic of Texas prior to their final battle with the Cherokee Indians. The home, billed as the only original two-story, pre–Civil War house still standing in Smith County, was built for War of 1812 hero Col. John Dewberry, who moved to the Tyler area in 1835.

Also noteworthy is the grand 1878 **McClendon House** (806 W. Houston St., 903/592-3533, www.mcclendonhouse.net, Tues.–Sat. 10 A.M.–5 P.M., tours $5). Once a hub for Tyler's eloquent Victorian society, the home was eventually purchased by the McClendon family, whose youngest daughter, Sarah, became a noted Washington, D.C., journalist with a presidential-coverage career spanning from Franklin Roosevelt to George W. Bush. The home is now primarily used as a wedding and events site, but is open to the public for tours. Drop-in tours should check in first at the adjacent Gipson Girl (625 Vine Street).

Caldwell Zoo

Big cities don't necessarily have the best zoos.

One of the best-run and highly acclaimed zoos in the state is Tyler's Caldwell Zoo (2203 W. Martin Luther King Jr. Blvd., 903/593-0121, www.caldwellzoo.org, 9 A.M.–5 P.M. daily Mar. 1–Labor Day, 9 A.M.–4 P.M. daily in the off-season, $8.50 adults ages 13–54, $7.25 seniors, $5 children ages 3–12). What started in 1938 as a backyard menagerie of squirrels and parrots for schoolchildren has evolved into an 85-acre zoo containing more than 2,000 animals representing species from East Africa, North America, and South America. Animals on display in naturalistic habitats include monkeys, rhinos, elephants, giraffes, cheetahs, and mountain lions.

Tyler Museum of Art

For a dose of traditional culture, visit the respectable Tyler Museum of Art (located on the east side of the Tyler Junior College campus at 1300 South Mahon Ave., 903/595-1001, www.tylermuseum.org, Tues.–Sat. 10 A.M.–5 P.M., Sun. 1–5 P.M., $7 adults, $5 seniors and students). The museum primarily showcases local and regional artists with an emphasis on contemporary works; however, occasional traveling exhibits feature centuries-old European paintings, Japanese artwork, and Native American pottery and ceramics. It contains three galleries on the main level, a smaller gallery for special exhibits upstairs, and a children's gallery.

Accommodations

Chain hotels are pretty much the only choice in Tyler; fortunately, the available options are safe, reliable, and relatively affordable. On the lower end of the price spectrum is **Days Inn & Suites** (2739 W. Northwest Loop 323, 903/531-9513, www.daysinn.com, $65 d), offering some decent amenities, including a free breakfast, free Internet access, and a fitness center. **La Quinta** (1601 W. Southwest Loop 323, 903/561-2223, www.lq.com, $75 d) features free Internet access, a free continental breakfast, and an outdoor pool.

Perhaps the best deal in town is the **Comfort Suites at South Broadway Mall** (303 E. Rieck Rd., 903/534-0999, www.choicehotels.

com, $99 d), offering rooms with free Internet access, microwaves, and refrigerators, and hotel amenities such as an exercise room, free continental breakfast, manager's reception (free happy hour drinks), and an indoor heated pool and whirlpool. The only drawback is its location: too far south of the downtown activity.

A bit farther north, on Broadway and about 10 minutes from downtown, is the city's largest hotel—the comfortable **Holiday Inn Select** (5701 S. Broadway Ave., 903/561-5800 or 800/465-4329, www.holidayinn.com, $99 d). The Holiday Inn features free Wi-Fi service, an outdoor pool, a full-feature fitness center, and free meals for kids 12 and under.

Food

Tyler's quality restaurant options are better than you'd expect, particularly for a smallish city in a largely rural area of the state. Perhaps it's the steady arrival of Dallas retirees demanding fine-dining establishments, but the end result is good news for everyone, from travelers to locals to newcomers.

AMERICAN

A stalwart on the scene is 【 **Rick's on the Square** (104 W. Erwin St., 903/531-2415, www.rix.com, $9–31), a swanky lunch and dinner joint and rowdy blues bar by night. Located in the heart of downtown in an old saloon and theater, Rick's is the kind of place that gets everything right—tempting appetizers (shrimp and oysters), gigantic juicy burgers with chunks of fried potatoes on the side, and exquisite entrées ranging from chicken dumplings to tortilla-crusted mahimahi to the indulgent yet highly recommended crawfish-stuffed filet mignon. Similar in approach menu-wise is the popular **Potpourri House** (3200 Troup Hwy., 903/592-4171, www.potpourrihouse. com, $8–27). This welcoming spot is combined with a retail establishment offering candles, antiques, jewelry, more candles, and probably even some potpourri. The restaurant's offerings range from club sandwiches to baked fish and chicken to prime rib.

A local legend and a must-experience for barbecue fans is **Stanley's Famous Pit Bar-B-Q** (525 S. Beckham Ave., 903/593-0311, www.stanleysfamous.com, $7–19). The smoked ribs here have been placed atop "best of" barbecue lists all across Texas, and for good reason—their tender, succulent taste will have you thinking about them for days. Try the smoked turkey and sausage, or sample a sliced brisket sandwich. Better yet, tackle the Brother-in-Law sandwich, teeming with sausage, chopped beef, and cheese.

MEXICAN

Tyler is pretty far away from the border, but that doesn't prevent it from having a few worthy Mexican restaurants. Among the most popular are the homegrown regional chains of Mercado's and Posado's.

If you're downtown, drop by **Posado's** (2500 E. 5th St., 903/597-2573, $6–14). The mission-style decor adds to the authentic Mexican taste, including interior-style dishes such as marinated quail fajitas and shrimp or fish platters. You can't go wrong with the classics here either, including chicken enchiladas and spicy beef tacos.

Locals also love **Taqueria El Lugar** (1920 1726 E. Gentry Pkwy., 903/597-4717, $6–15). As the name implies, tacos are the specialty here, and they're listed on the menu by number (up to 16). Order anything with the amazing guacamole and tasty beef (the cabbage isn't quite as recommendable), and be sure to ask for it on a corn tortilla.

Information and Services

The **Tyler Convention & Visitors Bureau** (315 N. Broadway Ave., 903/592-1661 or 800/235-5712, www.visittyler.com) is located just a few blocks north of the downtown square on the first floor of the historic Blackstone building. The friendly staffers will provide brochures, maps, and general information to help you get around the Rose Capital.

JEFFERSON

Jefferson (population 1,869) is nestled among the forests of far northeast Texas and certainly

ROSENWALD SCHOOLS

Rosenwald schools represent a brief yet far-reaching cultural phenomena that impacted the lives of thousands of underserved East Texans. These rural facilities were built throughout East Texas and the entire South in the early 1900s to benefit the African-American population thanks to Julius Rosenwald, a Chicago philanthropist and former president of Sears, Roebuck and Co.

Rosenwald felt compelled to address the educational needs of African-Americans in the rural South, who had previously attended makeshift schools in churches, shacks, and cabins. Rosenwald intended his facilities to serve as models of modern schoolhouse construction.

The Rosenwald program provided standardized-plan facilities that attracted qualified teachers and became community educational centers. These schools served as models for rural African-Americans to develop quality facilities and a better-educated population. To be comparable with the education in Anglo communities, Rosenwald required his schools to have certified college-educated teachers and a calendar year of at least five months. State and national funding paid for educational supplies, lesson plans, and, more importantly, additional high school levels. With the establishment of African-American colleges throughout the state, black students were able to complete 12 years of public school and go on to receive a college education, ultimately allowing them the freedom of working for themselves.

The last Texas Rosenwald building was constructed in 1931. School district consolidation and desegregation rendered most of the facilities obsolete by the late 1950s, but by that time, 527 Rosenwald schools had been built in Texas. Due to abandonment and neglect of these largely rural buildings, only 30 of them remain standing.

worth visiting for a pleasant escape to the Piney Woods' past. In its glory days of the mid-19th century, Jefferson was a burgeoning boomtown containing a kaleidoscope of cultures, from entrepreneurial East Coast shop merchants to newly freed slaves to Westward-moving pioneers. For more than a decade, Jefferson welcomed a steady flow of steamboats bringing worldly influences and people.

In 1870, Jefferson had a population of 4,180 and was the sixth-largest city in Texas. Between 1867 and 1870, steamboats became a tremendous factor in the town's commercial trade, which grew from $3 million to $8 million. By 1870, only the port of Galveston exceeded Jefferson in volume.

In 1873 things changed dramatically for Jefferson. The destruction of the Red River raft, a natural dam on the river, lowered the water level of the surrounding lakes and streams, making navigation to Jefferson via steamboat nearly impossible. Also that year, the Texas and Pacific Railway, which bypassed Jefferson, was completed. Without steamboat or railroad access, people started leaving Jefferson in droves.

In the mid-1900s, locals began looking at Jefferson's distinctive past as a way to preserve and promote the town's heritage, particularly its remarkable 100-plus state and nationally recognized historic structures. Known as the Bed and Breakfast Capital of Texas, tourism is now Jefferson's most important economic base.

Historic Buildings

With so much Southern heritage in such a small town, it's necessary to visit some of the sites that make Jefferson so historically significant. One of its crown jewels is the amazing **House of the Seasons** (409 S. Alley St., 903/665-8000, www.houseoftheseasons.com, tours available at 11 A.M. Mon.–Sat., $7.50 per person). Built in 1872 by Col. Benjamin Epperson, a prominent businessman and friend of Sam Houston, this magnificent home contains architectural elements representing styles ranging from Greek Revival to Italianate to Victorian. The house gets its name from the glass encasement on top of the house, featuring colored glass representing each season of the year.

A visit to Jefferson is incomplete without a stop at the fascinating **Jefferson General Store** (113 E. Austin St., 903/665 8481, www.jeffersongeneralstore.com, Sun.–Thurs. 9 A.M.–6 P.M., Fri.–Sat. 9 A.M.–10 P.M.). Walking through the creaky front screen doors offers a true step back in time, with vintage trinkets and current-day souvenirs mingling in a historic 1870s mercantile setting. Touches of bygone days are everywhere, from the signature five-cent cup of coffee to the homemade pecan pralines to the soda fountain. Jams, salsas, T-shirts, and candy round out this unique experience.

Also well worth a visit is **The Grove** (405 Moseley St., 903/665-8018, www.thegrove-jefferson.com, call for tour information, $6 admission). Referred to as "the most haunted house in Jefferson," The Grove is a private residence built in 1861 that was listed on the National Register of Historic Places. An hour-long tour offers a fascinating glimpse into the home, along with stories about the supernatural experiences of the owners, including a lady in a white dress who always takes the same path through the house when she appears. Its paranormal activity is so legendary, *This Old House* placed it on its list of Top 12 Haunted Homes, and it graces the cover of *A Texas Guide To Haunted Restaurants, Taverns, and Inns.*

Just outside of town is the stately **Freeman Plantation** (Hwy. 49 W., 903/665-2320), built on nearly 1,000 acres in 1850 by Williamson M. Freeman. Guided tours educate visitors about the Victorian antiques and the family who occupied the home during the antebellum period.

The Atalanta Railroad Car

The Atalanta (210 W. Austin St., 903/665-2513) was a private rail car used by railroad tycoon Jay Gould. It's rather odd that this elaborately designed and elegantly furnished car ended up in Jefferson since the city rejected Gould's plans to bring a railroad through the town. Upon being spurned, he hightailed it out of there, predicting Jefferson's demise (he was partly right, since the town never regained its steamboat-era splendor of the 1860s). The Atalanta features nearly a dozen rooms containing opulent interior materials such as mahogany, crystal light fixtures, and silver bathroom accessories. Located downtown across from the Excelsior Hotel, it remains a major attraction in Jefferson's heritage tourism industry.

Scarlett O'Hardy's Gone With the Wind Museum

If you're still pining for historic ties to the Old South, drop by the campy and somewhat strange Scarlett O'Hardy's Gone With the Wind Museum (408 Taylor St., 903/665-1939, www.scarlettohardy.com, Thurs.–Sat. 10 A.M.–5 P.M., $3 adults, $1 children 12 and under). The jam-packed museum contains everything imaginable related to the classic film, including posters, photos, costume reproductions, dolls, and seats from the Atlanta theater where the movie premiered in 1939. Perhaps most interesting is the collection of autographs from the movie's stars, most notably Clark Gable and Vivien Leigh, Leslie Howard, Hattie McDaniel, and Butterfly McQueen.

Lake o' the Pines

The nearby Lake o' the Pines is just as charming as its name implies. This popular destination is particularly known for its fishing, with bass, catfish, and crappie the main biters. Recreational boating is another common activity, especially waterskiing, sailing, or relaxing on pontoon boats, party boats, and "floating cabins," all available at several lakeside marinas. Campers also flock to Lake o' the Pines, pitching tents and parking RVs at one of the four U.S. Army Corps of Engineer parks or privately owned campgrounds. Other options include guesthouses, cabins, or motels. For more information about lake services, contact the local chamber of commerce at www.lakeothepines.com or 903/755-2597.

Caddo Lake

Just downriver from Jefferson is Caddo Lake, the only natural lake in Texas (all the others were created by dams). Stringy Spanish moss and outstretched cypress trees surround this mysteriously beautiful and sometimes-marshy lake. Caddo Indians claimed a giant flood formed the lake, but scientists believe massive logjams blocked the Red River, causing it to back up into the Cypress Bayou watershed, which formed the lake. Popular lake activities include camping, hiking, swimming, fishing, and boating. Among the many attractions at Caddo Lake is the Texas Parks and Wildlife–operated Caddo Lake State Park (take State Hwy. 43 to FM 2198, 903/679-3351, www.tpwd.state.tx.us). The park offers access to diverse fishing, canoe rentals, and quaint cabins, built by the Civilian Conservation Corps in the 1930s.

Accommodations

BED-AND-BREAKFASTS

Jefferson is the Bed and Breakfast Capital of Texas, so if you were ever going to stay in a B&B, this is the place to do it. It's practically required. The nearly 40 B&Bs far outnumber the measly hotel options, and the town is a Victorian-era playground, so you may as well go all the way.

Among the popular choices is the **Claiborne House Bed & Breakfast** (312 S. Alley, 903/665-8800, www.claibornehousebnb.com, $119–179), a stately Greek Revival home built in 1872. The Claiborne House offers six rooms—four in the main house and two in the carriage house, each named after romantic poets (Yeats, Wilde, Dickinson, etc.). All rooms have a framed poem, book of the poet's work, wireless Internet access, private baths, and color TVs. A full Southern gourmet breakfast is served at 9 A.M., and a day spa is available featuring massages, body wraps, hot rock treatments, and salt scrubs.

Guests make regular returns to the remarkable **McKay House Bed & Breakfast Inn** (306 E. Delta St., 903/665-7322, www.mckayhouse.com, $139–149). The McKay house is famous for its attention to detail (Victorian nightgowns, sleep shirts, and period hats await on guests' beds) and its Gentleman's Breakfast (French toast, bacon, shirred eggs with ham, pineapple zucchini muffins, strawberry cheese blintzes). Seven rooms feature period furnishings, private baths, and Wi-Fi access, and the B&B provides lemonade, fireside coffee, a Packard pump organ, and a lush garden.

The **Old Mulberry Inn Bed & Breakfast** (209 Jefferson St., 903/665-1945, www.jeffersontexasinn.com, $89–169) is recommended by *Southern Living* magazine and even the *New York Times,* and for good reason. This antebellum home contains five guest rooms and two cottages with private baths featuring footed tubs, family heirlooms, cable TV, and free wireless Internet access. The three-course gourmet breakfasts include delectable items such as artichoke quiche, baked pears with cranberries, Rocky Mountain grits, and mulberry almond coffee cake.

HOTELS

For those who insist on staying in a normal plush-free hotel in the B&B Capital of Texas, there's really only one option in town: the independently owned **Inn of Jefferson** (400 S. Walcott St., 903/665-3983, www.hotel-jefferson.com, $89 d). There's nothing fancy about this place, but it's certainly pleasant, with a free full hot breakfast, an outdoor pool, and free 24-hour beverage service. A word of caution: The loud whistles from the trains across the highway can be quite distracting. Especially at 3 A.M.

The historic **Excelsior House** hotel (211 W. Austin St., 903/665-2513, www.theexcelsiorhouse.com, $119 d) is technically a hotel but feels like a B&B (not a surprise in this town). It's rich in history and ghosts, however, and has hosted guests since the 1850s. Fans of paranormal activity claim this is one of the most haunted locations in town. During Jefferson's prosperous days, famous people such as Ulysses S. Grant, Rutherford B, Hayes, and Oscar Wilde stayed here, and its 150-plus years of operation make it one of the oldest establishments of its kind still in business in Texas.

Food

Because of its modest size, most restaurants in Jefferson are within walking distance of the historic downtown shopping and lodging attractions. One of the stalwarts is the tremendous **Riverport Bar-b-Que** (201 N. Polk St., 903/665-2341, $7–16). This is traditional East Texas–style 'cue, with sweet spicy sauce covering savory smoked meats, including pork ribs, brisket, and chicken. The turkey and chopped beef sandwiches are amazing, and the sides (potato salad, coleslaw, beans) are way better than average. Drop by Friday night for a catfish feast.

Another popular local eatery is **The Hamburger Store** (203 N. Market St., 903/665-3251, www.hamburgerstore.com, $4–14). It should be called the Pie Store, however, since it's best known for its incredible homemade pies. Call in a custom order (it takes about four hours) or pick up an individual slice while strolling through downtown. Of course you can also try to save room for pie after devouring one of the restaurant's enormous juicy burgers. Go full-throttle and order a jalapeño chili cheddar burger followed by a piece of chocolate pie.

For a fancier dining experience, make reservations at the top-notch **Stillwater Inn** (203 E. Broadway St., 903/665-8415, www.stillwaterinn.com, $8–27). Located in a 1890s Victorian house, this busy upscale restaurant is famous for its grilled seafood and steak, veal specials, and roasted rack of lamb.

Information and Services

To find out more about the dozens of available B&Bs or other area attractions, pick up a map or brochure from the kind folks at the **Marion County Chamber of Commerce** (101 N. Polk St., 903/665-2672, www.jefferson-texas.com).

THE GULF COAST

Stretching more than 350 miles along the Gulf of Mexico, this region of sun, sea, and sand offers the ultimate escape from cities, suburbs, and small towns. Its moderate beaches and waves don't attract crowds the way Florida's mighty surf does, but the call of the ocean draws casual beachcombers, salty fishermen, and frolicking families.

Occasionally referred to as the country's "Third Coast," the gulf region offers something for everyone: quiet natural seashores, crazy spring break parties, and world-class museum facilities. The constant breeze off the ocean keeps sailors and windsurfers blissfully cruising along the shore and the temperatures down a few degrees (though the humidity is always hair-curling). The warm ocean water is almost always inviting, though it sometimes approaches an uncomfortable souplike temperature in the summer, and it's technically responsible for stirring up horrific hurricanes far out at sea. Unfortunately, the gulf region has been making headlines the past few years for less-than-appealing reasons. Hurricane Ike (2008) wreaked havoc on Galveston, and the Deepwater Horizon oil spill (2010) caused visitors to avoid the beaches, albeit temporarily.

All along the Gulf Coast you'll find anglers of different stripes, from solo artists casting lines off a pier or from the surf's edge to groups of tourists on charter deep-sea boats with professional guides. Regardless, the promise of a fresh catch—flounder, trout, bull reds, snapper, and even shark and tuna—is a rewarding prospect and one of the region's main draws.

Naturalists flock to the area for the

HIGHLIGHTS

The Strand: Experience Galveston's thriving historic district in all its New Orleans-style splendor, including hotels, restaurants, art galleries, and boutiques (page 273).

The *Elissa*: Get a feel for seafaring life by walking across the sturdy wooden decks of this remarkable historic ship, the second-oldest operational sailing vessel in the world (page 277).

Texas State Aquarium: Visitors experience Texas's Gulf Coast from the ground down at Corpus Christi's Texas State Aquarium, starting with birds and gators at sea level and descending to oil-rig depths with menacing sharks, a colossal grouper, and hundreds of other slippery species (page 288).

USS *Lexington* Museum: Hop aboard the massive USS *Lexington* in the Corpus Christi Bay, where this decommissioned World War II naval aircraft carrier transports visitors back in time with vintage aircraft, tours of its 11 decks, and an impressive collection of historical memorabilia (page 288).

Padre Island National Seashore: Not to be confused with its rambunctious little sibling to the south, Padre Island National Seashore is the longest remaining undeveloped stretch of barrier island in the world (page 292).

King Ranch: This 825,000-acre "birthplace of American ranching" evokes the majesty and mystique of Texas culture, from Longhorn cattle to wide-open spaces to genuine cowboys on a vast expanse of coastal plains larger than Rhode Island (page 303).

Port Isabel Lighthouse: It's well worth the 74-step climb up the lighthouse's tight spiral staircase to experience the breathtaking views—from the bug-size cars passing over the gorgeous Laguna Madre Bay to the remarkable view of historic downtown Port Isbell, the vantage point from this historic lighthouse is truly a sight to behold (page 309).

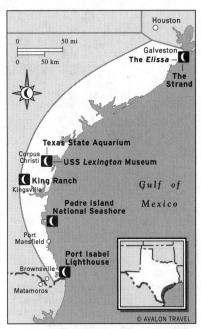

LOOK FOR **I** TO FIND RECOMMENDED SIGHTS, ACTIVITIES, DINING, AND LODGING.

abundant birding opportunities. The Great Texas Coastal Birding Trail ties together all 300-plus miles of shoreline, from hummingbirds near Galveston to whooping cranes and tropical species on Padre Island. Two major migratory flyways intersect along the Gulf Coast, allowing birders to potentially capture (on a camera viewfinder) an elusive species on their "must-see" list.

Though it's hard to imagine why anyone would want to abandon the recreational opportunities along the shoreline (perhaps your skin is already too parched), the cool air-conditioning at numerous Gulf Coast museums offers a welcome cultural respite. Galveston's Moody Gardens and several Corpus Christi attractions are world-class facilities for learning about regional history, wildlife, and art.

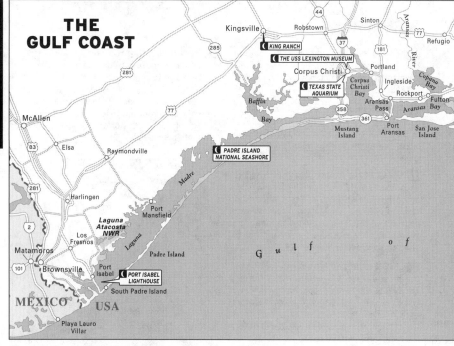

THE GULF COAST

Top your day off with a fresh catch from one of the seaside restaurants for a perfect ending to a Gulf Coast day.

Aside from the festive annual springtime activity in Galveston (Mardi Gras) and South Padre (spring break), most of the Gulf Coast is a year-round, slow-moving vacationland, where the biggest challenge is determining the day's activities—swimming, fishing, shell collecting, sunbathing, surfing, boating, or sand-castle building. Visitors responding to the call of the sea find the region to be as low-key as the gulf's lightly lapping waves.

PLANNING YOUR TIME

Coast-bound travelers tend to stay for a weekend in one area—Galveston, Brazosport, Corpus, or South Padre—to lay claim to a beach condo or hole up in a fishing village as opposed to roaming the entire region. In fact, parking yourself on one beach is the best way to

do it, unless you have time and money to spare and can enjoy your experience cruising along the coast in a boat (rentals are available).

In general, there are two types of Gulf Coast travelers: busy families looking for a getaway from the 'burbs and grizzled fishermen looking for a getaway from the family. The South Padre Island beaches are considered the nicest, so if quality sand and surf are your top priorities, that's the best place to start. Plan to spend at least two to three days soaking up the sun, soft white sand, and gently rolling surf.

As you make your way up the coast, the beaches tend to be less scenic—the sand is a bit darker and the infiltration of civilization is more apparent (oil rigs, trash, tankers, commercial buildings, etc.). Regardless, the scent of salt water and intrinsic lure of the sea are just as strong; you just have to deal with more traffic and city folk. It's worth spending a long weekend in Corpus Christi to soak

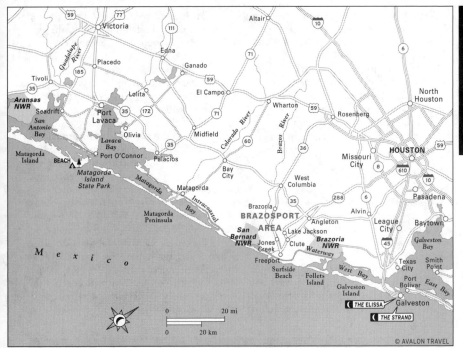

up the pleasant scene on Mustang Island or nearby Padre Island National Seashore. The city's USS *Lexington*, Texas State Aquarium, and Museum of Science and History are well worth visiting for a family-friendly, air-conditioned change of pace.

The Brazosport Area offers fewer cultural amenities than its coastal cousins, which is precisely the reason anglers prefer spending quiet weekends here sans water parks and booming car stereos. Things are more low-key and less commercial in this unassuming corner of the coast, where retirees, fishermen, and professional beachcombers peacefully coexist.

Galveston is where the big-city Houston folk go to spend their money and get their beach and seafood fix. It's the least-stunning of all the Gulf Coast beaches, but the waves are still welcoming, and the shopping and restaurant scene in the historic Strand district are certainly deserving of two travel days.

INFORMATION AND SERVICES

Most communities along the Gulf Coast have visitors bureaus where tourists can inquire about directions, equipment rental, and other travel-related assistance. Contact the following entities before your trip with questions about logistics or scheduling. Physical addresses and hours of operation are included at the end of each destination section in this chapter.

Brazosport Area Chamber of Commerce (979/285-2501, www.brazosport.org), **Corpus Christi Area Convention & Visitors Bureau** (361/881-1800 or 800/766-2322, www.visitcorpuschristitx.org), **Galveston Island Convention & Visitors Bureau** (409/763-4311 or 888/425-4753, www.galvestoncvb.com), and **South Padre Island Convention & Visitors Bureau** (956/761-6433 or 800/767-2373, www.sopadre.com).

A couple of helpful websites provide more

detailed information about the coast, including maps, resources, and notices about current conditions and events. The **Texas General Land Office** offers a Beach and Bay Access Guide with links to environmental reports and downloads (www.glo.state.tx.us/coastal/access/), and the Texas Gulf Coast Real Estate organization has compiled a handy website with general information about coastal geology, beaches, parks, and map links (www.texasgulfcoastonline.com).

GETTING THERE AND AROUND

Most travelers arrive to the Gulf Coast by car from other locales within the state; however, airline service is available via Corpus Christi International Airport and at Brownsville near South Padre.

Since the majority of the coastline is undeveloped, there aren't any major freeways linking major cities. State Highway 35 is the closest option—a primarily rural road stretching between Houston and Corpus Christi passing through dozens of small towns along the way. The lengthy Padre Island National Seashore is only accessible by a park road near Corpus Christi; otherwise, the trek to South Padre beaches is more than 20 miles offshore via U.S. Highway 77 through Kingsville, Harlingen, and Brownsville.

To reach the beach in a hurry, get on the next flight to **Corpus Christi International Airport** (1000 International Blvd., 361/289-0171, www.cctexas.com/airport), offering service from American Eagle, Continental, and Southwest Airlines. South Padre is accessible via the **Brownsville/South Padre Island International Airport** (700 S. Minnesota Ave., 956/542-4373, www.flybrownsville.com), served by Continental and American Eagle. Galveston is about an hour-long drive from Houston (see entry in the *Houston and East Texas* chapter for information about the city's two airports). Rental car service is available at each airport.

Galveston

Located on an island about 50 miles southeast of Houston, Galveston (population 56,148) is a hotbed for Texas history. Most people remember the Alamo, but they don't realize Galveston was once Texas's largest city and busiest port, with thousands of immigrants arriving each year. Unfortunately, recent hurricanes (2008's Ike, in particular) have been historic for all the wrong reasons, with devastating winds and waves destroying property and driving thousands of residents permanently out of town.

Galveston was founded in 1839, and the island town was emerging as a burgeoning commercial center until the Civil War put the brakes on its progress. An interesting historical side note: On January 1, 1863, Confederate troops recaptured the city, while, on the same day, Abraham Lincoln signed the final draft of the Emancipation Proclamation. Word didn't make it to Galveston until June 19, 1865, when enslaved Texans officially (finally) received their freedom. Afterward, Galveston became the birthplace of the now-national Juneteenth celebration, which commemorates the June 19 announcement.

After the war, Galveston resumed its steady growth due to the hundreds of immigrants, primarily German, disembarking from ocean liners each day. Trade was prosperous, especially cotton exports, and for a while, Galveston was known as the "Wall Street of the South" due to its robust economy and cosmopolitan amenities such as electric lights, telephones, and modern streetcars.

The stately mansions and downtown business buildings constructed during this era still stand as the heart of Galveston's historic district. Tourists from across the globe flock to the island to experience these intricate homes (most are now history museums) and ornate commercial architecture.

Galveston's fate was forever altered in 1900 when a massive hurricane decimated nearly a third of the island's buildings. The torrential 120-mile-per-hour windstorm caused an estimated 6,000 deaths, an inconceivable number of casualties in these 24-hour live-weather radar days. As a result of the devastation, Galveston's industrial and residential populations shifted to Houston.

Galveston eventually recovered from its economically challenging times—thanks in part to the construction of a massive seawall to protect the northern part of the island—to become one of the state's top tourist destinations. Although Hurricane Ike caused widespread damage in 2008 (mainly from flooding), most of the island's cultural and historical attractions survived the storm and have reopened for business. The beach remains the island's main draw, especially for surf-seeking Houstonians, but its rich historic fabric provides a pleasant slice of Victorian-era life for international visitors.

SIGHTS

Most of Galveston's attractions are heritage related, but they're well worth checking out since they're some of the highest-quality cultural sites in the state. The historic commercial buildings along The Strand and the century-old mansions showcase a distinctive and fascinating time in Texas history that visitors won't find throughout the inland regions.

◖ The Strand

The heart of Galveston's thriving business district in the late 1800s and early 1900s, The Strand (Strand and Mechanic Sts. between 20th and 25th Sts.) still captures the essence of the city's "Wall Street of the South" era. This 36-block National Historic Landmark District features New Orleans–style hotels, restaurants, art galleries, and boutiques, most of which escaped the devastation of the 1900 hurricane. Today, visitors flock to the antiques and clothing shops, art studios, and seasonal

festivals, including the popular Dickens on the Strand and Mardi Gras celebrations. For information about recommended shops, lodging options, and eateries throughout The Strand district, consult the corresponding sections in this chapter.

Museums

Most of Galveston's museums are located in historic buildings, offering an ideal opportunity to authentically experience the city's fascinating heritage. The 19th-century house museums, in particular, provide an intimate glimpse into the lives of prominent residents of the time through original furniture, heirlooms, artwork, and informative tours.

BISHOP'S PALACE

Grand. Stately. Ginormous. However you choose to describe it, the spectacular 1886 Bishop's Palace (1402 Broadway St., 409/762-2475, www.galvestonhistory.org, Mon.–Sat. 11 A.M.–4 P.M., Sun. noon–4 P.M., guided

Bishop's Palace

tours every hour, $10 adults, $7 students) is the centerpiece of Galveston's historic Broadway Street. The American Institute of Architects designated Bishop's Palace as one of the 100 outstanding buildings in the country, and it's easy to see why. This Victorian castle exudes elegance, from its ornate fireplaces (one is lined with pure silver) to its grand stairway to its stained-glass windows and intricately carved furnishings and details. The Bishop's Palace is Galveston's most visited historical attraction for good reason—its stately design and detailed furnishings transport visitors to another era, offering an escape to the past unmatched in this part of the country.

MOODY MANSION

Nearly as impressive in its opulence is the nearby Moody Mansion (2618 Broadway St., 409/762-7668, www.moodymansion. org, daily 11 A.M.–3 P.M., tours held on the hour 10 A.M.–3 P.M., $7 adults, $3.50 students). Renowned Galveston entrepreneur and businessman W. L. Moody Jr. purchased the four-story, 32-room, 28,000-square-foot limestone and brick mansion a week after the 1900 hurricane. The stately home features rare hand-carved wood, coffered ceilings, stained glass, and heirlooms from the Moody family, who established one of the country's most heralded financial empires through various entrepreneurial endeavors (cotton, banking, ranching, and insurance). Marvel at the manicured grounds, exquisite furnishings, the expansive ballroom, and the dining room's gold-leaf ceiling.

ASHTON VILLA

Also of interest to history enthusiasts is the remarkable 1859 Ashton Villa (2328 Broadway St., 409/762-3933, www.galvestonhistory. org, call in advance about hours of operation, tours, and admission fees). This stately mansion, built for one of Texas's wealthiest businessmen, James Moreau Brown, set the standard for the exquisite Galveston homes that followed. Experience the Victorian lifestyle through the home's grand entryway,

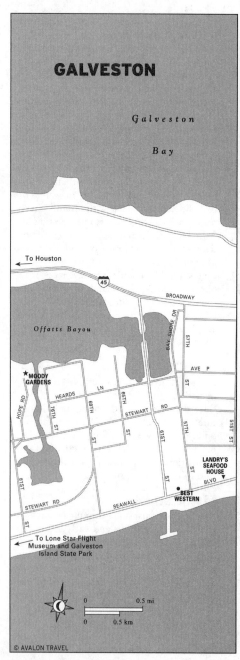

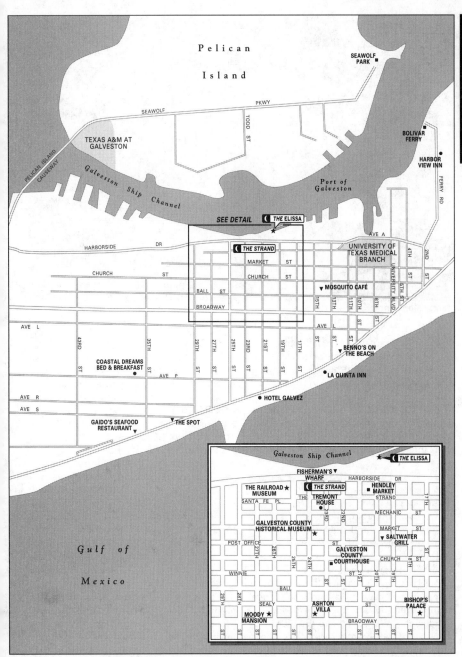

Moody Mansion

life-size paintings, and beautifully landscaped grounds. The house contains many pieces of artwork, furniture, and mementos the family acquired during its travels to the Far East. Ashton Villa now houses the city's Heritage Visitors Center, which is open daily, but, as of early 2011, tours of the mansion are still on hold as Hurricane Ike–related work continues on its interior.

LONE STAR FLIGHT MUSEUM
Located on the island's west end, the Lone Star Flight Museum (2002 Terminal Dr., 409/740-7722, www.lsfm.org, daily 9 A.M.–5 P.M., $8 adults, $5 seniors and students) features an impressive collection of vintage warbirds, including a rare operational SBD Dauntless, a AT-6/SNJ Texan trainer, and a mighty B-17 Flying Fortress. Children will marvel at the vintage planes that carried bombs and fought enemies from the sky, and their parents (or grandparents) are welcome to experience the planes authentically from the cockpit as part of the museum's flight program. Most of the

airplanes are operational, and the flights (with a trained pilot) are a once-in-a-lifetime experience for the World War II buff in your family. Check the website for pricing and details.

THE RAILROAD MUSEUM
Anchoring Galveston's historic downtown Strand district is the former Santa Fe Union Station, home to The Railroad Museum (2602 Santa Fe Pl., 409/765-5700, www.galveston-rrmuseum.com, call ahead regarding hours of operation and admission). More than 20,000 railroad items and several dozen vintage passenger, dining, and kitchen cars provide fascinating views of railroad life from the late 19th and early 20th centuries. The main terminal, located at the heart of this impressive art deco building, contains interactive exhibits and a collection of unique plaster sculptures depicting "ghosts of travelers past." Kids will love the miniature model trains and the historic rail cars behind the passenger depot. Note: The museum suffered damage from Hurricane Ike and remained under construction in early

2011—visitors should call ahead to determine accessibility.

GALVESTON COUNTY HISTORICAL MUSEUM

The best way to get a full appreciation of Galveston's past is at its remarkable downtown history museum (2219 Market St., 409/766-2340, www.co.galveston.tx.us, call regarding hours of operation). Housed inside the spectacular 1921 City National Bank building, the museum contains more than a dozen exhibits showcasing the region's history, all beneath a remarkably ornate barreled ceiling. Learn about the Native Americans, European explorers, and Civil War battles that shaped Galveston Island, and be sure to look for a small television screen offering an extremely rare view of the havoc caused by the 1900 hurricane. Known simply as the "Edison video," this grainy black-and-white archival movie footage was commissioned by Thomas Edison to use his new invention, the "motion picture camera." The rough images show ravaged boats and docks, bringing to life the utter destruction that befell the island. Note: As of early 2011, the museum was still "temporarily" closed due to damage from Hurricane Ike—visitors should call ahead to determine accessibility.

◖ The *Elissa*

One of the city's most treasured landmarks is the 1877 ship *Elissa* (Pier 21, 409/763-1877, www.tsm-elissa.org, 10 A.M.–5 P.M. daily, $8 adults, $5 students ages 6 and up). This remarkable historic ship is the second-oldest operational sailing vessel in the world and one of the three oldest merchant boats still afloat. Get a feel for seafaring life by walking across the sturdy wooden decks under massive masts and 19 sails, and exploring the sleeping quarters and mechanical room. While below deck, be sure to take a few minutes to view the professional documentary about the boat's dramatic shipyard rescue. Incidentally, the *Elissa* was one of the few historical attractions in Galveston that was largely unharmed by Hurricane Ike, losing only a few sails while

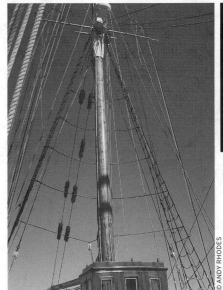

the *Elissa*

© ANDY RHODES

remaining anchored to the seafloor. For those interested, the ship has been designated an American Treasure by the National Trust for Historic Preservation.

To learn more about *Elissa*'s history and subsequent restoration, visit the adjacent **Texas Seaport Museum.** The portside facility features informative exhibits about maritime culture, a fascinating movie about Galveston's port-based heritage as the "Ellis Island of the West," and a computer database with the names of more than 133,000 immigrants who entered the United States through Galveston.

Moody Gardens

Natural wonders await beneath three enormous glass pyramids at Moody Gardens (1 Hope Blvd., 409/744-4673, www.moodygardens.com, daily 10 A.M.–6 P.M., $40 for a one-day pass, $10 average for individual attractions). One of Galveston's most popular and prominent attractions, Moody Gardens offers an elaborate and stunning collection of plants, animals, and educational exhibits inside

HURRICANES: DEADLY TROPICAL CYCLONES

Hurricane season is a tumultuous time for Gulf Coast residents. These devastating tropical cyclones can come ashore anytime between June and November, though most strike in the hot summer months of August and September.

Hurricanes originate when ocean waters reach their highest temperatures, leading to thunderstorms with winds of up to 40 miles per hour (officially a tropical storm). At this point, the National Hurricane Center names the storm, working from a predetermined alphabetical list of names. Tropical storms get their energy from warm, humid air over the ocean, and the release of this force is what drives the powerful winds of a hurricane.

Traditionally, the probability of a hurricane hitting Texas hasn't been too severe, but the past few years have been a different story. In September 2005, Hurricane Rita, a Category 5 storm with intense 120-mph winds, made landfall near Sabine Pass on the Texas-Louisiana border. It ultimately caused more than $11 billion in damage and is linked to seven deaths. Even more devastating size wise was Hurricane Ike, which slammed into Galveston Island in September 2008, leaving an enormous swath of destruction in its wake. Ike completely leveled several nearby communities, and its 110-mph winds ripped apart hotels, office buildings, and countless homes in Galveston, Houston, and the surrounding area.

In general, however, the statistical possibility of Texas being hit by a hurricane is not too severe (one every six years along any 50-mile segment of the Texas coast). The recent experiences, plus the fresh memory of 2005's devastating Hurricane Katrina in New Orleans, is serious enough to make residents tune in to the weather radar every time the words *tropical depression* surface. More often than not, the storm bypasses the gulf or dissipates by the time it reaches the Texas coast. According to weather researchers, annual probabilities of a hurricane striking a 50-mile segment of the coast range from roughly 30 percent near Port Arthur to nearly 40 percent at Matagorda Bay northeast of Corpus Christi.

That being said, some of the strongest hurricanes to hit the U.S. coast have come ashore in Texas. Unlike the overwhelmingly destructive effects of Hurricane Ike in Galveston, however, the storms that historically ravaged Texas are typically in uninhabited areas. In 1970, meteorologists recorded wind gusts of 180 miles per hour near Aransas Pass, and in 1961, Hurricane Carla brought 175-mph winds to Port Lavaca. By comparison, Katrina's wind speeds were 140 miles per hour at landfall, but its extremely low barometric pressure made it improbably intense.

In the wake of the devastating losses associated with Hurricane Ike, Texas officials have organized emergency plans and evacuation routes for coastal cities. Public awareness campaigns focus on the importance of being informed and prepared. The unpredictable nature of these storms makes evacuation planning a challenge, but an increasing number of Gulf Coast residents are erring on the safe side when an intensifying tropical storm is on the horizon by packing up and moving inland until the tempest subsides.

its colossal 100-foot-tall structures. The all-access day pass carries a hefty price tag, so if you'd rather choose just one area to explore, go with the Rainforest Pyramid. The Aquarium Pyramid has more animals and features, but the Rainforest environment is a unique experience, where you'll find yourself face-to-face with African jungle animals, tropical birds, and colorful reptiles. Massive plants, cascading waterfalls, and the constant chatter of birds and insects transport you across the planet to these exotic habitats. Be sure to check out the bat cave, with various species of bats hanging upside-down, nibbling on fresh fruit.

The Aquarium Pyramid takes you on a journey across the world's oceans, viewed at two levels—surface and underwater. Marvel at penguins as they waddle and dive, and catch an up-close view of sea lions as they glide and play. Sharks, sea turtles, rays, and tropical fish await below the surface, viewable in a traditional aquarium tank setting or from the underwater tunnel surrounded by one million gallons of water.

Other notable attractions include the Discovery Pyramid, featuring science and nature exhibits; three IMAX "ridefilm" theaters; kids' activities aboard the *Colonel* Paddlewheel Boat; seasonal recreation at Palm Beach (swimming lagoons, whirlpools, volleyball, and paddleboats); formal gardens; nature trails; and the esteemed Moody Gardens conference center, hotel, and spa.

SHOPPING

Shopping is one of Galveston's main draws, with abundant fashion boutiques and knickknack shops throughout the historic downtown area. Keep in mind, this is where wealthy Houstonians come to play, so items are often priced for this clientele.

The Strand

The gas-lit street lamps, ornate architectural detailing, and lofty display windows along the 36-block Strand district even attract nonshoppers with their Victorian-era charm. One of the first places many people start their browsing is the eclectic **Hendley Market** (2010 Strand St., 409/762-2610, www.hendleymarket.com). This fascinating emporium contains a little bit of everything, from Mexican imports to vintage jewelry to kitschy knickknacks to antique medical instruments. Kids will love the baskets filled with hand-crafted toys and plastic novelty trinkets. Not quite as charming yet equally beguiling with its amazing array of objects is **Big House Antiques** (2212 Mechanic St., 409/762-0559). Shoppers will find many estate-sale pieces here, including furniture, jewelry, decorative items, and books. For a modest increase on the price and quality scale, step into the **Front Parlor** (2111 Strand St., 409/762-0224, www.thefrontparlor.com), where the sign out front promises Books, Gifts, and Surprises. Though the store specializes in fancy Lampe Berger lamps imported from Paris, the Front Parlor also features home accessories and women's clothing.

This being Texas, shoppers may want to mosey through **Way Out West** (2317 Strand St., 409/766-7837). Like most Western-themed gift shops, some of the items here get a bit hokey (garish Lone Star State posters and T-shirts), but for the most part, Way Out West offers tasteful gifts, including silver jewelry, home decor objects, wind chimes, and hand-carved woodwork.

If you forgot your flip-flops or lost your sunglasses on the beach, drop by the **Jammin Sportswear** (2314 Strand St., 409/763-4005). Every beach town needs a few good T-shirt shops, and Jammin Sportswear is one of the most popular on the island. Pick up towels, caps, sunscreen, or even one of those bitey alligator toys here. A step up is **Surf Styles** (2119 Strand St., 409/763-0147), where you can get a T-shirt for the beach and some stylish cruisewear for a night on the town. Brands include Stussy, Miss Me Denim, Converse, and Lucky Brand.

A mandatory stop on The Strand is the venerable **Old Strand Emporium** (2112 Strand St., 409/515-0715). The longest-running spot in the district, the Old Strand Emporium offers fresh fudge, ice cream, deli sandwiches, and cold drinks, including beers and wine. Texas foods are the specialty here, so be sure to grab a jar of salsa, a pecan praline, or some tangy barbecue sauce.

ACCOMMODATIONS

Galveston's popularity as a tourist destination means there's no shortage of lodging options. From cheap beachside motels to luxurious resorts, the island has something for everyone.

Seawall Boulevard

For most visitors, the best way to experience an island vacation is on the shoreline. Though the following selection of hotels aren't technically on the beach—you'll have to cross busy Seawall Boulevard to get your toes in the sand—they're close enough to smell the salty air and see the sailboats and barges.

At the affordable end of the scale is the no-frills yet dependable **Gaido's Seaside Inn** (3700 Seawall Blvd., 409/762-9625, www.gaidosofgalveston.com, $79 d). Gaido's is perhaps best known for its incredible adjacent seafood restaurant, but the hotel has some tasty amenities, too, including a free continental breakfast, an outdoor pool, and free coffee and juice in the lobby. Another well-regarded local establishment is the nearby **Commodore on the Beach** (3618 Seawall Blvd., 409/763-2375, www.commodoreonthebeach.com, $109 d). The Commodore features rooms with balconies facing the beach, a large pool with a welcoming cascading fountain, and several complimentary services, including wireless Internet access, continental breakfast, coffee and juice, and late-afternoon cookies.

Some travelers value the comfort and familiarity of chain hotels, and, although the corporate options are nearly outnumbered by independent establishments on Seawall, there are several offering competitive rates and reliable service. Among them is **La Quinta East Beach** (1402 Seawall Blvd., 409/763-1224, www.lq.com, $64 d), featuring an outdoor pool along with a free continental breakfast and Internet access. Though the accommodations aren't luxurious, there's something very appealing about the comfy beach-town vibe here and especially the ocean view (and smell) directly outside your hotel room door. Another option farther down the island is the more expensive and fancier **Best Western Beach Front Inn** (5914 Seawall Blvd., 409/740-1261, www.bestwesterngalveston.com, $159 d), offering a free continental breakfast, Internet access, and free cappuccino and hot chocolate. The Best Western also claims to have the only heated pool on the island.

Those willing to drop some extra cash for a truly memorable vacation experience should consider the remarkable ◖ **Hotel Galvez** (2024 Seawall Blvd., 409/765-7721, www.wyndham.com, $197 d). Known as the "Queen of the Gulf" when it opened in 1911, the Galvez is stunning in its Victorian elegance. Luxurious amenities include a pool with swim-up bar, marble bathrooms, wireless Internet access, and an impressive spa and workout facility. Not nearly as historic yet similarly stylish is the **Galveston Island Hilton** (5400 Seawall Blvd., 409/744-5000, www.galvestonhilton.com, $295 d), featuring large rooms with plush robes, Wi-Fi service, gulf view rooms with private balconies, a tropically landscaped pool, and a fitness center.

Strand Area

If you'd rather be within walking distance of shopping than seashells, make reservations at the exquisite ◖ **Tremont House** (2300 Ship's Mechanic Row, 409/763-0300, www.wyndham.com, $179 d). Located in the heart of The Strand historic commercial district, the Tremont is a stunning 1879 Victorian hotel that transports guests to Galveston's heyday as the "Wall Street of the South." The first things you'll notice in the rooms are the lofty ceilings and incredibly tall windows. Wrought-iron beds, marble bathrooms, antique furnishings, and a stylish black-and-white color scheme add to the elegant environment. Modern touches include free wireless Internet access and Web TV. Just down the street is the **Harbor House** (28 Pier #21, 409/763-3321, www.harborhousepier21.com, $195 d), which is fancy in a completely different way. It's not historic, but the Harbor House offers an amazing vantage point of the busy harbor and bustling marina activity. One of the best seafood restaurants in town (Willie G's) is across the street, and the hotel provides free passes to a nearby fitness center. Amenities include wireless Internet access and a free continental breakfast.

Bed-and-Breakfasts

With so many impressive historic structures in a pedestrian-friendly vacation environment, Galveston is an ideal place to stay in a B&B. One of the more popular options is **The Inn at 1816 Postoffice** (1816 Post Office St., 888/558-9444, www.inn1816postoffice.com, weekend rates start at $159), located in the heart of the East End Historic District. This 1886 Victorian home is an elegant sight to behold, and its amenities are equally impressive, including wireless Internet access, a game room with a pool table and board games, bikes for an island cruise or trip to the beach, and packed picnic baskets (for a small fee). Another commendable option is **Avenue O Bed and Breakfast** (2323 Ave. O, 409/762-2868, www.avenueo.com, rooms start at $99), just a few blocks away from the beach. This 1923 Mediterranean-style home sits on a sizable piece of property surrounded by tropical foliage. Breakfasts are hearty here, and snacks are available throughout the day. Avenue O also provides bikes for island excursions. Just down the street is **Coastal Dreams Bed & Breakfast** (3602 Ave. P, 409/770-0270, www.coastaldreamsbnb.com, rooms start at $139). Built in 1887, this remarkable home boasts 12-foot ceilings and stained-glass windows, and an inviting pool. Breakfasts feature stuffed French toast, thick bacon slices, and omelets, and daytime treats include fresh baked cookies, brownies, and other sweets.

Camping

If you prefer lodging in an RV or tent, you'll enjoy **Galveston Island State Park** (14901 FM 3005, 409/737-1222, www.tpwd.state.tx.us, daily entry fee $5 per person ages 13 and older, camping fees $15–25 per night). Though portions of the park were damaged by Hurricane Ike, most of the campsites and facilities have reopened. Located on the west end of Galveston Island about 10 miles from town, Galveston Island State Park offers 2,000 acres of natural beauty along the Gulf Coast. Even if you aren't planning to spend the night, the park is a great place for swimming, hiking, birdwatching, and mountain biking. Educational tours of the coastline's native plants and animals are available by appointment—contact the park to make arrangements. Expect to encounter and learn about trout, redfish, croaker, and flounder as well as tropical birds, ducks, marsh rabbits, and armadillos.

Park facilities include four miles of hike and bike trails, an interpretive center and nature trail, concrete boat ramp, fish-cleaning shelter,

campsites with water and electricity, screened camping shelters, restrooms with showers, outdoor showers, picnic sites, and Wi-Fi access. The park contains 140 campsites with electricity and water hookups, and 10 screened shelters.

Less scenic yet more centrally located is the **Bayou Shores RV Resort** (6310 Heards Ln., 409/744-2837). Located just off the causeway, the RV park offers standard hookups as well as a fishing pier and exercise facility.

FOOD

There's no excuse to not eat seafood in Galveston; fortunately, the city is brimming with quality restaurants, and almost all of them survived Hurricane Ike. After you've had your fill of shrimp, oysters, and snapper, try some of the Southern-style comfort food at one of the island's tremendous neighborhood joints.

Downtown
AMERICAN

The Strand is filled with confectioners' shops and small eateries that come and go, but several have become mainstays for lunch breaks during prolonged bouts of shopping. Among them is the aptly named **Lunchbox Cafe** (213 23rd St., 409/770-0044, www.thelunchboxcafegalveston.com, $6–18), a family-friendly spot with character that specializes in healthy sandwiches and salads. Sandwiches are a step beyond expectations, with nice touches like fresh organic apple slices on the turkey and Brie. The Cape Cod salad is also excellent, with a flavorful blend of field greens.

Step back in time at the charming and moderately priced **Star Drug Store** (510 23rd St., 409/766-7719, www.galvestondrug.com, $5–10). The historic neon/porcelain Coca-Cola sign out front sets the tone for this establishment, featuring an ancient (well, more than a century old) horseshoe-shaped lunch counter with soda fountain. Not surprisingly, the menu options are typical old-time lunch fare: burgers, Reubens, pimiento cheese sandwiches, chicken salad, dilled pasta salad, and ice-cream floats. The drugstore's signature item is a tasty tomato-basil soup.

SEAFOOD

What else are you going to eat in Galveston? Put aside your craving for Mongolian or Canadian cuisine for a few days and savor the local flavor. Fresh seafood is everywhere in Galveston, and several of the best places are right on the bay just a few blocks from The Strand district.

There's something about arriving in a seaside town that creates an instant yearning for enjoying a plate of shrimp or oyster or snapper—sometimes all three—while overlooking the water. If you're in the downtown area, satisfy this urge at the low-key yet high-quality **Willie G's** (2100 Harborside, 409/762-3030, www.williegs.com, $9–31). Opt for bayside seating and let your ocean vacation begin. Order some peel-and-eat shrimp to start—squeeze fresh lemon on top and dip them in tangy cocktail sauce—and proceed to the fresh catch of the day, from blackened snapper to grilled flounder to fried trout. Welcome to Galveston! Next door is the larger and consistently dependable **Fisherman's Wharf** (Pier 22 and Harborside Dr., 409/765-5708, $9–30). Red snapper is the specialty here, but feel free to cast your eyes and teeth at everything on the menu—shrimp kisses, oysters on the half shell, calamari, and even the steak and pasta are all tempting and tasty. Be sure to ask for a table with a view of the bay, where you can sit on the deck and watch the shrimp boats slowly glide by.

About a half mile inland you'll find one of the finest (and most expensive) restaurants in town. The fabulous 【 **Saltwater Grill** (2017 Post Office St., 409/762-3474, $12–42) feels urban and spare like Houston but tastes fresh and flavorful like a Gulf Coast restaurant should. At Saltwater, *fresh* isn't just an appealing adjective, it's a genuine approach to food preparation. The restaurant utilizes a bizarre yet effective steam-kettle device that's linked to a large heater, pipes, and steel buckets that cause water to boil in merely three minutes. The result is rapidly cooked fresh seafood as opposed to reheated or perpetually boiling (and soaking) fare. Enjoy the results on a plate of mussels, clams, or shrimp, and be sure to order

the grand gumbo. Another must-taste is the appetizer dish with fried asparagus topped with crabmeat and entrées such as the grilled yellowfin tuna, red snapper, and seafood linguini. It's worth dropping by the next day for a big bowl of gumbo. Reservations are recommended.

Seawall and Vicinity
AMERICAN

One of the best restaurants in the entire region is just a few minutes from the shore at 【 **Mosquito Café** (628 14th St., 409/763-1010, www.mosquitocafe.com, $6–19, open at 11 A.M. Tues–Fri., 8 A.M. on weekends). You'll definitely want to have breakfast here at least once, and you may find yourself returning for each meal since the flavor-packed, creatively inspired, healthy food makes such an impression. Grab a hot mug of strong coffee and try to decide among the delectable options such as Mosquito Benedict (a fresh-baked scone covered with portabello mushrooms, sautéed shrimp, sun-dried tomatoes, artichoke hearts, asparagus, and poached eggs topped with serrano hollandaise sauce), cinnamon-tinged French toast, fluffy pancakes, or bagels and lox. Lunch items include hearty bowls of pasta with homemade pesto, olives, and feta cheese, or tasty sandwiches on delicious fresh-baked bread with hickory-smoked bacon, avocado salsa, and goat cheese.

For a simple, low-key breakfast, lunch, or dinner, drop by the nearby neighborhood stalwart **Sunflower Bakery and Cafe** (512 14th St., 409/763-5500, $4–10, closed Sun.). You'll find warm, soft, fresh-made bakery items (breads, pastries, desserts) and flavor-packed sandwiches (the turkey, bacon, and avocado on honey wheat bread is especially tasty) along with healthy salads and even a few eclectic daily specials. Along with its newer (and less charming) location in a retail center, the Sunflower has expanded its options, offering a fresh and full menu complete with crab cakes, burgers, and po'boys. Incidentally, this is the perfect place to order a to-go lunch for the beach—just don't forget to include brownies and their legendary strawberry lemonade.

SEAFOOD

If you're staying in a hotel on Seawall Boulevard, your inaugural meal should definitely be at **Gaido's Seafood Restaurant** (3800 Seawall Blvd., 409/762-9625, $8–29). This venerable institution has been serving memorable meals since 1911, and its legendary reputation is evident everywhere, from the time-honored trimmings to the traditional menu to attentive service. The shrimp bisque is exquisite, the garlic snapper is succulent, and the crab cakes are outstanding.

For an amazing lunch with an outstanding view you gotta hit **The Spot** (3204 Seawall Blvd., 409/621-5237, www.thespotgalveston. com, $8–19). After a morning or afternoon of beachcombing, this is a spot-on place for a shrimp po'boy, fish-and-chips, or even a big ol' burger. The breading and bread are what set this spot aside from others, with their perfectly crispy texture encasing fresh-flavored seafood and top-notch sandwiches. A big bonus: The second-floor deck offers panoramic views of the gulf almost as tasty as the food in front of you.

Although it's a regional chain, **Landry's Seafood House** (5310 Seawall Blvd., 409/744-1010, www.landrysseafoodhouse.com, $6–27) is a respected eatery, even in a Gulf Coast town known for its local legends. Opt for the fresh catch Lafitte, gulf red snapper, or broiled flounder. Landry's also does shrimp well, including a fried option stuffed with seafood.

Specializing in the Cajun variety of seafood is **Benno's on the Beach** (1200 Seawall Blvd., 409/762-4621, www.bennosofgalveston.com). This is a very unassuming place—guests order at the counter beneath dim fluorescent lights

JELLYFISH JAM

The "jellies" on Texas's Gulf Coast aren't tasty fruit-filled breakfast treats. They're jellyfish, and despite their iridescent and wiggly appearance, they'll cause much more pain than pleasure.

One of the most common creatures washed up on the shore isn't technically a jellyfish, despite its translucent air bubble and blue tentacles. The Portuguese man-of-war (aka the bluebubble, bluebottom, or man-of-war) is actually a colony of organisms, each with its own distinct function. Its name comes from the air bubble's resemblance to the sails of an ancient Portuguese war vessel.

The man-of-war floats on ocean currents and is deposited ashore on Texas beaches during the spring to late summer. These crafty carnivores feed on small fish and other small animals that get caught in their venom-filled tentacles. The other washed-up organisms visitors may encounter on the shoreline are traditional jellyfish – gelatinous invertebrates with varying-size tentacles hanging from the main "body" of the organism (technically referred to as the mollusk).

You won't find an abundance of these bizarre animals on a typical beach stroll, but it's worth keeping an eye out for them because their stings pack quite a wallop. They're much harder to see in the water, but a good indication of their presence is the appearance of any washed-up organisms on the beach. The man-of-war is especially difficult to see since it's translucent and often blends in with wave foam.

Aside from avoiding areas of the ocean where you see beached jellies, you'll have to make sure you don't step anywhere near the washed-up variety, since their stinging cells remain toxic even when the rest of the body has died. Often, the tentacles are nearly invisible, though you'll definitely feel the sharp shot of pain jetting up your leg.

If this happens, scrape the tentacles off with a driver's license or credit card. If you're stung by a jellyfish, place the affected area under hot water and apply hydrocortisone cream to relieve the itching. For a man-of-war sting, splash the area with saltwater, then apply vinegar or a diluted bleach solution (1 part bleach to 10 parts water) to the sting site without pressing too hard on the skin. The pain should go away within an hour.

and sit on hard plastic booth chairs, but as soon as the food arrives, it's apparent where Benno's focuses its resources. The shrimp dishes are spectacular, bursting with flavor and perfectly seasoned with Cajun spices. You also can't go wrong with Benno's crawfish étouffée, jambalaya, spicy crab, or oysters.

RECREATION
Beaches

There are two main beaches in Galveston: the mellow family beach and the raucous singles beach. Both serve important purposes, but it's probably best they're separated. The family-friendly spot is **Stewart Beach** (6th St. and Seawall Blvd., 409/765-5023, $8 admission per car—cash only, open Mar.–mid-Oct.), where you'll find moms, dads, and kids building sand castles, playing volleyball, and body surfing. Nearby amenities include a children's playground with water slides, umbrella and chair rentals, concession area, souvenir shop, restrooms, and a bathhouse. Things get a bit crazier at **East Beach** (1923 Boddeker Dr., 409/762-3278, $8 admission per car—cash only). This is where Houston's younger crowd comes to party, a rare surfside treat since East Beach is one of the few places where drinking is legal on the beach. As a result, you'll find more concerts, promotions, and festivals than other public stretches of shoreline. Up to 7,000 cars can pack the beach (parking and drinking/sunbathing is a popular activity), and the bar area is a magnet for partygoers. East Beach also includes restrooms with showers, volleyball courts, chair and umbrella rentals, and a souvenir shop.

INFORMATION AND SERVICES

The **Galveston Convention and Visitors Bureau** offers brochures and maps with friendly staff on hand to answer questions. Visit the CVB at 523 24th Street or call 866/505-4456. You can also visit their information-packed and user-friendly website at www.galvestoncvb.com. Contact the **Galveston Historical Foundation** at 502 20th Street

(409/765-7834, www.galvestonhistory.org) for information about the island's impressive historic attractions.

GETTING THERE AND AROUND

The island's unique public transportation service, **Galveston Island Trolley** (409/797-3900, www.islandtransit.net, $1.25 adults), was damaged in Hurricane Ike but plans to be back on the rails soon. Call ahead to determine if it is offering similar services to its pre-Ike days: transportation from the Seawall to The Strand district and Pier 21. The cars are charming replicas of those used in Galveston from the late 1800s to the 1930s.

BRAZOSPORT AREA

Brazosport isn't a town name, but a collection of eight Brazoria County communities southwest of Galveston offering a strange mix of lightly developed beachfront and petrochemical plants. For the record, the Brazosport communities are: Clute, Freeport, Jones Creek, Lake Jackson, Oyster Creek, Quintana Beach, Richwood, and Surfside Beach.

The area is rich in Texas history, with the state's earliest explorers landing on nearby beaches nearly 500 years ago and Stephen F. Austin's first colony settling along the rich bottomlands of the Brazos, Colorado, and San Bernard Rivers in the early 19th century. The venerable Texas term Old Three Hundred refers to the 300 settlers who received land grants for Austin's first colony, where each family received up to 4,000 acres of fertile farm and ranch property in the area.

The massive Gulf Intracoastal Waterway carves a path along the coastal lowlands. This commercial boating canal, constructed in the 1940s, is considered the most valuable waterway in the country, transporting as much tonnage annually as the Panama Canal. The protected waterway stretches more than 1,000 miles from Brownsville to Florida.

Visitors to the Brazosport region enjoy the small-town specialty and antiques shops, beach home rentals, and casual ocean-based recreation. Drive, walk, or swim along the 21-mile stretch of beach or watch the seagulls and ocean barges lazily glide by. Other popular recreational activities include fresh- and saltwater fishing, boating, crabbing, and surfing.

Sights and Recreation

A must-see attraction in the Brazosport Area is the spectacular 〔 **Sea Center Texas** (300 Medical Dr. in Lake Jackson, 979/292-0100, www.tpwd.state.tx.us, Tues.–Sat. 9 A.M.–4 P.M., Sun. 1–4 P.M., free admission). Sea Center Texas is a multiuse facility combining several aquariums, an education center, and a fish hatchery along with an outdoor wetland exhibit and a kids' fishing pond. The education center's main exhibit is a 50,000-gallon aquarium containing Gulf of Mexico marine animals such as nurse sharks, Atlantic spadefish, red drum, gray snapper, and an enormous moray eel. Other large aquariums house tropical species found in area slat marshes, coastal bays, jetties, and artificial and coral reefs. Kids will love the center's "touch pool," where they can gently handle marine animals such as several varieties of crabs, snails, and anemones. Outside, the wetland exhibit is accessible by a long boardwalk over several marsh areas. Families can bring along a nature checklist and activity book to identify species in the area, including green tree frogs, turtles, and a wide variety of birds. The adjacent hatchery has the capacity to produce 20 million fingerlings each year (mostly spotted sea trout and red drum) for release into Texas coastal waters. Tours are available by reservation only.

Regional culture converges at the **The Center for the Arts & Sciences** (400 College Blvd. in Clute, 979/265-7661, www.bcfas.org, Tues.–Sat. 10 A.M.–4 P.M., Sun. 2–5 P.M., free admission). This all-inclusive facility is home to the Brazosport Art League, the Brazosport Museum of Natural Science, the Center Stages Theater, and Brazosport Planetarium. With so many cultural activities sharing space under one roof, you'll find an amazing array of attractions, from a colossal collection of seashells to an art gallery and studio to a theater staging regional productions. Perhaps most impressive is the natural science museum, containing wildlife, fossils, and an aquarium. Be sure to check out the exhibit featuring the Lightening Whelk (Texas's state shell) and the planetarium, which offers public viewings and occasionally serves as a training facility for astronauts from NASA's nearby Johnson Space Center.

Beaches
SURFSIDE BEACH
If you don't mind a petrochemical plant as your scenic backdrop, Surfside Beach is a delightful getaway for some low-key recreational activity. Though most of the folks here are Houston residents looking for a respite from the Galveston crowds, you'll find other beach lovers here from across the state seeking similar solace. Popular Surfside Beach pastimes include fishing, swimming, sailing, camping, and shell collecting. For information about the village of Surfside Beach, including restaurants, shops, and lodging links, visit www.surfsidebeachtx.org or call 979/233-1531.

BRYAN BEACH
Just a few miles away near the community of Freeport is Bryan Beach, another casual, scenic stretch of surf and sand. Grab a bucket for some sand dollar collecting, a pole for shallow surf fishing, or a towel and sunscreen for sunbathing. Primitive campsites are available nearby. To reach the beach from Freeport, travel two miles southwest of town on FM 1495, then head three miles south on Gulf Beach Road.

Brazoria National Wildlife Refuge
This sizable wildlife refuge (24907 FM 2004 in Angleton, 979/964-4011, www.fws.gov) contains protected habitats offering safe harbor for animals, particularly birds. Its prime location on the Gulf Coast draws more than 200 bird species, one of the highest counts in the nation. In winter, more than 100,000 snow geese, Canadian geese, teal, ducks, and sandhill cranes fill the numerous ponds and sloughs. In summer you'll find herons, egrets, white ibis,

spoonbills, seaside sparrows, and scissor-tailed flycatchers. Alligators occupy the refuge year-round on Big Slough and in ponds. Look for their trails thorough the mud and "gator holes" in dryer months.

San Bernard National Wildlife Refuge

The other major refuge in the Brazosport area is San Bernard (6801 County Rd. 306 in Brazoria, 979/849-6062, www.fws.gov). This 24,000-acre protected area is a haven for snow geese, warblers, herons, egrets, ibis, gulls, and terns. Most of the refuge is closed to the public, but the accessible three-mile car tour and several miles of hiking trails offer access to high-quality wildlife viewing.

Fishing

The Brazosport area offers a multitude of facilities for fishing, either inshore or deep-sea. If you choose to keep your feet on the ground, there are plenty of jetties, piers, and beaches where you can cast a line for speckled trout, flounder, redfish, sheepshead, and gafftop. Nearby marinas and beachside shacks sell tackle and bait. For deep-sea fishing, you can hire a service to provide charter boats to take you out farther for big-time catches including snapper, marlin, king mackerel, and sailfish. Two reputable outfits are **Easy Going Charters** (979/233-2947, www.easygulffishing.com), which can accommodate up to six people on its 35-foot-long boat, and **Johnston's Sportfishing** (979/233-8513).

A popular place to spend a weekend of fishing, camping, and lounging is **Quintana Beach County Park** (330 5th St., 979/233-1461 or 800/872-7578, www.brazoria-county.com), located on a picturesque barrier island near Freeport. The park's multilevel fishing pier is a favorite among anglers, and the day-use facilities include shaded pavilions, restrooms, showers, and the historic Coveney House, containing a museum and natural history display. The camping sites include full hookups, showers, and laundry facilities. From Freeport, take FM 1495 south nearly two miles to County Road 723, then head east three miles to the park entrance.

Accommodations

Here's a nice change of pace: The Brazosport area is overrun with local lodging options, with nary a garish hotel chain sign in sight. Independently owned hotels are the norm, and many travelers opt to rent a beach house or cabin for the weekend.

HOTELS

Those looking for a clean, comfy place to stay within walking distance of the beach should consider the **Cedar Sands Motel** (343 Beach Dr. in Surfside Beach, 979/233-1942, www.cedarsandsmotel.net, $75–150, depending on room size and season). One-bedroom options are available, but you may want to splurge for the kitchenettes, including pots and pans, a queen-size bed, and pull-out bed. All rooms have refrigerators, microwaves, and free wireless Internet access. More casual and representative of many of the sun-bleached, wind-worn, slightly shabby beach hotels is **Surfside Motel** (330 Coral Ct. in Surfside Beach, 979/233-4948, www.surfside-motel.biz, $65–120). The motel offers kitchenettes with two queen-size beds, one twin bed, and a full kitchen, or two-room suites with one queen-size bed, a pull-out bed, small refrigerator, and microwave. Check with the front desk if you need beach towels, board games, or horseshoes.

Of course, chain hotels provide reliable consistency for some travelers; so, if slightly shabby isn't your thing, you'll have to venture four miles off the coast to the nearby community of Clute. The best option is **La Quinta** (1126 Hwy. 332 W., 979/265-7461, www.lq.com, $69 d), featuring free wireless Internet access, a free continental breakfast, and an outdoor pool. Another fine choice is **Holiday Inn Express** (1117 Hwy. 332 W., 979/266-8746, www.hiexpress.com, $107 d), offering wireless Internet access, a workout facility, and a free continental breakfast.

BEACH HOME RENTALS

Hundreds of rooms are available in cabins and

beach homes along the gulf in the Brazosport area. The best way to find something that fits your specific needs (pets, kids, weekends, beach access, etc.) is to contact a rental locating service. Two of the more commendable outlets in the area are **Beach Resort Services** (800/382-9283, www.beachresortservices.com) and **Brannan Resort Rentals, Inc.** (979/233-1812, www.brri.com). For a comprehensive list of companies, visit the following visitor-related sites: www.visitbrazosport.com and www.surfsidetx.org.

CAMPING

Families and RVers make repeated returns to **Quintana Beach County Park** (979/233-1461, www.brazoriacountyparks.com, $15–27), featuring 56 paved and level camping sites, full hookups, primitive tent sites, a bathhouse with restrooms, showers, and laundry facilities. Cabins—complete with TVs, microwaves, kitchenettes, and charming wooden detailing—are also available for rent, ranging from $135 to $160, depending on the season.

A popular option for anglers is **Surfside Beach RV Park** (102 Fort Velesco Dr., 979/233-6919, www.surfsidebeachrv.com, $25–30), offering full hookup RV sites, free parking for fishing boats, an on-site laundry, and free wireless Internet access.

Food

Let's assume you'll be spending most of your time at the beach. And we can presume you'll also be hungry at some point. The good news is, Surfside Beach has several good vacation-style eateries. The best of the bunch is the **Red Snapper Inn** (402 Bluewater Hwy., 979/239-3226, www.redsnapperinn.com, $9–21). This quality surf-and-turf restaurant is best known for its seafood items, including the grilled boneless flounder stuffed with crabmeat dressing, the fried soft-shell crabs with rémoulade sauce, bacon-wrapped oysters, and sautéed garlic shrimp. Turf-wise, most diners opt for the spaghetti and charbroiled Greek-style meatballs or the classic chicken-fried steak.

You can't miss **Kitty's Purple Cow** (323 Ocean Ave., 979/233-9161, www.kittyspurplecow.com, $4–9). The food isn't quite as attention-grabbing as the restaurant's facade, a distractingly purple building on the beach; regardless, Kitty's specializes in tasty meaty burgers and even a little seafood (boiled shrimp) from the unfortunately named "app-moo-tizers" menu. Breakfast is also available (after 10 A.M. on weekdays), with hearty portions of biscuits and gravy and standard egg dishes.

Locals loiter at the low-key **Jetty Shack** (412 Parkview St., 979/233-5300, $5–11), a beachside dive offering a tasty Angus burger, plenty of fried food, grilled cheese, and cold beer.

Any beach town worth its weight in sand dollars has a classic burger joint—in Surfside, it's **Castaway Bar & Grill** (979/233-7270, www.castawaybar.net, $5–12), where you can order a big ol' greasy burger and fries in-house or take out to complement the tasty waves.

Information and Services

The **Brazosport Visitors and Convention Council** (main office at 300 Abner Jackson Pkwy. in Lake Jackson, 979/285-2501 or 888/477-2505, www.brazosport.org) provides details on area attractions, accommodations, and restaurants, and brochures and maps to help you find your way around.

Corpus Christi and Vicinity

Corpus Christi (population 285,267) is the largest city on Texas's Gulf Coast, and it's one of the most popular destinations in the state for seaside recreation, including fishing, sailing, swimming, and windsurfing.

The city has experienced a precipitous history, with drought, conflicts with Native American tribes, and various wars preventing settlements from taking hold until the mid-1800s, when a trading post was established and a small village developed that eventually became known as Corpus Christi, which translates as "the Body of Christ." Just when the town started growing, a yellow fever epidemic decimated the population, and it was subsequently plagued for decades by the lack of a deepwater port.

In 1916 and 1919, torrential storms destroyed portions of the city, erasing grand hotels and palatial homes. As a result, Corpus Christi, dubbed the "Sparkling City by the Bay," can appear historically lackluster, with a deficiency of significant structures reflecting its heritage. Regardless, historic homes and churches still exist in downtown neighborhoods unaffected by hurricanes and wrecking balls.

By the middle of the 20th century, Corpus, as it's known throughout the state, became a major petroleum and shipping center, with coastal shipments of gasoline, crude petroleum, and natural gas bringing increased corporate activity. Also contributing to the economy were the military bases and the petroleum and petrochemical industry, particularly the six refineries making good use of the approximately 1,500 oil wells in the area.

Despite its fairly large population, Corpus retains the feel of a small city, albeit one with remarkable museums and top-notch seafood restaurants. Corpus Christi's mild year-round temperatures and inviting tropical climate draw visitors from across the country to its cultural and recreational opportunities and abundant sunshine glistening on this "Sparkling City by the Bay."

SIGHTS
(Texas State Aquarium

The magnificent Texas State Aquarium (2710 N. Shoreline Blvd., 361/881-1200, www.texasstateaquarium.org, daily 9 A.M.–5 P.M., $15.95 adults, $14.95 seniors, $10.95 children ages 3–12, parking $4) offers an ideal way to take a quick break from the beach while still being surrounded by the region's fascinating natural resources. The layout of the aquarium is rather clever, leading visitors into Texas's marine world at sea level with exhibits containing birds, alligators, and stingrays, and proceeding to explore the Gulf of Mexico at sequentially deeper levels. One of the aquarium's main exhibits showcases menacing sharks, a 350-pound grouper, and hundreds of other species as they slither and glide around the barnacle-encrusted poles of a replicated offshore oil rig. The 350,000-gallon Dolphin Bay habitat uses seawater from Corpus Christi Bay for the Atlantic bottlenose dolphins that cannot live in the wild. A shaded seating area provides respite from the relentless sun for daily interpretive programs, and a lengthy viewing window allows visitors to get nose to nose with the dolphins. Other popular exhibits include Otter Space, featuring the frisky fellas cavorting on slides and in pools, and Living Shores, allowing kids to handle nonthreatening sea creatures. The aquarium expanded to include terrestrial critters, particularly in the Amazon rain forest exhibit, containing boa constrictors and poison dart frogs, and in the bird theater, featuring "flight performances" by hawks, falcons, and parrots. In 2010, the aquarium introduced Swamp Tales, an exhibit dedicated to conservation efforts in the region, especially with American alligators like Bo, the museum's featured 10-foot 'gator.

(USS *Lexington* Museum

You can't miss the massive USS *Lexington* Museum (2914 N. Shoreline Blvd., 361/888-4873, www.usslexington.com, open 9 A.M.–5 P.M.

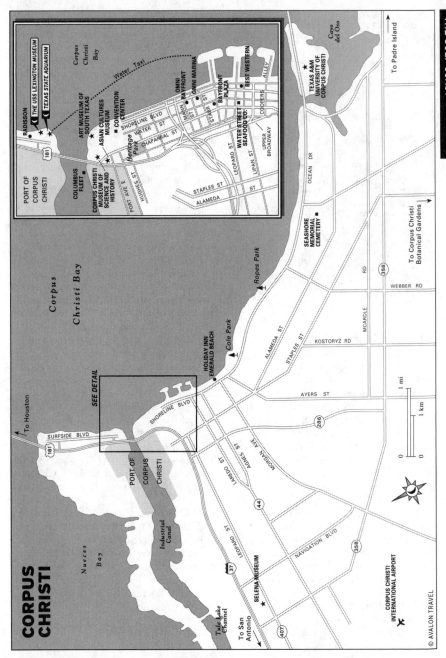

CORPUS CHRISTI

© AVALON TRAVEL

© ANDY RHODES

the USS *Lexington*

Science and History (1900 N. Chaparral St., 361/826-4667, www.ccmuseum.com, Tues.–Sat. 10 A.M.–5 P.M., Sun. noon–5 P.M., $12.50 adults, $10 seniors, $6 children ages 5–12). The museum features myriad educational exhibits emphasizing the Gulf Coast's relation to the natural and cultural world. Particularly fascinating is the Ships of Christopher Columbus exhibit, featuring authentic reproductions of the *Niña, Pinta,* and *Santa Maria.* The three vessels, located outside the museum and accessible to visitors, were built in Spain to commemorate the 500th anniversary of Christopher Columbus's voyage to the New World. Each ship was made with authentic 15th-century materials such as hand-forged nails and wood from the same forests used for Columbus's ships. The museum's other noteworthy exhibits are also maritime related, including an interactive shipwreck display containing artifacts from three Spanish treasure ships that ran aground on Padre Island in 1554, an exhibit featuring artifacts related to French explorer Robert Cavelier, Sieur de La Salle's ill-fated *Belle* shipwreck, and the Children's Wharf, a bustling learning area for youngsters. The remainder of the museum contains a comprehensive collection of more than 28,000 objects (shells, Native American crafts, bird and reptile eggs) representing the history and culture of South Texas.

daily Labor Day–Memorial Day, until 6 P.M. in the summer, $12.95 adults, $10.95 seniors/military, $7.95 children ages 4–12). Looming large in the Corpus Christi Bay, the USS *Lexington* is a decommissioned World War II naval aircraft carrier now serving as a 33,000-ton floating museum transporting visitors back in time with tours of the ship's decks and quarters, educational exhibits, restored aircraft, a high-tech flight simulator, and a collection of historical memorabilia. The music and voices blaring from speakers and interaction with the ship's docents gives an authentic feel for life aboard the nation's longest-serving aircraft carrier. The best way to experience the *Lexington* is via one of the five self-guided tours covering 100,000 square feet on 11 decks. Afterward, take some time atop the flight deck to soak up the view of the bay, the city skyline, and the impressive vintage aircraft.

Corpus Christi Museum of Science and History

To get a better sense of the area's colorful past, drop by the Corpus Christi Museum of

Heritage Park

Just down the street from the science museum is the city's Heritage Park (1581 N. Chaparral St., 361/826-3410, www.cctexas.com, Mon.–Thurs. 9 A.M.–5 P.M., Fri. 9 A.M.–2 P.M., Sat. 11 A.M.–2 P.M., guided tours Mon., Thurs., Fri. at 10:30 A.M., $6 adults, $2 children 12 and under). These 12 restored Victorian-era historic homes were moved to the city's cultural area to protect them from being demolished and to showcase the city's diverse past. The centerpiece is the Cultural Center's Galván House, open for free tours.

Asian Cultures Museum

Also located in the city's cultural district is the

Asian Cultures Museum (1809 N. Chaparral St., 361/882-2641, www.asianculturesmuseum.org, Tues.–Sat. 10 A.M.–4 P.M., $6 adults, $4 students, $3 children 12 and under), offering an interesting array of objects and artwork from across the Pacific. What started as a local resident's personal collection of cultural objects has evolved into a full-fledged museum containing thousands of items representing nearly a dozen Asian countries. Billie Trimble Chandler spent decades as a teacher and art collector in Asia, and brought items back to share with Corpus residents and educate them about faraway lands. Since then, the museum has grown to include clothing, furniture, paintings, dolls, statues, and other art objects from Japan, Korea, China, the Philippines, Taiwan, and other Asian countries. The museum also features international traveling exhibits and offers educational classes for students and the general public.

Selena Museum

Latin-music fans often make a pilgrimage to the Selena Museum (5410 Leopard St., 361/289-9013, www.q-productions.com, Mon.–Fri. 10 A.M.–4 P.M., $2 admission 12 and up, $1 children). It's not an easy place to find, however. The museum is located downtown just off I-37 in a warehouse-type building with no sign (look for the painted mural of Selena on the outside) and was created by Corpus resident Abraham Quintanilla to honor the memory of his daughter, the famous Tejana singer who was killed by the president of her fan club in 1995. The museum showcases many of Selena's personal memorabilia, including the outfits and dresses she designed and wore at concerts, her red Porsche, penciled sketches, her prized egg collection, and letters of sympathy from fans across the world.

Art Museum of South Texas

Culture converges at the Art Museum of South Texas (1902 N. Shoreline Blvd., 361/825-3500, www.stia.org, Tues.–Sat. 10 A.M.–5 P.M., Sun.

LA SALLE'S LEGACY

French explorer Robert Cavelier, Sieur de La Salle left an enormous legacy in Texas. Though he's well known for his exploration in the Great Lakes region, La Salle's ambitious nature and tremendous hubris ultimately led to his demise after a doomed colonization effort on the Texas Gulf Coast.

In 1684, La Salle embarked on a mission to build forts along the mouth of the Mississippi River to attack and occupy Spanish territory in Mexico. His expedition proved to be a series of failures, beginning when one of his ships was captured by pirates in the West Indies and continuing with sickness, misdirection, and shipwrecks.

While searching for the mouth of the Mississippi, La Salle missed his target (by a wide margin – nearly 500 miles) and instead landed at present-day Matagorda Bay in the central Gulf Coast of Texas. One of his ships was lost offshore, and another, La Belle, became stranded on a sandbar during a storm.

La Salle made several more attempts to find the Mississippi, but they ultimately proved unsuccessful. Though he eventually established Fort St. Louis near the coast, his subsequent attempt to lead a party in search of reinforcements proved to be the last adventure this famed explorer would take – he was killed by his own men near present-day Navasota, Texas.

La Salle's legacy would be rekindled nearly 300 years later when his wrecked ship La Belle was discovered by marine archaeologists with the Texas Historical Commission. Considered one of the most important shipwrecks ever discovered in North America, the excavation produced an amazing array of finds, including the hull of the ship, three bronze cannons, thousands of glass beads, and even a crew member's skeleton. The artifacts have been carefully cleaned and preserved, and are currently displayed at numerous Gulf Coast museums.

1–5 P.M., $6 adults, $4 seniors and military, $2 students 12 and older). The three-story building is unmistakable, with bright white concrete walls and 13 rooftop pyramids overlooking the bay. Inside, you'll find several galleries showcasing the museum's 1,300 works of art, primarily paintings and sculpture representing the Americas with a focus on Texas, Mexico, and the Southwest. The museum also contains an interactive kids' playroom, classrooms, studios, a gift shop, and an auditorium.

Corpus Christi Botanical Gardens and Nature Center

Those who want to appreciate the area's natural beauty beyond the beach should visit the botanical gardens (8545 S. Staples St., 361/852-2100, www.stxbot.org, daily 7:30 A.M.–5:30 P.M., $6 adults, $5 seniors and military, $3 children ages 5–12). Exotic gardens and perfectly landscaped lawns await visitors at this popular attraction, which takes full advantage of its tropical climate to produce vibrant colors and lush landscapes. One of the center's showpieces is the Rose Garden, featuring 300 roses, a large pavilion, and beautiful lightly lapping fountain. Other noteworthy areas are the hummingbird garden, orchid garden with 2,500 flowering plants, and the hibiscus garden.

RECREATION
Beaches
CITY BEACHES ON THE BAY
If you're staying downtown and need a quick beach fix, go to **Corpus Christi Beach** (just north of the USS *Lexington,* 361/880-3480). It's not quite picturesque, and the shoreline sand is pretty coarse, but it's great for a leisurely stroll or swim with a pleasant view of Corpus Christi Bay. You'll see lots of local families playing in the sand or flying kites, and there are several spots offering rinse-off showers, restrooms, and small cabana huts with picnic tables. Much smaller in size yet within walking distance of downtown hotels is **Magee Beach** (Shoreline Blvd., at Park St., 361/880-3461). This 250-yard stretch of sand on the bay isn't designed for shell collecting, but it's a

good place to get your feet wet without worrying about them being pulled away by the undertow you'll encounter on the larger ocean beaches. Showers and restrooms are located on the north end of the beach.

ISLAND BEACHES ON THE GULF
Serious beachcombers and bodysurfers skip the bayside beaches and head straight to the long stretches of sand on the barrier islands 10 miles east of town on the Gulf of Mexico. Don't miss the beautiful shoreline along **Mustang Island State Park** (17047 State Hwy. 361, 361/749-5246, www.tpwd.state.tx.us, $4 daily ages 13 and older). Named for the wild horses that escaped from Spanish explorers and roamed free across this 18-mile long island, Mustang Island park comprises five miles of the pristine outstretched beach, perfect for swimming, fishing, sunbathing, hiking, biking, and even low-intensity surfing. Birding is another popular activity along this 4,000-acre island, notable for its distinctive ecosystem based on 20-foot-high sand dunes that protect the bay and mainland, and can reduce powerful hurricane-driven waves. To get there from Corpus, take South Padre Island Drive (Highway 358) to Padre Island, then head north on Highway 361 for five miles to the park headquarters.

◖ Padre Island National Seashore
Just south of Mustang Island is Padre Island National Seashore (3829 Park Rd. 22, 361/949-8068, www.nps.gov/pais, $5 entry fee for walkers and bikers, $10 fee for vehicles, passes valid for seven days). Don't let the name fool you. This low-key, nature-oriented, protected shoreline is not to be confused with the commercial-minded party atmosphere of South Padre Island, a nearly three-hour drive to the south. Padre Island National Seashore is the longest remaining undeveloped stretch of barrier island in the world and appeals primarily to naturalists who delight in its primitive shoreline and birding and fishing opportunities. Birdwatchers arrive in droves during the fall and spring migration seasons when thousands of birds drop by the island, including sandhill

SAVE THE SEA TURTLES

Padre Island National Seashore is undertaking extensive efforts to protect an endearing creature that nests along its shoreline and glides among its gentle waves. The Kemp's ridley is the most endangered species of sea turtle, and it was nearly lost forever in the 1960s when a massive exploitation of eggs and meat occurred at its primary nesting beach in Mexico. The 16-mile stretch of sand at nearby Playa de Rancho Nuevo, Tamaulipas, Mexico, was home to nearly 40,000 Kemp's ridleys in 1947. Fewer than 5,000 currently nest each year.

Named for Richard M. Kemp, a fisherman who submitted the first documented specimen in 1906, the Kemp's ridley has been making a slow resurgence thanks to the devoted scientists with the National Park Service, which operates the Padre Island National Seashore between Corpus Christi and South Padre.

To help save the turtle, the U.S. and Mexican governments have been working together to reestablish a nesting beach at Padre Island National Seashore, utilizing the theory that turtles will return to the beach where they were born to lay their own eggs. For 10 years (1978-88), scientists collected more than 22,000 eggs at Rancho Nuevo and transported them in Padre Island sand to a lab at the national seashore for incubation. The hatchlings were released on the beach, where they then crawled to the surf with the hopes they'd be naturally imprinted with the location in their memories for future reference.

Park officials still incubate turtle eggs and release the little guys into the gulf each summer. The public is invited to view this fascinating natural event — for release dates and directions to the site, call the Hatchling Hotline at 361/949-7163.

Biologists have attempted to gauge the turtles' successful rate of return by marking their shells and fins with identification tags and even GPS devices. Their efforts appear to be productive, since each year more turtles revisit their birthplace. In fact, nearly 60 percent of the species' eggs are now found on Padre Island, making it the most important Kemp's ridley nesting beach in the United States.

Visitors who see a live or dead turtle on the beach are encouraged to immediately contact a park ranger or the seashore's turtle biologist at 361/949-8173. Messing with these endangered turtles in any way is considered a felony, with fines ranging up to $20,000. Many Kemp's ridleys have been identified and protected as a result of visitors' efforts, so perhaps your next stroll on the beach will yield a finding far more valuable than an intact sand dollar.

---

cranes, hawks, and songbirds. The park is also considered the most important nesting beach in the country for the most endangered sea turtle in the world (Kemp's ridley). Park officials incubate sea turtle eggs found along the coast and release the hatchlings into the gulf during the summer. The public is invited to view this fascinating natural event—for release dates and directions to the site, call the Hatchling Hotline at 361/949-7163. Other popular activities at the park include swimming, fishing, windsurfing, and beachcombing. Visit the website for detailed information about camping locations and fees. To reach the park from Corpus, take South Padre Island Drive (Highway 358) to Padre Island, then head south on Park Road 22 for 13 miles to the Malaquite Visitor Center.

Fishing

Corpus is a major destination for anglers, and there are plenty of locations and services to accommodate them. You'll find anglers with poles anchored in the sand at several city beaches, including Corpus Christi Beach, where fishers often gather at the Nueces Bay Pier at the end of Hull Street. Lines are also cast along the bay on the massive concrete downtown piers (known locally as T-heads), several spots along the seawall, and at lighted breakwater jetties. Another popular spot is Bob Hall Pier at Padre Balli Park on North Padre Island. Its prime location and abundance of fish species (tarpon, mackerel, redfish, and even shark) have drawn anglers to this venerable and productive location since the 1950s. Bait and tackle are available at a nearby shop.

If you'd rather get out to sea for some big-game fishing, contact a charter or rental company to set you up with all the gear, guides, and good advice you'd ever want. Deep-sea boats are available for those who want to troll for Gulf of Mexico species such as marlin, sailfish, tuna, and kingfish. Reputable companies include **C&T Bay Charters** (4034 Barnes St., 888/227-9172, www.ctbaycharters.com) and Port Aransas–based **Deep Sea Headquarters** (416 W. Cotter Ave., 361/749-5597, www.deepseaheadquarters.com), providing private excursions to anglers of all ages and skill levels.

Windsurfing

Thanks to its constant easy breeze (averaging 15–20 mph), Corpus is a mecca for windsurfers. Although some try their sails on the bay at city locales like **Cole Park** (near the 2000 block of Ocean Dr., restrooms available), most windsurfers head to North Padre Island, particularly Bird Island Basin at the Padre Island National Seashore. This half-mile stretch of beach is internationally recognized as one of the top windsurfing sites on the U.S. mainland. If you've never grabbed hold of a sail, this is the best place to learn since there's always a breeze a blowin'. To set yourself up with all the gear, contact **Worldwinds Windsurfing** (11493 S. Padre Island Dr., 361/949-7472, www.worldwinds.net) or **Wind & Wave Water Sports** (10721 S. Padre Island Dr., 361/937-9283, www.windandwave.net).

Horseback Riding

Have you ever wanted to ride a horse on the beach, with the waves gently crashing at your trusty steed's feet as the ocean breeze whips through your hair? Then gallop over to **Horses on the Beach** (16562 S. Padre Island Dr., 361/443-4487, www.horsesonthebeachcorpus.com, several rides offered daily, reservations required), located just north of Padre Island National Seashore. Horses are available for first-timers, children, and experienced riders, and the stable owners also handle lessons. You're welcome to walk, trot, or ride your horse into the surf.

ENTERTAINMENT
Bars and Clubs

Though many visitors choose to sip their cocktails on the beach or in the hotel bar, there are options available for the adventurous souls who want to see some live music or perhaps even mingle with the locals. The best place to soak up the local scene without feeling like an outsider is the downtown **Executive Surf Club** (309 N. Water St., 361/884-2364, www.executivesurfclub.com). Located adjacent to the Water Street Seafood Co., the Surf Club's decor reflects its name, with vintage surfboards on the walls and refurbished as tables. The scene is lively yet casual, with live music most nights (mainly Texas rock and blues acts, often with a cover charge), more than 30 beers on tap, and a kitchen serving up tasty grub. Another visitor-friendly spot is the decidedly more upscale **Republic of Texas Bar & Grill** (900 N. Shoreline Blvd., 361/886-3515, www.omnihotels.com/republic). Sitting atop the 20th floor of the Omni Bayfront hotel, the Republic of Texas bar is dimly lit and heavily wooded in a welcoming way. The views of the bay and city are outstanding, the drinks are expertly made, and the pianist provides a perfect soundtrack. Grab a Scotch, margarita, or a draft beer and soak up the surrounding scenery.

Veering in a local direction is the younger and more boisterous **Dr. Rockit's Blues Bar** (709 N. Chaparral St., 361/884-7634, www.dr.ldescher.com). Located along a formerly vibrant stretch of Chaparral Street in the heart of downtown, Dr. Rockit's is still thriving, and it's still all about the blues. Live bands from Corpus and across the state play here nightly, and the place can get pretty rockin' when the bands get rollin'. Check the website for a live music schedule and cover charges. Just down the street is another laid-back locale, **Bourbon Street Bar and Grill** (313 N.

Chaparral St., 361/882-2082), a New Orleans–style establishment with Cajun food and free-flowing drinks. The activity kicks up a notch in Bourbon Street's Voodoo Lounge and next door at **Porky's Saloon.**

SHOPPING

Corpus has several malls that don't differ much from others across the country, and many of the vacationers looking for trinkets and T-shirts opt for the souvenir shops in Port Aransas. However, there are several places in town worth checking out that offer quality clothing and jewelry, imported goods, and beach gear. Among them is **Pilar Gallery** (3814 S. Alameda, 361/853-7171), a colorful shop with quality women's clothing, tapestries, rugs, and imported jewelry and folk art from Mexico and across the globe. You'll also find an amazing array of imports and curios at **El Zocalo Imports** (601 N. Water St. in the Omni Bayfront hotel, 361/887-8847). Though the primary focus here is Mexican jewelry, shoppers will find an interesting mix of objects, from crosses and candleholders to books and belt buckles.

Every beach city needs a good surf shop, and Corpus has several rad options to choose from. Hodads to heroes will find boards, surf wear, kayaks, skateboards, and surf and skate accessories at **Wind & Wave Water Sports** (10721 S. Padre Island Dr., 361/937-9283, www.windandwave.net) or **Worldwinds Windsurfing** (11493 S. Padre Island Dr., 361/949-7472, www.worldwinds.net).

ACCOMMODATIONS

There's no shortage of lodging options in Corpus, and most have decent views with easy access to the bay and fairly reasonable rates for a vacation destination. For those interested, there are plenty of budget options available in the airport/greyhound race track area, but most leisure travelers feel it's worth dropping the extra cash to stay in a place by the sea. If you're looking for a nice spot away from the city, consider a condo (nightly rates available) on alluring Mustang Island or North Padre Island, about 10–15 miles from downtown directly on the Gulf Coast.

$50-100

You can do the beach on a bargain, if you consider lodging in the $90s a good deal. Not surprisingly, the more affordable hotels tend to be farther down the shoreline, but for many visitors, the key word is *shoreline,* so proximity isn't a concern. One of the better deals in town is the **Budget Inn & Suites** (801 S. Shoreline Blvd., 888/493-2950, www.budgetinnandsuitecc.com, $65 d), located within walking distance of Cole Park, one of the city's premier windsurfing spots. The hotel's amenities include a free continental breakfast, free wireless Internet service, and an outdoor pool and sundeck. A bit closer to the action is **Knights Inn** (3615 Timon Blvd., 361/883-4411, www.knightsinn.com, $94 d), located just a couple blocks off the bay and offering private balconies, several ocean-view rooms, free wireless Internet access, refrigerators, microwaves, and an outdoor pool.

Closer to downtown is the **Plaza Inn** (2021 N. Padre Island Dr., 361/289-8200, www.plazainnhotels.com, $99 d), offering a nice range of complimentary eats, from hot breakfast in the morning to popcorn and soda in the afternoon, and beverages and appetizers in the evenings. The Plaza Inn also has an outdoor pool, free Wi-Fi service, and is pet friendly. The best deal in the $100 range is **Quality Inn & Suites** (3202 Surfside Blvd., 361/883-7456, www.qualityinn.com, $99 d), thanks to its prime location on Corpus Christi Beach in the shadow of the USS *Lexington* and Texas State Aquarium. The hotel also features an outdoor beachside pool and hot tub, free continental breakfast, and rooms with microwaves and refrigerators.

$100-150

A reasonable deal in the heart of downtown is the **Bayfront Plaza Hotel** (601 N. Water St., 361/882-8100, www.bayfrontplazahotelcc.com, $109 d). The 10-story atrium lobby and interior corridor is pleasant, unless you're trying to get to sleep while a jazz band is enthusiastically playing in the bar. You can walk to restaurants and nightclubs from here, and even stroll down to the T-head piers or tiny Magee Beach. The hotel's amenities include a free breakfast, a large outdoor swimming pool, wireless Internet access, and free covered parking. A bit farther up the road in location and price is **Days Inn** (4302 Surfside Blvd., 361/882-3297, www.daysinn.com, $119 d), a block off Corpus Christi Beach. Amenities include rooms with microwaves, fridges, and free Wi-Fi access, along with a complimentary continental breakfast and outdoor pool.

A bit farther away from the bay is **Staybridge Suites** (5201 Oakhurst Dr., 361/857-7766, www.staybridgecc.com, $118 d). Features include a "sundowner reception" (Tuesday –Thursday) with complimentary light meals along with beer, wine, and soft drinks, as well as a free hot breakfast. Other amenities include a fitness center, whirlpool, outdoor pool, and free Wi-Fi service. Next door is the **Holiday Inn Express** (5213 Oakhurst Dr., 361/857-7772, www.hiexpress.com, $118 d), offering free Wi-Fi service, a complimentary hot breakfast bar, and a fitness center with an indoor pool and whirlpool.

A bit farther east is **Hilton Garden Inn** (6717 S. Padre Island Dr., 361/991-8200, www.hiltongardeninn.hilton.com, $119 d), offering a heated outdoor pool with Jacuzzi, complimentary high-speed Internet access, a microwave and minifridge in each room, and 32-inch flatscreen LCD TVs. Just off the busy South Padre Island Drive is **Hampton Inn** (5209 Blanche Moore Dr., 361/985-8395, www.hamptoninn.com, $119 d), which features free Internet access, a complimentary breakfast, to-go breakfast bags (on weekdays), an outdoor pool, and a fitness center.

Another downtown option is the **Best Western Marina Grand Hotel** (300 N. Shoreline Blvd., 361/883-5111, www.bestwestern.com, $139 d), offering rooms with private balconies and marina views, wireless Internet access, microwaves, refrigerators, a free continental breakfast, and an outdoor pool and exercise facility. Farther south along the bayside is **Holiday Inn Emerald Beach** (1102 S. Shoreline Blvd., 800/465-4329, www.ichotelsgroup.com, $143 d). Also located along a nice stretch of beach, the Holiday Inn contains an indoor pool and fitness center along with an indoor recreation area for the kids (heated pool, Ping-Pong tables, billiard tables, vending machines, etc.). The hotel offers wireless Internet access and free meals for children.

The best choice for those who want to stay directly on the beach is the (**Radisson** (3200 Surfside Blvd., 361/883-9700, www.radisson.com, $149 d). Step out the back doors and onto the sand of Corpus Christi Beach, a pleasant stretch of shoreline on the bay that hosts a large number of frolicking families, flotsam and jetsam, and the USS *Lexington*. Though the interior corridors are somewhat dark, the rooms are bright and cheery, with private balconies, microwaves, refrigerators, and free Internet access. The hotel features a splendid outdoor pool with swim-up bar service, a full-fledged fitness center, and a decent restaurant, the Blue Bay Grill.

$150-200

For something more intimate and less corporate, consider the new yet cozy **V Boutique and Hotel** (701 N. Water St., 361/883-9200, www.vhotelcc.com, $189 d). Located among the bayside businesses, the V features modern decor with a residential feel, including flatscreen TVs, free Internet access, fancy bedding, minibars, and a fitness center.

Looming large along the Corpus Christi Bay are the (**Omni** towers, the Marina and Bayfront (707 and 900 N. Shoreline Blvd., 361/887-1600, www.omnihotels.com, $159 d). Located within a block of each other, the towers are connected by a walkway to form a deluxe complex. They're similar in price and amenities, although the Bayfront Tower offers additional upscale room options. Both towers provide rooms with wireless Internet access, free meals for kids, a fancy fully equipped health club, an indoor/outdoor heated swimming pool, an in-house massage therapist, bike rentals, and free covered parking.

Camping

An ideal spot for RVers looking to set up shop in town is **Puerto Del Sol RV Park** (5100 Timon Blvd., 361/882-5373, $25–35 nightly rates), located at the northern edge of Corpus Christi Beach. Amenities include full hookups, a rec room, laundry facilities, restrooms with hot showers, Internet access, and a book exchange. Farther out of town at the entrance of Padre Island is **Colonia Del Rey** (1717 Waldron Rd., 361/937-2435 or 800/580-2435, $25–35 nightly rates), offering a heated pool, hot tub, a recreation facility, laundry room, convenience store, and wireless Internet service. Nearby is the minimal yet affordable **Padre Balli Park** (15820 Park Rd. 22, 361/949-8121, $10–18 nightly rates), containing 54 paved campsites with water and electric hookups, 12 hardtop campsites for pitching a tent with water and electric hookups, and primitive camping on the beach. A bathhouse and laundry facility are also available.

FOOD

Seafood is the favored item on the menu for most Corpus Christi diners, and the variety of restaurants in the downtown area offers plenty of options. Since the city has such a large Hispanic population, you'll also find high-quality (and quantity) Tex-Mex restaurants.

American

By nature, beach towns are populated with casual eateries catering to flip-flopped families and sun-soaked seamen. Still, vacations are often an opportune time to celebrate the special occasion of being away from home in an exciting unfamiliar locale. A fancy meal is one of the best ways to commemorate a well-deserved break, and in Corpus, it doesn't get much fancier than the **Republic of Texas Bar & Grill** (900 N. Shoreline Blvd., 361/886-3515, $10–42). Located on the 20th floor of the Omni Bayfront hotel, this restaurant serves upscale Texas fare in a refined environment with incredibly stunning views. Meat is the main event here, and the range of options and methods of preparation are as impressive as the surrounding scenery. Can't-miss menu items include Chateau steak with sautéed asparagus and broccoli, pork rib chops in an apple-ginger glaze, Texas crab cake with lobster and cognac sauce, and perfectly prepared venison, buffalo, and redfish.

One of the newer entries to the Corpus upscale food club is **Katz 21 Steak & Spirits** (317 N. Mesquite St., 361/884-1221, www.katz21.com, $13–39, closed Sun.). A traditional steak house specializing in prime grade-A beef, Katz's features quality cuts of beef as well as fresh seafood, veal, and lamb. Unlike many traditional stuffy steak houses, however, Katz's offers a lighter lunch menu with soups, salads, sandwiches, and pastas. Popular menu items include the prime rib served au jus with horseradish sauce, the bone-in rib eye, the rack of lamb, and veal picatta. Reservations are encouraged.

Slightly more trendy is **Dragonfly** (14701 Park Rd. 22 S., 361/949-2224, $8–23), offering a fresh take on seafood and other standard fare. The salmon has a wonderful curry seasoning and is accompanied by a tasty side of baby bok choy and carrots, while the cheesy lasagna somehow manages to be hearty without being overly filling. Other menu highlights include the slightly spicy shrimp skewer and tasty grilled tuna. Parents take note: Dragonfly doesn't officially have a kids menu, but they'll whip up a bowl of creamy mac and cheese upon request.

Okay, enough with the fancy stuff. Two of Corpus Christi's most venerable downtown eateries specialize in comfort food in a casual atmosphere. The 1950s-style **City Diner & Oyster Bar** (622 N. Water St., 361/883-1643, $6–16) is known for just about everything on the menu except its unremarkable oysters. From greasy burgers to zesty peppercorn ranch onion rings to classic chicken-fried steak to snapper smothered in a creamy crab and shrimp sauce, this retro establishment gets home-style regional fare right. Just a few blocks down the street is another esteemed local hot spot, the tourist-friendly **Executive Surf Club** (309 N. Water St., 361/884-7873, www.executivesurfclub.com, $7–16). This is an ideal place to grab a big ol' juicy cheeseburger and a Shiner Bock while you contemplate your next beach activity. Standard bar fare is the main draw here, and the Surf Club delivers with fish-and-chips, fried shrimp, tortilla wraps, and chicken-fried steak, all served on tables fashioned from old surfboards. Stick around after dinner for some local hot blues and rock bands.

Asian

Corpus has a long-standing connection with Asian cultures, reaching back nearly a century to the days when shrimpers and rice farmers arrived in the developing coastal town. Only recently, however, have Thai, Chinese, and Japanese restaurants come to the general public's awareness. Among the most popular is **Yalee's Asian Bistro** (5649 Saratoga Blvd., 361/993-9333, www.yaleesasianbistro.com, $6–18). The counter-service approach may lower expectations, but the food at Yalee's is top-notch, featuring popular menu items such as the spicy Ma Po tofu and flavorful standards like Kung Pao shrimp and General Tso chicken. Sushi fans should head directly to **Ichiban Japanese Seafood Buffet** (1933 S. Padre Island Dr., 361/854-6686, $7–19). There's something for everyone here, from classic tuna and shrimp rolls to more elaborate options such as octopus, unagi, hamachi, and squid. Since this is a buffet, diners also have the option of choosing oysters, crab legs, seaweed salad, and tasty barbecued short ribs.

Barbecue

Corpus isn't known as a barbecue mecca, but there are a couple noteworthy restaurants where out-of-staters can experience the mystique and magnificence of Texas-style 'cue. One of the better options is **Miller's Bar-B-Q** (6601 Weber Rd., 361/806-2244, $7–15). Miller's is known for its tender brisket and beef ribs, along with pork, chicken, and sausage. The sides here are better than average, so be sure to load up on the sweet potato salad and coleslaw.

Mexican

Unlike its seafood restaurants, most of Corpus Christi's Mexican spots are not on the waterfront. Regardless, several are worth the inland drive, particularly **La Playa** (5017 Saratoga Blvd. and 7118 S. Padre Island Dr., 361/986-0089, www.laplaya.cc, $7–18). This is the place to go for a top-notch traditional Tex-Mex meal. Feast on chicken enchiladas in a tangy tomatillo sauce or savor the sizzling beef fajitas. You won't regret ordering the stuffed fried avocados, either. This being a seaside town, you can also order Tex-Mex–style dishes featuring fresh fish and gulf shrimp. Another commendable spot offering some coastal flair to the Tex-Mex offerings is **La Costenita** (4217 Leopard St., 361/882-5340, $7–15, closed Sun.). This downtown eatery is small in size yet huge on taste, particularly the shrimp dishes and traditional enchilada and taco plates. Try not to fill up too quickly on the amazing chips and perfectly spicy homemade salsa.

Locals flock to **Kiko's** (5514 Everhart Rd., 361/991-1211, $6–15) for the enchiladas. Cheese enchiladas with zesty ranchero sauce are the specialty here, but you can't go wrong with most menu items, including the green chile burrito, guacamole salad, and tortilla soup. Better yet, sample all the goodness the restaurant has to offer with the Kiko's platter, offering a signature cheese enchilada, beef fajita tacos, and a crispy chalupa.

Also drawing Corpus crowds is **Solis Mexican Restaurant** (3122 Baldwin Blvd. and 5409 Leopard St., 361/882-5557, $6–14). This classic taqueria is known for its tasty tacos and enchiladas, all prepared with fresh homemade tortillas. Locals love their stuffed breakfast tacos (served all day) and *liquados* (fruity Mexican drinks).

Standard Tex-Mex is also the main draw at **Café Maya** (2319 Morgan Ave., 361/884-6522, $6–15), where you'll find massive plates of flavorful favorites such as beef enchiladas, chicken tacos, and cheesy quesadillas. For over-the-top goodness, order the shrimp-stuffed avocado.

Seafood

You'll catch the city's best seafood at ◖ **Water**

Street Seafood Co. (309 N. Water St., 361/882-8683, www.waterstreetrestaurants. com, $8–19). In fact, if you're in Corpus for more than a day, it's practically required to eat a meal at this legendary downtown locale or at its adjacent sister location, Water Street Oyster Bar. Water Street takes everything tasty in the region—fresh seafood, Mexican influences, Cajun flavors, and good ol' Southern cooking—and combines it on the menu for the ultimate Texas Gulf Coast eating experience. For first-timers, the best place to start is the big blackboard, where you'll find fresh catches and daily specials (think blackened snapper, broiled flounder). The regular menu is equally appetizing, featuring consistently in-demand items such as crab cakes served with a spicy rémoulade and mango salsa; seafood jambalaya packed with shrimp, chicken, sausage, and crawfish tails in a creamy tomato sauce; and Southern-fried catfish stuffed with shrimp. Slightly more upscale and not quite as family oriented is the next-door **Water Street Oyster Bar** (309 N. Water St., 361/881-9448, www. waterstreetrestaurants.com, $8–22). This is a great spot to have a few cocktails and order some freshly shucked gulf oysters on the half shell. The menu is virtually the same as the Seafood Company's, so the aforementioned recommendations apply; you'll just be able to enjoy them in a more refined atmosphere. Two additional recommendations: Order your salad with the walnut-based tangy dressing, and try to save room for the hot chocolate brownie with ice cream.

One of the fanciest places in town to delight in a dish of succulent seafood while gazing upon its place of origin is the **Yardarm Restaurant** (4310 Ocean Dr., 361/855-8157, $10–30, Tues.–Sat. 5:30–10 P.M. only). This modestly sized, cozy spot (snug, even) offers tantalizingly fresh seafood, including succulent oysters, flavorful shrimp, a snappy snapper papillote, and thick, juicy steaks. Due to its limited size and popularity, reservations are recommended. On the opposite end of the sophistication scale is the consistently tasty yet way casual **Snoopy's Pier** (13313 S. Padre Island Dr., 361/949-8815,

www.snoopyspier.com, $6–19). Located on the bay, Snoopy's is an ideal place to grab a cold beer and a plate full of fried or boiled shrimp. Watch the sun set as you lazily peel shrimp or enjoy the flaky goodness of fresh catches such as flounder or mahimahi.

If you're staying on Corpus Christi Beach, you'll find two quality laid-back seafood restaurants within walking distance of your hotel and the beach. **Pier 99** (2822 N. Shoreline Blvd., 361/887-0764, $7–21) is a Corpus Christi stalwart on the beach across from the massive USS *Lexington*. The portions here are nearly as big, particularly the combo plates overflowing with shrimp, crab legs, oysters, crawfish, and catfish. Be sure to order a bowl of the fresh seafood gumbo. Mellow live music keeps the atmosphere spirited most nights, providing a perfect Margaritaville moment for your tropical getaway. Not quite as aesthetically pleasing yet reliable in its good food is the misleadingly named **Blackbeard's On the Beach** (3117 E. Surfside Blvd., 361/884-1030, www.blackbeardsrestaurant.net, $6–19), located across the street from the Radisson and a couple blocks away from the ocean. This is another casual, family-friendly place where you'll find a bar full of bric-a-brac and hearty helpings of fresh seafood and Tex-Mex specialties.

INFORMATION AND SERVICES

The **Corpus Christi Area Convention & Visitors Bureau** (101 N. Shoreline Blvd., 361/881-1800 or 800/766-2322, www.visitcorpuschristitx.org) contains scores of brochures, maps, and helpful information on local attractions and recreation. Similar information is available at the bureau's downtown Corpus Christi Tourist Information center (1823 N. Chaparral St., 800/766-2322).

GETTING THERE AND AROUND

Located five miles west of downtown, the **Corpus Christi International Airport** (1000 International Blvd., 361/289-0171, www. cctexas.com/airport) offers service from several major airlines (Southwest, Continental, and American Eagle), including service to Monterey, Mexico. The city's bus system, **Regional Transportation Authority** (1806 S. Alameda St., 361/883-2287, www.ccrta.org), provides citywide service. Check the website for updated fare and route information.

PORT ARANSAS

When people say they're going to Corpus Christi to hit the beach, they're often referring to adjacent Mustang Island. Located at the northern tip of Mustang Island is Port Aransas (or Port A, as it's known locally), a charming little beach town with services catering to everyone from beach bums to big spenders.

Port Aransas's (population 3,905) origins are traced to an English farmer who used the area as a sheep and cattle grazing station in the mid-1800s. Decades later, New Jersey entrepreneur Elihu Ropes attempted to organize a massive project to dredge a 30-foot shipping channel across Mustang Island to allow access to the deep waters of the gulf. He was ultimately unsuccessful in his quest, but his efforts resulted in the town briefly being named Ropesville in his honor.

By the mid-20th century, Port Aransas became synonymous with recreation, drawing tens of thousands of anglers, swimmers, boaters, and beachcombers to its magnificent open beaches and charming seaside village atmosphere. The town's population swelled from 824 residents in 1960 to several thousand by the end of the century. As many as 20,000 vacationers descend on Port Aransas during peak periods, packing the island's motels, cottages, beach houses, condos, resorts, seafood restaurants, tackle shops, and boutiques.

To get there from the mainland, you'll have to travel across the South Padre Island Drive causeway from Corpus on the southern edge of the island, or, if you have the time and interest, take the 24-hour ferry from nearby Aransas Pass. It's well worth the effort. Look for dolphins behind the ferry as they tumble over each other in the bay snatching up fish in the boat's wake.

Marine Science Institute

At the risk of learning something on your beach vacation, consider a visit to the Marine Science Institute (630 E. Cotter Ave., 361/749-6729, www.utmsi.utexas.edu, Mon.–Fri. 8 A.M.–5 P.M., free admission). The oldest marine research station on the Texas Gulf Coast, the institute is dedicated to sciences (ecology, biochemistry, physiology, etc.) relating to plants and animals of the sea. Its visitors center offers educational movies (Monday–Thursday at 3 P.M.) and self-guided tours of marine related research project exhibits, stunning photographs, and seven aquariums containing offshore artificial reefs, black mangrove marsh, and Spartina, often over an open seafloor.

San Jose Island

If you're seriously into beachcombing—we're talking shell collections, mounted driftwood, maybe even a metal detector—then San Jose Island is your paradise. This privately owned property across the bay from Port Aransas is the definition of pristine—it's almost as untouched as it was when Karankawa Indians occupied the place nearly a thousand years ago. In the 1830s, locals found the remains of a pirate camp on the island, and rumor has it pirate Jean Lafitte's Spanish dagger with a silver spike is still somewhere guarding his booty of silver and gold. These days, "Saint Joe" is safe for visitors, who can access it via a short boat ride to partake of its premier swimming, fishing, sunbathing, and treasure hunting on this beautiful unspoiled property. To arrange transport, drop by Port A's **Fisherman's Wharf** (900 N. Tarpon St., 361/749-5448, www.wharfcat.com, call for seasonal rates).

Fishing

Port Aransas is a fishing mecca. Some claim the area is overfished, but it's clear to see why so many anglers are angling to get here— easy access to the bay and deep-sea gulf fishing provide species aplenty throughout the year. Those looking to keep their feet on solid ground or wooden dock can take advantage of the free fishing from beaches, jetties, or one of the three lighted piers (Charlie's Harbor Pier, Ancel Brundrett Pier, and J.P. Luby Pier) extending into the Corpus Christi Ship Channel. You'll have to pony up a dollar to use the popular and well-lit Horace Caldwell Pier, offering access to the gulf via Magee Beach Park. The pier is more than 1,200 feet long and open 24 hours day, with bait, tackle, rental equipment, and munchies available at a nearby concession stand.

Many anglers prefer the challenge of the larger deep-sea species, including kingfish, mackerel, red snapper, tuna, shark, and even mahimahi. Group boats offer bay and deep-sea fishing, and popular fishing tournaments take place throughout the summer. The Deep Sea Roundup, held each July, is the oldest fishing tournament on the Gulf Coast. As a testament to the overwhelming allure of fishing in Port A, the town has several hundred fishing guides. Inquire about group fishing at **Fisherman's Wharf** (900 N. Tarpon St., 361/749-5448, www.wharfcat.com), or to arrange a private rental, contact **Woody's Sports Center** (136 W. Cotter Ave., 361/749-5252, www.woodysonline.com).

Swimming

The best swimming in the area is at Mustang Island State Park, but visitors can still access portions of the wide and welcoming beach among the condos and private property just off the island's main road (Highway 361). Visitors can also swim and camp at the northern tip of the island just outside Port A at **Magee Beach Park** (321 North on the Beach, 361/749-6117, www.nuecesbeachparks.com). This 167-acre park isn't quite as breathtaking as other portions of Mustang Island or San Jose Island, but it's a good spot to dip your toes in the water and soak up the salty sea air. A park office offers limited visitor information, and the beach bathhouse contains publicly accessible showers.

Accommodations

INNS

For a truly memorable experience in this quaint seaside village, stay at the charming **C** **Tarpon Inn** (200 E. Cotter Ave., 361/749-5555, www. thetarponinn.com, $89–195, depending on room size and season). An "inn" in every sense of the term, this historic establishment offers a slice of life in the late 1800s. In fact, it's so authentic, you won't even find a TV (or phone!) in your room. Fortunately, Wi-Fi service is available, so if you prefer, you can get online and avoid doing old-fashioned things like book reading, relaxing in a rocking chair, playing croquet and horseshoes, or even talking. The rooms are small, but the lack of stuff in them—vintage beds and furniture notwithstanding—is imminently refreshing. Be sure to check out the old tarpon fish scales on the wall in the lobby, including those autographed by famous actors and politicians. The trolley stops out front every day to take guests to the beach or nearby shops.

Not quite as charming yet just as appealing in its localness is **Alister Square Inn** (122 S. Alister St., 361/749-3000, www.portaransas-texas.com, $89–189). Though it's a bit rough around the edges, this welcoming accommodation appeals to families and anglers alike with its various lodging options (two-bedroom apartments, kitchenette suites, and standard hotel rooms), each featuring microwaves, refrigerators, and wireless Internet access. Alister Square is within walking distance of the beach, shopping boutiques, and restaurants.

HOTELS

In Port Aransas, visitors have to pay more for the comfort of a familiar chain hotel than a local inn. Among the corporate options are **Best Western Ocean Villa** (400 E. Ave. G, 361/749-3010, www.bestwestern.com, $179 d), located within walking distance of beaches, fishing piers, and local shops. Amenities include rooms with microwaves, refrigerators, and Internet access, along with a free continental breakfast and an outdoor swimming pool. Closer to the beach (just a couple blocks away) is the **Holiday Inn Express** (727 S. 11th St., 361/749-5222, www.ichotelsgroup.com, $225 d), offering a fitness center, a pool and spa area, a free continental breakfast, and rooms with microwaves, refrigerators, and Internet access.

CONDOS

Condos proliferate Mustang Island's shoreline like barnacles on a shrimp boat. Albeit really nice barnacles. Condos make perfect sense in a beach environment—visitors can traipse back and forth between the surf and their temporary home, sand gathers guiltlessly on all surfaces, and beers and pizza fill the fridge. Perhaps most popular among the dozen or so options is **Beachgate CondoSuites & Motel** (2000 On The Beach Dr., 361/749-5900, www.beachgate.com, $230–310, depending on room size and season). Situated adjacent to the sandy shores of Mustang Island—meaning boardwalks or long trails through the dunes aren't necessary—Beachgate offers everything from efficiency-size motel rooms to full-size three-bedroom condos, accommodating everyone from the solo fisherman to the sizable family reunion. Larger options contain fully equipped kitchens, and all units have small refrigerators, microwaves, and coffeemakers. Additional amenities include a fish-cleaning facility, boat parking, and washers and horseshoe sets for fun on the beach.

Another commendable option is the **Sand Castle Condominium** (800 Sandcastle Dr., 361/749-6201, www.sandcastlecondo.com, $125–295), offering 180 units (efficiencies, one, two, or three bedrooms) with complete kitchens and laundry and maid service. The Sand Castle also features a fitness center, large outdoor pool and hot tub, a boardwalk to the beach, and a fish-cleaning facility.

Also drawing hordes of regulars is **La Mirage** (5973 Hwy. 361, 361/749-6030, www.lamirage-portaransas.com, $110–350), with clean and comfortable units in a three-story building surrounding a tropical courtyard. Options include studio efficiencies; one-, two-, or three-bedroom condos, each offering fully equipped kitchens; free Internet access; a laundry room; and living and dining areas.

Food

ITALIAN

There are two kinds of Italian restaurants in many coastal communities: beach grub and upscale cuisine. Port A has both. For a quick slice of pizza in an ultra laid-back environment, check out the immensely popular **Port A Pizzeria** (407 E. Ave. G., 361/749-5226, www.portapizzeria.com, $5–15, daily 10 A.M.–2 P.M., 5–9 P.M.). The biggest draw is the buffet, allowing diners to immediately devour hot slices of cheesy goodness. Some diners even choose to wait a few minutes for the tasty calzone. The big crowds usually ensure a quick turnaround on the pizza varieties.

The fancy Italian option in town is the consistently top-notch **Venetian Hot Plate** (232 Beach Ave., 361/749-7617, www.venetianhotplate.com, $8–31, Tues.–Sat. 5–10 P.M.). Named for the sizzling iron plates some of the meals arrive on, this upscale spot specializes in tender and succulent meats, including filet mignon medallions, veal, and lamb. The wine selection is excellent, and the desserts are spectacular. Reservations are recommended.

SEAFOOD

One of the best seafood restaurants on the Gulf Coast is the unassuming yet spectacular ◖ **Shells Pasta & Seafood** (522 E. Ave. G, 361/749-7621, www.eatatshells.com, $9–31, Wed.–Mon. 11:30 A.M.–2 P.M., 5–9 P.M.). Housed inside a modest blue building, Shells is a tiny place—nine tables with plastic chairs—with an enormous reputation for quality fresh seafood and pasta dishes. Order from the daily blackboard specials or the regular menu, featuring classic and perfectly prepared seafood dishes such as the signature pan-seared amberjack, grilled shrimp, blue crab cakes, or sumptuous shrimp linguine in a delightfully creamy Alfredo sauce. This is elegant food in a casual shorts-wearing environment. Finding Shells will be a highlight of your trip to Port A.

Not quite as fancy yet well worth a visit is **Lisabella's** (224 E. Cotter Ave., 361/749-4222, $7–20, Mon.–Sat. 5:30–10 P.M.). Locals love Lisabella's mermaid soup, a tasty concoction of lobster, shrimp, coconut milk, curry, and avocado. The crab cakes and sautéed grouper are similarly enticing.

If you're looking for an ultracasual spot where you can wear T-shirts and flip-flops while gazing upon old fishermen's nets, mounted marlin, and the ocean itself, head to **Trout Street Bar & Grill** (104 W. Cotter Ave., 361/749-7800, www.tsbag.com, $8–24). Sit outside on the covered veranda to gaze upon the marina and ship channel activity while feasting on jumbo fried shrimp, grilled amberjack, snapper, tuna, or steak. A bonus: Trout Street will cook your fresh-caught fish as long as it's cleaned and ready for the kitchen.

Another venerable seafood spot is the "downtown" **Pelican's Landing Restaurant** (337 N. Alister St., 361/749-6405, www.pelicanslanding.com, $7–26). The portions are enormous here, and shrimp is the specialty. Go for the gusto and order one of the Mambo Combos (fried shrimp, steak, crab cakes, beer-battered fries) and savor the flavor on your surfboard table.

Information and Services

Pick up a handy brochure with island visitor info and a map of the trolley route at the **Port Aransas Chamber of Commerce and Tourist Bureau** (403 W. Cotter St., 361/749-5919, www.portaransas.org). The **Island Trolley** (aka "The B" and "The #94 Shuttle") will take you pretty much anywhere you want to go in Port A, from the beach to the wharf to shops and back to your hotel. For only 25 cents. It's particularly handy when you're on beer number four and dinner is calling. For more information on the trolley, contact the city at 361/749-4111.

The **Port Aransas Ferry System** provides free marine transportation service year-round at all hours of the day. The 15-minute ride connects Port Aransas with the mainland at Aransas Pass, north of Corpus Christi. There are six ferries in operation, each carrying up to 20 vehicles per trip. During the busy season, particularly holidays and some summer weekends, you may have to wait up to 30 or 45 minutes for a transport, but typically the wait is no longer than 5–10 minutes. For more information, call 361/749-2850.

KINGSVILLE

Located about 40 miles southwest of Corpus Christi, Kingsville (population 24,394) is the birthplace of the American ranching industry. It's the main commercial center of the legendary King Ranch, which sprawls across 825,000 acres and boasts 60,000 head of cattle.

The community is named for the famous riverboat baron and rancher Richard King, who used his business profits to purchase the vast piece of property that would become the legendary ranch. Kingsville's roots as a city are traced to the St. Louis, Brownsville and Mexico Railway, which put the town on the map when its tracks were laid in the early 1900s. Most of Kingsville's early business activity, however, was related to the King family, who started a weekly newspaper and built a hotel, an ice plant, and a cotton gin. Kingsville went on to become a busy trade center for ranching families across South Texas.

Kingsville's population grew significantly when Exxon relocated a district office here in the 1960s. A surge in enrollment at the Texas College of Arts and Industries (now Texas A&M Kingsville) brought even more folks to town, numbering nearly 30,000 by the late '70s. Exxon closed its regional office in 1985, and the population has slowly declined since then.

Regardless, Kingsville remains a major draw for birders and naturalists, who delight in the area's million acres of habitat. Visitors from across the state and the country travel to the historic downtown area to learn about the heritage of King Ranch and to shop at the boutiques and antiques stores.

(King Ranch

For many Texas visitors, King Ranch is the embodiment of the Lone Star State's legacy. Longhorn cattle, vast ranchlands, and genuine cowboys evoke a sense of mystique and grandeur that Texas alone can claim.

As improbable as it may seem, America's ranching legacy was revolutionized by a man who arrived as a preteen stowaway on Texas's Gulf Coast. Richard King, who escaped from New York City in 1835 aboard a cargo ship, went on to become a steamboat baron along the Rio Grande before overseeing his ranching empire.

The origins of King Ranch, now an esteemed National Historic Landmark, date to 1853 when Richard King purchased 68,500 acres of property that had been Spanish and Mexican land grants. Between 1869 and 1884, King sent more than 100,000 head of livestock from his ranch to northern markets on now-legendary routes like the Chisholm Trail. Many of these herds were marked with the iconic symbol for the King Ranch, the Running W brand, which first appeared in the 1860s. Though the origins of this distinctive shape aren't known, local legends claim it represents the sweeping horns of a longhorn bull or a slithering diamondback rattlesnake.

One of King Ranch's biggest claims to fame is its development of the Western Hemisphere's first strain of beef cattle: Santa Gertrudis. Based on the name from the property's original land grant, this breed of cattle was developed in the 1920s to produce cows that could withstand the oppressive South Texas conditions—heat, humidity, and biting insects. To accomplish this, breeding experts (including Richard King's grandson) crossed Indian Brahman cattle with British Shorthorns.

King was also one of the first ranchers to move Texas Longhorns from Mexico to markets in the Midwest, and the innovations developed at his ranch, from cattle and horse breeding and disease control to improving the blood lines of the quarter horse to well drilling, earned it the proud title "birthplace of American ranching."

Today, King Ranch sprawls across 825,000 acres, an area larger than the state of Rhode Island. The **King Ranch Visitor Center** (2205 Hwy. 141 W., 361/592-8055, www.king-ranch.com, Mon.–Sat. 11 A.M.–4 P.M., Sun. noon–5 P.M., $8 adults, $4 children ages 5–12) offers daily guided tours along an old stagecoach road past majestic Longhorns with the iconic Running W brand on their hindquarters, and a 100-year-old carriage house with a mission-style roofline and distinctive arches. Other highlights include the Victorian-era cabin homes of King's working families (known as Kineños) and a horse cemetery with graves of famous racing thoroughbreds from the 1950s. Bring plenty of water, since it gets plenty hot out on the ranch. Special tours devoted to birding, native wildlife, and agriculture are available in advance by reservation.

To learn more about the fascinating history of the King family and property, move 'em up and head 'em a couple miles down the road to the **King Ranch Museum** (405 N. 6th St. in Kingsville, 361/595-1881, www.king-ranch.com, Mon.–Sat. 10 A.M.–4 P.M., Sun. 1–5 P.M., $4 adults, $2.50 children ages 5–12). Housed in a historic downtown ice plant, the museum contains stunning 1940s photos of the ranch by award-winning photographer Toni Frissell, fancy saddles and firearms, antique coaches and carriages, and other historic ranch items. One of the most intriguing objects on display is "El Kineño," a custom-designed 1949 Buick Eight hunting vehicle—complete with rifle holders and a shiny Running W hood ornament—made by General Motors especially for Congressman R. M. Kleberg Sr.

Another must-see (and smell) is the restored 1909 Ragland Mercantile Building that now houses the leather-filled **King Ranch Saddle Shop** (201 E. Kleberg Ave., 877/282-5777, www.krsaddleshop.com, Mon.–Sat. 10 A.M.–6 P.M.). Originally used to supply gear exclusively to the King Ranch cowboys known as Los Kineños (King's people), the store now offers leather goods and clothing to the world (its website does brisk business). The charming downtown shop also contains exhibits and photos on ranch history and information about the governors, presidents, and foreign dignitaries it has outfitted.

1904 Train Depot and Museum

Located a block away from the saddle shop is the restored 1904 Train Depot and

KING'S PEOPLE

© TEXAS HISTORICAL COMMISSION

the gates of the legendary King Ranch

At the heart of the King Ranch are the Kineños (King's people), a group of several hundred ranch employees whose families have dedicated their lives to operating the property for generations. From training horses to clearing fields to promoting the King Ranch's original cattle breed, the Kineños provide a vital link with the ranch's past and are responsible for maintaining its ongoing legacy.

If you schedule a visit to the ranch or take part in one of the tours, you'll likely get a chance to visit with one of these Kineños. Several now serve as visitor guides, even though they occasionally take on some of their traditional ranch-hand duties. By the way, many of these are men in their 80s.

Some of these men spent their early days "breaking" thoroughbred horses. In the 1940s and '50s, King Ranch trained racing horses and developed many well-known and successful thoroughbreds. The Kineños also worked extensively with the ranch's quarter horses, using the handling techniques passed down through generations of *vaqueros* (Mexican cowboys).

Other Kineños worked closely with the Santa Gertrudis cattle breed, specifically developed and marketed by the ranch. They helped promote the breed by attending livestock shows across the world and even slept in the barns with the animals and woke up early to clean, feed, water, and brush the cattle in preparation for the shows. Kineños also worked with the breed by administering vaccinations, helping in the pastures, and maintaining records.

Some of these stories have been captured for posterity's sake in print. For a fascinating collection of colorful Kineño tales, pick up a copy of Alberto "Beto" Maldonado's book *The Master Showmen of King Ranch* (University of Texas Press, 2009).

Kingsville's 1904 Train Depot and Museum

© TEXAS HISTORICAL COMMISSION

Museum (102 E. Kleberg Ave., 361/592-8515, www.1904-depot.kingsvilletexas.com, Mon.–Fri. 10 A.M.–4 P.M., Sat. 11 A.M.–2 P.M., free admission), offering a glimpse into Kingsville's bustling past. Photos and artifacts, including an operational telegraph, highlight the historical significance of this hub of regional activity.

Kenedy Ranch Museum of South Texas

Richard King isn't the only famous rancher in these parts. His longtime pal Mifflin Kenedy also accumulated great wealth and property thanks to his successful commercial and ranching endeavors. His legacy is on display at the Kenedy Ranch Museum of South Texas (200 E. La Parra Ave., 361/294-5751, www.kenedyranchmuseum.org, Tues.–Sat. 10 A.M.–4 P.M., Sun. noon–4 P.M., $3 adults, $2 seniors and children ages 13–18). Located 20 miles south of Kingsville in the little town of Sarita, the museum showcases Kenedy's illustrious past through exhibits

dedicated primarily to family, particularly his wife's, Petra Vela de Vidal, of prominent Mexican heritage. Through his successful business ventures, Kenedy accumulated 400,000 acres of Gulf Coast property and was among the first ranchers to hold cattle inside wire fences. Housed in the 1927 Kenedy Ranch headquarters, the museum also details the family's many successful philanthropic programs.

John E. Conner Museum

Regional history and the natural world are the main areas of interest at the John E. Conner Museum (905 W. Santa Gertrudis Ave., 361/593-2810, www.museum.tamuk.edu, Mon.–Fri. 9 A.M.–5 P.M., Sat. 10 A.M.–4 P.M., free admission). Located on the campus of Texas A&M-Kingsville, this modest museum offers exhibits devoted to the cultural groups that have historically occupied the area, from Native Americans to Spanish to Mexican and pioneer settlers. Native plant and animal species and their environments are also on display, as well as artwork from students and Texas artists.

Accommodations

If you find yourself making an overnight trip to Kingsville, there are only a few options available for lodging. Fortunately, one of them is the **Holiday Inn Express** (2400 S. Hwy. 77, 361/592-8333, www.hiexpress.com, $99 d), offering a free hot breakfast bar, Wi-Fi access, and a heated outdoor pool. If you want to experience "rustic" ranch lodging, check out the **B Bar B Ranch Inn** (325 E. County Rd. 2215, 361/296-3331, call for rate info), which sits on property that was originally part of the King Ranch. This B&B on a working ranch provides "rugged pampering," with its hearty gourmet breakfast and 16 guest rooms decorated in South Texas style. The B Bar B draws a good number of people who enjoy using the surrounding ranchland to hunt for antelope, turkey, and quail.

Food

AMERICAN

Kingsville isn't a highly regarded destination for fine dining, but there are a few places worth dropping by if you're visiting King Ranch or even headed down to South Padre. One of the best places to eat in the entire region is about 20 miles south of Kingsville in a tiny town called Riviera. **King's Inn** (1116 S. County Rd. 2270, 361/297-5265, $12–24, closed Sun. and Mon.) is billed as one of the best seafood restaurants on Texas's southern Gulf Coast, and for good reason. It doesn't look like much from the outside, and the outdated ambience isn't really charming either, but that matters not as soon as your food arrives. Be sure to order the lightly breaded fried shrimp, filled with freshly caught flavor and accompanied by the restaurant's famous spicy tartar sauce (the waiter claimed to be sworn to secrecy, though he eventually let it slip that the tartar sauce contained bread crumbs, "lots of eggs," and serrano peppers). This stunning sauce enhances everything from the interesting choice of fish (drum) to the homemade

bread to the avocado salad with accompanying slices of fresh, juicy tomatoes. It's absolutely worth the 20-minute detour to eat like a King.

Just south of the downtown area is an ideal lunch spot, the occasionally rowdy **Big House Burgers** (2209 S. Brahma Blvd., 361/592-0222, $5–10). The sports bar atmosphere can be a bit overwhelming on weekends (reminding you there's a college in this town), but it's worth enduring the noise and blaring TVs for the immense and flavorful burgers. Try the quadruple burger if you dare. These juicy treats will fill you up, but it's still worth splitting some of the crunchy fries or crispy onion rings with a pal.

MEXICAN

One of the most popular places in town to grab an authentic Tex-Mex meal is **El Tapatio Mexican Restaurant** (630 W. Santa Gertrudis St., 361/516-1655, $7–14), on the edge of Kingsville A&M campus. Though most of the food is standard Tex-Mex fare, there are a few items that set El Tapatio apart from other spots in town. The carne guisada, in particular, is spectacular, with a hearty gravy that brings out the rich flavor of the beef. Like the salsa, it has an extra kick and afterbite that leaves your mouth feeling warm and satisfied.

Another worthy local eatery is **Lydia's Homestyle Cooking** (817 W. King Ave., 361/592-9405, www.lydiasrestaurant.com, $6–16, Mon.–Sat. 5 A.M.–1:30 P.M.). Lydia's is known throughout town for its tremendous breakfast taquitos (try the potato, eggs, and sausage) and the machacado plate, featuring shredded dry beef scrambled with eggs along with grilled onions, tomato, and serrano peppers. Lydia's lunches are legendary, too, including the barbacoa plate, tamales, and chicken flautas. If necessary, you can also order gringo fare (burgers, sandwiches, etc.).

Another reputable Mexican restaurant is **El Dorado** (704 N. 14th St., 361/516-1459, $6–13). There's nothing too fancy here, but the traditional Tex-Mex fare is consistently decent, including the beef tacos, chicken enchiladas, and burritos.

Information and Services

For information about other area attractions, accommodations, and restaurants, visit the **Kingsville Convention and Visitors Bureau** (1501 Hwy. 77, 361/592-8516, www.kingsvilletexas.com, Mon.–Fri. 9 A.M.–5 P.M., Sat.–Sun. 10 A.M.–2 P.M.).

South Padre Island

The massive 130-mile-long Padre Island is home to the longest sand beach in the United States. Never stretching more than three miles wide, the island was formed by the methodical process of sea erosion and deposition. The northern portion, adjacent to Corpus Christi, has a modest collection of hotels and residences, and is mostly recreation oriented; the central portion is the natural protected wonderland of Padre Island National Seashore; and the southern tip is a major resort area lined with hotels and restaurants catering to a thriving tourist industry.

South Padre Island isn't technically a separate island; rather, it's the name of the resort community at the southern portion of the big island. The town is flanked by the Gulf of Mexico to the east, a narrow ship channel to the north, and the Laguna Madre, the narrow bay leading to the Texas mainland.

Spanish explorers visited the area in the 1500s, but the resort community remained a barren stretch of pristine seashore until the 1950s when a causeway bridge connected Port Isabel to South Padre Island. Although it provided access to the nicest beaches on the Texas coast, the community remained a low-key resort destination until the late 1970s, when insurance companies were required to provide hurricane coverage and the population increased rather dramatically (from 314 to 1,012 residents) thanks to the increased emphasis on tourism. For the past two decades, it's become a major spring break destination for college students, who descend on the small town in the thousands for revelry and recreation each March.

SIGHTS

Island time is good for the soul. Everything slows down, priorities shift to beach activities and seafood options, and even the tightly wound lay off their car horns. It may take a day or two to assimilate to South Padre mode, but once you're there, you won't want to leave.

South Padre is the ultimate beach vacation in Texas. Its soft, smooth sand is far more inviting and picturesque than the grainier, darker versions farther north along the coast. The resort community offers everything seaside travelers seek—beachcombing, fishing, parasailing, dolphin viewing, biking, snorkeling, and scuba diving. Lodging options range from opulent resort condos to pitching a tent on the beach, and restaurants offer gulf-harvested oysters, shrimp, and fish.

If you're visiting in the winter, you'll be surrounded by Midwestern license plates and polite retirees taking advantage of restaurants' early-bird specials. In the summer, Texas families flock to the island to play in the gentle waves and devour fried shrimp. Any time of the year is a good time to visit South Padre, since the beach is always pleasant and the vibe is always mellow (except during spring break).

The islanders take their enviable natural resources seriously, offering opportunities for visitors to experience the wonders of this region. Make a point of taking a dolphin tour and visiting the sea turtle research center to get a true appreciation of the sea life that doesn't end up on your dinner plate.

Though it takes some effort to get to South Padre, once you're there, maneuvering around the small town is a breeze. After crossing the Queen Isabella Causeway, take a left onto Padre Boulevard to reach the main drag, with hotels, shops, and restaurants. Take a right off the causeway to reach the public beaches and seaside attractions.

Sea Turtle, Inc.

A heartwarming experience awaits at Sea Turtle, Inc. (6617 Padre Blvd., 956/761-4511, www.seaturtleinc.com, Tues.–Sun. 10 A.M.–4 P.M., $3 donation requested), an unassuming little spot at the end of South Padre's main strip. Inside, you'll find tanks full of various types and sizes of sea turtles, several native to the nearby Gulf Coast. Try to arrive at 10 A.M. for the informative presentation offering context about the several dozen friendly and fascinating creatures on-site. Kids can feed the turtles, and everyone has a chance for a photo op. Marvel at these prehistoric animals—some can reach 450 pounds—and toss an extra few dollars in the box for this organization that works tirelessly to protect and promote these endangered sea creatures.

Dolphin Research and Sea Life Nature Center

Kids aren't the only ones who'll learn something at the nearby Sea Life Nature Center (110 N. Garcia St. in Port Isabel, 956/299-1957, www.spinaturecenter.com, daily 10 A.M.–6 P.M., $3 donation requested). This low-key locale just across the causeway from South Padre contains about 20 aquariums filled with sea creatures from the gulf waters. Shrimp, starfish, rays, and eel await at the center, which offers a children's program at 11 A.M. and 2 P.M. allowing youngsters to handle and feed some of the nonthreatening species in the touch tanks. Knowledgeable staffers educate visitors about environmentally responsible ways to enjoy their time on the island.

◖ Port Isabel Lighthouse

It's well worth the 74-step climb up the tight spiral staircase to experience the breathtaking views from the Port Isabel Lighthouse (421 E. Queen Isabella Blvd. in Port Isabel, 800/527-6102, www.tpwd.state.tx.us, summer hours: Sun.–Thurs. 10 A.M.–6 P.M., Fri.–Sat. 11 A.M.–8 P.M., winter: daily 9 A.M.–5 P.M., $3 adults, $1 students). From the bug-size cars passing over the gorgeous Laguna Madre

a rescued sea turtle at South Padre's Sea Turtle, Inc.

© ANDY RHODES

the Port Isabel Lighthouse near South Padre

Bay on the San Isabella Causeway to the remarkable view of adjacent historic downtown Port Isbell, the vantage point from this historic lighthouse is truly a sight to behold. Constructed in 1852 at the request of sea captains frustrated by visibility issues along the low-lying Texas coast, the lighthouse was a prominent and necessary fixture in the region until the early 1900s, when newer, more efficient, and more powerful towers were constructed. Sixteen similar lighthouses graced the Texas coast at one time, but the Port Isabel structure is the only facility remaining open to the public.

Pan American Coastal Studies Laboratory

Not quite as family oriented as other area attractions, the coastal studies lab (100 Marine Lab Dr., 956/761-2644, www.utpa.edu/csl, Sun.–Fri. 1:30–4:30 P.M., free admission) is designed more with researchers in mind than kiddos. Regardless, you'll learn things here about the plant and animal life in the Laguna

Madre and Gulf of Mexico through interactive displays (shark jaws, turtle shells) and limited aquariums.

Schlitterbahn Beach Waterpark

Despite the fact real waves are lapping at the shore just minutes away, families still flock to the water rides at Schlitterbahn Beach Waterpark (33261 State Park Rd. 100, 956/772-7873, www.schlitterbahn.com, open 10 A.M.–8 P.M. daily April–Sept., $40–48). Without any pesky sand and saltwater to worry about, kids and adults can spend the day gliding and cruising along water trails and rides, including popular attractions such as tube chutes, the Boogie Bahn surfing ride, uphill water coasters, and the Rio Ventura. Unlike the original Schlitterbahn in New Braunfels, which is far more spread out with more meandering, lazy inner tube rides, the South Padre version is more compact and beach oriented, with a five-story sand castle fun house and a surprisingly good restaurant (the Shrimp Haus).

RECREATION
Swimming

The beach is everywhere at South Padre, so you won't have any trouble finding a place to park and tote your gear to the soft, white sand (don't forget to bring plenty of sunscreen and bottled water). Look for public beach access points every few blocks along Gulf Boulevard. For a few more amenities—pavilions, picnic tables, and playgrounds in addition to the restrooms and showers—go to one of the county beach parks on the southern or northern ends of the island.

Fishing

Like most coastal communities, fishing is a huge draw in South Padre. Everywhere you look, you'll see men (and the very occasional woman) with a fishing pole standing on a beach, jetty, or pier. If they aren't standing on shore, they're in a chartered boat. Shoreline anglers tend to snag redfish, speckled trout, and flounder, while deep-sea adventurers seek

SPRING BREAK AT SOUTH PADRE

This low-key, unassuming beach community turns into a high-octane, raucous party town for several weeks each March. Nearly 100,000 students from across the country descend on South Padre Island from approximately March 10 through March 20, prompting locals to skedaddle from their quiet seaside homes quicker than a college kid can chug a beer.

Rivaling Florida's Daytona Beach as the nation's ultimate spring break destination, South Padre has become party central for college students primarily from Texas and the Midwest. Though the town doesn't quite have the infrastructure to handle the hordes – eight-hour waits on the causeway are common on peak arrival days – it ultimately benefits from the millions of dollars spent on lodging, food, and DWI tickets (be forewarned: take the Wave shuttle if you've had a few drinks).

Speaking of drinking, one of South Padre's biggest spring break assets is its on-the-beach consumption policy – unlike most American seashores, it's completely legal here if you're 21 or older. The undercover TABC (Texas Alcoholic Beverage Commission) agents are out in full force looking for MIPs (minors in possession), so make sure you're of legal age or at least extremely discreet. In other drinking-related news, visitors may want to consider renting a hotel with kitchenette or, even better, a condo for easy access to a fridge, ice, and countertops. For a comprehensive list of condo options, visit www.service24.com.

Spring breakers often take advantage of the various package deals offered by travel agencies. Most involve flights and lodging, but several feature miniexcursions around the area for those seeking a brief respite after four or five days of constant drinking and sunbathing. One of the most popular activities is a professionally operated surfing lesson, complete with board, wet suit, and individual instruction. Those in search of a change of scenery while downing drinks can sign up for a party yacht cruise originating at Tequila Frogs, one of South Padre's most famous bars.

---

tarpon, marlin, kingfish, mackerel, red snapper, and wahoo.

Many anglers use the services of the venerable **Jim's Pier** (209 W. Whiting St., 956/761-2865), which bills itself as the original South Padre Island fishing-guide company. Jim's provides boat slips, fueling docks, a launching ramp, and fish-cleaning facilities. The company also offers two bay fishing trips daily on its renowned 40-person-capacity party boat. To find out more about fishing locations and services, consult the **Port Isabel/South Padre Island Guides Association** at www.fishspi.com, offering a lengthy list of endorsed professional fishing guides.

Dolphin Viewing

Even though you don't technically get in the water to take on this activity, it's ocean based and certainly worth experiencing. The Laguna Madre Bay is home to myriad bottlenose dolphins, and there's nothing like the thrill of seeing them up close in their natural environment. The best way to get an intimate experience is through an independent tour company like **Fins to Feathers** (tours operate from Port Isabel's Sea Life Center, 956/299-0629, www.fin2feather.com; tours run daily 7 A.M.–sunset and cost $22.50 or $45 per person depending on the amount of time desired). Enjoy the quiet, smooth ride from a smaller boat allowing up-close views and facilitated interaction with the knowledgeable guide. Anticipate the surge of excitement you'll feel when that first dorsal fin ascends from the water and the sun glistens off the smooth gray surface of these magnificent and elegant creatures.

Snorkeling and Scuba Diving

With its clear water and fine sand, the South Padre Island area is a haven for scuba divers and snorkelers. The fish aren't as varied and colorful as you'll find in more exotic tropical

© ANDY RHODES

dolphin tour in Laguna Madre Bay

locales, but the marine life is certainly intriguing, and you never know what you might find among the reefs and rigs.

Those interested in snorkeling and shallow shore dives can explore the underwater action at the Mansfield Jetties, the beach at Dolphin Cove (look for sand dollars here), and the adjacent Barracuda Bay. Scuba divers will enjoy the artificial reef (a wreck dive known as "the tug") located seven miles southeast of the Brazos Santiago Pass Jetties. Farther out and most compelling to experienced divers are the oil rigs, where fish of all sizes are plentiful.

South Padre has several full-service dive shops offering equipment for rent and sale, organized excursions to prime spots, instruction, and service. One of the most reputable companies is **American Diving** (One Padre Blvd., 956/761-2030, www.divesouthpadre.com).

ACCOMMODATIONS
Hotels and Resorts

Lodging rates in a beach town are akin to those in a ski village—they can be mile-high in the busy season and downright affordable the rest of the year. The following South Padre accommodations include prices for a weekend stay in midsummer (the busy getaway season in Texas, despite the fact it's 93 degrees and humid).

Among the affordable options is **South Beach Inn** (120 E. Jupiter Ln., 956/761-2471, www.southbeachtexas.com, $49–149, depending on room size and season), an independently owned 12-unit establishment nestled among the palms just a block from the beach. One of the oldest hotel buildings on the island (1961), South Beach offers mostly efficiency-style kitchenettes with full-size stoves, refrigerators, microwaves, and toasters. Pets are welcome, and Wi-Fi service is available. Also in the affordable range is **Beachside Inn** (4500 Padre Blvd., 956/761-4919, www.padrebeachside.com, $99 d), featuring clean, simple rooms within walking distance of the beach, an outdoor pool with hot tub, and kitchenettes with microwaves and refrigerators.

The next step on the price ladder gets you a bit closer to the action with some added amenities. One of the more popular and reliable options is the **Ramada Limited** (4109 Padre Blvd., 956/761-4097, www.ramadasouthpadreisland.

com, $139 d), offering a free hot breakfast, an outdoor pool and hot tub, and rooms with microwaves, fridges, and free wireless Internet access. Closer to the Queen Isabella Causeway is the casual yet consistent **Super 8** (4205 Padre Blvd., 956/761-6300, www.super8.com, $153 d), offering a heated outdoor pool, free continental breakfast, free Wi-Fi access, and mini microwaves and refrigerators. Another trustworthy chain option is **Holiday Inn Express** (6502 Padre Blvd., 956/761-8844, www.hiexpress.com, $179 d). What sets it apart from the other corporate choices is the massive aquarium in the lobby with dozens of colorful fish darting about. Otherwise, the amenities here are pretty standard, including an outdoor pool, a fitness center, beach access, Wi-Fi access, and rooms with microwaves and refrigerators. The **Travelodge** (6200 Padre Blvd., 956/761-4744, www.southpadretravelodge.com, $184 d) offers a large outdoor pool and hot tub, a private walkway to the beach, free wireless Internet access, a deluxe continental breakfast, and microwave and refrigerators in each room.

Occupying 15 tropical beachside acres is **Sheraton South Padre Island Beach Hotel** (310 Padre Blvd., 956/761-6551, www.starwoodhotels.com, $179 d), a comfortable yet fancy spot with ample amenities and several types of accommodations. Choose from standard guest rooms, kitchenettes, suites, or even fully equipped two- and three-bedroom condominiums, all with private balconies. Other amenities include an enormous 6,000-square-foot swimming pool complete with waterfall and swim-up bar, a separate oversize Jacuzzi, volleyball nets, an exercise and weight room, and seasonal parasailing. Another option is **Best Western La Copa Inn & Suites** (350 Padre Blvd., 956/761-6000, $149 d), offering free Internet service, a free deluxe continental breakfast, and nightly happy hour with beer, wine, and snacks. Just down the street is the upscale **Peninsula Island Resort & Spa** (340 Padre Blvd., 956/761-2514, www.peninsulaislandresort.com, $280 d), featuring one-, two-, and three-bedroom units with kitchenettes, a swim-up pool bar, large edgeless pool, hot tub, rooms with fancy Brazilian furniture, a gym, and an on-site convenience store.

Among the most luxurious choices on the island is the **Isla Grand** (500 Padre Blvd., 800/292-7704, www.islagrand.com, $279 d), boasting perhaps the best beachfront location in town with excellent services. Rooms include free Internet access, microwaves, and refrigerators. Consider upgrading to a condo suite—the spacious rooms, living area with a couch and second TV, fully equipped kitchen, and separate bathrooms (a godsend for those with kids) provide a perfect home away from home. It's the hotel's grounds, however, that keep guests coming back for repeated recreational relaxation. Enjoy the direct beach access, two outdoor swimming pools with a cascading waterfall, three whirlpools, four lighted tennis courts, shuffleboard courts, and plenty of lounge chairs.

Camping

Beachfront property is too valuable to allow for many camping options in the commercial area of South Padre. In fact, there's really only one main option for serious RV-style campers, and fortunately it's a swell one. The **South Padre Island KOA** (1 Padre Blvd., 800/562-9724, www.southpadrekoa.com, $30–60 nightly) is geared toward RVs and mobile homes, but it also has a few cabins and lodges available. Site amenities include an outdoor pool, a fitness center, recreation room, and free wireless Internet service. Those looking for a more rustic, natural experience have the option of pitching a tent (or parking an RV) on the vast unpopulated stretch of sand north of all the major recreational activity. Local officials caution campers to drive on the wet sand to avoid getting stuck in the soft tractionless powder farther away from the surf. Also, be sure to bring your garbage back with you (there aren't any trash cans in these remote areas) and take the No Trespassing signs seriously.

FOOD
Seafood

One of the first places many beach-town visitors go is a seaside seafood restaurant. Even before you check in to your hotel room you may want to drop by a low-key local eatery like **Palm Street Pier Bar & Grill** (204 W. Palm St., 956/772-7256, www.palmstreetpier.com, $7–18), known for its tantalizing seafood and sunsets. Overlooking the scenic Laguna Madre Bay, Palm Street Pier specializes in tasty shrimp dishes, including admiral shrimp (sautéed in a sweet potato–jalapeño puree), honey chipotle shrimp, and the standard crispy fried variety. Other popular dishes include the tilapia fillet and rib eye steak. Don't miss the cheap margaritas and summertime Friday-night fireworks over the bay. Another bonus: the "you hook it, we'll cook it" policy, allowing diners to bring in their own fresh catch and have it expertly prepared—blackened, grilled, or fried with two sides—for $6.

Also drawing regular return customers is the venerable and well-regarded **Blackbeard's** (103 E. Saturn Ln., 956/761-2962, www.black-beardsspi.com, $7–20), a swashbuckling-themed spot with surprisingly refined food. Fresh gulf catches are the main draw here, including flounder and tilapia, but the landlubber options are equally commendable, including the charbroiled steaks and grilled chicken. Incidentally, the burgers here are the best on the island.

For the ultimate sampling of seafood, belly up to the buffet at **(Louie's Backyard** (2305 Laguna Dr., 956/761-6406, www.lbyspi.com, $9–26). Choose from boiled shrimp, crab legs, fish, and scallops along with ribs, pasta, and salad. The full menu has even better options, including a buttery and flaky red snapper fillet and crispy, flavorful fried shrimp. Top off your experience with a stunning view of the sunset over the bay while sipping Louie's signature cocktail, the multiliquored and aptly named Whammy.

South Padre also has a couple highly recommended seafood restaurants that are more upscale in nature. In a casual town like this, however, that simply means the quality and prices are higher—you can still wear shorts and sandals. One of the most popular is the remarkable **(Sea Ranch Restaurant** (1 Padre Blvd., 956/761-1314, www.searanchrestaurant.com, $9–40), the kind of place where you can't go wrong with anything on the menu, be it "from

the sea" or "from the grill." The options change regularly, but the mantra of the Sea Ranch remains constant: serving quality "local wild-caught" seafood directly from the gulf. Signature dishes include grilled red snapper, boiled king crab legs, gulf shrimp and bay oysters, and an amazing ahi tuna served rare with soy sauce and wasabi. Topping it all off is an exceptional view of the sea. Reservations are suggested.

Another popular semiupscale seafood spot is **Scampi's Restaurant & Bar** (206 W. Aires Dr., 956/761-1755, www.scampisspi.com, $8–39, open for dinner only), an old-school seafood and steak restaurant that's been around for decades thanks to its consistent high-quality food and service. Scampi's proves that venerable doesn't have to mean boring, with several innovative and unexpected dishes on the menu. The best of the bunch is the shrimp Marco Antonio, featuring sautéed shrimp with coconut milk, mango, apples, and a touch of habanero pepper. Locals love the peanut butter shrimp, an Asian-inspired recipe with ginger, garlic, soy sauce, and peanut butter. Other featured entrées include pecan redfish, crawfish penne, and local flounder, pompano, and amberjack.

Beach Grub

If you've somehow exhausted your craving for seafood, your next best bet is some standard beach fare—burgers, pizzas, fried stuff, and, in South Padre, Tex-Mex. One of the best places in town to combine all these things with a cold glass of quality suds is **Padre Island Brewing Company** (3400 Padre Blvd., 956/761-9585, www.pibrewingcompany.com, $6–17). Not surprisingly, beer is the main theme here, with home-brew supplies such as kettles, burlap sacks, and vintage bottles serving as surrounding scenery. It's a refreshing change of pace from the ubiquitous corporate light-beer signs in most beach establishments. Fortunately, the handcrafted beer is commendable, particularly the Tailing Red Amber. There's food, too, including traditional bar fare like burgers, nachos, ribs, and sandwiches. Look for a seat on the second-floor outdoor deck.

Slightly more upscale yet equally inviting

is **Amberjack's Bayside Bar & Grill** (209 W. Amberjack St., 956/761-6500, www.amberjacks-spi.com, $9–34), offering incredible views of Laguna Madre and a wide range of delectable menu items. Choose from oysters Rockefeller to chicken-fried chicken to rasta shrimp (prawns sautéed in curry sauce) to pecan-crusted chicken. Pull up directly to the restaurant in your boat and take advantage of Amberjack's "we'll cook your catch" policy.

For a tasty burger and cold beer, head to **Tom & Jerry's Beach Bar & Grill** (3212 Padre Blvd., 956/761-8999, $6–18). The seafood dishes here are commendable, but the beach grub is the main draw, from the burgers to the chicken plates to the chicken-fried steak and club sandwich. After your meal, head to the raised bar, where friendly staffers will gladly pour you a cold draft beer or expertly mix a frozen concoction.

Finally, if you're in the mood for some traditional Tex-Mex, head to the extremely popular and immensely satisfying **Jesse's Cantina & Restaurant** (2700 Padre Blvd., 956/761-4500, $7–15). Jesse's is famous for its potent margaritas and top-notch traditional dishes such as tacos, enchiladas, carnitas, and quesadillas. Naturally, they serve fried shrimp here, too, and it's some of the best on the island.

INFORMATION AND SERVICES

The incredibly friendly and helpful people at the **South Padre Island Convention & Visitors Bureau** (600 Padre Blvd., 800/767-2373, www.sopadre.com, Mon.–Fri. 8 A.M.–5 P.M., Sat.–Sun. 9 A.M.–5 P.M.) will provide you with brochures, maps, and information about area attractions. You can also check with them about activities and events related to fishing, boating, and other ocean-based recreation.

GETTING THERE AND AROUND

The Brownsville South Padre Island International Airport (700 S. Minnesota Ave., 956/542-4373, www.flybrownsville.com) is the closest airport to South Padre. At 27 miles away, it's not too far, especially if you need to get to the beach in a hurry and don't feel like making the nearly nine-hour drive from Dallas or approximately five-hour trek from Houston and Austin. The airport offers several American Eagle and Continental Airlines flights daily to and from Houston. Rental car services are available at the airport.

Once on the island, feel free to ditch the car in favor of the city's reliable and often-necessary **Wave transportation system** (866/761-1025, visit www.townspi.com for schedule and stops). If you plan to have a beer or six during spring break, you'll be glad these small buses are there to cart your impaired body safely home. Though the Wave typically operates 7 A.M.–7 P.M. among local businesses and services, it's also available during spring break to shuttle late-night revelers. Incidentally, the belligerent scene on the ride back from the bar at 3 A.M. is one of the most insane experiences imaginable.

EL PASO AND WEST TEXAS

Mention the word *Texas* to most people, and this region of the state is likely what they envision. West Texas is hot, dry, largely flat, and, yes, occasionally dotted with cactus and cow skulls.

The Chihuahuan Desert extends north into West Texas, accounting for its arid environment and temperature extremes. Portions of the region receive as little as eight inches of rain annually (compared to an average of 50 inches in East Texas), and temperatures typically range from the 40s overnight to daytime highs in the 80s. There's something to be said for the dry heat—most Texans find it a welcome respite from the oppressive humidity along the Gulf Coast and into the central prairies.

This region has been home to Native American tribes for more than 10,000 years,

and several settlements date to the 17th century (considered ancient by Texas standards). The Ysleta and Socorro missions east of El Paso were established after the Pueblo Indian Revolt of 1680 sent Native Americans and Spaniards from present-day New Mexico south along the Rio Grande.

Centuries later, westward expansion would forever affect the region as thousands of people from the eastern United States braved the frontier in search of opportunity. Military personnel erected frontier forts along existing trade routes, ranchers explored the area in search of open land, and post offices popped up to serve the bourgeoning communities. Travelers in West Texas can still see the natural splendor the region's settlers initially encountered—majestic mountains, dramatic river canyons, and

HIGHLIGHTS

◖ El Paso Mission Trail: The mesmerizing missions transport visitors to an era of 1600s Spanish colonialism via these three fascinating architectural structures (page 321).

◖ Franklin Mountains State Park: Offering a stunning natural backdrop to El Paso's urban landscape, Franklin Mountains State Park is a physically astonishing playground featuring a thrilling gondola ride with incredible views of the desert landscape (page 328).

◖ Hueco Tanks State Historic Site: Marvel at the park's mythological rock art and colorful animal figures and painted masks, representing the lifeways of the region's prehistoric cultures (page 329).

◖ Guadalupe Peak Trail: Located in Guadalupe Mountains National Park,

Guadalupe Peak Trail leads hikers to stunning views of the colorful canyon walls and rugged surrounding outcroppings from the summit of the highest point in Texas (page 341).

◖ The Petroleum Museum: This enormous structure in Midland showcases every possible aspect of the product and industry that forever altered the fate of West Texas, from prehistoric geological conditions and historic drilling equipment to current trends in oil recovery (page 342).

◖ Monahans Sandhills State Park: A true otherworldly experience, Monahans Sandhills State Park rises out of the West Texas desert scrub with miles of blindingly white sand dunes, where families flock to sand-surf among the critter tracks of snakes, birds, and lizards (page 346).

LOOK FOR ◖ TO FIND RECOMMENDED SIGHTS, ACTIVITIES, DINING, AND LODGING.

the outstretched sky—as they zoom along at the posted speed limit of 80 mph on I-10 or U.S. Highway 90.

The residents of this far-reaching region tend to be fiery and independent minded. Many live on large ranches and value their solitude without intrusion from neighbors or particularly the "gub-mint." With such a low population

density, West Texans are often ignored and disassociated with the rest of the state, and it's not surprising that people in El Paso have more in common with New Mexico and Old Mexico than Texas. The western portion of the region is even in a completely different time zone (Mountain) than the rest of the state.

The Wild West spirit thrives in this sun-

EL PASO AND WEST TEXAS

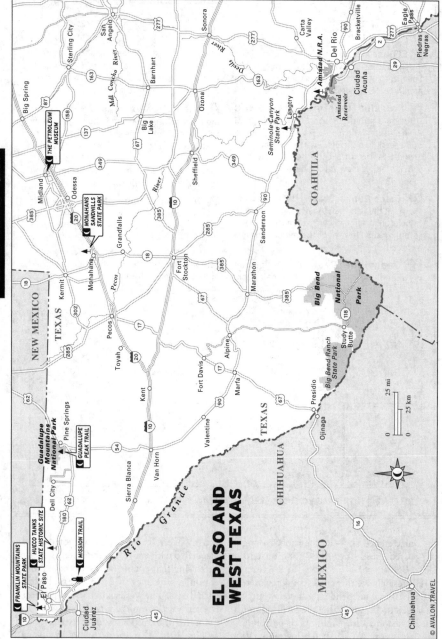

EL PASO AND WEST TEXAS

© AVALON TRAVEL

baked region, where visitors can still find traces of the Old West in its charming, wind-swept communities. Oil derricks remain a common sight in the Midland/Odessa area, and breathtaking views of sheer cliffs, rock towers, and mountain passes prevail in Guadalupe Mountains National Park. This mythical part of the state draws visitors from across the world seeking the fabled image of Texas's rugged and independent spirit.

PLANNING YOUR TIME

There's nothing compact about West Texas. In fact, locals consider the nearly four-hour drive between El Paso and Odessa a quick jaunt down the road. Visitors may find the trek extensive, however, especially considering that one of the most enticing carrots on Odessa's cultural stick is a statue of the world's largest jackrabbit.

El Paso doesn't draw too many visitors as they zoom along busy I-10 on their way across the country, but it's worth spending a couple days in the Sun City to experience its intriguing mix of cultural influences. The centuries-old missions, the Tigua Indian tribe, and the distinctive variety of Mexican food deserve exploration.

Set aside another couple of days to soak up the natural beauty of Guadalupe Mountains National Park, an underappreciated Texas treasure. Visitors are drawn to the park's dramatic peaks and deep canyons for day hikes and overnight camping excursions.

For an all-inclusive West Texas experience, make the four-hour journey across the desert and into the Permian Basin for a day or two in Midland and Odessa. Known primarily for its petroleum and presidents, these cities put the *Friday Night Lights* and George Bush phenomena into perspective.

INFORMATION AND SERVICES

Visitors will find several information centers in West Texas where they can inquire about maps, brochures, directions, equipment rental, and other travel-related assistance. The biggest of the bunch is **El Paso Convention Center and Visitors Bureau** (1 Civic Center Plaza, 915/534-0600, www.elpasocvb.com, Mon.–Fri. 8 A.M.–5 P.M., Sat.–Sun. 10 A.M.–3 P.M.). The Texas Department of Transportation operates a **Tourist Information Center** (8799 S. Desert Blvd., 915/886-3468, daily 8 A.M.–5 P.M.) five miles west of town on I-10 with an extensive selection of Texas-related maps and publications.

If you're heading to Guadalupe Mountains National Park, contact the visitors center at Pine Springs on U.S. Highway 62/180 (915/828-3251, www.nps.gov/gumo, daily 8 A.M.–4:30 P.M. Mountain Time).

For those planning a trip to Midland, contact the **Midland Convention & Visitors Bureau** (109 N. Main St., 432/683-3381, www.visitmidlandtexas.com) or drop by the **George & Gladys Hanger Abell Old Rankin Highway Visitor Center** (1406 W. I-20, 432/687-8285). In Odessa, get in touch with the **Odessa Convention and Visitors Bureau** (700 N. Grant, Suite 200, 800/780-4678, www.odessacvb.com).

For general information about cities and attractions in the region, the **Texas Mountain Trail** is a helpful organization under the direction of the Texas Historical Commission covering the six westernmost counties of far West Texas. Its regional office is based in Van Horn (432/284-0002, www.texasmountaintrail.com), and its website is packed with useful tidbits about the region. Another handy resource for exploring regional destinations is the **Texas Travel Information Center** (8799 S. Desert Blvd. in Anthony, 915/886-3468), on the New Mexico border, where you'll find travel professionals ready to assist you with road conditions, trip planning, routings, points of interest, and events.

GETTING THERE AND AROUND

If you have a few extra days, consider making the drive to West Texas from points east (as opposed to flying). Marvel at the topographic transformation as the Hill Country slowly blends into basin and desert terrain complete with minimesas and a surprising amount of color thanks to the wildflowers and stratified rock terrain. If you're pressed for time, hop aboard a cheap Southwest Airlines flight to **El Paso International Airport** (6701 Convair Rd., 915/772-4271, www.elpasointernation-alairport.com), located about five miles east of downtown. The airport operates international flights from most major airlines, including American, Continental, Delta, Southwest, and United.

The airport also has several taxi stands and staff members representing the major car rental companies. Since it's so close to I-10, cab fare to downtown El Paso can run as little as $10–15. Renting a car is typically the best option, however, since most travelers will want to traverse the sprawling metropolis and the Wild West environs beyond its city limits.

The city's public transportation service, **Sun Metro** (915/533-1220, www.elpasotexas.gov), provides bus routes from the airport to downtown. Call or check the website for information about rates and routes to your destination.

Once in town, Sun Metro is a cheap way to get around as long as you're familiar with the stops and neighborhoods. A day pass costs $3.50. Dozens of bus lines run to all parts of the city, typically every 20–45 minutes. There is no public transportation across the border to Ciudad Juarez.

To cross the border, you can walk or take a cab. Contact the following companies to get around town: **Border Cab Taxi** (915/533-4245), **Checker Taxi Cab Company** (915/532-2626), or **Yellow Cab** (915/532-9999).

For those heading straight to Guadalupe Mountains National Park, the closest airport is nearly 60 miles north in Carlsbad, New Mexico. Though service is provided only by Mesa Airlines from Albuquerque, it's an hour closer than El Paso. For Carlsbad flight information, contact **Cavern City Air Terminal** (505/887-1500, www.airnav.com). The El Paso airport is approximately 110 miles west of the park on U.S. 62/180.

Midland is a good four-hour drive from El Paso, and Southwest Airlines flights are pretty cheap to this oil-based community occasionally referred to as the "tall city of the plains." **Midland International Airport** (9506 Laforce Blvd., 432/560-2200, www.flymaf.com) lies approximately 10 miles west of Midland and 10 miles east of Odessa, and offers flights from American, Southwest, and Continental Airlines. Located at a former army airfield in the heart of the petroleum-rich Permian Basin, the Midland airport typically has more private jets than commercial airliners on its dusty runway.

El Paso

In some ways, El Paso (population 609,415) doesn't really belong in Texas, and there are residents of this remote border town who would wholeheartedly agree. Culturally and geographically, El Paso has more in common with New Mexico and even Old Mexico, but the fiery Wild West spirit that permeates the town makes it a perfect fit for independent-minded West Texas.

The city's history is marked by renowned outlaws like Pancho Villa and Billy the Kid. One of the more colorful local legends claims Billy the Kid once broke *into* a jail just east of town, pointed a six-shooter at the jailer's face, and demanded he set his friend free. Afterward, he locked the jailer in the cell, threw away the keys, and rode off on horseback across the Rio Grande into Mexico.

The most significant aspect of El Paso's history, however, lies along the magnificent Mission Trail east of the city. These significant structures have a rich heritage dating to the 1600s, and several are still active parishes. The seemingly ancient past they represent—Spanish colonial efforts to convert the native population to Catholicism—is nearly as fascinating as their compelling whitewashed adobe walls and rustic timber-laden interiors.

Despite their magnitude, the missions only represent a slice of El Paso's vibrant history. For centuries the city's fate has been tied to Mexico, particularly the cross-border town of Ciudad Juarez. Commercial activity has existed for hundreds of years along the traditional north–south trading routes for Spaniards and Indians. The city's name, originally El Paso del Rio del Norte (the pass of the river to the north), is a geographical reference to the accessible location used by traders and travelers.

Throughout the 1900s, El Paso and Juarez significantly impacted each other's development, especially with industry and manufacturing endeavors such as mining, natural gas, and clothing production providing labor and administrative jobs on both sides of the border. The population of both cities shifted rather dramatically in the 20th century—El Paso had a population of approximately 100,000 in 1930 while Juarez had about 45,000 residents. Juarez currently has nearly 1.7 million people while El Paso has a population of approximately 600,000. Locals note that 50 years ago, El Paso was considered an Anglo town with a strong Hispanic flavor; now it's thought of as a Hispanic town with an Anglo flavor.

Though residents used to freely cross the bridges over the Rio Grande to visit family and conduct business, this has virtually ceased to occur since the drug cartels escalated violence. In fact, upward of 40,000 Mexicans have moved to El Paso in the past several years to flee the gunfire and kidnappings associated with the cartels and smaller groups exploiting the fear factor in Mexico. The massive influx has had a significant impact on El Paso—construction was omnipresent in 2010 at a time when the rest of the country was mired in the Great Recession. Though some have questioned the source of funding for all these new building projects, others have welcomed the restaurants and businesses that previously were only accessible by making a treacherous border run.

SIGHTS

In the past (before 2008), visitors were drawn to El Paso primarily for its proximity to Ciudad Juarez—the largest city along the Texas-U.S. border, where they could spend the day shopping for bargains and eat a cheap and tasty authentic meal. Now that the drug cartels have scared everyone off (including tens of thousands of fellow Mexicans), many potential visitors are also wary of El Paso due to its proximity to Juarez. Never fear—incredibly, El Paso was named America's safest city in 2010 by independent research firm CQ Press. So tourists are still encouraged to visit El Paso to experience the area's distinctive history—from Native Americans to Spanish conquistadors to Mexicans and Wild West outlaws, the people of El Paso's past left a cultural legacy and related tourist attractions unique to Texas and the United States.

◖ The Mission Trail

Even if you're only in El Paso one day, make a point of traversing The Mission Trail, an eight-mile route southeast of the city (accessible via

Mission Ysleta

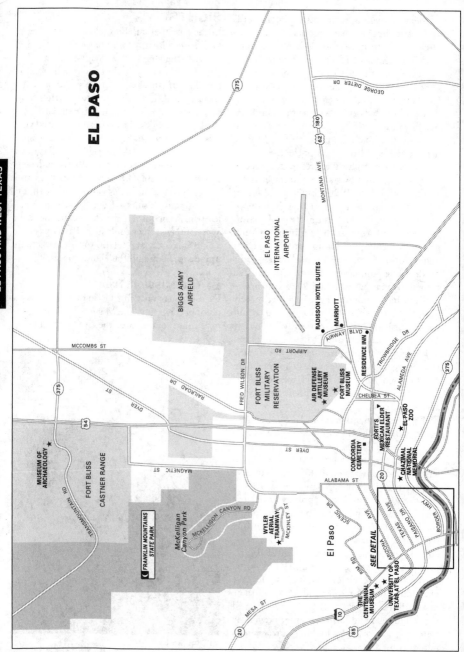

EL PASO

- 375
- GEORGE DIETER DR
- 180
- 62
- MONTANA AVE
- EL PASO INTERNATIONAL AIRPORT
- BIGGS ARMY AIRFIELD
- RADISSON HOTEL SUITES
- MARRIOTT
- AIRWAY BLVD
- RESIDENCE INN
- TROWBRIDGE DR
- AIRPORT RD
- MCCOMBS ST
- RAILROAD DR
- FRED WILSON DR
- DYER ST
- 375
- FORT BLISS MILITARY RESERVATION
- AIR DEFENSE ARTILLERY MUSEUM
- FORT BLISS MUSEUM
- CHELSEA ST
- FORTI'S MEXICAN ELDER RESTAURANT
- EL PASO ZOO
- ALAMEDA AVE
- 375
- 54
- DYER ST
- MAGNETIC ST
- CONCORDIA CEMETERY
- MUSEUM OF ARCHAEOLOGY
- FORT BLISS CASTNER RANGE
- ALABAMA ST
- CHAZIMAL NATIONAL MEMORIAL
- 20
- TRANSMOUNTAIN RD
- FRANKLIN MOUNTAINS STATE PARK
- McKelligon Canyon Park
- MCKELLIGON CANYON RD
- WYLER AERIAL TRAMWAY
- McKINLEY ST
- SCENIC DR
- ARIZONA AVE
- TEXAS AVE
- PASANO DR
- ARMY
- BORDER HWY
- SEE DETAIL
- El Paso
- RIM RD
- MESA ST
- 10
- 20
- 85
- THE CENTENNIAL MUSEUM
- UNIVERSITY OF TEXAS AT EL PASO

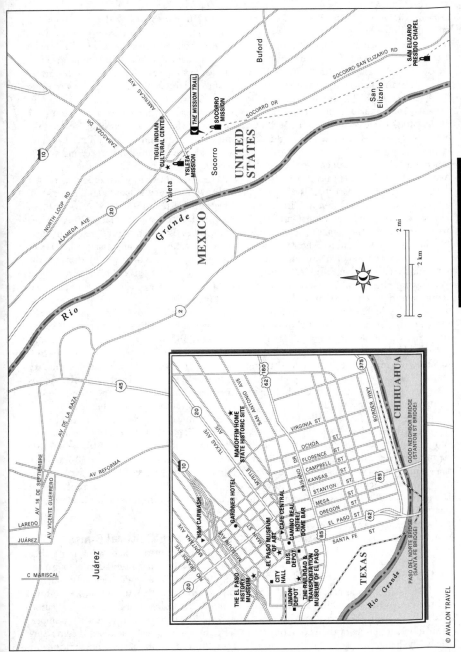

© AVALON TRAVEL

marked exits on I-10, 915/534-0677, free admission, call for hours of public access) containing three fascinating historic structures. The centuries-old and still active missions of **Ysleta** (131 S. Zaragosa Rd., 915/859-9848, www.ysletamission.org) and **Socorro** (328 S. Nevarez Rd., 915/859-7718) and the presidio chapel of **San Elizario** (1521 San Elizario Rd., 915/851-1682) were constructed in the 1800s, but their original settlements date to the 17th and 18th centuries.

Serving as lasting testaments to the Spanish colonial influence on the American Southwest, the missions originated as chapels designed to convert the native population to Catholicism. The success of the missions' mission may not be enduring, but these magnificent adobe buildings are truly a sight to behold.

The Ysleta and Socorro missions have a particularly rich heritage. In 1680, Native American tribe members and Spaniards fled present-day New Mexico to the El Paso area after the Pueblo Indian Revolt of 1680. Subsequently, they established the communities that would become Ysleta (the foundation of the Ysleta del Sur Indian Pueblo) and Socorro two miles east. The first Catholic Mass in Texas was celebrated near present-day Ysleta on October 12, 1680, to commemorate the perilous trek across the desert.

Throughout the following century, flooding affected the mission's adobe structures, some ultimately destroyed and relocated by the ravaging waters. The fragile adobe material—comprised of sun-baked mud bricks and straw—was particularly susceptible to water damage. Painstaking efforts have been made to repair the structures—at Socorro, in particular, where experts and volunteers hand made more than 20,000 adobe bricks and conducted extensive structural repairs.

Fort Bliss

Fort Bliss is an integral part of El Paso's past and present. What started in 1849 as an isolated frontier military post has become a 1.1-million acre home of the U.S. Army's air defense headquarters.

In 1916, Fort Bliss served as the command center for the country's extensive efforts to capture Mexican revolutionary leader Pancho Villa, and during World War II, the fort transformed from the country's largest horse-cavalry post to its largest antiaircraft artillery training center. Fort Bliss has several interesting museums worth visiting, especially for military and history buffs. A forewarning: To access the museums and buildings, you'll need to have a driver's license, auto insurance, and vehicle registration.

The most intriguing attraction is the **Air Defense Artillery Museum** (Building 5000, Pleasanton Rd., 915/568-5412, www.bliss. army.mil, Mon.–Sat. 9 A.M.–4:30 P.M., free admission). Antiaircraft guns are the main attraction here, with an impressive collection of equipment from World War II through the present. Exhibits showcase the advance in military technology in the United States and enemy countries.

The focus shifts to airplanes and army history at the **Fort Bliss Museum and Study Center** (Building 1735, Marshall Rd., 915/568-4518, www.bliss.army.mil, Mon.–Sat. 9 A.M.–4:30 P.M., free admission). For serious military enthusiasts, the reference library here contains volumes of material about the army's significant role along the Mexican border.

Also showcasing the history of the base is the **Old Fort Bliss Museum** (Pershing and Pleasanton Rds., 915/568-4518, www.bliss. army.mil, Mon.–Sat. 9 A.M.–4:30 P.M., free admission). Experience life at the fort as it was in the mid-1800s through replicas of original adobe fort buildings, outdoor displays, and military artifacts.

Tigua Indian Cultural Center

Don't be fooled by the unassuming appearance of the Tigua Indian Cultural Center (305 Yaya Ln., 915/859-7700, www.ysletadelsurpueblo. org, Wed.–Sun. 10 A.M.–3 P.M., free admission). At first glance, the Tigua's reservation and cultural complex may appear to be empty. The streets are often quiet, and the area surrounding the cultural center's museum and gift

NATIVE TEXANS

El Paso's Tigua Indians live southeast of downtown on a small reservation known as the Ysleta del Sur Pueblo (island of the south). These tribe members are descendants of the Isleta Pueblo's refugees, who fled from their home in present-day New Mexico with Spanish colonists during the Pueblo Revolt of 1680. Now, as the Tiguas' Texas home is being encompassed by a larger city, the Tiguas' reservation remains an island attempting to maintain its proud heritage.

Fortunately, the tribe has managed to keep its culture, traditions, and language intact for more than 325 years. Their pueblo and associated Spanish mission originated in 1682, allowing the Ysleta del Sur community to stake a claim as Texas's oldest town. The Tiguas are one of only three Native American tribes (aside from the Alabama-Coushatta and Kickapoo) living on reservations in Texas.

The Tiguas are working diligently to preserve their legacy by retaining vital customs of their past. They are keeping their vanishing Tiwa language alive through classes for the reservation's children and teaching them traditional skills like pottery, painting, ceremonial dancing, and bread baking.

The Tiguas have long relied on the natural world to sustain them, and the tribe flourished when irrigation ditches from the Rio Grande allowed them to grow corn, pumpkins, and beans. To celebrate their agricultural heritage, the Tiguas hold the ceremonial Feast of Saint Anthony every June with a corn dance, traditional food preparation, and other cultural activities.

Although most of the tribe's customary rituals were eventually incorporated with Catholic holidays, its members still share a belief system with their forefathers – a way of living in unity and harmony with the forces of nature. They pay attention to the natural world around them and recognize their significant role in the universe beyond the borders of the Ysleta del Sur Pueblo.

EL PASO AND WEST TEXAS

shop is typically vacant. Upon entering the site, however, the resounding life of this steadfast tribe's fascinating legend becomes apparent.

Founded in 1682, the Ysleta del Sur Pueblo, aka the Tigua Indian reservation, houses descendants of New Mexico's Isleta Pueblo's refugees who accompanied the Spanish during the Pueblo Revolt of 1680. Their reservation is physically surrounded by the city of El Paso, but the tribe has managed to keep its culture, traditions, and language. Despite the threats of declining numbers and encroaching development during the past three centuries, the Tiguas remain strong survivors.

The tribe's legacy is on display at its cultural center, where a modest museum showcases past leaders, proud accomplishments, documents, photos, and artifacts, including ceremonial costumes, handmade cooking items, and interpretive exhibits. An adjacent gift shop offers crafts, pottery, jewelry, and artwork made by tribe members along with educational books and brochures. A Tigua representative is usually on hand to provide insight about the tribe's history.

On many weekends, the Tigua youth dance group performs social dances, and seasonal special events feature traditional bread baking and powwows. Call ahead to confirm events are taking place.

El Paso Museum of Art

Experience acclaimed regional and European works of art at the El Paso Museum of Art (1 Arts Festival Plaza, 915/532-1707, www.elpasoartmuseum.org, Tues.–Sat. 9 A.M.–5 P.M., Sun. noon–5 P.M., free admission). The diversity of the museum's collection is rather impressive, ranging from European works from the 13th–18th centuries to Mexican colonial art to contemporary pieces from the southwestern United States. Take your time strolling through the museum's five permanent galleries, offering a remarkable sampling of the more than 5,000 works in its collection. Temporary exhibits often showcase up-and-coming regional artists, and the museum offers a respectable schedule of lectures, films, and educational programs.

Magoffin Home State Historic Site

The stunning 19-room Magoffin Home State Historic Site (1120 Magoffin Ave., 915/533-5147, www.visitmagoffinhome.com, Thurs.–Sun. 9 A.M.–4 P.M., $3 ages 13 and older) was built in 1875 by El Paso politician and businessman Joseph Magoffin. Now located in the heart of downtown, this adobe home is considered a prime example of Territorial-style architecture, a distinctively Southwestern approach combining local adobe (sun-baked bricks composed of mud and straw) and then-fashionable mid-Victorian wood trim. The one-story U-shaped compound, acquired by the Texas Historical Commission in 2008, was constructed around a central patio with a plastered exterior to provide a masonry appearance. Inside, visitors will find historic photographs, antique furniture, and vintage artifacts representing the upscale yet down-home lifestyle of this prominent and popular El Pasoan who served four terms as the city's mayor. Note the exposed fireplace, revealing adobe bricks, traditional red bricks, and fancy Victorian wallpaper, an ideal representation of the mix of cultural influences on this significant heritage site. Note: Magoffin Home has undergone an extensive restoration project; call in advance to determine accessibility.

El Paso Zoo

El Paso doesn't have an abundance of kid-friendly attractions, so you'll find most of the younger crowd running around at the small yet satisfying El Paso Zoo (4001 E. Paisano Dr., 915/544-1928, www.elpasozoo.org, Mon.–Fri. 9:30 A.M.–4 P.M., Sat.–Sun. 9:30 A.M.–5 P.M., $10 adults, $7.50 seniors, $6 children ages 3–12). This 18-acre site just east of downtown is home to nearly 1,000 animals representing 240 species from across the world. The Animals

of Asia area is the most impressive, with tigers, orangutans, tapirs, and an endangered leopard. Highlights of the Americas area include the must-see sea lion exhibit and a cage full of spindly spider monkeys. For a city of half a million people, the zoo seems rather limited in scope, but the effective use of desert foliage and squeals of delight from children make this a worthwhile experience.

The Centennial Museum and Chihuahuan Desert Gardens

This University of Texas at El Paso museum (500 W. University Ave., 915/747-5565, www.museum.utep.edu, Tues.–Sat. 10 A.M.–4:30 P.M., free admission) is one of those old-school facilities with exhibits dedicated to history and culture that harkens back to the days of being a kid on a field trip. Judging by most of the dated dioramas and stuffed animals on display, nothing's changed much here since, but a few new exhibits (with video screens and fancy graphics) are a sign that things are slowly but surely progressing. Still, what's on display is pretty intriguing, dedicated primarily to the heritage of native groups and the cultural history of the southwestern United States and northern Mexico. The most compelling exhibits are on the top floor, particularly the artifacts from the Pueblo, Apache, and Navajo Indian tribes.

For some reason, the university prioritized upgrading the outdoor Chihuahuan Desert Gardens rather than the indoor exhibits. As a result, the Centennial Museum features a nice collection of distinctive flora surrounding the building. The gardens' 600-plus species in multiple areas are fascinating, especially for those unfamiliar with the diversity of desert plant life. The educational component here is the importance of water conservation while landscaping in this arid region.

Worth noting: Since the museum is located on a busy college campus, parking is problematic. There are several places to park behind the building, but you'll have to deal with the slight hassle of heading upstairs to find someone to give you a parking pass, since the campus police are aggressive about ticketing permit-less people.

The El Paso History Museum

If the aforementioned Centennial Museum is old-school in the approach to exhibiting the past, then the new school is represented by The El Paso History Museum (510 N. Santa Fe St., 915/351-3588, www.elpasotexas.gov/history, free admission). A relative newcomer on the city's cultural scene (2007), the two-story history museum is packed with informative displays and fun features. Visitors experience maps, artifacts, and photos related to all aspects of El Paso's past—from regional Native American tribes to the Wild West days to the city's role in the Mexican Revolution. The museum offers numerous eye-catching displays and interactive exhibits, including computer touch screens with video clips, an amusing pop-culture trivia game, audio stations with recordings about significant entrepreneurs, and hands-on architectural activities for the kids.

The Railroad & Transportation Museum of El Paso

Just a few blocks away from the history museum, The Railroad & Transportation Museum (400 W. San Antonio Ave., 915/422-3420, www.elpasorails.org, Tues.–Sat. 11 A.M.–5 P.M., Sun. 1–5 P.M., free admission) showcases another important aspect of El Paso's history. The railroad's arrival in 1881 played a major role in El Paso's development over the past century, bringing people and money from east–west and north–south. The museum offers an impressive collection of historic photos along with its main attraction, a rare restored 1857 steam engine used by the El Paso and Southwestern Railroad. Note: The museum can be somewhat inconsistent with its hours, so it's a good idea to call ahead to make sure it's open.

El Paso Museum of Archaeology

Though located fairly far away from downtown, it's worth setting aside some time on your way to/from the Franklin Mountains State Park to visit the El Paso Museum of Archaeology

© TEXAS HISTORICAL COMMISSION

the El Paso Museum of Archaeology

THE ROYAL ROAD

Most of the western United States' traditional transportation corridors were established along wagon routes and trails associated with westward expansion. However, El Paso boasts the distinction of hosting a rare north-south route, the historically significant El Camino Real de Tierra Adentro (the Royal Road of the Interior Lands).

The road, now roughly represented by I-25, played a significant role in the Southwest and in Mexico as a trade route supporting cultural exchange and interaction among Spaniards, Native Americans, Mexicans, and Americans. Considered the earliest Euro-American trade route in the United States, El Camino Real de Tierra Adentro stretches more than 1,600 miles from Mexico City through El Paso to northern New Mexico. Based on ancient footpaths tying Spain's colonial capital at Mexico City to ancient Native American settlements in distant New Mexico, the route hosted historic *parajes* (camping grounds) created by

the Spanish colonists that formed the basis for several modern cities along the Rio Grande and into New Mexico.

In 1598, Don Juan de Onate established the general route of El Camino Real de Tierra Adentro when he crossed the Rio Grande at El Paso del Rio del Norte (the pass of the river to the north), which eventually became the town of El Paso. He then followed indigenous routes along the river, eventually leading vast herds of livestock, traders, and settlers into New Mexico. The activity along the trail greatly affected the cultural development of the greater Southwest for nearly three centuries.

Although the route itself has been internationally designated, it doesn't yet contain a comprehensive interpretive element. Efforts are under way to incorporate signage and an organized educational component. To access a Geographic Information System interactive map or to find out more about tourism efforts, visit www.nps.gov/elca or call 505/988-6888.

(4301 Transmountain Rd., 915/755-4332, www.elpasotexas.gov/arch_museum, Tues.–Sat. 9 A.M.–5 P.M., Sun. noon–5 P.M., free admission). Since this part of Texas is so rich with Native American heritage, this museum is stocked with intriguing history of regional tribes (especially from the southwestern United States and northern Mexico) in dioramas, artifacts, and pottery. Make a point of strolling through the 15-acre garden that surrounds the building, with more than 200 species of cacti and other flora representing the biodiversity of the Chihuahuan Desert.

◖ Franklin Mountains State Park

A trip to El Paso is incomplete without experiencing the country's largest urban park (1331 McKelligon Canyon Rd., 915/566-6441, www.tpwd.state.tx.us, daily 8 A.M.–5 P.M., $4 ages 13 and older). At 24,247 acres and covering nearly 37 square miles, the Franklin Mountains provide a stunning natural backdrop to El Paso's

urban landscape. The Franklins are considered Texas's largest sustained mountain range, with a top elevation of 7,192 feet at the summit of North Franklin Peak. A pronounced gap in the range offering "the pass" through this rugged terrain provided the inspiration for the city's name. For more than 12,000 years, Native American groups, Spanish conquistadors, international traders, and adventurers have traversed the pass, and evidence of these ancient travelers remains in the form of rock art pictographs in several natural shelters throughout the park. Rangers offer tours on the first and third weekends of the month. Reservations are suggested. In addition, the park contains two pleasant hiking trails (accessible from Loop 375/Transmountain Road) and established rock climbing areas in McKelligon Canyon. A limited number of primitive tent-camping and RV sites are also available.

The most popular park activity, however, is the thrilling **Wyler Aerial Tramway** (tickets

© TEXAS HISTORICAL COMMISSION

Franklin Mountains State Park just north of El Paso

and boarding at 1700 McKinley St., 915/566-6622, $7 ages 13 and older, $4 ages 12 and younger). The Swiss-made gondolas travel on a 2,600-foot-long cable offering striking views of 7,000 square miles encompassing three states and two countries. Your gondola guide will describe the desert flora, intriguing wildlife, and rock formations during the five-minute ride.

⬛ Hueco Tanks State Historic Site

It's well worth the 45-minute drive to witness the prehistoric wonders of Hueco Tanks State Historic Site (32 miles northeast of El Paso on U.S. Hwy. 62/180, then head north on RR 2775, 915/857-1135, www.tpwd.state.tx.us, $4 daily ages 13 and older). The 860-acre park is named for the massive granite basins or "huecos" that provided priceless collected rainwater to Native Americans and travelers for thousands of years in this parched region of the country. These days, the invaluable attraction is the park's fascinating collection of pictographs created by area tribe members during the past several thousand years. Marvel at the

mythological drawings and white- and rust-colored animal figures, each representing the lifeways of the region's bygone eras. Though the human and animal figures can be somewhat cryptic, the hundreds of masks—some clownlike, others menacing—painted by the ancient Jornada Mogollon culture are captivating and compelling. Park guides offer highly recommended pictograph tours, allowing visitors access to areas with rock art representing three distinct cultures. Tours are conducted primarily by reservation, so call a few days beforehand to let them know you're coming. Guides are available Wednesday–Sunday at 9 A.M. and 11 A.M. (May 1–Sept. 30) and 10:30 A.M. and 2 P.M. (Oct. 1–April 30).

Other park attractions include an interpretive center housed in a historic ranch house, ruins of a 19th-century stagecoach station, and abandoned ranch buildings. Visitors can also picnic, hike, camp, and rock climb. To reduce the threat of damage to the prehistoric pictographs, park officials limit the number of visitors to Hueco Tanks; therefore, advance

FROM ROBIN HOOD TO REVOLUTIONARY

Born with the nonthreatening name Doroteo Arango, **Pancho Villa** was a notorious Mexican revolutionary who endeared himself to the country's poor and scared the hell out of countless Americans along the Texas border near El Paso.

As a teenaged cattle rustler in the late 1800s, Doroteo took the name Pancho Villa (reportedly after a lesser-known bandit named Pancho Villa died). His ability to evade the local law enforcement and his occasional tendency to pull off Robin Hood-style escapades made him a hero to poor folks across Northern Mexico.

Villa officially became a revolutionary when he joined with Francisco Madero's opposition forces against Mexico's Porfirio Diaz-led government in 1910. A year later, Villa made his first trip to Texas to meet with revolution sympathizers. After escaping from a Mexico City jail in 1913, he returned to El Paso to recruit followers and plot against Mexican general Victoriano Huerta. Villa's presence was welcome in El Paso, where he purchased an abundance of supplies and even temporarily relocated his family.

That changed in 1916, when the U.S. government recognized and supported Venustiano Carranza's regime in Mexico. Villa retaliated by raiding towns along the U.S.-Mexico border. He was no longer revered in El Paso; rather, he was exceedingly feared for his vindictive and violent tendencies.

In fact, U.S. President Woodrow Wilson even dispatched two punitive expeditions to capture Villa. Both were unsuccessful, ultimately endearing him to some Mexicans who viewed him as a triumphant menace to the meddling U.S. government.

In 1920, the Mexican government accepted Villa's surrender and bought his retirement by giving him an estate and a general's salary in his home state of Durango. Three years later, he was assassinated in Parral, Chihuahua.

reservations are required. For camping or tour reservations, call 915/849-6684. For other day-use reservations, call 512/389-8900.

ENTERTAINMENT AND EVENTS

Visitors to El Paso may not find the legendary saloons they've envisioned from the Wild West of yesteryear, but they'll discover surprisingly top-notch performing arts organizations and memorable border-spanning live music and international annual events.

Performing Arts

The cream of the city's cultural crop is the renowned **El Paso Symphony Orchestra** (1 Civic Center Plaza, 915/532-3776, www.epso. org). Established in the 1930s, the symphony bills itself as the oldest performing arts organization in town and the longest continuously running symphony orchestra in the state. The organization is respected among its peers for its ability to recruit highly qualified talent and international soloists. The symphony performs 12 classical concerts annually and hosts a variety of special events and educational programs drawing attendees from West Texas, southern New Mexico, and northern Mexico. Equally grand in artistic ambition is the **El Paso Opera** (310 N. Mesa St., 915/581-2252, www.epopera.org), featuring national and international talent. The respected company stages several productions annually, with past performances including well-known masterpieces such as Mozart's *Così fan Tutte* and Puccini's *Tosca*.

Another venerable institution on the city's cultural landscape is **Showtime El Paso** (shows at the Abraham Chavez Theatre, 1 Civic Center Plaza, 915/544-2022, www.showtimeelpaso.com). In existence since 1934, the group has evolved from exclusively classical concerts to a broader range of similarly sophisticated shows, from Broadway musicals to jazz concerts to dance performances. Newer to the scene is **El Paso Pro Musica** (915/833-9400, www.elpasopromusica.org), a chamber orchestra and choir group holding a series of concerts October through April at the El Paso Museum of Art (1 Arts Festival Plaza) and the University of Texas at El Paso's Fox Fine Arts Recital Hall (500 W. University Ave.). Pro Musica features instrumental and vocal ensembles, and hosts a popular annual Chamber Music Festival showcasing acclaimed artists from across the country.

If you're planning in advance, check to see if there's a show at the venerable **1930 Plaza Theatre** (125 Pioneer Plaza, www.theplazatheatre.org, 915/534-0600). This remarkably restored venue was once advertised as the largest theater of its kind between Dallas and Los Angeles. It was particularly well known for its fancy interior design and pioneering high-tech features (the Mighty Wurlitzer Organ rose from below the stage and provided sound effects for silent movies). Thanks to a spirited fundraising campaign, the theater was spared the wrecking ball in the 1980s and continues to host events, including the symphony, pop acts like Boz Scaggs, country greats like George Jones, and themed movie nights.

Bars and Clubs

El Paso's bar scene is fairly widespread, but the major centers of activity are downtown and near the UTEP campus. Don't expect too much from the university bars, a small collection of nondescript venues congregated near an intersection (misleadingly referred to as "the strip") packed with indifferent college students. The best place to start is in the heart of downtown at the █ **Dome Bar** (101 S. El Paso St., 915/534-3000), on the ground level of the historic Camino Real Hotel. This semi-swanky spot begins the evening as a restaurant but transforms into a low-key bar drawing a comfortable mix of young professionals and singles. Named for the colossal and colorful Tiffany cut-glass dome presiding over the establishment, the Dome Bar is an ideal place to have a predinner cocktail or an evening-ending nightcap. Pony up to the circle-shaped bar for

a Scotch or order a top-shelf tequila for sipping at a table while listening to the blues band in the corner.

Just down the street you'll find the polar opposite scene in an equally compelling establishment. **The Tap** (408 E. San Antonio Ave., 915/532-1848) is the ultimate dive bar, with faded black and red velvet surroundings, recessed lighting, and so-bad-it's-good music on the jukebox (Journey, Loverboy, Bee Gees). It's dark and dank in here with the occasional questionable character (members of the industrial rock band Ministry have reportedly paid a visit), but that's exactly what a good dive bar should be. The Tap solidifies this reputation with its cheap drinks and mediocre food.

"The strip" is comprised primarily of generic dance clubs where college kids gather to not dance. However, there are a couple places where you can order a quality beer or even just hang out and have a conversation without yelling. **Hemingway's** (214 Cincinnati Ave., 915/532-7333) prides itself on its microbrews and imports, which are fairly limited by big-city standards but a welcome change of pace for this Bud Light–infused area. Next door is the comfy **Crawdaddy's Bar & Grill** (212 Cincinnati Ave., 915/533-9332), where you can order a cheap draft beer with a side of gumbo in a refreshingly laid-back environment.

Live Music

Geared toward the younger alternative crowd is **Club 101** (3233 N. Mesa St., 915/544-2101), a warehouse-type establishment featuring local and national acts. Hard rock, goth, and indie bands take the stage most weekends.

A couple of traditional venues are located within a few blocks of each other on a strip of highway northwest of town. For country and western dancing, drop by **Stampede** (5500 Doniphan Dr., 915/833-6397). For blues, rock, and occasional Tejano bands, go to **Aceitunas** (5200 Doniphan Dr., 915/581-3260).

Gay and Lesbian

El Paso's only prominent gay bar is the **Old Plantation** (301 S. Ochoa St., 915/533-6055).

This dance club is known for its foam parties, strippers, and open-mindedness.

Events

FIESTA DE LAS FLORES

One of El Paso's most beloved annual events is Fiesta de las Flores (at El Paso Coliseum, 4100 E. Paisano Dr., 915/755-2000), held on Labor Day weekend each year. This popular event features a beauty pageant, live music, plenty of food, and the World Championship Huacha Tournament (a washer-pitching contest).

PILGRIMAGE TO MOUNT CRISTO

In 1934, a 12-foot wooden cross was placed on the summit of Mount Cristo, where Texas, New Mexico, and the state of Chihuahua, Mexico, meet. Later that decade, a shrine and an enormous limestone statue of "Christ the King" were erected. At more than 42 feet high, the monument is considered the largest of its kind in North America. Since the first pilgrimage in 1934, faithful worshippers have gathered each October at the base of the mountain (at the end of McNutt Road) to ascend the 5,650-foot, two-hour-long trek. Some carry wooden crosses, others walk barefoot over the rough path, and a few even climb on their knees. The anniversary Mass each October is observed at noon on the mount's summit and is performed in both English and Spanish.

THE SOUTHWESTERN INTERNATIONAL LIVESTOCK SHOW AND RODEO

The rodeo (915/755-2000) has been a customary event in El Paso since 1940. Referred to as the oldest sporting event in the city and the 17th-oldest rodeo in the nation, this venerable attraction is held each September at Cohen Stadium (9700 Gateway North) with the Franklin Mountains serving as a picturesque and appropriately rugged backdrop. The event features traditional rodeo activities such as bull riding, barrel racing, and roping.

SUN BOWL PARADE

More than a hundred floats and marching bands take to the streets (Montana Street, specifically) for this annual Thanksgiving Day event. Held since the 1930s, the parade draws more than 200,000 revelers basking in El Paso's sunny winter weather.

SHOPPING

Portions of El Paso's downtown feel like marketplaces in Mexico, with discount clothing retailers and cheap trinkets lining the storefronts. They're interesting to browse, and they're pretty much the only way to do some authentic thrift shopping since a border run is no longer a safe option. Since this is the Wild West, you'll also find several reputable stores in El Paso offering quality Western wear and imports.

Boots and Western Wear

El Paso is one of the best places in Texas to find authentic Western wear. Boots and hats are required apparel as opposed to fashionable accessories in this sun-baked, wind-swept region. Besides, genuine cowboys live on surrounding ranches, so they need a place to get their work gear.

It's not the oldest place in town, but **Starr Western Wear** (two locations—112 E. Overland Ave., 915/533-0113, and 11751 Gateway Blvd., 915/594-0113, www.starrwesternwear.com) is the real deal. Ranching families and their workers have been outfitting themselves at this small store in the historic downtown shopping district for nearly 50 years. Starr's also carries ladies' and kids' Western wear and their durable line of Starr brand jeans and shirts. Look for traditional jeans (as opposed to fashionable) on the racks along with Wranglers, Levis, and Carharts.

For boots, there's no excuse not to drop by one of the **Tony Lama Factory Stores** (particularly 7156 Gateway E., 915/772-4327, www.tonylamabootshop.com). A legendary boot maker for more than 80 years, Tony Lama is one of the most recognized names on the Western-wear scene. Specializing in high-end handcrafted boots, Tony Lamas are made in El Paso and have been worn by famous customers such as Travis Tritt, the Texas Tornadoes, and ZZ Top. The factory outlets feature men's and ladies' boots and work boots, along with cowboy hats, belts, and Western-themed gifts. Another established and beloved local institution is **Champion Attitude Boots** (2100 Wyoming Ave., 915/309-4791, www.caboots. com). This fourth-generation boot-making family primarily operates as an Internet company these days (call for an appointment), but their legacy continues with hundreds of different styles of boots, for cowboys, bikers, and kids to custom-made varieties fashioned from alligator, ostrich, python, stingray, and lizard. Fun fact: Champion's once outfitted many of the 1980s hair metal bands, including Bon Jovi and Motley Crue.

Yet another venerable Texas boot maker has been operating a factory store in El Paso for decades. San Antonio–based **Lucchese Boots Outlet** (6601 Montana Ave., 915/778-8060, or 40 Walter Jones Blvd., 915/778-3066) features high-quality footwear at significantly marked-down prices. For sheer volume, drop by **Cowtown Boots** (11401 Gateway Blvd., 915/593-2929), a 40,000-square-foot outlet store with an enormous selection of cowboy boots, leather goods, brand-name clothing, and accessories with affordable price tags.

Imports

For warehouse-style imports, be sure to set aside at least an hour to browse the massive **El Paso Saddleblanket** (6926 Gateway E., 915/544-1000, www.elpasosaddleblanket. com). This one-acre megastore features stacks, rows, and cases of items from Mexico and the Southwest. Colorfully patterned blankets and rugs are the main draw here, but you'll find just about anything else under the hot sun— furniture, pottery, jewelry, clothing, housewares, and artwork to name a few. A more traditional import shop, with a strong emphasis on foreign goods, is the eclectic and intriguing **Galeria San Ysidro** (801 Texas Ave., 915/544-4444, www.galeriasanysidro.com). Located in a three-story downtown gallery, San Ysidro specializes in Mexican primitive and folk art but offers a worldwide collection

of treasures, including clothing, home decor items, and pottery. Keep an eye out for the amazing Moroccan objects—the fabrics and mosaics, in particular.

SPORTS AND RECREATION

With more than half a million residents, El Paso is one of the largest cities in the country with no major professional sports teams. However, much like Austin, fans are content to get their quality gamesmanship fix via Division 1–level college athletics (University of Texas at El Paso sporting events) and minor league teams.

Minor League Sports

The most popular sporting event in town, aside from the UTEP teams, is the **El Paso Diablos** (9700 Gateway Blvd., 915/755-2000, www.diablos.com). El Paso residents love their minorleague baseball team, which regularly draws 10,000 fans to Cohen Stadium, considered one of the finer ballparks in the state. The Diablos play rival American Association teams from May through August.

The **El Paso Patriots** (6941 Industrial Ave., 915/771-6620, www.elpaso-patriots.com) soccer team draws a surprisingly large crowd (several thousand fans) to its games at Patriots Stadium. Considered a veteran organization at 20 years old, the team plays in the U.S. Premier Development League against teams from Texas and Louisiana.

University of Texas at El Paso

Most of the sports talk in town centers on the **UTEP Miners** (http://utepathletics.cstv. com), a nickname passed down from the school's origins as the State School of Mines and Metallurgy. Like the rest of Texas, football reigns supreme here, and fans experience the bonus of attending games at Sun Bowl Stadium, nestled among the sheer cliffs of the Franklin Mountains. The 52,000-seat stadium also hosts the venerable Sun Bowl game in late December each year.

The other major crowd-drawing UTEP athletic events are men's and women's basketball games. Both teams are perennial contenders on the brink of achieving national acclaim. The basketball teams have played games at Don Haskins Center since 1976, but their new state-of-the-art facility, the Foster Stevens Basketball Center, opened in April 2009.

ACCOMMODATIONS

The majority of El Paso's lodging options are chains adjacent to the airport and Fort Bliss just northeast of downtown. Fortunately, most of the choices there and in the urban core are quite affordable (in the $100 range). El Paso's downtown used to have several historic hotels, but they've either closed their doors or declined to the point of not being recommendable.

Downtown

Budget travelers may want to consider the **Gardner Hotel** (311 E. Franklin Ave., 915/532-3661, www.gardnerhotel.com, $55 d), reportedly the oldest continually operating hotel in the city. Unfortunately, historic doesn't always mean quaint, as evidenced by the old furniture and bedding. Regardless, it's inexpensive and in a prime location. Amenities include Internet access and a fancy (in a dated way) lobby with memorabilia dating to the 1930s. For just a few dollars more per night you'll find newer and cleaner accommodations a few miles away at the **Holiday Inn Express** (409 E. Missouri Ave., 915/544-3333, www.ichotelsgroup.com, $82 d), featuring a free continental breakfast, free wireless Internet access, a small fitness center, and an outdoor pool.

Unless you need to be right next to the airport, there's no reason you shouldn't be staying at the magnificent **C Camino Real Hotel** (101 S. El Paso St., 915/534-3000, www.caminoreal. com, $89 d). Located in the heart of downtown within blocks of Mexican-style shopping and eateries, this 1912 towering structure is a true gem. The Camino Real features upscale amenities—notice the fancy chandeliers, marble detailing, and grand staircase in the lobby—without charging luxury prices. The large, clean rooms include free Internet access and offer top-notch views of the Franklin

Mountains and the not-as-picturesque border town of Ciudad Juarez. Be sure to enjoy a cocktail at the hotel's famous Dome Bar, featuring a beautiful 25-foot-wide Tiffany cut-glass dome. Just a few miles away on the edge of the University of Texas at El Paso campus is the commendable **Hilton Garden Inn El Paso** (111 W. University Ave., 915/351-2121, www. hiltongardeninn.com, $119 d). The Hilton offers free wireless Internet access and refrigerators and microwaves in the rooms, as well as a fitness center and outdoor pool.

Airport Area

The best bang for your buck in the airport vicinity is **Hyatt Place** (6140 Gateway Blvd. E., 915/771-0022, www.hyatt.com, $89 d), offering a slew of amenities, including rooms with 42-inch high-definition TVs, oversized sofa sleepers in a separate area, and free Wi-Fi Internet access along with a free continental breakfast and a fitness center. A bonus for cyclists (or those who just support cycling): Hyatt Place is a proud member of the Texas Mountain Trail Cycle Friendly Accommodations Program. Older yet still reliable is the nearby **Quality Inn & Suites** (6099 Montana Ave., 915/772-3300, www.qualityinn.com, $72 d), featuring a free full hot breakfast, an outdoor pool, free Internet access, and refrigerators and microwaves in each room.

Another worthy option is **Radisson Hotel Suites** (1770 Airway Blvd., 915/772-3333, www.radisson.com, $89 d), offering rooms with Internet access, refrigerators, and microwaves, as well as indoor and outdoor swimming pools, an exercise facility, and a nightly reception with complimentary cocktails. Not quite as fun yet similarly priced is the **Marriott** (1600 Airway Blvd., 915/779-3300, www. marriott.com, $89 d), with an indoor/outdoor pool, sauna, whirlpool, and exercise facility, and Internet for a daily fee.

Popular with the business crowd and longer-range visitors is **Residence Inn** (6355 Gateway Blvd. W., 915/771-0504, www.marriott.com, $99 d), offering a free hot breakfast buffet daily, an evening social hour Monday through

Thursday, a mini "market" with 24-hour access to snacks and drinks, large rooms with separate living areas, fully equipped kitchens with full-size appliances, and free wireless Internet access. A bonus: Leave your grocery list at the front desk in the morning and come back to a fully stocked kitchen at night.

Camping

One of the nicer RV parks in West Texas is located 10 miles outside of town just over the New Mexico border. **El Paso West RV Park** (1415 Anthony Dr. in Anthony, New Mexico, 575/882-7172, $20 nightly) offers free wireless Internet access, laundry facilities, and clean grounds with trees (a rarity in the desert). Another reputable option is **Mission RV Park** (1420 R.V. Dr. via exit 34 on I-10, 915/859-1133, www.missionrvparklp.com, $20 nightly) features free Wi-Fi service, an enclosed heated pool, and an on-site Laundromat.

FOOD

Not surprisingly, Mexican food is the most popular type of cuisine in El Paso; surprisingly, there isn't an abundance of high-quality locales to choose from. In fact, for a city of its size, El Paso is somewhat lacking in top-notch restaurants, but its commendable midrange Mexican and down-home cookin' spots are plentiful.

Mexican

One of the most memorable places you'll ever have a Mexican meal is **H&H Car Wash** (701 E. Yandell Dr., 915/533-1144, $5–11, Mon.–Sat. 7 A.M.–3 P.M.). That's not a misprint—it's a real car wash. Let the professionals outside make your rig sparkle while their indoor counterparts whip up a spectacular Mexican feast. The decor is interesting if somewhat uninspiring—a 1960s-style coffee shop with minimal furnishings situated in the concrete desert just east of downtown. Regardless, most folks are here for the food, a tantalizing selection of fresh-made El Paso–style specialties such as chile relleno burritos, red enchiladas (made with stacked or rolled tortillas filled with cheese and smothered in a spicy chile sauce), and carne picada—minced steak with diced jalapeños, onions, and tomatoes. One of the best menu items in town is the West Texas/New Mexico–style chile relleno, and H&H does 'em right, with a distinctive flavor bonus. Since the breaded chiles are heated on the same grill as the tasty (and greasy) burgers and sausage, the chiles' thin outer crust soaks up the goodness and adds an extra-flavorful kick.

For old-school Mexican food, head to downtown mainstay **G&R Restaurant** (401 E. Nevada Ave., 915/546-9343, $6–14), a traditional spot that's blissfully operating in the past—you won't find any low-cal options or California influence here. G&R is an ideal place to order stacked red enchiladas, a regional specialty with layered tortillas, meat, and cheese that becomes even more of a local custom when you add a fried egg on top (it tastes way better than it sounds). G&R is also known for its creamy and spicy chile con queso and exquisite chile relleno. Another classic Mexican joint just north of downtown is **Amigos Restaurant** (2000 Montana Ave., 915/533-0155, $7–15). The food here is spicy New Mexico style (hot chiles), a welcome jolt for some but an unwanted kick for others. To be fair, not everything is four-alarm level here, but consider yourself warned about the enchiladas or anything else with chiles in the description. The crispy beef tacos, with the regional custom of potatoes mixed with the seasoned meat, are mild, and the chicken tampiquena, though spicy, offers a delightful blend of fresh flavors.

Locals are more likely to frequent the venerable Mexican restaurants outside of downtown, such as **L&J Cafe** (3622 E. Missouri Ave., 915/566-8418, $5–11, closed Sun.). Occasionally referred to as the "place by the graveyard" due to its location adjacent to Concordia Cemetery, the L&J is an El Paso institution renowned for its cold beer and traditional Chihuahuan Desert–style dishes—caldillo, a flavorful beef, potato, and chile stew, and the green and red enchiladas with chicken, cheese, and multifaceted sauces.

If you only try one item at a Mexican restaurant in El Paso, make it the chile relleno at **Griggs Restaurant** (9007 Montana Ave., 915/598-3451, $6–12). These tasty delicacies are distinct to El Paso—an Anaheim chile (the long, green, and mild pepper) lightly fried in egg batter and filled with a velvety white cheese. They've perfected these supreme items at Griggs, so do yourself a favor and load up on them while you're here.

To truly eat like a local, head to the eastern edge of downtown for the authentic taste of (**Forti's Mexican Elder Restaurant** (321 Chelsea St., 915/772-0066, $8–24). Located in a slightly run-down part of town in a somewhat dated hacienda-style building (like the best undiscovered local gems), Forti's is all about flavor—especially heat. Bordering on too spicy, some of the dishes (the red enchiladas, in particular) will test your heat index, but most are packed with local-style goodness. The chile relleno offers a perfectly smooth blend of velvety cheese and tangy pepper, and the gorditas are meaty and savory. Other menu highlights include the mole chicken enchiladas and pork al pastor tacos. If you're lucky, your meal may even be accompanied by a small band of musicians in the corner to perfectly complement your borderland experience.

Another popular spot is **Avila's Mexican Food** (6232 N. Mesa St., 915/584-3621, $5–11), known for its semispicy chile dishes. To get an authentic sampling of local cuisine, order the tricolored enchilada plate, containing red, green, and sour cream enchiladas (the colors of Mexico's flag). Savor the flavors of these hearty desert chiles, coupled with the better-than-they-should-be beans and rice.

If you're simply looking for a quick bite to eat, drop by one of the several locations of **Chico's Tacos** (5305 Montana Ave., 915/772-7777, $4–7), a local chain with a rabid following. The main draw here is their rolled taco—order two singles (three tacos per order) and gorge on the cheesy goodness. Strangely enough, Chico's is also known for its hot dogs, served on a hamburger bun with chili beans, pickles, and mustard.

If you're looking for that rare combo of high-quality food with a ridiculously low price tag (who isn't?), head straight to **Los Colorines** (201 E. Main Dr., Suite 114, 915/544-5565, $4–9, breakfast and lunch only). As strange as it sounds, this is an easy yet difficult place to find. The physical landmark—the high-rise Chase bank building downtown—is pretty obvious, but the restaurant inside . . . not so much. You have to enter the building lobby and head past the escalators and around a corner to find the restaurant. It's definitely worth it. Since it's in an office building, Los Colorines is all about lunch—most tables are two-tops occupied by one businessperson—and therefore lunch specials (typically about $4–5). The tortilla soup is top-notch, with crunchy strips of fried tortilla accompanying a hearty chicken stock with fresh avocados, shredded chicken, and tasty cheese. Beef items are especially good here—the flautas are highly recommended—as are the guacamole and salsa. Top your meal off with a Mexican Coke and a smile.

American

El Paso's finest restaurant, (**Cafe Central** (109 N. Oregon St., 915/545-2233, www.cafecentral.com, $11–38) serves haute cuisine in a remarkable art deco building in the heart of downtown. Known for its impressive wine selection and sophisticated menu, Cafe Central is an ideal place for a fancy night on the town in a contemporary environment. Locals love the cream of green chile soup, the subtle yet savory sea bass, and the hearty grilled Angus tenderloin. Other popular menu items include the grilled pork chop with roasted brandied apples and the seared saku tuna crusted in sesame seeds.

For a thick steak with heaping sides of family activities, make the worthwhile trek to **Cattleman's Steakhouse** (30 miles northeast of El Paso in Fabens, 915/544-3200, www.cattlemanssteakhouse.com, $10–39). Out here in the Wild West, a 30-minute drive is just down the street, so locals drop by often to celebrate special occasions with the whole gang. Start your gastric juices flowing with the fluffy, buttery rolls, proceed to the ranch-style beans, and delve into the main attraction—the meaty, juicy prime beef. Attempt to choose from tantalizing options such as the T-bone, rib eye, New York strip, and filet mignon. Meanwhile, the kids will enjoy the outdoor petting zoo, snake pit, maze, playground, and livestock.

Breakfast

It's well worth making the five-minute drive from downtown to experience El Paso's **Bowie Bakery** (901 Park St., 915/544-6025, $2–5, daily 6 A.M.–9 P.M.). This small spot (note: there are no tables, so plan to take your items to go) is in the city's segundo barrio, a resurgent neighborhood near downtown filled with historic adobe homes and charming corner stores. The baked goods are the big draw here, particularly the traditional Mexican pastries. Bowie Bakery is a favorite among locals who line up every morning for hot coffee and perfectly prepared empanadas de pina (delectable pineapple turnovers), esponjas, and a cream-filled swan pastry that tastes as sweet as it looks.

INFORMATION AND SERVICES

To gather maps, brochures, directions, and other travel-related assistance, visit the **El Paso Convention Center and Visitors Bureau** (1 Civic Center Plaza, 915/534-0601, www.elpasocvb.com, Mon.–Fri. 8 A.M.–5 P.M., Sat.–Sun. 10 A.M.–3 P.M.). Five miles west of town on I-10 is a handy **Tourist Information Center** (8799 S. Desert Blvd., 915/886-3468, daily 8 A.M.–5 P.M.) operated by the Texas Department of Transportation. It's not quite as heavy on the El Paso info, but the selection of Texas maps and publications is extensive.

GETTING THERE AND AROUND

The quickest way to get to El Paso is via the **El Paso International Airport** (6701 Convair Rd., 915/772-4271, www.elpasointernationalairport.com), located about five miles east of downtown. The airport operates international flights from most major airlines, including American, Continental, Delta, Southwest, and United.

The airport offers taxi and car rental services (cab fare to downtown runs as little as $10–15), and El Paso's public transportation service, **Sun Metro** (915/533-1220, www.elpasotexas.gov), provides bus routes from the airport to downtown.

Once in town, Sun Metro is a cheap way to get around ($2 for a day pass), with dozens of bus lines running to all parts of the city.

Guadalupe Mountains National Park

Beckoning high in the distance to a surprisingly low number of travelers, the Guadalupe Mountains are an underappreciated natural wonder straddling the Texas–New Mexico border. Located 110 miles east of El Paso and 56 miles south of Carlsbad, New Mexico, Guadalupe Mountains National Park contains more than 86,000 acres with elevations ranging from 3,650 to 8,749 feet—the summit of Guadalupe Peak, the highest point in Texas. Travelers who make the effort to visit this remarkably rugged and remote park are rewarded with deep canyons, the world's finest example of a fossilized reef, a rare mixture of plant and animal life, and West Texas's only legally designated wilderness.

Historically, this was the land of the Mescalero Apaches before western-bound settlers arrived in the mid-1800s. Though a proposed transcontinental railroad line through Guadalupe Pass never transpired, the Butterfield Overland Mail route traversed the area—look for the stainless-steel monument documenting the route's significance near the summit of Guadalupe Peak. By the late 1800s, ranchers and the military had established a presence in the mountains, driving away the Mescalero Apaches for good.

In the early 1920s, geologist Wallace Pratt with the then-tiny Humble Oil and Refining Company (now enormous Exxon) became captivated with the area while scouting for oil in the nearby Permian Basin. In subsequent decades, he bought a significant amount of property in the McKittrick Canyon and eventually donated nearly 6,000 acres that became the nucleus for Guadalupe Mountains National Park. The federal government purchased an additional 80,000 acres of adjacent property, and by 1972, the park was dedicated and formally opened to the public.

The park remains a compelling destination for hikers, backpackers, and campers who appreciate its solitude and challenging terrain. From jagged peaks to smooth sand dunes, deep canyons to sparkling springs, Guadalupe Mountains National Park is a distinctive destination offering inspiration in its remote and rugged beauty.

LAND AND CLIMATE

Rising upward of 8,000 feet above the Chihuahuan Desert, the Guadalupe Mountains occupy a traditionally arid landscape. Summertime temperatures regularly reach the mid-90s, while winter lows can dip into the teens.

Several hundred million years ago, this area was a vast sea, and the impressive rock formations currently on display—particularly El Capitan peak—are a result of a large leftover reef formed by sponges, algae, and the skeletal material of numerous aquatic organisms. In fact, the park's Capitan Reef, as it's known in geological world, is recognized as one of the premier fossil reefs of the world. Incidentally, the millions of years of heat and pressure associated with the decomposition of this organic matter, most notably in the adjacent Permian Basin, transformed it to oil and gas.

Otherwise, the park's terrain is fascinatingly varied, shifting from dry creek beds to tree-lined ridge tops to dramatic canyons and rippling springs. The resulting plant and animal life associated with each area is distinct to this region of the state, offering visitors the intriguing experience of viewing various exotic species.

Guadalupe Mountains National Park

TAKE A PEAK

One of the few categories where Texans can't brag about having the biggest or best is mountains. Regardless, the mere fact the state boasts actual peaks – snow can even accumulate at its mile-and-a-half-high altitudes – is pretty impressive for a place typically associated with a flat, dry desert environment.

Geologically, the state claims 18 mountain ranges, all part of the rugged outcroppings of far West Texas. The most significant peaks are west of the Permian Basin between the New Mexico state line and the Rio Grande. Much of this uplifted area, particularly the Guadalupe Mountains on the New Mexico border, containing Texas's highest elevation (8,749 feet), is considered the far eastern edge of the Rocky Mountain system.

Guadalupe Peak, the tip of Texas's top, is easier to access than most people realize. A well-maintained trail provides a somewhat-gradual ascent to the summit, where visitors are rewarded with breathtaking views of the majestic El Capitan peak, the colorful surrounding canyons, and diverse vegetation. One of the more bizarre items you'll find near the peak is a large steel pyramid erected in 1958 by American Airlines as part of a centennial celebration for the nearby Butterfield Overland Mail stagecoach route.

El Capitan is perhaps the most recognized peak in Texas. With its distinctive blocky crown and sheer rock face, the mountain, at 8,085 feet tall, is the eighth-highest peak in the state. Unlike Guadalupe Peak, however, there isn't a trail to the top, so any attempts to ascend its summit should be cleared with the park's visitors center (a backcountry hiking permit is required). Expect plenty of loose rock, cactus, difficult terrain, and incredible views.

Although the most dramatic and picturesque mountains are in the Guadalupe and Big Bend National Parks, more Texans are familiar with the Davis and Chinati Mountains in the visitor-friendly Marfa and Fort Davis area just north of Big Bend. Historic hotels and lodges, fancy bed-and-breakfasts, and civilized campgrounds (potable water, electricity) draw visitors from across the state who enjoy less-strenuous hikes in Davis Mountains State Park (topped by 8,206-foot-tall Mount Livermore). Even easier is the scenic drive to nearby McDonald Observatory, atop the stunning Mount Locke (6,781 feet).

Don't forget about the Franklin Mountains, providing an attractive natural backdrop to El Paso's urban landscape. Referred to as Texas's largest sustained mountain range, the Franklins boast a top elevation of 7,192 feet at the summit of North Franklin Peak. Ditch the hard-core hiking boots and even the car in favor of Franklin Mountain State Park's Wyler Aerial Tramway, a peak-ascending gondola offering prime views of the surrounding scenery.

The desert environment is a land of extremes, so visitors should plan accordingly—bring sunscreen and water in the summer and hats and gloves in the winter. Rain is fairly uncommon, but random showers can occur at any time, so sleeping under a tent or tarp is advisable. August and September are the rainiest times of the year (averaging about four inches monthly), and the mild temperatures of October and April draw the largest crowds. October is especially busy since Texans relish the rare opportunity to see vibrant fall colors on display.

FLORA AND FAUNA

Because of the uncommon intersection of desert, canyons, and highlands, the park is home to a variety of ecosystems serving as habitat for 60 species of mammals, 289 types of birds, and 55 species of reptiles as well as 1,000-plus varieties of plants.

Many of the park's animals are nocturnal, so you probably won't witness an abundance of scurrying critters during daytime hikes. At night, however, the desert comes to life when cooler temperatures prompt foxes, bobcats, badgers, bats, and even some howling coyotes to emerge from their dwellings in search of food. Early-morning and late-evening creatures include mule deer, javelina, and black-tailed jackrabbits.

Reptiles thrive in the Guadalupe Mountains' harsh daytime conditions, so be on the lookout for lizards (varieties include collared, prairie, and crevice spiny) and snakes (western diamondback rattlesnake, bull snake, and coachwhip). Snakes tend to congregate in rocky areas like dry streambeds, so keep an eye and ear out for their presence. The park's rocky canyons are home to ring-tailed cats (a raccoon relative), rock squirrels, and a variety of reptiles including rock and black-tailed rattlesnakes and tree lizards. Also, don't be surprised if you come across one of the few dozen Rocky Mountain elk descended from a herd brought to the area in the 1920s.

Plant wise, the desert/mountain climate provides a diverse environment for a wide range of flora, from desert-floor cactus species (prickly pear, yucca, and sotol) to pine forests (ponderosa, Douglas fir) that thrive in the cooler elevations. The significant geographical variations in this rugged landscape result in various tress, grasses, and scrub brushes spanning across thousands of acres with more than 6,000 feet of elevation difference.

You'll find some deciduous trees near water sources in the park's higher elevations that mimic the environment in northern climes, but much of the landscape is hardscrabble and arid. These areas produce hearty plants that can withstand severe temperature extremes, powerful winds, and a minimal water supply. Cactus have thick stems that store moisture and spines that help reflect the sun's radiant heat. The park's annual wildflowers grow during the rainy summer season—August and September—with a compacted life cycle to maximize the region's minimal moisture.

CAMPGROUNDS

Two of the park's most popular campgrounds, Pine Springs and Dog Canyon, are accessible by car, but the remaining nine wilderness sites are only reachable by foot. Those interested in roughing it to these remote areas are required to obtain a free backcountry use permit at the Pine Springs Visitor Center or Dog Canyon Campground, where detailed maps are also available. Due to the isolated nature of these sites, it's essential to bring at least a gallon of water per person per day, ample food (open fires are prohibited so a camp stove may also be necessary), and emergency gear such as a first-aid kit, compass, and extra batteries.

For those who enjoy a little potable water with their wilderness camping experience (and who doesn't?), spend the night at either the Pine Springs or Dog Canyon campground. Upon arrival, select a tent or RV site (no hookups or dump station are available) and pay at the self-registration board near the restrooms. The fee is $8 per night per site.

Pine Springs

Located near the park's headquarters and visitors center, Pine Springs is the largest of the two main campgrounds, featuring 20 tent and 19 RV sites in a simple desert camping area at the base of the mountain. Small trees shade most of the graveled tent sites, but the RV area is basically a big ol' paved parking lot. The campground features safe drinking water, accessible flush-toilet restrooms (no shower facilities), a utility sink, pay telephones, and a drink machine.

Dog Canyon

Sitting more than 6,200 feet above the desert, Dog Canyon campground is in a secluded, tree-filled canyon on the north side of the park. Its higher elevation and sheltered location beneath steep cliff walls result in cooler temperatures than Pine Springs. However, the canyon also protects the area from strong winds that blast through this part of the park in winter and spring. Dog Canyon campground has nine tent sites and four RV sites along with restrooms containing sinks and flush toilets but no showers. Cooking grills are available for charcoal fires since the area isn't quite as dry and windy as other parts of the park.

HIKING

If you're not up for an overnight stay, the best way to appreciate Guadalupe Mountains State Park is by putting boot to rocky terrain on one of the breathtaking hiking trails. More than a dozen options are available (check with the park's visitors center about length and difficulty), but visitors can experience several of the most popular treks—or at least the most scenic portions—in a day. In addition, smaller self-guided nature trails are available at the park's headquarters, McKittrick Canyon, and at Dog Canyon.

McKittrick Canyon Trail

To fully experience the majesty of McKittrick Canyon, considered by some to be one of Texas's most captivating natural wonders, allow most of the day to reach the high ridges. Start at the McKittrick Canyon Visitor Center, where you'll descend two miles into the canyon before reaching the first significant milestone— Pratt Cabin, a 1929 structure constructed for geologist and land donator William Pratt. Continue another mile to the gorgeous Grotto Picnic Area, one of the most scenic areas in the entire canyon. If you have the extra time and stamina, continue four more miles to McKittrick Ridge for magnificent views of the colorful canyon walls and rugged surrounding outcroppings.

◖ Guadalupe Peak Trail

Accessible from Pine Springs Campground, Guadalupe Peak Trail is highly recommended for the stunning views atop the highest point in Texas. Fortunately, the trail is in good shape, and despite the seemingly daunting task of ascending to an elevation of more than 8,000 feet, the trek isn't overly strenuous. At four miles long (one-way), the trail is more than just a quick day hike. A campsite located about a mile before the summit is a good spot to take a break and eat a picnic lunch among the breezy pines and sun-drenched mountain ridges.

El Capitan Trail

Beginning at Pine Springs Campground, this trail offers a compelling experience of desert savanna and a tremendous view of the dramatic El Capitan peak. The trail doesn't lead to the summit—the distinctive formation is sheer vertical rock wall—but it gradually climbs along its base. Hikers can choose to descend farther into the canyon after skirting the peak, but the hike is rigorous. Consider heading back to Pine Springs after experiencing the grandeur of El Capitan.

INFORMATION AND SERVICES

To get started on your journey, drop by the park's headquarters/visitors center at Pine Springs, accessible via U.S. Highway 62/180 (look for the signs on the highway—there isn't much else out here). Pick up a stack of maps and brochures, find out the current weather forecast, view an orientation slide show and interpretive exhibits, browse the bookstore, and talk to the knowledgeable and friendly park staff about your plans. Adjacent to the center is the Pinery Trail, a paved pathway with scenic views and educational panels providing information about the native plants. The short trail leads to the Butterfield Overland Mail stage station's historic ruins.

The visitors center is open daily 8 A.M.– 4:30 P.M. (Mountain Standard Time) in the winter and until 6 P.M. in warmer months— generally April through October. Chat with the helpful park ranger, browse the impressive book selection, purchase a T-shirt, and check out the adequate exhibits dedicated to the park's history and natural assets. The entrance fee is $5 per person ages 16 and older, and the park pass you'll receive is valid for seven days. For more information, call the visitors center at 915/828-3251 or visit www.nps.gov/gumo.

Midland and Odessa

It may not be fair to lump these two distinctly different cities together, but they have more in common than they're willing to admit. Both cities can lay claim to the three p's: petroleum, pigskin, and presidents. Still, there's a fierce Midland vs. Odessa rivalry befitting of fiery West Texans, and like most neighboring communities in rural America, the competition between the two is hashed out on the football field. Unlike typical towns, however, the intensity of this gridiron action has been documented in the essential *Friday Night Lights* body of work (book, movie, and TV show).

The entire region is known as the Permian Basin, a reference to the vast Permian Sea that once covered much of the area nearly 300 million years ago. Native American tribes populated the region for much of the past 12,000 years before pioneer settlers arrived in the mid-1800s. The dry, dusty landscape appealed to only the hardiest of frontier settlers, who braved the conditions to (barely) make a living in ranching. In the late 1920s, oil was discovered deep beneath the sedimentary layers of the Permian Basin, forever altering the fate of Midland (population 96,573) and Odessa (91,113).

Thanks to the foresight of an entrepreneur named T. S. Hogan, who commissioned the construction of a stately 12-story office building in anticipation of the oil boom, Midland became the business center of the region. Though momentum slowed briefly during and after the Great Depression, exploration and drilling began again in haste in the 1950s, setting the big boom in motion. At one point, there were more than 600 oil companies, and the numerous multistoried corporate offices popping up downtown earned Midland the nickname "the tall city of the plains."

It was during this time that the two communities began taking on distinct identities. Midland became the white-collar town, with banks and businesses picking up where Hogan had left off by eagerly processing and

capitalizing on the abundance of cash that flowed in conjunction with the precious black gold. Conversely, Odessa became the blue-collar city, where many of the roughnecks (oil workers) resided.

These able-bodied men who handled the massive oil rigs and drilling equipment became fathers of equally brawny teenage sons, who excelled on the gridiron. These hulkish kids—some topping out at six feet five, 300-plus pounds—became local heroes, playing college-caliber ball for crowds of 20,000 strong. The phenomena was eloquently captured in H. G. "Buzz" Bissinger's captivating book *Friday Night Lights,* which eventually became an equally compelling movie and television show.

Another source of local pride is the Bush family presidential legacy. Though neither of the Georges were born in the Permian Basin, they spent formative years here, and both cities are eager to lay claim to the title of the Bushes' hometown. The family spent several years shuffling between Odessa and California before finally settling in Midland (and ultimately Houston). Their lives and times in West Texas are on display at Odessa's presidential museum and both cities' George W. Bush childhood homes.

SIGHTS
◖ The Petroleum Museum

You'll learn everything you ever needed (or wanted) to know about the industry that forever changed the lives of millions at The Petroleum Museum (1500 I-20 W. in Midland, 432/683-4403, www.petroleummuseum.org, Mon.–Sat. 10 A.M.–5 P.M., Sun. 2–5 P.M., $8 adults, $6 seniors and students, $5 children 6–11). This enormous, lofty-ceilinged structure contains information and exhibits related to every possible aspect of the oil industry, from prehistoric geological conditions and historic drilling equipment to current trends in oil recovery. Though the immense number of

© TEXAS HISTORICAL COMMISSION

the Permian Basin Petroleum Museum

artifacts and technical information about the minutiae of the industry can be overwhelming at times, there are gems that offer fascinating insight. For example, there's a rotating drill bit in one exhibit room that dug a 5.6-mile-deep (!) well over the course of three years, requiring 166 replacements, including 21 diamond-infused bits. Other museum attractions include several galleries devoted to Western art and children's activities, and an area called "the oil patch" that features thousands of objects, from antique drilling equipment to modern machinery, in a 40-acre exhibit area behind the museum.

American Airpower Heritage Museum

Depending on how you arrive to the region, the American Airpower Heritage Museum (9600 Wright Dr., 432/567-3010, www.airpowermuseum.org, Tues.–Sat. 9 A.M.–5 P.M., $10 adults, $9 seniors and teens, $7 children 6–12) is either extremely convenient or somewhat inconvenient to visit. Located on the grounds of the Midland International Airport, the museum is certainly worth experiencing, primarily for its extensive dedication to World War II events and artifacts, and its impressive collection of vintage aircraft. Visitors pass through the American Combat Airmen Hall of Fame before entering the museum's main exhibit space, a large hall presenting the events of World War II in chronological order. Vintage photos, uniforms, and weapons tell the story of the war's origins, major events, and chilling conclusion. Highlights include a fascinating Pearl Harbor video and exhibit, several large-scale dioramas featuring battle scenes and home-front activities, and a somewhat-unsettling area called "the awful weapon" dedicated to the atomic bombs and their devastating impact.

Another interesting portion of the museum is the gallery area, particularly the exhibit devoted to aircraft nose art. Giant slabs of steel from the front section of bombers and fighters feature pinup-style paintings of women with double-entendre titles such as *Night Mission, Sloppy But Safe,* and *Sack Time.* Despite being

MOJO WORKING

High school football is a religion in Texas, and in Odessa, the faithful worship at the shrine of Ratliff Stadium. This megasize monolith, with an astoundingly enormous capacity of 19,500, inspired the title of H. G. "Buzz" Bissinger's 1991 book *Friday Night Lights,* a fascinating story about the Permian High School (Odessa) football team's unforgettable 1988 season.

The book became a cultural phenomenon, spawning a successful movie and inspirational TV show chronicling the life of a football-crazed town dealing with typical issues in a rural America: family relations, religion, and especially racism. Bissinger's account of Odessa was so detailed — his journalism background inspired him to intensively research and report his findings — it upset many locals, who objected to a seemingly unflattering portrayal of their community. Upon release of his book, Bissinger became persona non grata in Odessa, despite the national attention Permian High School received for its football program.

The Odessa/Midland area holds a unique distinction when it comes to producing gridiron giants. The kids here are exceptionally big, many spawning from brawny oil riggers and burly roughnecks who operate the heavy equipment in the nearby oil fields. It's common in these parts to see 300-pound teenag-ers towering over standard-size six-foot-tall mortal men. Step into a local burger joint at lunchtime on Friday, and you'll find tables full of hulking kids in letterman jackets devouring plates of gigantic burgers in just a few bites.

They're just as ravenous when they take the field. The Permian Panthers and cross-town archrivals the Midland Lee Rebels are two of Texas's most successful high school football programs. Their supersize students often play college-caliber ball, and their achievements are the stuff of legend among Texas's gridiron geeks. Permian claims two national championships (1972 and 1989) and six state championships (1965, 1972, 1980, 1984, 1989, and 1991), while Midland Lee boasts three consecutive state championships (1998-2000). The schools' most famous football alumni are NFL stars Roy Williams (Permian) and Cedric Benson (Midland).

In the late 1960s, Permian fans began using the term "mojo" to describe the magic and emotion associated with their beloved Panthers' prowess, and the term quickly became an enthusiastic rallying cry representing the intensity of the ferocious players and fans. A testament to the power of the word permanently graces the high school's front facade, which boasts four enormous black letters requiring no explanation around here: MOJO.

in a gallery, the artwork isn't museum quality, but it represents a significant aspect of the lives of World War II soldiers; namely, the importance of inspiration, fun, luck, and individual expression. The Airpower Museum's tour ends at a colossal hangar, containing a rotating fleet of vintage aircraft in various stages of repair. The on-site Commemorative Air Force owns an impressive collection of historic planes, many of which are still in great demand at air shows across the country. Among the fascinating aircraft on-site are the massive B-29 Superfortress bomber known as *Fifi* and a huge cargo plane (C-46) called the *Tinker Belle.*

The Presidential Museum and Leadership Library

This museum (4919 E. University Ave. in Odessa, 432/363-7737, Tues.–Sat. 10 A.M.–5 P.M., $8 adults, $5 seniors and children) was conceived well before both George Bushes ascended to the presidential throne. Originating after the 1963 assassination of John F. Kennedy, the museum was located in Odessa's main library before moving to fancy new digs in the early '00s. Visitors first encounter a large rotunda area featuring a life-size replica of the presidential seal rug that lies in the real Oval Office, and then proceed through an intriguing exhibit

The Presidential Museum

area containing profound quotes from past commanders in chief, the presidents of the Republic of Texas (natch), and separate display cases devoted to each of the U.S. presidents in chronological order. The individual Plexiglas boxes contain fascinating artifacts and memorabilia, including coins, printed mementos, and campaign buttons representing the past 230 years of American history. Perhaps most popular, however, is the plain little house behind the museum. This modest postwar structure was home to the Bush family (George H. W., Barbara, and George W.) in the late 1940s and was moved from its original location to the museum grounds in 2006. The museum proudly claims to have the only home to ever be occupied by two presidents and a first lady, which was painstakingly restored and decked out to its authentic 1948 appearance.

The George W. Bush Childhood Home

Regardless of political leanings, it's quite compelling to learn personal details about a leader of the free world. Get a glimpse of this type of domesticity at the George W. Bush Childhood Home (1412 W. Ohio St. in Midland, 432/685-1112, www.bushchildhoodhome.org, Tues.–Sat. 10 A.M.–5 P.M., Sun. 2–5 P.M., $5 adults, $3 seniors, $2 students). Built in 1939, the plain yet comfy home was the Bush family residence from 1951 to 1955, when George W. was roughly 5–9 years old. Like the Odessa house, it's been redecorated based on photos and personal recollections to authentically represent the family's surroundings at the time. The highlight is little George's room, filled with '50s memorabilia depicting the activities he was involved with at the time, namely Little League, Cub Scouts, and the Roy Rogers fan club. Other rooms replicate the homey feel of the kitchen and den, and the remaining spaces contain computer screens with '50s TV shows and commercials, as well as photos and informative panels putting the family's life and Midland history in context.

Odessa Meteor Crater

The Odessa Meteor Crater (five miles west of Odessa off I-20, exit 108, 432/381-0946, self-guided tours daily 9 A.M.–6 P.M.) is an . . . out-of-this-world experience. Billed as the second-largest crater in the United States (only the Arizona Crater is bigger), it was formed nearly 50,000 years ago when a shower of nickel-iron meteorites crashed into Earth, resulting in a 100-foot-deep, 550-foot-wide depression. Over time, accumulated sediments filled the crater to within six feet of the level of the surrounding plain, but visitors can still easily discern the recessed area on the flat West Texas prairie. In the 1940s, scientists dug a 165-foot-deep shaft in the center to try to find the big meteorite they assumed was still buried. They didn't find anything, supporting the subsequent theory that the 350-ton meteor was traveling so quickly, it exploded and vaporized upon contact with Earth. An interpretive center provides exhibits and a video related to the exploration of the Odessa Meteor Crater and related scientific facts.

The Haley Library and History Center

Though it's set up for serious researchers of Western heritage, The Haley Library and History Center (1805 W. Indiana Ave. in Midland, 432/682-5785, www.haleylibrary. com, Mon.–Fri. 9 A.M.–5 P.M., free admission) is worth dropping by for a quick visit. Named for overachieving rancher and writer J. Evetts Haley, who interviewed more than 700 Southwestern pioneers, the facility contains a modest yet impressive collection of Western artifacts and a tremendous archive of books and documents dedicated primarily to ranching culture. Visitors interested in Texana will delight in seeing the historic bell that once hung at The Alamo as well as the numerous saddles from regional pioneer families and the remarkable collection of silver spurs. The building also hosts occasional exhibits featuring the work of local and regional artists.

Museum of the Southwest

Housed in a sprawling 1937 mansion is the misleadingly grand-sounding Museum of the Southwest (1705 W. Missouri Ave. in Midland, 432/683-2882, www.museumsw.org, Tues.–Sat. 10 A.M.–5 P.M., Sun. 2–5 P.M., free admission). The magnificent home is the main attraction here, offering a glimpse of a rich oil baron's homestead during Midland's boom years. Constructed on 12 contiguous lots, the 5,300-square-foot palace exudes opulence, with nearly a dozen fireplaces and ornamental architectural details. The art exhibits scattered throughout the rooms and added galleries aren't quite as impressive, featuring a smattering of Western paintings and pottery. The expansive complex also includes a decent yet small children's museum and one of the only planetariums open to the public in West Texas.

Ellen Noel Art Museum

For a blue-collar town, Odessa has a rather impressive cultural facility in the Ellen Noel Art Museum (4909 E. University, 915/550-9696, www.noelartmuseum.org, Tues.–Sat. 10 A.M.–5 P.M., Sun. 2–5 P.M., free admission). The museum's three main galleries contain permanent and traveling exhibits typically showcasing modern art, historic paintings, and installation work. Even more intriguing is the outdoor portion of the museum, a "sculpture and sensory garden" designed with visually impaired children in mind. Everything in the garden is dedicated to senses other than sight—particularly touch, sound, and smell. A flowing fountain provides soothing sounds and cool tactical sensation, while various herbs offer fragrant and soft or scratchy leaves.

◖ Monahans Sandhills State Park

For a true otherworldly experience, visit Monahans Sandhills State Park (exit 68 on I-20 W., 432/943-2092, www.tpwd.state.tx.us, daily 8 A.M.–10 P.M., $3 admission fee). Rising out of the West Texas desert scrub are miles of smooth, rotund, blindingly white sand dunes. These seemingly out-of-nowhere formations are a result of desert winds exposing ancient layers of sediment left behind by Pecos River erosion. Nowadays, families flock to the park with

© TEXAS HISTORICAL COMMISSION

Monahans Sandhills State Park

their saucer sleds to "sandsurf," which is exactly what it sounds like—cruising down a steep hill with the help of a plastic contraption. It's kind of like snow sledding, just without the snow or subfreezing temperatures. Unfortunately, the idea of it is more fun than the reality—ice is much slicker by nature than sand. Traversing the dunes is an experience unto itself (wear sandals or shoes with some stable support), and it's especially fascinating to keep tabs on the myriad critter tracks, including snakes, birds, and lizards. Camping and picnic areas are available, and the park store offers sleds for sale or rent.

ACCOMMODATIONS
Midland

Travelers shouldn't have to spend a lot of money on a hotel room in the middle of nowhere, but many Midland accommodations don't adhere to this philosophy. Fortunately, there are several worthy options in the semiaffordable range, including the **Plaza Inn** (4108 N. Big Spring St., 432/686-8733, www.plazainnmidland.com, $83 d). Though it caters largely to a business crowd, it's still a decent home away from home for a few nights. The Plaza offers Internet access and a free continental breakfast. Another notable spot near downtown is **La Quinta Inn** (4130 W. Wall St., 432/697-9900, www.lq.com, $85 d), featuring free Internet access and breakfast, as well as an outdoor pool.

For those looking to experience the upper echelon of Midland society, make reservations at the (**Hilton Midland Plaza** (117 W. Wall St., 432/683-6131, www.hilton.com, $124 d). Located in the heart of the downtown business district, the 250-room Hilton offers panoramic views of the wide open plains and the city skyline. The Hilton's amenities include free Internet access, a large fitness center and pool, and a swanky rooftop bar overlooking the city's Centennial Plaza.

Odessa

Odessa has more affordable rates than Midland, but most of the sub-$50 options are older hotels and motels badly in need of an

WRANGLING THE WORLD'S FIRST RODEO

Attempting to lasso the legend of the world's first rodeo is almost as tough as roping an ornery steer in a dusty arena. Many western U.S. cities claim to have hosted the first rodeo-style event, but the West Texas town of Pecos appears to have the strongest case for this distinction.

Eyewitness accounts gathered in 1928 by a Pecos journalist detail the firsthand experiences of cowboys who participated in the 1883 event that's now referred to as the first rodeo. According to these reports, several men were hanging out at a local saloon when discussion turned to steer roping and bronco busting abilities. After some hemming and hawing, plans were made to host a July 4th competition to coincide with the crowds in town for a holiday picnic. What sets the Pecos event apart from other "first rodeo" claims is its distinction of being held in town for spectators and with prizes awarded to the winning cowboys.

By laying claim to hosting the world's first rodeo, Pecos has encountered its fair share of naysayers. Communities in other Western states – Colorado, Arizona, and Oklahoma, to name a few – have disputed the title, but Pecos has fought diligently to prove its authenticity.

In an effort to make things official, an appeal was made to *Encyclopedia Britannica* in the 1930s by providing signed affidavits from Pecos residents who'd attended the rodeo event. Although encyclopedia researchers were eventually convinced about the authenticity of Pecos's claims, the official documents were lost in the process.

Another twist in this serious saga came in the mid-1980s, when the board game Trivial Pursuit included a question about a "rough-and-tumble Western sport" being first formalized in Arizona. Not surprisingly, the quiz card reference wasn't a trivial matter to Pecos residents, who reportedly threatened to sue the game company if the information wasn't changed. Ultimately, the wording wasn't changed since the game company decided the word *formalized* accurately applied to the Arizona event.

Regardless, Pecos maintains its claim to the title, and the community still hosts its annual West of the Pecos Rodeo each summer, drawing some of the sport's most accomplished athletes and thousands of spectators from across the country. The event has been held at its present location since 1936, and even though the memories of the first rodeo have long since faded into the vast, panoramic sky, the spirit of the 1883 competition endures in this proud West Texas community.

---

upgrade. For a bit more money, travelers can lodge in comfort with all the necessary amenities. The best value in town (and virtually a required stay if you're traveling with children) is the **(MCM Grande Hotel and Fun Dome** (6201 E. I-20 Business, 432/362-2311, www.mcmgrande.com, $79 d). The Grande, also referred to as the "fundome," caters to families with its indoor atrium area containing a playscape, nine-hole minigolf course, indoor/outdoor pool, and game tables. The rooms feature genuinely comfortable beds, and the free specials are equally impressive: hot breakfast, free Internet access, and complimentary drinks at happy hour. Similarly priced yet not quite as fun is **La Quinta** (5001 E. I-20 Business, 432/333-2820, www.lq.com, $92 d). Located about 10 miles west of the Midland airport, La Quinta offers free Internet access in all rooms, a complimentary continental breakfast, and an outdoor pool with a large sundeck.

Billing itself as West Texas's "only four-star hotel" is the **MCM Elegante** (200 E. University Blvd., 432/368-5885 or 866/368-5885, www.mcmelegante.com, $99 d). The Elegante prides itself on top-notch service not always found at run-of-the-mill establishments in town, with luxuries such as a bellman, a spa and salon, and an extensive recreation area (jogging track, putting and chipping green, practice fields, horseshoe pits, and a playground), as well as free Internet access and quality bedding.

Camping

Conveniently located between Midland and Odessa is the **Midland KOA** (exit 126 off I-20, 432/563-2368, www.koa.com). Tent sites are available for a fairly hefty fee ($17), as are full hookup spots ($25). For those not wanting to rough it too much, the campground offers cabins for around $35. For a truly distinctive camping experience, consider spending the night among the sand dunes at **Monahans Sandhills State Park**.

FOOD
Midland
AMERICAN

Midland's white-collar sensibilities are on full display at the (**Wall Street Bar and Grill** (115 E. Wall St., 432/684-8686, $10–29). Located on the city's big-money street with all the tall buildings, this well-heeled and high-quality restaurant caters to the business crowd with copies of the *Wall Street Journal* in the bar area and a stock ticker running over the entryway. The food reflects the tony surroundings, with hearty flavorful steaks and succulent seafood dishes the menu items of choice. Also notable is **Café at the Gardens** (3300 Fairgrounds Rd., 432/687-1478, www.alldredgegardens.com, $8–20), located outside of town at Alldredge Gardens, one of Midland's premiere greenhouse and nursery operations. Locals have long been taking root at the café for the tasty wraps and gourmet pizzas at lunch and the seafood entrées (snapper étouffée, crab cakes) for dinner.

MEXICAN

One of the top choices for Mexican food in Midland is **La Bodega** (2700 N. Big Spring St., 432/684-5594, $6–13). Known for its remarkable interior Mexican food, the restaurant's specialty is its chile relleno, prepared with seasoned beef stuffed in a not-too-spicy chile, which is peppered with raisins and pine nuts. An added bonus: The margaritas here are some of the best in town. Note: Smoking is still allowed in the restaurant, so you may get a mouthful of smoke with your chips and salsa.

Another popular Mexican *restaurante* is the deceptively named **Caramba's Spanish Inn** (3116 W. Front St., 432/520-9724, $6–12). Despite the name, there are no Iberian specialties here, although many of the waitstaff speak the Spanish language. Caramba's specialties include traditional Mexican fare such as enchiladas (try the green chile chicken), tacos, burritos, and nachos.

Odessa
AMERICAN

Odessa doesn't have a reputation as a cuisine capital, but several restaurants in town do a respectable job with the basics, which around here means meat. One of the best representations of Odessa eats is **The Barn Door Steakhouse** (2140 Andrews Hwy., 432/580-7019, www.odessabarndoor.com, $9–20). There's something endearing about the hokey Western decor and theme, probably because it's the way things have been here for decades, offering the same kind of familiarity as the comfort food on the menu. Meals begin with a big block of cheese and a fresh loaf of bread, and there's more homey goodness to be found among the entrées—charbroiled steaks are the main draw here, but the chicken dishes and fried shrimp are popular, too.

Barbecue is a safe bet in a town like Odessa, and one of the best places to sample the local flavor is **Jack Jordan's Bar-B-Q** (4605 Oakwood Dr., 432/362-7890, $7–13). West Texans are a fiery bunch, so it shouldn't come as a surprise that they like their barbecue spicy. The sauce here has a nice bite, orders come with jalapeños on the side, and a big bottle of Tabasco sauce is on each table. Despite the fact it's located in an uninspiring locale, people come here for the food, and in West Texas, that means beef. When they say ribs around here, they don't mean pork.

MEXICAN

For a Texas town of nearly 100,000, there are surprisingly few options for quality Mexican food in Odessa. One of the consistently reliable choices is **La Bodega** (1024 E. 7th St.,

432/333-4469, $7–14). Operated by the same crew as the Midland outfit, La Bodega offers the same quality Mexican cuisine, including the famous chile relleno. Another noteworthy spot is **Dos Amigos Bar & Grill** (4700 Golder Ave., 432/368-7556, www.dosamigoscantina. com, $7–14). Housed in an old horse stable, Dos Amigos has become better known as a live music and bull riding venue lately than as a restaurant, but their food remains decent, and it tastes even better when a band is accompanying the meal from the large stage across the large courtyard. You can't go wrong with the chicken enchiladas or anything else smothered in the New Mexico–style green chile sauce. Incidentally, the queso here is outstanding.

INFORMATION AND SERVICES

Midland and Odessa each have a convention and visitors bureau promoting attractions and events in their communities. To find out everything you need to know about Midland, including maps, brochures, and advice, contact the **Midland Convention & Visitors Bureau** (109 N. Main St., 432/683-3381 or 800/624-6435, www.visitmidlandtexas.com). For Odessa, get in touch with the **Odessa Convention and Visitors Bureau** (700 N. Grant, Suite 200, 800/780-4678, www.odessacvb.com).

GETTING THERE AND AROUND

The **Midland International Airport** (9506 Laforce Blvd., 432/560-2200, www.flymaf. com) is located exactly 10 miles between both cities and offers service from several major airlines. Although some hotels offer shuttle service, you'll be stuck there since the public transportation systems are virtually nonexistent. Renting a car from the airport is the best option for getting around, especially since there are several interesting places worth visiting (Monahans Sandhills State Park, in particular) that require 20-plus miles of driving.

BIG BEND REGION

Everything about the Big Bend area is vast—the sky, the views, the mountains, the canyons, and especially the sense of wonder. It's a true getaway to a relatively untouched land, where the natural elements dominate the landscape and the visitors simply marvel at its beauty.

What sets this region apart from the rest of Texas is the presence of mountains. The relatively accessible Davis Mountains in Fort Davis are fairly impressive, featuring giant outcroppings of red rock rising thousands of feet into the West Texas sky, but the state's magnificent mighty peaks are in Big Bend's Chisos Mountain range. A portion of Big Bend even invokes the Rocky Mountains in Colorado, with sheer vertical drops looming right outside the car window and tight switchbacks providing an element of suspense.

Though Marfa has landed on the radar of the international art community, the rest of the Big Bend area is desolate and unknown to most people outside the region. One look at a map reveals the lack of civilization, with vast areas of empty space dotted only by small towns with strange names like Study Butte, Balmorhea, and Van Horn.

It's this desolation, however, that makes the Big Bend region so appealing. The solitude and seclusion amid a gorgeous backdrop of rugged beauty are ultimately soul cleansing. You never realize how many utility poles, wires, and billboards surround you in everyday life until they're removed from your environment. Only then do you begin appreciating the sight of milk-white clouds and fascinating native flora, and the endearing sound of chattering birds.

© TEXAS HISTORICAL COMMISSION

HIGHLIGHTS

◖ **Santa Elena Canyon:** One of Big Bend's most dramatic natural features, Santa Elena Canyon's sheer cliffs—more than 1,500 feet high on each side of the Rio Grande—are absolutely mesmerizing (page 360).

◖ **Lost Mine Trail:** Considered one of the ultimate Big Bend hikes, Lost Mine Trail offers an ideal combination of moderate grades, extraordinary vantage points, and stupendous scenery (page 361).

◖ **Terlingua:** The liveliest ghost town you'll ever experience, this Big Bend neighbor draws tourists from across the globe in search of its quality restaurants, trendy lodging, funky gift shops, and historic cemetery (page 363).

◖ **Chinati Foundation:** Marfa's world-renowned art museum and artist compound, housed in a former army camp, features some of the world's largest permanent installation artwork (page 369).

◖ **Marfa Lights:** The mysterious Marfa Lights are bouncing, splitting, and disappearing ethereal orbs with no apparent source, unless you believe the theorists who claim they're UFOs, Native American spirits, or swamp gas (page 371).

◖ **McDonald Observatory:** Sitting nearly 7,000 feet high atop the Davis Mountains, the McDonald Observatory offers spectacular views of the heavens via its massive telescopes and famous stargazing parties (page 376).

LOOK FOR ◖ TO FIND RECOMMENDED SIGHTS, ACTIVITIES, DINING, AND LODGING.

These elements have been appreciated by the region's inhabitants for more than 10,000 years. From early archaic native groups to Spanish colonists to Apache and Comanche tribes, people have sought out the area's natural resources—water from the Rio Grande and mountain streams, wild game, rock shelters, and native plants. By the time European settlers arrived in the late 1800s, the Native American groups were displaced, and communities evolved around military posts and railroad stations.

Of the hundreds of thousands of visitors who make the long trek to the Big Bend region annually, the vast majority are Texans. Though you'll see an occasional Midwestern license plate in Big Bend National Park or hear a German accent in Marfa, the natural beauty of the area continues to be a source of fascination and wonder for Texas residents, who find the region equally as compelling and faraway as foreigners do.

PLANNING YOUR TIME

There's a good chance travelers won't find themselves in this remote region of the country too often, so maximizing time in this distinct part of the world is important. The popular West Texas triangle of Marfa–Alpine–Fort Davis is a natural place to start. Plan to spend two

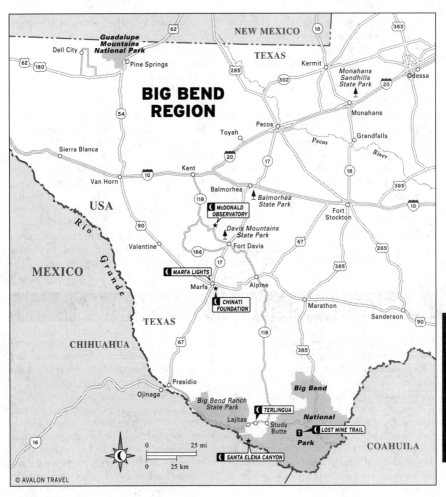

to three days in these towns, with at least half a day set aside for the incomparable Chinati Foundation in Marfa. Fort Davis is a charming Old West town with a day's worth of activities, but Alpine, despite its evocative name, only takes a morning or afternoon to appreciate.

Depending on your comfort level (tolerance for extreme topographical and climactic conditions), plan on spending two to four days in Big Bend National Park and its surroundings. Some visitors never leave the car, choosing instead to soak up the park's natural beauty on scenic drives, but hiking or camping is definitely the best way to appreciate this amazing topographical treasure.

INFORMATION AND SERVICES

For a regional perspective on where to go and how to get there, get in touch with the **Texas Mountain Trail Region** (432/284-0002, www.texasmountaintrail.com, Mon.–Fri.

9 A.M.–5 P.M.), a subsidiary of the Texas Historical Commission's heritage tourism initiative. Their staff members and website will lend a hand with navigating the rocky roads in this rugged part of the state.

For specific advice and printed materials related to the individual communities, contact the **Marfa Chamber of Commerce** (207 N. Highland Ave., 432/729-4942, www.marfacc. com), the **Fort Davis Chamber of Commerce** (#4 Memorial Square, 432/426-3015, www. fortdavis.com), and the **Alpine Chamber of Commerce** (106 N. 3rd St., 432/837-2326, www.alpinetexas.com).

GETTING THERE AND AROUND

For those not making the long haul from another part of the state, this region of West Texas is best accessed by plane. Southwest Airlines offers extremely reasonable rates to the area (occasionally less than $100 one-way) from most major cities in Texas. The best option for affordable rates and proximity to sites is **Midland International Airport** (9506 Laforce Blvd., 432/560-2200, www.flymaf.com), where you can rent a car and be in Big Bend or Marfa within three hours. The other option is **El Paso International Airport** (6701 Convair Rd., 915/780-4749, www.elpasointernational-airport.com), which offers a few more flights; unfortunately, it takes nearly five hours to get to Big Bend and about four hours to Marfa. There is no public transportation available to Big Bend or in the smaller surrounding communities, but the local chambers of commerce can suggest a private shuttle service to provide transportation within the region.

Big Bend National Park and Vicinity

The namesake bend in the Rio Grande isn't the only enormous thing around here—this colossal park encompasses more than 800,000 acres of spectacular canyons, mesmerizing Chihuahuan Desert, awe-inspiring Chisos Mountains, and unexpectedly temperate woodlands. It's the kind of place that words can't quite describe, and photos can't even do it justice. Phrases like "majestic peaks" and "rugged beauty" barely begin to illustrate the Big Bend experience, but they at least offer a glimpse into this ultimate "seen to be believed" destination.

Big Bend is the kind of place where you feel compelled to pull your car over every half a mile to snap a photo of the endless succession of stunning scenes. Avoid the temptation—you can return to the spots later once you've processed their context—and just soak up the natural beauty through your own eyes rather than a viewfinder. Play some appropriate West Texas soundtrack music (Willie Nelson complements the scenery quite nicely) and marvel at the jagged peaks, desert cacti, and sweeping vistas. Just be sure to occasionally keep your eye on the road—the switchbacks on the way to Chisos Mountain Lodge are dramatic hairpin turns with a 10 mph speed limit.

Speaking of speed, other parts of the park are much more open, and it's easy to find yourself cruising at 70 mph en route to the hot springs or the dramatic Santa Elena Canyon. It's okay to slow down. One of the best things about being in Big Bend is leaving the city and daily routine behind you. If the old couple in front of you is plugging along at 40 mph, resist the temptation to pass them and pay attention instead to the javelina lurking in the desert brush or the volcanic rock formations. Unfortunately, just when you've tempered your commute-minded driving habits, you'll be headed back home to rush hour traffic.

It may also be tempting to set an itinerary with goals of hikes or destinations to accomplish within a certain amount of time, but try not to get too caught up with an agenda. Some of the best experiences you'll have will be just sitting on a mountainside or relaxing at

© ANDY RHODES

entrance to Big Bend National Park

your campground. The absence of power lines, utility poles, billboard ads, and litter is cathartic, and the cleansing effect on your mind is equally therapeutic.

Sometimes it's necessary to get in touch with civilization (keeping up with your favorite blog, sports team, or office gossip doesn't count), and there are a few places in the park where this is possible. Wi-Fi service is often accessible on the porch of the Chisos Mountains Lodge, and mobile phone service is slightly more reliable—just not in low-lying areas or around mountain peaks.

Aside from missing your email or favorite TV show, the only negative thing associated with Big Bend is its remote location—a blessing and a curse, since it's inconvenient to get to but wonderfully isolated and peaceful. Once you've experienced its many unique charms, you'll be able to justify the long drive for many future visits to this unrivaled natural masterpiece.

LAND AND CLIMATE

Several lengthy books are dedicated to the dynamic geography and climate of Big Bend, so summarizing the myriad scientific descriptions of this vast property is somewhat challenging. Geologists have referred to the diverse terrain as a paradise and a nightmare due to its complex collection of stratified rock, volcanic formations, and windblown sand dunes.

The park's topographical features run the gamut from mountains to canyons to the Rio Grande. However, it's the desert climate that dominates the landscape, with 98 percent of Big Bend classified as part of the Chihuahuan Desert. The key word associated with deserts is *contrast,* as in 50-degree daily temperature extremes, old and new natural erosion from water and wind, and dry stretches punctuated by violent flash flooding.

Though water and deserts aren't typically associated with each other, Big Bend is unique in its access to the Rio Grande and seasonal rains. Water affects all aspects of plant and animal life in the park, and the cycle of wet and dry periods make Big Bend the fascinating natural landscape it's become, supporting intriguing and unfamiliar species ranging from cacti and agave plants to javelina and lizards.

The most obvious contrast in the park is

elevation—the Chisos Mountains rise nearly 8,000 feet tall while the banks of the Rio Grande sit approximately 1,000 feet above sea level. An interesting fact: Air temperature changes by five degrees for every 1,000 feet of elevation, so temperatures in the upper reaches of the Chisos can be more than 20 degrees cooler than they are along the Rio Grande.

On paper, this variation in elevation and temperature makes Big Bend appear to be an ideal year-round park, but in reality, it's only comfortable about seven months a year (October–April). Summertime is ridiculously hot—this is the Chihuahuan Desert, after all—and despite the increased elevation and low humidity, triple-digit temperatures are still brutal. May and June are considered the hottest months since periodic rainstorms later in the summer help ease the intensity (and pain) of the heat. In fact, the park experiences a "rainy" season—typically less than a foot of moisture in the summer months. Because of the complete lack of water from the previous season, there's a mini growth spurt in early fall when colorful blossoms and grasses emerge among the dry landscape.

Some hearty souls aren't deterred by the park's harsh summer conditions, delighting in brisk morning hikes and nippy overnights in the mountains. Big Bend's rainy season even brings occasional heavy thunderstorms and flash flooding. Winter is the most volatile season in Big Bend, with generally mild temperatures, though extremes are possible, from 85°F scorchers to periods of light snow.

FLORA AND FAUNA

With its remarkably diverse geography and climate, it's not surprising Big Bend has a similarly varied collection of plants and animals. Containing more than 650 species of animals (plus 3,600 different kinds of bugs) and 1,000-plus species of plants, the park represents a fascinating laboratory of living things.

While hiking along any of the park's trails—from the short paved loops to the major mountain excursions—be sure to take a moment to physically stop moving and look around. Make

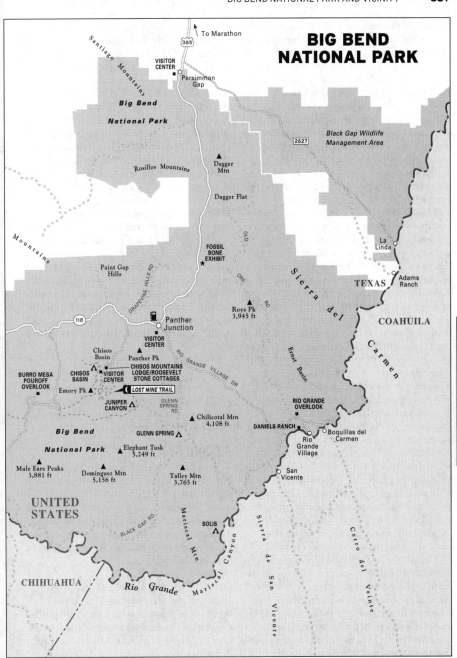

a slow 360-degree turn and take in every detail—it's absolutely unbelievable how many little things you'll notice: bizarre bugs on cactus blossoms, exotic insects on a tree leaf, a round sherbet-orange flower peeking from behind a spiky agave plant. And that's just looking straight ahead. Look down and you'll see giant red ants clamoring into a hole. Look up and you'll find puffy cotton clouds mimicking the shape of the nearby mountain peak. Though it's tempting to forge ahead on the trail and think about where you'll place your next step or how much farther you have to go, you'll truly benefit from a five-minute observation break.

Though Big Bend's animals can be elusive, particularly in the heat of day, its plants are omnipresent and completely intriguing in their variety and just plain weirdness. The Chihuahuan Desert dominates the landscape, so the flora is largely of the scrub and cactus variety. Not surprisingly, Big Bend is home to more species of cacti (65) than any other national park. The tremendous diversity in landscape accounts for the enormous range of cacti, including the ubiquitous prickly pear, pitaya, and claret cup. Those visiting the park in spring or late summer will experience the bonus of seeing cacti in bloom, a colorful display of vivid yellow, red, and pink flowers.

Aside from cacti, one of the most eye-catching species in Big Bend is the century plant, an enormous agave with an equally gigantic distinction: It blooms only once in its 20- to 50-year life, but it makes the most of the situation by producing a colossal 15-foot-tall stalk with bright yellow flowers. Other agave in the park include the lechuguilla, unique to the Chihuahuan Desert, and the gracilipes. Incidentally, agave plants are the source of a natural ingredient found in most tequila.

Trees thrive in Big Bend's higher elevations, particularly oak and juniper. The cooler climate at these heights (upwards of 7,000 feet) mimics the weather in northern states, so it's common to see Douglas fir, quaking aspen, and ponderosa pine, a rare treat for Texans accustomed to the limited varieties of trees associated with arid and subtropical climates.

Animals in Big Bend are a different story. They're equally as intriguing yet far more difficult to find. Two species in particular—mountain lion and black bear—draw the most attention due to their natural ferocity. Several dozen bears and a handful of mountain lions are reported each month, and some of the park's most popular trails (Lost Mine and Window) are hot spots for sightings of both creatures. Park officials advise hikers to ward off bears and mountain lions by intimidating them with loud noises, rock throwing, and plenty of arm waving (seriously).

It's far more fun to catch a glimpse of the javelina, a piglike creature with coarse black hair unique to the deserts of the American Southwest. Also known as the collared peccary, this fascinating fella is active in the cooler times of day, when it can be found munching mainly on prickly pear cactus and agave plants. They've also been known to invade campsites and investigate tents for food, so be sure to safely store everything edible in a vehicle or one of the many bearproof metal boxes located throughout the park.

Other interesting creatures roaming, scuttling, or flying throughout Big Bend include bats (representing the largest portion of the park's mammal species), 31 kinds of snakes, 22 types of lizards, roadrunners, tarantulas, owls, and myriad noisy insects.

RECREATION

There's no shortage of activities in Big Bend National Park, from extreme raft and canoe trips to low-key scenic drives to moderate day hikes. Without a cell phone or TV tethering you to the routines and clockwork of the real world, you can get away at your own pace and spend an entire day outside. It's practically the definition of *recreation*.

Driving in Big Bend

Some people may want to start out at full speed—the mountains can be so inspiring, it's tempting to turn your enthusiasm into energy by hiking or rafting. Others may want to take things slow and get their bearings.

For unbelievably dramatic mountain scenery, it's imperative to make the drive to Chisos Mountains Lodge. Your ears will pop and your jaw will drop as you ascend the road into the mountain range, with the famous formations of Casa Grande and Emory Peak acting as a beacon to the basin. Be sure to keep an eye on the road as you navigate the tight turns amid the stunning surroundings.

An ideal introduction to the complex range of natural wonders at Big Bend is a jaunt along Ross Maxwell Scenic Drive in the western portion of the park. The vast vistas slowly transform to striking views of volcanic rock formations reminiscent of an otherworldly scene straight out of a *Star Trek* episode. Be sure to drop by the historic village of Castolon and set aside about an hour for exploring the small museum exhibits in the charming century-old military structures. This is a good place to grab a snack and a cold drink at the old general store—sit on picnic tables out front to soak up the cliffs of Mexico across the river. Incidentally, the convenience store still feels much like general mercantile shops from the olden days. Unfortunately, you can't buy screwworm medicine or fox pelts here anymore, but you can buy a T-shirt, frozen burrito, or Pepto-Bismol. Nearby, there's a historic adobe house worth walking down the hill to admire, and be sure to step inside the small structures near the general store to see the interesting heritage exhibits.

A few miles down the road is the must-see Santa Elena Canyon. If you're driving a high-clearance vehicle, tackle the nearby Old Maverick Road for the rare chance to experience the invigorating sensation of plowing through rugged terrain just like they do in SUV ads.

Not quite as dramatic yet certainly worth experiencing is the 20-mile drive to Rio Grande Village. The terrain slowly descends as you approach the river, and the charms of the Chihuahuan Desert are in full effect in the blooming cacti, gentle mesas, and occasional javelina. For a little more excitement, take on the narrow mini-overhangs along the short road to the hot springs.

A word of advice: If you're heading out for evening (perhaps for dinner in Terlingua or Marathon), make an effort to get back to the park before sundown. Driving on park roads at night can be somewhat treacherous—especially when critters are out grazing on the roadside. Deer, javelina, and jackrabbits can jump out in front of your car at any time. Also, if you're staying in the basin, you'll have extra motivation to get back in time to catch the amazing view of the sunset through The Window formation near the lodge.

Navigating the Rio Grande

Once you've mastered the scenic drives and hiking trails in Big Bend, you may want to experience the park from a different perspective—by boat. Seeing the canyon walls from the source is imminently rewarding, and many options are available depending on your skill level and spirit of adventure, from Class IV rapids (on a I–V scale) to quiet canoe trips. For a comprehensive list of choices, consult Big Bend's website: www.nps.gov/bibe.

One of the most popular options is Santa Elena Canyon (downstream from Lajitas), a 13-mile adventure featuring easy desert paddling and severe rapid navigating. This stretch of the river is considered the most dramatic, with enormous 1,500-foot-tall cliffs towering overhead and the largest rapid, a class IV run known as Rock Slide. For an easier day trip, consider the "boomerang" jaunt upstream and back to the canyon.

A portion of the park known as **Rio Grande Wild & Scenic River** features several other trips appealing to beginner and intermediate boaters. The 10-mile-long Mariscal Canyon trek provides stunning scenery with 1,400-foot-tall limestone cliffs and some moderately exciting Class II–III rapids. For a longer excursion (2–3 days), consider the 33-mile-long trip through Boquillas Canyon, an ideal choice for beginners, since there aren't any rapids higher than Class II. Even longer (up to 10 days) is a trek through the lower canyons, where floaters can experience true solitude in the wilderness since they often won't encounter another human being for days at a time.

BIG BEND REGION

To find out more about shuttles, equipment rental, and guided trips, contact **Big Bend River Tours** (800/545-4240, www.bigbendrivertours.com), **Desert Sports** (888/989-6900, www.desertsportstx.com), or **Far Flung Outdoor Center** (800/839-7238, www.ffoc.net).

HIKING AND BACKPACKING

Big Bend offers more than 200 miles of hiking trails ranging from short, easy nature walks to primitive mountain trails for experienced hikers. There's truly something for everyone here—families can take their time on moderate trails with printed interpretive brochures as a guide, while hard-core backpackers have the option of taking backcountry trails into the desolate wilderness for challenging treks at their own pace.

Day Hikes
C SANTA ELENA CANYON

Talk about dramatic. You can see the massive walls of Santa Elena Canyon from miles away, but the effect of witnessing these sheer cliffs—more than 1,500 feet high on each side of the surprisingly narrow gap forged by the Rio Grande—is utterly mesmerizing up close. And it only gets better as the trail progresses. It's a 1.6-mile trek, so plan about two hours to fully appreciate the experience. You'll be drawn to the wide swath of river flowing from the massive canyon walls, but the difficult-to-find trail entrance will be off to your right. Look for the crude stone pathway across the shallow creekbed (your feet may get a bit wet), which leads to the trailhead. You'll encounter a series of tight switchbacks and concrete steps before ascending a rocky trail that eventually descends into the canyon. When you reach the end of the trail, you'll be surrounded by the stunning vertical cliff walls, which echo with the sounds of birds and kids (even adults) playing in the water. This is one of the few places in the park where swimming is safe and generally tolerated. Note: In late summer/early fall (after the "rainy" season drops up to a foot of moisture on the park), there will be more

Santa Elena Canyon was carved by the Rio Grande.

© ANDY RHODES

water in the Rio Grande, which affects access to Santa Elena Canyon trail. Instead of being able to walk across the stone pathway, you'll be faced with the not-very-recommended option of wading through several feet of murky water to get to the trail. Never fear—you can still get a sense of wonder just from being at the base of canyon, but you won't get the full experience of being within sheer-cliff walls. There's always next time . . . .

☾ LOST MINE TRAIL

If you're staying at Chisos Mountain Lodge, this is an ideal trail for a nearby morning hike. The cool temperatures are invigorating, and the scenery is stupendous. Considered one of the ultimate Big Bend hikes, Lost Mine Trail offers an ideal combination of moderate grades, a wide range of vegetation, extraordinary vantage points, and a handy interpretive brochure at the trailhead. If you happen to be at the park in late summer or early fall (following the summertime rains), you'll get the bonus experience of seeing the Lost Mine Trail's environs in a mini growth spurt with plenty of subtle colors and emerging flora. Look for red, yellow, orange, and blue blossoms on bushes, trees, cacti, and stems around every bend. Be sure to take a few minutes to stop hiking and do a 360-degree turn, absorbing all the fresh-green growth of new leaves and blooming cactus. If you look (and listen) closely, you'll see unfamiliar insects buzzing over new flowers, completely unaware of your presence.

The trail's 4.8-mile round-trip (roughly four hours) will get you back in time for a much-needed hearty lunch at the lodge's restaurant just a mile down the road. Those looking for a shorter venture are in luck: The most incredible view along the trail (and perhaps in the entire park) is about a mile into the trek—find a comfy rock to lean against and absorb the magnificent far-reaching view of Juniper Canyon. The untouched vista is absolutely mesmerizing—soak up the hundreds of miles of undulating terrain that's offered the same panoramic scene for fortunate viewers for thousands of years.

© ANDY RHODES

a view of Juniper Canyon from the Lost Mine Trail

RIO GRANDE VILLAGE NATURE TRAIL

This short excursion will introduce you to just about everything you'll need to know about Big Bend. It's just under a mile round-trip, but set aside an hour to fully absorb the dramatic vistas and desert intricacies. The trail starts in a somewhat bizarre fashion, with a boardwalk crossing over a body of water originating from the wetland natural spring. It's a strange sight to see, especially since it's immediately followed by a hot and hardscrabble trek across rocky terrain among myriad cacti and desert scrub brushes (a handy guide at the trailhead provides interesting information about the different plants). The highlight is the view from the top of the moderately sloped hill, where you'll find sweeping vistas of the Rio Grande and Mexico. Look for the blocky bright-white adobe buildings about a mile away in the Mexican village of Boquillas. The mighty Chisos Mountains loom in the background, presiding over a natural scene that is unlike any other you'll experience.

Backpacking Trails

Once visitors have experienced the awe-inspiring day hikes, they often feel compelled to take things to the next level. A popular follow-up excursion is to one of the backcountry campsites in the High Chisos Mountains along the trail system to the South Rim. These campsites, varying from one to eight miles each way, are accessible only by foot, and most involve an overnight trek.

For these trips, an overnight backcountry permit is required ($10), available only in person up to 24 hours in advance at all park visitors centers. Park staff can assist you with trip planning based on your needs and current trail conditions.

At 14 miles in length, the South Rim trek takes at least eight hours to complete. The Laguna Meadows trail traverses through a dense forest popular with birders thanks to the abundant oak, maples, junipers, and piñon pine. Be sure to bring plenty of water (at least a gallon per person daily), food, sturdy shoes, and sunscreen.

Another popular backpacking trip is to the Emory Peak campsite, located 3.7 miles from the trailhead via the Pinnacles Trail. Since it's the highest elevation in the park and therefore a quest to be conquered, Emory Peak is a natural draw for many hikers. Not surprisingly, it's rocky and steep, but the payoff comes in astounding views of Boot Canyon and the backside and summit of Emory Peak.

ACCOMMODATIONS AND CAMPING

Many people travel to Big Bend for the amazing camping opportunities (more about those in a bit), but others just want to experience the great outdoors during the day with a reliable roof, walls, and bed frame surrounding them at night. Fortunately, the park offers the **Chisos Mountains Lodge** (432/477-2291, www.chisosmountainslodge.com, rooms average $120 nightly). Situated nearly a mile high in a cozy little basin surrounded by mountain peaks, the lodge offers a no-frills experience befitting of its remote and rugged location. The two-story lodge buildings are thankfully unremarkable in appearance and amenities, prompting guests to spend most of their time on hiking trails or on the sparse porches. In fact, one of the lodge's best amenities is its lack of a TV—you may have to read a book or (gulp) just talk to your fellow travelers while sipping on a tequila or glass of wine. The rooms include tile baths, tubs, and showers; hair dryers; coffee pots; refrigerators; microwaves; and housekeeping service, so you don't have to worry about being too far removed from the comforts of modern civilization.

If you plan far enough in advance (almost a year ahead of time), you can snag a coveted spot in the park's premier accommodations: the **Roosevelt Stone Cottages** (432/477-2291, www.chisosmountainslodge.com, $147 nightly). These five stone cottages are removed from the hub of activity at the main lodge, and each cabin features stone floors and three double beds, showers, hair dryers, coffee pots, refrigerators, microwaves, and ceiling fans (no a/c is available, which isn't usually a problem at this elevation). The cabins are highly recommended, since it's likely you won't be out here very often and the appeal of staying in your own private quarters in this beautiful park is unparalleled. These historic (1940s) cottages are oozing with mountain character, from the regional art and photos on walls, to the welcoming porches, to the big windows that capture a nice gentle breeze. Keep them open at night for perfect sleeping weather—you won't even need to turn on the ceiling fan.

The park also offers three developed campgrounds—**Rio Grande Village, Chisos Basin,** and **Cottonwood Campground** (877/444-6777, www.recreation.gov, sites average $10 nightly plus service fees) for tent camping, trailers, and RVs. Rio Grande Village, located on the far eastern edge of the park among trees (and insects) near the river, has the only available hookups for RVs. The campground has 100 sites, flush toilets, running water, and a dump station. The Basin Campground is the most scenic of the bunch (and closest to the full-service restaurant). It's rugged and hilly, and not recommended for RVs. If you want to wake up in the morning and be immediately greeted by a scenic mountain view, this is the place to be. Cottonwood Campground, on the west side of the park, is in the lowlands of the Rio Grande. It's appealing for its namesake cottonwood trees and proximity to the historic Castolon village and Santa Elena Canyon. Big Bend also offers dozens of primitive camping sites (many are only accessible by high-clearance vehicle or four-wheel drive). These sites typically consist of only a flat gravel pad, and a backcountry permit is required from Park Headquarters.

FOOD

The only place to order a meal in Big Bend National Park is the **Chisos Mountains Lodge Restaurant** (432/477-2291, www.chisosmountainslodge.com, $5–15, open 7 A.M.–2 P.M., 5–8 P.M.). Fortunately, the food here is much better than expected for a remote national park, with a surprisingly varied menu offering regional fare (Tex-Mex, prickly pear cactus

sauces, etc.), standard dishes (sandwiches, pastas), and hearty breakfasts to fuel a long morning trek. "Hikers lunches" are also available as to-go options. The views of the mountains (particularly The Window formation) are stunning through the floor-to-ceiling windows, and it's always nice to know a decent meal is available daily with enough variety (along with beer and wine) to make things interesting for several days' worth of eating.

NEARBY COMMUNITIES AND SIGHTS

The Big Bend region is rife with fascinating communities offering a unique perspective on the region's heritage (the silver mine ghost town of Terlingua) and culture (the desert resort oasis in Lajitas). Consider planning an extra day or two for exploring these areas, or, if you're pressed for time, set aside an evening or afternoon for an excursion to these one-of-a-kind communities.

(Terlingua

This is the liveliest ghost town you'll ever experience. Quality restaurants, trendy lodging, and funky gift shops are just a few of the things you'll encounter in the small community of Terlingua. Even the cemetery here is a major tourist attraction. The town was abandoned after its mercury mines closed in the 1940s (leading to its distinction as a ghost town), but it has since been revitalized as a tourist attraction with several hundred permanent residents.

Some of the souls laid to rest at the cemetery were workers at the Chisos Mining Company, a major quicksilver producer established in 1903. The liquid metal, eventually called mercury, was mined as cinnabar ore and recovered via a baking process to its metallic state. The mining company became one of the nation's leading producers of quicksilver, peaking during World War I when 40 percent of the mercury mined in the United States came from Terlingua.

By World War II, mining operations ceased, leaving Terlingua as a ghost town until the late 1960s, when the village became famous

MINING FOR MERCURY

Unlike most traditional burial sites, the barren and rocky Terlingua cemetery contains above-ground graves covered in shards of stone, with crude wooden crosses often serving as the only adornment. Most of these sites mark the final resting place of the region's quicksilver (mercury) miners, who largely fell victim to the region's harsh environment, mercury poisoning, and disease – all hazards of working for Terlingua's mining companies.

The largest operation by far was the Chisos Mining Co., which owned the town of Terlingua and was operated by mining magnate Howard Perry, a Chicago industrialist. Perry was respected among businessmen but largely despised by the workers, many of them Mexicans who fled to Texas to escape cultural turmoil and the country's revolution. Miners were reportedly paid only $12 daily (or with coupons for Perry's company store) and often received only a bucket of water a day while having to carry 80-pound sacks of ore.

From its opening in 1903 until its bankruptcy in the mid-1940s, the Chisos Mining Co. supplied nearly a third of the country's mercury supply. Initially mined as an ore called cinna-bar, the silver liquid metal that became known as quicksilver (and eventually mercury) is ultimately recovered through a simple baking process completed on-site. The work was arduous – mercury poisoning could be fatal or have devastating side effects, including brain damage and tooth or hair loss.

As demand for mercury escalated, Perry increased production by incorporating more industrialized methods, including a massive furnace and deeper exploration of the mountain ranges, resulting in the discovery of one of the richest veins of cinnabar ore in the Terlingua district. The discovery coincided with the outbreak of World War I, where the U.S. military demand for mercury was high, resulting in the Chisos Mining Co.'s most successful period.

Before vehicles arrived on the scene, the company used mules to deliver the mercury via wagon to the railroad in Alpine. Production declined in the late 1930s, and by 1942 the company filed for bankruptcy. Several years later, the company's buildings and installations were demolished and sold for scrap. Its remaining legacy is represented by the mounds of rock and soil at the Terlingua Cemetery.

for its annual chili cook-off. In 1967, the Chili Appreciation Society named Terlingua the "Chili Capital of the World," and the event continues to draw thousands of people to this deserted desert community.

If you only have a short amount of time to spend here, be sure to visit the **Terlingua Trading Company** (100 Ivey St., 432/371-2234, www.historic-terlingua.com) and adjacent Starlight Theater. These two buildings perfectly capture the Terlingua vibe, with enough lively folk art, friendly locals, and spicy border-influenced food to rouse the spirits at the famed cemetery just down the road. You can easily spend a half hour in the Trading Company, browsing the impressive book collection featuring national, statewide, and regional titles (including the entertaining *Tales from the Terlingua Porch*); Mexican-themed artwork; local snacks; toys; and the requisite Viva Terlingua! T-shirts. And it's almost mandatory to grab a beer at the counter (they're sold by the bottle from a room in the back) and take it out to the porch, where you can enjoy stunning views of the Chisos Mountains while being regaled with colorful stories from the local characters who gather on the porch each evening to do just that (drink and talk).

Plan to have a meal at the adjacent **Starlight Theater** (432/371-2326, www.starlighttheatre.com, $8–27). This historic 1930s theater now serves as a restaurant featuring hearty American fare, regional dishes (the chipotle-glazed pork medallions are a must), and some of the best margaritas you'll ever experience. Also, the filet mignon is well worth the $26.95 (a pricey tag by West Texas standards), especially the grilled option with sautéed garlic and some of the tastiest mushrooms you'll ever experience. A troubadour often accompanies your meal with lonesome Western songs from a small stage in the main dining area.

Other noteworthy eateries in town include **Phat Cafe** (Hwy. 170, 432/371-2520, open for lunch Tues.–Sat. 11 A.M.–2 P.M., dinner Wed.–Sat. at 7 P.M., reservations required, $10–32), a fairly upscale and tiny Asian fusion restaurant featuring fresh vegetables and a perfect pad thai. For a true taste of local flavor and culture, check out **La Kiva Restaurant and Bar** (Hwy. 170, 432/371-2250, www.lakiva. net, daily 5 P.M.–midnight, $6–19). This rustic eatery is known for its top-notch barbecue and mediocre Mexican food—the best bet is the Terlingua Trio, a combo plate of smoked chicken, ribs, and brisket.

Unless you're visiting Terlingua during the raucous chili festival held the first week of November each year, you shouldn't have trouble finding a room. Surprisingly, there are several decent lodging options in and around this tiny village, but the best choice by far is **La Posada Milagro Guest House** (100 La Posada Ln., 432/371-3044, www.laposadamilagro.net, $145 d). The historic stucco and stone facility offers luxury in the midst of the harsh desert climate via its four suites with large comfy beds, air-conditioning, sundecks, fire pits, hammocks, and Wi-Fi service.

Presidio

Located approximately 60 miles west of Big Bend, Presidio (population 4,167) is known for its stunning scenery and its status as the only legal border crossing between El Paso and Del Rio.

Evidence of Native American tribes farming the fertile floodplains in the area dates to the 1200s, and the Spanish had a presence here beginning in the 1500s. As was the case in other areas of Texas, the Spaniards felt is was their mission to "civilize" the native groups, despite their proven ability to successfully cultivate crops, construct sturdy adobe homes, and practice their own religions.

The 1800s saw the arrival of Anglo settlers,

including the controversial frontiersman Ben Leaton, who constructed a large fortress and ostracized locals. In recent decades, Presidio has gained a reputation as the end point of perhaps Texas's most scenic drive, the breathtaking River Road (FM 170), featuring dramatic canyon views and stunning topographic changes along the Rio Grande coming from Lajitas. Presidio's other claim to fame is not quite as enjoyable—its distinction as the hottest town in Texas. In June, temperature-gauge capacities are put to the test with astronomical highs *averaging* 103°F.

Presidio's only real tourist attraction is **Fort Leaton State Historic Site** (FM 170, 915/229-3613, www.tpwd.state.tx.us, daily 8 A.M.–4:30 P.M.), an enormous adobe home built by Leaton in 1848 on the site of former Spanish settlement known as El Fortin de San Jose. Leaton is still considered a controversial figure by Mexican Americans. Originally employed by the Mexican government as a Native American scalp hunter, Leaton reportedly later encouraged Native American raids on Mexican

Fort Leaton's remarkable adobe architecture

© TEXAS HISTORICAL COMMISSION

villages by trading weapons and ammunition for stolen livestock. To this day, some locals of Mexican descent refuse to call the site Fort Leaton, opting instead to use its original name, "el Fortín."

Regardless, the impressive structure is still worth visiting, with more than half of its 40-plus original rooms featuring fully restored adobe walls and roofs with cottonwood beams and rails. It's easy to spend a few hours here just absorbing the fascinating adobe architecture—exposed walls reveal the sun-baked earthen bricks with straw and rocks, and stark wooden door and window frames. Outside, be sure to notice how the sun illuminates the soft corners of the plastered walls, casting evocative shadows and sunrays. Experience West Texas history through the informative exhibits and the region's vernacular architecture in the home's charming living and guest quarters, kitchen, dining room, and outbuildings.

Lajitas

Ever fed a beer to the mayor and watched him try to eat the can afterward? It used to happen regularly in Lajitas (population 150), where the esteemed mayor—a goat known as the Honorable Clay Henry III—held court at the Lajitas Trading Post. Unfortunately, Clay Henry III is no longer with us, but that doesn't mean you can't still honor his legacy.

Located at the far southwestern edge of Big Bend National Park, the tiny village (pronounced La-HEE-tas) draws visitors for its rugged natural beauty and fancy resort complex. Lajitas, Spanish for "little flat rocks," was inhabited by Native Americans for centuries before Anglo settlers arrived. Its namesake smooth rock river bottom was considered one of the best crossings on the Rio Grande between Del Rio and El Paso. In 1916, Lajitas became a center of intense military activity when Gen. John J. Pershing's troops established a major cavalry post to protect the U.S. border against Pancho Villa and his bandits.

By the late 1970s, the town was virtually abandoned until entrepreneurs arrived to construct a luxury resort complex, drawing

travelers from across the world who enjoy a little pampering with their hiking and rafting. The area has also become popular with movie producers who savor the incredibly untouched 360-degree vantage points.

Aside from chugging beers with the mayor, one of the few activities available in Lajitas is the **Barton Warnock Environmental Education Center** (one mile east of town on FM 170, 432/424-3327, www.tpwd.state.tx.us, daily 8 A.M.–5 P.M., $3 admission), showcasing the archaeology, history, and natural wonders of the Big Bend region. The center serves as the eastern gateway to Big Bend Ranch State Park and features exhibits and displays dedicated to 570 million years of geological history and the biological landscapes of the Chihuahuan Desert. A self-guided botanical garden highlights the desert's characteristic flora.

Those looking for a bite to eat in town are in luck since the two restaurants located in the Lajitas Resort and Spa feature high-quality regional fare. On the upscale side is **Ocotillo,** with a surprisingly extensive wine list and a menu offering exquisite West Texas wild game dishes, including the requisite rattlesnake cakes. The **Candelilla Café** features contemporary Southwestern cuisine enhanced with local ingredients like prickly pear cactus, indigenous peppers, and homegrown herbs.

For lodging, there's nothing else like the remarkable **Lajitas Resort and Spa** (FM 170, 877/525-4827, www.lajitas.com, $150–370). This 25,000-acre private estate boasts more than 100 rooms, ranging from modest hotelsize quarters with cowboy chic decor to spacious and elegant hacienda cottages, all with coffeemakers, satellite television (a rare luxury out here), refrigerators, and luxurious amenities. The resort offers myriad packages to choose from, combining lodging options with meals, activities, spa treatments, and day trips. Check the website for available options.

Big Bend Ranch State Park

Located west of Big Bend National Park is the less distinguished "little" cousin known as Big Bend Ranch State Park (432/358-4444, www.

ADOBE WALLS

The Big Bend region qualifies as America's desert Southwest, so the abundance of adobe structures in the area should come as no surprise. But for many Texans and out-of-staters, their presence is beguiling and intriguing.

Considered one of the oldest building technologies, adobe is as natural as it gets – bricks comprised of earth, straw, and water are formed in wooden molds and dried in the sun for up to two weeks. A lime-based whitewall plaster is often applied to the walls to help deflect the sun and protect the bricks from the harsh desert elements. Unlike traditional oven-fired bricks, adobe is considered a low-strength product and therefore can only support minimal weight – most structures are no more than two stories tall.

The large bricks – typically between one and two feet thick – used in adobe structures provide ideal insulation against the extreme desert conditions of far West Texas. The roofs are typically flat, with tile or wooden *canales* (gutters) providing drainage off the sides of the building. Because the *vigas* (beams) supporting the roof tend to be restricted in length, the corresponding rooms are also narrow.

Archaeological evidence suggests adobe originated in the ancient Middle East, and it's typically associated in the United States with Native American tribes in present-day New Mexico and Arizona, particularly the impressive pueblos in Taos and Acoma. Spanish explorers brought a similar adobe tradition, resulting in now-iconic structures such as missions, presidios, and dwellings across the South and West Texas landscape.

Many of the region's adobe buildings are endangered due to erosion, but others remain in good shape thanks to dedicated restoration efforts and continual maintenance to repair crumbling bricks and deter moisture. The best examples of historic adobe architecture in the region include the Castolon historic district in Big Bend, the Sauceda Ranch in Big Bend Ranch State Park, Fort Leaton State Historic Site in Presidio, the Hudspeth County Courthouse in Sierra Blanca, and the Sacred Heart of Jesus Catholic Church in Ruidosa.

tpwd.state.tx.us). The park's east entrance is located at Barton Warnock Environmental Education Center, one mile east of Lajitas on FM 170, and the west entrance is located four miles southeast of Presidio at Fort Leaton State Historic Site on FM 170.

Relatively new on the scene, this enormous chunk of property—more than 300,000 acres of remote Chihuahuan Desert wilderness—is the largest state park in Texas. Though it's far more limited in amenities, the park is best known for its spectacular views along River Road between Lajitas and Presidio, and has become quite popular with those in search of a genuinely solitary natural experience.

Containing some of the most isolated and rugged terrain in the state, Big Bend Ranch includes two mountain ranges with ancient volcanoes and sheer-cliffed canyons. Though some of the property is still being developed for public access, there are currently more than 100 miles of trails available for hiking and biking, with a goal of ultimately offering 236 miles on 65 interconnected trails. Maps with updated routes are available on the park's website or at ranger stations. Big Bend Ranch features 23 miles of Rio Grande frontage, offering an ideal starting point for boating excursions. Other popular park activities include horseback riding, fishing, stargazing, and birding.

If primitive backcountry camping and cooking doesn't sound appealing, the park provides access to civilization with food, lodging, and Wi-Fi service at its Saucedo Complex for $100 a night. The three-bedroom Big House accommodates eight and has a full kitchen. Meals are available with advance reservations.

INFORMATION AND SERVICES

Big Bend National Park includes several visitors centers offering maps and, most importantly, informed guides who help enhance visits by suggesting the perfect activities for travelers' particular comfort levels. The main center is at the park's headquarters at **Panther Junction,** about 26 miles from the north entrance gate (arriving from Marathon) and 25 miles from the western gate. The renovated visitors center offers interpretive exhibits and scores of books, brochures, and maps. The park's other visitors centers—**Chisos Mountains, Castolon,** and **Rio Grande Village**—are slightly smaller and are typically closed in the summer, but they're still packed with valuable information and helpful professionals.

A handy way to plan your trip to the Big Bend Region is via the **Visit Big Bend** website (www.visitbigbend.com), offering interactive maps and handy resources for food, lodging, and activities. Another helpful option is the **Texas Mountain Trail Region** (in nearby Marfa, 432/284-0002, www.texasmountain-trail.com, Mon.–Fri. 9 A.M.–5 P.M.), a subsidiary of the Texas Historical Commission's heritage tourism initiative.

Marfa and Vicinity

During the early 2000s, the small railroad stop of Marfa (population 1,916) became an unlikely cultural hotbed for artists and visitors from across the country and the world. With the current Great Recession, things have slowed down somewhat, but the growth and international exposure left indelible marks on the community. Though it may seem like a positive thing—national exposure brings valued tourism dollars and puts a spotlight on the region's natural beauty and quirky charm—it brought concern to the independent-minded residents who weren't too keen on the higher property taxes and curious outsiders.

The town was established in 1883 as a railroad water stop and was reportedly named by a railroad executive's wife who suggested the name based on a character from Fyodor Dostoyevsky's *The Brothers Karamazov,* which she was reading at the time. Two years later, a magnificent three-story Renaissance Revival courthouse was built downtown, providing a jarring contrast to the surrounding barren West Texas landscape. Refurbished to its original glory with the help of the Texas Historical Commission, the courthouse remains a downtown focal point and one of the state's architectural gems.

In 1911, the U.S. military established a presence in Marfa in response to the nearby Mexican revolution, and troops remained in the area for several decades with the establishment of the Marfa Army Air Field and Camp Albert (later renamed Camp Marfa, then Fort D. A. Russell, and now the home of the fascinating Chinati art foundation).

Another of Marfa's most compelling properties, the exquisite El Paisano Hotel, served as the operations base for the epic 1956 film *Giant,* starring Rock Hudson, Elizabeth Taylor, and James Dean. With its sweeping vistas and spectacular sky, Marfa continues to draw filmmakers, most notably as the backdrop for many scenes in two Oscar-nominated movies: *No Country for Old Men* and *There Will Be Blood.*

With its lofty elevations and spectacular scenery, Marfa is also a popular spot for outdoor recreational activities, including the links at Marfa Municipal Golf Course, the highest golf course in Texas, and glider excursions, benefiting from the area's strong thermal updrafts and unparalleled views. When visitors aren't enjoying the cooler temperatures, they head to the trendy art galleries, boutiques, and coffee shops in the historic downtown area. Worth noting: Much of Marfa is closed on Monday and Tuesday, so be sure to check ahead with restaurants and attractions to make sure they're open before making plans for early in the week.

SIGHTS

Despite being a tiny town in the absolute middle of nowhere, Marfa is packed with activities. The enormous sky is an attraction unto itself, but many visitors are captivated by the mysterious Marfa Lights and the Chinati Foundation, a worldwide destination containing avant-garde installation artwork housed in historic army barracks.

◖ Chinati Foundation

There's nothing else in the world quite like the Chinati Foundation (1 Cavalry Row, 432/729-4362, www.chinati.org, open Wed.–Sun. for tours, $10 adults, $5 students and seniors, 11 and under free). This unconventional art museum and artist compound is housed in nearly a dozen historic structures (barracks, artillery sheds, prisoner of war compounds) of the former Camp D. A. Russell army base. Based on the ideas of minimalist artist Donald Judd, Chinati features an amazing array of artwork, from Judd's large-scale pieces—most notably, a mammoth artillery shed containing stark metal boxes of varying size—to patterned fluorescent light sculptures, to sketches and paintings, to a large metal sculpture by famous Swedish-born artist Claes Oldenberg.

Judd's vision for the foundation was to blend art, architecture, and nature in an environment far different from traditional metropolitan art spaces. Artists and art lovers from across the world journey to this spectacular location to experience this fascinating confluence of elements, perhaps best represented by the compelling dichotomy presented in the barrack buildings: On one end of the room you'll find a bright pink fluorescent light sculpture, while the window on the opposite wall reveals the rugged beauty of the West Texas desert landscape.

Chinati offers one official tour Wednesday–Sunday, starting at 10 A.M., featuring the foundation's permanent installations by Judd, John Chamberlain, Ilya Kabakov, Richard Long, and David Rabinowitch. After a noon-ish lunch break, the tour resumes at 2 P.M. with a focus on permanent installations by

BIG BEND REGION

© TEXAS HISTORICAL COMMISSION

A former artillery building now houses art at the Chinati Foundation.

BUILDING 98

© TEXAS HISTORICAL COMMISSION

historic Building 98 near Marfa

For those interested in Marfa's Chinati Art Foundation, there's another hidden gem housed inside former army barracks in this little West Texas town.

This one is known by its institutional-sounding military name, Building 98. What awaits inside, however, is anything but ordinary. In fact, the building's multifaceted art and history are an international phenomenon.

Constructed in 1920, the adobe structure was home to the officers club and bachelor officers quarters for the army's Fort D. A. Russell. But it's much better known for its occupants during World War II – the German prisoners of war (POWs) who painted colorful panoramic murals on many interior walls.

The widespread canvases represent the largest collection of POW art in the United States. The colorful and detailed murals are incredibly stunning, especially considering they were created with house paint by war prisoners. The POWs, inspired by their time in far West Texas, devoted most of their murals to capturing the surrounding wide-open landscapes, including scenes of cowboys cooking and the desert vegetation.

When the property was procured nearly a decade ago by representatives of the art-based International Woman's Foundation, the murals were in danger of disappearing – there were holes in the wall, and the rooms were filled with debris. Restoration artists and preservationists helped shore up the buildings and provide a stable environment for the paintings. Visitors and artists travel from all over the world to experience this unique aspect of art. And, perhaps most compelling, the descendants of the original artists were discovered and invited to Building 98 to experience the artwork. Appropriately, one is a well-known children's illustrator in Europe.

Those interested in seeing the artwork for themselves can schedule a tour of Building 98 by calling 432/729-4826.

Carl Andre, Dan Flavin, Roni Horn, Claes Oldenburg, and John Wesley, as well as the museum's current temporary exhibition. A separate tour, held Thursday–Sunday at 3:45 P.M., showcases Judd's permanent installation of 100 untitled works in mill aluminum.

◖ Marfa Lights

Drawing even more tourists than Chinati are the mysterious Marfa Lights (about 8 miles east of Marfa on U.S. Hwy. 90, 915/729-4942), typically visible just after dusk on clear evenings. These bouncing, splitting, and disappearing ethereal orbs have confounded people for more than a century (but mostly in the past six decades), and the viewing center just off the highway hosts thousands of curiosity seekers annually who flock to the site for a chance to see the mystifying white, yellow, and orange lights suspended in the air with no apparent source. Adding to the intrigue is their distance—at any given time they appear to be either 100 yards away or 10 miles away. There are many theories about the unexplained phenomenon, from Apache Indian folklore to UFO sightings to vehicle headlights; however, a scientific explanation has yet to emerge.

First documented in 1883, explanations for the lights range from swamp gasses to bizarre bouts of electrostatic discharge to moonlight shining on shiny rocks in the Chinati Mountains. Scientists acknowledge their existence but take some of the fun out of the phenomena by suggesting the lights are a miragelike visual effect caused by the interaction of cold and warm layers of air, causing light to bend and move. Regardless, the absence of a valid and accepted explanation is ultimately the Marfa Lights's main draw. They defy explanation, and that's exactly why people continue to marvel at their mysteriousness.

Prada Marfa

Perhaps not surprisingly, one of the most popular attractions in the area is an enormous piece of art: *Prada Marfa* (about 37 miles west of Marfa on the south side of U.S. Hwy. 90). A permanent art installation mimicking a small

© ANDY RHODES

the Presidio County Courthouse in downtown Marfa

DONALD JUDD IN MARFA

Far West Texas and New York City don't have much in common. In fact, they have nothing in common. When contemporary artist Donald Judd arrived in Marfa in the early 1970s, he saw two things that had been missing from his metropolitan environs: the sky and affordable land. He also saw the immense beauty of the West Texas terrain.

Judd set to work using the wide-open and rugged landscape as his canvas. He purchased several buildings in and around Marfa, most significantly the barracks, hangars, and gymnasium of Fort D. A. Russell, an abandoned army base. The hangars, which once held German prisoners during World War II, along with barrack buildings and artillery sheds, became galleries for modern art. The entire facility was ultimately developed as the Chinati Foundation, drawing art lovers and artists from across the world to experience the fascinating installation projects and educational seminars.

Judd spent much of the late 1970s and early '80s developing and creating some of the world's largest permanent contemporary-art installations at Chinati. Most famous is *100 untitled works in mill aluminum*, installed in two former artillery sheds. The massive garage doors were replaced with windows, which disperse the omnipresent West Texas sunlight onto scores of metal boxes with the same outer dimensions yet completely different interior designs. The other large-scale piece, *15 untitled works in concrete*, was the first to be installed at the museum (1980–84) and was cast and assembled on-site. The individual units have the same measurements – 2.5 by 2.5 by 5 meters – and are made from 25-centimeter-thick concrete slabs.

Though his art was deemed puzzling by locals, Judd attempted to connect with Marfa residents by hosting an annual party with Mexican food and bagpipes (his favorite music). Despite the bizarre nature of the artwork, most Marfa residents welcomed Judd's peculiarities and especially the money Chinati brought to the community.

Judd died in 1994, leaving behind his foundation that would continue to attract international visitors intrigued by his vision for incorporating art with the environment. Though a few Marfa residents are complaining more loudly these days about the impact Chinati and its international spotlight has had on rising property values, they appreciate Judd's dedication to the incomparable charms of far West Texas.

Prada retail store, this adobe and plaster structure features display windows showcasing handbags and shoes with atmospheric interior lighting. Depending on who's doing the critiquing, the artwork is either mimicking the trendy visitors and artistes who descend on this remote landscape or it's just "dumb," as vandals painted on the walls soon after its opening. Regardless, it's well worth the half-hour drive for the unique photo op and to participate in the tradition of leaving behind a business card or shoe for the next round of pop-art aficionados to admire.

Presidio County Courthouse

Marfa's exquisite three-story courthouse (320 N. Highland St., 432/729-4670, www.co.presidio.tx.us) was built in 1886 and was restored with the help of the Texas Historical Commission's Texas Historic Courthouse Preservation Program. The building is a remarkable example of Second Empire architecture, featuring a light pink exterior of stone and local brick along with the stylish detailing and mansard roofs fashionable in Europe at the time of its construction. If you're in town during weekday business hours, pop in for a look at the intricate interior woodwork and impressive attention to detail in the light fixtures and windows.

Hotel Paisano

Even if you're lodging elsewhere, it's worth dropping by the elegant Hotel Paisano (207

THE MOST TREACHEROUS ROAD IN THE STATE

If you have a sense of adventure (and a four-wheel-drive vehicle), be sure to set aside a morning or afternoon to experience Pinto Canyon Road. Traversing the rugged canyon land in the Chinati Mountains, this roughly 50-mile road stretches between Marfa and the border ghost town of Ruidosa.

If you're starting from Marfa, you'll sail smoothly on the first 32 miles of paved highway before encountering the treacherous/fun part. This stretch of rocky road is technically a county road, but it twists and turns through private ranch property and across purely untouched desert landscape.

The sights and sounds you'll encounter are fascinating, from colorful cacti to screeching birds to spiky ocotillo plants to leaping lizards. And those are just your immediate surroundings. Even more mesmerizing are the majestic mountains behind these objects, providing a scenic and solid backdrop to the entire panoramic vista.

Though it's tempting to keep your gaze on the peaks and natural wonders, it's important to pay attention to the rocky roadway before you. The route makes steep dips and unexpected turns, with massive gaps in the roadbed, random low-water crossings, and long-forgotten guardrails.

Rest assured, it's perfectly normal to be cruising along at a speedy clip of 10 miles per hour. And be sure to make occasional stops to capture the astounding scenery on a camera or even just in your memory bank. It's not like you'll find yourself in the neighborhood again

sometime soon. Just don't wander too far off the road, since private-property owners in this part of the country take their privacy and property very seriously.

Another occasionally disconcerting experience on the road is the overwhelming sense you've somehow drifted off the official roadway and onto a barely used ranch trail or historic driveway of some sort. Rest assured, it's just part of Pinto Canyon Road's charm. As soon as you round the next rocky elevation or ascend from a dry creekbed, you'll see signs of what passes for civilization out here – tire tracks from sometime in the past two days, a rusted sign, or a cattle guard.

By the time you get to the end of the road (plan about three hours for the entire trip), you'll be fairly exhausted yet exhilarated from the experience. You'll also be rewarded with a remarkable structure waiting in the ghost town of Ruidosa. The Sacred Heart of Jesus Catholic Church (circa 1914) is recognized as one of Texas's most significant adobe structures – its three major arches are considered the largest existing round-structural adobe arches in the state.

Though the church is in partial ruins, its architectural and historic importance have inspired people to organize several restoration efforts over the past decade. The Marfa-based Ruidosa Mission Project has helped stabilize the church by replacing its roof, fortifying the foundation, and grading the site for drainage. Regardless of its condition, the church is a divine ending (or beginning) to this treacherous trek through the desert.

BIG BEND REGION

N. Highland Ave., 800/662-5517, www.hotel-paisano.com). Opened in 1930, the hotel was a gathering place for cattlemen and ranchers as well as a destination for railroad travelers between San Antonio and California. The Paisano's Spanish colonial–style architecture features colorful ceramic tile, ornate woodwork, and wrought iron. It became legendary in the 1950s when it served as headquarters for the classic movie *Giant* starring Rock Hudson, Elizabeth Taylor, and James Dean. Several

suites are named in their honor, and a display case in the lobby contains movie memorabilia. Visitors can enjoy a cocktail at the Paisano's courtyard patio, with its soothing fountain and pleasant atmosphere. The restaurant is also a major draw, featuring upscale dishes of contemporary and Southwestern fare.

Marfa Book Store Co.

A bookstore isn't typically a major tourist attraction, but most bookstores aren't like

Marfa Book Store Co. (105 S. Highland Ave., 432/729-3906, www.marfabookco.com, daily 10 A.M.–7 P.M.). The store is a magnet for the town's creative community, with an incredible selection of regional and intellectual-themed books, a small art gallery, and numerous readings and events. Its focus is on art and architecture, and you can get lost browsing through the sections devoted to photography, folk art, interior design, and other creative pursuits. The bookstore also showcases contemporary and regional writers and poets, and offers gifts, occasional coffees, and one of the few public Wi-Fi spaces in town.

ACCOMMODATIONS

Marfa's lodging options are limited but eclectic—there's something (except large chain hotels) for everyone. Visitors have the good fortune of choosing from the magnificent Hotel Paisano, the chic Thunderbird, or the standard Riata Inn. And don't forget the funky trailer park with outdoor showers.

For the ultimate West Texas lodging experience, book a room at the historic **Hotel Paisano** (N. Highland Ave., 800/662-5517, www.hotelpaisano.com, $99–149). This charming and classy hotel lies just a block away from the majestic downtown courthouse and harkens back to the days of upscale accommodations for cross-country travelers and cattle traders. The Spanish colonial architecture adds a touch of regional elegance to the experience, and guests have a wide range of room options, from the smaller quarters in the original part of the hotel to larger suites with balconies, kitchens, and plasma TVs. Call well in advance to reserve the popular James Dean room, where the movie icon stayed during the filming of *Giant.*

Equally as extraordinary for completely different reasons is the trendy and sleek **Thunderbird Motel** (601 W. Hwy. 90/San Antonio St., 432/729-1984, www.thunderbird-marfa.com, $130–180 d). Built in 1959 as a classic horseshoe-shaped roadside motel surrounding a swimming pool, the building has been tastefully remodeled with stylish stucco

the Hotel Paisano in downtown Marfa

© TEXAS HISTORICAL COMMISSION

and accompanied by native flora. Rooms feature polished concrete floors, locally built pecan furniture, quality bedding, minibars with specialty beverages and organic and local snacks, Wi-Fi service, access to vintage Stack-O-Matic record players and a vinyl library, and a thermos of coffee in a cloth bag placed on the doorknob at 7 A.M.

If these options offer too much character (or, more realistically, a strain on the wallet), the only "standard" choice in town is the commendable **Riata Inn** (1500 E. Hwy. 90, 432/729-3800, www.riatainn.com, $59 d). The Riata features extra-large versions of typical hotel rooms, each containing Internet access, flat-screen TVs with cable, and access to an outdoor pool.

One of the newest, funkiest, and most popular lodging options in town is **El Cosmico** (802 S. Highland Ave., 432/729-1950, www.elcosmico.com, $110–150 nightly for fully equipped trailers). This "campground hotel" consists of a cool collection of renovated vintage trailers, a tepee, a few ecoshack yurts, and several regular ol' campsites. The stylishly redecorated 1950s-era trailers include stoves, small fridges, fans, floor heating, and bathrooms with hot water. Bedding materials and cooking provisions are provided, and Wi-Fi access is available in the lobby lounge. Be aware that most trailers include an outdoor shower, which seems strange at first but is ultimately quite liberating without sacrificing privacy or comfort (strategically placed walls protect you from public view and the steady breeze).

El Cosmico is more than just a trendy/quirky place to spend the night, it's a concept—the goal is to build a sustainable community environment that "fosters and agitates artistic and intellectual exchange." Guests are encouraged to attain this by participating in the communal space (an elm grove filled with hammocks, outdoor kitchen and dining spaces, and a community lounge and mercantile). Plans are also in the works for adding art shacks and hosting cultural workshops and events.

FOOD

With the influx of out-of-towners and money, it's not surprising that Marfa's culinary scene is a bit more diverse than other Texas communities of its size. Fortunately, the new arrivals are respectful of local cuisine, and even if some of the prices are approaching New York or L.A. levels, the atmosphere and variety of food are purely West Texan.

A great place to kick off the day with a hearty meal is **Austin Street Cafe** (405 N. Austin St., 432/729-4653, www.austinstreetcafe.com, weekends only, 8 A.M.–3 P.M., $5–12), a low-key spot with high-quality fare. Austin Street is known for its welcoming large windows and screen porch, and its sumptuous egg dishes. For breakfast, sample the curried eggs or the green eggs (blended with cheese and spinach). At lunch, go with the tomato basil soup paired with one of the large, healthy salads. Be sure to grab a fresh fruit smoothie to go.

For an incredibly fresh and full-flavored meal, be sure to stop by **Marfa Table** (109 S. Highland Ave., 432/729-3663, www.marfatable.com, $7–16, closed on weekends). Located

in the heart of downtown, Marfa Table feels like it could be in Austin but doesn't feel out of place in Marfa. The space is open and contemporary, and the food is locally grown and packed with flavor. Sandwiches and salads are bursting with fresh ingredients and homemade goodness, and the warm soups and coffee make you want to grab a book and curl up in a comfy restaurant chair for the rest of the day. At the very least, you can extend your pleasant experience by lingering with a homemade pastry or a Mexican Coke. Or just come back the next day (or next meal) for another round . . . .

Visitors can still order traditional small-town food in Marfa, too. A popular choice with locals and families is the **Pizza Foundation** (100 E. San Antonio St., 432/729-3377, www.pizzafoundation.com, Thurs.–Mon. noon–9 P.M., $5–14). Located at the intersection of the only stoplight in town, this comfy eatery in a former gas station building is a welcome destination. The thin-sliced pie is perfectly prepared from scratch with a hearty tomato sauce and a fresh variety of toppings. The healthy salads and frozen limeade are necessary pairings with a slice or four of this tasty pizza—enjoy all of it inside or out on the small patio.

If eating outside is up your alley, head to the mobile trailer called **Food Shark** (typically located under the pavilion near the railroad tracks, 281/386-6540, www.foodsharkmarfa.com, typically open Tues.–Fri. 11:30 A.M.–3 P.M., $5–9). Not surprisingly, the menu is somewhat limited at this restaurant-on-wheels, but the available options are creative and filling, skewing toward Mediterranean-style versions of West Texas favorites (burritos, barbecue, etc.).

One of the only other downtown establishments within walking distance of the Thunderbird and Paisano hotels is **Carmen's Cafe** (317 E. San Antonio St., 432/729-3429, $5–11). Refreshingly nontrendy, Serving up diner-style goodness with a Mexican twist, Carmen's is an ideal place to go for a hearty breakfast. The eggs with green chiles are a perfect way to jump-start your day, the breakfast burritos are flavorfully wrapped in an astounding homemade tortilla, and the coffee is just as hot and bland as you'd expect from a no-frills local joint.

When you're downtown marveling at the Presidio County Courthouse or checking out the art galleries, be sure to drop by the tucked-away **Squeeze Marfa** (215 N. Highland Ave., across from the courthouse, 432/729-4500, Tues.–Sat. 10 A.M.–5 P.M.). There's much more on the menu than just drinks, but the flavorful fruit juices and satisfying smoothies are the main draw. Other highlights include the perfectly grilled paninis, the homemade soups, and the chocolate corner featuring high-quality Swiss chocolate.

INFORMATION AND SERVICES

The **Marfa Chamber of Commerce** (207 N. Highland Ave., 432/729-4942, www.marfacc. com) provides information about the community's limited yet interesting resources. Another handy resource is **www.marfa.org,** containing news about upcoming cultural events and links to city services and amenities.

FORT DAVIS

Fort Davis (population 1,041) truly feels like the Old West. Nestled among the Davis Mountains—therefore dubbed "the highest town in Texas"—Fort Davis exhibits the charm of an authentic Western community, with wide wind-swept streets containing flat-faced and sun-faded buildings under an enormous sky.

Fort Davis was established in 1854 by Secretary of War Jefferson Davis as one of the key army posts in West Texas's development and defense. The fort was briefly abandoned during the Civil War, allowing Native Americans to strip much of the buildings' wood for fuel, but it was reoccupied in 1867 and by the mid-1880s was a major operation with more than 600 men and 60-plus adobe and stone structures.

During this time, Fort Davis was home to several regiments of Buffalo Soldiers, African-Americans who earned distinction as brave fighters who served alongside Anglo soldiers,

a rare case of desegregation in the late 1800s. As settlement increased in the area and native populations dispersed, the fort's original purpose became obsolete, and it was abandoned in 1891.

The town's remote and rugged location made it a difficult destination to reach, resulting in slow growth throughout the 1900s. These days, its mild climate and natural beauty draw thousands of visitors annually from Austin and other urban areas in search of a high-altitude respite from the grueling summer heat. Fort Davis's intrigue lies in its proximity to attractions like the fascinating McDonald Observatory and breathtaking Davis Mountains State Park, as well as its refreshingly unspoiled allure, particularly compared to the "discovered" towns of Marfa and Alpine.

Sights
FORT DAVIS NATIONAL HISTORIC SITE

Be sure to set aside an hour or two for Fort Davis National Historic Site (on Hwy. 17 in Fort Davis, 432/426-3224, www.nps.gov/foda, daily 8 A.M.–5 P.M., $3 admission). Considered one of the country's best remaining examples of a 19th-century frontier military post, Fort Davis draws visitors from across the country. Families and history buffs can spend as much time as they like on the self-guided tour, showcasing the post's 20 buildings and more than 100 ruins. Of particular interest are the restored barrack buildings and officers quarters with period furnishings and military equipment, offering a slice of life on a frontier base in the late 1800s. Opened in 1854, Fort Davis played a key role in the history of the Southwest by protecting settlers, mail coaches, and travelers on the San Antonio–El Paso Road. The fort is especially notable for serving as the base for several regiments of African-American troops known as Buffalo Soldiers, who helped maintain peaceful settlement in the region.

◀ MCDONALD OBSERVATORY

Another must-see attraction in Fort Davis is the remarkable McDonald Observatory (on Hwy. 118, 16 miles west of Fort Davis,

FIGHTING FOR SURVIVAL

A Buffalo Soldier isn't just the name of a Bob Marley song. These fierce warriors were named by the Plains Indians who admired the bravery of the African-American troops that served on the frontier in the post-Civil War army.

Buffalo Soldiers were stationed at several forts in western Texas, but they are perhaps best known for their service at Fort Davis, where they spent nearly 20 years (1867-1885) protecting settlers. Several infantries and cavalry units earned distinction for their work at the fort, despite the lack of high-profile battles or significant military incidents.

The primary mission of the Buffalo Soldier regiments was to protect the established mail and travel routes, control movements of area Native American tribes, and scout the terrain. One of the few military-related highlights oc-

curred in 1879, when the army was waging a campaign against the Apaches who were attacking settlers in West Texas. Apache leader Victorio had fled to Mexico and was attempting to rejoin his tribe in the Fort Davis area when the Buffalo Soldier units were dispatched to prevent the regrouping. According to historians, several major confrontations occurred in the region, forcing Victorio to retreat to Mexico, where he was later killed by Mexican troops.

Otherwise, life for all the soldiers at Fort Davis was somewhat tedious. Routine duties and fatigue details occupied most of their time, with occasional excursions to patrol the frontier, guard water holes, and escort government survey crews, wagon trains, and mail coaches.

432/426-3640, www.mcdonaldobservatory. org, open 10 A.M.–5:30 P.M., $8 adults, $7 children ages 6–12, additional charge for star parties). Sitting high atop 6,791-foot-tall Mt. Locke, the observatory makes good use of its position approaching the heavens. Three large domes beckon visitors to the facility, which opened in 1939 with the world's second-largest telescope and has served astronomers and visitors ever since. The observatory's impressive equipment includes the massive Hobby-Eberly Telescope, with a 36-foot-wide mirror composed of 91 laser-aligned segments, and two other telescopes to monitor the sun, stars, and planets. Visitors have the option of attending informative guided tours (11:30 A.M. and 2:30 P.M.), solar viewings (30 minutes before the tours), and dramatic star parties (after dusk every Tuesday, Friday, and Saturday), but the spectacular views of the surrounding mountains and valleys are reason alone to make the journey.

OTHER SIGHTS

Overlooking the area's signature red-hued outcroppings is **Davis Mountains State Park**

(Hwy. 118, 432/426-3337, www.tpwd.state. tx.us). The park boasts 1,000 feet of elevation change and is a popular destination for hikers and campers who relish the natural beauty and cooler temperatures. Considered one of Texas's most scenic areas, the park showcases its namesake mountains, the most extensive range in the state. The park draws mountain bikers and hikers from across the state who marvel at the incredible views of the park's picturesque canyon formed by Keesey Creek. Hard-core campers also appreciate the park's Limpia Canyon Primitive Area, with 10 miles of backcountry hiking trails and primitive tent campsites. Other popular activities include bird-watching, stargazing, and cruising Skyline Drive, a paved road with two spectacular overlooks showcasing the Chinati Mountain Range, located 75 miles to the southwest. The park is also home to the famous Indian Lodge, a historic adobe hotel still in operation.

Check out the mystique of the region's surroundings at the **Chihuahuan Desert Visitor Center** (43869 Hwy. 118, 432/364-2499, www. cdri.org, Mon.–Sat. 9 A.M.–5 P.M., $5 adults, $4 seniors, children 12 and under free). Visitors can experience the wonders of the Chihuahuan Desert region firsthand by exploring the fairly strenuous Modesta Canyon trail, a one-hour hike, and the scenic Clayton's Overlook hike, offering amazing views of the area's diverse topography. The center's succulent greenhouse features more than 200 species of Chihuahuan Desert cacti as well as other attractions, like the 20-acre botanical garden, an interpretive center with indoor and outdoor educational exhibits, and educational programs.

It's worth the 38-mile drive north of Fort Davis to experience the spectacular scenery and distinctive allure of **Balmorhea State Park** (Hwy. 17, 432/375-2370, www.tpwd.state.tx.us). If you have the time, book a night at the historic adobe motel, featuring spacious rooms with cable TV but no phones. The park's centerpiece is San Solomon Springs, gushing up to 26 million gallons of refreshingly cool water daily into a large man-made swimming pool. The deep artesian springs offer an ideal spot for scuba diving, so it's fairly common to see divers in the far corner of the pool exploring the unique aquatic life in the crystal-clear water. The springs also feed a fascinating desert wetland, proving a habitat and life source for scores of uncommon birds and plant life. The viewing areas—a large wooden overlook and subsurface water window—are especially intriguing.

Accommodations
HOTELS AND MOTELS

If you plan far enough in advance, you may have the good fortune of staying at the immensely popular **⟨ Indian Lodge** (Park Rd. 3, 432/426-3254, www.tpwd.state.tx.us, $90 d). Built in the 1930s by the Civilian Conservation Corps, the multilevel pueblo-style hotel is nestled among the ridges of Davis Mountains State Park. The rustic cedar furnishings and woodwork coupled with the whitewashed-covered 18-inch-thick adobe walls provide a distinctly Southwestern visceral experience. The lodge also features a full-service year-round restaurant and an outdoor swimming pool.

Another popular lodging option in Fort Davis is **Hotel Limpia** (100 Main St., 432/426-3241, www.hotellimpia.com, rooms start at $99), a beautifully restored 1912 hotel containing period furnishings, four buildings, and a cottage. The charming guest rooms and welcoming courtyard garden with rocking chairs and lush vegetation offer a pleasant respite from city life.

Those in search of a newer facility will find solace at the downtown **Harvard Hotel** (109 N. State St., 432/426-2500, www.harvardhotelandlodge.com, $95–125). This rustic-looking yet modern-feeling facility offers rooms with DVD players, refrigerators, microwaves, and Internet access.

BED-AND-BREAKFASTS

With its quaint downtown and abundant natural beauty, Fort Davis is an ideal place to stay in a B&B. One of the best in town is **The Veranda** (210 Court Ave., 432/426-2233, www.theveranda.com, $95–125). Located just a block away from the beautifully restored Jeff Davis County Courthouse, The Veranda's 13 antiques-bedecked suites feature 12-foot-tall ceilings, private baths, and free Wi-Fi service. The inn also boasts walled gardens and quiet courtyards with rocking chairs and tables in the shadow of Sleeping Lion Mountain.

Just down the road are the cozy and comfortable **Butterfield Inn Cottages** (201 State St., 432/426-3252, www.butterfieldinn.com, $80–150). Each of these minihomes contain fireplaces, recliners, refrigerators, microwaves, and private baths with Jacuzzi tubs.

CAMPING

Aside from Big Bend, the best camping in the region is at **Davis Mountains State Park** (Hwy. 118, 432/426-3337, www.tpwd.state.tx.us). The park's northern section is the Limpia Canyon Primitive Area, a special-use district with 10 miles of backcountry hiking trails and primitive tent campsites. The park's developed facilities are south of Hwy. 118 and include restrooms with showers, campsites with water, electricity, sewer, and cable TV connection, and nine miles of hiking trails, some leading to Fort Davis Historic Site.

Those traveling in RVs may want to hook up in downtown Fort Davis at the **Overland Trail Campground** (307 N. State St., 432/426-2250, www.texascamping.com) offering cable and Wi-Fi service, a laundromat, showers, tent areas with water and electric, fully equipped cabins, and a biker camping area with accessible facilities.

Food

A good place to kick off your limited Fort Davis culinary tour is the low-key and down-home **Fort Davis Drug Store** (113 N. State St., 432/426-3118, $6–11). This old-fashioned soda fountain and restaurant is known for its comfort food, namely, chicken-fried steak, thick burgers, and hearty breakfasts. Top your meal off with a root beer float and a souvenir from the attached old-fashioned drugstore.

The only place in town with a full Tex-Mex menu is the commendable **Cueva de Leon Cafe** (611 N. State St., 432/426-3801, closed Sun., $4–12). Located in the heart of the tiny downtown area, the restaurant is known for its spectacular chiles rellenos (perfectly breaded and not too spicy) and its flavorful chicken enchiladas with tangy green sauce.

The best place in town for a high-quality yet casual dinner is the **Hotel Limpia Dining Room** (100 Main St., 432/426-3241, $8–24). If you want to start off with a cocktail at the upstairs bar, you'll have to pay a few bucks for a "membership" to comply with local liquor laws (it's worth it). Opt for the unique appetizer called the Texas Cheesecake, a tasty blend of cheeses and peppers, and proceed to the recommended main course: a hearty char-grilled Angus steak. Be sure to save room for the homemade pies.

Information and Services

For a small town, Fort Davis has well-organized and extremely helpful visitor service. The best way to start planning your trip is via the handy website hosted by the **Fort Davis Chamber of Commerce** (#4 Memorial Square, 432/426-3015, www.fortdavis.com). Drop by the office for brochures, maps, and helpful advice.

ALPINE

Don't be fooled by the town's name. Alpine evokes images of snow-capped peaks and lofty magnificence. You won't find that here. Instead, you'll encounter plenty of West Texas charm and fantastic food along the extra-wide streets of this historic community that serves as the economic hub of the Big Bend region.

Alpine's (population 6,460) origins date to 1882 when workers pitched their tents at a mountain base while working on the transcontinental railroad that traversed the region. The town slowly added residents until 1921, when the opening of Sul Ross State Normal College (now Sul Ross State University) resulted in a significant population increase. The university, railroad, and ranching industries solidified Alpine's status as the stable economic core of far West Texas.

Since Big Bend's opening in the 1940s, Alpine has become a destination for travelers who often schedule an extra day or two in town on their way to or from the park to enjoy the mild climate and cultural resources, including several noteworthy museums, restaurants, and year-round recreational activities. The Alpine visitors center offers a handy brochure with a map featuring a walking tour of historic downtown buildings. Popular annual events include the Texas Cowboy Poetry Gathering and Trappings of Texas in February, Cinco de Mayo celebration in May, and Big Bend Balloon Bash on Labor Day weekend.

Sights

Alpine's most significant cultural attraction is the **Museum of the Big Bend** (1000 E. Sul Ross Ave., 432/837-8730, www.sulross.edu/~museum, Tues.–Sat. 9 A.M.–5 P.M., Sun. 1–5 P.M., free admission). Located on the Sul Ross State University campus, the museum's impressive collections showcase the confluence of cultures in the region—Native American, Spanish, Mexican, and Anglo settlers. Visitors learn about the cultures that have occupied the area for thousands of years via ancient tribal artifacts, historic frontier items, and life-size dioramas. Be sure to check out the fascinating

BIG BEND REGION

CIVILIAN CONSERVATION CORPS

The Civilian Conservation Corps left an indelible mark across Texas, particularly in the Big Bend region. Step into one of the area's local, state, or national parks, and you're bound to encounter signage and literature chronicling the hard work CCC members contributed to the site's roads, drainage systems, and permanent facilities.

The CCC's origins were in President Franklin Roosevelt's New Deal legislation, which addressed the country's economic crises through myriad federal proposals providing relief and reform. In Texas, CCC projects helped develop the burgeoning state park system and with soil conservation and erosion control.

Much like other parts of the state, far West Texas's construction projects included buildings, bridges, dams, culverts, stone steps, and trails. The buildings and support systems were designed to tie in closely with their rustic sites by using natural materials such as native stone and timber. To this day, nearly half of the 56 state parks that incorporated CCC work in the 1930s remain in the state parks system.

Some of the most remarkable examples of the CCC legacy are in the Big Bend region. Most notable is Indian Lodge in Davis Mountains State Park in Fort Davis. The multilevel pueblo-style hotel remains a stunning work of architecture, with its stark whitewashed adobe walls encompassing rustic cedar woodwork offering a distinct Southwestern visceral experience.

Another significant CCC contribution is the remarkable adobe motor lodge and spring-fed swimming pool at Balmorhea State Park, where visitors can enjoy the spacious rooms and inviting water at the edge of the Chihuahuan Desert. In Big Bend National Park, the CCC projects have less of a visual impact but are just as important. The scenic road traversing through and winding among the Chisos Mountains was designed and constructed by corps members, along with several rustic stone cottages at the Chisos Mountains Lodge.

Chihuahuan Desert Cactus Garden near the museum's entrance.

For some visitors—baseball fans, in particular—the city's cultural highlight is the amazing **Kokernot Field** (at the intersection of Hwy. 223 and N. 2nd St.). This beautiful historic ballpark is a baseball fan's dream, featuring unexpected details around every corner, such as the wrought-iron fencing with baseball-shaped patterns, the lamps with handmade stitched-baseball themes, and spectacular views of the mountains looming beyond the outfield. The park opened in 1947 when legendary rancher and philanthropist Herbert Kokernot used his fortune to bring semipro baseball to Alpine. Kokernot spared no expense, investing more than $1.5 million on the park—an exorbitant amount at the time—to make his dream a reality. The minor-league Alpine Cowboys played at Kokernot Field from 1947 through 1958, drawing capacity crowds who appreciated the architectural gem and the quality of talent on

the diamond. Since the ballpark is currently home to the Sul Ross State University Lobos, the field is typically closed to the public unless a game is scheduled (February–April, check www.sulross.edu for game times).

It's a bit of a drive—everything out here is—but worth the effort to experience **Woodward Ranch** (18 miles south of Alpine on Hwy. 118, 432/364-2271, www.woodwardranch.net, call for times and fees). The ranch offers several recreational activities, including hiking, scenic drives, bird-watching, and stargazing, but it's primarily known as a gemstone collection destination. The 3,000-acre property contains more than 60 kinds of naturally occurring agates and gemstones that visitors can hunt and gather. Discover desirable (but not necessarily valuable) Texas agates such as red plume and pompom, as well as opal, jasper, and calcite. Upon returning to ranch headquarters, visitors can consult with staff about identifying and appraising their finds. Guide services are available, and a lapidary (stone) shop is on-site.

Accommodations

HOTELS AND MOTELS

If rustic casual is your style, consider the **Antelope Lodge** (2310 W. Hwy. 90, 432/837-2451, www.antelopelodge.com, double-occupancy cabins $60–80). Built in the late 1940s as part of the national "motor lodge" trend, this decidedly unmodern lodge revels in its historic charm. Cottages and guest rooms contain kitchenettes with two-burner stoves, mini refrigerators, and available microwaves and utensils (call in advance). Each cottage has a stone porch with weathered chairs for enjoying the cool mountain air.

For those in need of just the basics, the **Highland Inn** (1404 E. Hwy. 90, 432/837-5811, www.highlandinn.net, $55 d) offers simple and stark rooms with charmingly mismatched furniture. Located directly across the road from Sul Ross State University, the Highland Inn features a microwave and fridge in each room, along with Wi-Fi access and an outdoor pool.

The best option in this price range, however, is the comfy and casual **(Maverick Inn** (1200 E. Holland Ave., 432/837-0628, www.themaverickinn.com, $90 d). This former motor court received an extensive renovation, with modern amenities like Wi-Fi service, flat-screen TVs, fancy linens, regional artwork, Saltillo-tiled floors, mini refrigerators, and microwaves.

One of the only chain hotels in far West Texas is the reliable **Ramada Inn** (2800 W. Hwy. 90, 432/837-1100, www.ramada.com, $101 d), offering free Internet access, a free hot breakfast, an indoor pool, hot tub, and fitness center.

For a truly memorable stay in Alpine, reserve a room or loft at the magnificent **(Holland Hotel** (209 W. Holland Ave., 432/837-3844, www.thehollandhoteltexas.com, $99–150). Built in 1912 for cattlemen and the occasional tourist, this impressive downtown hotel will charm you from the moment you enter the ornate front doors, where your room assignment awaits in an envelope (it's taped to the door). There aren't any standard rooms at the Holland—they range from tiny to sprawling—but you can get a sense of what's available by previewing options on the hotel's website. All rooms feature eclectic furnishings and colors, along with private bathrooms, refrigerators, and microwaves. Incidentally, free earplugs are available at the hotel office (open 8 A.M.–5 P.M.) to help silence the trains that occasionally blast through town in the middle of the night. For fancier digs, consider the Holland Guest Lofts ($115–195), the misleadingly named ground-floor suites in the adjacent historic building. Guests access the rooms via a welcoming landscaped courtyard, and the spacious accommodations include Internet access, coffeemakers, free juice, and pastry baskets.

BED-AND-BREAKFAST

A mountain getaway is often a good excuse to stay at a cozy B&B like the **White House Inn** (2003 Fort Davis Hwy., 432/837-1401, www.whitehouseinntexas.com, $89–139). The large house offers several rooms with fancy linens, cable TV, microwaves, refrigerators, stoves, and cooking utensils. The upstairs suite is worth considering for its privacy and access to a balcony—perfect for relaxing with a coffee in the cool, dry air. The inn also offers small cottages with kitchenettes.

Food

AMERICAN

Alpine isn't known for its abundance of tourist attractions, but its quality restaurants are a major draw for visitors to the Big Bend region. One of the city's most famous eateries is the fantastic **(Reata Restaurant** (203 N. 5th St., 432/837-9232, www.reata.net, $10–38). Named for the iconic ranch depicted in the classic 1956 movie *Giant* filmed in the area, this upscale cowboy cuisine with a West Texas flair even inspired a second location in Fort Worth. Start things off with a hot bowl of jalapeño cilantro soup, and proceed with any of the tantalizing menu items, from the renowned tenderloin tamales to the carne asada to the double pork chop stuffed with pears. Not nearly as upscale is **Penny's Diner** (2407 E. Hwy. 90, 432/837-5711, $6–15). Locals love the down-home diner atmosphere and the heapin' helpings of traditional favorites like chicken-fried steak, pork chops, and grilled chicken. The breakfasts here are hearty and flavorful, and you can order any time of the day or night since Penny's is the only 24-hour spot in town.

MEXICAN

The best Tex-Mex in town is in an unassuming little house on the other side of the railroad tracks. Aptly named **La Casita** (1104 E. Ave. H, 432/837-2842, $5–11), this no-frills eatery focuses its efforts on flavorful food—hearty and spicy salsa, perfectly seasoned verde sauce on the chicken enchiladas, crispy jam-packed beef tacos, and satisfying chicken quesadillas.

A great way to start the day is with a huge breakfast taco at the tiny **Alicia's Burrito Place** (708 E. Ave. G, 432/837-2802, $3–6). Stuff it full of eggs, potatoes, cheese, bacon, and veggies before heading out for a hike or back to your room for a nap.

COFFEE AND BAKERIES

An ideal place to accompany the crisp mountain morning air is the **Bread & Breakfast Bakery Cafe** (113 W. Holland Ave., 432/837-9424, $4–9, closed Mon.). Not surprisingly, pastries and coffee are the main draws here, but they're extra tasty in a quaint location like this. The most popular item by far are the cinnamon rolls, but it's worth saving some room for a fresh doughnut or three.

Finally, **La Trattoria** (901 E. Holland Ave., 432/837-2200, www.latrattoriacafe.com, $4–13) started out as a modest espresso bar but has evolved into a legitimate restaurant (after 11 A.M.). In the morning, it retains its humble roots as the town's best coffee shop, with an impressive selection of quality java and fresh pastries offering the right combination of fuel to get you through your most challenging endeavors.

Information and Services

For brochures, maps, and travel assistance, contact the **Alpine Chamber of Commerce** (106 N. 3rd St., 432/837-2326 or 800/561-3735, www.alpinetexas.com). To get a handle on what's going on in town, pick up a copy of the *Alpine Avalanche* at one of the rack boxes throughout town or drop by the downtown office (118 N. 5th Street) to grab your own personal copy of this commendable community newspaper.

PANHANDLE PLAINS

The Panhandle region of Texas is rather desolate, but the cities that sprung up among the wind-swept plains are distinctive in their identities—independent and hardy, with a flair for the artistic. Robust residents have forged a living off the land in this unforgiving climate for thousands years, and despite the difficulties of dealing with snowy winters and 100°F summers, these proud Panhandlers are dedicated to maintaining their family ranches and agriculture-related businesses.

Historically, the Panhandle Plains have been home to these types of self-reliant people who lived off the land, from Native Americans to Spanish explorers to farmers and oilmen. Apaches ruled the region for several hundred years until the Comanches arrived in the 1700s. Other tribes (Kiowa, Southern Cheyenne, and Arapaho), collectively known as the Southern Plains Indians, occupied portions of the region until 1874, when the U.S. Army launched a "successful" campaign to permanently move them onto the reservations in present-day Oklahoma. With Native Americans no longer in the area, Hispanic sheepherders from New Mexico known as *pastores* arrived on the scene. Livestock roamed the open ranges of the Panhandle until the 1870s, when barbed wire was introduced to the region.

Soon after, two other significant advances—the windmill and the railroad—forever altered life in the area by promoting its settlement. Windmills tapped into underground aquifers for water and irrigation, while railroads provided farmers and ranchers with improved access to remote markets.

HIGHLIGHTS

◖ **Buddy Holly Center:** This cultural hotspot in Lubbock showcases their native son's brief life and significant contributions to rock music through informative exhibits and distinctive memorabilia, including his signature horn-rimmed glasses discovered at his death scene (page 387).

◖ **American Wind Power Center:** Who knew windmills could be so interesting? The unexpectedly compelling American Wind Power Center in Lubbock features more than 100 vintage windmills from across the world in a giant barn, and dozens more punctuate the surrounding grounds (page 389).

◖ **Cadillac Ranch:** This bumper crop of 10 Cadillacs buried nose-down in a field west of Amarillo is one of the premier art installations and photo ops in Texas, if not the country (page 398).

◖ **Palo Duro Canyon State Park:** The stratified colors of America's second-largest canyon are stunning, with sheer cliffs and rock towers displaying muted hues of red, yellow, and orange exposed by water and wind erosion (page 404).

◖ **Frontier Texas!:** Abilene's innovative history museum features spectral image movies (holograms) and interactive technology offering a realistic slice of life in the Panhandle Plains from 1780 to 1880 (page 406).

◖ **Fort Concho National Historic**

Landmark: Relive the life of an army soldier in the late 1800s through nearly two dozen renovated and well-maintained barracks, stables, and officers quarters at this compelling San Angelo destination (page 412).

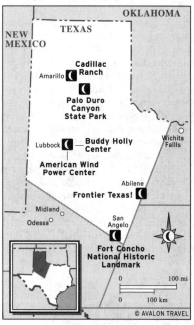

LOOK FOR ◖ TO FIND RECOMMENDED SIGHTS, ACTIVITIES, DINING, AND LODGING.

One of the region's most important cultural contributions of the 20th century was Route 66, which traversed the Panhandle through Amarillo with cafés and motor lodges catering to Americans in the 1940s and '50s in search of adventure and opportunity. The iconic Cadillac Ranch, a collection of classic cars buried hood-first in a field outside Amarillo, is a testament to the legacy of the Mother Road and a legendary contribution to Americana.

The Llano Estacado, an elevated ridge of ancient caprock in the western portion of the

Panhandle, geographically defines much of the area. The most commonly held belief is that *estacado* translates from Spanish as "stockaded," defining the steep rock walls at the edge of this enormous mesa. Its escarpment ridges, some dropping nearly 1,000 feet, create its namesake cliffs. The stunning Palo Duro Canyon near Amarillo along the edge of the Llano Estacado is one of Texas's most magnificent physical features.

This area of the state doesn't draw a steady stream of visitors, but those who make the

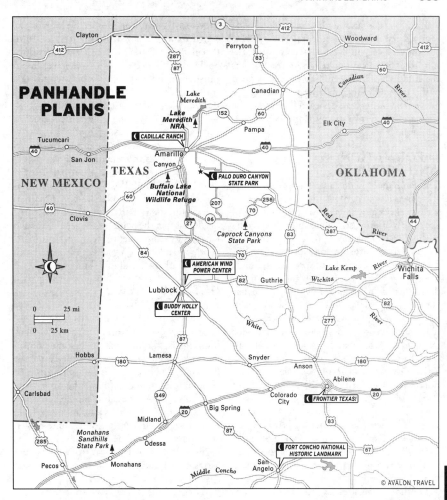

PANHANDLE PLAINS

effort to visit the region are rewarded with memorable vistas, compelling heritage, and uncommon adventures.

PLANNING YOUR TRIP

Plan on spending at least three or four days in the Panhandle, especially since it will take several hours to travel between cities. The topography isn't as enchantingly diverse as it is in far West Texas, so instead of enjoying/enduring the long drive from points east, some visitors choose to fly to Lubbock or Amarillo to begin their High Plains escapade.

To experience the best the Panhandle has to offer, set aside at least two days for Amarillo-area adventure. Plan a day of hiking or biking in beautiful Palo Duro Canyon and an overnight in the park's campground. Spend the next day or two exploring legendary Route 66 locales in nearby Amarillo and in the small towns east and west of the city just off I-40 (the Mother Road's soulless replacement).

Plan to spend another day in Lubbock, the region's economic and cultural hub. This is the only place you'll ever have an opportunity to experience such diverse attractions as the Buddy Holly Museum and the American Wind Power Center. Abilene and San Angelo are worth visiting for a day each if you have the time and interest in discovering Texas's frontier heritage.

INFORMATION AND SERVICES

The Panhandle Plains are widespread, so the travel services here focus on specific cities as well as entire portions of the region. One of the offices offering statewide and regional data is the Texas Department of Transportation's **Texas Travel Information Center** (9700 E. I-40, 800/452-9292, www.dot.state.tx.us, daily 8 A.M.–5 P.M.). This extensive and accommodating office near downtown Amarillo has "professional travel counselors" on hand to welcome visitors and provide free literature, information, and suggestions for local and statewide excursions. Also advocating a wide-scale approach is the Texas Historical Commission's **Texas Plains Trail Region** office, 50 miles northeast of Amarillo in the community of Borger (600 N. Main St., 806/273-0920, www.texasplainstrail.com, weekdays 9 A.M.–5 P.M.). Although the program focuses primarily on heritage tourism attractions, the friendly folks at the Plains Trail Region office can provide a wealth of information and brochures about all types of area activities.

For individual cities, a good starting point is the helpful **Amarillo Convention and Visitor Council** (offices at the Bivins Mansion, 1000 S. Polk St., and the Amarillo Civic Center, 401 S. Buchanan St., 800/692-1338, www.visitamarillotx.com, Mon.–Fri. 9 A.M.–6 P.M., Sat.–Sun. 10 A.M.–4 P.M., call about scaled-back winter hours). Drop by for city maps, brochures about area attractions, and assistance with planning an excursion along old Route 66.

To find out everything you'd ever need or want to know about visiting the Lubbock area, go to the **Lubbock Convention &**

Visitors Bureau (on the sixth floor of the downtown Wells Fargo Center at 1500 Broadway St., 806/747-5232, www.visitlubbock.org). Likewise, you'll find travel literature and friendly folks in the restored historic train depot that now houses the **Abilene Convention and Visitors Bureau** (1101 N. 1st St., 325/676-2556, www.abilenevisitors.com, weekdays 8:30 A.M.–5 P.M.).

One of the state's most impressive travel service offices is the remarkable **San Angelo Chamber of Commerce Visitors Center** (418 W. Ave. B, 800/375-1206, www.sanangelo.org, Mon.–Fri. 8:30 A.M.–5:30 P.M., Sat. 9 A.M.–6 P.M., Sun. 10 A.M.–5 P.M.). Located in a facility on the banks of the scenic Concho River, the visitors center features enormous windows and cascading waterfalls along with helpful staff and bundles of brochures.

GETTING THERE AND AROUND

Driving to the Panhandle Plains from Dallas, Austin, or San Antonio isn't very exciting. Unlike the majestic mesas and mountains greeting travelers to far West Texas, the Panhandle Plains are about as inspiring as their flat-sounding name implies. The drive from San Antonio to Lubbock is more than seven hours, and it's almost two hours more from there to Amarillo. As a result, some travelers choose to take a cheap Southwest Airlines flight (around $100 each way from most major Texas cities) and rent a car to save time and gas money.

As the Panhandle's largest city and economic hub, Lubbock is a good place to start, especially since most of the region's other major cities are only a few hours away. Book your flight to **Lubbock International Airport** (5401 N. Martin Luther King Blvd., 806/775-204, www.flylia.com), located northeast of the city, approximately 10 minutes from downtown. The airport offers service from American Eagle, Continental Express, and Southwest Airlines, and travelers can book reservations there with most of the major car rental companies. Lubbock's cab services include **City Cab** (806/765-7474) and **Yellow Cab** (806/765-7777).

Those focusing their travels exclusively on Amarillo and Palo Duro Canyon should use **Amarillo International Airport** (10801 Airport Blvd., 806/335-1671, www.ci.amarillo.tx.us). Situated seven miles east of downtown, the airport hosts arrivals and departures from American Eagle, Continental Express, and Southwest Airlines, and car rental service from **Avis** (806/335-2313), **Enterprise** (806/335-9443), **Hertz** (806/335-2331), and **National** (806/335-2311). Amarillo's cab companies include **Bob & Sons Taxi Service** (806/373-1171) and **Yellow Checker Cab** (806/374-8444).

The region's smaller cities also provide airport and transportation service, even though flights are limited to Houston and Dallas. If you're Abilene bound, consider flying to **Abilene Regional Airport** (2933 Airport Blvd., 325/676-6367, www.abilenetx.com), offering flights from American Eagle and Continental Express, and car rentals from Avis, Enterprise, and Hertz. Cab service is available via **Classic Cab Co.** (325/677-8294) and **Abilene Yellow Cab** (325/677-4334). For San Angelo travelers, there's **San Angelo Regional Airport** (8618 Terminal Cir., 325/659-6409, www.sanangelo-texas.us), providing service from American Eagle and Continental Express, and car rentals from Avis, Budget, and Hertz. The city's cab companies are **Red Ball Taxi & Shuttle** (325/942-8899) and **Yellow Cab Co.** (325/655-5555).

Lubbock

Lubbock (population 212,169) is distractingly flat. In fact, the lack of topography is a bit disconcerting—there should be a hill or a creekbed or some geographical feature somewhere in the city; instead, you can just see miles and miles of Texas. There's nothing wrong with that; in fact, it's an engaging and defining characteristic of Lubbock's nature.

The ranching culture is ingrained in Lubbock residents, and they take pride in their hard-working, sensible heritage. Settlers began taking root here in the late 1800s but were occasionally displaced by the nasty, dust-storm inducing winds. The hardy folks toughed it out.

Eventually a railroad arrived, and the city slowly emerged as the marketing center of the South Plains. By 1923, the Texas legislature authorized the establishment of Texas Technological College (now known as Texas Tech University), which went on to play a key role in establishing Lubbock's identity.

Another character-defining aspect of Lubbock's personality is its contribution to American popular music. Native son Buddy Holly helped revolutionize rock 'n' roll in the late 1950s, and other influential Lubbock-area country/rock artists include Roy Orbison, Waylon Jennings, Mac Davis, and Joe Ely.

Still, it's Texas Tech that makes locals the most proud, and their hometown academic institution brings worldly culture to the High Plains. Texas Tech has a healthy enrollment of nearly 27,000 students, and its agriculture and engineering programs continue to have a major impact on the economy and life of residents in the Panhandle and the entirety of West Texas.

SIGHTS
◖ Buddy Holly Center
At one point, Buddy Holly was the single most influential creative force in early rock 'n' roll. Visitors will find a testament to this legacy at the fascinating Buddy Holly Center (1801 Crickets Ave., 806/767-2686, www.buddyhollycenter.org, Tues.–Sat. 10 A.M.–5 P.M., Sun. 1–5 P.M., $5 adults, $3 seniors ages 60 and older, $2 children ages 7–17). Holly's enormous impact on rock music is compounded by the fact that his professional career lasted merely 18 months. In that brief time, his distinct "Western bop" sound—a blend of country, blues, gospel, and bluegrass—had a major

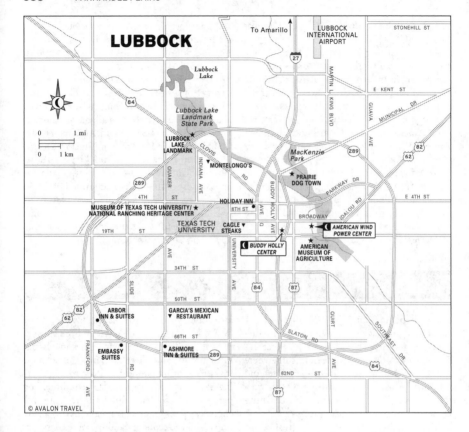

LUBBOCK

To Amarillo

LUBBOCK INTERNATIONAL AIRPORT

STONEHILL ST

Lubbock Lake

Lubbock Lake Landmark State Park

LUBBOCK LAKE LANDMARK

MONTELONGO'S

MacKenzie Park

PRAIRIE DOG TOWN

E KENT ST

MUSEUM OF TEXAS TECH UNIVERSITY/ NATIONAL RANCHING HERITAGE CENTER

HOLIDAY INN

E 4TH ST

TEXAS TECH UNIVERSITY

CAGLE STEAKS

AMERICAN WIND POWER CENTER

BROADWAY

BUDDY HOLLY CENTER

AMERICAN MUSEUM OF AGRICULTURE

ARBOR INN & SUITES

GARCIA'S MEXICAN RESTAURANT

EMBASSY SUITES

ASHMORE INN & SUITES

SLATON RD

© AVALON TRAVEL

impact on rock legends, including the Beatles, the Rolling Stones, and Bruce Springsteen. Paul McCartney claims the Beatles meticulously studied Holly's work and used it as a basis for their first hit song, "Love Me Do," and Holly's 1958 tour of England was a watershed moment for future British Invaders.

Holly and his band, the Crickets, developed an influential sound evident on classic hit songs such as "That'll Be the Day," "Oh Boy!," "Peggy Sue," "Maybe Baby," and "Rave On." Holly's life came to a tragic end with other music legends Ritchie Valens and J. P. "Big Bopper" Richardson when their plane crashed in an Iowa cornfield on February 3, 1959, famously referred to as "the day the music died" by songwriter Don McLean.

These stories and more take center stage at the Buddy Holly Center, which showcases the Lubbock native's brief life and significant career through informative exhibits, an enlightening film, and distinctive memorabilia (the signature horn-rimmed glasses found at his death scene are at once nostalgic and chilling). Other items, including childhood artwork, handwritten notes, and personal knickknacks, provide additional insight into this influential Lubbock musician whose noteworthy life was cut tragically short.

Aside from having a major city street renamed in his honor, Holly's legacy is evident in several Lubbock locales. The Buddy Holly statue near the corner of Avenue Q and 8th Street (just past the entrance to the

the Buddy Holly Center

Lubbock Civic Center) is a lasting reminder of the city's celebrated native son, and its surrounding Walk of Fame pays homage to other famous Lubbock-area musicians, including Roy Orbison, Sonny Curtis (a member of the Crickets), Waylon Jennings, Mac Davis, and Joe Ely.

Holly's gravesite is also a popular attraction for die-hard fans. Located just inside the entrance of the Lubbock Cemetery (at the east end of 31st Street), it contains admirers' mementos and the original spelling of his last name, "Holley"—the *e* was inadvertently omitted on his first recording contract, and the mistake was somehow never corrected.

American Wind Power Center

Who knew windmills could be so interesting? Apparently the owners of the unexpectedly compelling American Wind Power Center (1701 Canyon Lake Dr., 806/747-8734, www. windmill.com, Tues.–Sat. 10 A.M.–5 P.M., and on Sun. May–Sept. 2–5 P.M., $5 per person, $10 per family), who do a surprisingly good job of conveying the intrigue of many different kinds of wind-powered machines.

More than 100 historic and last-of-its-kind windmills from across the world reside in the center's giant barn, and dozens more punctuate the surrounding grounds. They range from the enormous (25 feet in diameter) to the strange (two-pronged whirligigs) to the inventive (models used to power most Great Plains homes during the early 20th century). Dominating the entire scene is the massive 164-foot-tall Vestas Wind Turbine, a metal giant with three imposing rotating fins that generate electricity for the museum.

Adjacent to the center is the associated **American Museum of Agriculture,** offering hundreds of antique tractors, equipment, and appliances related to the region's ranching heritage. The back room contains hundreds of tiny model tractors and vintage riding tractor toys. Visitors with kids are in luck—instead of being taunted by untouchable artifacts, kids are allowed to ride the mini tractor toys to test their future farming abilities.

PANHANDLE PLAINS

WIND POWER

Residents of the Panhandle Plains have been harvesting the wind for more than a century, using the natural element to power water-pumping windmills atop underground wells. These days, the ubiquitous wind currents on the high plains can generate electricity via massive turbines on quaintly named wind farms.

Lubbock, a hotbed for wind harvesting, is home to the American Wind Power Center, a museum dedicated to windmills and related energy issues. The center showcases these fascinating machines, primarily from the mid-1800s to 1920, that represent the "ingenuity, hardship, success and failure of the early settlers as they applied a new technology to conditions in an environment with which they were barely familiar."

These self-governing windmills had an enormous impact on the development of Texas and the entire western two-thirds of the country. In their heyday, more than 700 companies manufactured tens of thousands of windmills to help westward-bound settlers tap into their subterranean groundwater supply for irrigation and home use. Incidentally, only two windmill companies remain, and one is in Texas (Aermotor Windmill Company in San Angelo).

According to the American Wind Energy Association, Texas has become the leader in wind power development in amount of electricity generated. The omnipresent winds of West Texas (and the Gulf Coast) have helped Texas surpass California by hosting some of the nation's largest wind farms, wind turbine supply companies, and utilities that use the most wind power for their customers.

To learn all you ever wanted to know about windmills and wind power, drop by Lubbock's compelling museum dedicated to these topics. The American Wind Power Center contains more than 100 historic and rare windmills inside a large barn and dozens more on the surrounding grounds, ranging from an enormous 25-foot-diameter model to inventive models used to power many Great Plains homes in the early 1900s.

Texas Tech Cultural Facilities
THE MUSEUM OF TEXAS TECH UNIVERSITY

This enormous museum (3301 4th St., 806/742-2490, www.depts.ttu.edu/museumttu, Tues.–Sat. 10 A.M.–5 P.M., Thurs. until 8:30 P.M., Sun. 1–5 P.M., free admission) is far more remarkable than its name. In fact, while strolling through its multiple wings and impressive collections, it's easy to forget you're in a remote area of the Texas Panhandle.

Fascinating sculptures from Africa, colorful Latin American pottery, and rare pre-Columbian artwork transport visitors to other worlds. The museum's collections contain more than three million objects, and the thousands on display represent the upper echelon of the visual arts and natural sciences.

The Panhandle region and the entire southwestern United States are well represented by exhibits featuring ancient dinosaur fossils from the area and galleries showcasing historic Western art. The museum also includes a remodeled planetarium, a natural science research laboratory, a public auditorium, and a sculpture court. Just a note: If you prefer experiencing museums at a leisurely pace and in a distraction-free environment, consider visiting on the weekend, when large groups of local schoolchildren aren't set loose in the facility.

LUBBOCK LAKE LANDMARK

Though it's seemingly modest in comparison, Lubbock Lake Landmark (N. Loop 289 and U.S. 84 on Landmark Ln., 806/742-1116, www.depts.ttu.edu/museumttu, Tues.–Sat. 9 A.M.–5 P.M., Sun. 1–5 P.M., free admission) showcases a similarly significant aspect of history than the artifact-rich Museum of Texas Tech by offering a window to 12,000 years of the region's past.

The landmark's inspiring interpretive center

puts the surrounding diverse geographic features—a rare sight in Lubbock—in full perspective. A spring-fed reservoir on the grounds has provided a source of life for plants, animals, and their associated human hunters for at least 12 millennia. The center walks visitors through the fascinating archaeological finds made during the past 75 years that document thousands of generations of humans, mammoth, bison, and even giant armadillo who habitually returned to the watering hole to sustain (and take) life.

A one-mile walking trail encircling the reservoir now known as Lubbock Lake provides context for this unique area. The lush green marshes and elevated river valley noticeably contrast with the surrounding High Plains' overwhelmingly flat topography.

NATIONAL RANCHING HERITAGE CENTER
The ranching center (3121 4th St., 806/742-0498, www.depts.ttu.edu/ranchhc, Mon.–Sat. 10 A.M.–5 P.M., Sun. 1–5 P.M., free admission) is a 16-acre mostly outdoor site featuring 36 authentic yet relocated ranching structures. Spanning 200 years, these American ranch-related buildings run the gamut from ramshackle barn to opulent home. Also included on the grounds are windmills, a locomotive, a blacksmith shop, school, and bunkhouse. Visitors can't enter most structures, but several have open doors and gated windows offering views of period furnishings.

Prairie Dog Town and Mackenzie Park
The small area of parkland known as Prairie Dog Town (inside Mackenzie Park, entrance at 4th Street and I-27, 806/775-2687, open year-round sunrise–sunset) isn't as charming as it sounds. Don't get too excited about seeing scores of cute little fellas romping around and eating treats right out of your hand. They're definitely visible, and they are pretty cute, but aside from standing up on two legs and scanning the surrounding prairie, they don't do much. They pop out of holes relatively far away

from the viewing area—you can get a better look at them if you have binoculars or a telephoto camera lens.

The prairie dogs remain in this part of Lubbock thanks to the efforts of one man, who spared their cute little lives in the 1930s when efforts were made to eradicate their overpopulation. Incidentally, they get their canine-influenced name from the little doglike barks they emit when danger—in this case, tourists—threaten on the prairie's horizon.

The surrounding Mackenzie Park is a welcome respite from Lubbock's flat environs, with hills and valleys offering an opportunity to experience actual topography. Also on the park's grounds is a small amusement park called Joyland (open on weekends from spring through fall), a disc golf course, a real golf course, an amphitheater, and a sculpture garden.

ENTERTAINMENT AND EVENTS
Depot Entertainment District
Lubbock's downtown has seen better days, but the city's Depot Entertainment District (just off I-27 and 19th St.) is a lively collection of bars and clubs near the Buddy Holly Center that draws young professionals, Tech students, and even a few ranchers in search of rockabilly and 'ritas. The soul of the district is the venerable and beautifully restored 1930s Cactus Theater, located across from the historic Fort Worth to Denver Railroad Depot building, now serving as a portion of the Buddy Holly Center.

Make a point of dropping by the remarkable **Cactus Theater** (1812 Buddy Holly Ave., 806/762-3233, www.cactustheater.com). Ideally, you'll be able to catch a show—check the website for scheduled performances—from live country and western acts (the Maines Brothers) to soulful singer-songwriters (Jerry Jeff Walker) to musicals and theatrical productions. The acoustics are amazing, and the wraparound caprock canyon mural is captivating. Next door is another noteworthy live music venue, the **Blue Light** (1808 Buddy Holly Ave.,

806/749-5442, www.thebluelightlive.com), featuring Texas country and rock acts Tuesday through Saturday. Grab a frozen concoction or cold bottle of Lone Star at the adjoining **Tom's Daiquiri Place** and settle in for a fine evening of High Plains–style entertainment.

Those seeking a mellower scene should visit **La Diosa Cellars** (901 17th St., 806/744-3600, www.ladiosacellars.com, closed Sun. and Mon.), billing itself as the first and only winery inside the city limits. La Diosa (the goddess) offers wines by the glass, bottle, or case and is known for its bistro menu of tasty tapas, its coffee bar, and gourmet desserts. Of note: Lubbock is primarily a dry city, so this is one of the few places in town you can purchase alcohol to go.

There's not a lot of holy activity happening in **Heaven** (1928 Buddy Holly Ave., 806/762-4466), where the kids come to mingle and dance to hip-hop, techno, and house DJs. Another popular Depot District spot for singles is **Melt** (1711 Texas Ave., 806/687-2034), where you can eat a tasty dinner and dance off the calories afterward.

Events
LUBBOCK ARTS FESTIVAL
Held each April at the civic center, the city's popular arts festival (806/744-2787) is a feast for the senses. Stroll among booths of regional, national, and international artists offering everything from Southwestern jewelry to colorful murals to stone sculptures. Grab a tasty yet politically incorrect Indian taco (a corn tostada with beans and rice) from the food court, listen to a chamber music trio, and delight in the Lubbock's arts scene.

NATIONAL COWBOY SYMPOSIUM AND CELEBRATION
One of the city's most highly anticipated and well-attended annual events is the cowboy symposium (806/798-7825, www.cowboy.org). Held at the civic center each September, this uniquely Texas event celebrates Old West cowboys through storytelling, poetry readings, music, art, and participation from honest-to-goodness cowboys. Attend readings, panel discussions, and performances by scholars and genuine cowpokes, along with a chuckwagon cook-off, horse parade, and trail ride.

LUBBOCK MUSIC FESTIVAL
Also held each September is the city's annual music fest (800/692-4035). The Depot Entertainment District becomes music central, with stages and food booths showcasing the best Texas has to offer—blues, barbecue, and beer. Past performers include Three Dog Night and Cross Canadian Ragweed.

SHOPPING
Western Wear
Lubbock is cowboy country, so the Western gear around here is genuine. A good starting point is **The Branding Iron Cowboy Outfitters** (3320 34th St., 866/312-0500, www.cowboy-outfitter.com), just south of the Texas Tech campus. This family-owned shop keeps things simple by focusing on quality Western brands and merchandise. Look for Stetson and Resistol hats (felt and straw), Justin and Tony Lama boots, and bunches of belt buckles. Another respected local Western shop is **Boot City Inc.** (6645 19th St., 806/797-8782, www.bootcity.com). Located west of town just outside the loop, Boot City specializes in boots (Tony Lama, Justin, Nocona, Anderson Bean, and Dan Post), cowboy hats, belts, buckles, and other Western apparel.

The Fort Worth–based **Luskey's/Ryons Western Store** (5034 Frankford Ave., 806/795-7100, www.luskeys.com) has five locations in Texas, and its Lubbock store is one of the most popular. Luskey's has a far more extensive selection than other Western shops in town, featuring the requisite boots, hats, and apparel, along with saddles, ropes, tack, and other leather goods.

Antiques
Some may call it junk, but others delight in the bric-a-brac and Americana crammed into Lubbock's peerless **Antique Mall** (7907 W. 19th St., 806/796-2166). Boasting 24,000

square feet of stuff, Antique Mall peddles in nostalgia as much as (perhaps even more than) valuable objects. Texas Tech and Lubbock-related items offer a charming regional flair, and shoppers may find a treasure or two among the Depression-era glass and furniture, vintage drugstore/pharmacy collectibles, and historic advertising memorabilia.

ACCOMMODATIONS
$50-100

Affordable rooms abound in Lubbock, which tends to draw most of its out-of-towners for Texas Tech University–related activities (sporting events, alumni gatherings, commencement ceremonies, etc.). Those looking for a cheap and consistent place to stay near campus often go with the no-frills **Super 8** (501 Ave. Q, 806/762-8726, www.super8.com, $49 d), featuring a free continental breakfast, free Internet access, and refrigerators in every room. To get the most bang for your buck, consider the popular and amenity-packed **Guesthouse Inn** (3815 21st St., 806/791-0433, www.lubbockguesthouseinn.com, $75 d), which strives for a homey atmosphere by offering suites with kitchenettes, living rooms with reading libraries, a free continental breakfast, and complimentary wireless Internet access, all just six blocks away from the Tech campus.

If you're looking to stay downtown within walking distance of the many Civic Center activities, book your room at the **Holiday Inn Hotel & Towers** (801 Ave. Q, 806/763-2656, www.ichotelsgroup.com, $89 d). The "tower" is a six-story building with rooms facing an open interior atrium featuring a large fountain in the center. The hotel includes free Internet access, a fitness room, swimming pool, whirlpool, and sauna.

Farther outside of town is the independently owned and very recommendable ((**Ashmore Inn & Suites** (4019 S. Loop 289, 806/785-0060, www.ashmoreinn.com, $99 d). Nothing here is over-the-top, but the service and amenities are better than expected, including spacious rooms with free Wi-Fi access, microwaves, and refrigerators, along with a free

continental breakfast, complimentary cocktails (Monday–Thursday 5:30–7 P.M.), an outdoor pool, and an exercise room and hot tub.

$100-150

Consider spending a little extra money for one of the finest accommodations in town, the amenity-filled ((**Arbor Inn & Suites** (5310 Englewood Ave., 806/744-1763, www.arborinnandsuites.com, $109 d). This memorable locale offers large rooms with full kitchens, free breakfast, and a late-day treat of fresh-baked cookies with lemonade and iced tea (4–9 P.M. daily). Other unexpected pleasantries include complimentary cold bottled water and a generous "owner's reception" every Tuesday 5:30–7 P.M. featuring dinner, beverages (beer, wine, iced tea, or lemonade), plus dessert.

Farther south of town is the fancy **Embassy Suites** (5215 S. Loop 289, 806/771-7000, www.embassysuites.com, $139 d), featuring a Tuscan-style atrium with tropical plants and pathways meandering around a koi pond and miniature waterfalls. The hotel provides free wireless Internet access, complimentary nightly manager's receptions with drinks and food, a free hot breakfast, exercise room, and heated indoor pool. Just down the road is the commendable **Fairfield Inn** (4007 S. Loop 289, 806/795-1288, www.marriott.com, $149 d). Catering primarily to business travelers, the Fairfield features free Wi-Fi access as well as a spiffy indoor pool and spa, and a free continental breakfast.

Camping

Lubbockites love **Buffalo Springs Lake** (9999 High Meadow Rd., 806/747-3353, www.buffalospringslake.net, $12–24 nightly rates), a recreation area eight miles southeast of town with rare commodities—water, grass, and trees. The camping options here range from sites with paved pads and water access to spots with electric hookups to plain ol' tent sites. All the campgrounds have trees, and the tent area features grass along the water's edge. Other Buffalo Springs activities include a golf course, hiking and biking trails, an amphitheater, party house, and pavilions. The campground takes a limited number of reservations and requires a three-night minimum stay.

RVers return regularly to the popular **Lubbock RV Park** (4811 N. I-27, 806/747-2366, www.lubbockrvpark.com, $24 nightly site fee), offering plenty of shade trees, an outdoor pool, laundry facilities, and showers.

FOOD
Mexican

Ask locals where to find the best Mexican food in town, and they're not likely to suggest the bright, busy eateries packed with ravenous students near Texas Tech University. More likely, you'll be directed to a satisfyingly authentic locale like ◖ **Montelongo's** (3021 Clovis Rd., 806/762-3068, $4–10), just northwest of downtown. The flavors here are *incredible*, particularly in the magnificent chicken mole, an exceptional dish featuring perhaps the best mole sauce in the Panhandle. Savor the rich yet delicate taste of the hearty sauce, with its buttery nut base and accents of spicy pepper and bitter chocolate. The chicken is tender, and the rice and beans are elevated beyond mere side-item status. If you only eat one meal in Lubbock, make the effort to experience this exceptionally authentic item. Not quite as satisfying yet still very tasty is **Garcia's Mexican Restaurant** (5604 Slide Rd., 806/792-0097, $6–12). Located in a fairly new strip mall-esque building southwest of downtown, Garcia's serves fresh Tex-Mex that's consistently fulfilling. You can't go wrong with any of the standards here, from fajitas and enchiladas to tacos and quesadillas.

Although **Abuelo's** (4401 82nd St., 806/794-1762, www.abuelos.com, $6–19) is a chain, it's well respected in these parts, and for good reason. The food here is far better than expected, and the atmosphere makes it even more recommendable. Abuelo's is always packed, especially for happy hour and dinner, when local bands play outside on the patio and margaritas flow freely. Be sure to sample the seafood dishes here, the grilled mahimahi in particular. Other popular menu items include the jalapeño-stuffed shrimp, the bacon-wrapped beef tenderloin, and the delectable dulce de leche cheesecake.

Steak and Barbecue

There's only one noteworthy restaurant in Lubbock's Depot Entertainment District, and it's certainly worth experiencing. **Triple J Chophouse and Brew Co.** (1807 Buddy Holly Ave., 806/771-6555, www.triplejchophouseandbrewco.com, $10–33, closed Sun.) is the city's only brewpub, and it serves several hearty steaks to accompany the refreshing handcrafted beers. Filet mignon is the specialty here, but don't overlook the rib eye or prime rib. Alternate options include the smoked salmon or pork chop and grilled chicken.

Locals love **Cagle Steaks** (1212 Ave. K, 806/795-3879, www.caglesteaks.com, $9–37, closed Sun.), a charmingly rustic spot with grade-A meat located just west of town in an old house displaced by the railroad. Kick-start your meal with a "pasture pickle," a cheesy steak finger with jalapeños, and continue with a heaping helping of barbecue (the ribs are spectacular) or one of the tender and delicious rib eye steaks, offered by thickness of the cut, at three-quarters of an inch, one inch (just the right size at about 16 ounces), or one and a quarter inches.

Another popular place for Lubbockites in search of quality steaks and meat is **Las Brisas** (4701 112th St., 806/687-6050, www.lasbrisassouthweststeakhouse.com, $10–36, closed Sun.), specializing in Southwestern specialties and prime cuts of beef including filet mignon, New York strip, pecan-crusted pork loin, blackened salmon, mesquite-smoked fajitas, chiles rellenos, grilled shrimp, and sea bass.

For barbecue, it doesn't get much better than **J&M Bar-B-Q** (3605 34th St., 806/796-1164, www.jandmbar-b-q.com, closed Sun., also J&M Express, 7924 Slide Rd., 806/798-2525, $8–19). J&M is known for its perfectly smoked and seasoned brisket, jalapeño sausage, and ribs topped with a tangy and spicy sauce. Be sure to save room for cobbler or banana pudding.

Lunch

Appropriately located in Lubbock's medical

complex is the health-oriented **Bless Your Heart Restaurant** (3701 19th St., 806/791-2211, $5–12). This deli-style eatery just south of the Texas Tech campus is known for its fresh, fast, and healthy offerings, including salads, light chicken dishes, sandwiches topped with sprouts, baked potatoes, and frozen yogurt. On the heartier side is the as-welcoming-as-it-sounds **Home Cafe** (3131 34th St., 806/687-1466, $5–16, closed Mon.), where virtually every menu item is freshly made in-store daily. From breads to sauces to soups, pastas, chicken, sandwiches, and pork chops, Home Cafe is an ideal place to drop by for a satisfying and healthy lunch. The homemade lemonade is known throughout Lubbock.

For a good ol' fashioned burger, head to **Buns Over Texas** (3402 73rd St., 806/793-0012, $4–9, closed Sun.). This traditional burger joint serves exactly what you'd expect—hot, juicy fresh-ground burgers on sweet hand-toasted buns accompanied by crispy onion rings or deliciously gooey cheese fries. Wash it all down with a thick chocolate shake.

INFORMATION AND SERVICES

To get a handle on all the travelers' services available in Lubbock, including brochures, maps, pamphlets, and other literature, drop by the **Lubbock Convention & Visitors Bureau,** on the sixth floor of the downtown Wells Fargo Center (1500 Broadway St., 806/747-5232, www.visitlubbock.org).

GETTING THERE AND AROUND

For those traveling to Lubbock by air, the **Lubbock International Airport** (5401 N. Martin Luther King Blvd., 806/775-204, www.flylia.com) is located about 10 minutes from downtown just northeast of the city. The airport offers service from American Eagle, Continental Express, and Southwest Airlines. Once there, ground transportation is available from most of the major car rental companies and Lubbock's cab services, including **City Cab** (806/765-7474) and **Yellow Cab** (806/765-7777).

Amarillo and Vicinity

Amarillo (population 185,525) is the most compelling destination in the Panhandle because it offers two distinctly uncommon resources—Palo Duro Canyon and Route 66. Both involve some extra driving and exploring, but it's well worth the effort to experience these uniquely Texas attractions.

Amarillo's cultural heritage reflects a variety of influences: Native Americans, Spanish conquistadors, buffalo hunters, American settlers, cowboys, and the railroad. This combination of the Old and New West provides a captivating draw to this remote region of the state.

The city's name originates from a large nearby playa (seasonal lake) and creek referred to as *amarillo,* Spanish for yellow, by New Mexican traders and shepherds, describing the color of the soil. Though Native American tribes and Spanish explorers had traversed

the area for thousands of years, the lack of a consistent water source prevented permanent settlements.

That changed in the late 1800s, when windmill-powered wells reached the deep water table, and particularly when the Fort Worth and Denver City Railway arrived in 1887, resulting in freight service to Amarillo and its subsequent status as a cattle-marketing center. Hundreds of herds from ranches in the Panhandle, South Plains, and eastern New Mexico were driven and corralled in holding pens near the railroad tracks for shipment to meat-packing centers in the Midwest and the eastern UnitedStates.

In the late teens and early '20s, Amarillo became a hotbed for the petrochemical industry when gas and oil were discovered in nearby fields, resulting in a mini boom of oil refineries

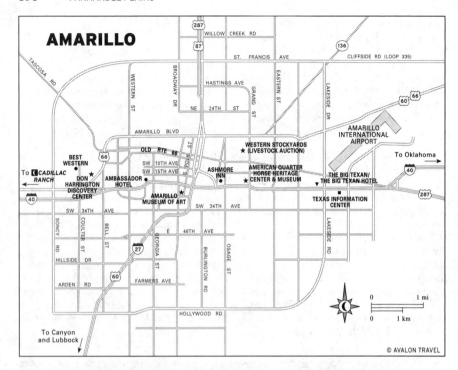

and oil-shipping facilities. The discovery of the helium-rich Cliffside gas field in 1928 led to the establishment of the United States Helium Plant.

By the 1930s, cross-country automobile travel kicked into high gear thanks to the newly established transcontinental highways, most notably the famed Route 66. Amarillo represented the Mother Road's only urban outpost between Oklahoma City and Albuquerque, and the city's unique blend of fiery, friendly folks endeared many travelers to its rich pioneer spirit and independence. Gas stations, motor lodges, and dance halls kept travelers served and entertained while passing through the Panhandle's largest city.

Throughout the remainder of the 20th century, Amarillo cemented its reputation as an economic hub for the petroleum, cattle, and agricultural industries (grain storage, processing, and feed). Though the city boasts several tourism-related attractions, including the iconic Cadillac Ranch just west of town, it's perhaps best known as the starting point for ventures beyond city limits to the alluringly desolate canyons and plains.

SIGHTS

Despite being hundreds of miles from nowhere, Amarillo has an artistic side that sets it apart from other cities in faraway areas of Texas and the United States. Cadillac Ranch and the helium monument are must-sees for pop culture enthusiasts, and the city's cowboy heritage is on full display at the American Quarter Horse Museum. Incidentally, while you're driving around town, keep an eye out for colorful fiberglass versions of this trusty steed. *Hoof Prints of the American Quarter Horse* is a city-wide public art display featuring more than 75 replicas of these horses, each painted or decorated by a local artist and displayed as a

THE MOTHER ROAD

Old **Route 66** has a distinctive urban presence in Amarillo, with its art deco-themed streetscapes and awnings of Spanish tile offering an endearing nostalgic charm compared to today's bland strip centers. For a true sense of the Mother Road's legacy, however, venture to the smaller Panhandle communities, where you'll discover authentic diners providing a welcome respite from franchise restaurant chains, and motor courts' neon signs crackling vacancy notices without promoting free Wi-Fi or announcing corporate seminars.

You'll find most of the historic small-town Route 66 buildings east of Amarillo, just off the 100-mile stretch of I-40 to the Oklahoma border. An essential stop is the city of McLean, home of the **Texas Old Route 66 and Devil's Rope Museums** (100 Kingsley St., 806/779-2225, www.barbwiremuseum.com, Tues.-Sat. 10 A.M.-4 P.M.). Though the barbed wire (aka "devil's rope") portion of the building is intriguing, the Texas Old Route 66 Museum offers a fascinating glimpse into the not-too-distant past, with vintage road signs, artwork from tourist traps – the enormous metal rattlesnake salvaged from the Regal Reptile Ranch is particularly amusing – and hundreds of mementos and souvenirs from the golden age of automobile travel. While in McLean, be sure to snap a few photos of the classic 1928 cottage-style **Phillips 66 station** on old Route 66 at the edge of town (westbound on Old Route 66 Hwy., two blocks west of Main St.).

Just east of McLean is Shamrock, home of Texas's most impressive Route 66 building. The **U-Drop Inn and Conoco Station** (intersection of Old Route 66 and Hwy. 83, 806/256-2516, www.shamrocktx.net) is a remarkable 1936 art deco landmark with a steeplelike spire that advertised food, gas, and lodging – three essential elements for Route 66 travelers. Refurbished to its original glory, this building, which inspired Ramone's detailing shop in Dis-

ney's animated *Cars* movie, now houses the Shamrock Chamber of Commerce.

West of Amarillo, the small town of Vega beckons travelers to the classic 1940s-era **Vega Motel** (1005 Vega Blvd., aka Old Route 66, 806/267-2205, www.vegamotel.com) still welcomes weary travelers and curiosity seekers, while the nearby **Dot's Mini Museum** (one block north of Old Route 66, 806/267-2828) features Texas memorabilia and Route 66 artifacts.

Farther west on I-40 lies Adrian, another little town that time forgot. It's best known for the **Midpoint Café** (on the south side of Vega Blvd., 866/538-6380, www.midpoint66.com), named for its location on Route 66 midway between Chicago and Los Angeles (each 1,139 miles away). The Midpoint Café is known for is delectable homemade pies (try the blueberry) and enormous hamburgers, but the best option on a chilly afternoon is a steaming bowl of hearty beef stew. Be sure to check out the Route 66-themed gift shop housed in the attached original café building, and don't forget to snap a photo in front of the famous Mid-Point sign across the street.

The end of the road for Route 66 in Texas is Glenrio, an abandoned community straddling the Texas–New Mexico border. You won't find empty saloons or bouncing tumbleweeds here, but it's a compelling place to get out of your car and explore. Check out the old gas station and post office buildings, and be sure to mosey by the vacant structure with a broken sign still announcing Last Motel in Texas on one side and First Motel in Texas on the other.

These communities are far removed from their heyday on Route 66, which once beckoned Americans with adventure and new beginnings around every bend of the highway. This sentiment was perhaps best captured by John Steinbeck in his classic 1939 novel *The Grapes of Wrath* in the passage, "They come into 66 from the tributary side roads, from the wagon tracks and the rutted country roads. 66 is the mother road, the road of flight."

tribute this animal integral to Amarillo's heritage and culture.

◖ Cadillac Ranch

One of the premier photo ops in Texas, Cadillac Ranch (approximately 12 miles west of downtown Amarillo between exits 60 and 62—exit Arnot Rd. on the south side of I-40) is a permanent art installation of 10 Cadillacs buried nose-down in a field. This bumper crop was originally planted in 1974 but relocated farther west 23 years later due to encroaching development. The cars, representing the golden age of American automobiles (1949–63) were positioned at the same angle as the pyramids in Egypt.

Cadillac Ranch is the brainchild of local eccentric Stanley Marsh 3, who inherited his family's oil and helium fortune and created pieces of compelling public art throughout the Panhandle. The 10 Cadillacs are covered with thick layers of paint and graffiti, a practice Marsh apparently encourages. At any given time, the cars may be painted in different colors or emblazoned with messages and signatures. To get there, park your car along the brim of the freeway and walk the well-worn path to the monument (open all hours). Be sure to bring a camera and/or a can of spray paint to document your visit.

© TEXAS HISTORICAL COMMISSION

Cadillac Ranch near Amarillo

American Quarter Horse Heritage Center & Museum

Horses are serious business in cowboy country, and nowhere else is this more apparent than at the American Quarter Horse Heritage Center & Museum (2601 E. I-40, 806/376-5181, www.aqhahalloffame.com, Mon.–Sat. 9 A.M.–5 P.M. year-round, Sun. noon–5 P.M. Memorial Day–Labor Day, $6 adults, $5 seniors, $2 children ages 6–18). This large and intriguing museum showcases the history and culture related to quarter horses, the country's most popular breed, revered for its skills on the ranch and its performance in rodeos. Museum visitors will learn everything they ever wanted to know about quarter horses through ranching and racing artifacts, interesting video clips,

and interactive exhibits. More than 1,000 objects depict the breed's rise to prominence in racing and recreation throughout the Americas and Europe, while art and photo galleries highlight its exquisite beauty. The museum's Grand Hall, an enormous area marked by an oversized medallion and hearty stone and timber columns, honors the people who shaped the quarter horse over the past several centuries. While at the museum, be sure to inquire about arena demonstrations featuring these exquisite equines in action.

Don Harrington Discovery Center

Families will love the delightful Don Harrington Discovery Center (1200 Streit Dr., 806/355-9547, www.dhdc.org, Tues.–Thurs. 9:30 A.M.–4:30 P.M., Fri.–Sat. 9:30 A.M.–8 P.M.,Sun. noon–4:30 P.M., $10 adults, $7 seniors and students ages 3–12). Science is the main attraction here, with dozens of fascinating exhibits and hands-on activities conveying the significance of biology, weather, and physics, to name a few. The center also features the region's only aquarium and planetarium, and an intriguing helium technology exhibit. Speaking of helium, the museum is home to the renowned **Helium Monument,** a four-pronged stainless-steel time column dedicated to the natural element found in great quantities near Amarillo. Three of the six-story-tall monument's columns form a tripod with four dangling spheres representing helium's molecular structure. Each column contains time capsules corresponding to natural resources to be opened 25, 50, 100, and 1,000 years from 1968, the year the monument was erected.

Amarillo Museum of Art

If you have a few hours to spare while in town, make a point of stopping by the Amarillo Museum of Art (2200 S. Van Buren St., 806/371-5050, www.amarilloart.org, Tues.–Fri. 10 A.M.–5 P.M., Sun. 1–5 P.M., no admission fee). Located on the campus of Amarillo College, the museum contains a worthy collection of paintings, photographs, prints, and sculptures representing a broad range of cultures and eras. The museum initially focused on early American Modernist paintings (four Georgia O'Keeffe watercolors represent this style), but it has since expanded to include centuries-old European paintings and an impressive collection of Asian art, including Buddhist and Hindu pieces from 200 B.C. to Khmer sculpture from the 1300s.

HIGH AND DRY

The Llano Estacado, a vast elevated mesa comprising the western portions of the Panhandle Plains region, literally translates as "staked plains" in modern Spanish, and the origins of this moniker vary wildly. Though some legends claim the words refer to wooden stakes jabbed into the ground to mark watering holes, or an allusion to the area's spiky yucca leaves, most historians agree it's a reference to the sharp cliffs of the mesa's eastern edge that resemble the walls of a stockade (*estacado*).

This high tableland, with elevations ranging 3–5,000 feet above sea level, slopes at a rate of nearly 10 feet per mile toward the southeast. Considered one of the largest mesas on the continent, the Llano Estacado comprises 33 Texas counties (four in New Mexico) and covers approximately 32,000 square miles, larger than the entirety of New England.

Coronado's description of the land's geographical features in a 1541 letter to the king of Spain reveals not much has changed here over the past several centuries. He wrote, "I reached some plains so vast, that I did not find their limit anywhere ... with no more land marks than if we had been swallowed up by the sea ... there was not a stone, nor bit of rising ground, nor a tree, nor a shrub, nor anything to go by."

The composition of this enormous physical feature is somewhat difficult to comprehend, but an unofficial geological comparison would be to a colossal river delta comprised of aggraded materials deposited from the activity associated with the Rocky Mountains' formation. Evaporation created a hard caprock, leaving this arid area isolated and impenetrable.

Because of its elevation, geographic location, and solid ground material, the Llano Estacado is in a precipitous situation regarding water availability. Though not heavily populated, the area uses a considerable amount of water for irrigation, causing many residents in the region to fear the ramifications of depleting a potentially finite source of groundwater.

Nearly three-quarters of the Llano Estacado's residents live in cities, mainly Lubbock and Amarillo, though Midland and Odessa are considered to be on the southern edge. Over the course of a century (1880–1980), the population of this area increased from approximately 1,000 residents to more than 900,000. Now, the more than one million people who call the Llano Estacado home are hoping they don't soon find themselves literally high and dry.

Amarillo Livestock Auction

If you're in Amarillo on a Tuesday, be sure to experience the livestock auction (100 S. Manhattan St., 806/373-7464, www.amarillolivestockauction.com, auctions typically begin at 10 A.M.). This is the real deal—steers and heifers are corralled into the auction ring and bid on by genuine cowboys and ranch owners. There's a palpable excitement to the proceedings, as hundreds of cattle trade hands while prospective bidders gauge the scene. By the end of the year, more than 100,000 head of cattle will be sold at the facility. The adjacent Stockyard Café offers tasty breakfasts and lunch for hungry visitors (no word on the origins of the beef).

ENTERTAINMENT AND EVENTS
Bars and Clubs

Amarillo's nightlife scene is relatively generic, with the exception of a handful of venues west of downtown on 6th Avenue, formerly Route 66. This stretch of road has some vacant pockets, but the areas of activity, including more than 100 independently owned antiques shops, restaurants, and memorable bars, are housed in charming art deco buildings on quaint cobblestone sidewalks. The most famous of the bunch is the spectacular **Golden Light Cafe and Cantina** (2908 W. 6th Ave., 806/374-0097, www.goldenlightcafe.com). This unassuming spot, built in 1946 and featuring a modest sign over the door that appears to have inspired the Hard Rock Café logo, stages live country and blues acts every weekend in a laid-back, casual environment (not surprisingly, actor Matthew McConaughey has been spied here). Returning acts include Stoney LaRue, Macon Grayson, and Cooter Graw. The cover charge is typically $5. Incidentally, the Golden Light runs a popular restaurant serving tasty down-home favorites like chicken-fried steak, burgers, and pork chops.

Another venerable venue on America's Main Street is **The Cattlemen's Club** (3801 E. Amarillo Blvd., 806/383-9053), a classic country and western bar featuring live music and cold beer. The lonesome sounds of twangy slide guitars provide an ideal accompaniment for the dark and low-key scene at Cattlemen's, where you can kick back with a Lone Star and let your troubles mosey away. Not quite as traditional yet equally intriguing is the newfangled **The 806** (2812 W. 6th Ave., 806/322-1806), a roadside café for the current generation. Named for the Panhandle's area code, this coffeehouse is a hotbed for Amarillo's Wi-Fi laptop crowd, who tap away while sipping on strong java drinks and listening to open mic acts in the shadow of avant-garde artwork.

Events
TEXAS OUTDOOR MUSICAL

With the colorful cliff walls of Palo Duro Canyon State Park just south of the city serving as a picturesque backdrop, this musical theater production depicts the historical romance of the Old West and Texas's 19th-century settlement years. Fancy lights and sound effects, along with traditional costumes, dancing, and music, tell the popular story to rapt audiences each summer. Performances are held Tuesday–Saturday June–August. A barbecue dinner is served 6–8 P.M. before each show. For more information, call 806/655-2181 or visit www.texas-show.com.

TRI-STATE FAIR

Drawing participants from Texas, New Mexico, and Oklahoma, the Tri-State Fair offers late-summer fun (mid-September in these parts) for area folks, with traditional activities such as rodeo and livestock shows, farming and ranching exhibits, and food and crafts booths.

NATIONAL OLD-TIMERS RODEO

This popular event, held most years in November at the city's civic center, features the country's finals competition for rodeo cowboys over the age of 40. Despite the "old-timers" moniker, these dudes can still move quickly while riding and roping.

SHOPPING

Amarillo's shopping scene is particularly noteworthy for its kitschy antique shops occupying charming historic retail stores along old Route 66. Since the city is entrenched in the agribusiness of the Old West, it's also a great place to find authentic boots, hats, and other Western gear.

Antiques

For a truly distinctive shopping experience, head on down to old Route 66 (now 6th Avenue, but referred to as 6th Street by locals) just west of downtown. Though some of the original charm has been "modernized," bulldozed, or abandoned, there are several pockets of America's Main Street offering a time warp to the road's busy heyday. The best stretch is between Georgia and Western Streets, where shoppers will encounter bright storefronts and cheery display windows in historic retail buildings, cafés, and service stations. One of the premiere antiques stores in the area is **Texas Ivy Antiques** (3511 W. 6th Ave., 806/373-1427), located in a quaint 1920s home. Specialties here include glassware, restaurant items, linens, toys, and retro furniture.

Antiques shops are by no means interchangeable, but the rotating nature of the stock makes it difficult to categorize them individually by content. The following 6th Street stores have been in business for a considerable amount of time, rendering them recommendable: **Sixth Street Antique Mall** (2715 W. 6th Ave., 806/374-0459) and **San Jacinto Antiques** (2900 W. 6th Ave., 806/372-3665).

Although most of its bustling antiques booths are gone, it's still worth dropping by the legendary **Nat Ballroom** (604 S. Georgia St., 806/236-6482) for a glimpse of history and some vintage volumes at the bookstore. The building opened as a natatorium (indoor swimming pool) in 1922 and was soon after converted into a "dine and dance palace," with a maple dance floor constructed over the pool. The Nat now serves primarily as a special-event venue with a modest yet interesting collection of books for sale.

Boots and Western Wear

Amarillo is known for its quality Western-wear stores, particularly its custom boot makers and abundance of cowboy hats and apparel. One of the legendary locales in town for exquisite custom-made boots is **Western Leather Craft Boot** (1950 Civic Cir., 806/355-0174). Specializing in top-notch working and dress boots for nearly a century, Western Leather outfits locals and visitors with work boots, art boots, wing tips, and flower inlays. Another popular spot for out-of-towners to browse is the aptly named **Boots & Jeans** (2225 S. Georgia St., 806/353-4368), a no-nonsense Western shop featuring brand-name cowboy hats, boots, shirts, and accessories.

Other stores in town offer similar products (hats, leather goods, jeans, snap-button shirts, buckles, and other accessories) in less-inspiring environs. Look for this cowboy gear with lower prices at **Los Tres Vaqueros Western** (1105 S. Grand St., 806/374-0000), **Horse & Rider** (2500 S. Coulter St., 806/352-5544), and **Cavender's Boot City** (7920 W. I-40, 806/358-1400).

ACCOMMODATIONS

Virtually all of Amarillo's decent hotels are chains located on I-40 that fall into the moderately affordable category. Unfortunately, most of the interesting historic hotels fell victim to the wrecking ball or are too run-down to recommend. The good news? The acceptable generic options are all within five minutes of the city's main attractions.

Hotels

If you don't mind a little wear and tear with your Texas kitsch, book a room at **The Big Texan Hotel** (7701 I-40 E., 806/372-5000, www.bigtexan.com, $69 d). This is not a place for those seeking sleek, new amenities, but it's certainly a memorable experience, with its Old West–themed building facades, Texas-shaped outdoor pool, faux cowhide bedspreads, and Texas flag shower curtains. It's Texas to the max. Far less interesting yet much more modern is **Baymont Inn & Suites** (3411 I-40 W., 806/356-6800, www.baymontinns.com, $69 d), offering free breakfast, a fitness center, free

Internet access, and an outdoor pool. Another fine option is **Best Western** (1610 S. Coulter St., 806/358-7861, www.bestwesterntexas. com, $99 d), featuring large rooms with free Internet access, an indoor pool, and a fitness center and spa.

Slightly more expensive yet worth the extra money is the independently owned ◖ **Ashmore Inn & Suites** (2301 I-40 E., 806/374-0033, www.ashmoresuites.com, $119 d). The Ashmore features a free continental breakfast, a complimentary happy hour (free booze and wine Monday–Thursday), microwaves, refrigerators, Internet access, an indoor pool, Jacuzzi, and fitness center. Another commendable option is **Hampton Inn** (1700 I-40 E., 806/372-1425, www.hamptoninn. com, $129 d), offering free Internet access, a free breakfast (including to-go bags), and an outdoor pool.

One of Amarillo's fanciest accommodations is the **Ambassador Hotel** (3100 I-40 W., 806/358-6161, www.ambassadoramarillo.com, $129 d). Though it's not quite as upscale as its website suggests, the Ambassador is nevertheless a comfortable and classy (for Amarillo) place to spend a few nights. Amenities include an indoor pool and whirlpool, a fitness center, and free Internet access.

The newest addition (late 2009) to Amarillo's hotel scene—and the first located in the historic downtown business district—is the **Courtyard Amarillo Downtown** (724 S. Polk St., 806/553-4500, www.marriott.com, $120 d). Occupying the historic (1927) Fisk Building, the hotel offers free Wi-Fi service, a restaurant (breakfast is not included in the room rate), a bar, free parking garage, 24-hour business center, and even a concierge.

Camping
There's really only one worthwhile place to camp in the Amarillo area (or even the Panhandle): **Palo Duro Canyon State Park** (11450 Park Rd. 5, 806/488-2227, www.tpwd. state.tx.us). Located about 15 miles south of Amarillo near the town of Canyon, Palo Duro is a true sight to behold. The park offers nearly

80 campsites ($12 nightly, $20 for sites with water and electric). If you plan ahead, you can snag a prized cabin—only seven are available, so they fill up quickly. Three of the cabins have two rooms ($100–115 nightly) and include two single beds and a queen bed, with linens and towels furnished. The park's four limited-service facilities ($55 nightly) contain two twin beds and a table and chairs, but no towels or linens.

For the RV crowd, the most popular option is **Amarillo Ranch RV Park** (1414 Sunrise Dr., 806/373-4962, www.amarillorvranch.com, $30), featuring an indoor heated pool, sauna, and hot tub; free coffee and doughnuts; and a private park.

FOOD
Mexican
Locals satisfy their Tex-Mex cravings at the consistently reliable **Jorge's Tacos Garcia Mexican Cafe** (1100 S. Ross St., 806/371-0411, $7–17). All the traditional favorites are here, from enchiladas to soft and crispy beef tacos to cheesy quesadillas. Jorge's margaritas and spicy salsa with chips are an ideal way to start your meal. Another popular spot is the commendable **Celia's** (2917 SW 6th Ave., 806/373-6522, $5–12), a classic Tex-Mex spot near downtown. You can't go wrong with the flavorful mole poblano, smothered in a thick, rich brown sauce, or the chile relleno, perfectly fried and just a bit on the spicy side.

For a more traditional Mexican meal, head to **El Bracero** (two locations: 2116 S. Grand St., 806/373-4788, and 2923 Bell St., 806/355-0889, $8–20). Meat is the main draw here, featured in exquisite dishes such as the tender cabrito (goat), tasty quail, and seasoned lamb chops. The seafood dishes are highly recommended, and be sure to save room for the velvety cinnamon-tinged flan.

Steaks and American
◖ **The Big Texan** (7701 I-40 E., 800/657-7177, www.bigtexan.com, $9–34) is a must, even if you don't plan to eat the 72-ounce steak, free of charge if you can consume the

entire placemat-size slab. It's a mighty challenge befitting of the restaurant's name, but before you tuck that napkin in your collar, be aware of a few minor details—you have to eat this mega meal, side dishes and all, in less than an hour. A few dozen hearty souls attempt the feat each month; of those, one or two earn the distinction of devouring 72 ounces of beef. The Big Texan's decor is perfectly kitschy—hokey cowboy themes and faux rustic timber—and the food is quite edible, uncommon for such a touristy place. Stick with the basics (a rib eye with baked potato, or a big bowl of chili) and be sure to browse the enormous gift shop afterward.

Amarillo's other legendary steak house is the **Stockyard Cafe** (101 S. Manhattan St., 806/342-9411, $8–24, open for breakfast and lunch Mon.–Sat., dinner on Fri. only). If you've ever considered ordering steak and eggs for breakfast, this is the place to do it. Located adjacent to the livestock auction warehouse, the Stockyard Cafe's booths are packed most mornings with hungry workers, primarily farmers and truckers enjoying heaping helpings of bacon, huevos rancheros, flapjacks, and steaming mugs of bland coffee. The sirloin is a popular lunch item, and the banana pudding is a must.

If you prefer a nice glass of wine with your beef, drop by the tasty and tasteful **Cafe Bella** (7306 W. 34th Ave., 806/331-2232, $9–28, Mon.–Fri. 11:30 A.M.–2:30 P.M., Thurs.–Sat. 5:30–10 P.M.). Cafe Bella specializes in Italian dishes, but the Kobe steak is excellent, and the bacon-wrapped pork tenderloin is equally commendable.

Most locals will tell you the best barbecue in town is at **Cattle Call B-B-Q Restaurant** (7701 I-40 W., 806/353-1227, www.cattlecall. com, $7–14). This crowded home-grown establishment is best known for its spectacular smokehouse ribs, but several other menu items are also worth sampling, including the sliced brisket sandwich, cheeseburger, and chicken-fried steak. Continuing in meat mode, you'll find one of the best burgers in town at the no-frills **Arnold Burgers** (1611 S. Washington St., 806/372-1741, $5–8). These enormous handmade beef patties are juicy and flavorful, and the crispy fries offer a perfect accompaniment. Arnold's is the kind of place that sticks with you the rest of the day (in a good way) since your clothes will soak up the smell of grilled goodness.

INFORMATION AND SERVICES

The Texas Department of Transportation's **Texas Travel Information Center** (9700 E. I-40, 800/452-9292, www.dot.state.tx.us, daily 8 A.M.–5 P.M.) near downtown Amarillo provides free literature, information, and suggestions for local and statewide excursions. For a more city-specific approach, head to the **Amarillo Convention and Visitor Council** (offices at the Bivins Mansion, 1000 S. Polk St., and the Amarillo Civic Center, 401 S. Buchanan St., 800/692-1338, www.visitamarillotx.com, Mon.–Fri. 9 A.M.–6 P.M., Sat.–Sun. 10 A.M.–4 P.M., call about scaled-back winter hours) for maps, brochures about area attractions, and assistance with planning an excursion on Route 66.

GETTING THERE AND AROUND

Amarillo International Airport (10801 Airport Blvd., 806/335-1671, www.ci.amarillo. tx.us) is located seven miles east of downtown and offers flights from American Eagle, Continental Express, and Southwest Airlines. Car rental service is available from **Avis** (806/335-2313), **Enterprise** (806/335-9443), **Hertz** (806/335-2331), and **National** (806/335-2311). Amarillo's cab companies include **Bob & Sons Taxi Service** (806/373-1171) and **Yellow Checker Cab** (806/374-8444).

CANYON

Located just 20 miles south of Amarillo, Canyon (population 12,875) is home to Palo Duro Canyon State Park, the most fascinating attraction in the Panhandle. The town's enormous historical museum is also notable, both for its impressive collection of Western art and artifacts and its striking art deco facility.

PANHANDLE PLAINS

COLORFUL CANYON

Aside from being the Panhandle's most stunning geographical feature, Palo Duro Canyon is the site of a significant battle (not necessarily in a good way) from the Red River War conflict between the U.S. Army and regional Native American tribes. In September 1874, U.S. colonel Ranald S. Mackenzie ordered a predawn attack on several Native American camps on the canyon floor. The surprise raid forced the tribe members to flee into the upper reaches of the canyon while army troops burned their villages and possessions.

While all this was happening, Mackenzie's partner in crime, Capt. Eugene Beaumont, rounded up more than 1,400 of the tribes' horses and mules, and drove them out of the canyon. He took all the animals to a nearby army camp, where nearly 1,000 of them were shot to death. With their provisions and means of mobility destroyed, the Native Americans' losses were catastrophic. Their will was ultimately broken, resulting in their surrender.

Employees at Palo Duro Canyon State Park have heard some fascinating legends about the battle and the tribes that lived in the area. One especially memorable tale was from an elder in the Kiowa tribe. The 80-year-old woman with reddish hair and light eyes talked about her great-grandfather being killed in the Battle of Palo Duro Canyon. He was a white man adopted by her ancestors after surviving a wagon attack as a child, and he was raised by the tribe to be a brave warrior.

The woman claimed he was a "dog soldier," the fiercest of fighters who would tether himself to a stake to defend his village and show loyalty by remaining there until released or even until death. Although records don't tell of the man's fate at the Palo Duro battle, the Kiowa elder took pride in her connection to the story of this brave warrior.

⬛ Palo Duro Canyon State Park

America's second-largest canyon is an absolute must. Palo Duro (11450 Park Rd. 5, 806/488-2227, www.tpwd.state.tx.us) offers colorful and topographical magnificence compared to the stark, level plains above. Though it's not quite as Grand as its Arizona relative, Palo Duro (Spanish for hard wood; namely, the abundant mesquite and juniper trees) features a vast expanse of colorful soil and spectacular geographic formations. The stratified colors are particularly intriguing, with sheer cliffs, rock towers, and canyon walls displaying muted hues of red, yellow, and orange exposed by erosion from a tributary of the Red River and the ubiquitous High Plains winds.

Visitors can experience Palo Duro's topographic splendor by foot, bike, car, or horse year-round. The park's 18,000 acres offer a topographical getaway unlike any other in the Lone Star State. In addition to hiking and biking, Palo Duro visitors enjoy picnicking and camping, wagon rides, and campfire breakfasts, along with the park's souvenir shop, interpretive center, and amphitheater.

People have inhabited Palo Duro Canyon for nearly 12,000 years, including the Folsom and Clovis groups who hunted mammoth and giant bison. The area was later occupied by Apaches, Comanches, and Kiowas who sought out the water and animals that gathered at the watering holes.

Early Spanish explorers are credited with "discovering" the canyon and providing its name; however, it wasn't until 1852 when an American first set eyes on its colorful walls. Two decades later, the canyon was a battle site during the Red River War with Native American tribes. Private owners deeded the property to the state in 1933, and for several years afterward, the Civilian Conservation Corps developed the property by building road access to the canyon floor, cabins, shelters, the visitors center, and the park headquarters.

The best place to start your Palo Duro adventure is the park's visitors center. Perched on the upper rim of the canyon, the building is one of several constructed by the CCC and contains an interesting museum with exhibits detailing the canyon's geographic and cultural history, as well as a store with books and gifts.

NATIVE NATURALISTS

For thousands of years, many different tribes of Native Americans (most notably the Kiowa, Comanche, and Apache) called the Panhandle Plains and Palo Duro Canyon home. The steady flow of water from the Red River tributary on the canyon floor typically resulted in an associated supply of animals (bison, elk, and bear) and vegetation.

This vegetation, in particular, was an important source of many elements that helped the tribes sustain themselves in the often-harsh climate. They would grind roots, beans, berries, and plants to make breads and natural remedies. Tribe members would also use the abundant mesquite trees for medicinal purposes. They could chew the leaves to relieve stomachaches and make tea out of the bark and sap.

Visitors to Palo Duro Canyon can still see where tribe members ground the berries and plants in the small depressions (known as mortar holes) on the canyon-floor rocks. Exhibits and markers in the canyon tell the tales of the tribes' lifeways.

There are several well-known legends about the canyon, including references to discovering mythical items such as Coronado's Spanish armor and Casner's lost gold. One of the most popular stories tells of the "ghost horses of Palo Duro," which appear as clouds on the canyon rim at dusk. When groups of schoolchildren visit the park, they often claim they can see the horses or hear them whinny as their imaginations get caught up in the colorful tales of the canyon.

The real fun begins as soon as you descend from the flat upper environs to the otherworldly scene below the tabletop surface. A paved road offers an initial glimpse of the canyon's colorful rock formations and rugged beauty, but the real adventure awaits off the asphalt, where you can get up-close views of bizarre and intriguing cacti, wildflowers, and wildlife (primarily lizards and snakes).

Hikers should make a point of taking the Lighthouse Peak Trail (maps are available at the visitors center—the trailhead is marked on the main road). The three-mile-long trail is perfect for a morning or afternoon hike, complete with interpretive panels and mesmerizing views, and culminating with a close-up look at lighthouse peak, the park's distinctive and oft-photographed rock tower.

Mountain bikers have several worthy options to choose from, most notably the Capitol Peak Mountain Biking Trail (recommended) and the Givens, Spicer and Lowry Running Trail, a law-firm-sounding yet imminently picturesque four-mile loop throughout the park. Both feature rugged terrain—plenty of loose rock, sand-filled holes, and narrow streambeds—so be sure to keep your eyes in front of you despite the irresistible urge to marvel at the spectacular natural surrounding scenery.

Many visitors choose to go old-school (in Palo Duro's case, Spanish explorers and cowboy settlers) by experiencing the canyon on horseback. The Old West Stables, located within the canyon, will take you on a guided tour to Timber Creek Canyon and the park's signature lighthouse tower. To make the required reservations, call 806/488-2180.

Panhandle-Plains Historical Museum

It's fitting that Texas's largest history museum is just a few miles down the road from the enormity of Palo Duro Canyon. The Panhandle-Plains Historical Museum (2503 4th Ave., 806/651-2244, www.panhandleplains.com, summer hours Mon.–Sat. 9 A.M.–6 P.M., Sun. 1–6 P.M., winter Mon.–Sat. 9 A.M.–5 P.M., Sun. 1–6 P.M., $10 adults, $9 seniors, $5 children ages 4–12) boasts "more than 500 million years of history across a 26,000 square mile expanse of the Panhandle-Plains." Indeed, the museum offers a far-reaching collection of diverse heritage-related exhibits, from dinosaurs to Native Americans to pioneers and petroleum. Science and art are also well represented, with displays focusing on archaeology, geology, and Southwestern art.

Particularly memorable exhibits include People of the Plains, showcasing ancient tribe members' use of the buffalo and an interactive pioneer home, a paleontology display featuring an impressive collection of 200-million-year-old fossils found in the Amarillo area (including a six-foot-long carnivorous amphibian), and an oil exhibit highlighting the importance of petroleum to the Panhandle.

Information and Services

To find out more about food and lodging options in Canyon, contact the **Canyon Chamber of Commerce** (1518 5th Ave., 800/999-9481, www.canyonchamber.org, Mon.–Fri. 9 A.M.–4:30 P.M.).

Abilene

Abilene (population 114,797) is known for its frontier heritage and cattle drives. Its name, in fact, is an homage to the famous Kansas cattle town at the other end of the rail lines, and this midsize Panhandle-area city (some refer to this region of Texas as the Big Country) remains an important destination for ranchers and tourists.

Like other towns in this region, Abilene's origins are traced to railroads and ranching. Initially inhabited by nomadic Indians and occasional westward-bound frontier families, the city didn't make it onto most maps until the Texas and Pacific Railroad established it as a stock shipping station in 1881.

Agriculture has been Abilene's major economic force since its inception, with cattle and farming making up most of the city's product base. By the mid-1900s, oil became another contributing factor, along with a sizable population boom resulting from a significant amount of federal funding and infrastructure related to World War II training.

With the increase in people came an added emphasis on education and religion (typically combined). The city boasts several bastions of higher education, including Abilene Christian University, Hardin-Simmons University, and McMurry University. The fact that these three institutions are Christian based has prompted some to dub Abilene the "Buckle of the Bible Belt."

SIGHTS
◖ Frontier Texas!

By nature, history museums aren't progressive places. That's why it's so refreshing to experience the innovative approach at Frontier Texas! (625 N. 1st St., 325/437-2800, www.frontiertexas.com, Mon.–Sat. 9 A.M.–6 P.M., Sun. 1–5 P.M., $8 adults, $6 seniors and military, $5 students, $4 children ages 3–12). For example: Comanche chief Esihabitu looks directly into your eyes as you hear his calm and measured voice tell a profound story about clashes with white settlers. In a flash he's gone, leaving an empty cave and vivid memories in the shadows. Esihabitu is one of eight "spirit guides," life-size spectral image movies (holograms) offering firsthand accounts of life in the Panhandle Plains from 1780 to 1880. These and other technology-based exhibits (intense 360-degree movies, educational computer games, and interactive displays) set Frontier Texas! apart from other history museums. Not surprisingly, kids love the experience and come away with stories of the historical figures they "met" rather than breezing past glass-enclosed artifacts with accompanying explanatory plaques. It's almost worth making the trip to Abilene simply for the *Century of Adventure* movie, where viewers sit on benches surrounded by screens and special effects depicting life on the Texas frontier in intense fashion, complete with an Indian

© TEXAS HISTORICAL COMMISSION

downtown Abilene

attack, buffalo stampede, violent thunderstorm, and firefly-filled evening.

National Center for Children's Illustrated Literature

Seemingly out of place in the remote city of Abilene is the National Center for Children's Illustrated Literature (102 Cedar St., 325/673-4586, www.nccil.org, Tues.–Sat. 10 A.M.–4 P.M., free admission). This contemporary urban-minded facility, located in a former hotel parking garage, showcases the unheralded artists whose work is featured in children's storybooks. From *The Very Hungry Caterpillar* to *The Berenstain Bears,* the museum highlights the achievements of artists typically recognized only by youngsters and their parents. Fortunately, the museum's important work is appreciated beyond Abilene, since each exhibition travels to other institutions, public libraries, and galleries across the country. The museum also offers families the opportunity to meet visiting artists, free art activities every Saturday afternoon, an annual summer art camp, and the popular ArtWalk,

featuring art exhibitions, live performances, movies, and interactive activities the second Thursday evening of each month.

Grace Museum

Across the street from the NCCIL is Abilene's best-recognized downtown feature, the Grace Museum (102 Cypress St., 325/673-4587, www.thegracemuseum.org, Tues.–Sat. 10 A.M.–5 P.M., Thurs. until 8 P.M., $6 adults, $4 seniors, $3 children ages 4–12). Housed in the magnificent four-story 1909 Grace Hotel, on the National Register of Historic Places, the Grace contains three museums showcasing regional history, international artwork, and interactive children's exhibits. Relive the fancy days of Abilene's history in the Grace's luxurious marble-filled lobby and grand ballroom before proceeding to the exhibits. Highlights include a replicated hotel room from the Grace's early days, a cluttered yet fascinating re-created boot shop, and a hands-on musical art exhibit. An interesting historical fact: The hotel was briefly known as The Drake, allowing the budget-minded owner to replace only two letters on The Grace's gigantic rooftop sign.

PANHANDLE PLAINS

the Grace Museum in historic downtown Abilene

Abilene Zoo

Billing itself as "one of the five largest zoos in Texas" is the popular and respectable Abilene Zoo (2070 Zoo Ln. in Nelson Park, 325/676-6085, www.abilenetx.com/zoo, daily 9 A.M.–5 P.M., until 9 P.M. Memorial Day–Labor Day, $5 adults, $4 seniors, $2 children ages 3–12). The zoo contains more than 500 animals representing hundreds of species, including monkeys, rhinos, zebras, bison, and jaguars. Popular exhibits include the Creepy Crawler Center, Wetlands Boardwalk, butterfly gardens, and the giraffe area, where visitors can occasionally pet and feed the exotic creatures via a bridge crossing over their habitat. The zoo also offers educational programs, summer camps, and interactive tours.

Fort Phantom Hill

Rising out of the earth like eerie spirits of the past, the lonesome chimneys of Fort Phantom Hill (11 miles north of Abilene on FM 600, 325/677-1309, www.fortphantom.org) stand as a testament to the region's frontier heritage. The fort was built in 1851 to protect settlers from Native American raids but was

abandoned three years later after a series of natural hardships. The Native American threat was largely unfounded, and the soldiers reportedly became so bored, they deserted the fort in increasing numbers until it was completely forsaken. Soon after, most of the buildings were mysteriously burned, though it's suspected that lingering disaffected soldiers were to blame. What remains at the fort are the forlorn chimneys, foundations of buildings, and even a few stone structures (most notably a commissary and guardhouse). Interpretive panels tell the story of this unique and oft-overlooked attraction. To get there, take exit I-20 at FM 600 and go 11 miles north. The main portion of the fort is located on the east side of FM 600.

Buffalo Gap Historic Village

Fourteen miles south of Abilene is the charming Buffalo Gap Historic Village (133 N. William St. in the small community of Buffalo Gap, 325/572-3365, www.buffalogap.com, Mon.–Sat. 10 A.M.–5 P.M., Sun. noon–5 P.M., $7 adults, $6 seniors and military, $4 students). This quaint living-history museum showcases the region's frontier heritage with historic artifacts, maps, interpretive events, and a dozen relocated historic buildings. The village's courthouse museum contains an impressive collection of arrowheads and weapons, and car buffs (and kids) will enjoy the pair of Model T Fords on the museum's grounds.

Abilene State Park

One of the most popular places for area residents to enjoy the outdoors is Abilene State Park (150 Park Rd. 32, 325/572-3204, www.tpwd.state.tx.us). Located 16 miles southwest of town, the 529-acre park is accented by rolling hills and sturdy rock structures constructed in the early 1930s by the Civilian Conservation Corps. Locals frequent the park for its sublime swimming pool and groves of shady pecan trees. Visitors drop by to catch a glimpse of the buffalo and the official Texas longhorn herd (a portion of the group is on-site). Camping, hiking, fishing, and biking are other popular activities.

SHOPPING

Abilene has several well-known authentic Western-wear shops specializing in custom-made leather goods. The city also has a surprisingly extensive collection of antiques stores, where visitors, particularly out-of-staters, will find plenty of Texas charm and maybe even a few treasures.

Boots and Western Wear

People travel hundreds of miles to experience the pleasure of ordering and purchasing boots from the legendary ◖ **James Leddy Boots** (1602 N. Treadaway Blvd., 325/677-7811, weekdays 8 A.M.–5 P.M.). Even if you don't order a pair of the perfectly designed and eminently comfortable cowboy boots, you can witness them being handcrafted in the store's workshop. Leddy family members are usually on hand to take visitors on personal tours, and the shop has a large section of boots available for immediate purchase if you find that perfect fit. Leddy's has outfitted the famous (George Jones, Jerry Lee Lewis, and Buck Owens) and the not so famous (local farmers and ranchers). Just a few blocks north is **Bell Custom-Made Boots & Repair** (2118 N. Treadaway Blvd., 325/677-0632). A friend of Leddy, Alan Bell operates a delightfully rustic workshop that welcomes walk-in customers. Though boots (and colorful stories) are Bell's specialty, he also designs custom belts.

For a truly distinctive custom-made leather item, head to **5D Custom Hats and Leather** (742 Butternut St., 325/673-9000, www.5dhats. com, Mon.–Sat. 9 A.M.–5:30 P.M.). Hats are the main draw here—owner Damon Albus will create any style, shape, or color you desire—but don't pass up the opportunity to order something unique, like a personalized belt, purse, or phone holder. Not quite as practical yet intriguing nevertheless is **Art Reed Custom Saddles** (361 E. South 11th St., 325/677-4572). The smell of leather is almost overwhelming (in a good way), and even if you're not in the market for a $2,000 saddle, you may find chaps or other cowboy gear to your liking.

Antiques

An Old West town like Abilene is a great place to buy old stuff. Start your search with a contemporary twist at **Stokes Chic Antiques** (855 Butternut St., 325/672-7777, Tues. 11:30 A.M.–5:30 P.M., Wed.–Sat. 11 A.M.–5:30 P.M.), a fun little shop with a range of items appealing more to the younger boutique crowd than grizzled treasure hunters. Sift through the dated and elegant collection of furniture, lighting, home accessories, and pictures. Another popular shop with a kitschy twist is **Fabulous Finds** (715 Grape St., 325/677-5110, www.stokeschicantiques.blogspot.com, Thurs.–Sat. 10:30 A.M.–5:30 P.M. or by appointment). You'll find plenty of antiques, glassware, and consignment items along with vintage costume jewelry and collectibles.

For an all-inclusive experience, head to the antiques mall at **Antique Station** (703 N. 3rd St., 325/675-6100). Items at the dozens of vendor booths include furniture, china, home accessories, and advertising memorabilia.

ACCOMMODATIONS
Hotels and Motels

Chain hotels are the name of the game in Abilene, so travelers won't find many charming independent options. Of the corporate choices, the most reliable and affordable include **Best Western** (350 I-20 W., 325/672-2696, www. abileneinnandsuites.com, $85 d), featuring free Internet access, a complimentary hot breakfast, an outdoor pool, and an exercise room. Also commendable is the **Holiday Inn Express** (1802 E. Overland Trl., 325/675-9800, www. ichotelsgroup.com, $93 d), offering free Wi-Fi service, a free continental breakfast, outdoor pool, and fitness center. Similar in price and amenities is the **La Quinta** (3501 W. Lake Rd., 800/531-5900, www.lq.com, $95 d), offering rooms with free Internet access, a free continental breakfast, and an outdoor pool.

Ascending to the next price (and quality) level, visitors will find **Courtyard Abilene** (4350 Ridgemont Dr., 325/695-9600, www. marriott.com, $100 d). The Courtyard's amenities include free wireless Internet access, a 24-hour market, an indoor heated pool, whirlpool, and fitness center. Just down the road is the worthy and reliable **Hampton Inn** (3917 Ridgemont Dr., 325/695-0044, www.hamptoninn.com, $109 d), featuring complimentary Internet access, an indoor pool, a free hot breakfast (and to-go bags), and a free beverage area. Occupying a former large chain hotel is the regionally operated and highly respected (€ **MCM Elegante Suites** (4250 Ridgemont Dr., 325/698-1234, www.mcmelegantesuites.com, $139 d). The welcoming lobby area contains a large naturally lit atrium where a free breakfast is served each morning, and the rooms include two separate areas, including a wet bar, refrigerator, microwave, and free wireless Internet access.

Bed-and-Breakfast

In a city overrun with chain hotels, it's nice to have the option of staying in an authentic environment—especially when it's just a few blocks from downtown. Many Abilene visitors opt to stay at the remarkable **Vintage House** (1541 N. 4th St., 325/677-8386, www.thevintagehouse.com, $75–105). This historic 1927 two-story brick home is comfortable and spacious, with four large antiques-bedecked rooms offering Internet access, cable TV, and private bathrooms. (If you forget your laptop, you can use the computer at the top of the stairs.)

Camping

The best place to pitch a tent (or rent a yurt) and enjoy a campfire in the Big Country is **Abilene State Park** (150 Park Rd. 32, 325/572-3204, www.tpwd.state.tx.us). Campsites are available with water and electric hookups, and the park added three yurts (defined as "enhanced shelters") containing double/single bunk beds with mattresses, a fold-out sofa, and a microwave, and range from $12–20 nightly; yurts are $40 nightly.

FOOD

This is cowboy country, so most locals consider Abilene's best restaurants to be steak houses. As always, the Mexican-food options are good; otherwise, fine dining is not one of Abilene's strong points.

Steaks

One of the best steaks you'll ever eat awaits at (€ **Perini Ranch Steakhouse** (3002 Farm Rd. 89 in Buffalo Gap, 325/572-3339, www.periniranch.com, $10–36). Tom Perini is a nationally respected expert on Texas cooking (he's appeared on numerous morning shows and Food Network specials), so it's a rare pleasure to be able to consume his exquisite creations at his charmingly rustic restaurant just south of town. The key to Perini's sublime steaks is his dry rub seasoning—a perfect blend of light spices that brings out the immense flavor of the prime beef. What puts this meal over the top are the unique side dishes, particularly the restaurant's signature green chile hominy, an ideal blend of grits, chiles, cheese, and bacon. Save room for the delectable bread pudding or jalapeño cheesecake.

If you're in downtown Abilene and have a hankerin' for a quality steak, head directly to **Lytle Land & Cattle Co.** (1150 E. South 11th St., 325/677-1925, www.lytlelandandcattle.com, $9–34). Lytle's specializes in superior heavy-aged, corn fed beef (impressive in steak-lover circles), and their steaks are cut on-site to ensure optimal flavor. Like Perini's, Lytle's adds a special cooking rub and prepares the meat over a hot mesquite fire to enhance the taste. The seafood options are prepared the same way, and the grilled portobello mushrooms are worth skipping dessert for. If you can't make up your mind on which tantalizing entrée to order, consider the all-encompassing mixed grill sampler, offering New York strip, chicken, quail, sausage, and bacon-wrapped shrimp.

Mexican

A bakery isn't the first place you expect to find amazing Mexican food, but that's exactly what's on the menu at **La Popular Bakery & Cafe** (1533 Pine St., 325/672-2670, $4–7), a hole-in-the-wall establishment near downtown. La Popular is a great place to go for brunch, since you can sample the tasty pastries (the gingerbread cookies and frosting-covered fruit Danishes are highly recommended) along with the lunch items. The burritos are legendary here, and you can't go wrong with anything made with their fresh tortillas—the beef tacos, in particular.

For a traditional Tex-Mex dinner, head to **Tamolly's Mexican Restaurant** (4400 Ridgemont Dr., 325/698-2000, www.tamollys.com, $6–15), a small regional chain. The personal mini bowl of salsa each diner receives is a nice touch, and the classic combo plates are pure comfort food—cheese enchiladas, chicken flautas, crispy tacos, and quesadillas. Top it all off with a strawberry crispito, consisting of fried tortilla strips smothered in fruit and whipped cream.

A couple other places in town also offer standard yet quality Tex-Mex fare. To get your fill of beef burritos, chicken enchiladas, carne asada, and loaded nachos, drop by **Enchilada Express** (790 S. Leggett Dr., 325/232-8682, $4–13) or **Alfredo's Mexican Food** (2849 S. 14th St., 325/698-0104, $4–13).

American and Barbecue

It's a bit hokey, but you won't experience too many other places like the **Ball Ranch** (south of Abilene at 525 S. Hwy. 83-84, 800/365-6507, www.theballranch.com, open Sat. night Apr.–Dec., $11–19). You'll find a big ol' open barnlike structure with several trees growing inside and accented with Western-themed items (saddles, ranching equipment). Ball Ranch serves an authentic and better-than-average chuckwagon supper, featuring mesquite-smoked barbecue meat (the brisket is mighty tender) with potato salad, red beans, biscuits, and peach cobbler. After dinner, the Ball family takes the stage and treats the audience to Western swing and country classics. Call ahead for reservations.

On the complete opposite end of the spectrum is the fancy downtown **Cypress Street Station** (158 Cypress St., 325/676-3463, www.cypress-street.com, open for lunch Mon.–Sat., dinner Tues.–Sat., $9–30). Start your meal by selecting from one of the best wine lists in town, and continue with a tasty appetizer of almond-crusted baked Brie with toast points, topped with honey and balsamic reduction. For the main course, consider the pork chop with apple demi-glaze, the filet mignon with stuffed crab and boursin cheese, or the seafood risotto with roasted red peppers.

An absolute must for fans of Texas barbecue is the legendary **Joe Allen's** (1233 S. Treadaway Blvd., 325/672-9948, $8–19). The perfectly smoked meat is consistently flavorful—try the brisket, pork rib, and sausage combo—and the sides are way above average (the potato salad and homemade corn bread in particular). The sauce sometimes needs an extra kick, so add a dash of Tabasco to it before dunking your brisket in it. Even when they're not craving 'cue, locals line up for Joe Allen's delicious mesquite-grilled steak and trout.

INFORMATION AND SERVICES

The **Abilene Convention and Visitors Bureau** and **Abilene Cultural Affairs Council** (1101 N. 1st St., 325/676-2556, www.abilenecac.org, weekdays 8:30 A.M.–5 P.M.) are worth visiting just to see the impressive facility they're both housed in—the beautifully restored Texas & Pacific Railroad Depot. Friendly staffers from both organizations will gladly offer assistance, suggestions, maps, and brochures.

GETTING THERE AND AROUND

The **Abilene Regional Airport** (2933 Airport Blvd., 325/676-6367, www.abilenetx.com) offers flights from American Eagle and Continental Express, and car rentals from **Avis** (325/677-9240), **Budget** (325/677-7777), **Enterprise** (325/690-9338), and **Hertz** (325/673-6774). For cab service, contact **Classic Cab Inc.** (325/677-8294) or **LeCoach Taxi** (325/673-3138). The city also offers bus service Monday–Saturday from the airport and throughout town via its **City Link** transit system (1189 S. 2nd St., 325/676-6287, www.abilenetx.com).

PANHANDLE PLAINS

San Angelo

The mystique of West Texas and the Panhandle Plains begins to unfold just beyond the Hill Country in San Angelo (population 88,300), where rolling hills tumble into outstretched vistas of vast sky. The city has grown slowly yet steadily since its early days as an outpost for the adjacent Fort Concho, established in 1867 to protect westward-moving settlers against Native American raids.

Like other frontier forts in the region, Fort Concho was well manned yet rather monotonous due to the lack of attacks. Historians have described the fort's typical experience as being "long periods of tedium interspersed with short blasts of excitement." The only significant activity occurred when encroaching Native American tribes caused a stir, resulting in minor skirmishes.

The army's presence at Fort Concho, however, was directly responsible for San Angelo's early growth. With plenty of federal funding arriving regularly for supplies and salaries, soldiers took to the streets in search of personal supplies, construction materials, and even some illegal activity. Businesses soon popped up to take care of the soldiers' needs for goods and services along with women and whiskey. Bordellos and saloons were almost as numerous as merchandise outlets.

After Fort Concho closed in the late 1800s, the arrival of the railroad helped establish San Angelo as a major ranching center; to this day, it remains one of the country's leading producers of mohair and wool production. The city continues to boast one of the state's most diverse industrial bases, with more than 120 manufacturing companies producing products ranging from denim to metals to oil field equipment.

San Angelo's distinct heritage, burgeoning arts scene, and welcoming combo of small-town charm and big-city services make for a unique getaway. The impressive art museum and better-than-expected restaurant scene allow tourists to enjoy impressive cultural amenities, while the wide downtown streets and charming historic buildings let them put a little West Texas swagger in their walk.

SIGHTS
◖ Fort Concho National Historic Landmark

The time-transporting Fort Concho (630 S. Oakes St., 325/481-2646, www.fortconcho. com, Mon.–Sat. 9 A.M.–5 P.M., Sun. 1–5 P.M., $3 adults, $2 seniors, $1.50 students) is considered perhaps the best preserved of Texas's frontier forts. Relive the life of an army soldier in the late 1800s through nearly two dozen renovated and well-maintained facilities such as barracks, stables, and officers quarters. Displays containing vintage artifacts and replica equipment effectively demonstrate the scene at Fort Concho, described as relatively active yet fairly mundane.

Constructed to protect settlers from Indian

Re-enactors portray the past at Fort Concho.

raids, the fort was much like a fire station: always poised for activity yet often encountering none. In fact, one of the more interesting aspects of Fort Concho is related to its soldiers rather than its enemies. An atypically diverse population (for Texas) emerged at the fort in the 1870s when Buffalo Soldiers, a colloquial name given to African-American troops, joined the ranks. In its 22-year history as an active post, Fort Concho hosted almost as many African-American soldiers as Caucasians. The exhibit dedicated to the Buffalo Soldiers is one of the highlights of a visit to Fort Concho.

San Angelo Museum of Fine Arts

Along with Fort Concho, the city's most significant cultural attraction is the San Angelo Museum of Fine Arts (1 Love St., 325/653-3333, www.samfa.org, Tues.–Sat. 10 A.M.–4 P.M., Sun. 1–4 P.M., $2 adults, $1 seniors and students). Boasting a hip physical address, this impressive museum showcases world-class exhibits and occasional regional shows. The building, with its dramatic saddle-shaped roof

designed by an architectural firm known for its restoration work at Radio City Music Hall, is a masterpiece unto itself. The museum features three galleries focusing on contemporary work and American ceramics, with a permanent collection of nearly 200 pieces, along with a research library, ceramics studio, and education wing. Visitors are allowed to view the artwork housed in storage, another unique opportunity at this one-of-a-kind facility.

Miss Hattie's Bordello Museum

Once home to "the most famous brothel in West Texas," this straight-out-of-a-Western-scene on historic Concho Avenue is now Miss Hattie's Bordello Museum (18 E. Concho Ave., 325/653-0112, www.misshatties.com, Tues.–Sat. 10 A.M.–4 P.M., tours available Thurs.–Sat. at the top of the hour 1–4 P.M., $5 adults). Cowboys, business travelers, and especially soldiers from nearby Fort Concho were quite familiar with the second floor of this downtown stone building, known simply as "Miss Hattie's." Vintage furniture and velvet drapes

San Angelo Museum of Fine Arts

recall San Angelo's Wild West era, when patrons would drink whiskey and play cards in the downstairs saloon and parlor house, then complete their evening of entertainment upstairs. The museum's rooms, complete with original furnishings, lace curtains, and gilded pressed-tin ceilings, are named for the women who worked at the brothel.

Concho River Walk

It's a far cry from the famous San Antonio River Walk, but San Angelo's version of a riverside stroll, the Concho River Walk (915/653-1206), is much more relaxing and natural. Though the entire trail spans more than six miles, the most interesting and accessible portions run through downtown, where walkers can experience manicured gardens and landscaped parks, fountains, miniature waterfalls, and stunning riverside homes. Watch out for the geese—they'll loudly demand a handout.

Railway Museum of San Angelo

Train buffs will be interested in the small Railway Museum of San Angelo (703 S. Chadbourne St., 325/486-2140, www.railwaymuseumsanangelo.homestead.com, Sat. 10 A.M.–4 P.M.). Located in the restored Santa Fe depot building just south of downtown, the museum features rotating displays of railroad-related artifacts, elaborate model-train exhibits (featuring a fascinating depiction of the city in 1928), and several railcars on permanent display. Unfortunately, the museum is only open on Saturday, so plan accordingly.

San Angelo State Park

Immediately west of town on the shores of Fisher Reservoir is San Angelo State Park (3900 Mercedes St., 325/949-4757, www.tpwd. state.tx.us, $3 daily ages 13 and older). This is where San Angeloans come to play, and there's plenty to enjoy; namely, 7,677 acres of mostly undeveloped property containing rolling hills, Native American pictographs, a portion of the Official Texas State Longhorn Herd, and many recreational activities. Park visitors can enjoy camping, hiking, mountain biking, and horseback riding on the trails, and fishing and boating on the lake. Tours are available to the ancient Permian animal tracks and rock art. Contact the park for a tour schedule and fees.

SHOPPING

For a small city, San Angelo has an impressive range of shopping options. The city is particularly proud of its unique Concho Pearls cultivated in its own waterways.

Concho Pearls

Not many places can claim to be a source for jewelry, so San Angelo residents are rightfully proud of their homegrown, naturally produced Concho Pearl. This stunning lavender-colored pearl is present only in freshwater mussel shells found in area lakes, rivers, and streams. These distinctive beauties range in color from light pink to dark purple and vary in size and shape from spherical to baroque. The pearls have been coveted for more than 400 years, when Spanish explorers sought the colorful iridescent treasures in nearby waterways. Incidentally, the word *concho* is Spanish for shell.

The best place to shop for Concho Pearls is **Legend Jewelers** (18 E. Concho Ave., 325/653-0112, www.legendjewelers.com), in the heart of San Angelo's historic downtown commercial district. Legend's boasts the largest collection of Concho Pearls in the country, offering various designs and settings in rings, necklaces, and earrings. While there, check out Legend's interesting selection of horned toad jewelry, produced from rubber molds made from the actual toads in the 1970s.

A more limited selection of Concho Pearls is also available at **Jewelry Expressions** (2009 Knickerbocker Rd., 325/224-4499).

Concho Avenue

Even guys won't mind browsing the charming shops along Concho Avenue in San Angelo's historic downtown commercial area. Consisting of a handful of shops in restored old buildings, this one-block area between Oakes and Chadbourne Streets is highlighted by **Eggemeyer's General Store** (35 E. Concho

Ave., 325/655-1166), a genuine mercantile shop. Eggemeyer's offers a true blast from the past, with homemade candy and fudge (highly recommended); specialty coffees; bins filled with toys, knickknacks, and souvenirs; plenty of kitschy Texas-style home decor items; and an entire room filled with kitchen gadgets and recipe books. Across the street is the exceptionally funky **J. Wilde's** (20 E. Concho Ave., 325/655-0878, www.jwildes.com), a bizarre collision of Haight-Ashbury and 1980s-era West Texas. Everything here—clothing, hats, furniture, toys—has a colorful psychedelic vibe, coupled with a Western flair straight out of *Dallas*. It's well worth a visit.

Boots and Western Wear

Most West Texas cities have a legendary boot maker, and in San Angelo it's **J.L. Mercer & Sons Boot Co.** (224 S. Chadbourne St., 325/658-7634, www.jlmercerboots.com). Located in the downtown commercial district since 1923, the company has been consistently producing high-quality cowboy boots for generations of satisfied San Angeloans. Mercer's claims to have outfitted such luminaries as Lyndon B. Johnson and John Wayne, along with slightly less legendary folks like Charlie Daniels, Barry Corbin, and Tom Wopatt. All of their boots are handmade on-site, from super ropers to cowboy boots with exotic skins and inlay work. Other popular Western-wear shops in San Angelo offering boots, hats, cowboy apparel, and accessories include **Blair's Western Wear Inc.** (4230 Sherwood Wy., 325/949-6287) and **M.L. Leddy's Boots & Saddlery** (222 S. Oakes St., 325/653-3397).

ACCOMMODATIONS

Chains dominate San Angelo's hotel landscape, with most commendable options located along Highway 87 northwest of downtown or on Highway 67 near San Angelo State University on the western edge of the city. Those looking for a unique lodging experience might want to take roost at the Inn at the Art Center, a former chicken farm turned B&B.

Hotels and Motels

One of the best deals in town, budget or otherwise, is **Days Inn** (4613 S. Jackson, 325/658-6594, www.daysinn.com, $50 d), featuring rooms with free Internet access, recliners, microwaves and refrigerators (upon request), an outdoor pool, and, most importantly, a coupon for free breakfast next door at Roxie's, a '50s-style diner serving omelets, pancakes, biscuits, and mediocre coffee. Located on the northwestern edge of downtown is the **Inn of the Conchos** (2021 N. Bryant Blvd., 325/658-2811, www.inn-of-the-conchos.com, $69 d). It's a bit rough around the edges, but the Concho is one of San Angelo's few independently operated hotels, as evidenced by its colorful slogan, "A darn good place to hang your hat." The hotel offers limited amenities but includes a large outdoor pool and free coffee in the lobby. Just down the road is **Ramada Limited** (2201 N. Bryant Blvd., 325/653-4482, www.ramada.com, $76 d), featuring rooms with free Internet access, refrigerators, a free continental breakfast, and an outdoor pool.

Slightly more expensive is the **Comfort Suites** (4450 W. Houston Harte Expwy., 325/944-8600, www.comfortsuites.com, $109 d), featuring free Internet access and a free hot breakfast. Also recommended is **Holiday Inn Express** (4613 Houston Harte Expwy., 877/863-4780, www.ichotelsgroup.com, $118 d), offering Internet access, a fitness center, and outdoor pool and spa near the San Angelo State University campus. Nearby is the fairly fancy **Fairfield Inn** (1459 Knickerbocker Rd., 325/482-8400, www.marriott.com, $119 d), offering a complimentary breakfast buffet, a fitness room, an outdoor pool and spa, and free Internet access.

Bed-and-Breakfasts

Offering a true alternative to traditional corporate lodging is the fabulously funky ◖ **Inn at the Art Center** (2503 Martin Luther King Blvd., 325/659-3836, www.chickenfarmartcenter.com, $75–110), near downtown. A former chicken farm, this 1970s-era compound contains a fascinating collection of artist studios, galleries, and a restaurant. The three rooms comprising the B&B portion of the art center are tastefully decorated with intriguing Western-themed works from the owner, and the whole place, with its colorful private gardens and meandering grapevines, has a Santa Fe via West Texas vibe. If you happen to be here on the first Saturday of the month, you'll be treated to live music performances and artists' demonstrations throughout the compound. For those seeking a more traditional B&B experience, consider **Angels Guest House** (121 E. Twohig Ave., 325/486-0739, www.angelsguesthouse.info). Located in the heart of downtown, this charming home offers all the customary amenities of a classic B&B—thick comforters, fluffy pillows, vintage furnishings, and a hearty homemade breakfast.

Camping

The best place to pitch a tent or park an RV is **San Angelo State Park** (3900 Mercedes St., 325/949-4757, www.tpwd.state.tx.us, $8–18 per night), just west of town on the Fisher Reservoir. The park features six air-conditioned and heated minicabins, sites with water and electricity, and tent sites with picnic tables and grills. Just southwest of town on Lake Nasworthy is the popular **Spring Creek Marina RV Park** (45 Fishermans Rd., 325/944-3850, www.springcreekmarina-rv.com, sites $25–38, cabins $50–70 nightly). The park contains 83 RV sites with full hookups, tent sites with water and electric hookups, and furnished cabins with air-conditioning, refrigerators, showers, and bathrooms.

FOOD
Steaks

San Angelo's legendary, if slightly outdated, steak restaurant is **Zentner's Daughter Steak House** (1901 Knickerbocker Rd., 325/949-2821, $9–33). Though it's not too inviting from the outside, the inside transports you back to the era of classic steak houses, with dimly lit rooms and well-worn furnishings. But that's not why people come here—it's for the thick, juicy steaks. The rib eye is tremendous, and the filet mignon is superb.

For an authentic West Texas steak house experience, go to the charmingly old-school **Western Sky Steak House** (2024 N. Chadbourne St., 325/655-3610, www.westernskysteakhouse.org, $10–34). Located in a generic-looking stand-alone spot with a large hokey mural painted on one side, Western Sky proudly bills itself as the "home of San Angelo's biggest steak." Indeed, the 52-ounce sirloin is mighty in presence, and the hardy patrons (ranchers and cowboys from the area) who devour the megasize meat claim it's equally large in taste. Meanwhile, the mere mortals tend to opt for the tender T-bone and rib eye, or one of the restaurant's specialties, like the Spanish steak—a tasty rib eye topped with ranchero sauce and served with beans, french fries, salad, and several flour tortillas.

Mexican

In Spanish, *el mejor* means the best. *Mejor Que Nada* translates as better than nothing. So it's fitting that the San Angelo restaurant officially named Mejor Que Nada is known around town simply as **El Mejor** (1911 S. Bryant Blvd., 325/655-3553, $8–16). What started out as a convenience store more than two decades ago has evolved into one of San Angelo's best and most popular restaurants, featuring classic Tex-Mex with a West Texas twist. Oft-ordered menu items include the tangy salsa-covered chicken enchiladas, the beef taquitos, and "karla," a fajita-like stir-fry concoction available with chicken or veggies. Rivaling El Mejor for top Tex-Mex in town is **Fuentes Cafe** (101 S. Chadbourne St., 325/658-2430, $7–14). Located in a charming downtown building, Fuentes is highly regarded for its fajitas, enchiladas (try the spinach option), and particularly its *guiso,* a tantalizing dish featuring tender stew meat simmered in a richly seasoned sauce.

If you like Western Sky Steak House, you'll love its Mex-themed sister restaurant, **Franco's Café** (2218 Martin Luther King Blvd., 325/653-8010, www.francoscafe.org, $5–13).

Like its *hermana,* Franco's is uninspiring on the exterior and tremendously tasty on the plate. Popular items include the burritos and fajitas, but one of the best options on the menu is their unconventional approach to the chile relleno. Combining the approaches of the Rio Grande Valley and far West Texas, Franco's version offers an egg-fried Anaheim pepper filled with beef and topped with ranchero sauce.

Lunch

When you're in the historic downtown commercial district shopping for Concho Pearls, make sure to grab some lunch at **Miss Hattie's Cafe & Saloon** (26 E. Concho Ave., 325/653-0570, www.misshatties.com, $7–20). Once home to a notorious brothel, the building now offers tempting dishes of American fare. The restaurant still maintains the feel of an Old West saloon, with dark wood furnishings and Victorian-era paintings and details, and the food is similarly welcoming, especially the hearty chicken and dumplings and fancy gourmet sandwiches. Also worth seeking out is the small yet satisfying **Tumble Weedz Deli** (2563 Sunset Dr., 325/944-3417, $4–9). It's somewhat difficult to find—look for the small Deli sign in the Southwest Plaza shopping center—but you'll be rewarded by the classic deli meats and sandwiches. Walk to the back and order an Italian combo "wedge" style (on a tasty herb-infused baguette) or a hearty Reuben.

INFORMATION AND SERVICES

The San Angelo Convention and Visitors Bureau stocks plenty of free brochures and maps at its impressive new **Visitor Center** (418 W. Ave. B, 325/653-1206, www.sanangelo.org, Mon.–Fri. 9 A.M.–5 P.M., Sat. 10 A.M.–5 P.M., Sun. noon–4 P.M.). This aesthetically pleasing facility, constructed with native materials—the limestone walls came from nearby quarries, and the floors and benches are constructed of local mesquite wood—is nestled along the Concho River, and its enormous windows and outdoor patio provide picturesque views of the river.

GETTING THERE AND AROUND

The **San Angelo Regional Airport** (8618 Terminal Cir., 325/659-6409, www.sanangelo-texas.us) offers service from American Eagle and Continental Express, and car rentals from Avis, Budget, and Hertz. San Angelo's cab options are **Red Ball Taxi & Shuttle** (325/942-8899) and **Yellow Cab Co.** (325/655-5555).

BACKGROUND

The Land

Texas defies geographic categorization, yet another reason for its residents to beam with pride. Most states easily fit into a comfortably accepted natural compartment, such as plains, coasts, or mountains, but Texas has as many as 13 distinct geographic regions, including prairies, mountains, basins, and a valley. Together, these various geographical areas make up a land area of 261,914 square miles, roughly the size of New England, New York, Pennsylvania, Ohio, and North Carolina combined. Not surprisingly, Texas's geography contains enormous extremes. The highest point in the state is Guadalupe Peak, at 8,749 feet above sea level, and the lowest point is, well,

sea level along the Gulf Coast. Texas occupies nearly 7 percent of America's land mass and boasts the distinction of being larger than any European country.

GEOGRAPHY

Attempting to pin down a decisive and accepted approach to Texas's geographical regions is challenging. A variety of factors—natural, physical, cultural, even political—contribute to the complexity. For clarity's sake, a good way to tackle the subject is from a fairly unbiased standpoint: natural and physical features. However, even this supposedly simplified method reveals the intricate

natural composition of the Lone Star State—its four main geographic regions (the Basin and Range Province, the Great Plains, the Interior Lowlands, and the Gulf Coastal Plain) contain more than 20 geographical subregions.

The Basin and Range Province

Texas's smallest geographic region is in far West Texas, bounded by New Mexico to the north, the Rio Grande to the south and west, and the Toyah Basin/Stockton Plateau to the east. Rain is very slight and erratic in this area—the average annual rainfall in El Paso is about eight miniscule inches—and most of the land is divided into large ranches.

The Basin and Range Province also contains a small portion of the Rocky Mountain system, though geologists continue to debate this claim. This entire area is also referred to as the mythical Trans-Pecos region, a rugged landscape that has captured the imagination of those who appreciate the beauty of nature in a panoramic and isolated setting.

This area is also home to the state's three main mountain ranges, the Guadalupe Mountains along the southern New Mexico border (home to the state's highest point, the 8,749-foot Guadalupe Peak), the Davis Mountains just north of Big Bend, and the Franklin Mountains in El Paso. Big Bend National Park, located along the biggest bend of the Rio Grande, contains the Chisos Mountains, where the highest elevation, Emory Peak, reaches a respectable 7,832 feet.

The basins of the region are noteworthy for not having a drainage outlet to the nearby Rio Grande. Instead, they channel the scant rainfall into "salt lakes." These areas are typically dry as a bone, and the exposed solid minerals in their beds were once a major source for commercial salt.

The Great Plains

In its entirety, this region extends all the way from Canada to Central Texas's Balcones Fault. It may seem like a stretch to connect these seemingly polar opposite regions of North America, but for the Panhandle residents who experience subfreezing temperatures when "blue northers" blow in, it's a chilling reality.

Because of its rocky surface composition, this region contains a variety of physical features, from the High Plains in the north to the Edwards Plateau in the south. The geologic structure of the Great Plains region also produces some of Texas's most breathtaking natural features. Palo Duro Canyon near Amarillo is a multicolored, otherworldly sight to behold, and the Hill Country's magnificent Enchanted Rock is a massive pink dome of solid granite that has beckoned people for centuries with its mystic aura.

This portion of the state is considered by many to be the most compelling and evocative region of Texas, especially in the southwestern area, which transforms into the fabled Trans-Pecos region. It's big sky country, where the surrounding natural beauty is astounding. Endless vistas, colorful rock formations, and the magnificent blue sky are tourist attractions unto themselves, drawing visitors from across the globe that consider wide-open spaces to be merely a myth.

The western portion of the Panhandle is known as the Llano Estacado, or Staked Plains. According to legend, Spanish explorer Francisco Vasquez de Coronado marked his trek through the region with wooden stakes since the area was (and still is) virtually void of physical landmarks.

The lack of water—rainfall and rivers are scarce in the area—has been problematic throughout the history of the High Plains. Perhaps as a concession, the region inherited mineral wealth in the form of oil and natural gas deposits. These petroleum gold mines were discovered in the 1920s in the Panhandle and in the Permian Basin area near the cities of Midland and Odessa.

The southern portion of this region, the Edwards Plateau, is marked by the Balcones Escarpment, a geologic rift in the underlying layers of rock stretching roughly from Del Rio eastward to Austin. This area has a thin limestone-based soil and is primarily used for cattle, sheep, and goat ranching, resulting in its distinction as one of the major regions for wool and mohair production in the country.

The Interior Lowlands

Much like Texas's Great Plains, the Interior Lowlands extend from North Texas through the Midwest all the way to Canada. An abundance of rivers, hills, and cultivable land tie Texas's Interior Lowlands to its midcontinent neighbors, resulting in its largely agricultural use. Unlike the arid conditions of the Basin and Range Province, this region averages up to 30 inches of rain annually.

Within the Interior Lowlands are several subregions, including the North Central Plains, which comprise roughly two-thirds of the entire region. This area is marked by rolling hills and the West Texas Rolling Plains, which are just as their name implies—pleasant yet unimposing.

Other subregions also reflect their natural nomenclature—the Western and Eastern Cross Timbers and the Grand Prairie. These three areas stretch eastward to Fort Worth and are primarily home to cattle ranches and crops such as wheat and cotton. The region's absence of a major water-producing aquifer necessitated the construction of several reservoirs for irrigation as well as strict conservation regulations. Two of Texas's major rivers, the Trinity and Brazos, also traverse the area, allowing agricultural production of cotton and grain to continue.

The Gulf Coastal Plains

The last of Texas's geographic regions is its largest, comprising the southern and eastern third of the state. This area has the lowest elevation in Texas—less than 1,000 feet above sea level—and contains several bands of physical features and soil types formed by the weathering of underlying rock layers. As its name implies, the Gulf Coastal Plains include Texas's entire coastline and the mouths of most of the state's major rivers.

The Pine Belt comprises the eastern portion of this region along the Louisiana border. Pine trees, hay fields, and cattle pastures dominate the area, which is home to several national forests and the state's lumber industry. The region's natural features also include two major oil fields—Spindletop near Beaumont and the East Texas Oil Field.

West of the Pine Belt lie the Post Oak and Blackland Belts. These regions are known for their fertile soil and rolling prairies, and cotton remains the major crop. Settlers coveted the clear streams and quality soil in the Blackland Belt, which stretches east from Del Rio and northward through San Antonio, Austin, Waco, and Dallas. The prime agricultural conditions fueled Texas's growth, and the region retains some of the state's most densely populated areas.

Texas's southern tip is mostly comprised of the Rio Grande Plain, which includes the Lower Rio Grande Valley, known throughout the state simply as "the Valley." The Rio Grande Plain extends southward into Mexico for several hundred miles. Much of the area is covered with cacti, mesquite trees, and wild shrubs. Cattle production is also significant in the southern Rio Grande Plains, including the famous King Ranch, located southwest of Corpus Christi. The Valley, meanwhile, thrives agriculturally, thanks to the rich delta soils and absence of freezing weather.

The region's Coastal Prairies stretch across the Gulf of Mexico coastline, reaching as far as 60 miles inland. The eastern portion of this region is thick with vegetation and supports crops ranging from rice to cotton. The southern portion contains grasslands, citrus fruits, and vegetables.

ENVIRONMENTAL ISSUES

Texas probably isn't the first place that comes to mind when talk turns to environmental responsibility, but the state has its fair share of activists and defenders. One of Texas's chief environmental concerns is air pollution, particularly from vehicle emissions.

Since most of Texas's big cities sprawl into outlying wide-open spaces, cars are the preferred method of transportation. The state's steady increase in population has become problematic for environmentalists. Air pollution concerns in Texas's cosmopolitan areas have prompted ozone alerts, and Houston has been jockeying with Los Angeles for the coveted title of "smoggiest city."

Other troublesome issues for Texas environmental activists are water pollution and unsafe waste disposal. The Texas Commission on Environmental Quality, a state agency dedicated to protecting Texas's natural resources, oversees a multitude of monitoring efforts and public awareness campaigns designed to maintain control over potentially dangerous environmental hazards. The agency's air monitoring endeavors, water conservation districts, and efforts to keep tabs on industrial waste are commendable but don't always reach citizens at the local level.

That's where grass-roots organizations like the Texas Campaign for the Environment come into play. The group's mission is to inform and mobilize Texans to maintain their quality of life and health. Their primary focus is improving trash and recycling policies to limit air, water, and soil pollution.

The indomitable Texas spirit is also represented in the environmental activism scene. PEER (Public Employees for Environmental Responsibility) spearheaded a project called the Texas Toxic Tour. It highlights more than 20 locations throughout the state identified as environmental problem areas. The group's informative and entertaining website—featuring a state map with site locations marked by skulls and crossbones—features stories from Texans living next to the chemical plants, toxic waste sites, and polluting industries. The organization's goal is to educate the public about ways environmental hazards impact individual Texas residents.

Flora and Fauna

The plant and animal kingdoms in Texas are a source of fascination. Thousands of plant varieties and more than 500 animal species call Texas home, and their compelling assortment is as diverse as the state's landscape. There's the expected (cacti, armadillos, and longhorn cattle) and the unexpected (pine forests, badgers, and cougars).

More than 750 miles separate the eastern and western portions of the state, and the northern and southern tips are nearly 800 miles apart; the resulting broad range of life throughout Texas is rather stunning. Texas's foliar variety mirrors its geographic regions, with 10 corresponding vegetational areas ranging from Gulf Marshes to High Plains. The state's wildlife is tied to its geography and climate. Most of Texas's mammals (aside from livestock) live in warmer, forested areas, and many exceptional birds and insects pass through the state on migratory routes.

TREES AND SHRUBS

Like most vegetation, the abundance and assortment of trees and shrubs in Texas is tied to the quality and quantity of soil and water. In West Texas, where annual average rainfall totals are often in single digits, only drought-resistant desert shrubs survive the arid conditions, and the main tree species—juniper and ponderosa pine—are found mostly in the higher elevations. As environmental conditions improve toward the east, tree species expand to include mesquite, live oak, and pecan, as well as colorfully named shrubs such as blackbrush, whitebrush, and greenbriar. The East Texas forests consist mainly of pine trees, with a healthy mix of oak, elm, and hickory.

GRASSES AND CACTI

Texas leads the United States in numbers of grasses, boasting more than 570 species, subspecies, and varieties. Cacti are not nearly as diversified (merely 106 species), yet they also represent a noteworthy aspect of Texas's ground-level vegetation. Found mainly in far West Texas, these spindly yet captivating plants—including the flowering prickly pear, agave, yucca, and even the hallucinogenic

a century plant in Big Bend National Park

more than 130 million years, and the different species are greatly affected by the differences in the state's soils (azaleas thrive in acidic East Texas soil but struggle in the chalky Central Texas earth). Central Texans are fortunate since they're in the middle of several overlapping ecoregions. This biodiversity results in a plethora of springtime wildflowers—nearly 400 varieties in all—and a majority are native species.

The scenery is just as good in East Texas, home to blooming azaleas, yellow jasmine, dogwoods, and wisteria. Texas's arid and sandy regions don't offer quite the same visual spectacle, but daisies, cacti, and yucca in West Texas offer dashes of color to the monochromatic natural surroundings.

MAMMALS

Nearly 150 animal species traverse Texas's terrain, yet only two are emblematic of the Lone Star State. Texas's official small mammal is the armadillo (fun fact: female armadillos always have four pups, and all four are always the same sex), and the state's official large mammal is the Texas Longhorn.

Though these iconic creatures can typically be seen from the road—in the armadillo's case, it's usually flat on the road—the animals lurking in forests and canyons are the most interesting. Cougars are still fairly common in southwestern portions of the state, and Texas-worthy mammals like the javelina (a feral, tusked piglike creature officially known as the collared peccary), the kangaroo rat, and the antelope-ish pronghorn roam the prairies and brush country.

Also of interest is Texas's bat population, which includes 33 of the country's 43 known bat species. The world's largest bat colony lives in Bracken Cave near San Antonio, and each summer, more than one million Mexican free-tailed bats emerge from beneath Austin's Congress Avenue bridge, much to the delight of tourists and townies. Texas's less distinctive yet still notable mammals include white-tailed deer (estimated at nearly four million), black bear, coyote, and beaver.

peyote—come in a fascinating variety of sizes, shapes, and colors.

Texas's grasses, meanwhile, are less viscerally intriguing and more botanically appealing. Although a fair number of native grasses have been lost to overgrazing, the several hundred remaining varieties endure in spite of Texas's variable weather and topography. Tolerant species such as sideoats grama (the official state grass), Texas grama, buffalo grass, and Indian grass still provide meals for livestock, while their hardiness also helps contain soil erosion.

WILDFLOWERS

Wildflowers in Texas are akin to fall foliage in New England. For most of March and April, nature puts on a brilliant display of iridescent blues, dazzling reds, and blinding yellows across fields and along highways throughout the state. The prime viewing area is the Hill Country, where landscapes are painted with bluebonnets, Indian paintbrush, Mexican poppies, and black-eyed Susans.

Texas's wildflowers have been around for

Wildflowers bloom across the state each spring.

© ANDY RHODES

BIRDS

Texas is a destination and crossing point for myriad bird species during migratory seasons. It's also home to hundreds of native varieties. More kinds of birds (approximately 600) are in Texas than any other state—primarily due to its south-central location. Feathered pals from the eastern and western part of the country occupy Texas's air space, and international travelers cross the Mexican border, drawing avid bird-watchers from across the United States.

Texas birds can be grouped into five major categories: permanent residents (mockingbirds, roadrunners, screech owls), migrants (snow geese, scarlet tanagers, various sandpipers), winter residents (common loons and terns, red-bellied woodpeckers), summer residents (purple martins, yellow-breasted chats, orchard orioles), and accidentals (greater flamingos, red-footed boobies, yellow-billed loons).

Spring is the prime time for bird-watching. Serious and amateur birders from across the country visit the Gulf Coast and Rio Grande Valley to catch a glimpse of migrating and native bird species. Pelicans, spoonbills, egrets, and herons are fairly easy to spot. Those looking for a unique birding experience can join a boat tour to spy whooping cranes, the massive white birds boasting a seven-foot-wide wingspan that were nearly extinct before efforts were made to revive the species. Now more than 100 spend their winters in the Aransas National Wildlife Refuge on the Gulf Coast.

Texas's other main endangered bird species is the golden-cheeked warbler, a migratory songbird that breeds only in ashe juniper woodlands in Central Texas. Its habitat was reduced by encroaching development by about a quarter, but highly publicized campaigns to protect the species have helped protect its nesting grounds.

MARINE LIFE

An amazing variety of marine animals live in the Gulf of Mexico, home to thousands of fish and shellfish that depend on the coast's diverse habitats for food and shelter. These environs are typically categorized by five distinct water areas—salt marshes, coastal bays, jetties, nearshore waters, and the Gulf of Mexico.

Fish and shrimp enter salt marshes looking for food or for a place to lay their eggs. They're joined by several species of crabs (fiddler, hermit, and stone), snails, mussels, and worms. Coastal bays and beaches are home to two types of jellyfish, the Portuguese man-of-war (stay away from these purplish baggy creatures with the poison blue tentacles) and the relatively harmless cabbagehead, which looks like its namesake and are occasionally used by dolphins as toy balls.

The beach area also supports oysters, spotted sea trout, and several species of catfish. Jetties, which are used to prevent ship channels from piling up with sand and silt, consist of large stones providing shelter and food for a wide range of sea life, including sea anemones, urchins, crabs, grouper, and sea trout. Artificial reefs (stone rubble, old ships, oil rigs) open nearshore waters to mussels, shrimp, crabs, and a host of other animals, including the fish that feed on them (tarpon, kingfish, and others).

The Gulf of Mexico is home to some of Texas's heaviest hitters. Great barracuda and hammerhead, lemon and bull sharks devour smaller varieties such as bluefish, striped bass, and tuna. When the currents and temperatures are just right, tropical species such as parrotfish, angelfish, and spiny lobsters also visit the Gulf waters.

REPTILES

Snakes slither across much of Texas's surface, and the state's range of reptiles is rather impressive. Texas is home to 16 varieties of poisonous snakes (including 11 types of rattlesnakes), which can be extremely hazardous to hikers and campers. Other dangerous snakes include cottonmouth, copperheads, and Texas coral snakes.

Snake bites from these varieties require a few basic first-aid techniques if medical care is not immediately available. The American Red Cross suggests washing the bite with soap and water, and keeping the bitten area immobilized and lower than the heart. Equally as important are avoiding popular remedy misconceptions: Do not apply hot or cold packs, do not attempt to suck the poison out, and do not drink any alcohol or use any medication.

© ANDY RHODES

a lizard in the Texas Panhandle's Palo Duro Canyon

Texas is also home to hundreds of nonvenomous snake species, some of which mimic their poisonous counterparts. The Texas bull snake realistically imitates a rattlesnake, all the way down to the rattling sound, and a milk snake and coral snake look disturbingly alike, with the same colors but in different orders. A time-honored Texas adage helps differentiate the two: Red and yellow, kill a fellow (the coral snake has red next to yellow stripes); red and black, friend of Jack (the milk snake has red next to black stripes).

Not to be overlooked are Texas's other distinctive reptiles. The official state reptile is the Texas horned lizard (charmingly referred to as the horny toad), which is primarily found in West Texas. The state's other noteworthy reptiles include alligators, sea turtles, gecko lizards, and spinytail iguanas.

INSECTS AND BUTTERFLIES

Nearly 100,000 different kinds of pesky insects buzz around Americans' heads and ankles, and a third of those bugs have been found in Texas. The Lone Star State proudly claims to have more different kinds of insects than any other state.

Texas also has more butterfly species than any other state. Its 400 varieties number more than half the butterfly species in the United States and Canada. The recognizable monarch butterfly makes its annual migratory flight through Texas en route to its wintering grounds in Mexico. Their southward flight in late summer and fall can be quite a spectacle, when monarchs fill the air and gather on trees by the thousands.

Texas's insects are just as numerous but not nearly as charming. Most of these winged and antennaed creatures are ecologically beneficial, but the two insects that creep immediately to most Texans's minds are the bothersome mosquito and the squirm-inducing cockroach.

AMPHIBIANS

Like most living things in Texas, amphibians are well represented due to the tremendous diversity in climate and temperature. Frogs, toads, and salamanders are common in all areas of the state, but the greatest abundance and diversity are in the relatively wet habitats of the eastern third of the state. Camping near lakes and streams in this area offers visitors an audio sampler of the various croaks and calls of Texas's native frog and toad species.

Perhaps the best-known Texas amphibian is the Barton Springs salamander, a tiny creature found only among the rocks of Austin's legendary spring-fed swimming pool. In 1997, the U.S. Fish and Wildlife Service added the Barton Springs salamander to the endangered and threatened wildlife list, and the city of Austin later caused a big stir when it adopted strict development guidelines to protect this pint-size creature.

Climate

A weather map in March or November tells the story of Texas's variable climate in a visually stunning way—the entire spectrum of colors is represented across the state. From icy 20°F blues in the Panhandle to balmy 90°F reds in the Valley, the rainbow of Texas's diverse climate is a revealing diagram.

When it comes to weather-related records, Texas's books are virtually off the chart. Consider these extreme extremes: The state's record temperatures range from -23°F (Seminole, in the southwestern Panhandle, 1933) to 120°F (Seymore, north of Abilene, 1936). Texas's greatest annual rainfall was 109 inches (Clarksville, in northeastern Texas, 1873), and the least was 1.8 inches (Wink, in far West Texas, 1956). Also of note, Texas's highest sustained wind velocity was 145 mph, when Hurricane Carla hit the Gulf Coast in 1961.

Otherwise, the state's average rainfall typically exceeds 56 inches annually in East Texas, while El Paso and other parts of West Texas typically receive less than 8 inches each year. The average annual precipitation in Dallas is nearly 35 inches, and Houston averages approximately 48 inches. One final note of interest: The Route 66 town of Vega in the Texas Panhandle receives an average of 23 inches of snow per year, while Brownsville, at the mouth of the Rio Grande, has no measurable snowfall on record.

Texas has two main seasons—a hot summer that lasts from approximately May through October, and a winter that starts in November and usually lasts until March. By the time summer is over, most of Texas's landscape is too crisp and dry for fall foliage. Some colors are visible in the East Texas forests, but most of the state settles into a brownish hue until rains bring life and greenery back to the state in March.

REGIONAL

When it comes to climate, meteorologists usually divide Texas into three areas—modified marine (aka subtropics), continental, and mountain. These climate types aren't divided by strict boundaries, but the vast majority of the state falls into the subtropics region (Central and East Texas), which can be further divided into four subcategories based on humidity. We'll just stick with the basics.

The subtropics region is primarily affected by tropical airflow from the Gulf of Mexico, and its four humidity-related subheadings delineate the moisture content of this northwest-moving air stream. The continental region is largely in the Panhandle and is similar to the U.S. plains states, with major temperature fluctuations, low relative humidity, and moderate amounts of randomly occurring rainfall. Cooler temperatures, low humidity, and arid conditions characterize the mountain climate in far West Texas.

Using these climate regions as a guide, it's safe to assume the following about Texas's weather: the eastern third of the state has a humid climate noted for its warm summers; the central region of Texas has a subhumid climate resulting in hot summers and dry winters; and most portions of West Texas tend to have semiarid to arid conditions, often with extreme differences in temperature throughout the year.

DANGEROUS WEATHER

Even the weather is extreme in Texas. Menacing hurricanes, treacherous tornadoes, and dangerous floods can strike at any time, and they wreak their havoc swiftly before clear skies and calm conditions return. Fortunately, Texans have learned from previous atrocities, resulting in evacuation plans and safety procedures. Though most of these events are seasonal, there's an unpredictable nature to Texas's nature, so visitors should be prepared for potential flash floods.

Historically, hurricanes have hit Texas's Gulf Coast about once every decade, usually in September or October. Most Gulf Coast communities have evacuation plans in place, along with reinforced buildings and homes to brace against the torrential winds. Many seaside structures are also raised on piers to help prevent damage from the crashing waves during a tropical storm.

In the past decade, however, the hurricane activity in the gulf has been much higher. In addition to the devastation brought by Hurricanes Katrina and Rita, Hurricane Ike slammed into Galveston Island on September 13, 2008, leaving an enormous swath of destruction in its wake. Ike completely leveled several nearby communities, and its 110-mph winds ripped apart hotels, office buildings, and countless homes in Galveston, Houston, and the surrounding area. Of the nearly 7,000 documented historic buildings in Galveston, upward of 1,500 were seriously damaged.

Things were quite different a century ago. Galveston experienced the most destructive storm in U.S. history (before Hurricanes Katrina, Rita, and Ike) in 1900, when a hurricane left at least 6,000 dead and leveled

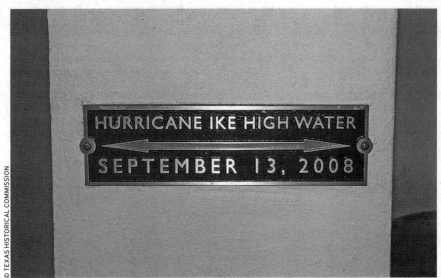

© TEXAS HISTORICAL COMMISSION

High water signs were placed throughout Galveston following Hurricane Ike.

most of the city. A storm of equal intensity hit Galveston in 1915, but the city was prepared with its new seawall. The death toll was a comparatively low 275.

Texas also lies in the path of Tornado Alley, with its central corridor running from the Panhandle north through Kansas. The state's worst tornado on record struck downtown Waco in 1953, killing 114 people, injuring 597, and destroying or damaging more than 1,000 homes and buildings. In 1997, a mile-wide tornado (as in *one mile wide*) wreaked havoc on the Central Texas town of Jarrell, leaving only the concrete slabs of dozens of homes in its wake.

Floods have also taken their toll on Texas. Thunderstorms are a major event—they typically come barreling in from the west, spewing lightning and firing occasional hailstones everywhere in their path. Appearing as massive, intimidating red blobs on the radar screen, they furiously dump heavy sheets of rain on Texas's lands, leaving saturated fields and overflowing rivers and streams in their wake.

One of the most destructive rainstorms in Texas history occurred in 1921, when floods in Central Texas killed 215 people. San Antonio was sitting under nearly nine feet of water, and 36 inches of rain fell north of Austin in just 18 hours (a U.S. record).

History

No place has a sense of place like Texas, and that sentiment is indelibly tied to the state's fascinating past. Texans are proud of their history, and for good reason. The state was once its own country, and many modern-day residents would likely welcome a return to the idea of isolationism. Above all, there's something reverential about the pride Texans take in their heritage, from the Native American contribution of the word *tejas* (meaning friends), to the state's nearly 400-year-old Spanish mission buildings, to the aforementioned Republic of Texas, to the role Texas played in the Civil War, to its ranching and oil heritage.

Being proud of what a state represents is somewhat distinctive to Texas. Not to take away anything from other states' history, but a term like "Rhode Island pride" or the concept of a proud Idaho heritage just don't resonate the way Texas Pride does. It's a badge of honor, and the state's rough-and-tumble past makes it a deserved title.

Everyone knows about The Alamo, but those who set out to discover Texas's dynamic heritage will encounter fascinating stories, like the 4,000-year-old Native American pictographs in a rock shelter along the Rio Grande, the discovery of the 1686 Gulf Coast shipwreck of French explorer La Salle, the influence of Mexican *vaqueros* on Texas's cowboys, and life in an oil boomtown in the 1930s. And that's just scraping the surface.

PREHISTORIC

Depending on the source, Texas's prehistoric past can be traced as far back as 13,000 years. That's 11000 B.C. That's a lot of years. Most archaeologists and historians divide the state's prehistoric era into three periods: Paleo-Indian, Archaic, and Late Prehistoric.

The Paleo-Indian period is significant for containing references to the earliest known inhabitants of the state (circa 9200 B.C.). Archaeologists have discovered numerous distinctive Clovis fluted points (a type of arrowhead) from this era, which were sometimes used for hunting mammoth.

The longest span of Texas's prehistory falls under the Archaic period (circa 6000 B.C.–A.D. 700). It's noted for the changes in projectile points and tools, and the introduction of grinding implements for food preparation. A significant weapon used during the Archaic period was a spear-throwing device known as an atlatl.

The bow and arrow was introduced during Texas's Late Prehistoric period (A.D. 700 to historic times). Pottery is present during this period among the hunters and gatherers in Central, South, and coastal Texas. Bison hunting was also very important to people living in most regions of the state's present-day boundaries.

NATIVE AMERICANS

Historians have identified hundreds of Native American groups in Texas. The validity of these names is problematic, however, because explorers used different languages (mainly Spanish, French, and English) to record what they heard to be the names of the newly "discovered" tribes they encountered.

Regardless, most historians agree that European diseases decimated Texas's native people. Anthropologist John C. Ewers identified at least 30 major epidemics (mostly smallpox and cholera) that wiped out as much as 95 percent of the state's Native Americans between 1528 and 1890. Until then, the four major tribes playing roles in Texas history were the Apache, Caddo, Comanche, and Kiowa.

The Apaches arrived in the area that would become Texas circa A.D. 1200. They were a nomadic tribe subsisting almost completely off buffalo, dressing in buffalo skins and living in tents made of tanned and greased hides. The Apaches were a powerful tribe that raided most groups they encountered. Eventually, their aggressive behavior turned their neighbors into enemies, and the Apaches eventually fled before the Comanches entered the region.

The Caddos were a collection of about 30 distinct groups, including the Tejas Indians, from whom Texas got its name, who had a similar language, political structure, and religious beliefs. Based in the current-day East Texas Piney Woods, the Caddos were mainly agricultural, living in permanent villages (as opposed to being nomadic). They weren't especially warlike, except for minor territorial conflicts they had with smaller nearby tribes over hunting grounds.

The Comanches were known as exceptional horsemen who played a prominent role in Texas frontier history in the 1700s and 1800s. They occupied much of what is now North, Central, and West Texas. Because of their trading skills, the Comanches controlled much of the region's commerce by bartering horses, buffalo products, and even captives for weapons and food. They lived in portable tepees constructed of tanned buffalo hide stretched over as many as 18 large poles.

The Kiowas acquired horses, slaves, and guns from the Spanish and eventually evolved into a nomadic, warring lifestyle until they became one of the most feared tribes in the region that became Texas. By the late 1700s, the Kiowas made a lasting peace with the Comanches and continued to live in the area until peacefully joining the Comanches with the Southern Cheyennes and Arapahos.

EUROPEAN EXPLORATION AND SETTLEMENT

The arrival (via shipwreck) of Spanish explorer Alvar Nunez Cabeza de Vaca in 1528 was one of Texas's first contacts with the Old World. His subsequent trek across the land that would become the Lone Star State offered Europeans some of the first clues about this newfound foreign region.

By 1685, the French were in on the action, dispatching explorer Robert Cavelier, Sieur de La Salle to find the mouth of the Mississippi River. He missed it by a long shot, ultimately wrecking his ship *La Belle* in a bay between

© TEXAS HISTORICAL COMMISSION

artifacts recovered from the 17th-century *La Belle* shipwreck

present-day Houston and Corpus Christi. More than 200 years later, the Texas Historical Commission discovered the contents and remains of *La Belle,* which offered a rare glimpse at a 17th-century New World colony—glass trade beads, dinnerware, gun flints, and even a human skeleton.

By the early 1700s, the Spanish solidified their presence in the region with four new mission buildings (The Alamo being one of them) used primarily to "civilize" the area's Native American tribes by converting them to Christianity. It didn't work as well as they'd hoped. By the early 19th century, European diseases had decimated most of the state's Native Americans, and many tribes had mixed in with other cultural groups, rendering the missions' objective obsolete.

Around this same time, the first wave of Germans arrived in Texas. Word spread quickly about Texas's bountiful land and ideal climate (perhaps they visited in springtime), prompting thousands of Germans to take root along rivers and streams in the state's fertile prairies and scenic hills.

THE REPUBLIC OF TEXAS AND STATEHOOD

An 1835 skirmish between colonists and Mexicans over ownership of a cannon is generally considered the opening battle of the Texas Revolution; subsequently, a provisional government was established in 1836 when delegates adopted the Texas Declaration of Independence on March 2 (which remains a state holiday). Texas's most famous battle occurred a week later with the 13-day siege of The Alamo. Mexican troops led by Gen. Antonio Lopez de Santa Anna eventually killed the remaining Texas defenders.

Later that month, about 350 Texan prisoners were executed by order of Santa Anna at Goliad. With these defeats in mind, the Texans, led by Sam Houston, defeated Santa Anna's Mexican army on April 21 with rallying cries of "Remember the Alamo!" and "Remember Goliad!" Houston reported 630 Mexican troops killed, with only nine Texan lives lost. The revolution's end became official in May 1836 when both sides signed the treaty of Valasco.

A year later, the United States, France, and England officially recognized the new Republic of Texas, and plots of land were soon sold in the republic's new capital, named for Stephen F. Austin, the state's preeminent colonist. In 1845, Texas became a U.S. state after U.S. Congress passed an annexing resolution, which was accepted by the republic's Texas Constitutional Convention and overwhelmingly supported by Texas voters.

From 1846 to 1848, Texas and Mexico engaged in a boundary battle known as the U.S.-Mexican War, which ultimately established the current international boundary. A decade later, the federal government moved Native American tribes in West and Central Texas to Indian Territory (now Oklahoma).

THE CIVIL WAR AND RECONSTRUCTION

Texas struggled with complexities during the Civil War. Some people supported the Union, including Governor Sam Houston, who refused to take an oath of allegiance to the Confederacy. It eventually cost him his office. For the most part, however, Texans identified with the rest of the southern United States, and in early 1861 it became official when Texas seceded from the Union and became the seventh state accepted by the provisional Confederate States of America government.

After four years of border skirmishes, gulf coast naval battles, and prisoner of war camps, Texas troops marked the true end of the Civil War with a battle near Brownsville, more than a month after the war officially ended (due to the time involved with news reaching Texas). In June, it was announced that slavery had been abolished, an event still commemorated today during Juneteenth festivals in African-American communities statewide.

Much of Texas's history during the late 1800s is centered around the arrival of railroads, which put towns on and off the map depending on the train routes. Cattle rustling was an important part of Texas's commerce and identity before railroads took over the responsibility of moving cattle northward. Texas's development was made possible by the railroads, and they continued to sustain the local economy for decades since so many areas of the state still needed railroad service, including the lower Rio Grande Valley, the South Plains, the Panhandle, and West Texas.

THE 20TH CENTURY

Texas's new century kicked off with a boom—a 100-foot oil gusher blew in at Spindletop near Beaumont in 1901, boosting Texas into the petroleum age. Oil wells would be discovered for several decades, turning small communities into boomtowns with tens of thousands of wildcatters and roughnecks arriving overnight to work on the rigs.

The Wild West arrived in West Texas when the Mexican civil war (1911–20) spilled across the border; as a result, supply raids and refugee harboring became common occurrences. The notorious Mexican general Pancho Villa was involved with some of these skirmishes.

By the 1950s and '60s, Texas was gaining a reputation for its intellectual resources, resulting in the Dallas-based development of the integrated circuit (used in semiconductors and electronics) and the opening of NASA's (National Aeronautics and Space Administration's) Manned Spacecraft Center in Houston.

In one of the darker moments of Texas and U.S. history, President John F. Kennedy was assassinated in Dallas. It marked the end of the country's optimism during Kennedy's presidency and ushered in a new president—Texan Lyndon B. Johnson, former vice president. Johnson would go on to play a major role in advancing the country's civil rights movement. The final two decades of the 20th century were notable for two additional Texans being elected to the U.S. presidency: George H. W. Bush and his son George W. Bush.

Economy and Government

Cotton, cattle, and crude (oil)—Texas's venerable "Three Cs" dominated the state's agricultural and economic development until the mid-20th century, and these land-based resources continue to support much of the state's wealth. Other factors contributing to Texas's economy are various industries not exclusive to the Lone Star State, such as retailing, wholesaling, banking, insurance, and construction.

Many national corporate headquarters have relocated to Texas (especially to the midcontinental location of Dallas), and petroleum companies continue to search for new sources of energy to provide fuel. In addition, Houston is home to many federal air installations and NASA's prestigious Lyndon B. Johnson Space Center, while Austin is home to Dell Computers and other esteemed high-tech companies. Tourism has also become a major business, particularly in San Antonio, and Texas has become a leader in the areas of medicine and surgery.

AGRICULTURE

Cattle and cotton remain staples of Texas's agricultural economy. The state's wide open spaces allowed both commodities to grow freely when settlers arrived in the mid-1800s, and Texas's remaining abundance of available land continues to make it the most important cattle-raising state in the country.

Nearly all of the state's 254 counties derive more revenue from cattle than any other agricultural commodity; those that don't almost always rank cattle second in importance. Cattle dominate Texas's livestock production, contributing approximately 70 percent of the state's livestock and products sales. And if those aren't enough agricultural accolades, consider this: Texas ranks first nationally in production of cattle, beef cattle, sheep, lamb, wool, goats, and mohair.

Cotton, meanwhile, became a prominent crop due to the immigration of settlers from the Deep South, who continued their plantation system of agriculture when they arrived in Texas. Cotton production grew steadily after 1900, and the crop became a major economic factor when suitable varieties were developed for the West Texas climate. Since that time, Texas has led all states in cotton production virtually every year, and it provides approximately one-quarter of the country's cotton supply.

In total value of farm crops, Texas consistently has ranked in the top five among the states since the mid-20th century and has been a leading producer of grain sorghums, peanuts (groundnuts), and rice. Incidentally, nearly all of the mohair produced in the United States comes from Texas's Angora goats.

MANUFACTURING AND INDUSTRY

Texas's manufacturing roots lie with its agricultural processing—cotton gins, cottonseed mills, meatpacking plants, flour mills, oil field equipment, and canning plants. These days, the state's largest employment sector is categorized as the "trade, transportation, and utilities industry," which includes jobs in retail, wholesale, and finance.

Jobs in the petroleum, construction, and service industries are also typically steady across the state. Texas's top exported products are chemicals, petrochemicals, and transportation equipment. The state's remarkable number of exports is attributed to its proximity to Mexico, which receives nearly half of Texas's products. Texas is also responsible for a large number of U.S. exports to Mexico (approximately 50 percent).

PETROLEUM

Oil changed everything for Texas. It transformed the state from a backwoods frontier to an industrial giant. In January 1901, a gusher blew in at Spindletop near Beaumont, and the Texas oil boom erupted into the nation's conscience. Thirty years later, an even more significant event occurred—the discovery of the enormous East Texas Oil Field. Within two

years, 5,600 wells were drilled near the cities of Kilgore and Longview, and 25,000 wells were in place by 1938.

Oil became the basis for Texas's mammoth petrochemical industry and provided the funding to develop the state's educational and highway systems. On the flip side, a massive drop in oil prices in the early 1980s resulted in a decline in Texas's economy.

Regardless, oil and natural gas remain the state's most valuable minerals, contributing nearly 20 percent of the country's oil production and 30 percent of its gas production in recent years. Texas leads all other states in oil and natural gas production. It also ranks first in oil-refining capacity.

TRAVEL

The state's official travel slogan aptly captures its allure: "Texas, It's Like A Whole Other Country." More than 200 million people visit Texas annually—70 percent are leisure travelers, and 30 percent are traveling for business. International travelers account for approximately 10 percent of Texas's total visitor spending.

The five countries with the highest visitation numbers are Mexico, Canada, the United Kingdom, Germany, and France. The top five destination cities for out-of-state visitors are Dallas–Fort Worth, Houston, various "rural Texas destinations," San Antonio, and Austin. The top five tourist sites are The Alamo, the San Antonio River Walk, outlet malls in San Marcos (south of Austin), SeaWorld of Texas (San Antonio), and the Six Flags Over Texas amusement park near Dallas.

GOVERNMENT

Texas was annexed to the United States as the 28th state on December 29, 1845. From Reconstruction (the late 1800s) through the early 1960s, the Democratic Party dominated Texas politics. Keep in mind, the Democrats of those days differed considerably from the current political party. For almost a century, Texas Democrats consisted mainly of white conservatives, who prevailed in almost all statewide elections.

A Texas-worthy phrase was used during this era to describe the especially dedicated party members: "Yellow Dog Democrats" were the state's die-hard partisan loyalists who would vote for a yellow dog if it ran on the Democratic ticket. The phrase is now used to describe any Democratic loyalist, although the recent stronghold of Republicans in Texas is rendering the term nearly obsolete.

Texas's bicameral legislature is comprised of 31 Senate members who serve for four years and the House of Representatives, with 150 members elected for two-year terms. The legislature meets for its regular session in the spring of odd-numbered years, but the governor may convene a special session for the legislators to address particular issues. The governor of Texas is elected to a four-year term in November of even-numbered, nonpresidential election years.

Texas is divided into a whopping 254 counties that average nearly 1,000 square miles in size. West Texas's Brewster County is especially enormous—at 6,169 square miles, it's roughly the size of Delaware and Rhode Island combined.

People

The people of Texas equally reflect and defy all stereotypes associated with their dynamic nature. For every good ol' boy set in his ways, there's a progressive genius building her Web-based empire. For every brash oilman making millions, there's a humble educator affecting lives. Intense football coaches coexist peacefully with environmental activists.

Like anywhere else, people in Texas have their differences, but there's one thing that transcends obstacles that is unique to this state—the common bond of being Texan. Not that it solves all problems, but most Texans look kindly upon their brethren and genuinely display the spirit of Southern hospitality. It's infectious—"Y'all come back" and "Well, bless your heart" become true expressions of kindness rather than silly stereotypes.

Transplants from the northern and eastern United States may initially be taken aback by random strangers in the grocery store commenting on their purchases, but they'll later find themselves doing the same thing. Offers of assistance are genuine rather than obligatory, and people make direct eye contact when they mutter a polite "Howdy."

There are many ways to categorize these Texans—by age, ethnicity, religion, income level, etc.—but labels don't capture the soul of the state's residents, who aptly represent the character of the word *friend* in the origins of the word *Texas*.

POPULATION

Texas's rate of population growth has exceeded the nation's in every decade since Texas became a state (1845), and recent population increases have been substantial. The state's population has more than doubled in the past 25 years, from roughly 11.2 million to more than 25 million. Estimates based on recent growth rates suggest the state is growing by nearly 500,000 people annually.

From 2000 to 2010, Texas led the country in growth, increasing in population by 20.6 percent (an addition of about 4.3 million people), which is more than twice as fast as the U.S. rate. Growth was generally concentrated in four areas: the Dallas–Fort Worth metroplex, Houston-Galveston, San Antonio–Austin, and the Rio Grande Valley.

Interestingly enough, this growth has been anything but uniform, with some counties in West Texas losing as much as 22 percent of their population while others around Dallas and Austin growing by more than 60 percent. In fact, recent demographic reports associated with the 2010 census reveal that nearly 85 percent of the state's population lives east of the I-35 corridor, which stretches north–south from Dallas to Laredo.

Austin's suburbs were among the state's leaders in growth, with Williamson County's (north of Austin) population increasing by 69 percent and Hays County (south of Austin) growing by 61 percent. A dramatic example of the population boom in Williamson County is found in the (formerly) small community of Hutto, the second-fastest growing city in Texas. From 2000 to 2010, the number of residents increased nearly tenfold, from 1,250 to a whopping 14,698.

ETHNICITY

Since the mid-1800s, most Texas residents have been of European descent, but for the first time in state history, their numbers are no longer the majority. Currently, about 49 percent of the population is of northern European ancestry; roughly 36 percent are Hispanic, and approximately 11 percent are African-American. The remaining 4 percent are listed under "other racial/ethnic groups," though most are of Asian descent.

The healthy pace of Texas's increased population is largely due to international immigration, which represented nearly 77 percent of the state's population growth in recent years. The Texas State Data Center projects that by 2020, Hispanics will represent the majority of the state's population. Of note is the rapid growth of foreign-born residents in Texas's major metro areas (112 percent) compared to border metro cities (51 percent). Austin witnessed the greatest increase in foreign-born population (172 percent), likely reflecting the city's economic growth in the technology sector.

Perhaps most significant are major population increases in the Lower Rio Grande Valley, with growth rates continually nearing 40 percent and birth rates significantly higher than the rest of the state. As a result, Texas has the country's second-highest Hispanic population, behind California.

According to reports from the 2010 census, Hispanics accounted for two-thirds of Texas's growth over the past decade and now represent about 37 percent of the state's total population

the Buu Mon Buddhist temple in Port Arthur

HOW TO SPEAK TEXAN

Texas boasts several accents within its own border, from the slowly stretched-out East Texas drawl, to border-hopping Spanglish known as Tex-Mex, to the tight twang of the Panhandle and West Texas. The distinctive West Texas lilt is perhaps the best representation of Texas talk, since you won't hear anyone speaking this way unless they're from this region of the Lone Star State.

Even though Texans like to brag about their accomplishments, they can't take credit for the Southern accent that prevails below the Mason-Dixon Line. However, the Lone Star State can claim some of the spice that makes the Southern dialect unique. For the most part, the following examples are found in rural areas of the state, though you'll occasionally hear a "yessir" or "fixin' to" in a downtown urban environment.

Let's start with the obvious: "Howdy, y'all." It's the quintessential Texas/Southern phrase, usually invoked by Yankees (jokingly referred to down here as anyone north and/or east of Oklahoma) with a mocking twang. The truth is, Texans actually say these words often, but usually not together. "Howdy" is typically muttered as a polite greeting as opposed to a garish welcome, and its use as a friendly salutation is one of many cultural traditions taught at Texas A&M University. As for "y'all," it just makes sense – why refer to a group of people (women and children, in particular) as "you guys"? The common Texas phrase "all y'all" takes things to whole nother level, however.

Texans also use "sir" and "ma'am" regularly, just not in a formal or subservient way. It's common to hear men respond to each other with a simple "yessir" or "nosir," and it's just plain polite to express appreciation to someone – a police officer, fellow pedestrian, or store clerk – with a simple "thank you, ma'am."

Up North, these terms take on military or Old Maid connotations, but in Texas it's just being cordial.

Like other Southerners, Texans of all ages refer to their parents as "mother" and "daddy." It's somewhat strange to hear a grown man talk about his "daddy's" influence, but it's charming, nevertheless.

Another Texas phrase that gets the Yankees giggling is "fixin' to." It's a handy term that's quintessentially Southern, indicating someone is getting ready to do something without fully committing to carrying out the task ("I'm fixin' to pay those bills soon."). Incidentally, the "fixin" also refers to food in Texas, garnishes in particular. If you order a burger or barbecue plate with all the fixins, you'll get onions, pickles, peppers, and any number of sides or sauces piled on the plate.

Speaking of food, occasional confusion arises when Texans refer to "dinner" and "supper." These are interchangeable in other parts of the country, but around here, "dinner" can mean lunch, while "supper" almost always refers to the evening meal.

Other examples of Lone Star speak are evident in the pronunciation of words. You can tell a Texan by the way they emphasize the first syllable in words like *umbrella* (UM-brella), *insurance* (IN-surance), and *display* (DIS-play.). Others are more subtle, like the tendency to flatten out the vowel sounds in words like *mail* (mell), *wheel* (well), and the double-whammy *windshield* (wenshell).

Finally, you'll occasionally hear Texans using traditional rural sayings like "over yonder" (over there), "pitch a hissy fit" (a dramatic reaction), and even "gaddum" and its derivative "dadgum." Fortunately, Texans are such a friendly bunch, they won't pitch a hissy fit if you sound like a dadgum Yankee.

(an increase from 32 percent in 2000). Also of interest is the considerably younger age of the state's Hispanic population (25.5 years for the median age versus 38 for Anglos). The effect on Texas's population is a statewide median age of 32.3, the second youngest in the country to Utah.

RELIGION

For the most part, Texas is a devoutly religious state, with Christianity dominating the spiritual scene. Although it mirrors national trends showing slightly declining congregation numbers, residents in the rural areas of the state remain committed churchgoers. In fact, a 15-county area in Texas's southeastern Panhandle is designated as a candidate for the "buckle of the Bible Belt," a wide band of the entire U.S. South where a majority of people identify themselves as Baptists.

The two primary religious groups in Texas are Baptist (approximately 22 percent) and Catholic (roughly 21 percent). The percentages are far lower for other religions—Muslim, Hindu, Buddhist, Jewish, and other faiths— which are mostly located in the state's urban areas. Texas's big cities also had the largest number of people claiming not to be affiliated with a religious group. In Austin, the percentage is roughly 55 percent, while Houston and Dallas–Fort Worth had approximately 50 percent and 48 percent, respectively, of nonaffiliates.

LANGUAGE

English speakers in Texas account for 68 percent of the population, with Spanish running a distant second, yet still notable (26 percent). People speak Vietnamese and German in a few small pockets of the state, but for the most part, it's Spanish and English (and a few interesting varieties of the two).

A fair number of Hispanics in South Texas speak an unofficial language known as Tex-Mex, which combines Spanish and English words without any rigid guidelines determining when to use each. It's a distinctive regional practice, resulting from an impulsive tendency to toss in an English or Spanish word when the translation isn't immediately on the tip of the tongue, and it's most evident on Tejano radio stations in Corpus Christi and the Lower Rio Grande Valley, where rapid-fire DJs pepper their announcements in Spanish with random yet instantly recognizable English words.

Learning to speak Texan is an entirely different endeavor. Though it sounds like a Southern accent on the surface, there are distinct dialects in different parts of the state. In East Texas, vowels are more drawn out, and the slower cadence includes inflections of the Deep South. People in West Texas, meanwhile, speak with more of a tight twang. Pronunciation of the word *Texas* is a prime example—in East Texas, it often sounds like "Tay-ux-us," and in West Texas it's pronounced "Tix-is."

Just to make things interesting, young adults in the state's metropolitan areas tend to combine elements of their own Texas dialect with California's "Valley speak." Dallas-born actor Owen Wilson's accent is the quintessential example of this style of speech.

Arts and Culture

One of the specialty license plates available to Texans features a bold image of the state flag with the phrase "State of the Arts" at the bottom. This motto might not be the first attribute people associate with Texas (California and New York immediately jump to mind), but it's absolutely befitting of the Lone Star State.

Hundreds of world-renowned writers, artists, musicians, and actors call Texas home, and their influences and styles are as far-reaching as the stars in the West Texas sky. Having three of the country's 10 largest cities also helps maximize exposure for artists and art aficionados. Premier exhibits and tours always include Texas on their schedule, and the dynamic magnetism of the state itself serves as an inspiration for a diverse mixture of creative endeavors. Anywhere that can claim Pulitzer Prize–winning (and Oscar-winning) writer Larry McMurtry and alternative rockers the Butthole Surfers is bound to be brimming with eclectic culture.

LITERATURE

Larry McMurtry, famed author of the cattle-drive epic *Lonesome Dove* and drama *Terms of Endearment,* as well as screenplay writer for *The Last Picture Show* and *Brokeback Mountain,* is emblematic of the literary state of Texas. He approaches his craft with the sweeping majesty of one of his favorite subject matters—the mythical old west, with Texas as a focal point.

Another celebrated literary genre in Texas is folklore, and J. Frank Dobie (1888–1964) was and still is considered the foremost figure in the field. Dobie painted fascinating portraits of cowboys, cattlemen, hunters, and countless other Texas characters and critters. From an intellectual perspective, many Texans cite Pulitzer Prize–winning journalist, essayist, short story writer, and novelist Katherine Anne Porter (1890–1980) as the state's most accomplished writer. She is perhaps best known for her acute insight about complex subject matters in her works *Pale Horse, Pale Rider* (1939) and *Ship of Fools* (1961).

An essential book about Texas by a non-Texan is H. G. Bissinger's *Friday Night Lights: A Town, A Team, A Dream* (1990), which accurately and compellingly chronicles the positive and negative aspects of Texas's passion for high school football. More recently, Texas journalist Molly Ivins (1944–2007) gained national fame as a sharp and scathing critic of the country's right-wing political movement in the early part of the 21st century. President George W. Bush was a frequent Ivins target, and her book *Bushwhacked: Life in George W. Bush's America,* was a success in liberal enclaves of the United States and especially in her hometown of Austin.

MUSIC

Texas has perhaps the most compelling music legacy in the country, and many of the state's artists have become influential figures in popular music history. Texans have contributed essential volumes to the world's music catalog by introducing and refining styles such as rhythm and blues, Western swing, Tejano, country, and rock. The state's musical giants are recognizable by a single name—Buddy, Janis, Willie, Selena, and Beyoncé—and each have influenced generations of future musicians while getting plenty of boots scootin' and toes tappin' in the process.

Texas's documented musical history begins with its initial wave of settlers in the late 1800s. A fascinating mix of cultures, including German, African-American, Czechoslovakian, Mexican, and Anglo, resulted in an equally intriguing blend of musical styles. The best-known types of music in the U.S. South—blues and country—evolved into new and intriguing genres when accompanied by a Texas twist. Appalachian "fiddle music" migrated westward with pioneers and merged with distinctly Texan influences such as yodeling, accordions, and 12-string guitar, resulting

TEXAS IN SONG

Texas is immortalized in song perhaps more than any other state. Several sources list nearly 100 tunes with *Texas* (or *Lone Star*, or Texas cities) in the title, a far cry from the number of songs heralding Idaho's contribution to the cultural landscape.

With all the options to choose from, it's unfortunate the official state song, "Texas, Our Texas," is unrecognizable by most people, including many Texans. Adopted by the legislature after being selected in a statewide competition, the song features inspirational (and poorly written) lyrics with simple rhymes like "all hail the mighty state" with "so wonderful, so great."

Our country's national anthem is rather difficult to sing due to its extremely wide tonal range and occasionally confusing lyrics, so Texas's official state song should be something recognizable and easy on the vocal chords. Some Texans have even proposed adopting an updated official tune to rouse the troops at athletic competitions and school or government events.

There are plenty to choose from, including iconic classics such as "Deep in the Heart of Texas," made famous by Gene Autry (and Pee Wee Herman); "The Yellow Rose of Texas," as performed by Bob Wills; Ernest Tubb's version of "Waltz Across Texas"; or even the fiddle-filled old-school dance craze "Cotton Eyed Joe." Collegiately patriotic Texans will insist their school fight songs are the most iconic Texas tunes, particularly "The Eyes of Texas" (University of Texas) and the "Aggie War Hymn" (Texas A&M University).

The 1970s were a golden time for Texas-themed songs, particularly in the country music scene. Though the following options haven't attained "official song" consideration status, they're known well enough in pop culture as ambassadors of Texas mystique. Highlights include Willie Nelson's adaptation of "San Antonio Rose," Marty Robbins's "(out in the West Texas town of) El Paso," "Streets Of Laredo" by Buck Owens, "Luckenbach, Texas (Back To The Basics Of Love)" by Waylon Jennings, Glen Campbell's "Galveston," ZZ Top's "La Grange," and a couple of George Strait classics, "Amarillo by Morning" and "All My Exes Live in Texas." Unfortunately, there's also Alabama's hit, "If You're Gonna Play in Texas (You Gotta Have a Fiddle in the Band)."

The Texas-themed songs haven't been quite as prolific lately, but the state's music scene remains vital. Perhaps in the near future we'll see a remixed version of a Texas classic or a new Lone Star legend penned by one of Austin's indie rock sensations. Stay tuned.

---

in unique styles such as Western swing, conjunto, and rockabilly.

One of Texas's most influential musicians was Blind Lemon Jefferson, who introduced his signature country blues in the 1920s with his raw, potent track "Black Snake Moan." Borrowing the flamenco-influenced guitar work he heard from Mexican migrant workers, Jefferson's fast fingers and ear for melody inspired fellow Texas blues legends Huddy "Leadbelly" Ledbetter and Lightnin' Hopkins. Their work paved the way for generations of Texas blues heroes, including Albert Collins, Freddy King, Clarence "Gatemouth" Brown, and Buddy Guy. Legendary Austinite Stevie Ray Vaughan led a blues revival in the 1980s with his soulful guitar wizardry, scoring national hits with albums *Couldn't Stand the Weather* and *In Step* before he was tragically killed in a 1990 helicopter crash at the age of 35.

A wholly distinct sound from Texas is conjunto music (aka Tejano, Tex-Mex, norteno), which combines accordion and 12-string guitar to produce lively dance melodies with South Texas soul. The style originated with Texas and Mexican working-class musicians who adopted the accordion and the polka from 19th-century German settlers. Conjunto music was popular along the Rio Grande and throughout Latin America for decades before artists began reaching larger audiences in the late 1960s. The genre's best-known artist is

Leonardo "Flaco" Jiménez, who has performed with renowned acts such as the Rolling Stones, Bob Dylan, Willie Nelson, Buck Owens, and Carlos Santana. An underappreciated Mexican-influenced style, dubbed "Chicano soul" or the "San Antonio West Side sound," emerged from the late-1950s influences of rhythm & blues and doo-wop. The instantly catchy sound represented an innovative blend of soulful Motown-style harmonies and melodies with Mexican-influenced accents from brass and reed instruments.

Although country music has its true origins in Anglo-based folk balladry, Texans took the style and made it their own. Several of country music's offshoots are Texas products, including Western swing, honky-tonk, and outlaw country. Bob Wills pioneered the jazz-based Western swing style of music in the 1920s, and Ernest Tubb's walking bass lines were a crucial component of 1940s honky-tonk country. In the late 1960s, Austin became the laid-back capital of outlaw country in response to the slick, produced material coming out of Nashville. A raw and loose version of country music emanated from the city's storied Armadillo World Headquarters, which regularly featured legendary outlaws like Willie Nelson, Waylon Jennings, and Jerry Jeff Walker. Overall, Texas's contributors to country music reads like a track listing from the style's greatest hits: Gene Autry, Buck Owens, George Jones, Kenny Rogers, Larry Gatlin, Barbara Mandrell, Townes Van Zandt, Kris Kristofferson, George Strait, Mark Chestnutt, Lyle Lovett, and Pat Green (and that's just volume one).

Rock 'n' roll also received a big ol' Texas brand on it during its formative years. Lubbock's Buddy Holly and the Crickets refined the country-blues style into a distinct rockabilly sound, which influenced the Beatles in ways far beyond their insect-inspired name. Another West Texan, Roy Orbison, made an impact in Memphis with a smoother approach to rockabilly. Port Arthur's Janis Joplin wowed Austin with her bluesy swagger in the late 1960s before moving to San Francisco, where she played a major role in solidifying the city's psychedelic sound. In the 1970s, Texas contributed to the future classic rock scene with artists such as the Steve Miller Band, ZZ Top, and Don Henley (of The Eagles).

During the past 20 years, Texans continued to make their marks on myriad musical styles. Selena Quintanilla-Perez (1971–95), known simply as Selena, led a surge in the Latino music scene's popularity in the early 1990s with her dancy pop tunes that drew thousands of converts to her spirited shows. The Dixie Chicks rose from relative obscurity to become one of the world's most popular country music acts with a sound inspired by traditional country, folk, and bluegrass. Their 1998 album *Wide Open Spaces* sold 12 million copies, becoming the best-selling album in country music history from a duo or group. Other significant Texas contributions to contemporary music in the early 21st century were Houston acts Destiny's Child (rhythm and blues) and Paul Wall (rap), along with alternative rock bands from Austin such as Spoon and . . . Trail of Dead.

FILM

More than 1,300 film projects have been made in Texas since 1910, including *Wings,* the first film to win an Academy Award for Best Picture (made in San Antonio in 1927). Film production in Texas has been a vital part of the state's economy for decades, bringing thousands of jobs and hundreds of millions of dollars to the state each year.

With mild winters and more than 267,000 square miles of diverse landscape to work with, Texas is an extremely versatile place to shoot movies, TV shows, music videos, commercials, and other independent film projects. Texas locations have doubled for the American Midwest; Mexico; Washington, D.C.; Vietnam; Afghanistan; Bolivia; Africa; Florida; and a host of other places throughout the world.

The Texas Film Commission, a division of the governor's office, lends filmmakers a hand by providing free information on locations, crews, talent, state and local contacts, weather, laws, sales tax exemptions, housing, and other

© TEXAS HISTORICAL COMMISSION

the Royal Theater in Archer City, inspiration for *The Last Picture Show*

film-related issues. The assistance certainly pays off, with the state receiving more than $2 billion in film-related expenditures during the past decade.

Filmmakers look kindly upon Texas because the state has experienced crew members, equipment vendors, and support services. On most features shot in Texas, 75 percent of the crew is hired locally, and the production company is 100 percent exempt from state and local sales taxes on most of the services and items they rent or purchase. In addition, Texas has several regional film offices that court the major studios and provide production assistance.

Dozens of acclaimed and influential films have been shot on location in Texas (of the hundreds of projects completed), and several have become celluloid classics. Most notable are the 1956 movie *Giant,* starring Elizabeth Taylor, Rock Hudson, and James Dean, and John Wayne's 1960 film *The Alamo. Giant* was filmed in West Texas, and its legacy is still celebrated in Marfa, where the stately 1930 Hotel Paisano served as home base for the cast and

crew. A glass case in the lobby displays movie-related magazine clippings and photos, and guests clamor to stay in James Dean's hotel room.

The Alamo isn't always remembered for its integrity as a dramatic film, but its set near the southwest Texas town of Brackettville remains a critical location for film projects and tourists. The Alamo Village bills itself as "Texas' most active and versatile movie set" and features one of the industry's largest and most complete backlots, boasting "no false fronts here." The site has hosted more than 200 major feature films, TV movies, miniseries, documentaries, commercials, and music videos.

Other significant film projects shot in Texas include *The Last Picture Show* (1971, screenplay by Texan Larry McMurtry), *The Texas Chainsaw Massacre* (1973), *Urban Cowboy* (1979), *Terms of Endearment* (1983, based on McMurtry's novel), David Byrne's brilliant *True Stories* (1986), McMurtry's *Lonesome Dove* (1990), Austinite Richard Linklater's generation-defining *Slacker* (1990), David Lynch's *Wild at Heart* (1990), Austinite Robert Rodriguez's groundbreaking

El Mariachi (1992), Linklater's classic *Dazed and Confused* (1992), Christopher Guest's hilarious *Waiting for Guffman* (1995), Dallas native Wes Anderson's masterpiece *Rushmore* (1997), Steven Soderbergh's *Traffic* (2000), Quentin Tarantino and Rodriguez's double feature *Grind House* (2006), Rodriguez's *Predators* (2010), and Terence Malick's *The Tree of Life* (2011).

In addition to its mighty movie credits, Texas has hosted noteworthy television shows. Perhaps most significant of them all is *Dallas* (1978–90), which entranced audiences across the globe with its Texas-worthy dramatic storylines centered around oil magnate J. R. Ewing and his family. Equally as remarkable yet more artistically viable is PBS's venerable *Austin City Limits* (1975–present), showcasing top-notch country, roots, and alternative music across America and spawning its thriving annual music festival. In 2011, the program made a dramatic venue change, from the University of Texas's communications building to a swanky new theater on the ground floor of the upscale W hotel. Other notable Texas TV shows include a season of MTV's *The Real World* shot in Austin (2005), NBC's critically acclaimed *Friday Night Lights* (2006–11), and finally, in the bizarro category, *Barney and Friends,* filmed in Dallas (1992–2010).

THE ARTS

The visual arts scene in Texas is particularly captivating, due in large part to available funding from the state's land and oil barons. World-class artwork is regularly exhibited throughout Texas in big cities and small towns, where art philanthropists give generously to construct ornate museums and draw exceptional exhibits.

In addition, the Texas Commission on the Arts state agency traditionally funded education and cultural programs (and it will hopefully continue to do so, if it escapes the state's proposed budget axe in 2011). Its grants help fund projects to educate Texas citizens about the importance of art, and the agency has been lauded for its work with at-risk youth and children with disabilities.

For the most part, Texas's fine arts opportunities are located in its metropolitan areas. Some of the country's best art museums are in Houston and Dallas–Fort Worth. Of particular note is Fort Worth's Kimbell Museum, where the facility housing the artwork is as impressive as the work it holds. Designed by architect Louis Kahn, its softly arching ceilings provide the perfect amount of natural light to complement the interior artwork by masters such as Picasso, Monet, Rembrandt, El Greco, Cézanne, and others in addition to its impressive collections of Asian and African art.

Other must-see art museums in Fort Worth are the Amon Carter Museum, showcasing high-quality Western art (Georgia O'Keeffe, Ansel Adams, Winslow Homer), and the Modern Art Museum of Fort Worth, a glass structure designed by famed Japanese architect Tadao Ando that seems to float in a surrounding shimmering pool. Inside are more than 26,000 works by renowned artists such as Picasso, Andy Warhol, and Jackson Pollock.

Dallas's premier art attraction, the Dallas Museum of Art, features an impressive $32 million two-acre sculpture garden showcasing the work of Miro, Rodin, Moore, de Kooning, and many others. The facility is also known for its Museum of the Americas, which showcases an impressive collection of historic art from North, Central, and South America.

Houston is the other main hub for Texas's fine arts, with nearly 20 major museums and galleries. The city's Museum of Fine Arts houses approximately 31,000 works of American, European, Latin American, Native American, and Asian art spanning 4,000 years. Its concentration is on Renaissance and impressionism, but there are treasures hiding around every corner, especially the primitive Native American pieces.

Other worthy Houston museums are the Contemporary Art Museum, which rotates exhibits every six weeks, offering visitors a fresh experience year-round. The Menil Collection also features rotating displays along with its permanent 10,000-piece collection, which includes a stunning mix of styles, from African and Byzantine to surrealist and contemporary.

ESSENTIALS

Getting There

Texas is far removed from the transportation hubs on the East and West Coasts, but it's easily accessible by plane and relatively accessible by car. The only problems travelers occasionally encounter when entering the state are at the Mexican border, where agents can take their sweet time checking vehicles and asking questions. However, with the recent unrest and violence associated with drug cartels, most travelers are avoiding Mexico entirely unless they absolutely need to go for business or family purposes. See the *Tips for Travelers* section for more information about crossing the border.

BY AIR

Texas is easy to get to by air because its two largest cities—Houston and Dallas—are primary hubs for major airlines (Continental and American, respectively). As a result, flights from all over the country wind up in the Lone Star State, often at affordable rates. Texas's other major cities—Austin, San Antonio, and El Paso—have international airports, but the nonstop flights from points beyond aren't nearly as frequent (or cheap). Even Texas's smaller cities (populations of 100,000 or greater) have airports, but you'll have to go through Dallas or Houston to get there.

BY CAR

The interstate highway system in Texas is pretty impressive—for a state this huge, you can get from most major cities to the others (excluding El Paso) by noon. The roads tend to be in good shape since they don't have to contend with icy conditions, but like most states, construction is a perpetual issue in Texas's metro areas. Increased truck traffic from Mexico has taken its toll on some of the freeways, and rural roads between smaller cities can get a bit rough, but that doesn't deter Texans from going 90 mph. The Texas Department of Transportation (www.txdot.gov) oversees all aspects of vehicular travel.

BY TRAIN

Be forewarned: Traveling by train in Texas is not nearly as charming as it sounds. Trains stop frequently between destinations and for long periods of time. The trip from Austin to Fort Worth can take as long as nine hours—the same trek is about three hours by car. Unfortunately, the fares aren't usually low enough to make the extra time worthwhile. One of the few trips recommended by some train travelers is the scenic trek to far West Texas (Alpine and beyond to El Paso), even though it can take up to 24 hours to get there. For more information, contact Amtrak at www.amtrak.com or 800/872-7245.

BY BUS

For the most convenient scheduling system and affordable fares from other parts of the country, leave the driving to **Greyhound** (800/231-2222, www.greyhound.com). The venerable Dallas-based bus line has an easily navigable online reservation system (not always the case with bus companies) and hosts bus stops in cities across the country. Fares tend to run about half the price of a plane ticket, often a welcome option for travelers on a tight budget (and willing to make the trip in more time with less glamour). Greyhound can assist travelers with fares and schedules via email (ifsr@greyhound.com) and can serve Spanish-speaking travelers via phone (800/531-5332) 5 A.M.–2 A.M. CST.

BY BOAT

Texas's Gulf Coast has several major shipping ports, including Houston, Galveston, Corpus Christi, Beaumont, and Brownsville. Virtually all the activity is industrial, but cruise ships occasionally dock in Houston and Galveston. Contact the cruise lines (Carnival, Royal Caribbean, etc.) to see if they plan voyages to the Lone Star State.

Getting Around

Texans love their cars. And trucks. In a state this big, a vehicle is virtually a necessity, despite some advances in metropolitan public transportation systems. Still, to get anywhere in Texas's sprawling cities and widespread landscape, a vehicle is the most practical approach. In fact, the state is so spread out, travelers occasionally hop on planes to get from place to place. The drive from Lubbock to Corpus Christi would take about 13 hours by car but only two hours via plane. Other small cities with airports include Tyler, Waco, San Angelo, Amarillo, and Brownsville.

BY CAR

Texas's major interstates are well maintained, and drivers are largely courteous, if a bit lead footed. The stretch of I-35 between Dallas and Austin is a racetrack, with cars and semi trucks regularly buzzing along at a 90 mph clip. That being said, some Texas drivers are notorious for hanging in the passing lane at 55 mph, forcing cars to line up behind them and pass on the right when there's a break in the "fast" lane. The true Lone Star autobahn experience is in far West Texas, where the posted speed limit is 80 mph, meaning drivers will go even faster since patrol cars are as abundant as trees out there. Incidentally, freeway ramps are unpredictable in Texas—some are only a few hundred yards short, while others seem to stretch for miles. Once you're off the interstate, be sure to keep an eye out for police, since some small Texas towns rely on speeding ticket fines to help fund their municipal budgets.

Toll Roads

Unlike other states with well-established turnpike and tollway systems, Texas is relatively new to the fees-for-freeways concept. Small stretches of highways in Dallas and Houston have charged tolls for decades, but only recently have other cities (Austin and Tyler) jumped on board.

For the most part, the tollways are welcome (unless they're placed or proposed on a previously public road) because they ease congestion on busy nearby interstates. Still, they rub some Texans the wrong way and can be underused due to perceived expense. The Texas Department of Transportation's system is surprisingly convenient and innovative (yet occasionally confusing), with electronic gates allowing drivers to cruise through the tolls and receive a bill in the mail several weeks later.

How does this work? It's fairly simple: Fancy cameras snap a photo of the car's license plate as it zooms through the toll booth; an automatic system reads the number and sends a bill to the car's registered owner. Fees are reasonable: from 75 cents to several dollars, depending on the length of the toll road.

If you're renting a vehicle, be sure to ask the rental company if they have a toll tag or if you can purchase a prepaid tag. Otherwise, you may be unpleasantly surprised to later find you've been charged a $50 "convenience" fee for the company to handle the arrangements. If you don't have a tag, be sure to look for the highway signs letting you know if there's an option for paying an actual person at a toll gate; otherwise, you may want to take a more convenient route on a true freeway.

For more information about Texas's toll roads, visit www.texastollways.com.

BY BIKE

Texas has a considerable number of bikers—including seven-time Tour de France winner Lance Armstrong—but its roadways aren't considered very bike friendly. Even Armstrong's own city (Austin) is a difficult place to get around on two wheels. The best places to ride are municipal and state parks, which contain well-designed and scenic hike-and-bike trails. The state's tremendous geographical diversity allows for a good variety of terrain, and several Texas locales—Palo Duro Canyon and the Hill Country, in particular—are major destinations for serious mountain bikers from across the country.

BY BUS

For those interested in traversing Texas by bus, it's worth contacting **Trailways** (319/753-2864, www.trailways.com). The company operates eight regional routes in Texas, offering passengers the option of making personalized trips using independently operated bus companies. This is an ideal option for travelers interested in exploring cities or smaller towns at their own pace without having to rely on a major bus tour operation with existing (and less-than-adventurous) itineraries.

PUBLIC TRANSPORTATION

With so many "new" cities (less than 150 years old), Texas is known more for its sprawl than dense metropolitan environs. Unlike long-standing urban areas on the East Coast and in the Midwest with well-established subway and train-based transit lines, Texas's cities have traditionally used buses for public transportation. Light rail can be a challenging system to incorporate on established traffic grids, but it's been successful in several cities, Dallas and Houston in particular. To find out more about public transportation options in Texas's major urban environments, visit the following websites: **Austin** (www.capmetro.org), **Corpus Christi** (www.ccrta.org), **Dallas** (www.dart.org), **El Paso** (www.elpasotexas.gov), **Fort Worth** (www.the-t.com), **Houston** (www.ridemetro.org), and **San Antonio** (www.viainfo.net).

Sports and Recreation

Texans spend a lot of time enjoying outdoor activities, despite the intolerably hot summers. For sports, football is the undisputed king, but baseball, basketball, and golf are also popular since they can be played year-round. The state's mild climate also allows nonprofessional (recreational) sporting activities to continue throughout the year. Campers, hikers, and mountain bikers flock to state and local parks year-round—in summer for the lower humidity and higher altitudes of far West Texas, and in winter for the warm tropical climate of the Gulf Coast and Rio Grande Valley. The *Sports and Recreation* and *Camping* sections for specific cities in this book provide detailed information about available resources.

Professional sports are a major attraction in Texas (the *Sports and Recreation* sections in the metropolitan areas contain detailed information). Most Texans are fans of the Dallas Cowboys, but loyalties are divided by region when it comes to professional baseball (the Houston Astros or Arlington's Texas Rangers) and basketball (Dallas Mavericks, San Antonio Spurs, or Houston Rockets).

High school football is a religion in Texas (it's the inspiration for *Friday Night Lights* after all), but the most passionate fans in the state follow college sports. The University of Texas versus Texas A&M University rivalry is one of the fiercest in the nation, and Texas's sheer size allows for serious intrastate competition among several large schools (Texas Tech University, Baylor University, University of Texas at El Paso, Texas State University, etc.).

ECOTOURISM

One of the most popular ecotourism destinations in the country is emerging in South Texas, particularly the Lower Rio Grande Valley. The Valley's immense biodiversity and ecological complexity make it a natural crossing point for migratory birds, which traverse the region each fall and spring en route to and from their winter homes in the tropics.

Much like the birds that arrive in the Valley from the East Coast and Midwest, the birders who track and document their feathered friends flock from across the country in search of their favorite and rare species. The McAllen area is home to several acclaimed birding sites catering to the thousands of ecotourists who arrive annually, including the World Birding Center's **Quinta Mazatlan,** the highly regarded **Santa Ana National Wildlife Refuge,** and the **Bentsen-Rio Grande Valley State Park.** These parks retain the region's natural state by maintaining the distinctive woodlands, which draw species popular with the birding crowd, such as the chacalacas, green jays, and broad-winged hawks.

Websites worth exploring to find potential ecofriendly travel options in Texas include www.ecotourism.org, www.Ecotravel.com, and www.texas.uscity.net/Eco_Tourism.

STATE PARKS

The Texas Parks and Wildlife Department operates nearly 100 state parks (including natural areas and historic sites), which may sound like a lot at first but doesn't represent much of the state's geographic area. At all. In fact, according to the state government, Texas has a total land area of 167.5 million acres, and the state parks' 586,501 total acres occupy one-third of 1 percent of that total.

Regardless, the state's enormous geographical diversity is aptly represented at the parks, from northern lakes to southern tropics, and western mountains to eastern forests. The largest park in the state's system is in the Panhandle region—the magnificent Palo Duro Canyon, at 26,275 acres (representing the country's second-largest canyon). The smallest is in West Texas—Balmorhea, at 46 acres (a spring-fed oasis near the Davis Mountains).

The most popular parks are in or near metropolitan areas. As of the late '00s, the state's most-visited parks were Cedar Hill State Park in Dallas County (531,153 annual visitors), San

© ANDY RHODES

camping in Big Bend National Park

Jacinto Monument Battleground and Battleship *Texas* in Harris County near Houston (415,817 visitors), and Goose Island State Park in Aransas County on the Gulf Coast (371,519 visitors). If you're planning to camp at these parks, it's highly recommended to make reservations several weeks in advance, since they're often fully booked and will turn away visitors at the gate. Incidentally, for those interested, the least-visited park was Devil's River State Natural Area in southwestern Texas (821 visitors).

Making Campground Reservations

Like many other states, funding for parks is scarce in Texas, but the Parks and Wildlife Department manages to run a decent operation with limited resources. For years, Texans complained mightily about the hassles of making campground reservations via antiquated systems such as phones. By 2010, TPWD finally implemented an online reservation system (http://texas.reserveworld.com/), which has provided added convenience, albeit with a few initial glitches.

Exploring Texas's Backcountry

For some, camping doesn't require a car or on-site gift shop. Backcountry camping is available across the state and, because of the varying geography, can be interpreted in different ways.

Traditionally, backcountry or primitive camping involves pitching a tent in an undeveloped, secluded area accessible only by foot without any amenities (except perhaps a fire pit). In Texas, this typically means an excursion in the western portions of the state (Bandera's Hill Country Natural Area is a particularly popular destination), where campers can experience nature without the interference of adjacent campers and nearby highways. The definition of *backcountry* is expanded a bit in far West Texas, where campers can take a secluded mountain trail in Big Bend State Park, or even along the coasts, where the term encompasses beach camping in undeveloped areas.

For these types of excursions, most state parks require backcountry campers to register at the reservation desk to ensure safety (if

Many birding centers and nature trails are found in South Texas.

campers doesn't return by the expected date/time, park rangers can check on them). To find out more about a park's policies, visit www.tpwd.state.tx.us.

FISHING

Like other outdoor activities in Texas, fishing is a popular recreational endeavor due to the mild year-round temperatures. The Lone Star State is also well known in angler circles for its freshwater reservoirs and streams packed with largemouth bass, smallmouth bass, crappie, panfish (bluegill, sunfish), and catfish, as well as the draw of the Gulf Coast's tarpon, amberjack, red drum, and spotted sea trout.

For recommendations about the best places to cast a line in Texas's fishing hot spots (along the Gulf Coast, the reservoirs in East Texas's national forests), consult the appropriate regional sections in this book. For detailed information about fishing reports, tides, and advisories, visit the Texas Park and Wildlife Department's comprehensive website: www.tpwd.state.tx.us.

Since Texas is so big and fishing is so popular, there are nearly 1,700 locations to obtain a license (a requirement). Anglers can purchase a license at most bait and tackle shops, as well as local sporting goods stores, grocery stores, and even some department stores. Recreational licenses are available on a daily basis (fees vary by location) or with an annual permit ($30 for freshwater, $35 saltwater, $40 "all-water"). These licenses can also be purchased in advance by phone (800/895-4248 Mon.–Fri. 8 A.M.–5 P.M.) or via TPWD's website. In addition, the site offers a handy service that identifies the nearest local license vendor based on the city.

HUNTING

Hunting is huge in Texas, and the state's sheer size provides countless opportunities to grab a gun and wait patiently for your critter of choice. Deer hunting is one of the biggest draws, and deer season has a major cultural and economic impact on much of the state. Pick up a community newspaper during the winter, and you'll find plenty of photos of hunters, ranging in age from 8 to 88, in the back of their pick-ups proudly displaying the rack of the buck they just killed.

In general, Texas offers something for every kind of hunter, from waterfowl along the Gulf Coast to quail and pheasant in South Texas to feral hogs in East Texas to antelope in the Panhandle. The best place to find all the information you'll ever need about hunting in Texas—seasons, permits, regulations, restrictions, hunting lodges, and hunting leases—is the Texas Parks and Wildlife Department's website: www.tpwd.state.tx.us.

Like fishing licenses, Texas's hunting licenses are required and can be obtained at 1,700 locations across the state. Hunters can purchase a license at a local gun shop, sporting goods store, grocery store, or department store. Resident licenses are available for $25 (fees for out-of-staters are slightly higher) and allow hunting of "any legal bird or animal (terrestrial vertebrates)." The licenses can also be purchased in advance by phone (800/895-4248

Mon.–Fri. 8 A.M.–5 P.M.) or via TPWD's website. Like the fishing licenses, the website offers a service that identifies local vendors based on the closest city.

Though most locals are well versed in the procedures associated with field dressing and transporting a deer after it's been killed, visitors may need a crash course on the state's requirements. To find out everything you need to know about appropriate tags, processing (four quarters and two backstraps), and keeping the deer in "edible condition," visit www.tpwd.state.tx.us.

Food

Food lovers love Texas. Turn on the Food Network, and you'll probably soon be watching a feature about Texas barbecue, the many varieties of Mexican food in Texas, or recipes for the perfect Lone Star chili. The following types of cuisine are represented in the *Food* sections of virtually every city in this book, but here's a quick overview of how they came to be culinary icons in Texas.

BARBECUE

The prime representation of Texas cuisine, barbecue is all about the meat—beef (brisket and ribs), pork (sausage, ribs, and chops), and turkey, chicken, mutton, goat, or anything else a Texan can put in a barbecue smoker. The tradition originated in the Caribbean as a method to cook meat over a pit on a framework of sticks known as a *barbacot*, and it eventually made its way across the southern United States, where it picked up various cultural influences on the way. Even in Texas there are several different methods for barbecuing meat, and there's plenty of debate about who does it the right way. Fortunately, everyone wins since all styles of Texas barbecue are exceptionally pleasing to the palate.

In general, the East Texas approach is aligned with African-American traditions of the South—the sauce is tomato based and somewhat sweet, and the sides (potato salad and coleslaw, in particular) are mayo based and extremely sweet. Central Texas–style 'cue is considered the ideal representative of the Lone Star State, originating in the German and Czech communities in the Austin area. Based on traditions from European meat markets,

a typical barbecue pit in rural Texas

© ANDY RHODES

the sausage and beef are smoked and served on waxed paper along with side items inspired by the former grocery store/butcher shops where they originated—bread slices, beans, tomatoes, cheese, and jalapeños. In West Texas, some restaurants and ranches still serve their meat "cowboy style," where an entire slab of beef is cooked over hot coals on open pits and basted with a "mop" of oil and vinegar.

TEX-MEX

For most people, Mexican food means tacos, burritos, and nachos. In Texas, Mexican food can mean a variety of things—cuisine from the interior of Mexico with savory sauces and various meats, Southwestern-style Mexican food with green chiles and blue corn, or border-inspired Tex-Mex with gooey cheese, seasoned beef, and tortillas.

Though interior Mexican food is certainly worth sampling if you can find an authentic restaurant, it's Tex-Mex that prevails in Texas, and it's not hard to find a good representation of this regional comfort food in most cities across the state. In fact, mom-and-pop Tex-Mex restaurants are much like Italian eateries on the East Coast and in the Midwest—the best food is often in the most unassuming spot, like a strip mall or small house on a side street.

The main ingredients in Tex-Mex are ground beef, chicken, cheese, pinto beans, and tortillas. These items are combined differently for tasty variations, including a crispy or soft beef taco; a beef, cheese, or chicken enchilada; a bean chalupa; cheese quesadilla; or beef and chicken fajitas. Salsa, guacamole, lettuce, tomato, and sour cream are typically added as flavorful accompaniments.

SOUTHERN

Texas doesn't hold exclusive rights to this category, but Southern food is considered somewhat exotic to more than half the country, and, like just about everything else, Texas puts its own distinct spin on this style of down-home country cuisine.

It's unfair to generalize Southern cooking as being mostly fried, even though a good portion of it is encased in crispy goodness (just not always of the deep-fried variety). One of the best examples of Southern cookin' done right in Texas is chicken-fried steak, a thin cut of cube steak that's tenderized, breaded in egg batter or a seasoned flour mixture, pan fried in lard or vegetable oil, and served smothered in peppered cream gravy. The name likely refers to the similar process used in frying chicken. Other fried favorites include pork chops, catfish, okra, and chicken.

Another Southern cooking tendency is to include meat in veggie dishes (vegetarians should consider themselves warned). Beans, greens, and black-eyed peas are often spruced up with ham hock or bacon, and lard or bacon grease can add an extra dimension of flavor to just about any vegetable or bread recipe. Incidentally, if you order tea in a Texas restaurant, you'll get iced tea (occasionally sweetened), and you should never skip an opportunity to order a fruit cobbler or pecan pie for dessert.

CHILI

Texans take their chili seriously. Maybe too seriously. But since Texans claim bragging rights to many things, it should be no surprise they profess to have the best chili, too. The main point of pride with the Texas variety is the absence of beans. It's meat and spices only. Beans are for wimps. And Yankees.

There's no denying the results, however. A meat-based chili puts the emphasis where it belongs, on tender beef (occasionally venison) enhanced by a blend of fiery peppers and flavorful seasonings like garlic, onions, and oregano. Chili cook-offs are traditionally cultural celebrations in Texas towns, and winners become local celebrities. In fact, the granddaddy of all chili competitions, the Original Terlingua International Championship Chili Cook-Off, held near Big Bend each year, draws hundreds of renowned chili "chefs" by invitation only from across the country, much to the delight of the thousands of chili-heads in attendance.

Not surprisingly, Texans claim to have the original chili recipe, though food historians trace the dish to Incas, Aztecs, and Mayan cultures. The Texas connection is tied to Canary Islanders, who arrived in San Antonio in the early 1700s with traditional meals of meat blended with herbs, garlic, wild onions, and other veggies, including pungent local peppers. These days, Texans typically opt to prepare their chili at home, since restaurants could never duplicate the perfect combination of ingredients passed down through the generations in family recipes.

Tips for Travelers

For the most part, traveling in Texas is similar to traveling in the rest of the United States, with the main exception being issues associated with crossing the Mexican border (which is avoided by most people these days). Otherwise, it's smooth sailing across state lines, with visitor information centers located on the Texas side of most major freeways entering the state.

BORDER CROSSING

Several years ago, people were able to easily cross the Rio Grande sans passport or auto insurance, free to roam Mexican border towns. These days, people in border communities are wary of the violence across the border associated with warring drug cartels, even though they remain safe on the Texas side. In fact, the border city of El Paso was named in 2010 as the country's safest city with a population of 500,000 or more.

As of early 2011, the violence and unrest in Mexico was severe enough to warrant statewide warnings against visits to the neighboring country. Since this affects most tourists, it is advisable for travelers in Texas to remain in the state for safety's sake. Even longtime residents of Texas's border communities are reluctant to cross the border, unless a family or business emergency necessitates it.

If the volatile conditions in Mexico subside (as most border communities hope, since their tourism has historically been tied to border hops), visitors will once again return to Mexico's *restaurantes* and *tourista* areas. Meanwhile, many of these destinations (restaurants, in particular) have addressed the drop in business by opening new locations on the Texas side of the Rio Grande. It may not offer the same international flavor, but it provides visitors with something equally as palatable: safety.

INTERNATIONAL TRAVELERS

Since Texas shares an enormous border with another country, international travel has traditionally been commonplace in the Lone Star State. Not anymore. With the recent rise in violence associated with the warring drug cartels, visitors are advised against traveling to Mexico.

Overseas travel is a different story—recent numbers compiled by state government show Texas ranks seventh as a destination point among mainland U.S. states for overseas travelers, with New York, California, and Florida taking the top spots.

Before international travelers arrive in Texas, they're encouraged to address several issues that will make their experience more pleasant and convenient. Suggested action items include: consulting their insurance companies to ensure their medical policy applies in the United States; making sure they have a signed, up-to-date passport and/or visa; leaving copies of their itinerary and contact info with friends or family for emergencies; and taking precautions to avoid being a target of crime (don't carry excessive amounts of money, don't leave luggage unattended, etc.).

SPECIAL CONSIDERATIONS
Travelers with Disabilities

Travelers with disabilities shouldn't have much trouble getting around in Texas; in fact, the only places that may not be wheelchair accessible are some outdated hotels and restaurants. Otherwise, parks, museums, and city attractions are compliant with the Americans with Disabilities Act, providing ramps, elevators, and accessible facilities for public-use areas.

Texas law requires cities to appoint one member to a transit board representing the interest of the "transportation disadvantaged," a group that can include people with disabilities. As a result, most cities have addressed accessibility issues in airports and public transportation services. For detailed information, contact the municipal offices in the city you're visiting or the Texas Department of Transportation's Public Transportation Division at 512/416-2810 or www.dot.state.tx.us.

Other handy resources for disabled travelers en route to Texas are **Disabled Online** (www.disabledonline.com), offering a page of links with travel tips; the **Handicapped Travel Club** (www.handicappedtravelclub.com), providing information about campgrounds with accessibility; and the **Society for Accessible Travel and Hospitality** (www.sath.org), containing a resources page with handy travel tips for anyone with physical limitations.

Senior Travelers

For seniors, it's always a good idea to mention in advance if you're a member of AARP or if you qualify for a senior discount (typically for ages 65 and older, but occasionally available for the 60 and older crowd). Most museums in Texas offer a few dollars off admission fees for seniors, and many public transportation systems also provide discounts.

If you haven't done so already, inquire about travel options through **Elderhostel** (877/426-8056, www.elderhostel.org,), an organization providing several dozen programs in Texas with seniors in mind. Excursions lasting 4–12 days are available, ranging from birding trails to heritage-based tours to art, nature, and fishing trips.

Gay and Lesbian Travelers

Texas's rural communities (and even some of its smaller cities) aren't quite as open-minded as its metropolitan areas. Houston, Dallas, and Austin have sizable gay communities, with bars, restaurants, and services catering exclusively to gay clientele.

To learn more about resources related to gay and lesbian travel in Texas, including accommodations, restaurants, and nightclubs, visit the following travel-related websites: www.gaytravel.com, and the McKinney, Texas–based www.gayjourney.com. For additional information, contact the **Lesbian/Gay Rights Lobby of Texas** (512/474-5475, www.lgrl.org).

Health and Safety

Texas isn't any more dangerous or safer than other U.S. states, but there are several environment-related issues (weather, animals) that set it apart. Travelers with medical issues are encouraged to bring extra supplies of medications and copies of prescriptions—local visitors bureaus can recommend the best pharmacy or medical center, if needed.

CRIME

Although it's still often considered a Wild West state, Texas is similar to the rest of the nation regarding crime statistics and trends. According to a recent (2009) report by the Texas Department of Public Safety, criminal activity in Texas was separated into the following categories: violent crimes (against people—robberies, assaults, etc.), which represented 11 percent of the reported offenses, and property crimes (burglary, car theft), representing the remaining 89 percent. The report also revealed that violent crime decreased by 1.5 percent from the previous year, while property crime increased 2.6 percent.

Also noted in the report were several interesting crime-related factoids (for those interested in crime tidbits), including: of the 1.2 million arrests made by Texas law enforcement officers, 11 percent were of people 16 years of age and under; residential burglaries accounted for 71 percent of all burglaries reported in Texas; and firearms were used in 68 percent of all murders reported.

As always, if you're a victim of a crime in Texas or witness any criminal activity, immediately call 911.

THE ELEMENTS

Texas's weather is as volatile as its landscape. Summers regularly reach triple digits, and winters are marked by vicious snowstorms in the Panhandle and Northern Plains. The biggest threat to travelers in winter is ice—bridges and overpasses become slick and are usually closed when a rare ice storm barrels through the state. Since Texans are unaccustomed to dealing with such slippery conditions, they often disregard the danger and plow across a patch of ice in their big, fancy trucks. The results are predictably disastrous.

Heat is by far the most serious threat to Texas travelers. From the sticky humidity of marshy East Texas to the dry desert conditions of the Big Bend region, the summer months (May–September in Texas) can be brutal. Hikers, bikers, and campers are encouraged to pack and carry plenty of water to remain hydrated.

WILDLIFE, INSECTS, AND PLANTS

Texas has some bizarre fauna and flora, which can occasionally pose a danger to travelers, particularly those who venture to the state's parks and natural areas. Of primary concern are snakes, which nestle among rocks and waterways throughout Texas (though rattlesnakes are largely found only in western portions of the state). Also of concern in the Big Bend region are black bears and mountain lions, which hikers and campers should intimidate with loud noises and rocks (seriously) to fend off their advances.

The most dangerous plant in Texas is cactus. There are many varieties in all regions of the state, and even though some appear harmless, they may contain barely visible needles that get embedded in your skin and cause major irritation. With cactus, the best approach is to look but don't touch.

Information and Services

The best way to find out about activities and services in the city you're visiting is through the local convention and visitors bureau, or in smaller communities, the chamber of commerce. Each destination in this book includes contact information for visitor services, and even the most rural areas have discovered the value of promoting themselves online thanks to the wonders of the Web.

MONEY

It's always a good idea to have cash on hand for tips, bottles of water, and parking or tollway fees, but you can get by in most Texas cities with a credit or debit card. Some smaller towns still don't accept them (old-fashioned restaurants and "convenience" stores, in particular), but they're typically modern enough to have ATM machines. Also available, yet not quite as accessible, are wire transfers and travelers checks. Call ahead for the bank's hours of operation since some institutions close at odd hours.

MAPS AND TOURIST INFO

Convention and visitors bureaus are the best resource for planning a trip to Texas. Call ahead to have maps and brochures sent before your trip, or check the town's website for electronic versions of walking tours and street maps available for download. It's also a good idea to check these sites or call in advance to find out if the city you're visiting is hosting its annual pecan days or biker festival at the same time. Depending on your outlook, this can enhance or hinder your excursion.

RESOURCES

Suggested Reading

GENERAL INFORMATION

Texas Almanac. Published annually, this handy book includes virtually everything you'd ever need to know about Texas—current and historical information about politics, agriculture, transportation, geography, and culture, along with maps of each county (all 254 of 'em).

Texas Monthly. With an upper-crust subscriber base, this monthly features some of the best writers in the state offering insightful commentary and substantive feature articles about the state's politics, culture, history, and Texas-ness. It's available at most bookstores, coffee shops, and grocery stores.

State Travel Guide. Each year, the Texas Department of Transportation publishes this magazine-size guide with maps and comprehensive listings of the significant attractions in virtually every town, including all the local history museums in Texas's tiny communities.

LITERATURE, FICTION, HISTORY

All the Pretty Horses, Cormac McCarthy, 1992. Tracing a young man's journey to the regions of the unknown (though it technically takes place along the Texas-Mexico border), this novel depicts a classic quest with plenty of good, evil, and Texas mystique.

Friday Night Lights, H. G. Bissinger, 1990. This book will tell you more about Texas than you could ever experience in a visit to the state. It's not just about football, but the passionate emotions involved with family, religion, and race in Odessa through the eyes of journalist Buzz Bissinger.

The Gates of the Alamo, Stephen Harrigan, 2001. This is gripping historical fiction, with detailed history about the actual people and events associated with the battle of The Alamo weaved with a dramatic narrative resulting in a completely compelling read.

Lonesome Dove, Larry McMurtry, 1985. Beautifully written by Pulitzer Prize–winning novelist Larry McMurtry, this period piece (late 1800s) chronicles two ex–Texas Rangers on a cattle drive, leaving readers with a yearning for the compelling characters and the Texas of the past.

Lone Star, T .R. Fehrenbach, 2000. Considered the definitive book on Texas history, this enormous book by a highly respected historian covers Texas's lengthy and colorful heritage in fascinating and accurate detail.

Tales of Old-Time Texas, J. Frank Dobie, 1955. Known as the Southwest's master storyteller, J. Frank Dobie depicts folk life in Texas unlike any other author, with 28 inspiring stories of characters (Jim Bowie) and culture (the legend of the Texas bluebonnet).

MUSIC AND FOOD

The Greatest Honky Tonks of Texas, Bill Porterfield, 1983. You'll likely have to so some searching to dig up a copy of this book, but it's worth it for the engaging text about the colorful culture associated with the state's iconic honky-tonks and historic dance halls.

Legends of Texas Barbecue, Robb Walsh, 2002. This book is as fun to read as it is to use—learn about the fascinating history of the many different styles of Texas barbecue while trying out some of the state's best recipes and cooking methods.

Meeting the Blues: The Rise of the Texas Sound, Alan Govenar, 1995. This thoroughly researched book provides fascinating insight about the development of the Texas blues through historical narrative, interviews, and photos.

The Tex-Mex Cookbook, Robb Walsh, 2004. Well researched and comprehensive in approach, this informative book includes cultural information about classic and unknown Tex-Mex dishes and plenty of authentic recipes.

The Wine Roads of Texas: An Essential Guide to Texas Wines and Wineries, Wes Marshall, 2002. Covering more than 400 Texas wines and the top wineries in Texas, this book offers a comprehensive sampling of wines from Big Bend to the bayous.

OUTDOORS

Birds of Texas Field Guide, Stan Tekiela, 2004. Designed for amateur birders, this handy guide is color coded (corresponding to the birds' feathers) with helpful photos, maps, and descriptions.

A Field Guide to Texas Snakes, Alan Tennant, 2002. This thorough guidebook provides essential information about understanding and appreciating Texas's venomous and nonvenomous snakes through identification keys and color photos.

Naturalist's Big Bend, Roland Wauer, 2002. If you ever wanted to know about the major and minor details of Big Bend's mammals, reptiles, insects, birds, trees, shrubs, cacti, and other living things, this is the place to find it.

Internet Resources

GENERAL TRAVEL INFORMATION
Office of the Governor, Economic Development and Tourism
www.traveltex.com
This indispensable site provides background and contact information for virtually every tourist attraction, major and minor, in the state.

Texas Department of Transportation
www.dot.state.tx.us
Visit this site for information about road conditions and travel resources (maps, travel info center locations, etc.).

Texas Monthly
www.texasmonthly.com
The site of this award-winning magazine offers samples of feature articles and recommendations for quality dining and lodging options throughout the state.

HISTORIC PRESERVATION
Texas Historical Commission
www.thc.state.tx.us
The official state agency for historic preservation, the THC provides helpful guidelines about its preservation programs and essential travel information about its popular historic properties across the state.

Texas State Historical Association, The Handbook of Texas Online
www.tshaonline.org/handbook/online
The *Handbook of Texas* has long been considered the definitive source for accurate information about Texas's historical events, sites, and figures.

OUTDOORS
Texas Parks and Wildlife Department
www.tpwd.state.tx.us
You can get lost (in a good way) exploring this site, with its comprehensive listings of state parks and detailed information about outdoors activities.

National Parks in Texas
www.nps.gov
Texas's national parks are astounding, and this site provides enough information to put these intriguing locales on your must-visit list.

Texas Campgrounds
www.texascampgrounds.com
Use this site to help find a commendable RV park or campground anywhere in the state.

Texas Outside
www.texasoutside.com
This site contains helpful info and links to outdoor activities in Texas such as hiking, biking, camping, fishing, hunting, and golfing.

Index

List of Maps

www.moon.com

DESTINATIONS | ACTIVITIES | BLOGS | MAPS | BOOKS

MOON.COM is ready to help plan your next trip! Filled with fresh trip ideas and strategies, author interviews, informative travel blogs, a detailed map library, and descriptions of all the Moon guidebooks, Moon.com is all you need to get out and explore the world—or even places in your own backyard. While at Moon.com, sign up for our monthly e-newsletter for updates on new releases, travel tips, and expert advice from our on-the-go Moon authors. As always, when you travel with Moon, expect an experience that is uncommon and truly unique.